Divine
Agitators

Divine Agitators

THE DELTA MINISTRY AND CIVIL RIGHTS IN MISSISSIPPI

By Mark Newman

THE UNIVERSITY OF GEORGIA PRESS
ATHENS AND LONDON

© 2004 by the University of Georgia Press
Athens, Georgia 30602
All rights reserved
Set in Monotype Janson by Bookcomp, Inc.
Printed and bound by Maple-Vail
The paper in this book meets the guidelines for
permanence and durability of the Committee on
Production Guidelines for Book Longevity of the
Council on Library Resources.

Printed in the United States of America
07 06 05 04 03 C 5 4 3 2 1
07 06 05 04 03 P 5 4 3 2 1

Library of Congress Cataloging-in-Publication Data

Newman, Mark.
Divine agitators : the Delta ministry and civil rights in
Mississippi / by Mark Newman.
        p.   cm.
Includes bibliographical references (p.) and index.
ISBN 0-8203-2526-0 (alk. paper) — ISBN 0-8203-2532-5
(pbk. : alk. paper)
1. Civil rights movements—Mississippi—History—
20th century.   2. Civil rights—Religious aspects—
Christianity.   3. African Americans—Civil rights—
Mississippi.   4. Delta Ministry.   5. Mississippi—
Race relations—History—20th century.   I. Title.
E185.93.M6 N49 2003
323.1'196073'09762—dc21   2003008497

British Library Cataloging-in-Publication Data available

In memory of my grandfather, John Harold Wear

CONTENTS

Mississippi provided the stiffest and most determined resistance to the demands of the civil rights movement for racial equality. In the early 1960s, the state's African Americans, particularly in the Yazoo-Mississippi Delta, also endured some of the nation's lowest levels of income, health, and education. The Magnolia State presented the greatest challenge to the movement but also its greatest opportunity, since a success in overturning discrimination in Mississippi would provide additional inspiration, improved morale, and perhaps even a model for civil rights activism in other states.

Movement activists appealed to the National Council of Churches (NCC), a New York–based organization that comprised most of America's mainstream Protestant and Orthodox denominations, to aid the struggle in Mississippi. Prominent National Council staff and leaders were eager to participate in the southern civil rights struggle in the belief that God was working through the movement. At the suggestion of and in cooperation with civil rights leaders in the Delta, in September 1964 the NCC inaugurated the Delta Ministry, a ten-year program of relief, literacy, voter registration, economic development, and community mobilization primarily in the Delta of Mississippi, with other projects in Hattiesburg and McComb. At its height in the mid-1960s, the Ministry had fifty-five staff and volunteers. By 1967, it maintained the largest contingent of civil rights field staff in the South, nearly half the number in the region. While civil rights groups such as the Student Nonviolent Coordinating Committee

(SNCC) and the Congress of Racial Equality (CORE) imploded in the second half of the 1960s and the Southern Christian Leadership Conference focused most of its efforts on the North and on opposing the Vietnam War, the Delta Ministry continued its work in Mississippi and filled the vacuum the other groups had left behind.

Historians have long recognized that Mississippi was vital in the civil rights struggle as a result of the strength of the state's resistance to the demands of the movement and of its large African American population. In recent years, the state has received considerable scholarly attention that testifies to its significance in civil rights history. Despite the importance of the Delta Ministry to the African American freedom struggle in Mississippi and the longevity of the group's active involvement, which stretched beyond its original ten-year mandate into the 1980s, there is no scholarly monograph about the Ministry. Yet the Delta Ministry's history and activities illustrate some of the key problems with which the civil rights movement grappled, not just in Mississippi but across the South. The Ministry's staff sought to act as facilitators so that the poor could take control over the direction of their lives and establish and fulfill an agenda of their own creation. It attempted to empower the most deprived and oppressed African Americans and stem the flow of Delta blacks to the ghettoes of northern cities, which by the late 1960s offered decreasing employment opportunities to the poorly educated migrants.

Operating in the South's most heavily black and racially repressive state, the Delta Ministry provides an insight into how African Americans, particularly the poorest and most deprived, sought to achieve genuine social, economic, and political equality in the wake of federal civil rights legislation. The organization's history illustrates the struggle of and divisions among blacks as they sought to establish a post-civil-rights agenda, the adoption by southern whites of more subtle means of maintaining their dominance, and the disengagement of the federal government from efforts to counter racial discrimination.

During its history, the Delta Ministry faced problems of entrenched white opposition, class divisions within the African American community, conflicts among civil rights groups, and the issue of Black Power. With few exceptions, white Mississippians within and outside the Church opposed the Delta Ministry from the outset. Fearful of white retaliation and oriented toward otherworldly religion, black churches in Mississippi generally held themselves aloof from the Ministry. Although clashes occurred between the African American community's traditional middle-class leadership and the poor over tactics and the right to represent the community, these disputes were often overridden by a shared desire to confront the common enemies of segregation and disenfranchisement. However, as blacks gained basic rights, conflicts emerged within the community over access to political office and federal poverty funds and jobs. Anxious to control power, moderate whites made some concessions to appeal to moderate blacks, divide the African American community, and maintain the substance of white domination. Typically, middle-class blacks, whether movement participants or not, took advantage of the opportunities opened up by the movement and emerged as the African American community's political leaders.

Concerned primarily with impoverished blacks, the Delta Ministry aligned itself at first with SNCC and CORE and, as these groups gradually faded from Mississippi, with the Mississippi Freedom Democratic Party (MFDP), which claimed to represent the poor. The primarily middle-class National Association for the Advancement of Colored People (NAACP), the nation's oldest civil rights organization, tended to be moderate and even conservative, whereas SNCC and the MFDP were more radical and oriented toward the indigent. But the divide between them often arose as much over competition for power and influence as over class or ideological differences. Local chapters of the NAACP sometimes pursued direct action campaigns. Some key MFDP figures were middle class and even college educated, and after 1964, the MFDP lacked either the organization or the numbers to sustain its claim to represent the poor.

Most impoverished African Americans were disinterested in or unaware of the conflicts between the NAACP and the MFDP but simply welcomed aid from whoever would assist them. Although the Delta Ministry held an unrealistic view of the representative nature of the MFDP and tended to favor it when it came into conflict with the NAACP, the Ministry worked with the NAACP and community advocacy groups in pursuit of shared goals. The Ministry found the poor much more willing than the middle class to engage in direct action protests. However, as the Delta Ministry's leadership moved in the direction of Black Power and the development of black community institutions in the late 1960s, most black Mississippians of all classes, both within and outside its staff, continued to favor integration. The Ministry's northern leaders, black and white, were often more radical than the impoverished blacks the group aided. Consistent with its desire to help the oppressed achieve goals of their own choosing, the Ministry sometimes had to subordinate its more radical impulses when they conflicted with those of local people. Poor rural African Americans were neither passive victims of racism nor obedient foot soldiers for established black leaders or the Ministry.

Historians have underestimated and often neglected the Delta Ministry's significant impact on the black struggle for equality in Mississippi. The Ministry experimented with alternatives to corporate capitalism, which was pushing African

Americans off the land, would not locate plants in the Delta, and increasingly could not offer southern black migrants jobs in northern industry. Furthermore, the group initiated and aided black manufacturing cooperatives, created the Delta Opportunities Corporation to train African Americans for employment, and supported striking farm workers who tried to organize for higher wages. The Ministry also founded Freedom City, a village built by displaced agricultural workers who made collective decisions and aimed to become economically independent by engaging in farming and small-scale industrial activity. Ministry workers hoped that the experiment would be emulated by others and would provide blacks with the means to remain and prosper in the Delta.

In addition to its economic programs, the Delta Ministry helped to register thousands of African American voters and operated workshops to train black candidates for office. It played a key role in inaugurating the Child Development Group of Mississippi, which organized Head Start centers for preschool children from poor backgrounds. By exerting determined pressure, the Ministry induced Mississippi state and county welfare officials to distribute free surplus federal foods to thousands of people who had not been receiving them. It allied with other advocacy groups to make health care available to many thousands of the needy, provided assistance in school desegregation cases, and worked to combat racial discrimination in education. The Ministry also helped to organize the Delta Foundation, which created jobs by channeling foundation and federal grants to small businesses that could not secure bank loans.

However, the Ministry was constantly underfunded, as many NCC denominations either did not make or failed to honor pledges. Consequently, the Delta Ministry had to restrict its activities and, on several occasions, to cut its programs and staff. Some of the Ministry's efforts were flawed in conception. It provided housing and support for Delta cotton-field workers who staged the region's first plantation strike in thirty years, but chronic agricultural employment meant the strike never had any realistic chance of success. Freedom City suffered from a lack of investment by industry, foundations, and the federal government, but its fundamental problem lay in the unsuitability of its many dependent, low-skilled, and poorly educated inhabitants for the training and autonomy that the experiment offered them. Despite some flaws in its approach, the Ministry could not have had a significant impact in creating alternative well-paid employment for deprived African Americans in the Delta for several reasons: the Ministry's budget was inadequate for the task, the federal government was insufficiently committed and was itself partly responsible for the Delta's unemployment problems, and industry was mostly averse to building plants in the region. That many of the economic and social problems with which the Ministry sought to grapple remain entrenched today is less an indictment of the Delta Ministry's efforts than of the failure of the state and federal governments to muster the political will to effect meaningful change in the Delta and the rest of Mississippi.

ACKNOWLEDGMENTS

Mattie L. Sink, a skilled and very knowledgeable librarian at the University of Southern Mississippi, suggested that I look at the Delta Ministry back in 1991, during a research visit for another project. Five years later, I returned to Starkville and, with her aid and enthusiasm, began work on the Ministry. I owe many thanks to Mattie and to all the other archivists who assisted me during my research.

Many other people also helped as I worked on the book. Richard H. King and Michael A. Simpson read the original proposal, and Richard also perused the first chapter. The following people provided essential aid regarding research trips: Bart and Sharon Bartleson, Bob and Joan Beech, Dan Carter, Frank and Linda Clover, Richard and Jennifer Damms, Leesha Faulkner, James F. Findlay Jr., Kees and Jean Gispen, David Levine, Peter J. Ling, Chris Lutz, Bill McCachren, Shay McDonnall, Shelia Moore, Arsha Rubyan, Mattie Sink, Jenny Walker, and Brian Ward.

A Small Project Grant from the University of Derby funded the research, while a sabbatical supported by the History Department and the Arts and Humanities Research Board provided time to write. The interlibrary loan staff at the University of Derby and Mark Shenise of the United Methodist Church Archives at Drew University obtained essential materials.

ABBREVIATIONS

CAP	Community Action Program
CDGM	Child Development Group of Mississippi
CEP	Citizenship Education Program
COFO	Council of Federated Organizations
CORE	Congress of Racial Equality
DOA	Delta Opportunities Association
DOC	Delta Opportunities Corporation
DRC	Delta Resources Committee
FMHA	Farmers Home Administration
FIS	Freedom Information Service
FSC	Federation of Southern Cooperatives
FSO	Forrest-Stone Opportunities, Inc.
GSA	General Services Administration
MACE	Mississippi Action for Community Education
MAMML	Mississippi Association of Methodist Ministers and Laymen
MAP	Mississippi Action for Progress, Inc.
MCHR	Medical Committee for Human Rights
MFDP	Mississippi Freedom Democratic Party
MFLU	Mississippi Freedom Labor Union
MMM	Mississippi Methodist Ministry
NAACP	National Association for the Advancement of Colored People
NCC	National Council of Churches
NSA	National Student Association
NWRO	National Welfare Rights Organization
OEO	Office of Economic Opportunity
PCUS	Presbyterian Church in the United States
SCLC	Southern Christian Leadership Conference
SEC	Shelby Educational Committee
SNCC	Student Nonviolent Coordinating Committee
UCMS	United Christian Missionary Society
UPCUSA	United Presbyterian Church in the United States of America
WCC	World Council of Churches
WCEC	Washington County Employment Committee

Divine
  Agitators

CHAPTER ONE

The Origins and Creation of the Delta Ministry

The National Council of Churches (NCC) comprised thirty-one Protestant and Orthodox denominations with forty-two million members, but, despite its size, it generally avoided direct involvement in the civil rights struggle until the 1960s. Except for sending the Reverend Will D. Campbell as a kind of roving but largely ineffectual ambassador to racial trouble spots in the South, the NCC confined itself to issuing statements in favor of desegregation. Yet between 1963 and 1964, the NCC created a Commission on Religion and Race, participated in the March on Washington, successfully lobbied members of the U.S. Congress on behalf of the civil rights bill, sent race relations mediators to several cities, and made a significant contribution to the civil rights struggle in Mississippi that culminated in the creation of a long-term project, the Delta Ministry. The National Council's belated but swiftly executed entry into civil rights activity reflected the predispositions of a new generation of NCC leaders. They and other liberal mainstream Protestants had been powerfully affected by the sustained direct action phase of the civil rights movement that began with the student sit-ins of 1960 and by the pleas of African American leaders in Mississippi to become involved in the ongoing struggle for equal rights in the Yazoo-Mississippi Delta.[1]

In the late 1950s and early 1960s, a new cadre of leaders and policy makers accepted high-level appointments in the NCC, which had experienced several years of consolidation after its creation in 1950 as successor to the Federal Council of Churches. R. H. Edwin Espy became the National Council's associate general secretary, its deputy administrative leader, in 1958. He assumed the general secretaryship five years later. Unencumbered by a long history of service in the NCC, which he had joined only in 1954, Espy proved open to new ideas and approaches. As general secretary, he had an important influence on NCC policy.[2]

Although the NCC was governed by a General Assembly of 734 clergy and laypeople elected or appointed by its member denominations, the assembly met only every three years. A General Board of 260 clergy and laypeople, elected by the General Assembly from its own membership, governed the National Council between its triennial meetings. The board met three times a year and bore responsibility for the NCC's program and administration. Espy reported to the board and held responsibility for administration and for recommending and implementing policy. Below him, associate general secretaries administered the National Council's four program divisions: Home Missions, Foreign Missions, Christian Education, and Christian Life and Work.[3]

Jon L. Regier, who was to play a key role in the Delta Ministry's creation and development, became executive secretary of the Division of Home Missions in 1958 at the age of thirty-six. He was the most prominent of a group of seminary-educated liberals who joined the NCC's staff in the late 1950s and early 1960s and made the National Council better equipped to address social issues. Educated at Huntington College, Indiana, and at McCormick Theological Seminary in Chicago, Regier received ordination into the predominantly northern United Presbyterian Church in the United States of America (UPCUSA) in 1947. After ordination, he worked in settlement houses in Chicago and Detroit and gained a master's degree in social work from the University of Michigan. Regier joined the NCC from Howell Neighborhood House, a Presbyterian-sponsored community center in Chicago; lacking previous ties to the National Council, he displayed a willingness to chart new directions. Familiar with urban problems and committed to social work, Regier also became attuned to the problems of the rural poor. As head of the Division of Home Missions, he oversaw implementation of a three-year citizenship-education project among two hundred thousand migrant crop pickers that was funded by a grant from the Schwartzhaupt Foundation.[4]

The increasing willingness of NCC staff to become involved in social programs was also shared by J. Irwin Miller, a successful Indiana businessman and Disciples of Christ layman whom the General Assembly elected in 1960 to a three-year term as NCC president. Miller urged the National Council to be responsive to national change and to adapt accordingly its programs and priorities.[5]

The desire of Miller and leading NCC staff to focus the National Council's social programs on current problems reflected some broader trends in religious thought that were also emerging in the World Council of Churches (WCC). Formed in 1948 to promote programmatic cooperation, the World Council comprised more than two hundred denominations in more than eighty countries. The WCC's Third Assembly, held in New Delhi in 1961, inaugurated a research project on "The Missionary Structure of the Congregation," which resulted in the creation of study groups, including a North American Working Group. Two members of that group, Colin W. Williams, who joined the NCC as director of the Department of Evangelism in 1962, and Harvey Cox, a professor at Andover Newton Theological School in Massachusetts, were to play a role in the creation of the Delta Ministry, which in part reflected their ideas about the Church's function in modern society.[6]

Williams, Cox, and Thomas Wieser, the North American Working Group's secretary and the American representative of the WCC, shared the view of an emerging group of Protestant theologians that the Church had become too preoccupied with its institutional growth and survival, limiting its mission to evangelism and the practice of religious ritual. By largely disengaging from the concerns of the secular world, the Church not only had lost its relevance for many outside its structures but also had lost sight of God's mission in the world. Members of the study group argued that the Church needed to identify and then contribute to God's mission by discovering what God was doing in the world. Williams articulated these views in two books, *Where in the World?* (1963) and *What in the World?* (1964) that were first published by and were influential within the NCC, while Cox wrote a best-seller, *The Secular City: Secularization and Urbanization in Theological Perspective* (1965).[7]

Williams and Cox argued that God was active in the world and had worked throughout history on behalf of justice. Consequently, the Church should not withdraw from the world but instead should go into the world to do God's bidding and aid those through whom he was working for social change. Church structures and theology were less important than discerning and then participating in the authentic work of God through missions in a servant ministry, where necessary, in cooperation with secular organizations. Cox later wrote, "The first premise is that for us, as for Moses, an act of engagement for justice in the world, not a pause for theological reflection, should be the first 'moment' of an appropriate response to God. Theology is important, but it comes after, not before, the commitment to doing, to what some still call 'discipleship.'" The emphasis on action over theology was to become characteristic of the Delta Ministry.[8]

Such ideas received a wide audience within the NCC and many of its member denominations, and some of those involved, like Williams and Cox, became convinced that God was working on the side of justice through the civil rights movement. Impressed by the Montgomery Bus Boycott, a yearlong struggle that ended successfully in 1956, Cox invited the boycott's spokesman, Martin Luther King Jr., to speak at Oberlin College in Ohio, where Cox served as chaplain. The visit produced a lasting friendship between the two men. As a member of the Southern Christian Leadership Conference (SCLC), created by King and a group of black ministers in 1957, Cox participated in civil rights demonstrations.[9]

The Montgomery Bus Boycott was the first major success involving public protest in the southern civil rights struggle. Direct action reemerged on a wider scale in the student sit-ins of 1960, which spread from North Carolina into many urban areas in the Upper South and into a few Deep South cities and led to the formation of the Student Nonviolent Coordinating Committee (SNCC). A year later, the Congress of Racial Equality (CORE), founded in Chicago in 1942, organized a Freedom Ride to test desegregation of terminals serving interstate buses, which the Supreme Court had ordered in *Boynton v. Virginia* (1960). Forced to intervene to protect the Freedom Riders from southern white violence, a reluctant Kennedy administration was similarly slow to act when a riot broke out as James Meredith desegregated the University of Mississippi in 1962. Belatedly, the Kennedys sent federal troops and a federalized state National Guard to quell the violence at the university. Civil rights demonstrations peaked in 1963 and reached a high point in the March on Washington, attended by 250,000 supporters of jobs, freedom, and the civil rights bill, through which the Kennedy administration sought to outlaw segregated public accommodations.[10]

Although the NCC dispatched the Reverend Will D. Campbell, a maverick white Mississippian, to racial conflicts in the late 1950s and early 1960s in an attempt to encourage peaceful white acceptance of change, the council otherwise avoided direct participation in the civil rights struggle and relied instead on issuing resolutions and pronouncements. The NCC's General Board adopted a resolution that endorsed the Supreme Court's 1954 *Brown v. Board of Education* school desegregation ruling, and in June 1960 the board adopted another resolution that supported the sit-ins. A year later, however, board members rejected a resolution approving the Freedom Rides. However, the growing intensity of civil rights action created pressure on and from some churchmen for active involvement. At the request of Martin Luther King Jr., seventy-four northern pastors, rabbis, and laymen marched at demonstrations in Albany, Georgia, in 1962. In January 1963, the NCC, the National Catholic Welfare Conference and the Synagogue Council of America cosponsored the National Conference on Religion and Race, which took place in Chicago and issued an appeal for equal rights, desegregation, and enfranchisement, although it did not produce any programs or lasting ecumenical organization. Aware that a more wide ranging and less individualistic approach to the escalating civil rights crisis was needed, the NCC gradually phased out the program of Will Campbell, one of the conference's speakers, and he left the National Council in August.[11]

Martin Luther King Jr. had also spoken at the conference, but he and the SCLC had a more direct impact on the NCC, when in April and May 1963 they staged a series of protests in Birmingham, Alabama, that were designed to overturn segregation and discrimination in employment. Police and firemen under the command of Public Safety Commissioner T. Eugene "Bull" Connor attacked the protesters with police dogs, fire hoses, and cattle prods. Imprisoned for his participation in the campaign and condemned for his involvement by local white ministers, King wrote his widely read *Letter from Birmingham Jail,* which sought to justify his efforts and excoriated white ministers for their failure to support the civil rights struggle. In a warning that resonated with important NCC leaders, the North American Working Group, and the liberal, seminary-educated staff that the National Council had been recruiting, King declared, "If today's church does not recapture the sacrificial spirit of the early church, it will lose its authenticity, forfeit the loyalty of millions, and be dismissed as an irrelevant social club with no meaning for the twentieth century." Although historian Henry J. Pratt overstated the case when he claimed that King's charges were "the *ultimate* cause" of the NCC's change from a race relations policy focused primarily on "preaching, teaching, and proclamations" to one of sustained, direct involvement in the civil rights movement, they certainly provided an impetus for the new direction.[12]

As Pratt noted, other contemporaneous events helped to transform the NCC's approach. Less than two weeks after the Birmingham demonstrations had ended in a negotiated settlement, the UPCUSA held its annual general assembly in Des Moines, Iowa. J. Irwin Miller, the NCC's president, urged strong action on civil rights in his address to the assembly and in private meetings with Presbyterian leaders. With strong support from Eugene Carson Blake, the denomination's stated clerk (highest administrative official), the assembly created the Commission on Religion and Race. Given an appropriation of five hundred thousand dollars, the commission was to design "a single comprehensive strategy" for the UPCUSA in race relations.[13]

Shortly after the Presbyterians' action, a group of prominent African American professionals and cultural figures, gathered around novelist James Baldwin, sought a meeting in New York with Protestant leaders to enlist their aid in the civil rights struggle. The group requested the meeting in a search for allies following an angry exchange with Attorney General Robert Kennedy in which Kennedy had defended the administration's record in civil rights. Espy, Regier, and leaders from several denominations emerged from the lengthy meeting with Baldwin and his associates convinced that they shared, as participant Robert W. Spike, an executive in the United Church of Christ, later explained, "a sense of personal guilt" and "personal responsibility" for the injustices African Americans suffered. The churchmen determined to enlist the Protestant community in "positive action" and approached the NCC's General Board, where they received a sympathetic response from Miller.[14]

Miller appointed a committee of six, including Spike and Regier, to suggest ways in which the National Council could aid the African American struggle for equality. The committee proposed the establishment of an NCC Commission on Religion and Race that would bypass the National Council's considerable bureaucracy by being responsible only to its General Board. Approved by the board on June 7, 1963, the new commission's purpose was to mobilize the NCC's resources behind the struggle for racial equality, including the "encouragement of negotiations, demonstrations and direct action in places of particular crisis." Because the struggle was "in the providence of God" and an example of God working in the world, the General Board authorized the commission "to make commitments, call for actions, [and] take risks" in support of civil rights. The new agency received a generous budget of $175,000 for the remainder of the year and almost $277,000 for 1964.[15]

The commission's rapid establishment after the meeting with Baldwin's group was possible because high-ranking officials in the NCC had already been seeking a way to involve the National Council in civil rights. Miller, Espy, and Blake, who served on the General Board and became the vice chairman and later chairman of the NCC's Commission on Religion and Race, enthusiastically supported the new agency. Regier and his Home Missions staff played an important role in suggesting its purview, and Regier headed the commission's emergency staff, pending permanent appointments. He worked closely with Colin Williams, whose ideas had influenced the commission's creation, and coopted Williams onto its staff.[16]

Five days after the General Board had approved the commission, segregationist Byron De La Beckwith assassinated Medgar Evers, Mississippi field secretary of the National Association for the Advancement of Colored People (NAACP), a long-established, mass-membership organization headquartered in New York. In its first act, the commission sent a group of Protestant leaders to Evers's funeral. At the funeral, Aaron Henry, state president of the Mississippi NAACP, invited the commission to send a delegation to his home town of Clarksdale, in the Delta county of Coahoma, to support an ongoing campaign against discrimination. The commission twice sent delegations to Clarksdale in July, but they were rebuffed by the mayor and local white clergymen, and the first group was served with injunctions forbidding them to demonstrate. The commission sent thirty-six clergymen to the city in August in support of a special prayer service in a black Baptist church, which local white ministers refused to attend. Clarksdale authorities issued injunctions against the visiting clergymen, barring them from participating in or inciting public protest and breaches of the peace.[17]

On July 15, Spike, a participant in the prayer service, had been appointed executive director of the NCC's Commission on Religion and Race. He concluded from the failure in Clarksdale that although the commission had been justified in becoming involved, it had been wrong to participate and then retreat, leaving local people to deal with the consequences. As a result of the experience, Spike recalled, "we determined to establish as soon as possible a long-term Mississippi-based ministry that would work at the basic roots of the problem—focusing particularly in the Delta of Mississippi where great numbers of Negro sharecroppers are disenfranchised, are displaced from their jobs by automation, and where the pressure is heavy to make it so uncomfortable for them that they will move north."[18]

Spike fitted the mold of the NCC's new young activist churchmen. Born in Buffalo, New York, in 1923, he received his theological training from Colgate-Rochester Divinity School and from Columbia University and Union Theological Seminary in New York City. His education convinced him of "the sociological mission of the Christian church." But his experience as pastor of Judson Memorial Church in New York's Greenwich Village between 1949 and 1954 completed his transformation from "conservative Baptist" to social activist. Conscious of the social injustice that surrounded him in Greenwich Village, Spike developed a social action program, and he served as chaplain of Youth House, a detention center for juveniles. Spike left the pulpit to become general secretary for programs at the Board for Homeland Ministries of the United Church of Christ. There, under the influence of Truman Douglass, his superior, he became an advocate of direct church involvement in civil rights. Eight years later, Douglass recommended Spike's appointment as head of the NCC's Commission on Religion and Race.[19]

Like Williams and Regier, with whom he worked at the commission, Spike was convinced that the Church had to be active in Christ's work in the world and that civil rights was part of that work. In a later assessment of the commission's role, Spike wrote, "What we have tried to do is to let the world set the agenda for our work—to take the world of the civil rights struggle seriously, and to develop a ministry in response to that." Consequently, the commission recruited between twenty-five thousand and forty thousand white church people to attend the August 1963 March on Washington. The commission chairman, Blake, addressed the march, alongside key civil rights leaders. Blake and the commission also lobbied Congress to support the civil rights bill. In the summer of 1963, commission staff attempted to mediate in racial conflicts in Savannah, Georgia; Danville, Virginia; and Wilmington, North Carolina; as well as in Clarksdale. Spike suggested to a commission meeting in September 1963 that the NCC "develop a comprehensive program of rehabilitation in the Delta area of Mississippi." The idea had several sources.[20]

The Reverend Andrew J. Young, a black United Church of Christ minister and director of the SCLC's Citizenship Education Program (CEP) that trained African Americans in political participation, claimed that the Delta Ministry was "a result of work that [the Reverend James] Bevel and I began in Mississippi in 1961." Born in the Delta town of Itta Bena in Leflore County, Bevel was a student at the American Baptist Theological Seminary in Nashville, Tennessee, and a leading participant in the city's sit-in movement before returning to Mississippi in 1961 as a Freedom Rider. He later joined SNCC, which had begun a voter registration campaign in southwestern Mississippi at the request of local NAACP leaders but then switched its efforts to the Delta. Bevel continued voter registration work when he became the SCLC's field secretary in Mississippi. In early 1963, Bevel proposed to Young that the SCLC create a center in the Delta to train community leaders. Although supportive of the idea in principle, Young noted the difficulty of securing financial support from mainline churches and foundations, with the result that the SCLC took no action. However, Young, who had worked for the NCC's Department of Youth Work until 1961, did not forget the idea, and he recommended it, along with a program of "area development for the Delta," to Spike and the NCC's Commission on Religion and Race. Young knew Spike through the United Church of Christ's Board for Homeland Ministries and had discussed the CEP directorship with him before accepting it. The two men remained in contact, as the Board for Homeland Ministries disbursed a grant from the Marshall Field Foundation that funded the CEP.[21]

Interest in the Delta also emanated from sources within the NCC. Since 1945, the National Council's Department of Town and Country and its predecessor in the Federal Council of Churches had conducted short annual programs to improve the pastoral training of rural African American preachers in Mississippi. In the late 1950s, five of the department's field workers had tried unsuccessfully "to enlist the interest and support of pastors and laymen in Mississippi in rural development." Department executives continued to discuss the Delta at their meetings and later evaluated and supported the proposal for a Delta project that emerged from the Commission on Religion and Race.[22]

Unidentified black Delta residents also approached the National Council for help. From them, the Commission on Religion and Race received a request early in the summer of 1963 "for the churches . . . to become involved in a program of community development." The commission referred the request to Regier, who assigned Henry A. McCanna, executive director of the Department of Town and Country, to investigate the needs of the Delta and to confer with local people. McCanna made several field trips and held consultative meetings with experts on rural problems, black and white Mississippians, and representatives from the Council of Federated Organizations (COFO), a statewide coalition of civil rights groups dominated by SNCC but also including CORE, the NAACP, and the SCLC. In September 1963, McCanna and NCC staff met with COFO workers as well as professors and students at Tougaloo College, a predominantly African American institution outside Jackson. A second meeting occurred in November at LeMoyne College, a black institution in Memphis, Tennessee, selected because of Mississippi's volatile racial climate. Two white Methodist ministers from Mississippi; representatives from eight denominations; SNCC's executive director, Jim Forman; and COFO's program director and assistant program director, Bob Moses of SNCC and Dave Dennis of CORE, attended the meeting with NCC staff.[23]

Although white Mississippians had generally expressed resentment at outside interference and urged caution, the meetings and field observations resulted in McCanna and his staff presenting a detailed December 1963 proposal to the Executive Board of the Division of Home Missions for a program of community development in the Delta that would last between five and ten or twenty years. The program, heavily influenced by ideas presented by Forman at LeMoyne, would encompass relief, education and training, self-help initiatives, economic and community development, and the fostering of indigenous leadership and leadership skills. It would also seek to establish communication between the African American and white communities. The program was to be staffed by a director and fifteen field workers, supported by a maximum annual budget of $260,000, to which the WCC would be invited to contribute. The proposal explained that a sustained commitment was needed to address the extensive economic, health and educational problems of the Delta's black majority population brought about by decades of white domination.[24]

The Delta's rich fertile soil, which extended two hundred miles almost from Memphis to Vicksburg and stretched to seventy miles at its widest point, had been created by alluvial deposits from the Mississippi River fifteen thousand years before. Settled primarily after the Civil War, the Delta became a center of cotton production. White plantation owners hired African Americans to work the land in return for a share of the crop produced. These blacks owned little beyond their own labor, and this sharecropping system further impoverished them, since as a result of fraud or overcharging, the cost of the supplies and tools they received from the owner to produce the crop and provide for their families usually exceeded the proceeds the sharecroppers received from the sale of their shares of the crop. Beginning in the late 1940s, machines increasingly replaced sharecroppers, who were reduced to picking and "chopping" (weeding) cotton. Sharecropper numbers in eighteen Delta and adjacent counties fell from 17,563 in 1959 to 8,788 in 1964. Growing use of machines and herbicides in the 1960s eliminated most of the need for pickers and choppers, leaving Delta blacks destitute. Mississippi provided little welfare assistance, encouraging African Americans to migrate through both parsimony and publicizing the more generous welfare benefits available in northern states. Young adults departed, leaving behind a black population that disproportionately comprised the very young and the very old. But the North offered little but ghettoes for the ill-educated and unskilled Mississippi migrants, who experienced difficulty finding employment.[25]

According to the 1960 census, nonwhites in eleven Delta counties had a median income of only $452. Between 1950 and 1960, economic conditions and white domination induced more than two hundred thousand blacks to leave eighteen Delta and adjacent counties, mostly for the North. Even so, African Americans constituted more than 60 percent of the region's 1960 population. A minority of wealthy whites dominated landownership. In Bolivar County, 5 percent of farms included more than 50 percent of the farmland. Unwilling adequately to support black schools and concerned with maintaining a docile, dependent agricultural workforce, whites restricted blacks to an inferior, segregated education. African American children had a shorter school year and finished their education earlier than whites, thereby making black children available for plantation labor alongside their families. In 1960, the median number of school years completed by children in six Delta counties was 10 for whites and 4.9 for African Americans, compared with national averages of 10.9 and 8.2, respectively. No black high school in the Delta had received accreditation from the Southern Association of Colleges and Secondary Schools.[26]

Poor education and low incomes brought African Americans a plethora of health and nutritional problems. Ten Delta counties recorded an average nonwhite infant mortality rate of 63.5 per thousand in 1961. Black homes, many of which were located on white-owned plantations, frequently lacked basic sanitary and washing facilities. In 1960, Sunflower County had 11,818 housing units, of which 6,264 lacked flush toilets, 7,265 lacked bathtubs and showers, and 4,593 lacked piped water. Tunica County had 5,130 homes, 4,005 of them without flush toilets and 4,134 without showers or bathtubs.[27]

Disenfranchisement deprived African Americans of political power to improve their position. The Mississippi state constitution, adopted in 1890, effectively barred most blacks from voting through a poll tax, a residency requirement, and a provision that voters should be able to read any section of the constitution chosen by the registrar (those who were unable to read were required to understand or interpret a section read to them). An amendment approved by voters in 1954 obliged registrants to complete written applications before the registrar without assistance; to read and write and interpret any section of the constitution; and to demonstrate an understanding of the duties of citizenship. A further amendment, adopted in 1960, required applicants to be "of good moral character," while a 1962 law mandated that applicants' names be published for two weeks in local newspapers, thereby inviting "character" challenges or retaliatory action by whites. By 1960, only 5.2 percent of Mississippi's eligible black population—twenty-two thousand people—had registered to vote. In the Delta, where blacks formed a majority in every county and therefore a potential threat to white political dominance, whites used their economic control as well as occasional violence, including murder, to ensure that black registration levels remained below the state average in most counties. In 1961, only 612 of 20,600 eligible blacks in Bolivar County were registered, only 472 of 16,933 eligible blacks were registered in Leflore, 2 blacks were registered in Humphreys, and none were registered in Issaquena.[28]

Living conditions for African Americans in the Delta approximated those of nonwhites in developing countries, where the wcc supported projects similar to the ncc's Delta proposal. Consequently, the Executive Board of the Division of Home Missions agreed in December 1963 that the National Council should solicit wcc support for the Delta project, which, if secured, would also put moral pressure on the National Council's General Board to accept the proposal. Never before had the World Council been asked to contribute to a project in the United States, a country proud of its prosperity and largely unaware of its own pockets of poverty. To seek wcc support for work in the Deep South, the heart of the Bible Belt, might also shame the region's churches into action—if it did not earn their scorn for outside interference. In December, Spike requested assistance for the Delta project in an address to the wcc assembly in Mexico City. Spike, Blake, Regier, and Williams also held discussions with wcc general secretary W. A. Visser 't Hooft, who expressed interest in the proposal. A January follow-up inquiry from Espy led Visser 't Hooft to offer wcc support and ask the ncc to specify "ways in which the World Council can best assist."[29]

Support from Visser 't Hooft and the World Council became crucial in securing NCC approval of the Delta project over the objections of southern denominations. In February 1964, the National Council's General Board overwhelmingly approved a detailed proposal for the Delta Ministry that Blake had presented on behalf of the Division of Home Missions and the Commission on Religion and Race. The General Board argued that "as the Delta area of Mississippi is now a symbol of the most hard core resistance to full racial equality, it must become a symbol of redemption and reconciliation." The approved proposal was essentially unchanged from that considered by the division two months before, except that the new document envisaged "a long term commitment of at least a decade and perhaps two." The board agreed to request funding for the Ministry from the WCC, with the expectation that the World Council would contribute 40 percent and that NCC denominations would voluntarily donate the remainder. The Delta Ministry would operate within the Division of Home Missions under Regier, detached from the Commission on Religion and Race, which would continue to focus on broad race relations issues. A committee of nationally prominent people and representatives from the Delta would be appointed to "mobilize competence and resources and to give guidance to the project."[30]

The proposal sought to allay criticism from southern white religious leaders by emphasizing that the Delta Ministry would be a "ministry of services of direct relief developed to relieve suffering" and a "ministry of reconciliation." It would establish communication between black and white communities, develop local leadership, and create community centers that would "assist in the process of literacy and fundamental education, manpower retraining, communications and planning." The words *service* and *reconciliation* recurred throughout the proposal, which made no mention of the civil rights movement, black disenfranchisement, or segregation. At the suggestion of Episcopal Bishop William Hargrave of St. Petersburg, Florida, and to reassure Mississippi's white religious leaders, the General Board voted to "invite representatives of the judicatorial bodies of our member communions in Mississippi to further collaborate with, and advise concerning development" of the Ministry and insisted on consultation with the state's relevant judicatory heads during the summer.[31]

Regier and the Delta Ministry's planners had originally expected that the Ministry would begin in the spring of 1964. However, the General Board's requirement for further consultations with Mississippi's religious leaders, the search for a director for the Ministry, and the time needed to secure official approval from the WCC resulted in a March decision to delay the Delta Ministry's start until September. Equally important in the Ministry's rescheduling were the other extensive commitments that the NCC had taken on in Mississippi, commitments that had begun in 1963 and grown with the group's involvement in the 1964 Mississippi Summer Project sponsored by COFO. The National Council's participation in Mississippi civil rights activities helped to change the shape of and provide the staff for the Delta Ministry, which commenced in September 1964.[32]

During their visits to Clarksdale in the summer of 1963, NCC representatives became aware that African American demonstrators arrested in Mississippi could not obtain bail funds from national bonding firms. The companies refused to take on civil rights cases out of fear that local offices would lose their state licenses. At the request of Jim Forman, the National Council's Commission on Religion and Race arranged bail in August for fifty-seven people who had been arrested for civil rights activities in Leflore County, with funds provided by the Board for Homeland Ministries of the United Church of Christ. The action marked the beginning of the commission's program of bail bond and legal assistance for civil rights protesters, with money obtained from voluntary donations from member denominations of the NCC and directed by the commission's lawyer, Union Theological Seminary graduate Jack Pratt.[33]

The Commission on Religion and Race maintained contact with each of COFO's four member organizations. But Regier, Spike, and the commission's members were particularly drawn to SNCC and CORE because of the dynamism and radicalism of their young activists and their willingness to undertake voter registration efforts in the most repressive areas despite harassment and violent opposition. Less than two weeks after the NCC had created the commission, Regier declared in a press release that SNCC "had taught American citizens the true meaning of commitment." He indicated the National Council's desire to work with SNCC, which had a representative on the commission.[34]

SNCC's extensive operations in Mississippi and consequent dominance of COFO, with the less well staffed CORE as a junior partner, also made SNCC attractive to the NCC as it sought to establish a long-term presence in the state. Although some local NAACP leaders, such as Henry and, before his death, Medgar Evers, had favored direct action in Mississippi, the organization's national headquarters had often discouraged such action, preferring its traditional approach of litigation and lobbying the federal government and Congress. The SCLC had little presence in the state and confined its activities to citizenship education.[35]

Begun in 1962, SNCC's voter registration efforts in the Delta drew particular NCC interest as it planned the Delta Ministry. Guided in Mississippi by twenty-eight-year-old Bob Moses, an African American native of New York state who held a master's degree in philosophy from Harvard University, SNCC was increasingly looking for national allies, such as the National Council. SNCC wanted to focus attention on Mississippi as a lever to force the federal government to protect civil rights workers from violent repression. The group took an innovative approach. In November 1963, SNCC organized a Freedom Vote, a mock election that paralleled the state gubernatorial election. More than eighty-three thousand blacks voted for COFO and NAACP president Aaron Henry for governor and Tougaloo College's white Mississippian chaplain, Ed King, for lieutenant governor, thereby demonstrating the desire to be involved in the political process. The presence of white volunteers from the prestigious universities of Yale and Stanford generated some national media attention for the Freedom Vote. Impressed by the efforts of SNCC and CORE, Spike recalled that in late 1963 and early 1964, "we tried to stay particularly close to the movement in Mississippi because here was located a concentration of the most militant, most capable, most competent of the young Negro leadership in the civil rights movement."[36]

SNCC initiated a Freedom Day in Hattiesburg, in southeastern Mississippi, in January 1964, while CORE arranged the first of a series of such voter registration days in Canton, the seat of Madison County, in February. At the request of the UPCUSA's Commission on Religion and Race, which began a project in Hattiesburg with Moses' encouragement, the NCC sent two men to the city, Art Thomas and Jack Pratt. Thomas, field representative of the National Council's Commission on Religion and Race, helped coordinate northern clergy participation, while Pratt spent two weeks providing legal assistance. The NCC's involvement cemented its growing working relationship with SNCC, which had sent its first field workers to the city in 1962. More than fifty northern ministers participated in Freedom Day under the auspices of the UPCUSA's commission, which continued to send short-term volunteer clergymen to aid the Hattiesburg movement until April. The involvement of the ministers in pickets, marches, canvassing, and general support activities provided an example and inspiration to the National Council, which in May took over sponsorship of the Hattiesburg Ministers' Project from the United Presbyterians. The NCC continued to dispatch clergymen to the city to help in civil rights work throughout the summer. As a consequence of this commitment, Hattiesburg became part of the Delta Ministry's operations when it commenced its work in September.[37]

Involvement in Hattiesburg's Freedom Day led the NCC's Commission on Religion and Race to take a sponsorship role in Canton's Freedom Days, organized by CORE, and to assist a SNCC voter registration drive in Greenwood during March and April 1964. The commission sent Thomas to coordinate the involvement of volunteer, northern ministers in the Canton protests, as in Hattiesburg. Thomas, aged thirty-two, was a native of Williamsport, Pennsylvania, and had been educated at Colgate University and at Duke Divinity School in Durham, North Carolina. An ordained minister in the Methodist Church, Thomas had organized the Covenant Community Church in Durham in 1960, one of the first integrated congregations in the South. Its members actively supported the city's civil rights movement. The experience Thomas gained in Durham, the cordial relations he established with the movement in Canton, and his roving role in Mississippi later brought his appointment as the Delta Ministry's director.[38]

By the time Thomas arrived in Canton, the NCC had also agreed to contribute to COFO's forthcoming Mississippi Summer Project. Inspired by the Freedom Vote of 1963, the project recruited about 650 student volunteers, 90 percent of them white. Mainly from prestigious northern universities, the volunteers assisted COFO workers in voter registration and helped to run forty-seven freedom schools, which taught African American history, citizenship rights, and other subjects neglected in black Mississippi schools and to organize thirteen community centers. Some whites also participated in an unsuccessful project that sought to gain white support for equal rights. SNCC, the prime mover behind the Summer Project, adopted four of Mississippi's five congressional districts, including the Delta, for its operations, with CORE taking the Fourth Congressional District.[39]

As a result of his close contact with SNCC, Spike was aware of the Mississippi Summer Project during its planning stage. In January 1964, he suggested that the Commission on Religion and Race operate an orientation program to prepare student volunteers for service in Mississippi. The commission appointed Bruce Hanson, assistant minister of the First Congregational Church in Washington, D.C., to coordinate the program, which took place in June at Western College for Women in Oxford, Ohio, with subsequent programs held at LeMoyne and Tougaloo Colleges. Drawing on its activist role in Hattiesburg, Canton, and Greenwood, the NCC recruited ministers to serve in the Summer Project, and from these ranks came most of the Delta Ministry's initial staff. Under National Council auspices, sixty-one ministers and rabbis served as counselors with the project, generally for periods of two to four weeks. They undertook a wide range of tasks that included "chauffeuring, teaching, counselling, 'spreading oil on troubled waters' in a project, visiting people in jail, going to jail, interceding with white members of communities where projects were located, talking theology, listening, building community centers, playing with children, participating in freedom days, getting villified, [and] getting beaten." An additional two hundred ministers served in voter registration projects for one or two weeks, while Pratt coordinated the efforts of 125 lawyers recruited to aid the volunteers by the Lawyers' Constitutional Defense Committee and the Lawyers' Committee for Civil Rights under Law.[40]

As director of its program in Mississippi, the Commission on Religion and Race hired forty-five-year-old Warren H. McKenna, the Episcopalian pastor of St. John's Church in Holbrook, Massachusetts. Since the 1950s, McKenna had been involved in work with the African American community of Boston's Rox-bury neighborhood, and had been arrested while participating in a civil rights protest in North Carolina in November 1963. Originally from Providence, Rhode Island, McKenna had been educated at Connecticut Wesleyan and at Episco-pal Theological School in Cambridge, Massachusetts. He had also studied social work. From his office in Jackson, McKenna provided orientation for NCC minis-ters. Although he had not expected to remain in Mississippi beyond the summer, McKenna stayed on as administrative assistant to the Delta Ministry's director.[41]

The Summer Project further strengthened the NCC's links with the movement in Mississippi. The Commission on Race and Religion's staff and many of the ministers it recruited for the Summer Project strongly favored the approach taken by SNCC and CORE, which believed in patient organizing. They sought to enable lo-cal African American communities to realize goals of their own creation in a form of participatory democracy. Rather than impose leadership from outside, activists worked with indigenous leaders or sought to foster their emergence. Once a local movement became self-supporting, SNCC and CORE workers intended to proceed to another community and begin the process of organizing afresh. Although SNCC and CORE worked with amenable local leaders regardless of class or affiliation, the organizations—SNCC in particular—championed and identified with the interests of the rural poor. The Delta Ministry was to share SNCC's outlook, and the group's influence was strongly evident in the proposal for the Delta project approved by the NCC's General Board in February 1964. The Summer Project's concern with voter registration, adult and child education, community centers, and converting local whites all became part of the Delta Ministry's program of operations.[42]

But by late 1964, SNCC activists in Mississippi had become disillusioned, with the result that they could not maintain and staff the freedom schools and com-munity centers that they had helped to create. CORE projects in Meridian and Canton had also entered decline by the fall. The Delta Ministry inherited and partially filled the vacuum left by the two groups' increasing disengagement from Mississippi.[43]

The causes of disillusionment in SNCC and CORE can be traced to the fed-eral government's failure over several years to provide the protection for civil rights workers and black communities that activists believed the U.S. Justice De-partment had promised. Violence and harassment plagued the Summer Project, which successfully registered only sixteen hundred of the seventeen thousand African Americans who made the attempt. One thousand people in the Missis-sippi movement were arrested, and eighty activists received beatings. Thirty-five of the sixty-five buildings bombed or burned during the summer were churches, and most of the remainder were homes of those who sheltered the volunteers or were otherwise active in the movement. Thirty-five firearm attacks occurred, and six people were murdered, including three activists in Neshoba County. The Neshoba murders finally forced the federal government to intervene, yet this only increased SNCC's bitterness toward the government, since the group believed, probably justifiably, that the government acted only because two of the three civil rights workers killed, Mickey Schwerner and Andrew Goodman, were white. James Chaney, the third victim, was a black Mississippian. Federal indictments eventually resulted in seven convictions for violation of the civil rights of those murdered.[44]

At its August 1964 national convention, the Democratic Party failed to seat the Mississippi Freedom Democratic Party (MFDP), thereby significantly increasing many SNCC and CORE activists' disillusionment with the federal government and with the civil rights movement's white liberal allies in the national Democratic Party and labor unions. Created by COFO in April 1964, the MFDP sought to displace the regular, all-white Mississippi Democratic Party's delegation to the national convention in Atlantic City because the regulars routinely excluded black participation. The MFDP organized meetings and elected delegates, including four whites, by following the procedures established by the national party. Supported by Robert Spike's statement to the Credentials Committee, the MFDP asked the national convention to seat the MFDP delegation in place of the regulars because, unlike them, the Freedom Democrats had followed the party's rules and pledged loyalty to the national ticket. Concerned that meeting the MFDP's demands would cost him crucial southern white votes, President Lyndon B. Johnson pressured the MFDP's allies to persuade the group to accept a compromise. The Freedom Democrats would receive two at-large seats at the convention, allocated to Aaron Henry and Ed King, and a promise that at the next convention, in four years' time, the party would enforce a nondiscrimination policy. The Atlantic City convention would treat other MFDP delegates as "honored guests."[45]

Vice presidential aspirant Hubert Humphrey, United Auto Workers president Walter Reuther, Spike, Jack Pratt, and, to a lesser degree, Martin Luther King Jr. tried to persuade the MFDP to accept the compromise, which Henry, its nominal leader, supported. However, Bob Moses and other SNCC workers and CORE activists strongly opposed the deal. The MFDP delegation included a few indigenous black SNCC activists, and most of the Freedom Democrats had been recruited into the movement by SNCC and CORE. A few NAACP-oriented delegates favored the compromise, but, after heated debate, the delegation decisively rejected it. Historian John Dittmer explains the resulting but long-brewing split between SNCC and the MFDP on the one side and the Mississippi NAACP on the other as a schism between the radical, rural poor and the moderate, urban middle class. However, fellow academic Alan Draper argues, more convincingly, that the MFDP included businesspeople and independent farmers alongside the rural poor and that the division between the MFDP and the NAACP was caused not by class-based ideological differences but primarily by competition for influence and power. By April 1965, the rivalry between SNCC/MFDP and the NAACP had led the state NAACP to withdraw from COFO, with strong encouragement from the association's national office in New York City, which had never liked the local group's involvement. Upset by his support for the compromise, the MFDP excluded Henry from its membership.[46]

Despite the support expressed by Spike and Pratt for the compromise in Atlantic City, there was no breach in the relationship between the NCC and SNCC/MFDP. The National Council's Commission on Religion and Race had played only a minor part in the discussions, and Spike, nursing injuries from a street accident, had been confined to Atlantic City Hospital for much of the convention. Spike tried unsuccessfully in September to mediate among representatives from the national NAACP, the SCLC, CORE, and SNCC at a meeting he called in New York. In the months following the national convention, SNCC and the MFDP directed their anger primarily toward the NAACP and liberal Democrats rather than at the NCC, which had given them substantial aid in the Summer Project. In any case, SNCC and the MFDP had a vested interest in the success of the forthcoming Delta Ministry, which shared a commitment to the poorest and most excluded African Americans. Spike met in Atlanta with Moses and other SNCC activists soon after the convention. Moses hoped to place the Delta Ministry within COFO, but he accepted the NCC's desire for independence.[47]

The leaders of the NCC's white member communions in Mississippi, rather than civil rights forces, provided the greatest potential opposition to the Delta Ministry. In accordance with instructions from the NCC's General Board, the Division of Home Missions had contacted twenty-seven judicatorial officials from the thirteen Mississippi denominations, black and white, affiliated with the NCC. This effort culminated in a meeting with NCC executives in St. Louis in late May 1964 to which all judicatorial heads received invitations. Nine communions, the division reported, expressed unreserved support for the Delta Ministry, and three agreed with its objectives but argued that the NCC was not the proper instrument for their implementation. Only one communion rejected the Ministry outright. The St. Louis meeting concluded that the Delta Ministry's objectives were "both necessary and valid" and that it "should begin with the existing groups that are in favor of the program and seek to involve other groups as it progresses." Aware that opposition to the civil rights movement would prevent some Mississippi judicatories from supporting the Ministry, the NCC decided not to press them for approval since "the risk of rejection is reduced and the Delta Ministry can at least function in a climate of toleration while seeking to maintain a climate in which consultation can continue."[48]

Although John M. Allin, bishop coadjutor of the Episcopal Diocese of Mississippi, had sent a representative to the meeting in St. Louis, Allin subsequently claimed that the NCC had announced the Delta Ministry without consulting the leaders of Mississippi's judicatories. He also complained that the Ministry excluded the state's denominational leaders. Allin was wrong about consultation but correct regarding exclusion from leadership in the Delta Ministry. The National Council's Division of Home Missions took the pragmatic view that to make the Ministry dependent on the approval or under the control of the state's white denominations and their leaders would effectively emasculate, if not doom, the project. Most white Mississippians, as Allin recognized, opposed the civil rights movement and could exert considerable pressure on their denominational leaders and the NCC. Many white Methodist churches stopped contributing to the National Council in protest at the proposed Ministry. In June 1964, the Mississippi Synod of the Presbyterian Church in the United States (PCUS) voted seventy-six to seventy-two to reject a resolution to cut off funds to the NCC because of its plan for a "Mississippi Delta project"; however, the synod then reversed itself and voted to withhold its money from the council. Allin's plea that Mississippi's denominations and churches be permitted to undertake a gradualist approach to improving race relations with NCC support offered little prospect of appreciable progress in ameliorating the everyday lives of African Americans in the state.[49]

Despite Allin's objections, the Delta Ministry officially began on September 1, 1964. Because the Ministry was unable to hire Andrew Young, who chose instead to become the SCLC's executive director, or another "qualified acceptable Negro," Regier initially served as the Delta Ministry's director, with Thomas as his deputy. Within a few months, Thomas received confirmation as director, with McKenna as his assistant. Regier retained administrative control of the program from his New York office in the Division of Home Missions. Negotiations begun in the summer of 1964 to lease Mount Beulah, a disused college near Jackson, from the Disciples of Christ as the Delta Ministry's headquarters dragged on into the new year. Consequently, the Ministry located its first head office in the Delta city of Greenville, Washington County, a site chosen because of the city's relatively progressive image and absence of racial violence. The Delta Ministry's purview encompassed the Delta and Hattiesburg, where the twenty-nine-year-old Reverend Bob Beech, a seminary-educated Presbyterian originally from Minnesota, had codirected the NCC's Hattiesburg Ministers' Project since May after resigning his two pastorates in Illinois.[50]

In late September, the Ministry added McComb in southwest Mississippi to its operations. McComb, SNCC's entry point into Mississippi community organizing in 1961, had been one of COFO's centers during the Summer Project of 1964. The NCC had supplied minister-counselors in July, including twenty-eight-year-old Harry J. Bowie, a black Episcopalian priest from New Jersey who had gone south for the summer as a COFO volunteer. McComb had long been subject to white racial violence. It erupted with particular force in a series of bombings that began in May 1964 and continued through much of the summer. The departure of many of COFO's summer volunteers when the Summer Project ended in late August led to an increase in bombings as racists targeted indigenous leaders in the black community. In response to falling black morale, COFO increased the size and strength of its operation in McComb. Appalled by the violence, the NCC issued an appeal in September for ministers to assist a COFO voter registration drive in the city. Thirty ministers from across the United States, all short-term volunteers, responded immediately. As a result of the emergency, McComb became a project of the Delta Ministry, with Bowie as director because of his experience working in the city.[51]

By October 1964, the Delta Ministry had tentatively begun to take shape, with a budget of $73,760, approved by the Division of Home Missions, for the remainder of the year. It had five staff members. Thomas played a roving role, working with COFO and frequently traveling to the NCC's New York office. McKenna ran the Ministry's headquarters in Greenville, from which the Reverend Larry Walker headed the Greenville Project. Walker, a thirty-five-year-old American Baptist minister from Thomasville, Georgia, had been educated at Mercer University, a white Southern Baptist institution in Macon, where he had helped organize interracial meetings, and at Andover Newton Theological School. After pastoring a church in Massachusetts, he had joined the Intercollegiate YMCA as chaplain to New York University students. The Greenville Project received additional help from Wilmina "Billie" Rowland, a white middle-aged ordained minister, originally from Georgia, who served as a volunteer while on four months' leave from the UPCUSA's Board of Christian Education. However, the Delta Ministry had still to recruit a full complement of staff for the remaining county projects it planned in the Delta. Furthermore, a commission to oversee the Ministry's program had yet to be appointed, and the NCC had not persuaded its member denominations, except the United Church of Christ, to help fund the Ministry's operations, although the WCC raised $48,000 in 1964 from its members.[52]

Despite these problems, Thomas remained confident in the mission of the Delta Ministry, which was to function, in many ways, as a religious equivalent of SNCC. He considered the Delta Ministry to be "challenging," "exciting," and "without parallel in contemporary American religious life." In a passage that reflected the thinking of Colin Williams, Harvey Cox, and Robert Spike, Thomas wrote to Jon Regier, "Understanding that the church is being the Church as it embodies the servant role of its Lord, the Delta Ministry is undertaking the responsibility of mission to a people long-suffering and too long in alienation."[53] The other members of the Ministry's staff shared Thomas's vision of its function as well as his motivation. Asked why he had gone to serve in Mississippi, Beech cited Luke 4:18: "The Spirit of the Lord *is* upon me, because he hath anointed me to preach the gospel to the poor; he hath sent me to heal the brokenhearted, to preach deliverance to the captives, and recovering of sight to the blind, to set at liberty them that are bruised."[54]

The five members of the Delta Ministry staff were similar in other ways. They were, with the exception of Walker, all northerners. Drawn from a range of mainstream Protestant denominations, the clergymen were mostly young; highly educated, with college and seminary degrees; male; and except for Bowie, white. Although the Ministry sought to develop indigenous leadership and expected local people to join its project staff, alongside staff and volunteers from NCC and WCC member denominations, Thomas warned that "We can get hung up trying to balance a staff as to Negro and white for political purposes." To maintain cohesion and purpose, he proposed that the staff members develop a "common discipline" in which they would "come together on a regular basis for worship and for study." In these meetings, they would discuss and increase their understanding of and common commitment to a servant ministry and find strength through communal worship. But, in practice, few such worship or study meetings occurred.[55]

In fact, so oriented did the Delta Ministry become to its role as a mission rather than missionary agency, common religious observation did not become part of its operations. Concerned with providing a practical, servant ministry that met the needs of the poor, the Ministry became a significant civil rights group in Mississippi. The opposition and rejection that it encountered from the state's white churches and denominations in the early years of its operations destroyed the hope of the NCC and Thomas that the Ministry might work with "all people of faith in the Delta" in a ministry of reconciliation and provided a further reason why religion played little overt role in the Delta Ministry's everyday operations and staff activities. The widespread hostility of Mississippi's white churches to desegregation and the civil rights movement and the general reluctance of black Mississippi clergy to support the movement, despite some important exceptions, made all religious but especially white institutions and ideas suspect in the eyes of some civil rights workers despite the religiosity of many black Mississippians. Consequently, the Ministry's staff members were reluctant to discuss or advocate their personal religious beliefs. Generally rejected by white churches, Ministry staff had little outlet through the state's black churches since, as one worker explained, "the black church saw the need for the Delta Ministry, but out of apathy and fear of intimidation gave little response."[56]

By October 1964, the Delta Ministry was under way in Greenville, Hattiesburg, and McComb with a complement of five paid staff members, one volunteer, and a confirmed budget for the remaining months of the year. The Ministry had been created by the NCC in response to suggestions from the civil rights movement and pleas from African Americans in the Delta. And it was made possible by new currents of thought in the WCC and the National Council about the Church's mission that had influenced a new generation of seminary-educated staff who had joined the NCC in the late 1950s and 1960s. Supported by key leaders in the National Council, Regier, Spike, and McCanna constructed a proposal that incorporated many of SNCC's ideas regarding relief, education, self-help, community building, and leadership development. By securing WCC support, maintaining consultations with Mississippi's denominational leaders, and emphasizing the Delta Ministry's commitment to service and reconciliation, NCC leaders managed to secure General Board approval of the Ministry in February 1964, despite misgivings and opposition from white southerners. As the Delta Ministry's programs began to take shape and their potential for bringing radical changes in race relations became increasingly apparent, the Ministry came under severe pressure from its southern opponents but nevertheless endured to become a significant civil rights presence in Mississippi.

CHAPTER TWO

External Relations,
Internal Policy, 1964–1965

In the months before the Delta Ministry's inauguration in September 1964, white Mississippi and southern opposition to the Delta Ministry and the NCC had mounted against the backdrop of the National Council's involvement in COFO's Summer Project. Unable to prevent the Ministry's launch and under pressure from their members, the leaders of Mississippi's white denominations affiliated with the National Council sought, with considerable success and support from other southern religious leaders, to persuade their ruling bodies to starve the Delta Ministry of funds. Underfinanced and heavily dependent on the WCC, a few northern denominations, and funds from the NCC's reserves, the Ministry nevertheless made good progress in facilitating relief for the poor, preschool education, community building, health care, citizenship education, and voter registration. However, the Ministry failed to secure funding from the federal government or charitable foundations for its literacy and economic development programs. Widespread clerical and secular opposition from white Mississippians prevented the Delta Ministry from having much opportunity to achieve reconciliation between the races. Furthermore, its close working relationship with COFO and the MFDP soon alienated some of its early supporters in Mississippi.[1]

John M. Allin, bishop coadjutor of the fourteen-thousand-member Episcopal Diocese of Mississippi, had been the Delta Ministry's most vociferous and influential clerical critic during its planning stage. Despite repeated meetings and correspondence in 1964 with NCC officials and Arthur E. Walmsley, executive secretary of the Protestant Episcopal Church's Division of Christian Citizenship, and an invitation to join a proposed Commission on the Delta Ministry, Allin continued to insist that the NCC had failed to consult him. He argued that the National Council was imposing a program on the state rather than assisting Mississippians in developing a plan and that the NCC's intervention only increased rather than alleviated racial tensions. Allin complained to Henry McCanna, executive director of the NCC's Department of Town and Country, "The project has been ill-defined, ill-planned, ill-timed, and ill-announced." Allin at first contended that most of Mississippi's denominations agreed with him, but when the NCC reminded him that nine of the state's judicatories had expressed support for the Ministry, he could name only two denominational leaders, both white, who shared his opinion. They were Edward J. Pendergrass, the bishop of the Jackson Area who led the state's white Methodists, and M. Maurice Grove, secretary-director of the Mississippi Christian Churches (Disciples of Christ).[2]

Allin made his objections to the Delta Ministry known to the Protestant Episcopal Church's highest officials. His views carried weight in the denomination, not only because the Delta Ministry operated within his diocese but also because Allin could not be dismissed as a segregationist. In accordance with denominational policy, he had asked Mississippi's Episcopal churches not to bar African Americans. In October 1964, the Protestant Episcopal Church's General Convention, which met every three years, commended Allin and his Mississippi coreligionists for their efforts on behalf of "brotherhood which is now embodied in the law of our land." While the General Convention met, Allin asked David R. Hunter, the NCC's deputy general secretary, if the Delta Ministry could be held back and the churches in Mississippi given an opportunity to develop an alternative program that would enlist the support of the state's white population. The bishop coadjutor insisted that he did not oppose the Delta Ministry's goals but contended that there was so much opposition to the NCC in Mississippi that the Ministry could not succeed. It would, he argued, only increase Mississippians' suspicions about the National Council.[3]

At the same time, Arthur C. Lichtenberger, the Protestant Episcopal Church's presiding bishop, informed Ed Espy, the NCC's general secretary, that the denomination could not "support the Delta Ministry in the terms along which it is developing." Accompanying Lichtenberger's letter was a memorandum from Bishop

Daniel Corrigan, director of the Home Department, setting out the denomination's reservations and outlining remedial measures required to secure Episcopal support. The memorandum reflected many of the grievances expressed by Allin, arguing that the Delta Ministry's civil rights work would conflict with the task of community development and complaining that the Ministry had expanded its scope beyond the Delta "to include the whole state." The project, Corrigan charged, lacked an appropriate methodology for its goals, a "properly trained professional leadership," and a set of "priorities of need." Furthermore, the Ministry had been planned without appropriate consultation with experts within and outside the Church. It had not identified "the nature of indigenous leadership and its relationship to volunteers from elsewhere." Episcopal support would be contingent on removing the Delta Ministry from civil rights activity and on the appointment of a task force to secure "competent professional leaders" and to "identify goals, methods, and techniques appropriate" for the project. Until then, the Ministry should be held in abeyance, with no volunteers "recruited or programs initiated."[4]

Stunned by the Protestant Episcopal Church's severe criticisms, Jon Regier, executive secretary of the NCC's Division of Home Missions, postponed the establishment of the Commission on the Delta Ministry that would serve as the Ministry's governing body. The normally diplomatic Regier wrote to Corrigan that his complaints were "invalid and unfair." Regier questioned whether civil rights could be separated from community development in Mississippi and wrote that until that issue was settled, it would be inappropriate to create a task force. While the Delta Ministry would not be stopped, Regier promised that it would "avoid major directional commitments" until the Division of Home Missions had held a special meeting with Episcopalian representatives to discuss their reservations and recommendations. The meeting was set for November 9 under the auspices of the division's Policy and Strategy Committee.[5]

Allin followed up his approach to Hunter at the General Convention by suggesting that the NCC send a delegation to Jackson, Mississippi, to discuss the Delta Ministry with "a representative group" of white and African American church and lay leaders. Allin hoped that in the interim, the NCC would withdraw the Delta Ministry and that after the meeting, the National Council would replace the Ministry with a program under the control of Mississippi churchmen assisted by the NCC.[6]

Hunter took Allin's suggestion to the November 9 meeting of the Policy and Strategy Committee, which decided that the Delta Ministry should proceed and that a Commission on the Delta Ministry should be established to provide direction and priorities for its program. The Ministry would focus primarily on the Delta, but its activities would not be rigidly confined by geography. The committee concluded that the distinction between civil rights work and community development was largely false. The civil rights work with which the Delta Ministry would be concerned, such "as education about voter registration, freedom schools, literacy education, and the development of community centers," was intrinsically part of community development. Confusion had arisen since "it turned out that in the minds of some, civil rights activity meant chiefly direct confrontations and demonstrations." The meeting's attendees agreed that the Delta Ministry's "point of entry" should be those it intended to serve, "particularly the impoverished people in the Delta area and specifically the Negroes in the area." The committee recognized that the NCC had "established deeply significant relationships" with the black community and accepted Allin's suggestion for a meeting with representative church leaders in Mississippi as a means of building on these connections and creating others.[7]

Hunter conveyed the meeting's decisions to Allin, who thus learned of the defeat of his efforts to scuttle the Delta Ministry. A heated exchange of letters between Allin and Hunter followed, with Allin repeatedly charging the NCC with failure to consult Mississippians. He also threatened to take his grievances to the press. In reply, Hunter listed the many occasions when Allin had been consulted about the Ministry and its development. Hunter also noted that Allin had refused to serve on the Commission on the Delta Ministry. Rebuffed, Allin denied that he had called for the NCC to end the Delta Ministry and replace it with a program under local church control. He agreed to make plans for a meeting between state denominational leaders and the NCC, but, in the meantime, he and other southern white Episcopal leaders pursued alternative means of undermining the Delta Ministry.[8]

The bishop coadjutor made several protests to Episcopal leaders about Warren McKenna's appointment to the Ministry and attempted to have him removed. Since the late 1940s, McKenna had supported many civil liberties and peace causes. Against the advice of the U.S. State Department, he had visited communist China with a party of students in 1957. Allin later claimed that he did not oppose McKenna's past actions but was concerned that the press might use them to discredit the Ministry. Supported, as McKenna noted, by "allies in the South as well as [by] unknowing and fearful Northern churchmen," Allin's protests led the Executive Council of the Protestant Episcopal Church to seek McKenna's dismissal from the Ministry. The attempt failed. Following a detailed study of his record, the denomination's Division of Christian Citizenship exonerated McKenna. But the issue of his past was to surface in the Mississippi press a few months later and provide further ammunition for the Ministry's opponents.[9]

Allin's efforts to undermine the Delta Ministry received a boost in December 1964. Southern members of the Executive Council of the Protestant Episcopal Church introduced and the council passed a resolution that no priest could work in a diocese with any group supported by the denomination's Church and Race Fund without the prior approval of the bishop of that diocese. Designed to aid Allin, the resolution gave him the power to block the Ministry's continued employment of McKenna and Harry Bowie and its recruitment of any other Episcopal clergy as staff or volunteers. Nearly half of the Council's members at the December meeting had been newly elected and were attending their first meeting. Many of them said that they had allowed the resolution to pass in the erroneous belief that they had been helping rather than undermining civil rights work. Over the opposition of its southern members, the Executive Council rescinded its action when it next met in February 1965. The denomination's new presiding bishop, John E. Hines, a South Carolinian who was an outspoken advocate of civil rights, encouraged the move. At the same time, the Executive Council voted to make the denomination's first financial contribution to the Delta Ministry, twenty thousand dollars.[10]

Many denominations were extremely reluctant to commit funds to the Ministry, leaving it heavily dependent on the wcc. In 1964, the World Council contributed $48,000 to the Delta Ministry's $73,760 budget. U.S. denominations provided $11,178, with $10,000 of this amount donated by the United Church of Christ and the rest given mostly by individual upcusa churches. Although the Ministry sought $415,000 in 1965, the ncc's General Board set the budget at $260,000, of which member denominations were asked to furnish 60 percent and the wcc's members were asked to provide 40 percent. But World Council denominations gave only 20.5 percent of the proposed $260,000 budget ($53,385) in 1965, after their large donation the previous year, and U.S. denominations contributed only 43 percent ($113,041), despite having given so little in 1964. Southern white opposition to the Delta Ministry inhibited contributions from overwhelmingly southern denominations, such as the pcus, or denominations with large southern contingents, such as the Methodist Church (which had 37 percent of its members in the South). The denominations that gave the largest donations to the project, the upcusa ($40,000) and the United Church of Christ ($37,000), had southern memberships of 5 percent and 6 percent, respectively. Many other denominations, even predominantly northern ones, did not contribute at all because of caution induced by southern white criticism of the Ministry. African American denominations gave nothing to the Delta Ministry during its first two years, while denominations from Australia, Europe, Asia, and Africa contributed $101,385 through the wcc during the same period.[11]

White southerners exhibited great hostility to the NCC because of its tradition of making progressive pronouncements on social issues, particularly race relations, and its civil rights activities. Denominational officials in the PCUS and the Methodist Church refused to support the Delta Ministry for fear that it would lead southern churches to stop contributing to the National Council. In April 1964, all three of the PCUS's presbyteries in Mississippi, which had a combined membership of 35,774, had asked the denomination's General Assembly to cut off funds to the NCC because of its planned involvement in the Delta and Mississippi. Although the assembly refused this request and recommended greater Presbyterian funding for the National Council, the body also adopted a report that called some of the civil rights activities of the NCC's Commission on Religion and Race "ill advised." The commission, the report argued, should consult and work with local ministers to solve "racial tensions." The report noted growing opposition to the NCC and the WCC among Presbyterians. James A. Millard Jr., the PCUS's stated clerk, or highest administrative official, feared that individual churches and presbyteries and ultimately the General Assembly would stop contributing to the National Council because of the Delta Ministry. Indeed, several Mississippi churches and then the state's presbyteries and the Synod of Mississippi declined to fund the NCC because of its sponsorship of the Ministry.[12]

Patrick D. Miller, executive secretary of the PCUS's Board of Church Extension, opposed the Delta Ministry in meetings of the NCC's Division of Home Missions. Much like Allin, T. Watson Street, executive secretary of the PCUS's Board of World Missions, complained in *Presbyterian Outlook,* the denomination's monthly magazine, that the NCC had failed to consult about the Ministry and that it had been imposed on Mississippi. Street's accusations were as groundless as those made by Allin. Although Miller had been invited to an early discussion about the project at LeMoyne College in Memphis in November 1963, neither he nor any official from the PCUS had attended. The NCC had also consulted with Mississippi judicatories on several occasions in 1964.[13]

With the Delta Ministry under way for nearly eight months, the PCUS's Standing Committee on Christian Relations firmly endorsed the project as "in the finest tradition of Christian love for one's neighbor" in an April 1965 report to the General Assembly. However, the delegates to the assembly voted by 228 to 111 to refer the statement to the assembly's Permanent Committee on Inter-Church Relations for study and a recommendation at the denomination's next General Assembly. William F. Winter, the Mississippi state treasurer, led the call for the investigation into the Delta Ministry. Pending the committee's recommendation, the PCUS provided no funding for the Ministry except for small amounts contributed by individual churches.[14]

The Methodist Church also provided no financial assistance for the Delta Ministry, but as the largest denomination in the NCC, with ten million members, this support was badly needed. Pressure from its southern constituency, and particularly from within Mississippi, dissuaded the Church from funding the Ministry during the first two years of its operation. In July 1964, the Southeastern Jurisdictional Conference of the Methodist Church, representing white Methodists in nine states, passed a resolution that praised the NCC's "many constructive cooperative endeavors." However, it also rebuked the National Council for having "irresponsible administrative procedures" that allowed it to act "without first consulting and conferring with local leadership of the member Protestant churches in the areas to be affected."[15]

More than two hundred Methodist churches in Mississippi voted to stop their financial support of the NCC in 1964, and many called on the Methodist Church to withdraw from the National Council. The state's two white Methodist conferences, the Mississippi and North Mississippi Conferences, appointed committees to investigate the NCC and report in 1965. Further pressure came from the Mississippi Association of Methodist Ministers and Laymen (MAMML), a segregationist group formed in 1955, which sought to withdraw white congregations from the Methodist Church and establish a new Methodist church in the South. Although MAMML included only between 3,000 and 5,000 of Mississippi's 185,000 white Methodists, the group's influence exceeded its numbers. The organization was highly critical of the national Methodist Church for its support of church integration and its attempts to dismantle the all-black Central Jurisdiction and integrate African American churches into white geographical jurisdictions. MAMML fiercely denounced the NCC and its support for the COFO Summer Project and the Delta Ministry.[16]

Marvin A. Franklin, Pendergrass's predecessor as Methodist bishop of the Jackson Area, had sought to avoid controversy. He refused to press for church desegregation after the General Conference, the Methodist Church's ruling national body, made that the official policy in May 1964, and he also offered no leadership to Methodists who opposed MAMML. As protests mounted against the NCC and the Delta Ministry, Franklin wrote to Methodist B. F. Smith, executive vice president of the Delta Council, which represented the region's planters, that he had not been kept informed about the NCC's plans in Mississippi. In fact, McCanna told Pendergrass, who became bishop in July 1964, that his predecessor had been "of good assistance in helping to evaluate the situation in Mississippi."[17]

In their many resolutions and complaints against the NCC, Mississippi's white Methodist churches frequently argued that the National Council's work in their state should not proceed without consultation with and consent from "the leaders of the Churches in Mississippi" and that the NCC was largely ignoring established churches in the Delta. In making such arguments, white Methodists neglected the fact that there were African American churches and judicatories that supported the Delta Ministry. The whites also did not understand that under its constitution, the NCC could not work directly with local churches. Ordinarily, it worked through state and local councils of churches. However, no such councils existed in Mississippi. Consequently, the NCC relied on contacting the leaders of the judicatories of its member denominations in the state. The National Council undertook substantial efforts to consult with and inform Methodist leaders about the Delta Ministry, but McCanna could not consult individual churches.[18]

However, McCanna did meet with Methodist officials during visits to Mississippi in 1963 and 1964. As he wrote to one of the NCC's Delta critics, "I have made several trips to the Delta and talked with as many local people as time would allow (including all of the interboard staff at Grenada [the executive body of the North Mississippi Conference], the Methodist pastor at Greenwood, your newspaper editor Hal De Cell [*Deer Creek Pilot*], and a lawyer in Greenville—to name just a few." He explained that most of the people he had met requested that "I not call attention to such visits," which gave the erroneous impression that the Delta Ministry "had been concocted from afar."[19]

In September 1964, McCanna and NCC staff members met in Cleveland, Mississippi, with John D. Humphrey, executive secretary of the North Mississippi Conference Interboard Council, and other leaders from the conference, which covered most of the Delta. Leading local Methodist clergy and laymen also attended. Although MAMML claimed that local ministers said nothing during the meeting, B. F. Smith stated that "Delta laymen and ministers . . . advised against orienting the Delta Ministry program with COFO, SNCC, or other 'radically oriented' organizations that were active in the area." Therein lay the crux of the problem: it was not that white Mississippi clergy and lay leaders had not been consulted and informed about the Ministry but that many of them simply did not support its approach and goals.[20]

A day after the meeting in Cleveland, McCanna met with Bishop Pendergrass in Jackson and reported that the meeting proved "helpful." However, Pendergrass was determined to prevent the national Methodist Church from funding the Delta Ministry. Consequently, he approved the creation of the Mississippi Methodist Ministry (MMM) in February 1965, a collaborative effort supported by the state's four African American and white Methodist conferences. Under the MMM program, two white Mississippi sisters, Louise and Mathilde Killingsworth, who had returned to the state after years of missionary service in Malaya, worked in Clarksdale to assist black Methodist churches in "Christian education, leadership training, and church extension" and to improve communication between black and white Methodists. With the program sponsored by the Methodist Church's National Division of Board of Missions, Pendergrass saw the MMM as a means of keeping Methodist funding from the Delta Ministry by channeling money into a state-run Methodist alternative. The bishop's strategy, alongside sustained Mississippi opposition to the Delta Ministry and the NCC, dissuaded the Methodist Church from contributing to the Ministry during 1965.[21]

M. Maurice Grove and members of the Mississippi Christian Churches were as opposed to the Delta Ministry as white Mississippi Methodists, but, unlike Pendergrass, Grove and his allies could not prevent their national organization from helping the Delta Ministry as it struggled to establish itself. The NCC began negotiations in the summer of 1964 to lease Mount Beulah from the United Christian Missionary Society (UCMS) of the Disciples of Christ. The National Council intended to use the twenty-three-acre site in Edwards, twenty-seven miles from Jackson, as a headquarters during the Summer Project and then transfer the facility to the Delta Ministry for its use. However, the UCMS's Board of Trustees, which controlled the site, was not prepared to lease Mount Beulah until September. Consequently, the Delta Ministry had to locate its headquarters in the Delta city of Greenville. Unable to find an alternative site for a conference center, in October the NCC reopened negotiations with the UCMS to lease Mount Beulah.[22]

Opposition to the NCC's role in the Summer Project and to the Delta Ministry led the majority of Mississippi's Christian Churches to withdraw financial support from the National Council. In November 1964, Grove and representatives from twenty-one of the state's Christian Churches raised their objections to leasing Mount Beulah to the Ministry at a meeting hosted by Jackson's First Christian Church. Disciples of Christ national officials and Jon Regier and Art Thomas, the Delta Ministry's director, also attended the meeting. As a result, the Disciples' national leaders allowed representatives from the First Christian Church to present their objections to the lease when it was considered for approval by the UCMS's Board of Trustees in January 1965. Despite a strong plea from Sutton Marks, chairman of the board of First Christian Church and a Mississippi state legislator, the UCMS agreed, with one dissenting vote, to lease the site to the NCC for five years for a nominal sum. The State Board of the Mississippi Christian Churches responded by passing a resolution in protest.[23]

The hostility of many white Mississippians and their religious leaders to the Delta Ministry presented the NCC with great difficulty in recruiting indigenous whites for the Commission on the Delta Ministry. Opposition to the Ministry from Bishop Allin and also for a time from the Protestant Episcopal Church's national leadership delayed the establishment of the commission, which did not meet until January 1965. Thomas devised most of the principles under which the commission operated. Its function was to advise Delta Ministry staff regarding policy and strategy. The commission would report directly to the NCC's newly created Division of Christian Life and Mission, which replaced the Division of Home Missions and was, like its predecessor, headed by Regier. The commission's membership was, Thomas wrote, to "be composed of those who by technical competence, specialized skills, or by residence have a direct relationship to the project." Commission members were to meet at least twice a year, with more frequent meetings of an executive committee drawn from the commission's ranks.[24]

In December 1964, the NCC appointed Paul Moore Jr., the suffragan bishop of the Episcopal Diocese of Washington, D.C., as chairman of the commission. Born to a wealthy East Coast family in 1919, Moore had been brought up with a sense of noblesse oblige. Educated at Yale, he had volunteered for the Marines before the Japanese attack on Pearl Harbor. Moore saw combat at Guadalcanal and received both the Silver Star and the Navy Cross. Acting on a long-felt desire, he entered the priesthood after the war. In 1949, Moore became pastor of Grace Church in Jersey City, New Jersey, where he created a social outreach ministry and recruited African Americans to the congregation. The injustice he saw blacks face in Jersey City led Moore to donate a large sum to the NAACP Legal Defense and Educational Fund, Inc. In 1951, the NAACP invited Moore to join a team it was sending to defend three African Americans accused of raping a white woman in Groveland, Florida. Moore likened the atmosphere he encountered there to that of "a police state." The three men had confessed under police torture and been convicted. They were subsequently murdered on their way to a retrial ordered by the Supreme Court. Moore recalled, "This was a turning point in my life. Never again would I trust the American system when it was dealing with African Americans."[25]

After serving for nearly six years as dean and rector of Christ Church Cathedral, Indianapolis, Moore was consecrated suffragan bishop of Washington, D.C., in January 1964. Later that year, he served one week as an NCC volunteer in Mississippi with the Summer Project. Moore visited ministers' projects in Hattiesburg, where he met Bob Beech, and McComb, which, like Hattiesburg, became part of the Delta Ministry. Moore's awareness of racial injustice, sympathy for the civil rights movement, and high office made him an obvious choice for the chairmanship of the Commission on the Delta Ministry. Explaining his acceptance, Moore wrote, "God is working through this [civil rights] movement, and it would be a blasphemy for the Church to stand outside of it."[26]

When Moore accepted the chairmanship, the commission had still not recruited a full complement of members, but the task was completed by late January 1965. In addition to Moore, the biracial, ecumenical commission had twenty-two members, five of them resident in Mississippi and another five living in the ten other states of the old Confederacy. The Mississippi residents included two African Americans: Aaron Henry, the state president of the NAACP who had invited the NCC to Clarksdale in 1963; and Marian Wright, a young Yale-educated lawyer from South Carolina who had joined the Jackson office of the NAACP Legal Defense and Educational Fund in 1964. The white Mississippians included one churchman, John Humphrey, the leading Methodist official in the Delta. The remaining Mississippians, Hodding Carter III and Ruth Brent, were both residents of Greenville, a Delta town renowned for its comparative moderation and lack of racist violence. Carter, an Episcopalian, had become editor of the *Delta Democrat-Times* in 1960, succeeding his father, who had won a Pulitzer Prize in 1946 for editorials "on the subject of racial, religious, and economic intolerance." Young Hodding continued his father's tradition of moderation and adopted a gradualist approach to racial change. Brent was a devout Methodist who believed that "we are all God's children." She served on the board of directors of the Mississippi Council on Human Relations.[27]

Prominent among the non-Mississippians who served on the commission were Harvey Cox, Gayraud S. Wilmore Jr., Dr. H. Jack Geiger, and W. Ray Kyle. Cox was a professor at Andover Newton Theological School in Massachusetts whose ideas about the Church's mission in the world had been influential in the Delta Ministry's creation. Wilmore, an African American, was executive director of the UPCUSA's Commission on Religion and Race, which had begun the Hattiesburg Ministers' Project in January 1964 before turning it over to the NCC. Geiger, a faculty member at the Harvard School of Public Health, served on the Medical Committee for Human Rights (MCHR), which had been founded with Art Thomas's participation in July 1964 to provide health care for civil rights workers. Kyle, director of Material Aid Services for the Brethren Service Commission, had extensive experience in relief services. The Commission on the Delta Ministry also included Bryant George, an African American who served as director of internal operations and administration at the UPCUSA's Board of National Missions, and Mae Yoho Ward, vice president of the UCMS, who, like Bishop Moore, had been a volunteer in Hattiesburg during the Summer Project. The Commission did not seek or provide representation for all of the NCC's denominations; rather, its members were chosen because of the "tremendous contributions [they had] made in the field of Race."[28]

Robert Spike, executive director of the NCC's Commission on Religion and Race, which had played a major part in the creation of the Delta Ministry, addressed the commission's first meeting in January 1965. Spike affirmed that the "Freedom Democratic Party in Mississippi is the factor in the national picture which represents the Negroes['] reactions in Mississippi." The Ministry, which shared Spike's view, had worked with the MFDP in voter registration campaigns in Hattiesburg and McComb. Delta Ministry staff and volunteers had also canvassed African Americans to vote for the party's congressional candidates, who opposed incumbent white Democrats in a Freedom Vote that paralleled the official election in November 1964. Although they had been defeated in the earlier Democratic Party primary elections, MFDP candidates overwhelmingly won the mock election. Three of the five MFDP candidates, Fannie Lou Hamer, Victoria Gray, and Annie Devine, decided to contest the election of Democratic congressmen from their districts on the grounds that most African Americans were disenfranchised and thereby excluded from the official ballot. Two weeks before the Commission on the Delta Ministry met, the three women took their challenge to the U.S. House of Representatives, where they demanded that Congress seat them in place of the incumbents. Spike's commission and the Delta Ministry endorsed the challenge to the congressmen, which lasted through the summer before finally being defeated in the House of Representatives in September by a vote of 228 to 143.[29]

In addition to the Delta Ministry's work in voter registration and in support of the MFDP, the commission's first meeting also reviewed the Ministry's progress in other aspects of its program areas of relief, community and economic development, and reconciliation. Although the Ministry had operated projects in Hattiesburg, McComb, and Greenville and their surrounding counties since its inauguration in September, insufficient staffing had prevented it from creating county projects elsewhere. Ray Kyle had initiated a pilot relief project in December 1964. The United Church of Christ, the Disciples of Christ, and the Church of the Brethren had collected food and clothing in three northern states, and the Delta Ministry had distributed the donations in Greenville, Clarksdale, and Issaquena County.[30]

Apart from its Greenville, Hattiesburg, and McComb projects, the Ministry's efforts in community development remained tentative. In October 1964, the NCC's Division of Home Missions had authorized negotiations with the New York–based Diebold Group, Inc., to supply the Delta Ministry with instructional materials for a basic literacy course, contingent on the Ministry securing adequate funding from foundations or federal government sources. Art Thomas told the Commission on the Delta Ministry in January 1965 that the literacy project would cost $250,000. Although both the federal government and the Ford Foundation had been approached for funding, neither had yet replied. A further problem was that Mount Beulah, where the Ministry intended to have Diebold staff train black Mississippians as literacy instructors, had still not been leased from the UCMS.[31]

Related to community development was the issue of proper medical care for African Americans in a state that had only fifty black doctors. The MCHR, which had expanded its interests to encompass African American health issues, worked closely with the Delta Ministry, serving as its health program in the state. Jack Geiger reported in January 1965 that the MCHR had two nurses in Mississippi, one in Hattiesburg and the other in Holmes County, which lay partly in the Delta. The group also had a medical director, Dr. Robert Smith, an African American who practiced in Jackson. Geiger had raised twenty-three thousand dollars for the medical program, which the Delta Ministry included in its budget. The commission agreed to expand the program to include the purchase of a mobile clinic and the hiring of additional nurses, who would operate primarily in Holmes County, providing care and facilitating the "organization of a county health improvement association to conduct demonstration clinics and to put pressure on the county and state for expanded, non-discriminatory health programs."[32]

The Delta Ministry had made little or no progress by January 1965 in the remaining parts of its mandate, economic development and reconciliation. Its efforts to work with the white community and with white churches and denominational leaders had been almost entirely rebuffed. Although John Humphrey had agreed to serve on the Commission on the Delta Ministry, he did not attend its first meeting or become an active member.[33]

In early March 1965, a meeting occurred between African American and white denominational leaders from Mississippi and other southern states and a contingent from the NCC and the Commission on the Delta Ministry. Bishop Allin, who had suggested the meeting in November 1964, invited fourteen denominational officials, telling them that the meeting would seek to determine whether the NCC's function was to help member churches coordinate their efforts in programs of their own making or whether the National Council could "launch independently specific projects in its own name." Allin, of course, held the former view. At the meeting, to which eleven judicatories sent representatives, he attacked the Delta Ministry as being a copy of COFO. The rift between Mississippi's white denominational leaders and the Ministry remained unaltered. Allin subsequently wrote in his diary, "To me there is still a lack of communication and coordination. It is apparent that the N.C.C.C., has chosen 'a side.' Their role is one-sided." Thomas subsequently invited Allin and Pendergrass to the next meeting of the Commission on the Delta Ministry, but they did not attend and remained determined opponents of the Ministry.[34]

The Mississippi and North Mississippi Conferences of the Methodist Church heard reports in June 1965 from their study committees on the NCC, which cleared the National Council of its most extreme opponents' charges of communism. However, the Mississippi Conference's report criticized the NCC for encouraging direct action protest and concluded that the council contained "a mixture of good and bad."[35]

The North Mississippi Conference attacked the Delta Ministry as "ill-conceived because no practical research undergirds its efforts." The conference also criticized the Ministry for working with COFO and claimed that the NCC had insufficiently consulted with white Methodist leaders in Mississippi and that the National Council had merely delineated its "plans and programs" rather than seeking cooperation. Nevertheless, the report conceded that the conference shared the blame for poor communication between Methodists and the NCC: "The participation of the white Methodist Church in the meetings within Mississippi was entirely lacking" because the whites had refused to collaborate. "These meetings," it continued, "were not successful because of lack of cooperation from leadership of the North Mississippi Conference." Hostility from the Conference's churches had "contributed to the association of the National Council of Churches with the Negro churches and explains the reason why meetings were held in Negro churches rather than in white churches."[36]

Nevertheless, the opposition of Mississippi's white Methodists and their state leaders to the Delta Ministry continued unabated. Garland H. "Bo" Holloman, superintendent of the New Albany District of the North Mississippi Conference, complained to Grover C. Bagby, associate general secretary of the Methodist Church's Division of Human Relations and Economic Affairs, that the Delta Ministry was not Christian and that it ignored the white community. Holloman lambasted the Ministry for "irresponsibly" trying to overturn Mississippi's economic system. Francis B. Stevens, lay leader of the Mississippi Conference, wrote to Bagby that the Delta Ministry had failed to communicate with local denominational leaders. He accused the Ministry of "far left" extremism for supporting the MFDP and of "seeking to destroy the existing governmental and economic structure" of Mississippi. Stevens also complained that the Ministry identified only with the black poor.[37]

Bishop Pendergrass, with whom Stevens frequently corresponded about the Delta Ministry, echoed Stevens's comments in letters to Ed Espy. Pendergrass also asked the NCC to investigate the Ministry. The bishop told Humphrey, who attended only one meeting of the Commission on the Delta Ministry, that the

Ministry was "a political football to agitate and destroy everything that we stand for." Pendergrass consistently refused to meet with Delta Ministry staff. He told two thousand white Methodists who had gathered in Jackson for the Mississippi Methodist Action Crusade, "I'm just as much opposed to the Delta Ministry as you are and I have been from the beginning." Many of Mississippi's Methodist churches continued to exclude the NCC from their budgets.[38]

The detractors were correct that the Delta Ministry sought to change Mississippi's economic and political system and that the Ministry identified with the aspirations and needs of the black poor and with the MFDP, which claimed to represent them. However, what these critics regarded as dangerously revolutionary the Ministry saw simply as "the democratizing of an oligarchic, paternalistic political and social system" that had long denied African Americans equal opportunities, particularly in the Delta. Although the Ministry sought to foster conciliation with the white population, its first priority was the black community and its most impoverished members. Furthermore, the white community and its religious leaders had repeatedly rebuffed the Ministry's efforts to work with them.[39]

The Delta Ministry's critics were particularly incensed by its support for an African American picket of Greenville Mill, a carpet factory, beginning in January 1965. Some Ministry personnel joined the pickets, who protested against the plant's refusal to hire black women and its restriction of black men to the lowest-paying jobs. Francis Stevens accused the Ministry of trying to "wreck the economy" of Greenville and compared its tactics with those of the segregationist Citizens' Councils, which had used economic boycotts against their opponents.[40]

Hodding Carter III, who had been an early supporter and defender of the Delta Ministry, attacked the Ministry editorially when the picket was extended to the home of the mill's manager, W. T. Wilcox, and when the picketers marched through a police line. Carter later claimed that Ministry staff "want revolutionary change, of a kind which goes far beyond the question of an equal chance for all men." Before the year was out, the editor had left the Commission on the Delta Ministry without ever attending its meetings. Carter, like his father, had been accustomed to speaking out on behalf of African Americans against racial discrimination and intolerance. He could not adjust to a situation in which blacks, aside from Greenville's African American middle class, which adopted a gradualist approach to change akin to his own, could represent themselves and pursue their own more radical and immediate challenges to racial inequality.[41]

Aaron Henry, who shared Carter's predilection for conciliation and was prepared to compromise along the road to equality, also left the commission. Henry had become estranged from the MFDP since he had supported and most of its delegation rejected the compromise offered by the Johnson administration at the Democratic Party's August 1964 national convention. Subsequently, Henry's NAACP and the COFO-MFDP coalition became rivals for the support of Mississippi's black community. Although the Delta Ministry sometimes worked with local chapters of the NAACP, it aligned itself with COFO and the MFDP in the belief that they best represented Mississippi's black poor, who formed most of the state's African American population. Paul Moore reported to the NCC's Division of Christian Life and Mission in June 1965 that "the Freedom Democratic Party . . . is the banner under which the local people are gathered. FDP represents to them their own indigenous, autonomous organization which reflects their own hopes and aspirations."[42]

When Henry and Carter left the Commission on the Delta Ministry, they were replaced by MFDP members Unita Blackwell and Fannie Lou Hamer. Moore and the Delta Ministry overestimated the degree of African American support for the MFDP and too easily dismissed the support that the NAACP enjoyed in the state. The Ministry largely accepted the MFDP's view that the NAACP was conservative in its goals and tactics and was concerned with the middle class to the exclusion of the poor. Although there was considerable truth to the MFDP's allegations, the NAACP was more diverse than its rival acknowledged. Despite the support it received from the Delta Ministry in its project areas, statewide the MFDP lacked strong local organization and the support necessary to justify its claim to represent Mississippi's black population.[43]

The Commission on the Delta Ministry's second meeting occurred at Mount Beulah, now under NCC control. The Ministry assigned Alfred R. Winham and his wife, Margery, to manage the site. A white New Yorker, Winham had resigned his United Church of Christ pastorate in Holyoke, Massachusetts, to join the Delta Ministry after a career spent pastoring churches in the northeast. At fifty-five, he was the oldest member of the Ministry's staff. Energetic and outspoken, Al Winham, accompanied by Margery, had served as an NCC minister-counselor in Moss Point and Pascagoula during the Summer Project in 1964. The Winhams eagerly embraced the opportunity to return to the state, spending two months with the Delta Ministry in Greenville before moving to Mount Beulah.[44]

In a poor state of repair and stripped bare by hostile members of the Mississippi Disciples of Christ before its handover, Mount Beulah required three months of expensive repairs and renovation. It became the Delta Ministry's headquarters and was intended to accommodate the Ministry's major summer 1965 training programs, including the Diebold literacy project, a Freedom Corps of young Mississippians, the newly formed Child Development Group of Mississippi (CDGM), and citizenship education. Mount Beulah's central location and the programs it conducted helped make the Delta Ministry more of a statewide organization. The Ministry also filled a vacuum left by the gradual withdrawal of SNCC and CORE from the state after COFO dissolved itself and turned over its resources to the MFDP in July 1965. Almost by default, the Delta Ministry became a major civil rights group in Mississippi.[45]

The unavailability of Mount Beulah had been one of the stumbling blocks in implementing Diebold's program of training Delta blacks to serve as literacy instructors in their communities. However, the company refused to begin operations until it had refined the system, a process it projected would take eighteen months. Consequently, the Ministry sought a grant from the federal government to fund the completion of Diebold's research and a demonstration project in Mississippi. Anxious to support a program ready for immediate implementation, the federal Office of Economic Opportunity (OEO) preferred instead to fund an alternative program, STAR, Inc., sponsored by the Catholic Diocese of Natchez-Jackson. The Delta Ministry approached OEO for funding again in January 1966, as STAR still had not implemented the literacy training component of its program six months after receiving a seven-million-dollar grant. Rebuffed once more by OEO, the Ministry, which had also failed to attract foundation grants for the Diebold program, had to abandon literacy training.[46]

However, the Ministry succeeded in creating a Freedom Corps of nineteen young black male and female Mississippians who served as community organizers in seven Delta and adjacent counties, Pike and Amite Counties in the southwestern part of the state, and Leake County in central Mississippi. The Delta Ministry chose the Freedom Corps from sixty-six applicants who underwent training at Mount Beulah in April and July 1965. Curtis Hayes, the Freedom Corps director, was a twenty-three-year-old native of Summit, near McComb, who had joined SNCC in 1961, when it began organizing in southwest Mississippi. Paid subsistence, Freedom Corps members made a one-year commitment and lived in the communities to which the Delta Ministry assigned them. However, they did not represent the Ministry. Instead, they worked with local people, regardless of affiliation, who sought their rights as citizens. Inevitably, some Freedom Corps workers were more effective than others. As a group, they partially offset the loss of field activists that resulted when SNCC and CORE workers either withdrew from the state or lapsed into inactivity during the summer of 1965. In some places that few COFO workers had visited, such as Yazoo County, Freedom Corps workers broke new ground.[47]

Apart from training the Freedom Corps, Mount Beulah also hosted an orientation program in July 1965 for the staff of the CDGM, a Head Start program funded by the OEO to prepare deprived preschoolers for entry into the education system.

Art Thomas and the Delta Ministry had played a central role in CDGM's creation.[48]

In early 1965, the Delta Ministry had found a recurring interest in day care services among community center workers in Mississippi. In March, Thomas met with Tom Levin, a New York psychoanalyst who had helped to found the MCHR, and other northern professionals and academics. The group discussed creating a small program of day care centers for the children of civil rights workers. Polly Greenberg, an OEO official in Washington, D.C., also attended the meeting, at Levin's invitation. Greenberg had contacted Levin to see whether he knew of any poor people in Mississippi who might be interested in the Head Start program. At Greenberg's request, Thomas agreed that the Delta Ministry would disseminate information about Head Start among poor communities. In April, the Ministry organized a statewide meeting at Mount Beulah to which more than twenty communities sent delegations that registered their interest in Head Start. The delegations formed CDGM to coordinate their approach. Sixty-four communities sent representatives to a second meeting at Mount Beulah in mid-April and, with assistance from the Delta Ministry, applied for OEO funds.[49]

OEO granted nearly $1.5 million to CDGM to operate Head Start centers during the summer. To place the grant outside the veto power of the state governor, the money was dispensed through Mary Holmes Junior College, an African American institution supported by the UPCUSA in West Point in northeastern Mississippi. Thomas persuaded D. I. Horn, the college's president, to accept the arrangement after George Owens, the acting president of Tougaloo College, had refused.[50]

Although CDGM received $3,100 in start-up aid from the Delta Ministry as well as assistance from Ministry staff, and although Thomas served on the Head Start group's board of directors, CDGM became an independent group with its own policies and administration. CDGM paid the Delta Ministry rent for its headquarters and staff housing at Mount Beulah and paid the Ministry to provide room and board for staff attending CDGM orientation sessions at the site. CDGM illustrated the Ministry's operating method of helping to initiate projects and achieving community mobilization without seeking to dominate or claim credit. Once CDGM began operations, the Ministry receded into the background while maintaining its interest and staff support both at Mount Beulah and in its county projects.[51]

CDGM was a very successful program that although open to whites attracted primarily African Americans. It operated eighty-four centers in twenty-four counties, enrolled six thousand children, and employed 1,100 people, most of them local black women, as teacher aides and trainees. Children received health care, nutritious meals, and educational support. However, U.S. Senator John C. Stennis of Mississippi opposed the program because it employed many people connected with the civil rights movement, bypassed state authorities by channeling money directly to the poor, and provided black people with better paying jobs than white employers did. Stennis, a member of the powerful Senate Appropriations Committee, on which OEO depended for funding and on which President Johnson relied for financing for the war in Vietnam, sent a team of investigators to scrutinize CDGM. Stennis's team alleged that the program misappropriated funds, lacked proper accounting procedures, and spent money on civil rights activity by CDGM staff in violation of the terms of its grant. The investigators also accused the Delta Ministry of overcharging CDGM for the orientation program because the Ministry had charged the group twice the daily rate it had asked from the MFDP when it held a conference at Mount Beulah. Stennis claimed that the Ministry used the excess received from CDGM to subsidize MFDP demonstrations in Jackson.[52]

Both CDGM and the Delta Ministry vigorously challenged these accusations, which were reiterated by OEO after conducting its own audit in July 1965. The Ministry argued that it had charged CDGM half the standard rate set by OEO and that it had billed the MFDP at an even lower rate to reflect ability to pay. CDGM was guilty of poor record keeping and inadequate administration, thereby making it difficult for either CDGM or the Delta Ministry effectively to refute Stennis's allegations. CDGM had also improperly recorded as bail money salary advances it had made to staff members arrested for participating in MFDP protests during their free time. The capital's leading newspapers, the *Jackson Clarion-Ledger* and the *Jackson Daily News*, both staunch opponents of the civil rights movement, eagerly reported Stennis's charges and demanded CDGM's eviction from Mount Beulah. The newspapers also attacked the Delta Ministry for its civil rights activities and published stories accusing Warren McKenna of communist sympathies because of his trip to China eight years earlier. Police and state highway patrolmen harassed Mount Beulah's residents and visitors with tickets for traffic offenses. George Shaw Jr., a Jackson attorney, received a one-year prison sentence after firing several shots at CDGM staff and children at Mount Beulah, who escaped injury by leaping behind some boxes.[53]

Despite strenuous opposition from Mississippi's politicians and the Jackson papers, OEO, which had conceded that the CDGM had run an excellent program, finally agreed in February 1966 to grant the Mississippi group $5.6 million to run an expanded program for six months through the summer. As a condition of the grant, CDGM's headquarters moved from Mount Beulah to Jackson. Thomas remained on the board of directors. After months of wrangling, the Delta Ministry reluctantly repaid OEO the balance of the amount that the agency accused it of overcharging CDGM in connection with the orientation program.[54]

White Mississippians' opposition to the activities at Mount Beulah was driven by the facility's strong association with the civil rights movement. During the summer of 1965, Mount Beulah hosted meetings organized by the MFDP, SNCC, CORE, and the SCLC. While SNCC and CORE began to withdraw from the state, the Delta Ministry expanded its activities and recruited additional staff. In September, Bob Beech began to divide his time between the Hattiesburg Project he directed and West Point, where he worked with the local civil rights movement and Mary Holmes Junior College. The Ministry assigned many of its new staff to county projects in the Delta, where they focused primarily on voter registration and community organizing. Their work was eased by the August 1965 passage of the Voting Rights Act, which outlawed literacy and other discriminatory registration requirements. The Ministry also conducted a series of citizenship education classes at Mount Beulah, with assistance from Tennessee's Highlander Research and Education Center, which had pioneered the idea. The classes taught local black activists constitutional rights, literacy skills, and community organizing and leadership techniques.[55]

The Delta Ministry made a conscious effort to recruit African Americans, particularly local people, to its staff. Owen H. Brooks, a thirty-six-year-old electronics engineer who held a degree from Northeastern University in Boston, joined the Ministry in May. An African American, Brooks had grown up in Boston's Roxbury ghetto. A longtime member of the NAACP who also helped SNCC's fundraising efforts in Boston, Brooks was recruited into the Delta Ministry by Warren McKenna, the former pastor at Roxbury's St. John's Church, where Brooks served as a lay associate. In June 1965, Brooks began the Ministry's fourth county project, in Bolivar County. A month later, the Reverend Solomon Gort Jr., a twenty-eight-year-old African American from Cleveland, Mississippi, returned to the Delta to work for the Ministry in Greenville. Gort's denomination, the American Baptist Convention, paid his salary. In September, the Delta Ministry recruited for its staff another African American Mississippian, Clarence Hall Jr., who eight years earlier had become the first African American to register to vote in his native Issaquena County. A forty-one-year-old Missionary Baptist layman who owned a farm, Hall took responsibility for Issaquena and Sharkey Counties, both in the Delta.[56]

The Delta Ministry's two other new staff recruits in 1965 were white, northern ministers in their thirties. Bruce Hilton, a thirty-five-year-old former newspaper editor, had worked for youth publications of the Evangelical United Brethren Church for ten years before joining the Delta Ministry as director of interpretation. Hilton's job was to promote and explain the Ministry and its activities to Mississippians, the NCC's national constituency, and the WCC. Frederick S. Lowry, a thirty-year-old United Church of Christ pastor on New York's Long Island, served in McComb as a volunteer in September 1964 and subsequently joined the Ministry's permanent staff. Four months after returning to McComb in March 1965, Lowry took over at Mount Beulah from Al Winham, who turned his attention to economic projects and liaison with the state's denominational officials.[57]

During its first year, the Ministry also attracted more than three hundred volunteers, both clergy and lay, from more than a dozen denominations. Almost exclusively northern and white, they were dispersed throughout the Delta Ministry's projects, with some serving at Mount Beulah. Two of the volunteers who joined the Ministry for a year in the summer of 1965, Rims K. Barber and Roger A. Smith, were later hired as permanent staff members. Both men had served as minister-counselors during COFO's Summer Project in 1964. Smith, a thirty-nine-year-old Methodist minister in North Dakota, became the Ministry's finance officer. Barber, age twenty-eight, left his Presbyterian pastorate in Davenport, Iowa, to return to Canton, where he had served a year earlier. He became the Delta Ministry's coordinator for Madison County.[58]

Unable to hire additional permanent staff, the Ministry subsidized civil rights work by making its facilities available to other groups. In September 1965, it agreed to provide room, board, and office space at Mount Beulah for the Freedom Information Service (FIS). Founded two months earlier, FIS "served the whole freedom movement in Mississippi with voter-registration materials, statistics, background information and scores of pamphlets for semi-literate people."[59]

Mount Beulah had also become a refuge for some of the people that FIS and the Delta Ministry served. The Ministry had supported, encouraged, and aided Delta agricultural workers who in May 1965 launched a strike for higher wages at the Andrews Brothers' Plantation in Tribbett, Washington County. Thrown off the land by their white employer, the strikers set up a picket while their families temporarily settled at Mount Beulah. Their presence gave added urgency to the Delta Ministry's goal of creating alternative economic opportunities in Mississippi and placed a considerable and unanticipated drain on the Ministry's resources.[60]

In September 1965, the Ministry helped create the Delta Opportunities Association, with leaders from eight Delta counties plus Madison and Yazoo Counties. Later incorporated as the Delta Opportunities Corporation (DOC), the nonprofit organization sought federal and charitable foundation grants and loans for low-cost housing, small-business opportunities, and agricultural development. Despite Winham's strenuous efforts, DOC did not receive substantial funding until 1967, when it obtained a grant from OEO followed by matching funds from the Ford Foundation. Objections from hostile Mississippi politicians and the greater priority OEO gave to funding Coahoma Opportunities, Inc., an antipoverty program promoted by Coahoma County resident Aaron Henry, accounted for the delay.[61]

Increasing agricultural unemployment made improved welfare provision an immediate concern. At the suggestion of the National Student Association (NSA), the Delta Ministry pressured six of the eighteen counties that did not participate in the federal government's surplus commodities program to sign up or to let the Ministry act as a distributing agency in their place. Federal regulations permitted private agencies to act in this capacity. Although the surpluses were free, the county authorities did not want to pay the handling costs involved. Even with the NSA's financial support, the Ministry lacked the resources to operate such a large-scale distribution program. Nevertheless, nine counties, all located outside the Delta, fell for this bluff and agreed to participate in federal food programs lest the Ministry become involved. Consequently, an additional sixty-four thousand poor people received food. By the end of July 1965, "all but two of Mississippi's 82 counties had some form of food distribution set up using government food," with the result that more than one hundred thousand additional people received food because of pressure exerted by the NSA and the Delta Ministry.[62]

The Ministry then offered to distribute surplus federal commodities in any county that did not do so. To forestall Ministry involvement, in August the state government proposed Operation Help, under which the Mississippi Department of Welfare would distribute twenty-four million dollars' worth of surplus commodities to seventy-six Mississippi counties, with distribution costs funded by a six-month OEO grant. The state's remaining six counties had been accepted for the federal Food Stamp program. Approved on November 23, Operation Help was to commence within sixty days. The Delta Ministry provided more immediate relief in November by distributing seventy-four tons of NSA-donated food to Delta communities.[63]

Although the year seemingly had ended on a high note, the Delta Ministry's future was precarious. The Ministry's 1965 General Board–approved budget of $260,000 was inadequate for its programs. Furthermore, donations by the NCC's and the WCC's member denominations fell $93,959 below the amount requested of them by the board. The Ministry spent $479,989. Its income totaled $318,573, including a crucial gift of $50,000 from a West German organization, Brot für die Welt; money raised from individuals, corporations, and foundations; and payment from CDGM for rent and services. More than half of the $161,416 deficit was accounted for by denominational underfunding of its agreed budget, and much of the remainder by the unanticipated costs of renovating Mount Beulah and the unexpected burden of supporting the Andrews Brothers' Plantation workers and their families. The NCC's Division of Christian Life and Mission "seriously depleted its reserves" by covering the deficit in "hopes that [greater] denominational support would be forthcoming." As the new year approached, the Ministry faced the prospect of substantial cuts in its program to bring expenses into line with income and to repay the division. Furthermore, in response to pressure from the Methodist Church and the PCUS, and at the request of the Commission on the Delta Ministry, which sought to secure a set of program priorities, the NCC decided to undertake an evaluation of the Ministry's entire program. The Delta Ministry's future was uncertain.[64]

Despite sustained opposition from Mississippi's white religious leadership and limited financial support from the NCC's member denominations, the Delta Ministry had become a key civil rights presence in the state within sixteen months of its inauguration. It had played a key role in the founding of CDGM; conducted voter registration, citizenship education, and community organizing activities in the Delta as well as in southwestern and southeastern Mississippi; dispensed food and clothing to the needy; sponsored a health demonstration project in Holmes County; and pressured state and local authorities into agreeing to distribute federal surplus commodities. The Ministry filled part of the vacuum created by the withdrawal of SNCC and CORE from the state and by the disintegration of COFO. But the Ministry had also suffered setbacks, particularly in failing to secure funding for a literacy program and for DOC. Although the unrelenting opposition of most white Mississippians to the Ministry had made the goal of reconciliation between the races unrealistic in the short term, the Ministry's identification with the MFDP and policy of supporting poor blacks, regardless of established black leadership, had also alienated Aaron Henry and Hodding Carter III. Nevertheless, many African Americans in its project areas appreciated the Delta Ministry's servant ministry, and these areas will now be considered.

CHAPTER THREE

Hattiesburg, 1964–1967

Although far from the cotton fields of the Delta, Hattiesburg became an important part of the Delta Ministry. At SNCC's invitation, more than two hundred northern white clergymen, mostly under UPCUSA direction, joined a voter registration drive in the city during the early months of 1964. The NCC took over the Hattiesburg Ministers' Project in May and, in effect, began applying the Delta Ministry's program in the city four months before its official launch in Mississippi. In September, the Ministry inherited "a going voter registration program, educational activities, community organization, and white community contacts," created by the combined efforts of COFO, the UPCUSA, and the NCC. Delta Ministry staff and volunteers helped the Hattiesburg civil rights movement maintain its momentum and played a crucial role in coordinating its activities. The Ministry also pressured county authorities into distributing federal surplus commodities to the poor, and, uniquely among Delta Ministry projects, made progress in working with the white population. Convinced that a sustainable, indigenous freedom movement had developed, the Ministry began phasing out the Hattiesburg Project in 1965. However, even before the project finally ended in 1967, the Hattiesburg movement had begun to unravel, divided by organizational rivalries, blunted by white authorities' co-option of African-American leaders, and increasingly neglectful of the interests of the black poor.[1]

Founded in 1884, Hattiesburg, the seat of Forrest County, lies midway between Jackson and the Gulf Coast cities of southeastern Mississippi. The county had a population of 52,722 in 1960, with 34,989 people living in Hattiesburg. African Americans comprised 14,752 (28 percent) of Forrest County's residents. With a median family income of $4,004, they were less poor than blacks in the Delta. Nevertheless, 31 percent of Forrest County's African American families earned less than $3,000 a year, and, according to the Mississippi Board of Health, malnutrition constituted "a major health problem" in the county. Agriculture consisted of small farms, mainly engaged in animal husbandry, with 85 percent of them owned by whites. Opportunities for independent farming in the countryside and for business in Hattiesburg's segregated black community had created an African American middle class, a phenomenon that was almost entirely absent from the Delta's cotton plantation economy.[2]

Despite their comparative advantage, African Americans in Hattiesburg and Forrest County suffered greater disenfranchisement than did Delta blacks. Only 12 of 7,406 voting-age blacks were registered in 1961. Their registration predated the election of Theron Lynd as county circuit clerk in 1959. Lynd, a member of the segregationist Forrest County Citizens' Council, refused even to allow blacks to try to register during his first two years in office. Only the filing of a federal government suit against him in January 1961, after Lynd had refused to allow the U.S. Justice Department to examine his records, led him to allow a few blacks to attempt the registration test. Even then, Lynd failed them. In July 1961, the Kennedy administration filed the first of a series of further suits against Lynd in an attempt to ensure equal treatment for black registration applicants. Lynd simply ignored court injunctions issued against him by the Fifth Circuit Court of Appeals after Federal District Judge W. Harold Cox, a Mississippi segregationist, consistently refused to support the administration that had appointed him. In July 1963, the Fifth Circuit found Lynd guilty of contempt and ordered him to register forty-three black applicants and cease discrimination. Lynd appealed the decision to the U.S. Supreme Court.[3]

Federal action against Lynd encouraged SNCC, which was looking for new project areas in Mississippi, to begin voter registration work in the Hattiesburg area in 1962. Vernon Dahmer, president of the Forrest County chapter of the NAACP, asked SNCC to send workers to Hattiesburg. Dahmer, a fifty-four-year-old father of eight whose light skin would have enabled him to pass as white, had prospered on his inherited two-hundred-acre farm. A tireless worker, he had added a sawmill and a grocery store to his inheritance. Committed to change but with his time taken up by business, Dahmer had extended an invitation to SNCC in frustration at the local NAACP's inactivity. His action cost him the chapter's presidency. SNCC sent to Dahmer Curtis Hayes and Hollis Watkins, residents of Pike County the group had recruited during a campaign in southwestern Mississippi a year earlier.[4]

Palmers Crossing, located five miles south of Hattiesburg, became a prime recruiting ground for SNCC after St. John's Methodist Church agreed to allow civil rights meetings. Victoria Gray was among a small group mustered by Hayes and Watkins to take the voter registration test. A thirty-five-year-old local woman who managed a family and ran a business selling beauty products, Gray was eager to challenge discrimination but had lacked an outlet through which to channel her energies. Although her brother co-owned a radio and television shop with J. C. Fairley, Dahmer's successor as president of the Forrest County NAACP, Gray had not been invited to join and had not sought membership in the male-dominated branch. At first the NAACP opposed SNCC's presence as a threat, but the two groups gradually began to work together.[5]

Lynd rejected Gray's application along with a group of others. By September 1962, one hundred African Americans had taken the test, and Lynd, conscious of federal pressure, had registered four of them as a token. When Hayes and Watkins transferred to SNCC's Delta project in the same month, Gray became project director in Hattiesburg. She began conducting citizenship education classes after attending a training session at the SCLC's Dorchester Center in Georgia. By 1963, the Hattiesburg movement had gained substantial momentum based on a working alliance between Gray, now president of the Forrest County Voters League, Fairley, and three SNCC staff members who had been dispatched to the city during the summer. Lynd's refusal to submit to the federal courts and continued pressure on him from the U.S. Justice Department made COFO choose Hattiesburg to employ a new tactic, Freedom Day.[6]

Held on January 22, 1964, Freedom Day occurred little over two weeks after the Supreme Court had denied Lynd's appeal of a lower court order to register forty-three blacks and to end discrimination against African American voter applicants. After a mass meeting the night before, more than 150 African Americans waited in line and attempted to register on Freedom Day, while movement supporters picketed the county courthouse in protest of Lynd's discriminatory practices. Leading activists in Mississippi converged on the city, among them Charles Evers, Aaron Henry, and Amzie Moore of the NAACP; Bob Moses, Lawrence Guyot, and Fannie Lou Hamer of SNCC; Dave Dennis of CORE; and Annell Ponder, state director of the SCLC's Citizenship Education Program. SNCC leaders Jim Forman and John Lewis also took part. At Moses' suggestion, SNCC had invited ministers from across the United States to Hattiesburg to help draw media attention to the project.[7]

Fifty-two clergymen participated in Freedom Day in an effort sponsored by the UPCUSA's Commission on Religion and Race with assistance from the Presbyterian Inter-Racial Council, the Episcopal Society for Cultural and Racial Unity, and the Rabbinical Assembly of America. The group comprised thirty-two Presbyterians, ten Episcopalians, two Jews, a Unitarian, and several Methodists and Disciples of Christ. All but one of the clergymen had come from the North and border South states. Most of the ministers were white, but a few, such as Gayraud S. Wilmore Jr. and J. Metz Rollins Jr., who served as executive director and associate director of the UPCUSA's Commission on Religion and Race, respectively, were African American. The group also included a Chinese American, the Reverend Larry Jack Wong of the Presbyterian Church in Chinatown, San Francisco. The clergymen's role was to help man the picket line outside the county courthouse.[8]

The NCC had declined to sponsor the event. According to historian Taylor Branch, Robert Spike, executive director of the National Council's Commission on Religion and Race, did not want to upset Paul B. Johnson Jr., Mississippi's incoming governor, by bringing clergymen to a civil rights protest in Johnson's hometown. However, at the Presbyterians' request, the commission sent its legal counsel, Jack Pratt, to assist the clergymen, who expected to be arrested. Spike also sent his commission's field representative, Art Thomas, to Hattiesburg to help coordinate the ministers' efforts.[9]

Although police ordered the pickets to disperse, the officers made no arrests when the order was ignored. City authorities feared that arresting the pickets, especially the visiting ministers, in front of reporters from the national media would tarnish Hattiesburg's image. Instead, authorities protected the protesters and the line of African Americans waiting to take the registration test. Police arrested only Moses at the demonstration, charging the well-known SNCC activist with breach of the peace. Freedom Day was the first time that a civil rights demonstration in Mississippi had lasted more than fifteen minutes without mass arrests occurring. Hattiesburg's authorities hoped that if they avoided a confrontation with civil rights forces, the movement would withdraw, starved of publicity, and move on to other areas. Lynd administered the registration test to the applicants one at a time to slow down the process, but even so, he could not halt it.[10]

Encouraged by its breakthrough, for the next three months, COFO organized canvassing in the African American community, voter registration attempts, and picket lines. The UPCUSA's Commission on Religion and Race coordinated clergy participation by creating the Hattiesburg Ministers' Project, under the leadership of Robert J. Stone, the commission's associate director. Pratt stayed in Hattiesburg for the first two weeks of the project. He provided legal counsel for Moses; Guyot, who had been arrested for allegedly urging a child to miss school and picket; and nine UPCUSA ministers arrested on January 29 for refusing to desist from pick-eting close to the courthouse. During the first four weeks of the project, more than five hundred African Americans attempted to register and more than one hundred passed the test. The Ministers' Project supplied more than one hundred clergymen during this time. They usually served for one week before returning home.[11]

Police authorities protected civil rights workers and their clergy supporters from being attacked on the street, although one minister, Tom J. Lasswell of the United Church of Christ, and several COFO workers suffered assaults from lo-cal white residents. However, the police arrested one visiting clergyman, Roy G. Smith of the Disciples of Christ, for assault after he bumped into a police officer and arrested several COFO workers on various charges. The Mississippi State leg-islature passed an antipicketing law in April to help the Hattiesburg authorities stem the protests. When COFO defied the new legislation, police arrested forty-four picketers, including eight ministers. Pratt defended them in court as they challenged the law's constitutionality. Seven more people, including five northern ministers, were arrested for picketing in May. COFO decided to end picketing and concentrate on voter registration as it prepared for the forthcoming Mississippi Summer Project.[12]

The Hattiesburg Ministers' Project entered a new stage when it came under NCC sponsorship in May, by which time 205 clergymen had passed through the project, most of them from the North but a few from Texas and Upper South states. The UPCUSA's Commission on Religion and Race had planned to end the project in mid-April. Recognizing its importance, Spike asked the commission to transfer it to the National Council so that it could be incorporated into the NCC's contribution to the Summer Project.[13]

The National Council appointed John E. Cameron and Bob Beech as codirec-tors of the Ministers' Project, which the council scheduled to last through Au-gust. Since February, Cameron, a thirty-one-year-old African American Baptist minister and NAACP member, had served as local project director for the UPCUSA under Stone. Cameron had been the only local minister among the eight arrested for picketing in April. Beech, aged twenty-nine, was a native of St. Paul, Min-nesota. A white Presbyterian minister, he had been educated at Carleton College in Northfield, Minnesota, the University of Minnesota, and McCormick Theo-logical Seminary in Chicago. While serving as pastor of a small church in Hebron, Illinois, and assistant pastor of a larger church in Harvard, ten miles away, Beech met Presbyterian ministers who had gone to Hattiesburg under the Ministers' Project. Swayed by their argument that the presence of visiting white clergymen helped reduce violence, Beech went to Mississippi for a week in March to assist a COFO voter registration drive in Greenwood. Arrested within two hours of his arrival as he passed out leaflets, Beech was released without charge. Although he was married and had three sons, he decided to make an extended commitment to the struggle and on his return to Illinois volunteered his services to Wilmore. Beech accepted the codirectorship of the Hattiesburg Ministers' Project, the only position Wilmore had available. Beech resigned his pastorates and left for Mississippi.[14]

After meeting Wilmore and Cameron in New Orleans, Beech arrived in Hattiesburg on May 19. The Ministers' Project rented space in J. C. Fairley's radio and television shop in the heart of the black community for a headquarters. COFO's office lay across the street. Sanford R. Leigh, a white twenty-seven-year-old from Connecticut who became COFO's (and SNCC's) Hattiesburg Project director, soon praised Beech for coordinating his work with that of COFO. Beech's open, easygoing manner also served him well as he made contacts with the local white community, which became more receptive after the cessation of picketing. He reported that he had been well received by city officials, including the mayor and sheriff. Beech and project volunteers also found that some faculty members at the University of Southern Mississippi and William Carey College, a Southern Baptist institution, were willing to discuss race relations and that some of these professors opposed segregation, even though both campuses excluded African Americans. However, moderate segregationists who were prepared to accept change and white integrationists were not willing to speak out publicly. The Ministers' Project put such people, who believed they were alone, in contact with each other and, in some cases, with local blacks.[15]

Most of Hattiesburg's white clergymen and their congregations were hostile to the Ministers' Project. Upset by a month of picketing, five Hattiesburg Presbyterians (PCUS), three ministers and two elders, had gone to a meeting at the First Presbyterian Church (UPCUSA) in Charleston, Illinois, in February 1964 to protest the participation of ministers from the area in the Hattiesburg protests. However, one of the Hattiesburg clergymen, Newton P. Cox Jr., the Pennsylvania-reared pastor of Westminster Presbyterian Church, subsequently became open to dialogue with Beech and his volunteers. The project made little progress with ministers from other Protestant denominations it contacted. The city's Protestant churches excluded African Americans, with the exception of Trinity Episcopal Church, which occasionally had black worshipers. Hattiesburg's Catholic priests generally opposed racial discrimination, which enabled the Ministers' Project to establish "a direct relationship" with them. The city's Catholic church, the Church of the Sacred Heart, welcomed worshipers and visitors regardless of race. The Rosary Catholic Mission Hall, located in a slum that housed poor whites and African

Americans, was integrated but mainly black. Beech also found Rabbi David Ben-Ami of Temple B'nai Israel, a transplanted New Yorker, open and supportive of the Ministers' Project's efforts.[16]

With the exception of Cameron's newly constructed Faith Tabernacle Baptist Church, most black Baptist churches remained aloof from the Ministers' Project and the civil rights movement. Black Baptist clergymen preached an otherworldly religion that stressed the rewards to be had in heaven after a life of struggle. Like white Baptist churches, they emphasized evangelism and dismissed social action. Methodist churches and clergymen were more supportive of the movement. Bishop Charles F. Golden of the Methodist Church's all-black Central Jurisdiction had directed Mississippi's black Methodist churches to allow civil rights meetings. However, most of Hattiesburg's black population belonged either to Baptist or Holiness churches. Consequently, the Ministers' Project reported that only "some" local black clergymen cooperated with the movement.[17]

Visiting ministers under the direction of Beech and Cameron canvassed African American neighborhoods to persuade blacks to attempt to register. The presence of these visitors had a galvanizing effect on many of those they approached. Chad Combs, pastor of Christ Presbyterian Church in Camp Hill, Pennsylvania, explained, "Being a minister makes a difference. The people in the rural areas are very religiously oriented. When a group canvassing calls on them, they address their words to the minister. A woman said to me, 'I'd be glad to sign anything that will help us.'" Appeals from the ministers were particularly effective in breaking down the fear felt by older people. The willingness of visiting clergymen to take the very real risk of arrest and assault for their activities emboldened African Americans to seek registration despite the danger of economic and physical harassment. And Beech noted, "There's a feeling on the part of Negroes that since the ministers have been here there's been a decline in violence and harassment and a slow but sure build-up of registered voters."[18]

However, even before Beech's arrival, the number of volunteer clergymen had begun to taper off. Throughout June 1964, Beech complained that the Ministers' Project lacked staff and volunteers, with the result that he felt "like a chief with no Indians." He appealed to ministers and laypeople to serve the project, which he said needed twelve volunteers each week rather than its current crop of between two and six. Project volunteers spent most of their time canvassing in the black community with COFO workers. Although the Ministers' Project was independent of COFO, staff of the two programs cooperated closely and held joint strategy meetings, focusing much of their effort on generating support for the MFDP and the precinct and county meetings it held as part of its challenge to the regular Democratic Party. In June, Victoria Gray and John Cameron ran as MFDP candidates in the regular Democratic Party's primary, from which most blacks were excluded. Gray received 176 votes in Forrest County and 4,703 votes statewide in her campaign against U.S. Senator John C. Stennis. Cameron secured 105 votes in the county and 883 votes overall in his bid to unseat Representative William Colmer from the Fifth Congressional District. On the same day as the primary, African Americans in Hattiesburg, as elsewhere in Mississippi, voted in a parallel freedom election to demonstrate their desire to be involved in the political process.[19]

Gathering support for the MFDP became one of the key aims of COFO's Summer Project, alongside voter registration, work in the white community, and the creation of freedom schools and community centers. During the summer, COFO's Hattiesburg Project became "one of the largest and most active in the state." The publicity generated by the Summer Project helped bring Beech the additional lay and clergy volunteers he sought for the Ministers' Project. Beech oversaw up to twenty volunteers each week, coming from a range of the NCC's member denominations and including some Jews. The volunteers played an important supporting role in COFO's efforts in and around Hattiesburg.[20]

During the summer, COFO created three freedom schools in Hattiesburg and two at Palmers Crossing. They had an average attendance of five hundred, with morning classes held primarily for grade school and high school children and evening classes for high school students and adults. COFO also established a community center on Hattiesburg's Dewey Street and another at Palmers Crossing. During the six weeks following June 21, COFO and NCC staff and volunteers accompanied seventy African Americans who took the voter registration test and persuaded almost 3,400 blacks to sign freedom registration forms to signal their wish to vote, thereby discrediting white authorities' claim that blacks did not want to be enfranchised.[21]

The inauguration of the Summer Project in Hattiesburg led to a resurgence of harassment of COFO and NCC people by the police and local white segregationists. Incidents recorded by Beech in late June included a white man firing shots into the engines of two cars owned by COFO volunteers, "a parade of hostile whites in cars" late at night along the main street that ran through Hattiesburg's black neighborhood, "some hate literature," and "the slapping of one of our college students by a deputy sheriff." Police also routinely checked volunteers' cars and driving licenses and handed out fines for alleged traffic violations. More seriously, in early July, Rabbi Arthur Lelyveld from Cleveland, Ohio, and COFO workers Dave Owens and Larry Spears were brutally beaten by two white men after returning from canvassing in the black community. Although the mayor condemned the attack, the police moved slowly on the case before eventually arresting the perpetrators, who received suspended sentences after pleading guilty at their trial. On July 20, freedom school teacher Peter Werner was kicked in the head while in a drugstore. However, compared with some areas of Mississippi, such as McComb, Hattiesburg's volunteers suffered relatively little violence and harassment. The city's only other major violent incident was the arson of the integrated Rosary Catholic Mission Hall in June 1964.[22]

Although Beech believed that he enjoyed good relations with the city authorities and the police, they were quick to arrest and prosecute him when an opportunity arose in July. Police charged Beech with attempting to obtain property under false pretenses after he had written a check that his account held insufficient funds to cover. Before the check was deposited, Beech realized his mistake and deposited two out-of-state checks to cover the shortfall. However, the bank refused to credit the money to his account until the checks cleared their home banks. Despite these circumstances, District Attorney James Finch pursued the case, for which conviction carried the prospect of a three-year prison sentence. However, the county dropped the charges in August, encouraged in part by the outrage at his arrest that some local whites expressed to the mayor, sheriff, and district attorney.[23]

Throughout the summer, the Ministers' Project continued to make progress in its work with the white community. Beech wrote in August that "one of the most exciting and rewarding new developments is the weekly get-together for local white citizens and some of the COFO staff, Freedom School students, and/or local Negro citizens." Milton Barnes Jr., a Hattiesburg native and black Baptist minister, argued that members of the Ministers' Project "have made their most effective contribution in the area of voter registration, in breaking through the white community, and also in increasing the exposure between Negroes and whites." But although the project had increased interracial contact and placed white moderates in contact with each another, they still remained too intimidated by segregationist white authorities to speak out publicly. Despite the passage of the Civil Rights Act in July 1964, most public facilities remained segregated.[24]

The civil rights movement in Hattiesburg stayed loyal to COFO's pledge not to test desegregation of public accommodations during the Mississippi Summer Project. Fear of heightening tensions with the white community lay behind COFO's decision, but this approach also made it easier for more cautious elements of the African American middle class to become involved in the struggle. Upper- and middle-income black businessmen and professionals formed the Hattiesburg Civic Improvement Association and twice met with the mayor during the summer to discuss their grievances. Although no breakthroughs occurred, the association's activities confirmed the high degree of unity that characterized the movement in Hattiesburg during 1964. Unlike in some other Mississippi communities, the NAACP and SNCC functioned well together within COFO. NAACP chapter president Fairley attended the Democratic Party's national convention in Atlantic City as a member of the MFDP delegation.[25]

However, relations between COFO and John Cameron worsened as the summer went on. Both Sandy Leigh and Cameron had quite forceful, almost authoritarian, approaches to their leadership roles, but the problems between COFO and Cameron went beyond a simple clash of personalities. SNCC, COFO, and the MFDP accused Cameron of acting independently and seeking personal recognition rather than working through the movement. Cameron, for his part, disliked the casual dress and freewheeling approach of many young movement workers. Beech tried to smooth over relations between COFO and Cameron, but the gap between them widened. Influenced by the problem as well as by Beech's skillful handling of his responsibilities and good relations with COFO, the NCC appointed the Minnesotan director of the Delta Ministry project in Hattiesburg, which began on September 1, 1964. Cameron, Beech announced, would "spend more time with his local responsibilities."[26]

The NCC's decision to add Hattiesburg to the Delta Ministry flowed from the National Council's eight-month involvement in the city, which had evolved from cautious initial support of the civil rights movement to sponsorship of the Ministers' Project. Nearly five hundred volunteers had served in the project by the time it concluded on August 31, 1964. The Delta Ministry inherited, Beech wrote, "a deep reservoir of good will on the part of the local Negro community, good working relationships with SNCC, COFO, FDP, NAACP, and the white community's leadership." However, the Ministry could play only a small supporting role in the local movement during the next few months because a series of bombings in McComb, sixty miles east, led the NCC to send most of its Hattiesburg volunteers to assist in that emergency. Beech provided volunteers reassigned to McComb with a short orientation.[27]

With more than a dozen staff members, SNCC maintained a strong presence in Hattiesburg. Freedom Schools were merged into the community center program. The two community centers on Dewey Street and at Palmers Crossing provided day care for preschoolers, recreation for schoolchildren, and evening classes for adults. In accordance with SNCC and the Delta Ministry's aim of developing local leadership, community center programs were generally staffed by local people, with assistance from SNCC and Ministry volunteers. The Delta Ministry also contributed to voter registration work. By the end of 1964, 236 African Americans had registered in Forrest County. However, the figure would have been far greater without Lynd's continued obstructionism. Beech and Ministry volunteers continued to take the lead in establishing contacts with moderate whites and sponsored informal, interracial gatherings of local people.[28]

Beech reported in the fall of 1964 that relations between the Delta Ministry and COFO in Hattiesburg remained excellent: "All of our staff are completely integrated into their staff and take an active part in the decision-making process by which COFO program and policy are hammered out." Beech worked closely with the movement. Untroubled by the Ministry's leaders in Greenville, Beech enjoyed virtual autonomy. In contrast to much of Mississippi, relations in Hattiesburg between SNCC and the NAACP were good. Sandy Leigh noted in his project report that J. C. Fairley "works closely with us."[29]

However, the already poor relations between COFO and Cameron worsened in September, when he took control of the distribution of several tons of clothing sent to him but designated for COFO. Leigh charged that Cameron had given "most of the best clothing to his friends, and the rest to those persons in the community whose support he sought to buy." Cameron, Leigh claimed, had handed out the remainder "in a grand manner from his church." COFO attacked Cameron's actions at a mass meeting. Cameron countercharged that he had stepped in because COFO's welfare and relief committee functioned inadequately. Beech, who usually worked with COFO in clothing and food distribution, had been out of town at the time of the shipment. In private, he agreed with the criticisms directed at Cameron by Leigh and by Gray at the meeting. The acrimonious public dispute between COFO and Cameron wrecked plans for a bus boycott in Hattiesburg.[30]

Apart from the Hattiesburg movement's internal problems, Beech faced harassment from elements of the white community. Unable to find anyone willing to rent him a house, Beech "bought a nice home in a white residential neighborhood" when he moved his family to Hattiesburg in September. Harassment began almost immediately. In October 1964, Beech wrote, "In the few weeks we have lived there we have had a cross burned in our yard, one neighbor to tell us that we may not under any circumstances entertain 'niggers' in our home[,] a series of threatening phone calls—several each day—varying from silence to obscene phrases to warning that we had better leave town." The parents of two neighborhood boys barred their children from continuing to play with Beech's sons after discovering their father's occupation. A local woman who regularly invited Beech's wife, Alice, to her home for coffee reluctantly stopped the practice at her husband's insistence. A private kindergarten dismissed Beech's youngest son, Russell, because of his father's civil rights work. Beech explained, "Only a very few people in the white community are even willing to associate with us. We're treated very much the same as some person who has been convicted of some serious crime and then returned to try to live in the community."[31]

After Beech and his family attended a Sunday service at Westminster Presbyterian Church in September 1964, Beech was confronted by its pastor, Newton Cox Jr., and a church elder. They explained that church members had besieged the pastor with protest calls and several of them had withdrawn financial support for a new church building because of a rumor that Beech had applied for church membership. The elder asked Beech not to come again. Although he had engaged in dialogue with visiting NCC ministers since the summer, Cox was not prepared to risk the material success of his ministry by defending Beech's right to attend his church.[32]

In October, M. W. Hamilton, the owner of Polk's Hardware Store, struck Beech and ripped his shirt after recognizing him as a civil rights worker when he signed a check for a stepladder. Beech, who had his three sons with him, pressed charges. The city court threw the case out for insufficient evidence because Beech lacked witnesses to support him. Two months later, Hamilton attacked Ed Hamlett, a white civil rights volunteer from Tennessee. Hamlett did not press charges because he would not be in Hattiesburg long enough to follow the case through.[33]

Diehard segregationists dominated the white community in Hattiesburg and its elected leadership. The Forrest County Citizens' Council held meetings at the county courthouse. However, the Delta Ministry continued to find additional white moderates, particularly on the faculties of the University of Southern Mississippi and William Carey College. Beech reported in November that although white moderates existed "in appreciable numbers," they still would not declare themselves publicly. "Those whose attitudes are discovered," he wrote, "are faced with social astricism [sic] at the least and financial ruin quite probably."[34]

Rabbi David Ben-Ami lost his job in December 1964 for engaging with the movement. In January, Ben-Ami had visited jailed clergymen who had come to Hattiesburg under the Ministers' Project. He had later befriended Beech. For a while Ben-Ami survived criticism from leaders of Temple B'nai Israel, who suggested that he look for another synagogue. In December, the rabbi attempted to enlist the city's clergymen in distributing Hattiesburg's share of twenty thousand Christmas turkeys donated by African American comedian Dick Gregory and syndicated columnist Drew Pearson for needy black and white Mississippi families. Temple leaders balked at Ben-Ami's involvement and firmly insisted that he leave.[35]

Violence remained the ultimate sanction against those who challenged racial discrimination. Citizens' Council members assaulted Jack Barlett, a United Church of Christ minister from California, and three COFO workers, all white, when they were recognized at a council meeting held in the county courthouse in January 1965. An editorial in the segregationist local newspaper, the *Hattiesburg*

American, implied that COFO had provoked the incident as a "money-raising gimmick." The four men filed assault-and-battery charges against their assailants, who again beat the workers outside the courthouse after the case was heard. Although present at the incident, the police intervened belatedly. "The people who had done the beating," Beech reported, "were treated by the police and others there at the city hall almost as if they were heroes." [36]

Many segregationists regarded the Civil Rights Act with contempt. The NAACP, led by Charles Evers, its Mississippi field secretary, tested Hattiesburg's compliance with desegregation in February 1965, following unsuccessful tests conducted by high school students from the local branch of the Mississippi Student Union. Seven establishments served the small NAACP groups that fanned out across the city, and four refused. Many facilities remained segregated. [37]

Lynd continued to keep most African American applicants off the voter registration rolls, despite the federal rulings against him. By February, only about three hundred blacks were registered. Some African Americans were deterred from attempting to register by the threat of losing their jobs with white employers and by the local welfare office's practice of denying help to those who took the test. [38]

The Delta Ministry and COFO continued to distribute food and clothing to the needy. After the problems with Cameron, the Ministry urged its donors to send supplies directly to Beech or to the NCC's headquarters in New York. The program's recipients became biracial when three poor white women from Purvis in neighboring Lamar County appeared at the Delta Ministry's office in search of food and clothing. They received supplies and returned with other members of their community to receive help. They eventually asked Beech to preach in their Holiness church. He was received warmly, except by the Ku Klux Klan members present. The Ministry maintained and strengthened its contacts with the community, some of whose members lost their jobs or were threatened because of their association with Beech. [39]

In February, at the suggestion of the NSA and with its financial support, the Delta Ministry submitted a plan to the U.S. Department of Agriculture to distribute surplus federal commodities to feed 7,900 needy people in Forrest County for a ninety-day period. Aware that federal regulations allowed private agencies to act as distributors and informed by the Ministry of its intention to become involved, state welfare authorities arranged for Forrest County to begin distribution of the commodities in May. In the program's first few days, county agents segregated waiting lines, spoke harshly to African Americans, and kept them waiting for hours in the hot sun. The county agents also called out applicants' names over a public address system in an attempt to humiliate them. Intervention by the

Jackson office of the public welfare department reversed most of these practices within a few days and created a more efficient service, but applicants continued to encounter racial discrimination when they registered for commodities.[40]

Encouraged by the Civil Rights Act of 1964, which had outlawed racial discrimination in employment, the Delta Ministry focused much of its effort on job opportunities. Hattiesburg's two largest industrial firms, the Hercules Powder Company and the Reliance Manufacturing Company, each of which employed more than one thousand people, began to hire African Americans in the summer of 1965 after the Ministry publicized the companies' legal obligation to end discriminatory hiring policies. Together with COFO, the Delta Ministry encouraged maids to seek a collective solution to their problems of low pay and unsocial hours. However, efforts to form a union foundered because of the wide dispersion of the maids and their places of work.[41]

Although the Delta Ministry sought to continue to work closely with SNCC, the MFDP, and the NAACP, during 1965 the three groups became increasingly ineffective. Cameron was supposed to direct an NAACP summer voter registration project, but he did nothing. Beech, an NAACP member, had agreed to serve as the project's assistant director. At the NAACP's request, the Delta Ministry lent some of its volunteers to the project, which, Beech noted, "netted few tangible advances" and achieved "no lasting mobilization of l[o]cal leadership." The breakthrough in voter registration came in July, when the Fifth Circuit Court of Appeals found Lynd guilty of civil contempt for his defiance of previous court orders to treat black applicants fairly. Thereafter, an average of twenty-five African Americans a day registered successfully, with Lynd ordered to help those who did not understand a question and to disregard spelling mistakes by applicants. By October 1965, about 2,500 of Forrest County's eligible black population of approximately 7,500 had registered.[42]

COFO, which had done much to mobilize the community behind voter registration in 1964, had done little in Hattiesburg since the Summer Project. Sandy Leigh left the city in October 1964. Hattiesburg's COFO descended into self-evaluation and internal bickering before Mississippi's COFO dissolved itself in July 1965 and turned over its resources to the MFDP. Although the MFDP had "strong community acclaim," it lacked extensive organization in Hattiesburg and its environs. Unduly dependent on Victoria Gray, the MFDP drifted without direction during her frequent absences from Hattiesburg as a result of her work for the SCLC's Citizenship Education Program and of her participation in the MFDP challenge to the seating of Mississippi congressmen. Of equal importance, Beech noted, "Much of the active FDP leadership was siphoned off into the Headstart program" run by CDGM, which the Delta Ministry had played an important part in creating.[43]

After the Hattiesburg Board of Education refused to participate, the Ministry helped organize five CDGM centers in and around the city. Staffed by local blacks, the program ran through July and August, enrolling 450 children, all of them African American, since efforts to recruit poor white children failed. In addition to education and health care, the program provided some children with their only "adequate meal" of the day.[44]

Apart from their work with CDGM and in voter registration, relief, and employment, Beech and his staff of volunteers, who numbered twelve throughout most of the summer, assisted local people in providing literacy and adult education classes. The Delta Ministry also encouraged black high school students to desegregate the University of Southern Mississippi and William Carey College by applying for admission after the two institutions ended discriminatory policies in the summer of 1965. Two of the students gained admission to the university. In addition, the Ministry continued a program, first instituted in 1964, of soliciting scholarship funds for students who wanted to study at high schools or colleges outside Mississippi.[45]

Hattiesburg's African American high school students proved particularly receptive to the civil rights movement. Many student activists belonged to the Mississippi Student Union, which resumed desegregation tests of public facilities during the summer of 1965. Some Delta Ministry personnel, such as volunteer David Nesmith, participated in the tests along with people from the Hattiesburg NAACP, MFDP, SNCC, and Head Start. The effort succeeded in integrating the Rebel Theater, although one Delta Ministry volunteer suffered a beating while waiting to enter. Nesmith and Beech narrowly missed being shot during a birthday party for Nesmith at Beech's house. Nesmith was also twice beaten by M. W. Hamilton, who had previously assaulted Beech. Desegregation attempts at restaurants and other establishments sometimes resulted in violent attacks on civil rights workers, although some businesses desegregated. During the summer, however, the chapter's main leader left for Chicago, and the Mississippi Student Union became largely inactive. Beech reported, "At present, no one in Hattiesburg seems to understand the full significance of working with the youth and therefore no one is taking this responsibility, other than DM."[46]

Apart from public accommodations, the Delta Ministry also addressed segregation in the public school system. In July 1965, the U.S. Office of Education approved the city's plan to desegregate grades one through four in September after rejecting an earlier plan for desegregation of only the first two grades. Two Delta Ministry volunteers responded by organizing local parent-teacher associations, which provided African American parents with the information they needed to register their children in formerly all-white schools under Hattiesburg's "freedom of choice" plan. Fear generated by the city's failure to offer protection or transportation for black children restricted the number entering previously white schools to twenty-nine. Desegregation occurred peacefully in September: "Now that the barrier has been broken," Beech wrote optimistically, "I expect that next year's enrollment will be much larger."[47]

In September, Beech began dividing his time between Hattiesburg and a new Delta Ministry project in Clay County, in northeastern Mississippi, centered on West Point. He sought to replicate the success of the Hattiesburg program, which he had recommended the Delta Ministry end by December 31, 1965. Beech argued that although much remained to be done in the Hub City, "existing indigenous groups are capable of performing all of these functions." His September 1965 report to the Delta Ministry noted the achievements of the Hattiesburg civil rights movement during the previous year and the Ministry's involvement in them. Yet Beech's report also documented the failure of the NAACP's summer project, the weaknesses of the MFDP in leadership and organization, and the inactivity of the Mississippi Student Union. It noted that only one community center remained in operation. Beech's belief that the indigenous movement was sufficiently strong to continue without the Delta Ministry's assistance was misplaced. Furthermore, since the Ministry had, as he noted, "provided a crucial communication function" by keeping the city's civil rights groups focused and "knitted together in a unified whole," its termination increased the danger of loss of cohesion.[48]

Nevertheless, the Delta Ministry agreed to phase out its Hattiesburg Project. Beech believed that local groups could complete the registration of Hattiesburg's African American population. Hattiesburg graduates of the SCLC's Citizenship Education Program, he argued, could use its techniques to teach others to use their votes effectively by holding citizenship classes under MFDP sponsorship. Beech also believed that the Hattiesburg Civic Improvement Association "contains the nucleus of much of the solid leadership that will come from the community." Inactive between June 1964 and May 1965, the association had begun to hold a series of community meetings, with assistance from the Delta Ministry, to discuss the creation of a Community Action Program (CAP), for which it would seek OEO funding.[49]

Beech's expectations for Hattiesburg proved to be too optimistic. City authorities and prominent white leaders made token concessions to placate African American moderates and divide the black community while maintaining the substance of white dominance. The city hired five black policemen and paved a few streets in the African American community. But it closed many public water fountains rather than desegregate them and converted others for use with paper cups. Once school desegregation no longer attracted publicity, some of the black parents involved suffered beatings. When whites created Forrest-Stone Opportunities, Inc. (FSO), to apply for CAP status, OEO rejected its application and urged it to meet with the Hattiesburg Civic Improvement Association to work out a compromise program. Although the association included many people who supported the MFDP, the FSO co-opted some controllable association members and other amenable blacks to achieve the racial balance required by OEO. In June 1966, OEO approved a grant for FSO. Beech, who still lived in Hattiesburg, worked throughout 1966 to broaden black representation within FSO, until he was satisfied at the end of the year that its board had become "truly representative," with a majority of poor people sitting on it.[50]

Another source of conflict within the African American community was also based on competition for power. The murder of Vernon Dahmer, the man who had invited SNCC into Hattiesburg and worked closely with COFO and the Delta Ministry, led to the breakdown of the hitherto good relationship between the Ministry and the Hattiesburg NAACP. In the early hours of January 10, 1966, Ku Klux Klansmen from Jones County firebombed Dahmer's home on the orders of Sam Bowers, their imperial wizard, who had also ordered the 1964 murder of Mickey Schwerner. Dahmer became a target because of his long-standing civil rights work. He had recently offered to collect the poll tax, necessary to vote, from African Americans at his grocery store to save them the trouble of paying at the courthouse. Dahmer had also declared his willingness to settle the tax for those too poor to afford it. During the attack, Dahmer stayed in his burning house, exchanging gunfire with the Klansmen while his family escaped. He died in hospital the following afternoon from burns to his lungs.[51]

Charles Evers led three hundred African Americans on a march to the county courthouse to protest Dahmer's murder. Evers remained in Hattiesburg for a week, leading mass marches and mass meetings. Roy Wilkins, the NAACP's national leader, and Gloster B. Current, the NAACP's director of branches and field administration, also came to the city. The Delta Ministry and the MFDP wanted the meetings to formulate a list of grievances to present to city authorities. Instead, Evers and the local NAACP Executive Board met privately and issued fifteen demands. They called for the desegregation of all city and county facilities, services, schools, and offices; the hiring of black firemen and transit bus drivers; the hiring of more black law officers; the appointment of blacks to local school boards; the improvement of black neighborhoods; the ending of police brutality; and compliance with the Voting Rights Act. Beech criticized Evers's autocratic approach, which drained "the community of trust" and deprived local people of their voice. Current insisted that Beech be excluded from the membership and meetings of the Executive Board of the Hattiesburg NAACP chapter. J. C. Fairley believed that "in this kind of situation[,] you can't let people decide for themselves what they want to do. You have to have a leader." At Current's instruction, Fairley permanently expelled Beech from the Executive Board.[52]

On his first day in Hattiesburg, Evers had threatened a boycott of white downtown stores. However, when the self-proclaimed Forrest County Movement, formed mostly from the ranks of MFDP members, instituted a boycott the next day, Evers condemned it as "irresponsible." Unaware of the boycott, most African Americans continued shopping.[53]

Although the Forrest County Movement was not representative of the African American community, the national and state NAACP had taken over Hattiesburg's civil rights movement without considering the wishes of local people, as Beech had charged. The NAACP excluded dissenting voices from speaking at the mass meetings it organized. Beech wrote to a former Delta Ministry volunteer that the NAACP had "managed to destroy in one short week all of the things Vernon Dahmer worked for in terms of cooperation in his local community for the whole of his life." There had been some tensions within the local movement that an informal meeting of local leaders in December 1965 had helped to overcome, but in the wake of Dahmer's murder, the NAACP had reopened and severely deepened divisions. "The attitudes which people have toward one another in the local community," Beech lamented, "are now fraught with distrust and tension, and all of this can be directly attributed to the invasion by outside NAACP staff people." The NAACP, he believed, was "attempting to capitalize" on Dahmer's murder to raise its profile "in the community and to raise money."[54]

Current denied Beech's charges and maintained that the NAACP had every right to intervene after the murder of one of its activists. Current attacked the MFDP, accusing it of trying to create a third political party rather than working through the two existing parties. Current told Beech that his membership in the Delta Ministry precluded him from sitting on the Executive Board of the local NAACP chapter because of the potential for "a conflict of interest and divided loyalties," although Beech had held both positions for more than a year. Beech's hitherto good relationship with Fairley was ruined by the intervention of Evers and Current. In March, Fairley gave the Delta Ministry notice to quit his premises, which had served as its headquarters in Hattiesburg.[55]

The NAACP's fifteen demands, Beech complained, produced "no tangible results," and the group had called off nightly marches after city officials agreed to a meeting. The authorities issued a general statement in which they expressed their willingness to cooperate and to address the concerns raised. White leaders placated the NAACP and its allies in the Hattiesburg Civic Improvement Association without taking any practical action. In any case, the NAACP's demands, Beech contended, reflected the interests of upper- and middle-income people rather than those of low-income earners and the unemployed, who formed "the large majority of the people in the Negro community."[56]

Although the MFDP sought to represent the interests of the poor and unemployed, Beech conceded that the new party was "not effectively organized" in Hattiesburg. "The biggest disappointment to me in the local community," he wrote, "is that the F.D.P. is not moving ahead as fast as I would like to see it move." Beech welcomed the progress made by Forrest County's upper- and middle-income blacks, to which the Delta Ministry had contributed. But he was "dismayed to discover that no concerted feeling of responsibility" existed among them for those who "remain behind them at the bottom of the ladder." With the MFDP largely ineffective, the Delta Ministry, Beech argued in March 1966, would have to focus primarily on helping the most excluded in Forrest County by organizing neighborhood meetings in which these people could express their concerns. At the same time, the Ministry would "continue to work on other fronts such as voter registration, citizenship education, the work with youth in Forrest County, and interracial communication."[57]

Beech had overestimated the strength, coherence, and resilience of the indigenous movement when, a few months before, he had called on the Delta Ministry to phase out the Hattiesburg project. With only one volunteer left in Hattiesburg and with Beech spending his time in West Point, there seemed little possibility that the Ministry could undertake the ambitious program that he now envisaged. Beech received no help from the Ministry, which increasingly focused its energies and resources on creating Freedom City, a new Delta community it proposed to develop for displaced agricultural workers. Furthermore, the Ministry's financial problems compelled it to make several cuts in its other programs in April 1966. The Clay County Project's budget was slashed, and the effort was subsequently terminated. Ironically, the end of the project gave Beech the opportunity to refocus some of his energies on Hattiesburg, although he also undertook other duties for the Delta Ministry across the state.[58]

His first priority in Hattiesburg was to raise funds to rebuild Dahmer's home and to provide college funds for Dahmer's school-age children. The Delta Ministry made a national appeal for the Dahmer family. Leading local white citizens were outraged by Dahmer's murder, which had been condemned by Mayor Paul E. Grady; Selby C. Bowling, president of the County Board of Supervisors; the Hattiesburg Chamber of Commerce; and the Forrest County Ministerial Association. The *Hattiesburg American,* which called the firebombing a "cowardly and despicable attack," publicized the establishment of a Dahmer Family Fund by local whites with the support of the Chamber of Commerce. Beech sat on the committee that coordinated the local effort. The NAACP, he noted, refused to participate, as it was unwilling to cooperate with other groups. "Through all of this Vernon Dahmer thing," wrote Beech, still shocked by the murder of his friend, "I have discovered a good deal of respect and open cordiality on the part of the white people here in town, which no doubt is a result of the work we have done here."[59]

The combined efforts of local black and white citizens, the Delta Ministry, and other groups, such as the Mennonites, enabled the Dahmer home to be almost completely rebuilt. However, plans to rebuild the Dahmers' grocery store and return their sawmill to production with an expanded capacity as a means of generating jobs in the community remained unfulfilled.[60]

Although some of Hattiesburg's whites had been cooperative in the wake of the Dahmer murder, Forrest County officials remained intransigent. In April 1966, the County Board of Education decided to sell twenty-seven and a half acres of land at Kelly Settlement, which the Dahmer family had deeded many years earlier to the trustees of a black school that was built on the site. The school had fallen into disuse in 1957. With the consent of local people, CDGM had used the site for a Head Start center in the summer of 1965 and the spring of 1966. With Dahmer deceased and his family's records destroyed in the fire that killed him, the County Board of Education laid claim to the land and put it up for sale. The Board was in dire need of funds because unlike the city school system, it had refused to desegregate and consequently had lost federal funding. Beech spearheaded successful efforts to prevent the sale, but the board padlocked the site, preventing its further use as a Head Start center.[61]

Another focus for the Delta Ministry in Hattiesburg was the creation of black-owned industries and businesses that would complement a similar effort at Freedom City. However, Beech could not raise adequate funds for the program, while the Delta Ministry increasingly focused on northwestern Mississippi, leaving him little part to play within the Ministry. Beech unsuccessfully sought to interest the UPCUSA's Commission on Religion and Race in supporting his work in southeastern Mississippi. The Delta Ministry redeployed him in several roles, including some work at Freedom City and in fund-raising. The Commission on the Delta Ministry reported in July 1967, "There is no program in Hattiesburg." Lack of resources had forced its closure. Selected for termination from the staff as the Ministry gave priority to citizenship education and political development, Beech resigned at the end of August to become chaplain at Mary Holmes Junior College in Clay County, where he had previously run a Delta Ministry project.[62]

As Beech recognized, the work in Hattiesburg was far from complete. There had been some significant breakthroughs regarding the white community. Beech had participated in a February 1966 panel discussion on race relations sponsored by the Newman Club, a Catholic youth group at the University of Southern Mississippi, something that he noted would have been inconceivable a year earlier. He had worked with the Chamber of Commerce to rebuild Dahmer's house. Beech's efforts to merge the city's black and white ministerial associations, begun in 1964, finally succeeded three years later. By May 1967, the formerly all-white Hattiesburg Ministerial Association had twelve African American members. The association's reluctance to integrate was in some ways ironic since the failure of all but a minority of black clergy to become involved in the movement had been an ongoing source of frustration for Beech.[63]

Many whites remained segregationist at heart. Some white pastors, most of them Baptist, left the ministerial association when it desegregated. Beech regarded school desegregation in Forrest County, which began in January 1967, as a failure since by March only twelve African Americans were attending formerly all-white schools. White teachers' and students' physical mistreatment of black children in predominantly white schools and the Ku Klux Klan intimidation that black parents suffered, including threats and cross burnings, led many parents either to withdraw their children from desegregated schools or to keep them in black schools. Another indication of white resistance lay in the fact that Klansmen arrested for Dahmer's murder addressed segregationist rallies while free on bond.[64]

White authorities accepted only such change as they could not avoid, and they sought to limit its impact by co-opting black leaders. Despite Beech's efforts, white authorities effectively maintained control of the FSO program by working with the upper- and middle-income African Americans hired as FSO administrators and program staff. Some of the African Americans whom whites co-opted had never been part of the movement but took advantage of the opportunities it created. Some blacks who had been at the movement's forefront joined with white moderates. They welcomed change away from rigid exclusionism as previously unimaginable progress.[65]

Black unity in the Hattiesburg civil rights movement fractured when the movement lost the common enemy of exclusion, disenfranchisement, and de jure segregation. White authorities divided blacks primarily along class lines by giving the semblance of inclusion and recognition to the black upper and middle classes while maintaining the substance of power. With 5,467 African Americans registered in Forrest County by 1967 (68 percent of those eligible), white leaders realized that they had to make some concessions to blacks. Beech explained, "The work with upper level Negroes has brought us now some perplexing problems. Some who were among the most militant two years ago now seem overwhelmed by being able to sit down + talk with white leaders. We find that they too quickly acquiesce to suggestions which leave the poverty level + presently militant Negroes out in the cold. Thus we find ourselves fighting those with whom we so recently were working!" Some of those who had been prominent in the movement, Beech observed, had now withdrawn because "they either lack expertise or ability to adapt to the new level of attack." More moderate persons replaced them, "many of whom are insensitive to the priorities felt by grass roots folk."[66]

In a limited way, the development of a working relationship between white and black leaders represented a success for the Delta Ministry's policy of bringing the two communities together. The Ministry had not sparked the civil rights movement in Hattiesburg but had provided valuable assistance, manpower, and publicity. The Ministry had also helped to ease tensions within the movement by acting as a reconciling force. Uniquely among the Delta Ministry's projects, the Hattiesburg operation made inroads into the white community by cultivating moderates, serving the white poor, and establishing communication with white authorities. However, the Ministry began withdrawing from Hattiesburg prematurely in the mistaken belief that a sustainable indigenous, inclusive movement had developed. Instead, the movement fractured once its chief goals of eliminating de jure discrimination had been achieved and as white authorities co-opted upper- and middle-class African Americans from within and outside the movement's ranks. Although the Delta Ministry could not have prevented divisions within the black community from widening, its dwindling presence provided ineffective aid for the neglected poor black majority. The Ministry's misplaced faith that the MFDP would represent the poor foundered on the party's failure to develop an organized base of support. Aware that the job remained incomplete, Bob Beech unsuccessfully sought ways to continue working in southeastern Mississippi, but, under financial pressure, the Delta Ministry refocused all of its efforts on the northwest part of the state.

CHAPTER FOUR

McComb, 1964–1966

The McComb Project, like that in Hattiesburg, had not been part of the Delta Ministry's original plan. After sending minister-counselors to support COFO's work in McComb during the Summer Project of 1964, the NCC withdrew when the project concluded in late August. Violent resistance, which had plagued the movement in McComb and surrounding areas throughout the summer, escalated with the departure of many of COFO's volunteers and the NCC ministers. Consequently, the National Council made an emergency appeal for clergymen to aid COFO's voter registration campaign and established a long-term project under Harry Bowie, who had served as a minister-counselor in the city during the summer. The NCC dispatched ministers to McComb for several months. Their presence helped deter violence, while Bowie worked closely with the MFDP. A skilled and committed organizer, Bowie solicited and managed bail funds for civil rights protesters, organized cooperatives, and, alongside local people, played a leading role in the creation of a CDGM Head Start program in Pike County and in the establishment of a community center. Financial problems forced the Delta Ministry to terminate Bowie's employment and the McComb Project in April 1966. The Ministry soon rehired Bowie to work on citizenship education in Mississippi, and he continued his residency and activism in McComb.[1]

Lying in southwest Mississippi, seven miles from Magnolia, the seat of

Pike County, McComb had a population of twelve thousand in 1960, with 42 percent African American. The city had a history of civil rights activism that began long before the 1964 Summer Project and NCC involvement. The Illinois Central Railroad, for which McComb had been founded as a repair station in 1872, served as a major employer of blacks and whites. The railroad's unionized African American workers could not simply be fired for speaking out against discrimination in the community. From their ranks came the leaders of the Pike County Voters League, founded by Nathaniel H. Lewis in 1946, and the McComb chapter of the NAACP, led since the 1950s by C. C. Bryant. Both organizations focused on voter registration, and some people belonged to both groups. But by 1960 these efforts had raised black registration in Pike County to only 207, subdued by a renewed campaign of white terror in Mississippi as blacks asserted their rights.[2]

At Bryant's invitation, Bob Moses of SNCC launched a voter registration project in McComb during August 1961. Moses worked closely with the NAACP's middle-class leadership of railway workers, operators of small businesses, and independent farmers. SNCC conducted registration classes to prepare African Americans for the voter application form and test. At the request of local blacks, SNCC extended its campaign into neighboring Amite and Walthall Counties, both notorious for racial violence. Moses received a beating in August outside the registrar's office in Liberty, the seat of Amite County, and in the following month, two other SNCC workers, Travis Britt and John Handy, were attacked in Liberty and Tylertown in Walthall County.[3]

SNCC worker Marion Barry favored direct action over voter registration. Inspired by his workshops, black youths and students began a sit-in protest and then marches in McComb, with Moses' reluctant support. SNCC workers, youths, and students were arrested and jailed. Burgland High School expelled two students for participating in a sit-in as well as those who refused to desist from protest. Appalled by SNCC's involvement of schoolchildren and its use of direct action, Bryant wanted the organization to leave town, but he later softened his opposition as parents rallied behind their children.[4]

White violence against the movement, including the murder of Herbert Lee, an Amite County farmer, in September and the beating of five CORE Freedom Riders at the McComb bus station in November, did much to bring the McComb movement to a standstill, because blacks would no longer attend voter registration classes. After completing their jail terms, SNCC workers left McComb in December 1961, following a campaign that had added only six African Americans to the voter registration rolls. SNCC's first attempt to establish a presence in Mississippi had failed. It moved on to conduct a sustained voter registration drive in the Delta.[5]

Factional divisions within McComb's black leadership, exacerbated by SNCC's campaign, paralyzed the movement in the city for the next three years. Older members of the black establishment, including Nathaniel Lewis and some ministers and teachers, took a conservative position. The moderate faction comprised Bryant and those NAACP members who continued to accept his leadership. The militants, who had been closest to SNCC in 1961, included young activists as well as some adults, such as Webb "Supercool" Owens and Aylene Quin, who were long-standing NAACP members. The McComb movement remained largely moribund until SNCC workers returned to encourage participation in the MFDP's Freedom Vote in November 1963. These activists also began voter registration workshops in January 1964.[6]

As a result of SNCC's renewed efforts, armed night riders fired on six black businesses, shot at two black homes, and wounded an African American boy on January 9. Worse followed on January 31 with the murder of Louis Allen, a witness to Lee's murder. In fear of his life, Allen had not incriminated Lee's killer, E. H. Hurst, a state representative, at the coroner's trial but had subsequently become a marked man after telling FBI agents the truth.[7]

The Ku Klux Klan, which had a stronghold in southwestern Mississippi and among members in the McComb police force, escalated its attacks on the city's black community as COFO's Summer Project drew near. Middle-class whites panicked not at the violence but at the prospect of the arrival of the summer workers in the city. On June 22, three black homes, including that of Bryant, were bombed. COFO workers arrived in McComb on July 5 and moved into a Freedom House owned by a local supporter. They were joined by NCC minister-counselor Don McCord, a white twenty-five-year-old Disciples of Christ clergyman and graduate of Yale Divinity School, from Stafford, Kansas. Three days later, a bomb thrown by Klan night riders destroyed the outside wall of one of the Freedom House's bedrooms, injuring two COFO workers. In response to the attack, the NCC sent McComb a second minister-counselor, Bowie, a black twenty-eight-year-old Episcopalian, who pastored the Chapel of Annunciation in Lawnside, New Jersey. J. Oliver Emmerich, the segregationist editor of the *McComb Enterprise-Journal*, declared that the community abhorred the bombings. Nevertheless, the attempt to wreck the project and intimidate African Americans soon widened into an indiscriminate campaign of violence that spread beyond McComb into Pike and Amite Counties and included bombings of several black churches, none of them involved in the movement. The terror dissuaded most African Americans from participating in the movement or attempting to register to vote.[8]

NCC minister-counselors, who came to McComb throughout the summer, usually for one week each, participated in COFO's voter registration drive and in general support activities. White NCC ministers also tried to establish communication with the white community. Alone among McComb's white clergymen, Colton Smith, a Vicksburg native who pastored a small Episcopalian mission, formed a good relationship with NCC and COFO volunteers. Smith introduced McCord to Albert "Red" Heffner, a successful local insurance salesman. Alarmed by the growing violence in the city and the atmosphere of intimidation, Heffner invited McCord to discuss race relations over dinner at the Heffners' home on July 17. With Heffner's consent, McCord brought Dennis Sweeney, a white COFO volunteer, with him. Although Heffner was a segregationist and a well-respected member of the white community, his house was soon surrounded by members of a local segregationist group, Help, Incorporated. No violence occurred against them, but the Heffners endured a campaign of harassment and ostracism that forced them to leave McComb on September 5. Not surprisingly, many of the city's white people and their ministers were hostile to COFO and to visits from NCC clergymen.[9]

White hostility made it unrealistic for Bowie to work in the white community. Except for contacts with Smith, with whom Bowie had attended the General Theological Seminary in New York City three years earlier, Bowie concentrated on the black community. He had grown up in Long Branch, a small town in New Jersey, largely oblivious to racial problems. After writing a seminary paper about black nationalism and then developing a greater awareness of racism through his pastoral work, Bowie began to gravitate toward the civil rights movement. He attended a symposium in Washington, D.C., that featured Martin Luther King Jr. and John Lewis of SNCC, worked on local housing problems, and joined a support group for SNCC. In July 1964, Bowie took a month's vacation from his church to work for COFO in the Summer Project. At the NCC's request, he became a minister-counselor.[10]

Bowie worked closely with the city's African American community and extended his stay, with a leave of absence from his church, for the entire two months of the Summer Project. He focused primarily on voter registration and canvassing for the MFDP as its candidates challenged the election of congressmen from the regular Mississippi Democratic Party. Bowie found a black church in McComb that was willing to accommodate a freedom rally and a freedom school. More than one hundred children enrolled in the school, which received assistance from NCC ministers. The children's attendance drew their parents into the movement.[11]

The turning point in securing black community involvement occurred in early August, when twelve African American businessmen secretly met with COFO people at a café owned by Aylene Quin. The businessmen offered the movement their support. Each man donated fifty dollars toward the cost of buying land for a community center, a project with which Bowie and the Delta Ministry were to become deeply involved. Attendance at COFO meetings picked up, and COFO scheduled a Freedom Day, a mass voter registration attempt, for August 18.[12]

Predictably, white extremists instituted a new reign of terror, with renewed bombing in the black community. Klansmen bombed the Burgland supermarket, which was owned by Pete Lewis, an African American supporter of the movement. They also burned crosses on the lawns of two whites who had expressed sympathy for the movement's efforts. Police raided the COFO Freedom House for illegal liquor; finding none, the officers stayed to search through files. Despite the intimidation, more than thirty African Americans attempted to register on Freedom Day, and each day for the next few days about fifteen blacks repeated the attempt at the county courthouse in Magnolia.[13]

The Summer Project ended in McComb on August 27. With most of the COFO volunteers gone and Bowie back in New Jersey, the bombings reached a new intensity. There were six bombings within a seventy-two-hour period in early September. Black morale slumped. In response, the NCC again recruited minister-counselors for McComb. Warren McKenna, administrative assistant to the Delta Ministry's director, drove three volunteers to the city in mid-September. On September 20, Quin's home was bombed, the thirteenth bombing in McComb in three months. Quin, targeted for attempting to register on Freedom Day and for opening her café to COFO meetings, was not at home, and her children, Jacqueline and Anthony, and their babysitter, Johnnie Lee Wilcher, survived the attack, although the children suffered minor injuries. On the same night, a fourteenth bomb destroyed the Society Hill Missionary Baptist Church, which hosted civil rights meetings. COFO workers managed to calm three or four hundred angry blacks who had taken to the streets, demanding revenge. Over the next few days, police jailed many blacks, including COFO organizers. Twenty-four African Americans were charged under a criminal syndicalism law, approved by the state legislature in May, that effectively made illegal any activity that might lead to social or racial change.[14]

A day after the Quin bombing, the NCC's Commission on Religion and Race flew her and two other women whose homes had been bombed during the summer, Ora Bryant and Matti Dillon, to Washington, D.C., for a meeting with Justice Department officials Burke Marshall, John Doar, and Lee White. Robert Spike, the commission's executive director, and other NCC officials argued vociferously at the meeting that President Lyndon B. Johnson should meet the women and thereby send a discouraging message to the terrorists in McComb. The NCC arranged a press conference at which Quin contemptuously rejected claims by Pike County Sheriff R. R. Warren that she and other black victims had bombed their own homes. Eugene Carson Blake, the commission's chairman and the stated clerk of the UPCUSA, declared that "nothing in the history of Christianity is comparable to the mass destruction of the houses of God in Mississippi." Two more homes were bombed in McComb on September 23, making a total of sixteen bombings and four burnings there since June 22.[15]

President Johnson met the three women for ten minutes on September 24. He made an ambiguous promise of action after Quin asked him to send federal troops to McComb. A day later, Blake presented a widely reported statement from the NCC's Commission on Race and Religion that called on Mississippi's white population to support law and order and to pressure state officials to ensure its restoration. The statement condemned the arrests on charges of criminal syndicalism. The commission also urged President Johnson to send former CIA director Allen W. Dulles to help restore order. The president had sent Dulles to Mississippi after the Neshoba County civil rights murders earlier in the summer. Johnson did not oblige on this occasion, but, on the same day, Emmerich broke his twelve-week editorial silence about racial terrorism and cautioned that "bombings create tension." Based on information planted by federal sources, Emmerich also warned that the city faced the threat of federal martial law. The editor appealed to the public to help bring the bombers to justice.[16]

To maintain national media interest in McComb, the NCC's Commission on Religion and Race, at COFO's request, issued an emergency national appeal for clergymen to serve as minister-counselors in the city. Within a few days, thirty ministers from nine denominations had arrived in McComb from around the United States, marking the beginning of the McComb Ministers' Project, which became part of the Delta Ministry. The project's immediate task was to support the African American community, aid COFO's voter registration project, establish communication with whites, and help focus national attention on McComb to bring federal intervention. At the request of local people, Bowie returned to McComb from New Jersey and became director of the Ministers' Project. The commission and the Delta Ministry chose him for the post because of his experience and good working relationship with COFO.[17]

Visiting clergymen immediately made their presence felt. A group of four Episcopal priests—three white and one black—tried to visit the twenty-four African Americans who been charged with criminal syndicalism and kept in the Pike County Jail at Magnolia, but county officials denied the ministers access. Undeterred, the ministers joined twenty-six other visiting clergymen in signing a statement that was published in the *McComb Enterprise-Journal* on September 29. This declaration endorsed COFO's program of citizenship education and voter registration and its desire to build a community center. The ministers stated their commitment to promoting reconciliation between the races and urged McComb's clergymen to recognize their moral responsibility to speak out "about racial justice and human freedoms." In a final plea, the visiting ministers called on "the peaceful and law-abiding majority elements in this community to exercise their responsibility to prevent any further violence and to work toward peace."[18]

The NCC continued to dispatch ministers to McComb for the next three months. Between September 1, 1964, and early January 1965, the National Council sent ninety-three clergymen, each of them serving for up to a week. Bob Beech, director of the Hattiesburg Ministers' Project, diverted its minister volunteers to McComb, observing that "since ministers have been coming in noticeable numbers, violence and harrassment have dropped off noticeably." Although the bombings stopped, police harassment of the movement still occurred. The presence of the clergymen and the actions of the NCC helped focus national media attention on McComb and thereby contributed to an atmosphere in which white moderates felt compelled and able to act.[19]

Adverse national publicity stymied business growth in McComb. Emmerich and two white moderates met with officials from the Community Relations Service, created by the Civil Rights Act of 1964 to advise communities facing racial problems. The officials recommended that McComb's leading citizens should publish in the local newspaper a statement calling for law and order. U.S. Justice Department officials warned Mississippi Governor Paul B. Johnson Jr. and the Pike County district attorney, Joseph Pigott, that federally imposed martial law was imminent. To preempt this threat, which may well only have been bluff, Johnson met with the leaders of McComb and Pike County. Johnson told them that he would send in the state National Guard to forestall federal intervention. However, he agreed to wait two days to give county officials the opportunity to restore law and order.[20]

The first arrests of Klan terrorists occurred within twenty-four hours and sent a warning to the white community to desist from violence. However, the light punishments the accused received weakened the cautionary effect of their apprehension. Nine Klansmen received suspended sentences after pleading guilty or no contest to a range of charges, including bombing, at their trial on October 23. Presiding Judge W. H. Watkins argued that the men had been "unduly provoked" by COFO workers and that, as "young men" from "good families," the accused deserved another chance. In fact, five of the nine men were older than thirty-four.[21]

A day after the Klansmen were released, McComb police officers raided the COFO Freedom House and charged those living there, including Bowie, with "operating a food handling establishment without a permit" because they served food to civil rights workers. Released on bail, they returned to their work organizing the black community. Bowie provided orientation for the rotating groups of volunteer ministers that continued to come to McComb at the request of the NCC. Many of these volunteers had been reassigned from the Hattiesburg Ministers' Project. Working alongside COFO, the visiting clergymen canvassed the black community to register people for the MFDP. They also encouraged African Americans to demonstrate their wish to be involved in the political process by participating in a Freedom Vote organized by COFO to parallel the November federal elections.[22]

COFO maintained its efforts to increase black voter registration levels in McComb and Pike County by organizing a Freedom Day on October 26. Beech and several other visiting NCC ministers accompanied African Americans as they tried to register at the courthouse in Magnolia. Bowie, who had helped COFO solicit bail funds and even contributed some of his own money, joined COFO in arranging bail for those arrested. In all, Freedom Day brought thirty arrests, including those of about a dozen NCC ministers, on charges of "trespass" or "resisting an officer." Two NCC clergymen were among those arrested during another voter registration attempt on the following day. With funds short by the afternoon, COFO and Bowie decided not to bail out anyone else who was arrested in the hope that incarceration of the protesters would force federal intervention. In the event, the authorities released those arrested in the afternoon without bail, fearing the publicity that might result if the protesters remained in jail. The arrests neither brought federal intervention nor broke the movement's momentum.[23]

Although the McComb movement did not depend on the presence of NCC clergymen, the visitors provided valuable assistance. Bowie commented that the "ministers' presence has exerted a positive influence. It has boosted the morale of the Negroes, who had seemed to have lost their initiative; and it helped the COFO staff, which is small and in need of support." Furthermore, Bowie noted, "There is reluctance among whites to bring about undue publicity to the town. If something should happen to [the NCC pastors], it would be difficult for McComb." As with the earlier civil rights workers, some of McComb's black ministers, particularly in the Methodist Church, welcomed the clergymen's intervention. Bishop Charles F. Golden of the Methodist Church's all-black Central Jurisdiction had ordered Mississippi's black Methodist churches to accommodate civil rights meetings. One black minister in McComb told a visiting white cleric, "It's good you're here. You can do things we could never do. We thank God for your coming." However, again as was the case with the civil rights movement, some of McComb's African American clergy remained aloof from the NCC ministers for fear of white harassment and violence.[24]

In addition to their work in the black community, NCC ministers tried to influence local white opinion by attempting to open up lines of communication. At the end of September, a group of visiting clergymen met with Mayor Gordon Burt Jr. and Police Chief George Guy but made no progress. Burt, who was chairman of the segregationist Pike County Citizens' Council, accused the ministers of interference. Guy, who headed the more extreme Americans for the Preservation of the White Race, also responded negatively. McComb police were routinely hostile to the clergymen. Pike County Sheriff R. R. Warren, who was also connected to Guy's group, told Walter J. Mehl, pastor of the Presbyterian church in Edwardsville, Illinois, "Why do you want to come down here where you don't belong and meddle?" before arresting him at the county courthouse as he accompanied blacks to the registrar's office.[25]

Successive cohorts of NCC clergymen visited local white pastors, generally receiving a hostile response. Many local ministers accused COFO and NCC of unwarranted interference and increasing racial tension. Bob Lynch, pastor of the Central Baptist Church, blamed outsiders for McComb's racial problems. Similarly, the Reverend Wyatt Hunter of the First Baptist Church denounced COFO and affirmed his opposition to integration. In contrast, some ministers were at least open to dialogue. Pastor Eldon Weisheit of Trinity Lutheran Church, who had been educated in the Missouri Lutheran system, declared his support for COFO's goals but accused COFO workers of having a slovenly appearance, drinking, and keeping house poorly. Weisheit urged the NCC to disassociate itself from COFO but expressed a willingness to meet with National Council and COFO staff. Native Mississippian David M. Ulmer, who pastored Centenary Methodist Church, contended that COFO had made race relations worse but conceded that its presence might be God's will and that confrontation might be necessary to achieve progress. Ulmer also confessed that the movement had made him reexamine some of his long-held beliefs about race.[26]

While the NCC ministers made their visits, McComb's moderate whites, who shared their clergymen's disdain for the presence of COFO and NCC, began an attempt to calm race relations. Emmerich published a series of editorials in October 1964 that condemned hate, appealed for peace, attacked resistance to federal authority and the civil rights movement, and called for "a new era of responsibility." Emmerich's words encouraged other moderates to take a public stand. More than 650 whites signed a statement, published in the *McComb Enterprise-Journal* on November 18, that called for the reestablishment of law and order and for "equal treatment under the law for all citizens regardless of race." The signatories condemned what they termed, "the extremists on both sides," warned against harassment arrests by the police, and declared, in a veiled reference to white supremacist groups, that no public official should have membership in a "subversive" organization. Acutely aware that the state NAACP was about to test McComb's compliance with desegregation of public accommodations under the Civil Rights Act of 1964, the statement called for obedience to "the laws of the land," even when they contradicted "our traditions, customs or beliefs."[27]

On the same day, Charles Evers, field secretary of the Mississippi NAACP, led a group of twenty black people into downtown McComb, where they entered four formerly white restaurants and motels without hindrance. Determined to avoid further adverse publicity from the national reporters who were covering the event, McComb's authorities had a large contingent of police and state highway patrolmen present to ensure order.[28]

Both the November statement and the success of the desegregation tests gave the impression, as intended, that McComb had entered a new era of racial progress. Consequently, the national media shifted its attention elsewhere and, with the bombings in McComb over, the NCC ended its emergency appeal for ministers. After the last cohort of visiting clergymen left in early January 1965, Bowie ran the McComb Project with just a secretary and one or two short-term volunteers.[29]

City authorities hoped to divide the resident black community from COFO by ending the worst excesses of racism but to avoid making substantive change. Despite the NAACP's desegregation tests, McComb's public facilities remained largely segregated. The Delta Ministry reported in January 1965 that "intimidation and bigotry" remained and that there had been "no significant gains for the people of McComb." The city's new image of moderation was "simply a paper curtain that would hide the blatant discrimination and oppression of half of its citizens."[30]

Divisions, temporarily submerged by common outrage at the wave of violence in September 1964, reappeared in McComb's African American community. More inclined to seek progress by establishing contacts with white leadership, the NAACP remained at odds with COFO, which had little faith in white moderates, tended to dismiss NAACP staff as "Uncle Toms," and focused instead on trying to empower the black community by working on behalf of the MFDP. Although he had always been closer to COFO, Bowie tried to act as a bridge between it and the NAACP. By April 1965, however, the state NAACP, with C. C. Bryant's support, had withdrawn from COFO. During the summer, COFO dissolved itself and turned over its resources to the MFDP. Bowie focused his energies and those of the McComb Ministers' Project primarily on helping COFO and subsequently the MFDP, which he believed best represented the interests of the majority of the black population.[31]

Bowie and the NCC ministers worked with COFO to turn out people for the November 1964 Freedom Vote, which saw MFDP candidates run against the official white Democratic Party nominees for the U.S. Congress. Approximately sixty thousand African Americans across the state voted in the mock election.[32]

As so often before in the city, the young—those not old enough to participate in the Freedom Vote—exhibited greatest enthusiasm for the movement. In late February 1965, African American students from three Pike County high schools organized and led demonstrations at the county courthouse against voter registrar Glen Fortenberry, who had continued to reject most black applicants. They also protested Mississippi's literacy test for registrants. The students called for a mobile registration unit to serve the black community. Bowie, COFO staff members, and some local black adults joined the protests. He and ninety others were arrested in early March while demonstrating. Bowie was released on bail after serving a night in solitary confinement. He handled bail for some of the other protesters arrested and again contributed some of his own money.[33]

The February and March courthouse protests encouraged the MFDP to run a candidate in a special election for selectmen, who served on McComb's city council and sat on committees that decided how taxpayers' money was spent on local services. The party secured the signatures required from fifty qualified voters to place L. J. Martin Sr. on the ballot. Martin, a fifty-two-year-old machine operator, was a deacon in the bombed Society Hill Missionary Baptist Church and a registered voter. The MFDP also ran a parallel Freedom Vote, in which McComb's disenfranchised blacks could protest their exclusion from the official ballot. Martin and Wilmer Dodds, who had failed the voter registration test, ran for two of the three selectmen vacancies. Bowie worked conscientiously in the campaign, for which the MFDP raised all money locally. In their campaign platform, the two MFDP candidates opposed a recently approved $1.47 million bond issue since the civic improvements it would fund, such as street and sewerage repairs, were centered on the white community. Most black areas of McComb lacked paved roads or sewer systems. The two men also campaigned against the bond issue because it would pay for the repair and construction of segregated public buildings. The MFDP candidates' platform included the employment of blacks as firemen, policemen, and city clerks; improvement of public services in the black community; and a review board "to consider complaints of police brutality and injustice."[34]

The election results disappointed Bowie and the MFDP. About two hundred of McComb's 3,410 registered voters were African American, yet Martin received only sixty-two votes in the official April 1965 election. Many blacks had not voted for Martin because they considered him unqualified. The small turnout in the Freedom Vote—only 560 of between 1,000 and 1,500 African Americans of voting age in McComb—indicated the MFDP's failure to establish a large base of support in the community. Bowie conceded a few months later that "no more than 10 per cent of the Negroes in McComb are really involved in the activities of the F.D.P."[35]

However, the fact that Martin was able to run for election indicated progress since the violence of 1964. He was the first African American from a town that included whites to run for local office in Mississippi since Reconstruction and the first ever black candidate in McComb. Bowie wrote, "The atmosphere is appreciably different. The basic problems have not been solved, but at least we are able to work more freely with local people." Now in control of McComb, white moderates maintained segregation and white dominance. They divided the black community by making a few token concessions, such as opening a few jobs to African Americans and creating an interracial committee. NAACP leaders and their supporters took encouragement from such incremental progress, believing that it justified their approach and laid the groundwork for further advances. By contrast, Bowie and the MFDP remained critical of white moderates for offering token concessions and of the NAACP for accepting them.[36]

As elsewhere in Mississippi, Bowie and Delta Ministry staff focused their efforts primarily on helping the black poor. In July 1965, they initiated an OEO-funded CDGM Head Start program in Pike County. The county's nine CDGM centers enrolled three hundred black children, despite opening three weeks after the public school system had begun its own Head Start program. CDGM centers employed African Americans as teacher aides, providing them with an alternative to working for whites as domestics and paying higher wages. Many of CDGM's employees, such as Quin, had been active in civil rights, and some had lost their jobs for being involved. Head Start proved to be a very successful program, both for the staff and for the children.[37]

The Sweet Home Center in McComb taught children to color and draw and to write their names. It had particular success in helping withdrawn children overcome their shyness. Sweet Home also taught children unfamiliar with the bathroom how to use it. Parents appreciated the help their children received. Mr. and Mrs. Frank Tucker wrote, "My children would not have been able to get any pre-school training it had not been for Head Start. They have learn to get along with other children and play new games. They have learn to regnise their name."[38]

Bowie assigned some of the sixteen volunteers that the McComb Project received in the summer of 1965, several of them ministers and laypeople from the Disciples of Christ, to work as assistants in the McComb Head Start program. He divided most of the other volunteers between "visiting businessmen to discuss racial discrimination in employment" and developing contacts with McComb's white clergymen. The Reverend Ned C. Gillum, a Disciples of Christ minister from Fairfield, Iowa, was refused admission to a Disciples of Christ church in July. Nevertheless, the Delta Ministry reported that in contrast to its efforts in the autumn of 1964, McComb's "ministers were more receptive [to] the possibility of dialogue, [and] some encouraged us to keep a man in contact with them." However, the local ministerial association balked at a Delta Ministry proposal "to place one of our volunteers in the white community to have a ministry of interpretation and reconciliation," although it expressed willingness to reconsider the idea at "a later date."[39]

Some of the volunteers canvassed African Americans to attempt voter registration. The Delta Ministry had neglected the task in recent months but resumed it in July 1965 when Pike County, ahead of time, began using a new state procedure that required applicants to complete a registration form with six rather than eighteen questions. In August, the state's voters approved a constitutional amendment, championed by Governor Johnson, that instituted the new procedure statewide and eliminated the rest of Mississippi's battery of requirements for voter registration. The governor had supported the measure in the vain hope that such action would place Mississippi in a better position to challenge the Voting Rights Act, which President Johnson had signed into law almost two weeks earlier. The new federal legislation suspended literacy tests in places where less than 50 percent of eligible adults had registered or voted in the 1964 presidential election and authorized the U.S. attorney general to send federal examiners to such areas. Bowie reported that more than 1,400 African Americans had registered to vote within six weeks of Pike County's adoption of a simplified application process, although the registrar had failed one-third of the applicants. The Voting Rights Act brought further substantial increases in the county's black registration.[40]

In addition to organizing Delta Ministry volunteers, Bowie had a busy summer on a personal level. In August, he married Eula Mae, an African American woman from Magnolia, and established what became permanent roots in McComb. The Bowies subsequently had two children, Harry and Rian, who later attended McComb's public school system.[41]

Bowie and the Delta Ministry helped recruit eleven African American children to attend four grades of McComb's white public schools when they voluntarily complied with federal laws mandating desegregation. The Ministry instituted workshops for the children and their parents to prepare them for any problems that might arise from integration, which took place without incident in September 1965. However, the North Pike County Consolidated School District refused to comply with desegregation and raised taxes to compensate for the loss of federal funds under the Civil Rights Act of 1964. A suit filed with the U.S. Department of Justice resulted in desegregation of two grades in North Pike under court order.[42]

The Delta Ministry hoped that in the long term, better educational opportunities would improve African Americans' economic position, but the Ministry also took more immediate action in an attempt to improve pay and employment conditions. Most black women in Pike County worked as domestics in the homes of white people, although some were employed by hospitals and hotels. The Ministry helped to organize a committee to press for employment of African American women at the McComb Manufacturing Company and Summit Mills, both of which were subsidiaries of Sears, Roebuck, and Company. The threat of the committee led the two companies to hire fifty black women full time on a regular basis and to begin employing a second group of applicants with the stipulation that their jobs would become permanent only if they met production standards. However, the companies set tougher production requirements for black employees.[43]

As an alternative to dependency on the whims of white employers, the McComb Ministers' Project devoted a great deal of its time to organizing black self-help cooperatives. They operated as part of the Poor People's Corporation, set up in 1965 by Jesse Morris of SNCC. The Poor People's Corporation comprised a network of cooperatives in Mississippi that marketed their produce through the Liberty House, a cooperative store in Jackson owned by the corporation, and another outlet in New York City. By the end of 1965, the Delta Ministry's McComb office had helped create a garment cooperative involving one hundred women, a furniture-making cooperative employing twenty men, and a leather goods cooperative with ten workers. Bowie secured a loan of five sewing machines for the garment workers from a Pennsylvania company and a financial loan for their cooperative from the NCC. An attempt to unionize maids and other workers at the Holiday Inn failed when the hotel dismissed them for going on strike and hired replacements.[44]

The community center project begun in 1964 also continued. Bowie was involved in efforts to solicit donations to add to the $600 the businessmen had contributed, and by February 1965, $8,000 had been raised. Although funds continued to come in, progress stalled because of the inability to find suitable, affordable land. Twelve months later, however, a five-acre site had been secured, along with a state charter and more than $20,000 in donations. The Mississippi State Sovereignty Commission, an investigative and propaganda agency designed to defend segregation and undermine the civil rights movement, sought to discredit Bowie, the center's treasurer. Commission agent L. E. Cole Jr. investigated Bowie for alleged misappropriation of funds. The allegation was entirely false.

Undaunted, Bowie continued to work on behalf of the community center, which in February 1969 received a federal Department of Housing and Urban Development grant of $193,000 toward the cost of a $289,000 building. In 1970, the Martin Luther King Center finally opened in McComb, providing meeting and recreational facilities. Bowie served on its board of directors.[45]

By the time the center was built, the Delta Ministry's McComb Project had been over for four years. Budget cuts had forced the Ministry to terminate several programs, including the McComb Project in April 1966 and, along with it, Bowie's employment. However, the Ministry rehired Bowie in October to organize a statewide voter education program. Although his new work took him across Mississippi, Bowie maintained his residence in McComb and remained involved in community affairs.[46]

At the time the McComb Project ended, much work remained to be done to achieve racial equality in the city. Racial discrimination in employment was commonplace. Most employed African Americans had low-paying jobs, and black men in particular were often unemployed or underemployed. School desegregation did not exceed tokenism, and most black children attended inferior, segregated schools. Although some public facilities were desegregated, many were not. The authorities closed the swimming pools in Percy Quin State Park when the park was opened to African Americans. None of McComb's white churches would admit blacks. The Head Start centers established by the Delta Ministry were transferred from CDGM to the control of moderate whites and moderate blacks in Southwest Mississippi Opportunity, Inc., in 1966, after OEO ceased funding many CDGM centers because of largely unfounded allegations of fraud and mismanagement by the group. Both the Citizens' Council and the Ku Klux Klan remained active. Only about half of eligible African Americans had registered to vote. Even then, Quin commented, "the trouble is to get them to vote." The MFDP enjoyed support from a small minority, and the long-standing division between the Freedom Democrats and the NAACP continued.[47]

Nevertheless, the civil rights movement had brought some significant changes to McComb, helping to end racial violence, registering blacks to vote, achieving the first breaches in school segregation, desegregating some public facilities, and opening up some jobs to African Americans. The NCC played a role in each of these gains, initially through its minister-counselor program during the Summer Project of 1964, then by sending nearly one hundred ministers to McComb between September 1964 and January 1965, and finally by inaugurating the McComb Project using these ministers and subsequent volunteers in civil rights work between 1964 and 1966. Summing up the role of the ministers and civil rights workers who came to McComb, Bowie argued, "We served as a catalyst. We were a triggering agent for the people of the McComb area to begin taking control of their own lives and destinies. Nothing would have happened unless we [had] played a catalytic function." Bowie fully acknowledged that local people constituted the movement's backbone in McComb, and the Delta Ministry was always careful to work with them in achieving their goals. Oriented toward activism and to the needs of the poor, the Ministry worked most closely with the MFDP, but it also cooperated, when possible, with other elements of the black community in pursuit of shared aims. The Delta Ministry's financial problems and primary focus on northwestern Mississippi led to its premature withdrawal from McComb. Given its short duration and small staff, the McComb Project made an important contribution to the African American struggle for equality in the city and its surrounding area.[48]

CHAPTER FIVE

Greenville and the Delta, 1964–1966

The Yazoo-Mississippi Delta in northwestern Mississippi contained some of the richest soil and poorest people in America. A majority of the region's population, most African Americans were impoverished, disenfranchised, and denied adequate education by a system of white-owned cotton plantations that limited blacks to unskilled agricultural labor. For decades, young adults and the most able had migrated to take jobs in the industrial North. But in the 1960s, automation of northern factories decreased opportunities for migrants, while federal funds and legislation led Delta planters to reduce acreage under cultivation and replace their workers with machines and chemicals. During its first eighteen months, the Delta Ministry established projects in five of the twelve Delta counties. By dispensing food and clothing and pressuring the state and federal government to distribute food, the Ministry eased but could not offset a rapidly deteriorating situation for many African Americans. Apart from seeking to relieve the immediate needs of poor people, the Ministry began a long-term strategy of trying to create black political power and economic alternatives, consistent with the program's policy of assisting the poor to fulfill goals of their own design. By aligning itself with the poor, the Delta Ministry also associated itself with direct action protests that alienated the NAACP and exacerbated divisions within the African American community.[1]

Greenville, in Washington County, became the Ministry's Delta headquarters because the city lay at "the heart of the Delta region" and had expressed less hostility to the NCC project than had other towns. Located by the Mississippi River, Greenville had a population of forty-seven thousand and was 48 percent African American. "Textiles, river shipping, gypsum and other industries" formed its economic base. The city's "liberal" reputation rested on its lack of racial violence, the presence of an educated white upper class, and the moderation of its newspaper, the *Delta Democrat-Times*, published by Hodding Carter II. Winner of a Pulitzer Prize in 1946 for writing editorials against intolerance, Carter still contributed to the paper, although he had turned over control to his son, Hodding III, who continued his father's tradition of speaking out for law and order and against segregationist extremists. African Americans had voted in Greenville since the 1940s, and the city had hired black policemen since 1950. City police protected COFO workers during the 1964 Summer Project and, uniquely in Mississippi, arrested and convicted Ku Klux Klansmen for burning crosses in a statewide show of strength. The city experienced no racial violence or arrests of civil rights workers. Although some whites supported the local Citizens' Council, it was not influential. Greenville's airport, bus and railroad stations, public library, and golf course desegregated, and Howard Dyer, a local lawyer, successfully defended an African American man, Oliver Lee Williams, accused of raping a white woman.[2]

However, much as William H. Chafe found in his study of Greensboro, North Carolina, Greenville's image of civility and good manners in race relations masked the realities of racial discrimination and convinced whites and some African Americans that there was little need for change. Greenville's white business leaders, Police Chief William C. Burnley Jr., and the *Delta Democrat-Times* sought to boost the local economy. To attract industry, they lauded their city's economic progress, stability, and seemingly good race relations. Delta Ministry volunteer Wilmina Rowland, on four months' leave from the UPCUSA's Board of Christian Education in Philadelphia, reported that "in Greenville just enough had been given to the leaders of the Negro community—a privilege here, a favor there, some concession at another point—so that they were unwilling to risk losing these crumbs." With most of black Greenville's middle-class leadership co-opted by white authorities, poor blacks had no one to represent their interests and aspirations.[3]

Despite Greenville's image as a beacon of liberalism in the state, the Delta Ministry soon discovered that discrimination blighted everyday life for the city's African American population. Segregated public schools provided blacks with an inferior education. Greenville spent $134.43 for each white student per year but only $34.25 for every African American pupil. Two of the city's black schools had no accreditation. Downtown stores would not hire African American cashiers. Greenville Mill, a carpet factory, employed black men only in lowly positions and refused to hire black women. Some white-run restaurants served African Americans, but many public accommodations remained closed to them. The General Hospital operated separate black and white wings, with air-conditioning available only to whites. No white house of worship other than the Roman Catholic church admitted African Americans. Although there was no overt harassment to prevent blacks from attempting to register to vote, only two thousand had registered. Those who attempted the voting test often failed because of their illiteracy, but many did not try because they feared economic retaliation by whites. Rowland found that "it was generally understood that the registration of large numbers [of African Americans] would not be acceptable." Blacks did not serve in the city government and, outnumbered by white voters, had no influence on it.[4]

The Delta Ministry discovered the shallowness of Greenville's reputation soon after opening the group's downtown headquarters, in line with its intention of engaging with the white community. The office housed Art Thomas, the Ministry's director; Warren McKenna, Thomas's administrative assistant; Laurice Walker, director of the Greenville Project; and Billie Rowland. While Thomas and McKenna took responsibility for the overall direction of the Ministry in Mississippi, Walker spent his first two months in Greenville, listening to and learning the concerns of the African American community. Beginning in November, he received assistance from Herbert O. Edwards, a thirty-five-year-old black Baptist minister and graduate of Harvard Divinity School, and Edwards's wife, Helen, a trained social worker. The couple, who lived in Baltimore, joined the Ministry for three months as consultants. Rowland accepted the job of interpreting the Delta Ministry to the white community with the hope that its more progressive members might "give us counsel, and perhaps even assistance."[5]

As its secretary, the Ministry hired Thelma Barnes, a thirty-nine-year-old African American who had grown up in Issaquena County and Greenville. College educated, Barnes had worked for ten years as a management analyst at the Greenville Air Force Base before spending a year as secretary in Nashville, Tennessee, to Bishop Charles F. Golden of the Nashville-Carolina Area of the Methodist Central Jurisdiction. Barnes left Nashville to return home and joined the Delta Ministry because she needed employment rather than because she was dedicated to its mission. However, as an active laywoman in Greenville's Revels Memorial Methodist Church, she found the Ministry to harmonize with her religious outlook.[6]

When Barnes took her desk at the front window of the Delta Ministry's office, local white businessmen and other white citizens asked that she be fired. A committee of white clergymen delivered the request. The Ministry refused to dismiss Barnes and rejected the churchmen's subsequent call for her desk to be moved out of sight of passersby. Soon thereafter, the Ministry's lease was rescinded. Evicted in November, the Ministry tried in vain to rent another downtown office, even placing an advertisement in the *Delta Democrat-Times*. The paper published an editorial that condemned the attempt to exclude the Delta Ministry as a "betrayal of our birthright." The *Delta Democrat-Times* also defended the Ministry's mission as "based upon brotherly love" and endorsed its advocacy of "meaningful action." Despite the Ministry's unpopularity, Hodding Carter III had agreed to serve on the Commission on the Delta Ministry. Unable to find another downtown office, the Ministry reluctantly relocated to Nelson Street, the main road through the heart of the black community.[7]

White hostility not only prevented the Ministry from staying downtown but also meant that Larry Walker spent three months before finding someone willing to rent him a house in the white community. Rowland similarly had considerable difficulty renting an apartment in a white neighborhood, and she encountered strong white hostility when she tried to explain the Delta Ministry's purpose. Rowland visited nearly all of Greenville's white ministers, some of them more than once. Only Harold Hermetz, pastor of Faith Lutheran Church, responded positively. His church included a large number of northern businessmen, and, under their influence, it had rescinded a policy of not seating African Americans. Rowland reported that other white clergymen "have been either highly reserved or actively hostile toward us and our mission." Some ministers had been pleasant to Rowland but had also expressed their opposition to the Delta Ministry. A few clergymen, she noted, "personally may feel sympathetic, but they all fear the wrath of their congregations were they to show any sign of cooperation with an agency of the National Council of Churches, which is widely regarded here as communist-inspired." While Hermetz, a minister of the non-NCC Missouri Synod Lutheran Church, proved "really friendly," other local white pastors from denominations that belonged to the National Council refused to endorse the Ministry.[8]

Rowland's visits to white clergymen produced an invitation for Delta Ministry staff members to attend one of the monthly meetings of the all-white Greenville Ministerial Association. However, the YMCA, which normally housed the association's meetings, refused to allow the Delta Ministry representatives to enter after discovering that the Ministry had a black secretary. The ministerial association switched the meeting to the Delta Ministry office, but only two local ministers came. The Ministry fared no better with Catholics. On several occasions, Walker talked with a local Catholic priest who indicated his desire to become involved in the civil rights movement. However, the priest could not participate because Bishop Richard O. Gerow of the Diocese of Natchez-Jackson had ordered clergymen in his diocese, which stretched across Mississippi, not to be drawn into the movement.[9]

The Delta Ministry suffered no harassment, other than losing its downtown office, but the white community as a whole adopted a policy of "massive noncooperation" that gradually turned into open hostility. Rowland reported that the white power structure was "unalterably opposed to anything that would change the status quo" and would make concessions only under pressure. It was, she said, "essential to them to say they changed because they *had* to." Outside of Greenville's artistic and literary community, few whites were ready to accept change. However, only a handful of people within the city's cultural elite were "ready to assist in bringing changes." Overt support came mostly from Hodding Carter III and from Ruth Brent, a leading member of Trinity Methodist Church. Brent's husband, Jesse, ran two businesses that left the couple economically secure from attack. A member of the board of directors of the Mississippi Council on Human Relations and the main organizer of the Greenville Day Care Center, which served the children of working black mothers, Ruth Brent joined Carter on the Commission on the Delta Ministry. Consequently, Brent's church friends ostracized her.[10]

Almost completely rebuffed by the white community, despite extensive efforts to establish dialogue, the Delta Ministry decided to concentrate primarily on Greenville's African American population. "Our early contacts with white clergy and the white community," Walker explained, "led to the conclusion that this was not the time for reconciliation. We could have talks, but with the Negro being subservient."[11]

Established African American leaders, the Delta Ministry found, were too beholden to white leaders to challenge discrimination. Rowland reported, "The Negro power structure is not willing to take the Delta Ministry to its heart; they are fearful of the white man's displeasure." Black municipal employees, including teachers, were "exceedingly cautious lest they lose their jobs." With few exceptions, most African American ministers remained aloof from the civil rights movement; only the Friendship Baptist Church, located in the heart of the black community, regularly allowed the movement to hold meetings. Herbert Edwards reported that no more than eighteen of the fifty-five members of the black Ministers' Alliance ever attended meetings with the Delta Ministry and that only three or four of them participated in the Ministry's weekly Freedom Church rallies. Some African American businessmen and professionals belonged to the Washington County chapter of the NAACP, but fear of economic retaliation from their white employers and the haughtiness and elitism of NAACP members kept other blacks away. Consequently, the NAACP, Edwards reported, was "practically non-existent."[12]

Riven by factionalism, fear, and apathy, the African American community lacked effective leadership. According to Herbert Edwards, "There are a number of leaders, some self-styled, others so designated by other persons, but a dearth of leadership. It seems that many of the so-called leaders are unable to get any real support and widespread backing in the community because of past betrayals, and now the people will hardly trust anyone." Distrust partly explained widespread black apathy, but other causes also existed. Edwards cited as important factors "fear of loss of jobs, of lack of support from others in the community, of being betrayed by 'Uncle Toms,' of making the most 'liberal' town in Mississippi show its less than liberal colors." Barnes, a member of the black middle class, believed that Greenville's progressive image made it difficult for that class to recognize the city's deficiencies.[13]

Without a disabling history of involvement in the fragmented African American population and respected because of its religious underpinnings, the Delta Ministry received black acceptance as "a good thing for the community." The Ministry concluded that the black population could be mobilized and unified by the creation of a community center, already under consideration by local people. Consequently, the Ministry contributed $2,800 toward the cost of buying land for what became the Herbert Lee Memorial Community Center. Most of the major local black organizations had representatives on the center's advisory committee. Barnes and Walker represented the Delta Ministry on the center's Executive Committee, alongside community leaders and COFO representatives. The Ministry hoped that the Executive Committee would mark "the beginning of the formation of a power structure group for the Negro Community and the base from which the Negro community at large may be organized."[14]

Dr. Matthew J. Page served as chairman of the community center. Page had grown up on the poor south side of Greenville but despite this handicap had graduated from Tougaloo College and Meharry Medical College in Nashville, Tennessee. Well respected by leading members of the white community, he had built a clinic with their financial support. Page pressured Greenville into improving recreational facilities for African Americans and played an active part in the NAACP. At a Freedom Rally held at Friendship Baptist Church in October 1964, Page urged blacks to apply for jobs at Greenville Mill. He pointed out that because the carpet mill had a federal contract, it would have to employ qualified blacks on an equal basis with whites. After the rally, Rowland and Walker spoke with Page about the mill. In her report to the Delta Ministry, Rowland suggested, "Here is something we might find a way to support."[15]

In his conversations with local blacks, Walker had found that employment discrimination was the "most evident grievance" in the community. Consequently, the Ministry called a meeting of black women upset by Greenville Mill's refusal to employ them. The meeting led to the formation of the Washington County Employment Committee (WCEC). The committee, which included Page, tried to persuade the mill to discuss its discriminatory employment policy, which had long been a source of contention among African Americans.[16]

The city's biggest factory, Greenville Mill had opened in 1953. The city had carefully courted the mill's owners, Mohasco Industries of New York City, constructing a $4.75 million building to house the mill. To secure black votes for the bond issue that funded the facility, Greenville authorities, including the Chamber of Commerce, had stated that the plant would have a nondiscriminatory employment policy and would offer jobs to African American women, a large segment of the available labor force. However, the mill never employed black women among its 1,100 workers and confined its 200 to 250 black male employees to low-paying jobs with no possibility of promotion. As he gathered evidence of inequity to present to federal authorities, Walker discovered that the General Services Administration (GSA), charged with ensuring that firms with federal contracts did not discriminate in employment, had awarded Greenville Mill a contract in March 1964 despite finding evidence of racial discrimination in January.[17]

Given time by the GSA to rectify discrimination, Greenville Mill hired six African American women in January 1965 as its federal contract came up for renewal. The Chamber of Commerce's Industrial Foundation announced in the same month that Greenville Mill would receive an award as "the best plant of the year." Herbert Shuttleworth II, Mohasco's president, planned to fly down to Greenville to receive the award. The WCEC sent Shuttleworth a telegram requesting a meeting with him while he was in the city, causing Shuttleworth to cancel his trip.[18]

Unable to persuade Greenville Mill to negotiate, the WCEC decided to picket the factory. The picketing continued for three months, with an average of thirty participants a day. Reports in the *Delta Democrat-Times* claimed that the Delta Ministry and COFO sponsored the picket, with Walker leading the protest. Although police protected the pickets, Police Chief Burnley accused out-of-state participants of shouting abuse at his officers. COFO and Delta Ministry staff, including Walker, joined the picket, but the Ministry contended that it was merely assisting local people in implementing a protest of their own choosing. Walker reported that the Ministry had shown locals how to set up a picket line because none had ever done so. Page told the *Delta Democrat-Times* that the white community "seem to be treating these events as isolated incidents which are unrepresentative of the feelings of the Negro community. Someday, I don't know when, they will realize that they are not." Other established black leaders also supported the picket. James Edwards, a funeral home owner and chairman of the board of the NAACP's Washington County chapter, chaired the WCEC. In February, he moderated a Freedom Rally that decided to continue the picket. Yet the *Delta Democrat-Times* focused its report on Walker's speech to the rally, even though he had been only "one of several speakers." The paper assumed that only whites could have generated and organized the protest.[19]

However, local black leaders subsequently joined in, forcing the *Delta Democrat-Times* to concede that they supported direct action. As a result of their involvement, the paper called for biracial discussions to resolve Greenville's problems and once again displayed its antipathy to the Delta Ministry and COFO. The paper warned that "incipient unity among a hitherto factionalized Negro community could make it impossible to separate the so-called 'good' local from the 'bad' outside organizations." The *Delta Democrat-Times* strongly condemned an attempt to extend the Greenville Mill pickets to the home of W. T. Wilcox, the mill's manager, and the newspaper report highlighted Walker's participation in the action. Although "the right to picket is guaranteed to all Americans," the paper declared, the picket should be confined to the mill and not used "to persecute an individual or his wife and children." Bernadine Young of the WCEC denied any intention to intimidate the Wilcox family and explained that Wilcox's home had been picketed because of his continued refusal to meet with the committee. Aggrieved by the *Delta Democrat-Times*'s hostile coverage and editorial comment, the protesters had police evict reporter John Childs from one of their rallies.[20]

The *Delta Democrat-Times* again condemned the pickets when they voted to march to the mill by a different route each day. Police arrested twenty-six demonstrators over three days for abandoning the previously agreed-upon path and marching through police lines. Walker, Delta Ministry volunteer Keith McNeil, and a few COFO workers were among the people arrested, but local people formed the bulk of those apprehended. Young explained that the demonstrators had hoped to recruit more protesters by walking to the mill through different parts of the community. However, the *Delta Democrat-Times* saw only a "calculated design" on the part of COFO, the Delta Ministry, and "their handful of local allies" to create "an incident to bolster their sagging campaign." Hodding Carter III condemned the two organizations as "phonies . . . who bleed so copiously for the failure of biracial progress, then do their damnedest to insure that the only progress will be on their terms." The arrests stopped after the protesters reached a compromise with the police.[21]

Although he was a member of the Commission on the Delta Ministry, Carter attended neither its first meeting in January 1965 nor its second meeting in April, when the commission endorsed the Ministry's participation in the attempt to end racial discrimination at Greenville Mill and its call for a national boycott of Mohasco Industry's products. Nevertheless, Art Thomas "attempted to keep in personal touch" with Carter, who said that he agreed with the Ministry's opposition to the mill's employment policy. However, Carter, Thomas noted, would not support the black community's challenge against the mill because of his "own employment situation and . . . unwillingness to discuss the internal practices of a business." Exasperated, Thomas wrote to Carter, "Instead you teamed up editorially with the persons in the community who attempted to distract from the real issue by the phony issue of the arrests and a march route."[22]

Picketing ended in late April 1965, when Mohasco officials requested talks under pressure from the GSA, which had refused to renew a federal contract until the mill acted against discrimination. City authorities led by Mayor Pat Dunne sought to choose the "negotiators for the picketers," while the pickets "appointed several 'established leaders' for their negotiating committee." As a result, the Delta Ministry reported, the "established leaders," including James Edwards and Matthew Page, "were expected on the one hand to deal with the situation as the white community wanted it handled, but on the other hand were expected to deal with it as the picketers hoped." The WCEC picketing and negotiating committees soon were at odds. The pickets became convinced that the mill was negotiating in bad faith after its officials and the mayor called a secret negotiating session without Henry Aronson, an NAACP Legal Defense and Educational Fund lawyer whom the WCEC had hired as an adviser. Consequently, the picketing committee called for an end to talks and had Aronson file suit against the mill. Undaunted, James Edwards declared that the talks would continue. Aronson responded that the negotiating committee was "negotiating out of stupidity rather than out of interest in the problem." Eventually, under pressure from the lawsuit and the GSA, the mill agreed to employ an equal number of black and white women, to promote qualified black men, and to desegregate its drinking fountains and snack area.[23]

The protest had been a great success, but white authorities had divided the African American community after the picket had initially united members in a common cause. Working-class black women, who had formed the bulk of the picketers, felt betrayed by traditional leaders from the black business class, such as Edwards and Page, whom the women had at first trusted. Through participation in pickets and committees, African American women discovered their voice and

agency. They, and some other members of the black poor, were no longer prepared to take direction from the African American elite. Black business and professional men, for their part, were more conservative. They would have preferred
negotiations with Greenville Mill at the outset, but the company had consistently
refused. When negotiations at last became possible, members of the black elite believed that they could succeed by working with the mayor and company officials,
in much the same way as the city had previously made concessions regarding
such issues as recreational facilities. According to Bishop Paul Moore Jr., chairman of the Commission on the Delta Ministry, the wcec negotiating committee
had "broken faith with the picketers by conducting a negotiation with the Mayor
without consultation with them." The negotiating committee's members were
prepared to compromise and accept gradual change at a pace decided by whites.
They dismissed the picketing committee's objections as those of a minority of
the wcec.[24]

Committed above all to the empowerment and self-actualization of the African
American poor, the Delta Ministry welcomed the success at Greenville Mill.
However, the Ministry had also become estranged from the city's black business
and professional leaders. Page charged that during the picket, the Delta Ministry had sought to induce federal intervention by adopting tactics that would
result in an incident in which people would be injured or killed. Although the
accusation was implausible, it indicated the depth of the breach between Page
and the Ministry. Page also claimed that the Ministry had sought to undermine
his leadership and that Thomas had threatened to destroy Page if he did not go
along with Thomas's plans or leave the movement. For its part, the Delta Ministry
contended that it initially had worked with Page, but the poor had rejected his
leadership. Consequently, the Ministry had "stood with the poor people in this
rejection."[25]

Convinced that the Delta Ministry represented a radical threat, Greenville's
white businessmen and professionals and their African American counterparts
began to work together. In May 1965, the Chamber of Commerce and a group of
black businesspeople, some of them affiliated with the NAACP, issued separate but
jointly published statements in the *Delta Democrat-Times* that supported equal employment opportunities. Hodding Carter III welcomed this "epochal joint declaration" and accused the Delta Ministry and COFO of trying to "sabotage the cooperative venture." Both groups denied Carter's accusation as well as the paper's
report that they had opposed the statements. Dismissing their objections, Carter
accused them of harboring a desire for a far-reaching revolution that they would
provoke by creating incidents that "will bring the two racial communities to the
battle lines in implacable hostility." His editorials received national publicity in

Time magazine and in a syndicated column by Nicholas Von Hoffman, bringing the NCC and the Delta Ministry complaints and anxious inquiries from pastors and laymen across the United States. At a time when the Ministry struggled to attract funds from many of the NCC's member denominations, the editor's charges proved especially damaging.[26]

Called to account for Carter's accusations, Walker explained to the Commission on the Delta Ministry that Page had convened a special session of the Herbert Lee Memorial Community Center's Executive Committee to discuss the employment statement issued by black organizations. Walker correctly claimed that most of the organizations represented "the same ten or fifteen persons." The Executive Committee had voted four to three against the statement because Page had tried to push it through without adequate time for discussion and consideration, particularly because participants had to share a single copy of the statement. Committee member Barnes had voted in favor of the statement, and Walker had voted against, but the Delta Ministry had taken no official position.[27]

Thomas believed that Carter's failure to attend meetings of the Commission on the Delta Ministry partly explained his "lack of knowledge." The Ministry's director also felt that the problem ran deeper because the editor could not accept that many local blacks no longer needed him to speak out for them against injustice. They also rejected the gradualism that he and members of the black elite, such as Page, favored. Carter accused the Ministry of "busily trying to discredit the same Negro leadership whose help they once welcomed." Yet several NCC and Delta Ministry staff reported that, in private conversations with them, the editor had welcomed the Ministry's presence. Carter had said that it deflected attacks away from him, thereby giving the editor more influence in the community.[28]

Members of the black elite shared Carter's publicly expressed hostility to the Delta Ministry, which they accused of trying to supplant their leadership. They resented the fact that the African American poor rejected them and, rather than recognizing this decision as having been made by the poor themselves, accused the Ministry of seeking to undermine and replace these leaders at the head of the community. There was a class division between the poor and the business and professional classes. Their differences were based not on different aspirations but on a struggle for leadership of the community and the right to represent it in discussions with white leaders. Levye Chapple, president of the all-black Washington County Democratic Club, had signed the black equal opportunity statement. He subsequently complained, in what the *Delta Democrat-Times* interpreted as an attack on the Delta Ministry and COFO, "The groups which make up the Herbert Lee Center should be consulted and allowed to participate in the decisions of the group and we have been ignored by those controlling the Center." Matthew Page agreed with Chapple: "I maintain that all major civil rights activities in the city should be directed by Greenville people. Outside help is welcome when it helps us do what we want to do but not when it tries to direct the operation."[29]

Another point of contention between Page and the Delta Ministry was the Ministry's support and encouragement of black agricultural workers in the newly formed Mississippi Freedom Labor Union (MFLU) who had chosen to go on strike. The union had emerged from discussions at a COFO Freedom School about how African American farm workers could improve their pay and working conditions. Tractor divers typically earned six dollars a day; cotton pickers a little less; and choppers—mostly women, children, and elderly men who weeded the cotton—only three dollars. The workday lasted from dawn to sundown. In April 1965, forty-five farm workers in Shaw, in Bolivar County, organized the MFLU, which demanded a $1.25 per hour minimum wage, an eight-hour day, sick pay, and health and accident insurance. The workers went on strike at the Seligmann plantation in support of their demands. Within two weeks, one thousand people in eight counties had joined the union, and at least two hundred of these Delta workers soon were on strike.[30]

By the time the first strike occurred in Shaw, Walker for several months had been spending two days a week with agricultural workers in Tribbett, ten miles east of Greenville. He had first gone to Tribbett shortly before Christmas 1964 to deliver some of the twenty thousand turkeys donated to Mississippi's poor by comedian Dick Gregory and syndicated columnist Drew Pearson. Walker found that the workers he met were unaware that African Americans could vote. Consequently, he organized regular meetings to discuss civil rights at Roosevelt Adams's grocery store, located on Adams's eighty-acre farm, two miles from Leland. Adams, the only black farm owner in the area, sympathized with the movement because white night riders had tortured one of his family members.[31]

Isaac Foster accompanied Walker to the meetings at Adams's store. Born in Sunflower County, Foster, a twenty-two-year-old African American, had grown up on Mississippi plantations. A white man had killed Foster's father in 1957 because he was about to buy his own farm from a black landowner. Foster had graduated from high school at age twenty-one and worked at the Greenville Mill. When picketing began at the mill, he tried to organize its workers in sympathy but soon lost his job. Consequently, Foster returned to plantation work to support his mother. He visited the MFLU in Shaw and told the Tribbett workers about the union and its demands. Prompted by Foster, twelve tractor drivers at the Andrews Brothers' Plantation joined the MFLU and, after a unanimous vote, went on strike at the end of May.[32]

Bill Sartor, a former *Delta Democrat-Times* reporter, wrote in a freelance story for *Time* that the Delta Ministry had incited and "ardently" promoted the strike. Walker, Sartor reported, had denounced "the man in the big white house taking food out of your wife's and your children's mouths and the clothes off your back." He implied that Walker had also stated that "the white man is your enemy." In fact, Walker, himself white and described by fellow staffer Bob Beech as "our radical—our revolutionary," had made only the first statement. Von Hoffman claimed in his syndicated newspaper column that Walker was the strike's "organizer and leader." However, the Delta Ministry declared that it had "neither planned nor incited this strike." It had supported the men in the decision they had made and helped them organize as Local 4 of the MFLU, with Foster serving as the local's chairman.[33]

A. L. Andrews evicted the tractor drivers and their families, who worked as cotton choppers, from the rent-free houses he provided on the plantation. Earl Fisher, chief deputy sheriff of Washington County, used inmates from the county jail to pile up the strikers' furniture and other belongings along the highway, damaging some of them in the process. The Delta Ministry provided food, medical care, and a large tent as housing for the expelled men on Adams's land while they picketed the plantation. The Ministry also fed and housed the drivers' wives and children—forty-eight people—at Mount Beulah for a week and then arranged accommodation for them at Greenville Industrial College, owned by the black Mississippi Baptist State Educational Association.[34]

A day after the strike began, Andrews obtained an injunction in the Washington County Chancery Court that limited picketing to four people. He hoped to render the tactic ineffective, since several roads entered his 1,300-acre plantation. Walker and Delta Ministry volunteers joined the picket and its largely successful efforts to persuade black Greenvillians not to ride the buses to work at the Andrews plantation or at another plantation where workers had also gone on strike. Andrews initially used labor supplied by sympathetic local planters before importing white workers from Arkansas to maintain operations. The strikers suffered several violent incidents, including shots fired over their heads, an ammonia spray attack, the slashing of their car tires, and an attempt to run over a striker. Justice of the Peace L. L. Hubbard of Leland refused to act on strikers' complaints about their treatment yet convicted in absentia David DeRienzis, a Delta Ministry volunteer, of assault and battery on James Mason, a black bus driver who carried workers to the plantations. DeRienzis, from New York City, had denied the charge before leaving the state at the Ministry's instruction.[35]

Citing unsanitary and overcrowded conditions, the local health department forced the eviction of the Andrews strikers' families from Greenville Industrial

College in late June. Walker believed that they had been evicted for their civil rights activity, since whites rented many homes to African Americans that had far worse conditions. The families joined the strikers on five acres of Adams's land, living in family groups. The Delta Ministry supplied them with tents, food, and clothing. The inhabitants called their encampment Strike City.[36]

This strike, like those at other Delta plantations, failed to achieve its demands. Across the Delta, strikers were evicted from their plantation homes and found themselves unemployed and unemployable. In the short term, the strikes improved conditions for some of those who did not participate. The *Memphis Commercial Appeal* reported that some planters increased wages, although they still remained far below the level demanded by the MFLU, and some planters had also made "extensive improvements in [the] homes and general living conditions" of the tractor drivers needed to run the farms. In the long term, the strike only encouraged more planters to dispense with cotton pickers and choppers, the poorest agricultural workers, and replace them with mechanical cotton pickers and herbicides.[37]

The Federal Food and Fiber Act of 1965 also hastened agricultural employment since it provided "a payment of 10.5 cents per pound on projected yields for land diverted from cotton production" and "required at least a 12.5 percent reduction in acreage and allowed up to a 35 percent cutback." Some planters allowed their unwanted workers to remain rent-free in plantation shacks, while others made the most of their reduced cotton acreage by evicting workers, demolishing their homes, and planting over them. Few if any planters shared federal payments with their employees. The MFLU staged a second wave of strikes in the fall cotton picking season, but, under such adverse conditions, the strikes proved abortive. The union soon withered away.[38]

Since the strikers could not obtain or maintain employment in Greenville once their backgrounds became known, the Delta Ministry continued to aid the people at Strike City. Foster joined the Ministry's Freedom Corps and lived at Strike City with three other corps members. The families struggled through the cold winter in their tents, making wooden nativity sets for sale to sympathizers through the Delta Ministry's national contacts. The effort marked the beginning of Freedomcrafts, a network of cooperatives with start-up funding provided by the Ministry that subsequently spread to Freedom City, Edwards, Shaw, and West Point in 1966. The Ministry also helped arrange for students from the University of Pennsylvania to build a community center at Strike City during Christmas 1965. Strike City residents accepted leadership from Frank Smith, an African American former SNCC activist and head of Neighborhood Developers, Inc., of Jackson, Mississippi, after he promised to build them houses with money from an anonymous northern donor. Consequently, the Delta Ministry and Foster withdrew from direct involvement with Strike City, but the Ministry remained a channel through which resources could be sent. By the fall of 1966, Strike City's residents lived in eight newly built houses on land bought from Adams. They had also found "decent paying jobs in Greenville."[39]

Delta planters, the state AFL-CIO, and Matthew Page roundly criticized the MFLU's strike action, correctly arguing that a strike had no chance of success in a glutted agricultural labor market and would inevitably hasten further unemployment. In meetings with the MFLU and the Delta Ministry, Claude Ramsay, president of the Mississippi AFL-CIO, also pointed out the impracticality of trying to organize thousands of tractor drivers and seasonal cotton pickers and choppers over such a vast area. Born of desperation, the MFLU had been unrealistic in its goals. The Ministry's enthusiasm for the both the union and the strike was misplaced and reflected its identification with the struggle of the poor rather than a hard-nosed appreciation of economic realities.[40]

For Matthew Page and Hodding Carter III, who shared a commitment to gradual evolutionary change, the Ministry's involvement in the Tribbett strike provided further evidence of its determination to foment revolution. Page saw a sinister design behind the Ministry's support for the striking farm workers, explaining, "These people would end up frustrated—they would have absolutely no hope, and they would become totally dependent upon the Delta Ministry, SNCC, and FDP and perhaps communist apparatus and become tools for the ultimate political coup that I think is still possible. This is part of their plans to create these frustrated dead-end groups." Carter focused particularly on Walker's role, telling Nicholas Von Hoffman, "If those suburban church ladies who pour their thousands of dollars in the ministry could hear Larry talk to the farm workers they would drop their teeth."[41]

The *Delta Democrat-Times*'s antipathy toward the Delta Ministry increased when its staff supported a three-month boycott against Stein Mart, Greenville's largest store, that the WCEC called in June 1965. Jake Stein, the store's owner, had been an outspoken advocate of nondiscriminatory employment, and Stein Mart had two African American employees. The *Delta Democrat-Times* condemned the boycott as "gangsterism" and defended Stein's record. The paper accused the boycotters of wanting a quota system for black employment. In private, Hodding Carter II sarcastically wrote, "These men of God in the Delta Ministry decided that Jake must go." Like his son, Hodding II assumed that local blacks could not have begun the boycott on their own initiative.[42]

However, Bruce Hilton, who joined the Delta Ministry as director of interpretation in July, described the WCEC's action as a "questionable choice" because other stores still would not hire African Americans despite the Chamber of Commerce's recent equal employment statement. Walker denied that the Ministry had had any role in the WCEC's choice of Stein Mart and reiterated that the Ministry saw its role as supporting local black people in their decisions, even if they were ill-advised. Furthermore, the WCEC had called the boycott only after a month of talks with Stein about hiring a black cashier had failed. Stein argued that he employed only family members in that position, but the committee subsequently discovered that he had lied. Distrustful of Stein and aware that blacks provided half his business, the WCEC decided to picket. Stein Mart rode out the boycott.[43]

Hilton, like other Delta Ministry staff members, found that Hodding Carter III privately expressed support for the Ministry. Yet the *Delta Democrat-Times*, Hilton lamented, "continues to attack DM on a rather irrational basis whenever it gets the chance." Carter's denunciations helped to encourage and legitimate other assaults on the Ministry because of his paper's moderate credentials and reputation for reliability.[44]

Several local white clergymen publicly attacked the Delta Ministry. Robert Glenn, pastor of the First Christian Church, told the East Greenville Kiwanis Club that the Ministry had "violated a professional code of ethics" by its uninvited presence and that it had "set things back about ten years." In an address to the Leland Rotary Club, Patrick Sanders, rector of Greenville's St. James Episcopal Church, lambasted the Ministry as "incompetent and not really Christian in its approach." He cited the Tribbett strike as an example and interpreted it as little more than an irresponsible publicity stunt to raise funds. T. Robert Fulton, pastor of the First Presbyterian Church, claimed that Delta Ministry staff "have made no effort to enlist people in their work" and that the NCC had not engaged in dialogue. The clergymen ignored the National Council's extensive consultations with the leaders of Mississippi's denominations both before and after the Ministry's launch.[45]

Some opposition to the Ministry was more sinister. After an absence of forty-two years, the Ku Klux Klan returned to Greenville, burning two crosses in the area in July 1965 and coming under suspicion for the arson of a black church in nearby Balewood. Arriving in Greenville, the Hilton family tried to rent a house in the white community, "but Klan agitation and leaflets calling us 'the filthy, immoral dregs of the earth' caused 55 families to pay rent on the house to keep us out." Appalled by the action and anxious to retain Greenville's reputation for "tolerant decency," the *Delta Democrat-Times* condemned such "cowardly intimidation." When the Hiltons finally rented a home, the Klan kept it under surveillance. Only two white couples ever visited the Hiltons. A white woman withdrew her invitation to Ginny Hilton, the pastor's wife, to join the local chapter of the

American Association of University Women after the act generated opposition. The Hiltons attended five white churches, but each of their pastors refused to call on them when invited. Their social life, like that of other Delta Ministry staff, was restricted to Ministry personnel and the African American community.[46]

The Hiltons enrolled one of their four sons in a local Head Start center, one of eight operated by CDGM in Greenville and nearby communities. Prompted by Art Thomas, Thelma Barnes had taken on the task of organizing and locating sites for CDGM in and around Greenville and hiring staff. As chairperson of the Herbert Lee Memorial Community Center's Head Start Committee, Barnes performed the work almost single-handedly, serving "as a local citizen and not as a Delta Ministry employee." Her efforts saw 367 children enroll in a seven-week program "of fun and excitement centered around learning experiences in song, play, academic work, personal recognition, wholesome food, good eating habits, improved health habits, complete physical examination, one well balanced meal and two snacks daily, [and] field trips." The eight centers, for which Barnes assumed responsibility, employed 105 people, paying all of them at least the $1.25 per hour that the MFLU had demanded for agricultural workers. Matthew Page praised Barnes's stewardship of CDGM, but he and the NAACP remained otherwise strongly critical of the Delta Ministry's involvement in Greenville.[47]

Unwilling to work together, the Washington County NAACP and the county MFDP conducted separate voter registration campaigns after Mississippi simplified and eased its voter registration requirements in the summer of 1965. The Delta Ministry jointly sponsored the MFDP's voter registration drive and lent dozens of volunteers to the project. Solomon Gort Jr., a native of Cleveland, Mississippi, who joined the Delta Ministry in July, worked among his fellow black clergymen in the Ministers' Alliance. "The clergy here in Greenville," Gort reported, are "in a gross state of lethargy, they listen, but [are] hard to activate." Nevertheless, the Ministers' Alliance supported the voter registration campaign. The NAACP, the MFDP, and the Delta Ministry registered a total of about three thousand new voters in the city during the summer of 1965. Gort rated the campaigns' success as "fair" and cautioned, "There is a great deal of work yet to be done in getting people registered to vote."[48]

The Delta Ministry carried out a simultaneous voter registration campaign in Bolivar County, where it had begun a new project under Owen Brooks in June, and in other counties to which it had assigned the Freedom Corps workers it had trained in late spring and early summer at Mount Beulah. Brooks, a well-educated electronics engineer from Boston, Massachusetts, spent his early months in Bolivar, the largest and poorest county in the Delta, assessing and trying to work with existing civil rights organizations. He found the NAACP "non-existent," with only a few members and no program. The MFDP fared only a little better. Brooks reported that "the FDP organization in Bolivar is decidedly weak in its leadership and resultantly lacking in program." After COFO disbanded in July 1965, its projects in Shaw, Cleveland, Rosedale, and Winstonville "passed over into the hands of either FDP or DM." The Ministry "completely" took over the administration of the COFO project in Winstonville, an all-black town. Brooks reported that most of the county's churches refused to become involved in civil rights activity.[49]

With the NAACP inactive and the MFDP ineffective, Delta Ministry staff and volunteers and Freedom Corps members played the leading role in registering 300 people in Cleveland and others in Rosedale and Winstonville, all within the boundaries of Bolivar County. During the summer, Freedom Corps staff and the MFDP helped 150 people attempt to register in Yazoo County, more than 300 in Holmes County, 200 in Tallahatchie County, and 15 in Sunflower County.[50]

At the request of local people, the Delta Ministry's Bolivar County Project also sent food and clothing to neighboring Tallahatchie County during the summer. In August 1965, it assigned Freedom Corps worker Ben Brown to assist in an economic survey of the county and in voter registration. The Delta Ministry helped black farmers organize the Tallahatchie County Improvement Association. Gort transferred from Greenville to begin the Ministry's Tallahatchie Project, which focused on "community organization, adult education, head-start, [and] voter education and registration."[51]

Tallahatchie was one of eight Delta counties that, along with Madison and Yazoo Counties, was included in the Delta Opportunities Association (DOA). Assisted by the Delta Ministry, fifty African Americans, nineteen of them independent farmers, formed DOA in September 1965 at the suggestion of Henry S. Reuss, a Democratic congressman from Wisconsin. DOA sought incorporation from the state of Mississippi as a nonprofit group, seeking federal and charitable foundation funds for jobs and economic development, low-cost housing, and small business opportunities. As an agency of the NCC, the Delta Ministry could not apply for federal funds because of the separation of church and state. DOA's all-black steering committee included Aaron Henry, state president of the NAACP and a member of the Commission on the Delta Ministry; Thelma Barnes; two clergymen; and several farmers. Already at odds with the Delta Ministry because of its support and close working relationship with the MFDP, the NAACP's rival in Mississippi, Henry soon left the steering committee and the commission. He secured OEO and U.S. Department of Labor funding for Coahoma Opportunities, which primarily operated adult education and Head Start programs in his home county. Henry's departure removed Coahoma County from DOA, which became a nine-county organization.[52]

Art Thomas asked Hodding Carter II to support DOA, which shared the Delta Ministry's office in Greenville. However, Carter believed that as a newspaper editor he should not become directly involved. However, he offered to serve the group in an advisory capacity and to write an editorial in its support. His cautious editorial stated that "we cannot see any reason, at first glance, to oppose the program as outlined if it does not collide with nor duplicate local or county projects which will also need money from the government." Mississippi at first refused to incorporate DOA, although, after litigation, it later secured recognition as the Delta Opportunities Corporation (DOC). DOC applied for OEO funding early in 1966. Opposition from Mississippi's political leaders and the priority OEO gave to Coahoma Opportunities delayed DOC's first federal grant until 1967. A few months later, it received matching funds from the Ford Foundation.[53]

Clarence Hall Jr., who farmed sixty-six acres in Issaquena County, served as DOC's chairman. He lost his part-time job as a flat grinder operator in Greenville when he returned late from a trip to Washington, D.C., with Delta Ministry staff to confer with federal officials about DOA. Consequently, in October 1965, the Ministry added the World War II combat veteran to its staff as director of a new project in Issaquena and Sharkey Counties.[54]

However, Greenville and Washington County remained the main focus of Ministry activity in the Delta. In September 1965, 146 African American children enrolled in formerly white schools in Greenville. The Delta Ministry had played an important role in school desegregation by calling a series of late 1964 meetings to discuss the issue, resulting in the Herbert Lee Memorial Community Center's establishment of a school desegregation committee. Barnes and Page were among the Committee's members. They forged a good working relationship that withstood the later tensions between Page and other members of the Delta Ministry's staff. Frustrated by lack of progress in its meetings with the Greenville School Board of Education, the committee organized a petition signed by 250 people. A week later, the board announced that it would voluntarily begin desegregation to avoid a federal lawsuit and withdrawal of federal school funds, which constituted 10 percent of the city's school budget.[55]

Dissatisfied with the school board's plan to desegregate only the first grade, the school desegregation committee demanded full desegregation and equalization of classroom teachers' salaries. The committee presented its demands to the school board and complained to the U.S. Office of Education about the limited desegregation plan. New federal guidelines forced the board to submit a revised plan that desegregated four grades. The board also equalized teachers' salaries. The Delta Ministry "supported intensive door-to-door canvassing" that encouraged African American parents to transfer their children to the city's white schools, all of which desegregated.[56]

By the time the schools desegregated, Larry Walker had resigned from the Delta Ministry because of "the physical strain which my work entails" and perhaps because of the vilification he had received in the national and local press. Thomas, who had early on detected leadership qualities in Barnes of which she had been unaware, appointed her as project director for Greenville and Washington County, replacing Walker.[57]

Despite Walker's departure, the *Delta Democrat-Times* continued to attack the Delta Ministry. With Hodding Carter III recently departed to Harvard as a Nieman Fellow and no longer even nominally on the Commission on the Delta Ministry, his father took up more editorial writing. Less than three weeks after half-heartedly supporting DOA in an editorial, Hodding II censured Warren McKenna for his 1957 trip to China against the wishes of the U.S. State Department. Carter stated that the trip made McKenna a poor choice for the Delta Ministry, since it made him a divisive figure, at odds with the Ministry's stated goal of reconciliation. The editor claimed that Ministry staff did not want to improve Mississippi's race relations. Instead, he argued, they divided the races and alienated the African American middle class. "If the Delta Ministry chooses . . . to advocate something akin to class warfare," Carter concluded, "the quicker the National Council of Churches gets the monkey off its back the better." He continued the theme three days later, arguing that the Ministry needed to abandon its confrontational tactics of "protest marches, boycotts, strikes [and] picketing" in favor of conciliation. Carter's wife, Betty, explained to Hilton, much as her son Hodding had done earlier, that the *Delta Democrat-Times* maintained its influence in the community by distancing itself from the Ministry.[58]

The provision of relief to the poor seemed on the surface to be a noncontroversial Delta Ministry program. During three months' service as consultants to the Ministry, Herbert Edwards had set up a relief program in Greenville, and his wife, Helen, had helped distribute food and clothing in Issaquena County. During its first winter, the Greenville Project provided nutrition and garments to 300 families including 2,400 people. The project dispensed nearly ten tons of food, but it acknowledged that people's needs far outstripped the available resources.[59]

Several Delta counties, including Washington, Sunflower, and Bolivar, ordinarily distributed federal surplus commodities to the poor but did so only during the winter months, beginning in December, when planters did not require large numbers of laborers. In the fall of 1965, more than seven hundred people were also on strike for higher wages under the banner of the MFLU. To help the impoverished of the three counties, the Delta Ministry in November 1965 distributed seventy-four tons of food donated by the National Student Association.[60]

Another relief effort, Operation Help, was approved by OEO and the Mississippi Department of Public Welfare on November 23, 1965, but the new program still had not yet started by late January 1966. OEO withheld its $1.6 million grant for Mississippi to distribute $24 million in federal surplus commodities for six months because the state had not established a biracial administrative board. At the same time, opposition from U.S. Senator John C. Stennis of Mississippi continued to hold up a second grant from OEO to CDGM. The state employment service had also announced that a 35 percent decrease in crop allotments by the federal government would throw 6,500 tractor drivers and mechanics and their families, some 30,000 people, out of work and off the plantations by the spring of 1966. The service accurately predicted that employment of cotton pickers and choppers would halve from 1965 levels. Alarmed by these developments, the MFDP, the MFLU, and the Delta Ministry called on Mississippi's poor to participate in a conference at Mount Beulah to discuss ways to obtain food, employment, and housing.[61]

Seven hundred people attended the three-day meeting, which began on January 29, 1966, calling themselves the Poor People's Conference. After waiting two days in vain for President Lyndon B. Johnson to reply to a telegram in which the participants described their plight and called for jobs and housing, the poor voted to send a contingent to occupy Greenville Air Force Base to protest their condition and demand the base for housing. Deactivated by the air force in March 1965, the base had a skeleton staff and better accommodations than were available to many of the poor. Forty protesters from the Poor People's Conference, including Isaac Foster, entered the base at 6:30 A.M. on January 31, 1966, driving by its surprised guards. The protesters were joined by several members of the MFDP and the Delta Ministry, including Thomas and Brooks. Other plantation workers and civil rights workers later joined the occupiers, as military and civil authorities discussed which of them had jurisdiction. The occupiers soon numbered about one hundred people.[62]

Bishop Paul Moore and Hilton, neither of whom had been present at the Poor People's Conference, and a contemporary Delta Ministry account claimed that the Ministry had not suggested the occupation. But they recognized that its staff had not attempted to dissuade the members of the Poor People's Conference from pursuing the idea. Once the poor had made their decision, Moore reported, the Ministry had decided to support it despite some staff members' reservations about its wisdom. However, Brooks later told an interviewer that he, Thomas, Hall, Barnes, and some MFDP leaders had met separately from the Poor People's

Conference, conceived the idea of occupying the air base, and then presented it to the Poor People's Conference for consideration.[63]

Whatever its origins, the occupation garnered local and national media coverage and the attention of the White House. On behalf of the Poor People's Conference, the group demanded food, jobs, job training, income, land, employment of the poor in Operation Help, and refunding of CDGM. The federal government offered to fly spokespersons from the occupying group to Washington, D.C., for negotiations, but the protesters refused to leave the base. On the morning of February 1, a contingent of 150 air police forcibly evicted the group. The occupiers were carried out quietly except for a few plantation workers and a group of embittered civil rights workers, who kicked and shouted abuse at the air police. The group took temporary refuge at Strike City before moving on to land owned by an African American farmer in Issaquena County. Sickness, freezing rains, and deep mud forced them off the land after a week. At the Delta Ministry's invitation, they moved to Mount Beulah while they searched for permanent accommodations.[64]

Predictably, the Mississippi press condemned the occupiers as lawbreakers. The *Delta Democrat-Times* singled out the Delta Ministry for particular criticism and reported that Thomas, Barnes, and McKenna had planned the air base occupation. The paper's editorial page declared, "If the Delta Ministry, whose members were with the squatters, supports such lawlessness[,] it, like the Ku Klux Klan, has misused the cross of Christ and set itself above the law." The Executive Council of the Protestant Episcopal Church and thirty-one white Methodist ministers from the Cleveland District of the North Mississippi Conference also condemned the occupation.[65]

Nevertheless, the occupiers induced the federal government to act. As a direct result of the incident, U.S. Attorney General Nicholas Katzenbach wrote to President Johnson, "I think it is essential that we deal with this problem expeditiously and directly through surplus food distribution, crash employment programs, and as many poverty programs as we can fund." OEO immediately released the grant needed to implement Operation Help. In February, 348,000 Mississippians received surplus commodities under the program, with 500,000 served before the completion of Operation Help on June 30. The Mississippi Department of Public Welfare appointed an administrative board acceptable to OEO so that the state could control the program. The U.S. Justice Department declined calls from Mississippi congressmen to prosecute the protesters. Partly as a consequence of the occupation, CDGM received a new grant of $5.6 million to operate Head Start centers for six months in twenty-eight counties. However, the federal government did not meet the group's other demands, and the protest had no long-term impact on federal policy. Furthermore, occurring ten days after the first meeting of an NCC evaluation committee to assess the Delta Ministry, the action endangered the Ministry's future.[66]

The Delta Ministry also faced the immediate practical problem of the responsibility it had assumed for the refugees from the occupation. For some time, it had contemplated creating a "New City" to which displaced plantation workers could relocate, build their own houses, and sustain themselves through farming and small-scale industry. The Ministry had presented the idea to the Poor People's Conference at Mount Beulah before the air force base occupation. With most of those evicted once again at Mount Beulah along with other plantation refugees, the idea of inaugurating New or Freedom City assumed priority. Aided by the Delta Ministry, DOC bought land twelve miles from Greenville for the creation of Freedom City and held it in trust for the Poor People's Conference. In April, a northern sympathizer provided a loan to cover the down payment on the site, while its future residents commuted daily from Mount Beulah to work the land and prepare the site.[67]

Freedom City marked a new avenue in the Delta Ministry's attempts to provide the rural poor with an alternative to outmigration as mechanization and federal agricultural policy displaced them from the land. By 1966, the Ministry had only just begun to grapple with these problems, inaugurating projects in the Delta counties of Washington, Bolivar, Tallahatchie, Issaquena, and Sharkey. It had supported the MFLU's unrealistic strikes and lent particular assistance to the Andrews strikers. The Ministry had been more successful in Greenville, where it had assisted in voter registration, school desegregation, Head Start, and action that ended discriminatory employment at Greenville Mill. But with few exceptions, the white community had from the outset recoiled from the Ministry, despite its efforts to establish communication. The Delta Ministry initially worked with the African American professional and business class and with Hodding Carter III. However, the Ministry's overriding commitment to working with the poor and the direct action techniques that the poor adopted soon alienated moderate blacks and the Carter family. By forcing the implementation of Operation Help and the refunding of CDGM, the Greenville Air Force Base occupation became one of the most successful Ministry-assisted protests. But it also provided the Ministry's many critics with further ammunition when they appeared before the NCC's Evaluation Committee on the Delta Ministry.

CHAPTER SIX

Under Investigation

Less than eighteen months into its operations, the Delta Ministry underwent an extensive evaluation by the NCC. The Evaluation Committee gave
the Ministry's critics a full opportunity to voice their objections to its
program and conduct. At the same time, the Methodist Church, which
did not fund the Delta Ministry, undertook a separate investigation of the
project. The NCC's Evaluation Committee made several harsh criticisms
of the Ministry yet still gave it a strong overall endorsement that convinced the NCC's governing General Board of the project's worth. Issued in
May 1966, the NCC's report, alongside a subsequent favorable report by the
Methodists' investigative committee, persuaded the Methodist Church to
begin funding the Ministry. Substantial Methodist support reduced the
project's deficit and secured its operations. The Delta Ministry emerged
from its period of scrutiny with a refined set of goals drafted by the NCC,
a solid financial base, and new leadership. During the summer of 1966,
Bishop Paul Moore Jr., chairman of the Commission on the Delta Ministry, and Art Thomas, the Ministry's director, resigned, and the National
Council fired Warren McKenna, Thomas's assistant.[1]

Officially, the initiative for the NCC's investigation came from the Commission on the Delta Ministry. The commission explained to the National
Council's General Board in December 1965 that "the first-year budget for
this pioneering program did not provide for a number of needs which were

impossible to foresee." In particular, the Delta Ministry had provided food and housing for families evicted from the Andrews Brothers' Plantation in Tribbett after they had struck for higher wages. Furthermore, the budget had "greatly underestimated the eagerness with which people in need would respond to Delta Ministry programs." Acutely aware that the needs of poor Mississippians far exceeded its budget of $260,000, which the Ministry hoped in vain would be increased to $400,000, the commission asked the NCC "to evaluate the program so far," to establish priorities, and to recommend "guidelines for future action."[2]

The investigation also had other sources. The NCC's General Board preferred "to have impartial examination of all its programs from time to time." Edward J. Pendergrass, the Methodist bishop of the Jackson Area and one of the Delta Ministry's most persistent Mississippi critics, welcomed the National Council's appointment of an investigative committee, which he had long sought. John F. Anderson Jr., executive secretary of the PCUS's Board of Church Extension, claimed that "it was at the behest of our denominational leaders in the General Board" that the NCC appointed the Evaluation Committee. In April 1965, the PCUS's General Assembly had ordered its own investigation of the Delta Ministry. A year later, with the National Council's study under way, the assembly agreed to allow its Permanent Committee on Inter-Church Relations an additional twelve months to complete its report on the Delta Ministry in "fairness" to the NCC's Evaluation Committee.[3]

Unaware of the National Council's investigation, the Woman's Division of the Methodist Church focused on the Delta Ministry at a conference in Frogmore, South Carolina, in February 1966. Impressed by the Delta Ministry's achievements, the Frogmore Conference adopted a resolution asking the Woman's Division to request that the Methodist Church's National Division aid the Ministry. Peggy Billings, secretary of the Section of Christian Social Relations at the Woman's Division, gave the Delta Ministry enthusiastic backing and consistently urged Methodist officials to support it. A white Mississippian originally from McComb, Billings had visited the Ministry in November 1965. She had examined its programs, talked with staff and volunteers, and spoken to local people the Ministry had assisted. The former missionary to South Korea wrote a glowing testimonial for Bruce Hilton, the Ministry's director of interpretation, to use for publicity purposes. But made aware of the NCC's Evaluation Committee on the Delta Ministry, the executive committee of the Woman's Division voted to take no action on the Frogmore statement until after the NCC committee had issued its report.[4]

Reuben H. Miller, the National Council's president, appointed Brooks Hays and A. Dale Fiers as cochairmen of the Evaluation Committee. Hays, a former president of the non-NCC Southern Baptist Convention, had lost his Arkansas congressional seat in 1958 after urging obedience to federal law during the Little Rock school desegregation crisis. Fiers was president of the UCMS of the Disciples of Christ. The Evaluation Committee had nineteen members drawn from twelve denominations. It included several African Americans, notably Dorothy Cotton, director of the SCLC's Citizenship Education Program, and George Wiley, associate director of CORE. Bryant George of the UPCUSA's Board of National Missions, who was also a member of the Commission on the Delta Ministry, served on the Evaluation Committee's staff. Delta Ministry opponents, such as Francis B. Stevens, lay leader of the (Methodist) Mississippi Conference, also sat on the committee. Hilton wrote gloomily that only five committee members were from denominations that gave financial support to the Delta Ministry. Moore expressed concern to Fiers that the committee had representation from white Mississippi but none from the state's African American community.[5]

At its first meeting in January 1966, the Evaluation Committee decided to divide its work between four subcommittees, charged with investigating the Delta Ministry's program, its administration, the Mount Beulah Center, and the Ministry's relationship with CDGM. Collectively, the subcommittees interviewed more than one hundred whites and African Americans, including such determined opponents of the Delta Ministry as Governor Paul B. Johnson Jr.; Bishop Pendergrass; Episcopal bishop coadjutor John M. Allin; B. F. Smith, executive vice president of the Delta Council; Greenville Mayor Pat Dunne; Greenville Police Chief William C. Burnley Jr.; and several white Greenville residents and clergymen. The Evaluation Committee interviewed disillusioned former Ministry supporters, such as Aaron Henry, president of the Mississippi NAACP, and Greenville doctor Matthew J. Page. NCC and Delta Ministry staff and residents at Mount Beulah and Strike City also answered the committee's questions. The investigation produced more than five thousand pages of written testimony, most of it from opponents and critics of the Delta Ministry, including Mississippi's two U.S. Senators, James O. Eastland and John C. Stennis; Mississippi Congressman John Bell Williams; the Mississippi State Sovereignty Commission; Hodding Carter III; and journalist Nicholas Von Hoffman. Bishop Moore complained accurately that the Evaluation Committee spent "little time . . . with the program staff," gave "little attention . . . to our future plans," and asked him to meet only with the subcommittee on administration.[6]

Some opponents accused the Delta Ministry of employing leftist staff, breaking the law, and promoting left-wing revolution. Consequently, the Evaluation Committee asked the U.S. Department of Justice to check out each member of the Delta Ministry staff, including McKenna, who had been widely criticized in

Mississippi for having visited communist China in 1957. The check found "no evidence of disloyalty." The committee also worked with police departments in Mississippi and discovered that Delta Ministry staff had no arrests or convictions other than those for "picketing, traffic violations and civil disobedience."[7]

Bishop Pendergrass presented the committee with some of the harshest criticisms of the Delta Ministry. He charged that it had made "no effort toward reconciliation" between the races and that its members identified only with poor blacks. Furthermore, the staff, Pendergrass insisted, "regard the civil rights movement as a war or class struggle between the underprivileged Negro and the whites or/and status quo Negroes." The Ministry's workers had, he said, violated the law by participating in the occupation of the Greenville Air Force Base. Both the staff and the Commission on the Delta Ministry were "completely intransigent" and would not accept criticism. Consequently, Pendergrass claimed, John D. Humphrey, a leading white Mississippi Methodist official, had resigned from the commission in February 1966. The Delta Ministry program was "not ecumenical in nature" since it did "not involve church people in Mississippi" and gave them "no voice or participation." What was needed, said Pendergrass, was for "men of goodwill of both races [to] learn to minimize their differences, to sit down at the conference table together and to work out their problems of human relations in a Christian spirit of love and concern for each other."[8]

Rather than overturning segregation, the bishop argued, the Delta Ministry perpetuated it by supporting CDGM, creating Strike City, and proposing to establish "a Negro community" at Freedom City. The Delta Ministry's claim that it sought to foster black self-determination and indigenous leadership were myths. The Ministry, Pendergrass suggested, simply appointed figureheads as leaders and manipulated them. Although it held meetings where "ignorant, uneducated people" reached decisions, they chose only from a "limited" range of options "formulated in the first instance by the Delta Ministry staff members."[9]

The Ministry, Pendergrass charged, had alienated local white and black Mississippians beyond its "extreme left wing civil rights compound" at Mount Beulah. "The arrogant judgmental attitude of the Delta Ministry staff members," he added, "is in direct violation of our concepts of Christian mission." Pendergrass directed his final criticism at the Ministry's material and financial support of the MFDP, which, he said, "violates the most fundamental principle of separation of church and State."[10]

Pendergrass repeated his criticisms when the National Division of the Methodist Board of Missions Church met in April 1966 to consider funding the Delta Ministry. He asked the National Division to continue sending money to Mississippi only through the Mississippi Methodist Ministry, which the state's white

Methodists had created little more than a year earlier as an alternative to the Delta Ministry. Although Henry A. McCanna, executive director of the NCC's Commission on the Church in Town and Country, gave a presentation about the Delta project, Pendergrass persuaded the National Division not to commence funding the Ministry. Instead, the National Division decided to appoint the Special Committee to Study the Relationship of the National Division to the Delta Ministry and to await its recommendations.[11]

Aware that Methodist support was essential for its survival, the Delta Ministry produced a detailed packet of material that rebutted Pendergrass's charges. The packet included a statement that Bishop Moore had made earlier to the NCC's Evaluation Committee. Moore readily admitted that the Ministry focused on empowering the African American poor by attending "to underlying needs—equal justice, education, political power, [and] economic development." Nevertheless, these efforts served its goal of reconciliation "by helping the poor to gain enough self-confidence, articulateness, and power to negotiate on a basis of equality of person with the powers that be. We feel true reconciliation between unequal and alienated groups is not possible without justice." The project, Moore claimed, was intrinsically Christian. He cited Luke 4:18, in which Jesus proclaimed that God "hath sent me to heal the brokenhearted, to preach deliverance to the captives, . . . to set at liberty them that are bruised."[12]

In an open letter to Bishop Pendergrass, Thomas firmly responded to the bishop's accusations, denying that CDGM excluded whites and noting that its director, John H. Mudd, was white. Thomas claimed that the Delta Ministry was developing indigenous leadership. Thirteen of its staff were Mississippians, and the chairman of the CDGM board, James F. McCree, was a black Mississippi pastor. The Delta Ministry had tried to work with white Mississippi Methodists, Thomas explained, but had been rebuffed. Humphrey had attended only one meeting of the Commission on the Delta Ministry before resigning. Rather than ignoring him, the commission had sought Humphrey's input at the single meeting he attended, but "he had no suggestions." Thomas dismissed Pendergrass's call for biracial discussions of problems by people of goodwill as "sentimental reconciliation" that ignored the realities of entrenched racial discrimination and injustice. Strike City and Freedom City, he asserted, were not born of a desire to perpetuate segregation. They were, instead, products of white rejection of African Americans. The families at Strike City had been refused jobs and housing in Greenville, and those who would build Freedom City had also been thrown off white plantations.[13]

Other articles in the Delta Ministry's packet of responses to Bishop Pendergrass detailed the failure of the bishop and white Mississippi Methodist ministers to respond to the Delta Ministry's appeals for involvement. Al Winham, for example, had tried and failed to get an appointment with Pendergrass on four separate occasions. The efforts made by Bob Beech in Hattiesburg and Bruce Hilton in Greenville to meet white ministers had largely been rejected. All of the Ministry's projects were open to white people, but very few whites were willing to become involved. The project helped African Americans register to vote and participate in the political process, since both "are necessary to end oppression." However, the Ministry made no mention of its support and tacit alliance with the MFDP, which, as Pendergrass charged, violated the separation of church and state.[14]

While the NCC's Evaluation Committee continued its investigation, the Delta Ministry's dire financial situation forced substantial program cuts. The Ministry had run up a deficit of $161,416 by the end of 1965. Its expenses escalated further in 1966 when Mount Beulah housed and fed approximately 120 refugees from the Greenville Air Force Base occupation and the plantation strikes. By the end of March 1966, the Ministry had spent 42 percent of its approved budget of $264,170 for the year. In April, the Commission on the Delta Ministry cut $69,000 from the Ministry's budget for 1966 and set aside $75,000 from that budget "as a partial repayment of the deficit incurred in 1965." To accommodate these cuts, the Ministry withdrew financial support from the Freedom Information Service (FIS), which produced voter registration materials and information pamphlets for the semiliterate, closed down the McComb project, and terminated its economics and health programs. It reduced support for the Clay County program, based in West Point, to $2,000, and halved the budget of its citizenship and Freedom Corps programs. The number of Freedom Corps staff members shrank to four, and the Delta Ministry terminated four of its own employees, including Harry Bowie, who ran the McComb project, and Al Winham, who was in charge of the economics program. If the Ministry were not to shrivel away amid dire warnings from the NCC that the cuts were insufficient, it needed a favorable report from the Evaluation Committee to induce the National Council's member denominations to increase—or, in most cases, commence—financial support.[15]

When the committee reported in May, it concluded that the Delta Ministry had outstripped the achievements of all other civil rights organizations in the state and become the premier group among them. The Ministry, the committee stated, had given hope to poor African Americans when the NAACP, the Church, and the federal and state Mississippi governments had failed to do so. Specifically, the Ministry had created CDGM and forced the increased distribution to the poor of federal surplus commodities. Furthermore, the Ministry had "developed models of hope-producing organization for the poor which will be copied in many parts of the country, if not the world."[16]

The report's criticisms sought to placate the Delta Ministry's opponents, both within and outside the committee. The Ministry, the committee asserted, had been "less than candid" with the NCC's constituency about its "purposes, goals, objectives and tactics" and had widened the "cleavage" between poor and middle-class African Americans. Furthermore, the Ministry had ignored poor blacks who did not agree with it, failed to enlist the help of sympathetic white Mississippi clergymen, and failed to promote reconciliation between the races. The Ministry had also failed to deliver an adult literacy program, which had been part of the Ministry's February 1964 mandate from the NCC. The planned development of Freedom City, the committee charged, had "the potentiality of promoting racial separatism."[17]

Some of the Delta Ministry's problems, the committee believed, stemmed from inadequate management and financial controls. Staff, rather than the Commission on the Delta Ministry, had made policy, such as the boycott of the Greenville Mill and the occupation of the Greenville Air Force Base. Consequently, the commission had served as "little more than a ratifier of staff decisions and actions." The Ministry's mounting deficit, the Evaluation Committee asserted, also demonstrated that its administration was inadequate.[18]

Despite these criticisms, the committee strongly recommended that the NCC continue its support of the Delta Ministry and that the project's budget for the year be raised to $300,000 to keep it operational. The committee urged the National Council to define more clearly the Ministry's goals and to ensure more rigid adherence to budgets through "responsible financial control." The Delta Ministry, the report stated, should involve the white and middle-class black communities in its work, hire more native Mississippians, and employ African Americans at its highest levels. The Commission on the Delta Ministry, the committee recommended, should have its function clearly defined and should draw half its membership from among black and white Mississippians. Other commission members "should represent a broad geographic spectrum and include a variety of skills" from the NCC's member denominations. Finally, the Delta Ministry should withdraw from Mount Beulah by July 1, 1966, because of its high operating costs, and the NCC should work with the UCMS of the Disciples of Christ and other denominations to create an adult educational and vocational institution on the site that would be "entirely separated from the Delta Ministry."[19]

On behalf of the Commission on the Delta Ministry, Bishop Moore welcomed the report's praise and added that the Ministry had also been responsible for registering twenty thousand African Americans to vote. Although he conceded that the Ministry had failed to create a literacy program, he did not, for the most part, accept the report's criticisms. The Delta Ministry, he noted, had made "continuous and intense efforts at communicating with the white community of Mississippi." Moore maintained that the Ministry had not increased the differences between the African American middle class and poor, as the report claimed; rather, it had simply " 'revealed' the cleavage already there." Freedom City did not seek "to promote racial separatism," which, in any case, already existed in Mississippi because of the legacy of Jim Crow. Instead, the settlement sought to provide the poor with housing and employment while the struggle for integration continued.[20]

Moore was justified in defending the Ministry against charges of failing to communicate with and involve the white community: Mississippi's white clergymen and denominational leaders had consistently refused to cooperate with the Delta Ministry, despite the Ministry's many attempts to explain its work. But repeated rejection inevitably hardened Ministry staff against virtually all of the state's white clergymen, making some of the staff dismissive of indigenous pastors. "Our attempted communication has been slapped down so often," Moore wrote to John Humphrey in March 1966, "that I think the staff has become discouraged about the possibility of it." Even then, important exceptions existed, including Bob Beech, who worked successfully with local whites, if not their pastors, as director of the Hattiesburg Project.[21]

It was nevertheless true, as Pendergrass and Stevens complained, that some Delta Ministry staffers were so sure of the righteousness of their cause that they would brook no disagreement or compromise. Such staff members did not appreciate the pressures that Mississippi's white clergymen faced from their overwhelmingly segregationist parishioners. Fifteen years after he first went to Mississippi, Moore wrote, "We had no patience with the feelings of the local Episcopalians. You were either a good guy or a bad guy. Looking back on it, despite the righteousness of the cause and the permanent liberating effect it had on race relations in the South, I realize that we were self-righteous, and I can well understand the feelings of moderates like Jack Allin. Over the years he had been trying to change attitudes in a peaceful way and at the same time preserve the life of the Church."[22]

The Ministry's complete identification with the African American poor and the militant COFO wing of the civil rights movement, which Moore argued represented the poor, alienated even moderate white Mississippians. Thomas told the Evaluation Committee, "From its inception the Delta Ministry took its stance with the community already engaged in movement. This group has been primarily Negro and basically poor. Our role has not been to act as a mid-channel or transmitting agent between these people and any other group. The Delta

Ministry is attempting to assist the poor Negro in organization for self-determination." Critics found the Ministry unbending. "The Delta Ministry," Thomas declared, "identifies with the poor Negro, his problems, his hopes, and his plans."[23]

The Ministry's perceived self-righteousness and identification with the African American poor partly explain the hostility it faced from elements of the black middle class. However, Moore was correct that the Ministry revealed rather than promoted differences between the black poor and middle class. Impoverished African Americans had greater needs and therefore were often more willing to engage in direct action and to make more far-reaching demands than was the middle class, which tended to prefer gradual change. Its members did not want to endanger their economic and community leadership positions, both of which often depended, to a significant extent, on white approval or acquiescence. Furthermore, traditional middle-class black leaders resented and resisted the challenge to their authority from the previously inarticulate poor, who had a more radical agenda. The Delta Ministry attempted to work with the middle class and the NAACP but gave priority to the black poor and the MFDP, which claimed to represent them.[24]

Freedom City was a prime example of the Ministry's concern for the dispossessed. The Evaluation Committee's accusation that Freedom City would foster racial separatism ignored the reality that segregation and white adherence to it forced the Ministry to operate programs that catered primarily to African Americans, since few whites would accept aid in an integrated setting. The Delta Ministry's projects in the Delta, Hattiesburg, and McComb primarily served African Americans—but not because the Ministry refused to accept white participation. Mount Beulah gave refuge to a poor white family in March 1966, but few other whites followed.[25]

Moore provided a weak and unconvincing defense regarding policy making in the Delta Ministry. He conceded that it was "an on-going problem," maintained that effective guidelines were being developed, and expressed satisfaction "with the staff's respect for Commission policy guidance." Moore argued that the boycott of Mohasco Industries, the Greenville Mill's owner, fell within NCC policy. He ignored the fact that the commission had endorsed the picket of Greenville Mill only after the Ministry had already begun to participate. However, the Commission later supported the Ministry's call for a national boycott of Mohasco Industries' products. Delta Ministry staff, in Moore's view, had felt compelled to take part in the occupation of the Greenville Air Force Base because the poor people with which the Ministry identified had made the decision. However, participant

Owen H. Brooks later claimed that the Ministry had, along with the MFDP and the MFLU, suggested the occupation, a claim that tends to support Bishop Pendergrass's charge that the Ministry directed and manipulated the poor by presenting them with a limited range of options for decision.[26]

The possibility that they might in some way be manipulating the poor, if only by dint of their greater education and organizing skills, was a constant concern among Delta Ministry workers. McKenna told the Evaluation Committee that the staff members "often discuss[ed] among themselves the question of how to work effectively *with* people and avoid *leading* them." The Ministry, he said, listened to the concerns of poor African Americans, such as employment discrimination at Greenville Mill, and then helped them find ways of addressing these issues. C. Richard Cox, a New York City Methodist minister who served as a Delta Ministry volunteer in early 1966, gave his church a vivid account of self-determination by the poor: "The D.M. is not doing things for the indigenous 'poor people.' All decisions are made by the 'poor' and responsibility lies with them. . . . Never have I seen such verbalization, insight, comprehension, depth and sound thinking as I've seen among these people. . . . D.M. philosophy is, generally, that you can't tell the poor what they don't know but that they can be helped to formulate what they do know!"[27]

Moore conceded that in helping the poor, the Delta Ministry overspent its budget. However, he added that Mount Beulah had required more than $30,000 in capital expenditures, and the Ministry had not received the level of donations from NCC member denominations that it had anticipated. "The mandate," he declared, "was too big for the budget." The evidence supports Moore's contention. American denominations contributed only $113,041 to the Delta Ministry in 1965, and just six of the NCC's thirty-one denominations donated at least $1,000. Furthermore, emergencies, such as the needs of the Tribbett strikers and those of the Poor People's Conference, many of whose members lived at Mount Beulah, could not be ignored, despite their expense, if the Delta Ministry were to fulfill its servant ministry.[28]

Bishop Moore accepted most of the Evaluation Committee's recommendations but rejected the proposed budget of $300,000 as inadequate, since a portion would have to be spent to pay back the Ministry's deficit. The Delta Ministry needed, he said, a net annual operating budget of at least $360,000 to continue "the very programs for which the ministry has been commended," or a total of $400,000, including debt repayment. Furthermore, Mount Beulah should not be sacrificed as the Delta Ministry's headquarters to save money. It provided a sanctuary for civil rights workers and dispossessed plantation workers, a training center, and a "visible sign of our presence," which, if lost, would demoralize the poor, encourage opponents of civil rights, and boost support for black separatists, who maintained that whites could not be trusted.[29]

The NCC's Division of Christian Life and Mission, to which the Commission on the Delta Ministry was responsible, approved Moore's report and recommendations. The Division urged the National Council's General Board to consider them alongside those of the Evaluation Committee when it met on June 2. After the General Board heard the two reports, Marian Wright, a lawyer for the NAACP Legal Defense and Educational Fund and a member of the Commission on the Delta Ministry, made an impassioned plea for the NCC to increase the Ministry's budget. She dismissed accusations that the Ministry's work had caused a breakdown in communication. Justifiably, she argued, "I think we're just beginning to have the first real communication Mississippi's had. The problem is that a whole lot of people just don't like what they're hearing, but we are communicating very well." Wright told the General Board that it was imperative that the Delta Ministry be supported and strengthened. She concluded: "Tactically, it's going to be far cheaper to support this Ministry and help people become useful citizens than to support them the rest of their lives on welfare or in prison because of crimes committed out of hopelessness and despair. And morally, anything we give will be cheaper than the cost to ourselves of the Church's failure to fulfill its mission in this world."[30]

Charles F. Golden, bishop of the Nashville-Carolina Area of the Methodist Church's Central Jurisdiction, sent a telegram to the General Board. The Board read Golden's message that the Upper Mississippi Conference of the Methodist Church, an African American conference, had endorsed the Delta Ministry in a unanimous vote and asked all churches financially to support the Ministry.[31]

After weighing the reports and presentations it had received, the General Board affirmed "its confidence in the purposes and direction of the Delta Ministry" and called on its denominations to begin making or to increase donations to the Ministry. The board instructed the Division of Christian Life and Mission to consider and commence implementation of the report and recommendations of the Evaluation Committee during the next six months. It also ordered the division to take immediate steps to bring Delta Ministry expenditures "within available funds and firm assurances of support."[32]

In June 1966, the division appointed a five-man committee to seek $100,000 in additional money for the Delta Ministry from NCC member denominations, in line with Moore's request for greater funding. The division deferred implementation of most of the Evaluation Committee's recommendations, including withdrawal from Mount Beulah, pending the appointment and report of a committee to determine the Delta Ministry's goals. The division approved a Ministry budget of $300,000 for the year and began implementing stringent financial controls. The Ministry continued to spend beyond its reduced monthly allowance of $19,200 in June and July but brought its expenditures under control in August.[33]

The Ministry was not profligate, as some of its critics charged; rather, the need it was designed to serve overwhelmed its resources. The Ministry cut its program drastically in June but still had overheads and staff to pay plus the costs of supporting ninety-four refugees at Mount Beulah and then moving them to Freedom City in July. Three staffers volunteered to take unpaid leave in July. The Ministry ended travel expenses and its program in Clay County and froze voter registration and community organization programs insofar as they incurred expense.[34]

On June 4, lack of funds forced Brooks, director of the Bolivar County Project, to end a voter registration drive that had added two thousand African Americans to the county's voter registration rolls in five weeks. Brooks subsequently helped persuade the organizers of the Meredith March to divert it through the Delta and to add a voter registration drive to its program. James Meredith, who had desegregated the University of Mississippi in 1962, had been shot and injured on June 6, on the second day of a lone march from Memphis, Tennessee, to Jackson, Mississippi. Meredith hoped that his self-proclaimed march against fear would inspire blacks to assert their rights. The leaders of SNCC, CORE, and the SCLC rushed to Mississippi to complete the march, which Meredith, after a stay in the hospital, rejoined at its conclusion. During the march, which ended on June 26, 4,077 black Mississippians registered to vote in counties visited by the marchers.[35]

Less than two weeks after the Meredith March ended, the Division of Christian Life and Mission approved a statement of goals for the Delta Ministry. Drawn up by a seven-man committee headed by Kenneth G. Neigh, general secretary of the UPCUSA's Board of National Missions, the statement represented a victory for Moore, an ex officio member of the committee. The new goals vindicated the Delta Ministry's approach despite the NCC Evaluation Committee's earlier criticisms. The Ministry's priority, the committee decided, would remain the African American poor because it was "essential to the Church's witness to her Lord that she should move out to identification with the poor and the dispossessed in faithfulness to her original mandate and her continuing faith in Christ's presence with the outcast." Designed as a servant ministry that would assist the dispossessed in achieving self-determination, the Delta Ministry, the committee resolved, should not seek to control their actions but should instead participate. When, in consequence, the Ministry followed directions beyond established NCC policy, it would have to clear its action with the chairman of the Commission on the Delta Ministry. The Division of Christian Life and Mission would determine the Ministry's policy, the commission would determine strategy, and the Ministry would determine tactics.[36]

The Evaluation Committee had criticized "a continuous difference" between the purposes of the Delta Ministry approved by the General Board in February 1964 "and the actual fact of the ministry." By contrast, the Goals Committee endorsed Moore's understanding of the meaning of reconciliation, a term that had been emphasized but not defined or its means of achievement explained in the Ministry's initial authorization. There could be no reconciliation, the Goals Committee stated, until injustice had been exposed and the oppressed helped to "become free and equal participants in a reconciled society." The process might entail "the painful release of long suppressed hostility." While the Ministry had tried to and would continue to attempt to work with all of the poor, the committee recognized that "many white poor are afraid to be related to a Ministry with Negro poor."[37]

After justifying the Delta Ministry's approach, the committee defined the Ministry's goals. It should focus primarily on the dispossessed, continuing to provide them with relief and to assist in their economic development, including the establishment of Freedom City as a model community. Freedom City would promote self-determination rather than black separatism. Voter registration, community organization, and the fostering of indigenous leadership remained crucial aims. While the Delta Ministry would assist African Americans as they necessarily pressed their claims against whites who held power, the Ministry's ultimate concern lay in helping Mississippians overcome the racial divide. While the NCC recognized the necessity of demonstrations and challenges to unjust laws, the Ministry should engage in such protests only under carefully prescribed circumstances. Chastened by the Delta Ministry's failure to develop a literacy program, the Goals Committee formulated a less demanding role in which the Ministry would act as an enabler and a participant with other groups and agencies in literacy, vocational training, and citizenship education programs.[38]

The Ministry would also continue seeking to work with other segments of the community in addition to the poor. The Goals Committee recognized that it was "at present virtually impossible" for the Ministry to work with both the dispossessed and the white middle class. However, the Ministry should, the committee decided, attempt to involve the privileged whenever possible—for example, as members of the Commission on the Delta Ministry or in particular programs. Most of the privileged, the committee believed, would remain resistant, and for them the NCC should consider developing a separate approach detached from the Delta Ministry. Although not part of its purview, the Goals Committee also endorsed Moore's call for the retention of the Delta Ministry's headquarters at Mount Beulah because of its practical and symbolic value.[39]

The Delta Ministry thereby emerged from its scrutiny by the NCC with its program and operating methods approved. Its goals were more precise than those outlined in February 1964, which had necessarily been more general and had emphasized offering service and facilitating reconciliation between the races to placate the project's opponents. Mount Beulah would remain at the hub of the Delta Ministry's operations. The proposal for a vocational college on the site fell by the wayside. Yet soon after the Ministry's vindication, the men who had overseen its development—Paul Moore, Art Thomas, and Warren McKenna—were no longer at its head.[40]

Moore submitted his resignation from the chairmanship of the Commission on the Delta Ministry on May 17, a day after the NCC's Evaluation Committee issued its report. Ed Espy, the National Council's general secretary, asked Moore to reconsider his decision, which seems to have been withheld from the Delta Ministry staff until after the Goals Committee reported on July 7. Thomas resigned immediately after the Division of Christian Life and Mission's executive committee approved the Goals Committee's report, the same day. Both men had endured considerable pressure as well as some harsh criticism of their work. Ready to move on and laden with other commitments, Moore denied that the evaluation process had brought about his resignation. And Thomas had quit, Moore believed, "because he is exhausted and feels that he can no longer give the energy and leadership which the Delta Ministry needs." However, the bishop also acknowledged that Thomas "resigned under pressure." Although Moore believed that Thomas had done "a most extraordinary job, combining great courage, stability, and common sense," some of the director's staff had strongly criticized his leadership.[41]

Bob Beech criticized Thomas in May 1966 for his "long-standing failure to facilitate a flow of key information, facts & resources to the staff so as to enable them to do their jobs efficiently." Everything, Beech wrote, funneled through Thomas, who assumed "more of the pressure for all parts of the program-policy, personnel, etc. on himself than is necessary or healthy." Such an approach undoubtedly contributed to Thomas's sense of exhaustion and alienated Bowie. In a letter to Jon Regier, associate general secretary of the Division of Christian Life and Mission, Bowie said that he had been "highly critical" of Thomas's "method of administering the staff and program, as well as the way in which he made decisions." After Thomas's resignation, McKenna wrote to Moore that "some of us cannot escape the feeling that Art has abandoned a sinking ship, leaving us to deal with all kinds of problems for which he was mainly responsible."[42]

Criticism of Thomas and, to a lesser degree, Moore also came from denominations on which the Delta Ministry depended for its financial survival. Bryant George wrote to Kenneth Neigh, his superior at the UPCUSA, in late May 1966 that the NCC evaluation report "is the mildest possible reproof of absolutely fantastic administration that I have ever seen." A firm supporter of the Delta Ministry, George nevertheless told Neigh, "I do not think that it is responsible *for the Presbyterian Church to invest any more money in this Ministry unless it gets a new administrative head (a replacement for Thomas), and a new head for the Commission (a replacement for Bishop Paul Moore).*" A day before Thomas resigned, George wrote to Neigh that "the present leadership (Thomas and Moore) are incapable of developing the 'orderly revolution' that is necessary in Mississippi with Church support." Several months after Thomas's departure, George wrote, "Arthur Thomas brought the Delta Ministry to the brink of ruin from which it was snatched back by the Presbyterians."[43]

The UPCUSA, the Delta Ministry's largest contributor, donated an additional $10,000 to protect it, but without financial support from the Methodists, the Ministry's program would wither. According to the *Washington Post*, some Delta Ministry staff and supporters believed that the Methodist Church demanded Thomas's resignation as the price of its support. J. Edward Carothers, associate general secretary of the National Division of the Methodist Board of Missions, denied that he had "demanded a certain person's head on a platter," but he conceded that "names were discussed" with NCC officials.[44]

McKenna was likely to have been one of the people discussed since the NCC terminated him from the Delta Ministry effective September 16, 1966. Rims K. Barber believed that the Methodist Church insisted on McKenna's removal, red-baiting him for his 1957 visit to China. "That's a rumor which could be true," Beech commented, "altho[ugh] I don't think it is." Colin Williams, the associate secretary of the Division of Christian Life and Mission, claimed that "we reluctantly released . . . Warren McKenna, sooner than we would have wished as the financial plight required further staff reductions." Although staffers' feelings about Thomas's departure were mixed, those in the Delta Ministry were angry to see McKenna fired and saddened by Moore's resignation.[45]

However, the staff changes and, equally if not more importantly, the NCC's endorsement of the Delta Ministry helped clear the way for Methodist financial support. After the NCC's General Board approved the Ministry in June 1966, A. Dudley Ward, general secretary of the Methodist General Board of Social Concerns, wrote, "The Delta Ministry was endorsed. The plain hard fact is we've gotta find some money for it." The board sent three thousand dollars to the Ministry. Ward encouraged the Methodist National Division to "do something," but it would not act until the National Division's Special Committee on the Delta Ministry, appointed in April, made its report.[46]

The special committee reported in September 1966 after an extensive investigation that had listened to the criticisms of the Delta Ministry leveled by Bishop Pendergrass, his area cabinet in Jackson, and Stevens. The report welcomed the Ministry's revised statement of goals and agreed, almost unanimously, that the "Methodist Church should give its united commitment to the Delta Ministry." With this recommendation, the National Division, over Pendergrass's outspoken opposition, voted to give forty thousand dollars toward the Ministry's indebtedness and thirty thousand dollars for its program. The bishop and the twelve district superintendents who comprised the Jackson-area cabinet strongly condemned the decision. Delegates representing Mississippi's more than one thousand white Methodist churches commended this stand. A few days later, the College of Bishops of the Methodist Church's Southeastern Jurisdiction met in Jackson and issued a statement criticizing the NCC for acting "without adequate consultation with a substantial segment of the Methodist churches in Mississippi." Impressed by the report of the National Council's Evaluation Committee, the Woman's Division voted in September to donate thirty thousand dollars to the Ministry in 1966 and another thirty thousand dollars in 1967. The Methodist Church thereby became the largest contributor to the Delta Ministry, followed by the UPCUSA, which donated sixty thousand dollars during 1966.[47]

The PCUS also made its first contribution to the Ministry when its newly created Division of Church and Society donated five hundred dollars in November 1966. The money went toward emergency expenses at Freedom City, where a storm had destroyed the temporary canvas tents that housed the residents. The issue of funding the Delta Ministry remained in abeyance while the denomination continued its investigation of the NCC project.[48]

When the National Council's General Assembly met in December 1966, it heard that the $405,000 the Delta Ministry needed for the year's budget, after further escalating expenses, had been approved and raised. Approximately $38,000 of this amount had been received during the previous six weeks. Ten American denominations had contributed $237,000, and members of the WCC had donated approximately $50,000, with other contributions coming mostly from individuals. With help primarily from the Methodists, the Ministry had paid off $62,670 of its debt to the Division of Christian Life and Mission but still owed nearly $100,000, which it planned to repay by the end of 1967 or mid-1968 at the latest. For 1967, the General Board set the Ministry's budget at $300,000 for staff and county programs, but the Ministry would have to continue separately raising money for Freedom City, which remained excluded from the regular budget funded by NCC and WCC member denominations. In his inaugural address to the General Assembly, Arthur S. Flemming, the NCC's new president, urged its members to support the Delta Ministry. Flemming, a Methodist who had served as secretary of Health, Education, and Welfare during the Eisenhower administration, declared that "having put its hand to the plow," the National Council could not afford "to turn back from this project just because of tensions it raises."[49]

The NCC's General Board commended the progress the Delta Ministry and the Division of Christian Life and Mission had made since June. However, the administrative reorganization of the Delta Ministry and its commission, although under way, had not been completed. Consistent with the Evaluation Committee's desire to see high-level African American appointments, Brooks had replaced Thomas in September. Brooks held only the title of acting director. Frederick S. Lowry assumed McKenna's role as administrative assistant. The Commission on the Delta Ministry remained unreformed. Henry McCanna took on the new title of executive secretary for the Delta Ministry in December 1966. The post entailed "the duties of New York liaison, finances, and denominational contacts" and the task of reorganizing the commission. The reconstituted commission held its first meeting in March 1967.[50]

Given the financial cutbacks it had sustained, the Delta Ministry had little to report in terms of program to the NCC's General Board in December 1966. Its major effort had been the creation of Freedom City, to which the plantation refugees had moved from Mount Beulah on July 25. The need to house and feed Freedom City residents had absorbed a significant part of the Delta Ministry expenditure. With the refugees' departure from Mount Beulah, the Delta Ministry reduced expenses at its headquarters to a minimum.[51]

The Ministry's support for an African American boycott in nearby Edwards constituted its major activity at Mount Beulah after July. Two-thirds of the town's 1,200 people were African Americans. They were confined to low-paid employment as maids, cleaners, providers of child care, and agricultural workers. The boycott's origins lay in the city's decision to sell its swimming pool after African Americans tried to integrate it. The pool's new private owners refused blacks admission. Consequently, some African Americans decided to picket the facility. The arrests of fifty pickets led the black community to adopt a boycott of white downtown stores that was more than 90 percent effective. The protesters formulated eighteen demands, calling for employment of African Americans in white-owned stores; higher wages for black employees in Edwards; sewers, sidewalks, paved streets, and improved street lighting and garbage collection in the black community; and the use of courtesy titles for blacks. Erle Johnston Jr., director of the Mississippi State Sovereignty Commission, accused Delta Ministry worker Charley Horwitz of triggering the boycott but conceded that "native Edwards Negroes are firm in their determination to bring about some improvements for Negro residents." Horwitz worked with the protesters but did not, as Johnston asserted, direct them.[52]

A thirty-one-year-old Jew from Chicago, Horwitz held a master's degree in international relations from the University of Chicago. He had worked as a reporter for *Newsweek* magazine in the Windy City before coming to Mississippi as a COFO volunteer in October 1964. After COFO's disintegration, Horwitz stayed on to work for the MFDP. He joined the FIS in 1965, operating from the Mount Beulah campus. The Delta Ministry provided FIS staff with salaries, room and board, office equipment and supplies, and travel and other expenses. After the Delta Ministry withdrew its funding from FIS—90 percent of FIS's budget—in April 1966, Horwitz joined the Ministry as a subsistence worker, remaining at Mount Beulah. Horwitz's work led to the creation of the Delta Ministry's Hinds County Project, which he also directed.[53]

In the summer of 1966, Horwitz organized political education classes with the aid of a volunteer MFDP teacher and worked on the Meredith March. Horwitz had close ties with the Edwards boycott, which began in August. Irene Thompson, one of the boycott's leaders although she was only seventeen, lived with her older sister, Mary White, who worked as a switchboard operator for the Delta Ministry at Mount Beulah. Horwitz kept in contact with Thompson during the boycott. Mayor Clark E. Robbins blamed the Ministry for "stirring up the niggers." According to a Sovereignty Commission source, the Delta Ministry aided the boycott by offering to transport African Americans to Vicksburg or Jackson to shop. Horwitz reported that the Delta Ministry "helped institute a law suit against the town of Edwards which levied unfair tax fees on almost the entire black community" in retaliation for the protest.[54]

African Americans sought ways to become independent of white employers in Edwards. Consequently, Horwitz and the Delta Ministry helped to create two Freedomcrafts cooperatives at Mount Beulah in 1966. Modeled on the first Freedomcrafts venture at Strike City, the male-staffed Freedomcrafts Wood Cooperative initially produced nativity sets. It later switched to making nursery school equipment for CDGM Head Start centers in Hinds County. A group of black women started a candy-making cooperative that operated a mail-order business that used the Ministry's network of contacts across the United States.[55]

Although the widely observed Edwards boycott continued unabated into 1967 and drove at least two white stores out of business, city authorities refused to give in. Johnston tried to find a basis for a settlement, but the city offered insufficient concessions to placate the protesters. African Americans eventually voted out the mayor and other white officials, replacing them with a black city government. The Delta Ministry had helped lay the groundwork for this political victory by conducting a voter registration campaign in Edwards during the summer of 1965.[56]

Financial difficulties caused the Ministry to freeze all expenditures on voter registration and citizenship education in June 1966. However, the Ministry was able to mount a five-week voter registration campaign in five counties during August and September, funded by a donation channeled through the UPCUSA by Rustum Roy, a professor at Pennsylvania State University in State College. The drive registered 2,865 African Americans. Brooks headed the effort in Bolivar County, which pushed the number of black voters there to more than seven thousand. African Americans now had a substantial voting majority in the county. In November, Clarence Hall Jr., director of the Delta Ministry's county projects in Issaquena and Sharkey, became one of eight African Americans to run for county office in Issaquena. Hall lost his bid for a seat on the school board, 208 to 102.[57]

The Delta Ministry began a citizenship education program in November 1966 with a nineteen-thousand-dollar donation from Herb McKinstry. A layman and, like Roy, a professor at Penn State, McKinstry had spent a week as a Delta Ministry volunteer in Hattiesburg during July 1964. Bowie rejoined the Ministry as director of the citizenship education program, which sought "to provide the many thousands of newly registered voters with the information they need to become responsible and effective voters." Bowie planned to organize workshops in thirteen counties—six in the Delta, four in the southeast, and three in the southwest. The Ministry chose them because they were "key counties in their geographical area" and places in which the Ministry had "been most active previously." Bowie intended his workshops to train local people to run their own seminars to prepare voters for the primary and general elections in August and November 1967, when a substantial number of African Americans would run for office in Mississippi for the first time since Reconstruction.[58]

Brooks cited Sunflower County in the Delta as a good example of the program's necessity. At the request of local people, Bowie and Joseph L. Harris, a black Freedom Corps worker originally from Holmes County, had since the spring of 1966 registered nearly 95 percent of the town of Sunflower's African American population. Bowie and Harris had also focused on citizenship education and "working to develop local people as candidates for local offices." The citizenship education program, begun in November, enabled the Delta Ministry to advance the work. A SNCC veteran who was active in the MFDP, the twenty-one-year-old Harris served as director of the Ministry's Sunflower County Project. He joined the Ministry's regular staff in early January 1967, after spending a few months as a subsistence worker.[59]

Able to resume its program, the Delta Ministry also enjoyed better staff relations. Beech wrote to Beryl Ramsay, a former secretary at the Delta Ministry's NCC office in New York, "Things down here are going much better since the directorship was assumed by Owen Brooks. Our staff meetings now evidence real openness and sharing and team spirit. The program seems to be slowly but surely moving ahead in a constructive direction." Al Winham also believed that the Ministry had improved under the direction of Brooks: "Have had more (and very welcome) chance to work with him, and the results, from my point of view, are swell. Like just about every other member of the staff—and definitely every white member—I sure hope he's made Director."[60]

By the end of 1966, Brooks led a group of Delta Ministry staff and volunteers that had been reduced from a high of fifty-five during the year to twenty-eight. The Ministry had also dissolved the Freedom Corps. Thirteen of the twenty-eight Ministry staff were black Mississippians, two were northern African Americans, and thirteen were white. The Ministry had projects in Bolivar, Forrest, Hinds, Issaquena, Sharkey, Sunflower, Tallahatchie, and Washington Counties; had begun a new project at Freedom City; retained Mount Beulah; and resumed its voter education and economics programs under Bowie and Winham, respectively. Although the ministry's debt remained at nearly one hundred thousand dollars, that amount had been reduced by more than sixty thousand dollars.[61]

After a perilous year in which budgetary problems and external investigations had seriously threatened its existence, the Delta Ministry had emerged with new leadership, improved finances, and a vote of confidence from the NCC and the Methodist Church. The NCC's Evaluation Committee recognized that with the collapse of COFO and the gradual withdrawal of SNCC and CORE from Mississippi, the Delta Ministry had become the state's main civil rights group by virtue of its personnel, scope, activity, and funding. The committee's largely positive report, tighter financial controls on the Delta Ministry, and the replacement of the Ministry's leaders encouraged the Methodist Church to become the project's largest contributor. Burdened for much of the year by debt, reductions in program, and investigations, the Ministry's new initiatives were limited to the creation of Freedom City, new projects in Sunflower and Hinds Counties, voter registration, and citizenship education. However, the Delta Ministry emerged with a refined set of goals and the NCC's approval of the Ministry's approach and methods. A disproportionate amount of the Delta Ministry's efforts during the next few years would be devoted to Freedom City, which, ironically, had been championed by the Ministry's former leaders—Moore, Thomas, and McKenna.

CHAPTER SEVEN

Freedom City

In July 1966, a group of African American families displaced from Mississippi plantations by mechanization and herbicides relocated to four hundred acres of land twelve miles southeast of Greenville. Aided and advised by the Delta Ministry, they hoped to create a model community. The ninety-four residents intended to pioneer a viable alternative to black migration to northern ghettoes by developing a self-sustaining agricultural and industrial cooperative. With financial aid from OEO and the Ford Foundation, the families received vocational training from DOC and began constructing their own homes. Yet the experiment failed. The residents built only twenty of the projected fifty houses. Freedom City lacked sufficient start-up money, and during the 1970s, it became a victim of growing federal and church indifference to African American problems. The residents lacked commitment to farming, while industrial firms proved unwilling to locate plants in the Delta because of its unskilled labor force. Many residents proved incapable of developing and sustaining disciplined work schedules, yet their newfound sense of freedom made them bristle at direction from others. Although some people acquired low-level skills, few employment opportunities existed.[1]

Communal experiments have occurred throughout U.S. history. Attempts to provide cooperative farming alternatives to sharecropping for African Americans and whites also predated the Freedom City exper-

127

iment. Two white southerners, Gene Cox and Sam H. Franklin Jr., organized the 2,700-acre Delta Cooperative Farm, near Tchula in Holmes County, Mississippi, in 1936. The farm, later renamed Providence, operated a credit union and provided medical care for both races. A mass meeting organized by the local Citizens' Council in 1955 ordered Cox and David Minter, Providence's doctor, to leave after they were accused of allowing biracial swimming at the farm. The two men denied the accusations, but an economic boycott, threats of violence and arson, and intimidation by the local sheriff forced them to leave Mississippi in 1956.[2]

Koinonia Farm, a communal experiment in southwest Georgia, suffered similar pressure and violent attacks but withstood them. Founded in 1942 by two white Southern Baptists, Clarence Jordan and Martin England, Koinonia occupied four hundred acres. It sought to teach farm workers scientific agriculture and to make them self-sufficient so that they could remain on the land rather than be forced by agricultural change to move to dilapidated cities in search of employment. Opposed to racial discrimination, Koinonia accepted African Americans as equals.[3]

However, the inspiration for Freedom City came not from Providence or Koinonia but from Israel's kibbutzim and moshavim, in which "people owned their own land but farmed it cooperatively." Warren McKenna, administrative assistant to Delta Ministry Director Art Thomas, placed a picture of a moshav on his office wall soon after taking up his post. McKenna championed the idea of a cooperative farm that, like many in Israel, would combine agriculture with industrial activity. Rising Delta agricultural unemployment as machines and chemicals increasingly did the work once performed by African Americans made it imperative to find an alternative indigenous source of employment for blacks.[4]

Influenced by McKenna, Thomas asked the U.S. Department of Agriculture in June 1965 to secure loans for the purchase of two thousand acres for a cooperative farming village and to provide training in "relevant agricultural techniques, credit association, and other cooperative facilities." The proposal envisaged dividing the land into seventy-five farming plots of twenty-five acres per family, with the remaining acreage set aside for community buildings, forestry, educational facilities, workshops, parks, and roads. The farm would involve "a total transformation in agricultural practices and in the values of the people who participate" as they created "a mutual aid cooperative structure."[5]

Within a month, the U.S. Department of Agriculture rejected the proposal. It argued that the family farming plots envisaged were too small to sustain either full employment or adequate incomes. Internal departmental documents expressed great skepticism that cooperatives could become self-supporting. Department staff argued that the small farms funded by the federal Resettlement Administration and the Farm Security Administration in the 1930s and 1940s had mostly failed, that mechanization and herbicides had made small-scale farming uneconomic, and that even with training, displaced plantation workers would be unlikely to develop the necessary "managerial capacity to operate such farms." Education and training should, the department believed, instead be directed at nonfarm jobs such as crafts.[6]

Despite the rejection, the Ministry pressed ahead with the idea of a cooperative farm. J. Oscar Lee, secretary for program services at the NCC's Division of Christian Life and Mission, held several meetings with American Jews knowledgeable about kibbutzim and also met with Abie Ben Ari, a former rural development planner in Israel. Marian Wright, a member of the Commission on the Delta Ministry, visited Israel and later cowrote an article proposing the creation of kibbutzim in Mississippi.[7]

The Delta Ministry supported strikes organized by the MFLU among Delta plantation workers in the spring and early summer of 1965. The strikes gave added impetus to the search for an alternative for agricultural workers. Ministry workers began discussing the idea of creating farming cooperatives with some of the strikers. Thomas told the Commission on the Delta Ministry in July 1965 that the Ministry regarded "The cooperative farming village . . . as an intermediate step in the development of long range solutions to the employment crisis in the Delta."[8]

Supported by Thomas, McKenna cultivated the idea of creating new communities that would develop small-scale industrial and agricultural cooperatives and provide their inhabitants with decent housing and a political base. The Ministry presented its idea to the Poor People's Conference, which the Ministry, the MFLU, and the MFDP helped to organize at Mount Beulah in January 1966. The conference sent a group to occupy Greenville Air Force Base to protest poverty and seek redress from the federal government. At a press conference after their eviction by the military, Isaac Foster, one of the occupiers' spokespersons and a leader in the earlier tractor drivers' strike in Tribbett, announced the group's intention of relocating to Strike City, where the ousted drivers had set up camp. Foster declared that "The people are going to . . . work on getting poor peoples to come out and build a new city. Because of the fact that we was refused by the federal government and evicted, it's important that we start planning our own government."[9]

In the wake of the air base incident, OEO asked the Delta Ministry "to submit a proposal for a self-help housing and education program." Despite qualms among some of the Ministry's staff about accepting federal money, the idea proved attractive. Overcrowded conditions and rain and cold had forced the air base group to relocate from Strike City to land owned by an African American farmer in Issaquena County. However, nearly half of the seventy people at the new site suffered from illness caused by bad weather. Unwilling to turn its back on those it was designed to help and encourage, the Delta Ministry offered to shelter the group members at Mount Beulah, where they were joined by other plantation refugees. By February 1966, an overstretched Ministry was providing for 120 displaced plantation workers. OEO's suggested program offered the Ministry a practical means of helping the poor at Mount Beulah, whose upkeep contributed significantly to the Ministry's worsening budget deficit.[10]

A church organization and therefore unable to accept federal funds, the Delta Ministry arranged for DOC, a spin-off organization designed to further economic development and opportunities for African Americans, to submit a proposal to OEO for a $555,745 grant. Submitted on March 1, 1966, the proposal, written largely by Tom Carter of OEO's Migrant Division, envisaged literacy and pre-vocational training for adult members of one hundred families, together with the materials and skills training necessary for them to construct their own houses. The proposed program included twenty families currently at Mount Beulah. DOC was to select the program's eighty other families from among the poor within its nine-county focus. The Delta Ministry, for its part, would help locate a site in Issaquena County for the proposed houses.[11]

In a very short time, McKenna's idea of creating new communities in Mississippi had been transformed into a practical possibility if land could be found to create the first "New City." But as Bruce Hilton, the Delta Ministry's director of interpretation, recalled, "Many of the staff flatly opposed the idea." Harry Bowie, director of the McComb Project, feared that the plan would simply transfer poor people from one form of dependency to another. He believed that the people at Mount Beulah, deprived of education and having depended all their lives on white planters for food, shelter, and work instructions, would lack the necessary self-discipline and initiative to make the New City a success. Some of the Delta Ministry's staff contended that the Ministry should not be making long-term plans and generating hope among the poor when its ability to see them through was threatened by its parlous financial situation and the NCC's ongoing evaluation of the Ministry's program. Freedom Corps staff refused to recruit for New City under these circumstances.[12]

The Ministry conceded that the pace of events had "prevented us from having as full a discussion as seems necessary." Consequently, McKenna tried to rally staff support for New City by circulating a document for discussion that explained the project's rationale. McKenna questioned whether freedom, which he defined as "control of one's own destiny," could "be equated with a middle class standard of life." Scathingly, he wrote that "most americans have homes and jobs but are not free." New City—or Freedom City, as it came to be called—would promote "self-determination of the Negro community" by creating a viable economic enterprise that would serve as a model for the establishment of others in Mississippi. It would mark a "declaration of independence" from government antipoverty programs, which did not end poverty and kept the poor dependent.[13]

McKenna argued that Freedom City would not become a new ghetto and that it was not utopian. However, the document was vague about how Freedom City would achieve economic success, and its solution exuded the kind of utopianism that McKenna claimed to reject. "Through planning and cooperative effort with whatever outside assistance is available," the document affirmed, "the Negro community will develop its own creative solution to the problems of jobs, houses, education and brotherhood." But, if it needed outside assistance, which in practice meant federal funding and grants from philanthropic foundations, Freedom City would inevitably become dependent on the controlling interest of "the white power structure" that McKenna claimed the settlement was designed to escape.[14]

Although he argued that Freedom City would not become a new ghetto, McKenna conceded that it would put "less emphasis on integration" and more on African American self-determination. In any case, he argued, "There is little evidence both north and south that American society is really prepared to accept anything more than tokenism." Nowhere did the document mention the possibility of Freedom City including poor whites. In arguing for black self-determination and community control, which would encourage "the dignity, self-confidence, and uniqueness of the Negro community," McKenna anticipated the arguments later propounded by the Black Power movement.[15]

However, neither Freedom City nor the Black Power movement could escape the fact that whites controlled most of the economic resources in Mississippi and across the nation. On April 7, 1966, OEO rejected DOC's proposal on the grounds that it was "not authorized under the law to make grants for the purchase of land or the construction of homes." In an irony, given the poverty of most black Mississippians and the opposition of the state's white politicians to the civil rights movement and the Delta Ministry, OEO declared, "The answers to questions of land, building requirements, financing arrangements and job opportunities that might make these applications realities rather than dreams must be found in Mississippi."[16]

Thomas made Freedom City the Delta Ministry's main priority. He insisted that all staff members devote some of their time to the project. The Ministry secured a $71,000 loan to DOC from Irving Fain, a Jewish philanthropist from Rhode Island, to serve as a down payment for land on which to build Freedom City. The Ministry also persuaded the Ford Foundation to send a team to Mississippi to explore the possibility of supporting the project. Attempts by the Delta Ministry to find an appropriate site for Freedom City foundered on the unwillingness of Delta whites to sell farmland to African Americans. However, on the day that OEO rejected its proposal, DOC purchased four hundred acres at Wayside in Washington County from J. B. Keel, a white farmer who was moving to Missouri. Thelma Barnes, director of the Delta Ministry's Washington County Project and secretary of DOC, held the land in trust for the Poor People's Conference until such time as the conference became incorporated. Anxious to keep the project moving, Clarence Hall Jr., DOC chairman and a Delta Ministry staff member, asked OEO to disregard DOC's request for "brick and mortar" money and instead to fund only the educational part of the proposal, amounting to $300,745. OEO refused.[17]

Al Winham, director of the Delta Ministry's economics program, engaged in protracted negotiations with federal officials while trying to interest the Ford Foundation in partly funding the development of Freedom City. Winham also tried to persuade food processing plants to relocate to the site. B. F. Smith, executive vice president of the Delta Council, a white planters' group, told the *Delta Democrat-Times* that most of the soil at Freedom City was "buckshot," unsuitable for growing vegetables. Winham countered that Freedom City would not grow vegetables but instead would process those grown by poor people across Mississippi.[18]

Until the Delta Ministry could arrange temporary housing at Wayside, the men of the families at Mount Beulah made a two-hour journey to the site each morning in buses and cars provided by the Ministry. The families made all the decisions regarding the land's use. Unwilling to grow cotton because of its link with their poverty, they asked Hall's advice and accepted the Issaquena farmer's suggestion that they plant soybeans. DOC intended that the proceeds from farming would meet the annual sixteen-thousand-dollar payment for the one-hundred-thousand-dollar ten-year mortgage on the land and equipment.[19]

Already an experienced organizer, the twenty-four-year-old Foster served as Freedom City's director. Foster had grown up working on Delta plantations with his family and understood the displaced people at Mount Beulah. He explained, "With a few exceptions, we were dealing with the discarded ruins of the plantations; it was really tough to rebuild enough spirit to get them to accept any responsibility. But that's really what we were trying to do during those days at Mt. Beulah." Most of the plantation refugees were used to planters making all decisions. "It took a few weeks," the Delta Ministry reported, "before some stopped calling DM workers 'Yes sir' and 'No sir.' " The Ministry provided classes each morning for women, children, and others not working the land at Freedom City. These classes included literacy training, African American history, citizenship education, and instruction in running cooperative businesses. Women also had sewing classes, where they learned to mend clothes and make new ones. The Mount Beulah families met three nights a week to discuss future plans and make group decisions, often in a contentious atmosphere.[20]

Leon Howell, a white Tennessean who served as literature and study secretary for the University Christian Movement, spent time observing the families. He attended an adult literacy class at Mount Beulah in June 1966. As he took his seat, Howell recalled, "a middle-aged Negro, eyes downcast, apology all over his face . . . said to me, a total stranger: 'Would you 'scuse me, mister? I'm just gonna get something to smoke. Be right back to class, I sure will.'" However, an older woman in the class later challenged Howell by asking, "Can somebody tell me what this strange white man doin' here?" Howell explained himself satisfactorily and later discovered that the woman had refused to speak in public when she first came to Mount Beulah. For every member of the group, like her, who gained in self-confidence, Howell estimated, two were "so broken, twisted, deprived, used up" by years of oppression that they could not overcome their condition.[21]

The Delta Ministry had planned to move the poor people to the land in early May. However, it had to delay until July 25, partly because of legal wrangles to gain title to the land as Mississippi refused to grant DOC a charter of incorporation, and partly because the Florida company from which the Ministry had purchased specially designed temporary homes postponed their delivery date. Twenty-two families including ninety-four people, sixty-seven of them children, made the journey to Freedom City from Mount Beulah. There were more than twice as many women as men. The group moved into twenty-four urethane plastic pre-fabricated houses, which had cost eight hundred dollars each, including transportation and the construction of wooden floors on which to erect the structures. The manufacturer expected them to last between four and seven years, depending on weather conditions. The residents would cook and eat communally in a large farmhouse that came with the land.[22]

Roy Reed, a *New York Times* reporter, called Freedom City "a desperate experiment" that was based "on neither intellectual curiosity nor idealism." With several months' experience working with the group behind him, Foster openly expressed pessimism: "I don't know," he said, "if they will ever learn to work for themselves." The preparatory classes he had helped teach at Mount Beulah had achieved only limited success. Barnes did not believe that a new community could be developed by the people who moved to the site, given their dependent backgrounds. Even McKenna privately conceded Freedom City's "experimental and thus tenuous character."[23]

Concerned about the Delta Ministry's growing deficit, the NCC forced the Ministry to exclude Freedom City from the regular budget funded by National

Council and wcc denominations. Consequently, the Ministry had to raise money for the temporary houses by appealing to sympathetic northerners for donations. Asked when permanent homes would be built at the site, McKenna replied, "We haven't a cent for that."[24]

While the men worked in the fields, the women sewed. The Delta Ministry organized a summer Freedom School for children, about thirty of whom had attended local schools in Edwards while at Mount Beulah. The school presented a great challenge since many of the children had limited education and some had no school experience. They were unused to classroom teaching and discipline, and many had never before seen a flush toilet. Naomi Long, an educator from Australia formerly with the Buffalo Council of Churches, served as the school's coordinator. Rims Barber, a former Ministry volunteer now on the staff as a subsistence worker, held overall responsibility for the education of children and adults at Freedom City. Barber had worked for the Ministry, helping the civil rights movement in Canton and Madison County, before moving to Freedom City in July 1966. He reported that the Freedom School had "some moderate successes."[25]

In September 1966, thirty-four children from Freedom City enrolled at Riverside High, a white school in Avon. Ironically, many white parents had just transferred their children to the school from Glen Allan, hoping to escape school desegregation. White pupils regularly attacked and harassed the Freedom City children. Some teachers mistreated their African American students, but most instructors were friendly. Freedom City children were not passive victims. They often fought back and stood their ground. The Ministry organized after-school tutoring sessions at Freedom City to help the students with their work. Two African American teachers from Greenville joined the project. Half the students finished the school year with passing grades. One nine-year-old boy advanced through the first three grades despite lacking previous schooling. Barber recalled that some of the children were quite intelligent but had been denied opportunity.[26]

Pat Mutch, a white twenty-eight-year-old Episcopalian woman from New Jersey, taught women at Freedom City. Formerly an administrative assistant at the NCC's headquarters in New York, she had joined the Ministry after serving as a volunteer. Mutch helped Barber run the tutorial classes for Freedom City's schoolchildren. Sue Geiger, a twenty-four-year-old Ministry volunteer from Davenport, Iowa, also shared in the work. Geiger had first come to Mississippi in March 1966 to report on the Delta Ministry for her local newspaper. She had become interested after reading reports sent back to Iowa by Barber, who had pastored a church in Davenport before becoming a volunteer. In September 1966, Geiger, a Lutheran, decided to become a Ministry volunteer herself and was assigned as Hilton's assistant for interpretation. She took a particular interest in the development of Freedom City and soon began to devote much of her time to the project.[27]

Problems beset Freedom City. According to their manufacturer, the insulated plastic houses would reflect the summer heat and be cheap to keep warm in winter. According to Winham, "The 'Plydom' homes we got them are a very slight notch above tents: no water (outdoor privies), no electricity (and few kerosene lamps), no heat—no windows & doors to contain it if it were available. Moreover, they are placed on the ground and our mud is DEEP when it rains. But they are nice & hot on a sunny afternoon." The parts of the houses often did not fit together properly. The structures let in dust during dry weather and water when it rained. Worse still, they had been positioned on what turned out to be the lowest and muddiest part of the site. Men hired to install electricity repeatedly failed to show up. Barnes wrote in September 1966 that the houses were "quite inadequate." She feared that they would not "last through the winter without excessive patch work and repair."[28]

However, a solution to the problem seemed in sight. Marian Wright wrote to Barnes in September 1966 that the Ford Foundation had agreed to grant DOC $125,000 to build fifty houses if OEO would cover the other costs involved. To satisfy OEO's nondiscrimination requirements, DOC persuaded sympathetic whites to join its all–African American Board of Directors. The new board members included reporters John Childs of the *Delta Democrat-Times* and Bill Sartor, a former journalist at the newspaper, and two other residents of Washington County, architect Bobby Sferruzza and STAR placement director S. J. Carroll. However, OEO continued to stall on making a grant while at other times hinting that it was imminent. Sources in Washington, D.C., told the Delta Ministry that Mississippi Senator John C. Stennis had opposed the grant, correctly regarding DOC as a creature of the Ministry, of which he was a persistent adversary. DOC shared the Ministry's office space in Greenville and included some Ministry staff among its officers. President Lyndon B. Johnson did not want to antagonize Stennis, whose Subcommittee on Preparedness could authorize or refuse his request for more troops for Vietnam.[29]

Funded by an OEO grant, Foster left Freedom City in August 1966 to study at Queens College in New York City. Foster had experienced difficulty in getting Freedom City's men to work, although the situation improved when men from Strike City, ten miles to the northeast, lent a hand. Self-starters who had lost their skilled jobs after striking for higher pay, the disciplined, hardworking example provided by the Strike City men influenced those at Freedom City. However, too much time had already been wasted. The delay in acquiring land and then two weeks spent arguing over what to grow meant that the soybean crop had been planted too late, when the land was dry instead of wet. By the time the people adopted more regular work patterns, the fields were covered with weeds. Unfamiliar with complicated farming machinery, they misused and did not maintain the machinery, which had been purchased along with the land. The men began harvesting the disappointing soybean crop in October.[30]

By then, John Bradford had become Freedom City's director. A twenty-six-year-old African American from Mound Bayou, Mississippi, with a degree in sociology from Ohio University, Bradford had worked for SNCC and CDGM. Asked why he had not stayed in the North, he explained, "My idea is that this is home to me, as I know it, and I think that if the problems here will ever be worked out, then we're going to have to do it." No one doubted his commitment. Nevertheless, according to Hilton, "Bradford wasn't the leader that Isaac was, but he stayed with the job through days that would have unbalanced somebody less tough." Hilton's wife, Ginny, a registered nurse, also joined Freedom City to run a health program.[31]

Freedom City's financial situation was so poor that its members voted to pick cotton for neighboring African American farmers who asked for help. Hall supervised the November planting of sixty acres of winter wheat in an attempt to raise money for the mortgage payment. T. B. Green from Strike City taught Freedom City residents to make cedar nativity sets by hand for the Christmas market, as he and others had done at Strike City a year earlier. Bob Beech, who had become Delta Ministry's Freedomcrafts director, searched for markets for the products produced at Freedom City and other Freedomcrafts sites that subsequently began at Edwards, West Point, and Shaw. Nash Basom, a Delta Ministry volunteer since October 1965 who was supported by the Evangelical United Brethren, took charge of production at Freedomcrafts shops and of housing at Freedom City. Although only twenty-four, the white native of Alexandria, Virginia, had already gained considerable experience after working at Strike City for six months.[32]

Freedomcrafts nativity sets could generate only seasonal money from northern sympathizers. The Delta Ministry had been aware from the beginning that Freedom City needed to attract industry. Winham's efforts to bring a food-processing plant foundered when the company's representative said that a four-year feasibility study would be needed. Although a firm that bred laboratory animals expressed interest in setting up at Freedom City, as did chair-making and sheet-metal companies, these businesses did not follow through. The site's poor conditions, the extensive training required by its workforce, and fear of a hostile business environment combined to deter potential employers.[33]

The Delta Ministry made extensive efforts to raise money for Freedom City.

After McKenna's termination from the Ministry's staff in September 1966, Barnes became the project's principal fund-raiser. "I am personally concerned," she wrote, "as these people are in our community." Donations from the Village Independent Democrats of New York City and the International Convention of Christian Churches (Disciples of Christ) enabled gas heaters to be installed in the residents' homes in October, ready for the onset of winter. Each house also had lighting added. A grain bin housed three showers, while freezers and a water heater, sink, and stove equipped the cafeteria.[34]

Disaster struck in the early hours of November 10, 1966, when a storm damaged virtually all of the houses beyond repair and blew two away like kites. The residents escaped without serious injury and through adversity developed a community spirit not seen before. Winham found them "rather more involved with their own fate than is usually the case" as they moved furniture and cleaned two tenant shacks for habitation. The residents moved into the cafeteria and two frame buildings on the site, while the Delta Ministry made an emergency appeal for aid.[35]

Hall telegraphed OEO and pleaded to no avail for DOC's proposal to be funded. Francis B. Stevens, a lawyer and lay leader of the Methodist Mississippi Conference, contacted the Red Cross and the Civil Defense Agency in Mississippi to alert them to the emergency at Freedom City. Civil Defense sent a representative, who promised to supply beds and timber to renovate the barn for use as housing. However, Evelyn Gandy, director of the Mississippi Department of Public Welfare, vetoed delivery of the materials, claiming that Freedom City's residents were wards of the NCC and therefore ineligible for assistance. Greenville's Red Cross did not respond to telephone calls, and, according to the Ford Foundation, the National Red Cross was closed for the Veterans' Day holiday and the weekend that followed it.[36]

However, some NCC denominations responded to the Delta Ministry's appeal. The national offices of the Methodist, Evangelical United Brethren, United Church of Christ, and Episcopalian denominations donated several thousand dollars within twenty-four hours. The Division of Church and Society of the PCUS sent five hundred dollars, the first money that the denomination's national office had given to a Delta Ministry cause. Several truckloads of food, clothing, blankets, and bedding arrived from the Church of the Brethren and the Disciples of Christ.[37]

The manufacturer of the destroyed homes promised sturdier replacements but refused to accept any further liability. Very frightened by their experience, Freedom City residents no longer wanted to live in plastic homes, which had afforded them no protection from the storm. Discouraged, some families moved out. One family, threatened by withdrawal of Social Security aid, left reluctantly. The Delta

Ministry used some of the emergency appeal money to revamp the barn, installing electricity and using partitions to divide the space into four apartments. Two families moved into each of the two disused tenant shacks.[38]

Both residents and many Delta Ministry staff became dejected. With the November 1966 addition of volunteer Bill Rusk from Chicago to the Freedom City staff, the Ministry had six of its twenty-eight staff members and volunteers working full time at the project and many more—including Clarence Hall Jr., Al Winham, Thelma Barnes, Sue Geiger, and Bob Beech—devoting part of their time to the settlement's needs. The maintenance of the displaced people before their move from Mount Beulah and the cost of their removal had substantially increased the Ministry's deficit and threatened its future. Time spent raising funds for Freedom City distracted the staff from other important tasks and distorted the Ministry's focus away from the whole of the Delta region. Freedom City had been a disaster. The soybean crop had been poor, OEO still would not grant funds to DOC, no progress had been made in building permanent houses, and little had been "accomplished toward making adults literate." Freedom City's residents were living in conditions little different from those they had hoped to escape. The Ministry abandoned the aim of creating a self-governing community, leaving Bradford, Hall, and Barnes to manage the project.[39]

Although some residents had left Freedom City discouraged by events, some of those who remained found solace despite their situation. Ora D. Wilson, a fifty-year-old mother of eleven who had spent most of her life in the cotton fields, told a reporter, "For the first time in my life I feel like I'm gaining something. For the first time I'm able to have some say-so in my life." Her thirteen-year-old son, Sammy Lee, now enrolled at Riverside High, also preferred his new life: "I used to go to the fields with my mama. We got up when it was still dark. We worked all day, except when we had lunch. We come home when it was dark, and it was too late to fix supper so we eat some cheese and light bread and go to bed cause we have to get up early in the morning."[40]

However, given the Delta Ministry's task of helping the poor across the Delta, staff time expended on Freedom City was justified neither by the small numbers who lived at the site nor by the project's disappointing results. Yet the Ministry felt compelled to keep faith with the experiment out of loyalty to its inhabitants and as a symbol of the Ministry's determination to remain in the Delta for the long haul. As staffers knew, the withdrawal of SNCC and CORE from the state and the collapse of COFO had caused some African American Mississippians to believe that the civil rights movement had deserted them. Brooks, the Delta Ministry's acting director, announced during the December 1966 meeting of the NCC's General Assembly that the Ministry would develop Freedom City by continuing to raise funds specifically for the project. The Ministry also asked delegates to send money to buy Christmas toys for the children at Wayside.[41]

Hodding Carter III of the *Delta Democrat-Times* made a strong editorial appeal for the people of Washington County to help those at Freedom City. Private and public relief agencies in the county, he noted, had ignored pleas for assistance because of the project's connection with the Delta Ministry. Local churches had also done nothing. "Deltans, in this time of celebration for Christianity," Carter lamented, "have demonstrated their brotherly love by turning away from desperate need." His editorial may well have shamed some Greenvillians into action, since local white merchants, like people from around the nation, donated toys and clothing. However, the merchants were desperate to keep their action anonymous.[42]

In one of his last acts before the Delta Ministry's financial situation forced his termination from the staff in January 1967, Winham helped solicit donations and loans to buy the old Elks Club in Greenville and relocate it to Freedom City. Divided by the Ministry into three separate buildings for accommodation, it still required funds for conversion into living quarters. Money raised by the Wild Goose Committee, a lay organization in the Netherlands, paid off debt on the new housing. The committee had made a radio appeal for donations after an hour-long program on Dutch television about Freedom City. Freedom City's families now had separate living areas and could undertake individual grocery buying and cooking, hitherto done collectively. The residents became eligible for welfare, which had previously been denied on the grounds that they were part of an institution and ate communally. Eight residents attended a federal-government-funded STAR literacy course in Greenville and received temporary income from the program.[43]

However, Freedom City's situation and prospects remained bleak. Bradford told a February 1967 Delta Ministry staff meeting that the project cost $2,500 a month to maintain. OEO had still not given DOC a grant, and everything, he said, was "at a standstill." Barnes noted that the $16,000 annual mortgage payment fell due on April 7, but Freedom City had only $10,000 on hand. Proceeds from farming the land had been inadequate. Furthermore, poor maintenance had rendered farm equipment inoperable. "The real problem," Barnes concluded, "is the people just don't like to farm."[44]

Charles Evers, who had succeeded his slain brother, Medgar, as Mississippi field secretary of the NAACP, told the press that Freedom City was "a disgrace." He attacked the Delta Ministry for initiating the project, charging, "They're destroying Negroes in the Delta. What they're doing is taking them off the plantation and putting them out there to starve. What have they accomplished?"[45]

Barnes reported Freedom City's parlous circumstances to the Commission on the Delta Ministry when it met in Greenville in late March 1967. Even if DOC's housing project materialized, she noted that money would still be needed to pay for sewerage and water. The commission decided that its in-state members and the Delta Ministry's staff should "make an immediate and thorough study of Freedom City and make a recommendation" as to whether it should be continued. On the day that the commission's meeting concluded, OEO announced that it was granting DOC $199,805 to provide literacy classes, pre-vocational education, and training in construction skills for seventy-five poor Delta families. The grant was contingent on the Ford Foundation paying the cost of materials for building fifty homes at Freedom City to be erected by program trainees, including family heads already living at the site.[46]

Freedom City received national publicity in April 1967, when Senators Joseph S. Clark of Pennsylvania and Robert F. Kennedy of New York visited the project as part of a Delta tour arranged by Marian Wright. The two men were in Mississippi conducting hearings in Jackson with the Senate Subcommittee on Employment, Manpower, and Poverty. Barnes showed Kennedy and Clark around Freedom City, and Clark later said that he had been impressed by Bradford. Nevertheless, he doubted that Freedom City would succeed without a large federal grant. Clark also commented, "I am a little concerned as to whether they can find an adequate market for the crops they intend to raise. It's a most hopeful enterprise, and I wish it well but I certainly couldn't say that as of this moment I would be very optimistic about it."[47]

The proceeds from the winter wheat crop and a private donation paid for seed and fertilizer, while funds from the WCC arrived just in time to meet the bulk of the costs of the mortgage payment in April 1967. On May 1, all of Freedom City's residents took to the fields to plant soybeans, wheat, and vegetables.[48]

Freedom City maintained a holding operation during the summer of 1967. Although DOC immediately submitted a revised housing proposal to the Ford Foundation after OEO announced that it would fund a training program, complications arose over the legal details. In the meantime, Barnes tried to raise funds to keep the farming operation going. She regretted that most of the donations she received came from whites, whom she recognized had greater resources. Nevertheless, Freedom City attracted gifts from African Americans, particularly after *Jet*, a black magazine, published an article about the Kennedy-Clark visit. Barnes wrote to a potential donor in June that although repairs had been undertaken on some of the farm machinery, they were still needed on the combine, which would soon be needed to harvest the wheat crop. Furthermore, there was no money for gas and oil for the tractors.[49]

A federal dollar-per-hour minimum wage law that had taken effect on February 1, 1967, led many planters to dispense with their remaining workers and replace them with machines and herbicides. Consequently, more and more displaced plantation workers, including for the first time some whites, sought refuge at Freedom City. During the first week of June, Barnes wrote, "We cannot accommodate other families who are continually requesting to become a part of this project. We have had to turn away two white families and one Negro family during the past month because of our limited housing." Freedom City had twenty families on its waiting list but felt obliged to accept people who had no other place to go.[50]

In July 1967, Jim Allen and his wife and five children became Freedom City's first white residents. Originally from Arkansas, the Allens had worked on the Andrews Brothers' Plantation at Tribbett after A. L. Andrews had evicted the striking African American tractor drivers and their families. Mistreated by Andrews, the family had left after six months for Leland, where an accident severely injured Jim Allen. Unable to find work, the desperate family turned to Freedom City as their last hope. After a heated debate, residents voted to accept the Allens, who moved into one of the tenant shacks. Allen's wife commented, "Jim and John Bradford gets along real well. I told 'em they are more like brothers than a white and a nigra." Bradford reciprocated and explained, "Everybody had to change their way of thinking. When something has always been said about somebody, it takes a lot of time to get that changed, but it can be done. The white family and the Negroes have learned to trust each other." A second white family, also from the Andrews Brothers' Plantation, moved to Freedom City two months later.[51]

Geiger saw little potential for change in most of Freedom City's residents. In July 1967, she wrote,

> If we are going to be honest and frank about what has happened, we cannot say that the people have been trained in many skills. A few of the women have learned to sew and are running a sewing room at Freedom City; some of the men work on the farm and have learned additional skills to those they already had; a few of the adults are enrolled in STAR, a federal job training program, and MDTA [Manpower Development and Training Act, a federally funded adult education and skill training program], but have learned little; Freedomcrafts operated at Freedom City only when they were making nativity sets—the people are basically unable to learned the more skilled jobs now required in Freedomcrafts products.

Freedomcrafts cooperatives at Shaw and Edwards had branched out into making furniture for CDGM Head Start centers, while the women at Edwards made candy. Geiger explained that the families that would be recruited for DOC's self-help housing project would "have male heads of household and will be people with more potential for education and job training." The Delta Ministry hoped that "the people who are at Freedom City now will fit into the new community in various jobs, etc., but probably few will actually be re-trained in construction jobs."[52]

Financial considerations and its increasing emphasis on voter registration, citizenship education, and political development forced the Ministry to terminate Hilton and Bradford in June 1967, with Barnes taking over Bradford's job as Freedom City's director. Although the Ford Foundation told DOC that it would announce a housing grant to the organization, it had still not done so by August 1967. However, during that month the PCUS sent the Delta Ministry twenty-five thousand dollars, most of which was earmarked for Freedom City. The grant assumed the costs of Barnes's salary, contributed to farming costs, and helped pay for a classroom building on the site that would become a community center after the DOC training program finished. In October, the United Church Women sponsored the salary of a nurse at Freedom City to replace Ginny Hilton, who had left Mississippi with her husband. The eight-thousand-dollar grant also paid for a Freedom City health program focused on nutrition and health education. After an inspection of Freedom City, the Ford Foundation told the NCC that the "DOC board appears to be working together harmoniously, and we are impressed with the energy and dedication that Mrs. Barnes has brought to the project."[53]

With a long-awaited $160,000 grant from the Ford Foundation finally secured, DOC hired McKinley C. Martin in October 1967 to direct the education and self-help housing project. Martin, an African American from Clarksdale, Mississippi, joined DOC from Coahoma Junior College, where he had been director of institutional development and public relations. He had previously worked as a private building contractor. Martin shared office space with the Delta Ministry in Greenville and hired eight other staff members.[54]

The Protestant Episcopal Church gave Freedom City a $9,110 grant to help relocate twenty-five families from the Delta for the DOC program and to provide for medical examinations and related health program costs. The federal Farmers Home Administration (FMHA) agreed to provide a loan of $30,000 to pay for half the cost of a water and sewerage system at Freedom City, with the Ford Foundation providing matching funds.[55]

DOC's adult basic education and self-help housing program began at the end of November 1967. Classes initially took place in temporary facilities in Greenville because poor weather had prevented the construction of a classroom building at Freedom City. Adults in nine of the fourteen families at the site enrolled in the programs; some other heads of household were too elderly to participate. DOC sought recruits throughout its nine-county focus, but only thirty of the two hundred people it interviewed reported for training. Twelve participating families came from outside Washington County and, with DOC assistance, relocated to the Greenville area. By February 1968, DOC had nearly fifty men enrolled, mostly heads of household. They received vocational training in brick masonry and carpentry, with classes in plumbing and electrical wiring planned. Trainees also included young adult men, who were eligible if they were married or provided the main support for their mothers. Enrollment numbers fluctuated, with a high dropout rate. Some men left the program because they were unable to support their families on the stipend DOC provided during the training period of eight to ten months. Others joined when they lost their plantation jobs. DOC expected enrollees to build fifty houses at Freedom City for program participants. The corporation planned to recruit and train twenty-five other men and then help them obtain FMHA loans to build homes for their families. DOC hoped that all enrollees would become equipped for employment in the Greenville area.[56]

All trainees and their families had medical examinations and appropriate treatment. Thirty-nine people received eyeglasses, paid for by the Protestant Episcopal Church. The wives of trainees and female heads of household attended health education classes, which focused on birth control methods as well as general health care and nutrition classes. Female heads of household received training in electrical wiring. Both men and women enrolled in the education program, which offered courses in literacy, mathematics, science, social studies, and home economics. Five people took the General Education Development (GED) examination in June 1968. By then, DOC had also used the High School Equivalency Program to place several former trainees and Delta residents in universities across the United States to prepare for the GED test.[57]

During its first seven months of program operations, DOC also conducted adult basic education classes in Yazoo and Madison Counties. It helped ninety-seven low-income families submit applications to the FMHA for low-cost home loans in Madison, Yazoo, Sunflower, and Issaquena Counties. In addition, the corporation operated a food and health program in Issaquena and Sharkey Counties.[58]

On May 31, 1968, DOC held a ceremony to break ground for house building at Freedom City. Although construction was originally scheduled to begin in early spring, bad weather had delayed the start. Fifty-one heads of household were receiving skills training to build houses, rather than the seventy-five that DOC had envisaged. The trainees headed families that comprised a total of 244 people, 94 adults and 150 children. By July, the community center had been built, and DOC moved its office to Freedom City. Plans for the site comprised fifty houses, "a complex for senior citizens, and a home for foster children and transient children as their family situations demand." A twenty-acre park, a church, and a school were also planned. A shopping center would be built, with a barber and beauty shop, "a grocery store, washerette, restaurant, clothing store, and service station." DOC also began training female heads of household in ceramics so that they could make a living. The PCUS donated another $25,000 to the Delta Ministry in 1968, most of it designated, as before, for Barnes's salary and Freedom City. The Ministry received $87,442 from WCC denominations as a memorial to Martin Luther King Jr., who was assassinated in April, allocating $10,000 from the memorial funds for the water supply at Freedom City.[59]

By the end of 1968, DOC had provided job training for approximately 120 people and placed 40 of them in industrial jobs. The corporation operated an adult basic education program one night each week in Yazoo, Sunflower, Madison, Bolivar, and Washington Counties. The corporation had furnished training in construction and business skills for twenty unemployed farm workers in Sunflower County. Fourteen houses at Freedom City, DOC reported, were nearing completion, although the work had been slow. Women at Freedom City had created a Freedomcrafts ceramics operation.[60]

DOC proudly reported and publicized its efforts, but significant problems beset the program. Gaile Noble, a Delta Ministry volunteer in the summer of 1968, described the people at Freedom City as "a demoralized group of families who have no place to go and are suspicious of each other as well as the DM staff." Although academically qualified, DOC staff, Noble believed, lacked the skills, patience, and understanding to help people from severely deprived backgrounds with significant social and behavioral problems. DOC trainees, she observed, were often inattentive in class, and many recognized that they would not obtain jobs using the skills the corporation taught.[61]

Nevertheless, in January 1969 OEO granted DOC a further $304,394 to fund the self-help housing program at Freedom City, training for twenty men to build and repair homes in nine counties, basic adult education programs at Freedom City and in several counties, partial college tuition support for thirty students, and other supportive services. The federal Department of Health, Education, and Welfare awarded DOC a $120,000 grant in the spring to expand its adult education program into all of the nine counties within its purview. DOC used a $25,000 federal Economic Development Agency grant to establish two farming cooperatives, one each in Sharkey and Tallahatchie Counties; a radio and television repair shop; and a dirt hauling business. Work continued into the summer on the first set of homes at Freedom City.[62]

The Delta Ministry acted primarily as a fund-raiser for Freedom City and for DOC programs that federal and private sources did not finance. Prompted by the Ministry, the United Methodist Church agreed in 1969 to help pay for streets and other community improvements at Freedom City. The project continued to rely on donations to meet its annual mortgage payment as its crops failed to produce sufficient revenue. Delta Ministry staff helped raise money for the mortgage and the Freedomcrafts ceramics project, furnished transportation for DOC trainees, and provided volunteer help for a day care center established at Freedom City. The United Methodist Church gave DOC four thousand dollars for ceramics training, and the Merrill Foundation provided twenty thousand dollars, six thousand of which would repay a start-up loan from the NCC.[63]

Ten families moved into new homes at Freedom City in August 1969, the same month that Martin resigned from DOC. In all but two of the completed houses, the ceilings collapsed. Eight other houses were in various stages of construction. Freedom City's families incorporated Freedom Village in August 1970, and DOC authorized trustee Barnes to transfer the property, land, equipment, and all debts held by DOC on behalf of Freedom City to Freedom Village, Inc., in September. The residents now assumed control of Freedom Village, which operated as a nonprofit cooperative with its own board of directors and leased 320 acres to a white farmer, abandoning its agricultural operations. Eleven of the twenty completed homes were occupied. Residents owned their houses by dint of their labor, the "sweat equity" they had contributed during construction. Those who wished to sell their houses would receive whatever balance was left after the cost of materials had been considered. Freedom Village planned to sell lots to those who obtained an FMHA or other loan to build a house. Proceeds from lot sales were to be used to repay a fifty-thousand-dollar loan from the Ford Foundation to install water and sewerage at the nine vacant homes and thus make them habitable. Although private funds had built a combined restaurant and grocery store at Freedom Village, there was no money left for house construction. The Delta Ministry continued to help raise funds to meet the annual mortgage payment for which Freedom Village became accountable.[64]

Still responsible for training Freedom City's inhabitants and other impoverished Delta residents, DOC suffered from poor administration and internal conflict. The corporation failed to follow proper accounting procedures. It appointed Rutledge A. Waker, an African American based in Boston, Massachusetts, but originally from South Carolina, as project director in May 1970. He replaced Robert Holmes Jr., a former Greenville schoolteacher who had served as acting director since Martin's resignation. Waker dismissed DOC's existing employees and put together a new staff. He claimed that the posts had become vacant with the expiration of OEO's previous grant to DOC and that he was entitled to hire a new workforce to implement a new $367,338 OEO grant approved in March 1970. The new director appointed Clarence Hall Jr. as administrative assistant in place of Holmes. Thelma Barnes succeeded Hall as DOC chair.[65]

Holmes and fourteen former DOC employees filed a list of grievances with OEO in June 1970, arguing that the Delta Ministry had slowed down DOC's program and "got rid of those who resisted their ideas, regardless of their position." Former Ministry staff members, they said, now occupied key salaried posts, and DOC staff had been fired in violation of the terms of OEO's grant to the corporation. The former employees also charged that the Ministry was trying to use DOC's new OEO grant almost solely to build more houses at Freedom City. The disgruntled former staffers pointed out that despite four years of work, DOC had completed only twelve houses, with eight still unfinished.[66]

Waker blamed Holmes for DOC's failure to complete the fifty houses the corporation had originally projected. The new director claimed that he had inherited a program that had become languid and unproductive and maintained that he was reinvigorating DOC. Within a month of his arrival, he said, two houses had been nearly completed at Freedom Village, most of its land had been put under cultivation, and two families had been taken "off the poverty level." Waker asserted that he would ensure that Freedom Village had fifty houses by July 1971.[67]

OEO took the charges made by Holmes and the other former DOC staffers very seriously and nearly withdrew financial support. However, OEO gave DOC a reprieve to improve its efficiency. In the three years before its refunding grant in March 1970, DOC had received more than $731,000 in federal funds as well as substantial private funding. However, the corporation had, according to a report in the *Memphis Commercial Appeal,* "trained about 150 displaced migrant farm workers during the last three years at a cost of more than $50,000 per trainee." The newspaper may have underestimated the numbers trained, but OEO was dissatisfied with DOC's results. DOC had also fallen far behind schedule in its goal of building fifty houses at Freedom Village by July 1971, five years after the Mount Beulah refugees had moved to the site.[68]

Barnes, who had worked so hard on behalf of DOC and Freedom Village while serving as director of the Delta Ministry's Washington County Project, took a one-year leave of absence from the Ministry in October 1970. She became field representative for Black Methodists for Church Renewal, an Atlanta-based organization, and remained there for ten and half years. She had become tired of raising money to keep Freedom City afloat as it slipped down the Delta Ministry's priorities, and she hoped that her absence would force Brooks, the Ministry's director, to turn his attention to Freedom Village.[69]

Poor performance by some employees continued to pervade DOC, which its planning officer, David M. Frank, commented "had a noticable deletrious effect on the work output of other staff members." Waker resigned. OEO funds for the self-help housing training program at Freedom Village ended in 1971. DOC, like

OEO, became a casualty of President Richard Nixon's policy of devolving program implementation and revenue to elected state and local authorities and dismantling some of Lyndon Johnson's Great Society programs.[70]

New priorities and budget cutbacks had gradually forced the Delta Ministry to withdraw staff from Freedom Village in the late 1960s and early 1970s. A severe budget cut in 1971 necessitated drastic cutbacks in most Delta Ministry activities. The Ministry and the NCC continued to try to raise funds for the settlement but could render little other assistance. Freedom Village shared the Delta Ministry's Greenville office in the early 1970s. A water and sewerage system was finally installed in 1972. Three families moved into new houses, bringing the total number occupied to fourteen. Freedomcraft Ceramics, which sold its products by mail order and through college campuses, made enough money to pay its fixed expenses but not employees' salaries. It remained dependent on financial support from sympathetic denominations. In 1972, the UPCUSA donated twenty thousand dollars to Freedomcraft Ceramics, which the Presbyterians reported "was the only source of income-employment reasonably near the Village." The town's inhabitants, the UPCUSA noted, constituted "one of the poorest communities in the nation." Not economically viable, Freedomcraft Ceramics, which employed seven residents, closed in February 1973. The United Methodist Church donated twenty thousand dollars to Freedom Village in 1972–73, and the PCUS gave nearly eighteen thousand dollars. The Ford Foundation wrote off its fifty-thousand-dollar loan to Freedom Village in March 1973 to enable further development of the site.[71]

A flood temporarily forced village residents to leave their homes in 1973, although they were later able to return. By March, sixty-eight residents occupied sixteen houses at Freedom Village, and three more houses neared completion. Toward the end of the year, the U.S. Catholic Conference's Campaign for Human Development awarded the Village a one-year grant to build forty new homes. However, the FMHA, which had already refused individual applications by residents for home improvement loans, declined to give the approval needed for further house construction because the houses were to be built on a floodplain. Consequently, the Campaign for Human Development withdrew its offer. Freedom Village paid its last mortgage installment in April 1976 and received full title to the land but subsequently had to take out another mortgage to pay its operating expenses. The site began hosting the annual Delta Blues Festival in 1977. There were fewer than twenty houses at Freedom Village a year later. The *Jackson Clarion-Ledger* reported in December 1980 that "few of the original residents remain, houses are in disrepair and the dream appears all but dead." Still living at Freedom Village, Ora D. Wilson declared, "People were really hopeful. I'm very disappointed."[72]

Influenced by the kibbutzim and moshavs of Israel, Warren McKenna conceived the idea of creating self-governing agricultural and industrial cooperatives for African American Mississippians forced from plantation jobs by agricultural change. He hoped that they would provide a viable alternative to black migration to northern urban ghettoes. Before it had time to consider McKenna's idea in depth, the Ministry began Freedom City as a solution to the burden it had assumed of supporting plantation refugees at Mount Beulah. The project reflected McKenna's utopian belief that oppressed, undereducated people who had been dependent on others all their lives could be remade into independent, self-supporting individuals who governed themselves within a cooperative. Tragically but understandably, few of Freedom City's residents could make that transition. Although the Delta Ministry managed to attract considerable federal and church money to the project, the funds were insufficient to bring it to completion, and industry would not locate plants in such unpromising circumstances. Freedom City distracted the Delta Ministry from the Delta's wider problems, and the drain on staff time was not justified by the small number of residents involved. The Ministry felt obliged to continue to support the people it had encouraged to create Freedom City, and the group's prestige became tied to the project's success. However, during the early 1970s, the Delta Ministry's mounting budget difficulties forced it to begin a gradual withdrawal from Freedom City, and a now indifferent federal government was unwilling to support further development of the site.

CHAPTER EIGHT

Changing Focus, 1967–1971

The late 1960s marked a period of transition for the Delta Ministry. From making mostly ad hoc responses to problems that involved assisting African American protests; pressuring local, state, and federal authorities; and operating virtually autonomous county projects, the Ministry under Owen Brooks's directorship moved toward a more focused long-term and statewide approach to improving the lives of Mississippi's poor. The Ministry continued to conduct voter registration and citizenship education programs but also trained black candidates for political responsibility. Its involvement in education broadened from Head Start to school desegregation and improving educational opportunities. The Ministry continued to provide direct relief and to try to make Mississippi's welfare offices more responsive to the needs of the poor, but the group also encouraged the poor to assert their rights to welfare assistance. The Ministry still supported cooperatives, but it also tried to generate labor-intensive, sustainable, profit-making businesses. Staffers supplemented the Ministry's small budget by raising additional funds for specific activities, but a massive cut in its regular NCC approved budget in 1971 necessitated drastic reductions in its programs and personnel.[1]

By January 1967, the Delta Ministry had become the largest civil rights group operating in the South. The *New York Times* reported that twenty-eight of the sixty-five civil rights field workers in the region were with the Ministry. SNCC and CORE had about twelve workers each in the South, while the NAACP had eleven and the SCLC twelve organizers there. Each of the major civil rights groups had shed staff during 1966 because of declining financial contributions from sympathizers, many of them northern whites. SNCC chairman Stokely Carmichael's call for Black Power, first made during the Meredith March in June 1966, had alienated many white supporters of the movement. Disaffected former white sympathizers associated Black Power, endorsed by SNCC and CORE, with separatism, violence, and hatred of whites. Annual summer riots in some black northern ghettoes, which first began in 1964, further drained white support and led SNCC, CORE, and the SCLC to refocus their energies and many of their staff on the North. Northern white support for civil rights also declined as civil rights groups began demanding that northern cities and suburbs desegregate housing and education and ensure equal job opportunities. Some former civil rights activists directed their energies into protesting U.S. involvement in the Vietnam War.[2]

The Delta Ministry had become a prominent civil rights group largely by default and despite its net loss of seventeen staff and volunteers between January 1966 and January 1967. Although its three-hundred-thousand-dollar regular budget made the Ministry the best-funded civil rights organization in Mississippi, fifty thousand dollars of that amount had to be assigned, at NCC insistence, toward paying off a deficit of nearly one hundred thousand dollars dating from 1965. Budgetary problems continued to force the Ministry to cut back staff in 1967. Al Winham left in January 1967, with the expiration of funds donated by a Midwestern sponsor that had kept him in his post.[3]

Shortly after Winham's departure, the Delta Ministry received the firm endorsement of an investigatory committee appointed by the PCUS's Council on Church and Society in September 1966. The committee, chaired by Joseph A. Norton, noted that steps had been taken to improve the Ministry following its earlier evaluation by the NCC. The committee was "very favorably impressed with the character and spirit of the DM staff we met" and described the Ministry's work as a "profoundly Christian, and genuinely evangelistic witness." Shamed that gifts to the Delta Ministry of $1,000 from the Christian Council of East Asia and $680 from the Evangelical Church in Cameroon had exceeded the PCUS's 1966 donation of $500, the Norton Committee recommended that the denomination's Board of Church Extension donate at least $25,000. In appointing the Norton Committee, the Council on Church and Society had forgotten about an ongoing investigation of the Delta Ministry by the Permanent Committee on Inter-Church Relations that the PCUS's General Assembly had ordered in 1965. Consequently, the Norton

Committee sent its findings, approved by the Council on Church and Society in February, to the permanent committee, which also recommended that the denomination contribute to the Ministry. Meeting in June, the General Assembly would decide whether to approve the permanent committee's recommendations.[4]

After a strong appeal from some Mississippi Presbyterians that the denomination not fund the Ministry, the PCUS's Board of Church Extension appointed a third Presbyterian investigatory committee in February 1967. The committee, chaired by Henry W. Quinius, was "to explore alternative possibilities for a ministry with the dispossessed in Mississippi" and report in August to the board, which would then decide "whether to support the DM or an alternative." The board would appropriate $25,000 for the Ministry, as the Norton Committee had recommended, unless it received a "firm and workable alternate plan" from the Synod of Mississippi and its three presbyteries.[5]

While the Southern Presbyterians grappled with the issue of funding the Ministry, a nineteen-thousand-dollar donation from Herbert McKinstry, a northern Presbyterian layman and former National Council volunteer in Hattiesburg, kept the Ministry's citizenship education program afloat. Begun in November 1966, the program became "the backbone of Delta Ministry operation" over the next twelve months. During the first half of 1967, citizenship education focused on "voter registration and workshops with local community workers and leaders" in preparation for the August Democratic Party primary and November general elections in Mississippi. The program operated in twelve counties, including parts of the Delta, southwestern Mississippi, and Hinds and Forrest Counties. It trained local community workers and leaders to hold workshops that taught African Americans the structure of local and state government, the nature of the electoral process, and their rights as citizens. The Ministry helped register more than eight thousand blacks by funding voter registration campaigns that local people conducted.[6]

The citizenship education program's first test came in Sunflower County, where Federal District Judge Claude Clayton ordered May 1967 special elections in the towns of Sunflower and Moorhead. The Fifth Circuit Court of Appeals set aside the June 1965 municipal elections in both towns after a suit by MFDP lawyers protested that white officials had denied blacks the opportunity to register. Harry J. Bowie, director of the Delta Ministry's citizenship education program, and Joseph L. Harris, the director of its Sunflower County Project, had been conducting voter registration and workshops for potential black candidates since 1966 at the request of local people and in anticipation of Clayton's decision.[7]

Running on the MFDP ticket in May 1967, blacks stood for six of the seven offices up for election in Sunflower and for all five available offices in Moorhead.

Although 98 percent of eligible African Americans voted in Sunflower and 85 percent cast ballots in Moorhead, no blacks won election in either town. The MFDP had anticipated possible defeat in Moorhead, where there were 418 white registrants and 412 African Americans registered. However, in Sunflower, where black registrants outnumbered whites by 185 to 154, whites had intimidated more than one hundred African Americans into voting for white candidates. White officials broke a preelection agreement allowing campaign manager Joseph Harris to help voters mark their ballots if they requested aid; instead, the whites themselves undertook that task. Consequently, many black voters were frightened into choosing white candidates. Some African American voters felt threatened even merely by going to the voting booth, where the white police chief greeted each one of them and another man photographed them. Whites milled outside the polling place with shotguns prominently displayed in their parked trucks. The experience in Sunflower was a foretaste of what was to come in the fall elections.[8]

Even before the May elections, the Delta Ministry had broken new ground in Mississippi by responding to a request for aid from the Yazoo County Voters' League in late February 1967. The league wanted to broaden its program beyond voter registration in a county that, apart from the efforts of two Delta Ministry Freedom Corps workers in 1965, had been largely untouched by the civil rights movement. The Ministry made Yazoo County a priority because it was the largest county in Mississippi and lacked movement involvement. Although based in Greenville, Rims Barber became the Ministry's Yazoo County Project director. He expended a thousand dollars in citizenship education monies, helping to register more than one thousand new voters in the county and funding citizenship education workshops. The project also pressured the Yazoo County Community Action Program Board, which ran Head Start, to include eight representatives of the poor and succeeded in opening public accommodations in the county to blacks.[9]

Yazoo became the eighth Delta Ministry county project, replacing Forrest County, from which the Ministry withdrew during the first half of 1967 as it focused its efforts primarily on the Delta and surrounding areas and on citizenship education. Bruce Hilton, the Ministry's director of interpretation, and his wife, Ginny, lost their posts in June, followed in the fall by the director of the Hattiesburg Project, Bob Beech; Owen Brooks's administrative assistant, Fred Lowry; director of Freedom City John Bradford; and a secretary in Greenville. Beech explained to Harvey Cox, an early supporter of the Ministry, "The choice of which staff to drop was decided on a priority bases considering the fact that those who are involved in voter registration, citizenship education, and political development were the most needed at the moment." Executive Secretary Henry

McCanna had warned the Ministry that if it finished the year with a deficit, the whole program would be under threat. Staff reductions were necessary to cut expenses.[10]

Program priorities and a limited budget also forced the Delta Ministry to contemplate relinquishing Mount Beulah. The Ministry had fought hard to keep the conference center in 1966, when the NCC's Evaluation Committee had called for withdrawal from the site because of high maintenance and operating costs. At the insistence of the Commission on the Delta Ministry, in June 1967 Brooks reluctantly asked the UCMS, Mount Beulah's owners, to reclaim the property because continued spending on it would severely hamper the Ministry's spending in other areas during the remainder of the year. The Delta Ministry hoped that the Disciples of Christ would keep Mount Beulah open since it housed the Ministry's finance and Hinds County Project offices, a Head Start program, and Freedomcrafts woodwork and candy cooperatives. The UCMS told the Ministry that it did not have the funds to keep Mount Beulah open and that it would have to close if the NCC surrendered the lease. Faced with this possibility, the National Council removed Mount Beulah from the Ministry's regular budget on July 1, 1967, and told the Ministry to raise the site's operating costs or lose it altogether.[11]

The Ministry responded by creating a fund-raising committee, the Ad Hoc Committee to Save Mount Beulah. The committee generated sufficient funds to keep Mount Beulah operational before the UPCUSA took over the lease in May 1968 with the intention that Mary Holmes Junior College in West Point would create an adult education college on the site. Most of the monies raised came from major denominations, particularly the UPCUSA and the Episcopal and Methodist Churches.[12]

Delta Ministry staff proved adept at raising funds for such specific projects as Mount Beulah, Freedom City, and citizenship education that lay outside its normal, NCC-approved budget. During 1967, the Ministry secured $123,887 in donations to spend in nonbudgeted areas. However, fund-raising consumed a great deal of time and diverted staff from program activities.[13]

Contributions generally came from major NCC denominations, northern and western churches and church associations, and nonsouthern laypeople and clergy. The Ministry occasionally received gifts from individuals living in the Upper South and Texas but almost none at all from Mississippians and other Deep South residents. Consequently, the decision of the PCUS, an almost entirely southern white institution, to endorse the Delta Ministry in 1967 marked a significant advance.[14]

In response to the Quinius Committee, in June 1967 the Synod of Mississippi approved a report that recommended that the PCUS's Board of Church Extension not grant any funds to the Delta Ministry. The synod charged that the Ministry was "not performing a proper church-related ministry," had fomented "dissension and conflict," had created "antagonism between classes of Negroes and between Negroes and whites," and had failed to develop "a primary emphasis on spiritual endeavor." Mississippi's Presbyterians urged the PCUS's Board of Church Extension to allocate twenty-five thousand dollars to be disbursed through existing Mississippi black churches as Presbyterian Service Centers. The centers would conduct evangelism, "training in responsible citizenship, literacy programs . . . Day-care centers for children, Health and medical aid, [and] Relief and social welfare, etc." The Synod commended the idea to the PCUS "as a possible alternative to the Delta Ministry."[15]

The Reverend Al Freundt, stated clerk of the Synod of Mississippi, presented his synod's rejection of the Delta Ministry and its alternative proposal to the PCUS General Assembly in June. Another Mississippi commissioner, the Reverend Lee M. Gentry of Cleveland, told the General Assembly that Freedom City was run by "outsiders and off-beats." Gentry conceded that the Delta Ministry was "not made up entirely of sex perverts, beatniks and people with an ax to grind over society," but he nevertheless asserted that the group inflamed blacks against whites.[16]

Influenced by the Norton Committee's positive assessment of the Delta Ministry and by the favorable report of the NCC's Evaluation Committee, the Permanent Committee on Inter-Church Relations urged the PCUS General Assembly to endorse the Ministry. The permanent committee argued that although the Ministry had made mistakes, the NCC had taken corrective action to improve the program. The permanent committee recommended that the Boards of Christian Education and Church Extension support the Delta Ministry without specifying an amount. But in an effort to appease the Synod of Mississippi, the committee also recommended that the two boards encourage and support the synod "and its Presbyteries in programs which they may develop to serve the human needs of all people in that Synod."[17]

The recommendation in favor of the Delta Ministry split the General Assembly down the middle, winning by just 214 votes to 200. Nevertheless, the denomination became the last major denomination to support the Ministry. Mississippi gubernatorial candidate and State Treasurer William Winter, who had led the fight against the Delta Ministry as a commissioner to the General Assembly in 1965, deplored the decision and pledged his continued opposition to the NCC project. "The Delta Ministry," he declared, "has been a great detriment to the people of both races in Mississippi and has broken down channels of communication and understanding among our people." Undeterred, the Board of

Church Extension decided in August to donate twenty-five thousand dollars to the Ministry.[18]

A committee from the PCUS Board of National Ministries, the Board of Church Extension's successor, met with representatives of the Synod of Mississippi. The PCUS agreed to fund a staff member for a Presbyterian Council of Special Ministries for three years and to supply matching funds up to twenty-five thousand dollars per year. The council would include at least three African Americans and provide the services the synod had suggested in its earlier Presbyterian Service Centers proposal. A sop to the synod, the council was "to serve the spiritual and social needs of all the people of Mississippi" and was forbidden from perpetuating segregation in its work. The council was to consult with, rather than be an alternative to, the Delta Ministry. In practice, the council, which began operations in the summer of 1968, focused primarily on traditional outreach programs, such as adult evangelism, and summer classes for African American children in Bible study, handiwork, sewing, and cooking. The synod provided little money for the PCUS to match. The PCUS's financial difficulties forced the Board of National Ministries to end the matching-fund agreement and to withdraw funding for the council's director after 1970. The Synod of Mississippi made a special appeal to its members for replacement funds, but insufficient money resulted. Consequently, the synod ended the Council in January 1971. White Mississippi Presbyterians had shown little commitment to the council because it had not served their intention of undermining the Delta Ministry.[19]

Although limited to twenty-five thousand dollars, PCUS funds were crucial to the Ministry's survival, helping to maintain its commitment to Freedom City and to stave off a potential deficit in the regular budget. The denomination designated half of its contribution for Freedom City, while the remainder paid the salary of Thelma Barnes, who had replaced John Bradford as Freedom City's director, and enabled the Ministry to hire Ed King as education director.[20]

The Delta Ministry made education one of its priorities during 1967. Its involvement in the creation of CDGM in 1965 had deepened the Ministry's "interest in the range of educational needs in communities." Furthermore, school desegregation under "freedom of choice" plans placed the burden of initiating desegregation on African American parents, who were frequently intimidated by whites. Consequently, fewer than 3 percent of Mississippi's black children attended formerly white schools in 1967, and those who did often suffered physical harassment. African American students sometimes also found the transition to white schools difficult because these pupils had received inadequate academic preparation in less well equipped black schools and from less qualified staff. Teachers in formerly all-white schools sometimes discriminated against black students and used teaching methods and approaches that differed from those with which African American students were familiar.[21]

Freedom City also stimulated the Ministry's interest in education. Barber organized a tutorial program for Freedom City children, many of whom had attended school either irregularly or not at all. The program continued when the children desegregated a local school. "Through this struggle of learning," wrote Barber, "we began to sense some of the greater educational needs for Black children in Mississippi." Consequently, Barber took on the portfolio of education in addition to his duties at Freedom City and as Yazoo County Project director.[22]

The Delta Ministry adopted several approaches to education. It used two volunteer black teachers from Greenville to provide Freedom City students with after-school "compensatory and remedial work" and located northern colleges that were prepared to dispatch their students on a rotating basis to help Mississippi children with educational problems. The Ministry worked with students from Smith and Amherst Colleges in Massachusetts and with Marian Wright of the NAACP Legal Defense and Educational Fund to formulate a successful proposal for an OEO-funded summer project that helped prepare African American children for entry into formerly all-white schools in the fall of 1967. Housed at Mary Holmes Junior College, the program provided residential tutoring for more than two hundred black students. In addition, the Ministry helped create a tutorial program for thirty-five students in Mayersville, the seat of Issaquena County, staffed by two students from Antioch College in Ohio. The Ministry also helped recruit volunteers for a tutorial center at Cleveland in Bolivar County that had been operated by students from Wisconsin's Beloit College with Delta Ministry support since May 1966. Concerned about adult education, the Ministry assisted an adult literacy program that served fifty people in Issaquena and Sharkey Counties.[23]

Local protests in favor of quality education received Ministry support. African Americans in Shelby, a majority black town in Bolivar County, formed the Shelby Educational Committee (SEC) in March 1967 to improve the local black school. At the request of Shelby's African American community, Brooks, the director of the Delta Ministry's Bolivar County Project, assisted the SEC, which mounted a school boycott that forced a change in the school's administration.[24]

Ed King became director of the Delta Ministry's education program in September 1967, taking over what had previously been Barber's duties. King was the first white Mississippian to join the Ministry. Born in 1936, he had grown up in a well-to-do Methodist family in Vicksburg, accepting segregation without question, like his parents and peers. But attacks on segregation by the national Methodist Church and its youth magazine, *Concern*, led him to question Jim Crow.

In 1953, a tornado ripped through Vicksburg, devastating its black section. King assisted the Red Cross and other groups in dispensing food and clothing to the needy. The experience convinced him that segregation was wrong: "For the first time we saw the terrible poverty and living conditions of many black residents of Vicksburg."[25]

King studied at Millsaps College, a Methodist institution in Jackson, receiving a bachelor's degree in sociology in 1958. He subsequently left Mississippi to study at Boston University and earned a bachelor's of divinity degree in 1961. King first became involved in civil rights when he went to Montgomery, Alabama, in March 1960 to serve as a liaison between protesters and local white church people. Arrested and fined for breaching the peace by eating in an African American restaurant, King only became more committed to integration. A second arrest three months later, when King took a black minister, Elroy Embry, to lunch in the restaurant of a white Montgomery hotel, brought King four days on a chain gang. Mississippi Bishop Marvin A. Franklin ordained King as a minister in the spring of 1961 but without affiliation to any conference of the Methodist Church because of his civil rights activities. The young minister returned to Boston University to earn a master's degree in theology while continuing to travel to the South for civil rights work.[26]

At the urging of NAACP Field Secretary Medgar Evers, King returned to Mississippi permanently in 1963 as chaplain of Tougaloo College. He became a prominent member of the Jackson movement. In May 1963, the Mississippi Conference of the Methodist Church voted eighty-nine to eighty-five to deny King the right to be appointed to any of its churches. However, African American Bishop Charles F. Golden of the Nashville-Carolina Area accepted King as a minister in the Central Jurisdiction of the segregated Methodist Church. King began seeking admission to services in Jackson's white churches with Tougaloo students and prominent visiting clergymen. He and group members were frequently barred from church entry and were sometimes arrested. In November, King ran as the MFDP's candidate for lieutenant governor. A year later, he served in the MFDP delegation that went to the Democratic Party's national convention in Atlantic City. King continued his involvement with the civil rights movement and ran unsuccessfully for Congress on the MFDP ticket in 1966. Disappointed by Tougaloo College's disengagement from civil rights under a new college administration and eager to work full time on school desegregation, King joined the Delta Ministry a year later.[27]

Brooks was keen to recruit King, who had acted as liaison between the MFDP and the Delta Ministry. Concerned that King might go north after leaving Tougaloo, Brooks wrote, "We are convinced that it would be [a] tragedy to lose such a symbol and the counsel of a man with such long-term contacts on a state-wide basis."[28]

After joining the Delta Ministry, King focused most of his efforts on public school integration. He had "numerous meetings with Negro students and parents and with local civil rights leaders discussing the conditions of the segregated Negro schools in Mississippi" as well as ways of improving black schools and integrating white schools. King was committed to the goal of an integrated society. He rejected Mississippi's adoption of token school desegregation as inadequate and harmful to African American students affected, since they would lack "a friendly peer group." King worked with the NAACP Legal Defense and Educational Fund and local civil rights groups in Rankin County in a monthlong campaign of community meetings and rallies to persuade black parents to transfer their children to the county's white schools. As a result, black enrollment in formerly white schools rose from 173 in 1966 to 311 by the fall of 1967. King regarded the Rankin County school desegregation drive as a model for work in other counties. However, desegregation of white schools raised the possibility that black schools might be undermined in their role as community institutions and disseminators of black identity and culture. Aware of the issue, the Delta Ministry did not take a position and instead deferred to the wishes of the African American communities in which it worked.[29]

Along with the Delta Ministry's other staff members, King participated in the Ministry's citizenship education campaign, which had entered a new phase after concentrating on voter registration during the first half of 1967. Between mid-June and November, the Ministry conducted workshops for more than 80 of the 108 African-American candidates who qualified to stand for public office. They had chosen to run for election partly as a result of the Ministry's earlier efforts to persuade blacks to become involved in the political process.[30]

As an NCC organization, the Delta Ministry was barred from engaging in partisan political involvement. The citizenship education program enabled the Ministry to help African American office seekers by claiming that it did so regardless of their political affiliation. Because the Ministry could not overtly support particular candidates, Brooks joined the steering committee of a new organization, Mississippians United to Elect Negro Candidates. Formed in July 1967, Mississippians United was, the Ministry conceded, "controlled by MFDP local organizations" and chaired by Joseph Harris, who served as both a Delta Ministry staff member and the MFDP's state office manager. The Ministry maintained that staff members who worked with Mississippians United and helped it raise funds for the campaigns of particular candidates did so "aside from their assigned duties."[31]

When Thomas Y. Minniece, a lawyer and PCUS layman from Meridian, Mississippi, complained that the Delta Ministry was engaging in political activity and supporting selected office seekers, McCanna denied the charge. He acknowledged that the Ministry had supported the creation of Mississippians United but pointed out that it did not fund the group or "any political party." McCanna's argument lacked candor. The Delta Ministry did not directly fund the MFDP but contributed staff time and worked closely with the group. In June 1967, the MFDP moved its state office from Jackson to Harris's Delta Ministry project office in Sunflower County. More than half of the Delta Ministry's staff were MFDP members, and some of the most active members on the state board of the MFDP were paid Ministry personnel. King was a MFDP national committeeman. The steering committee of Mississippians United met in the Delta Ministry's Greenville office and used it as a mailing address.[32]

Rivalry between the MFDP and the NAACP weakened the impact of the African American vote in Mississippi. The MFDP's strongholds were in the Delta, whereas the charismatic Charles Evers, who had succeeded his slain brother, Medgar, as the NAACP's Mississippi field secretary, commanded the support of blacks in NAACP-dominated southwestern Mississippi. In the November 1966 senatorial election, NAACP supporters had, at Evers's prompting, voted for Republican Prentiss Walker as a protest against Senator James O. Eastland rather than MFDP candidate Clifton R. Whitley. Consequently, Whitley, who ran as an independent, garnered only 27,863 votes and finished third behind the winner, Eastland, and Walker.[33]

Evers fiercely criticized the MFDP. In January 1967, he declared, "The FDP? I don't even know they exist. They'll run a candidate for office with no body registered. That's crazy." Evers was equally scathing about the Delta Ministry's efforts at Freedom City, exclaiming, "I am tired of the good white folks from the North running down here to help us poor Negroes and then running off again leaving us worse off than before they came. That Freedom City is a mess. They are using my people just like they did after the Civil War, and they aren't going to get away with it." Despite his harsh criticisms, Evers invited the MFDP and the Delta Ministry to a March 1967 meeting of the state's black leaders in an attempt to overcome their differences in preparation for the forthcoming state elections.[34]

A month later, the Delta Ministry announced that it would cooperate "with predominantly Negro groups like FDP, NAACP, in attempts to unify [the] vote on state offices in upcoming elections." Although the Ministry had always been closer to the MFDP than the NAACP and had sided with the MFDP when the two groups clashed, the Ministry also had previously worked with the NAACP. The Ministry had assisted Charles Evers when he led a boycott of white downtown stores in Natchez during 1965 and a year later had conducted a voter registration campaign in southwestern Mississippi with the NAACP, aware that many African American registrants would vote as Evers suggested.[35]

With approximately 175,000 African Americans registered to vote by March 1967, the MFDP, like the Ministry, began to recognize the importance of trying to unify the black community. During the summer, Mississippians United announced that it would support all black candidates for election, including those of the NAACP. Brooks, Harris, MFDP Chairman Lawrence Guyot, and MFDP activists Charles McLaurin and Hollis Watkins signed the declaration. The statement also indicated the political differences that separated the NAACP and the MFDP. The NAACP chose to run candidates in the Democratic Party's primaries in the belief that "political power can be realized within the structure of the Mississippi Democratic party." By contrast, the MFDP, which would, in many cases, offer candidates only in the general election, had concluded that "the Black community must build and solidify its own political base before there can be any significant and substantive political inter-action between Black and White political forces in Mississippi." Rebuffed in 1964 by the Democratic Party's national convention, in 1965 by the Democratic-controlled House of Representatives, and continually by the Mississippi Democratic Party, the MFDP had decided to focus its efforts on building what its activists called "a powerful, community-oriented, grass-roots political movement" that would be "capable of unified action on the state level."[36]

Both the NAACP and the MFDP chose to focus primarily on local offices in the upcoming elections, since these positions had the potential to "bring about some concrete changes in the lives of Black Mississippians." The two groups would field candidates mainly in communities in which blacks enjoyed "a two to one voting majority." The fact that the NAACP had chosen to offer candidates in the southwest and the MFDP in the Delta, their respective areas of strength, had helped make possible "an informal and unarticulated agreement among the differing political camps within the Black community to co-exist throughout the election year."[37]

Working with the MFDP and Tennessee's Highlander Research and Education Center, the Delta Ministry offered workshops for candidates who ran in the August Democratic Party primaries and for those who entered the elections in November as independents. The workshops explained "the duties and functions of the various offices" and taught campaigning techniques. The Delta Ministry claimed that it "did not run campaigns," but staff members were closely involved in several efforts to run for office. Brooks assisted the successful campaign of Kermit Stanton, a mechanic from Shelby, for a place on the Bolivar County Board of Supervisors. Shelby's African American community rallied behind Stanton, who had played a leading role in a boycott of the local black school a few months earlier. Thelma Barnes and Delta Ministry secretaries Maxine Maxwell and

Juanita Rogers helped in Joseph H. Bivins's unsuccessful campaign for a seat on the Greenville City Council. Mississippians United raised nearly eleven thousand dollars, five thousand dollars of which came from the Executive Council of the Protestant Episcopal Church. Mississippians United dispensed funds to campaigns in eight counties, half of them either wholly or partly in the Delta.[38]

In a breakthrough for black political representation, twenty-two African Americans won election to office, six of them as independents from the MFDP. Robert Clark from the MFDP stronghold of Holmes County was foremost among the victors. Elected to the state House of Representatives, Clark became the first African American to sit in the Mississippi Assembly during the twentieth century. Eighteen of the African Americans elected had attended one of the Delta Ministry's workshops. But disappointingly for the Ministry, most of the black victories occurred in southwest Mississippi.[39]

Given that more than half of eligible African Americans were registered to vote and that 108 blacks had run for office in twenty-eight counties, the results were discouraging. Although blacks constituted 24 percent of Mississippi's registered voters, they had won approximately 1 percent of the offices up for election in 1967. Fifteen of those elected had won the minor posts of constable and justice of the peace. Only four African Americans had secured election to any of the powerful five-person county boards of supervisors, which set and spent property taxes, maintained roads and recreational facilities, selected jury rolls, and set the boundaries of election precincts. In addition to Clark, two blacks had succeeded in countywide contests, but they had been elected to the minor posts of chancery clerk and coroner in non-Delta counties.[40]

The Mississippi Assembly had changed the state's electoral laws a year earlier, significantly undermining the impact of the black vote and making it difficult for African Americans to win office. Nineteen independent candidates in eight counties, most of them affiliated with the MFDP, had been disqualified from standing because of obstacles created by the legislation. Eleven counties had made the position of county superintendent of education elective instead of appointive, discouraging blacks from running for that office. Twenty-two counties had changed from district to at-large elections for county school boards, and fourteen had done so for county boards of supervisors, thereby deterring African Americans from running for some offices, creating white majorities, and undermining the effectiveness of black votes. Fourteen of the sixteen African Americans who ran for at-large county posts lost, whereas nineteen of the twenty-two blacks elected won in supervisors' districts with black majorities.[41]

Whites, unlike African Americans, voted as a bloc for candidates of their own race. Deference, economic dependence on whites, and threats and intimidation deterred many blacks from voting or led them to vote for white candidates. In some cases, fraud reduced the vote for African American office seekers. According to a civil rights lawyer, the election in Yazoo County featured "ballots dropped on the floor, voters turned away for frivolous reasons, an unfair count, one pistol-packing white election manager, and an ominous crowd of 100 whites with guns gathering around (one) polling place."[42]

At its November 1967 meeting, the Commission on the Delta Ministry, impressed by the group's contribution to the black political struggle, determined that the Ministry's citizenship education program should be extended in 1968. The commission also directed the Ministry to expand its welfare and education programs and to work on economic development.[43]

Meeting immediate human needs had been part of the Delta Ministry's mission since its inception. In practice, this effort had taken the form of providing clothing, food, and shelter. Thelma Barnes, project director for Washington County, coordinated the Ministry's emergency relief program, which served Washington, Bolivar, Sunflower, Humphreys, Issaquena, and Sharkey Counties in 1967. However, the large degree of autonomy that Delta Ministry staff enjoyed to run county projects and pursue their particular interests had prevented a coordinated approach to welfare and relief. Consequently, Solomon Gort Jr., the director of the Ministry's Tallahatchie County Project, wrote the section on welfare and relief in the Ministry's annual report for 1967. Gort focused much of his work in Tallahatchie County on welfare and relief. In addition, Charley Horwitz reported arranging for the distribution of food and clothing in Hinds County, his project area.[44]

In an attempt to streamline operations, Brooks told the Commission on the Delta Ministry in November 1967 that the welfare and relief programs in Washington and Tallahatchie Counties should become the model for all the counties in which the Delta Ministry was involved and that Greenville should become the central office for such programs. The commission recommended that the programs should not simply provide material assistance but "should have the goal of creating representation of indiginous groups through welfare rights organizations." The intention was that the poor should be made aware of and encouraged to claim their rights to assistance from local and county welfare offices, which frequently discriminated against African Americans. The Ministry would then help coordinate welfare rights groups across the state and link them with other groups nationwide.[45]

The welfare needs of African Americans had become even more acute during 1967 because of the implementation of a dollar-an-hour minimum wage for agricultural workers in February and a switch by many counties from the federal surplus commodities program to food stamps. The federal minimum wage law, passed in 1966, accelerated black agricultural unemployment and displacement from the land as plantation owners found it more economical to replace workers with machines and herbicides. The region experienced a net outmigration of twelve thousand people during the year, generally from the ranks of the most able young adults. Although many planters permitted unneeded workers to remain rent-free in plantation shacks, other landowners reclaimed the land on which these dwellings stood for cotton acreage.[46]

Under the Food Stamp Act of 1964, counties could obtain state approval to shift from free federal surplus commodities, distributed to the poor at county expense, to federally funded food stamps, which the poor bought and spent in designated grocery stores. When they bought food stamps, the poor received additional stamps at no charge. The federal government believed that the program would boost the spending power of the poor and encourage them to adopt improved dietary and work habits. By the end of March 1966, only six Mississippi counties had switched to food stamps, but more than thirty did so during late 1966 and early 1967, including most of those in the Delta.[47]

Many poor people found the stamps too expensive to buy, and some people had no cash income at all. A family of six with a monthly income below thirty dollars had to buy twelve dollars in food stamps per month to participate in the program. A month's stamps had to be bought at one time, but many people did not have sufficient money to make a lump sum purchase. In some cases, those who had jobs obtained loans from plantation owners, thereby increasing indebtedness and dependence. Planters often certified their workers' income, which determined their eligibility for food stamps, and thus retained a powerful influence over the workforce. Some grocery owners accepted food stamps only for the most expensive brands of food and refused to issue a "due bill" as change, thereby forcing people to buy goods they did not want. Stores sometimes raised prices when the county entered the food stamp program.[48]

As early as February 1966, Henry McCanna asked the U.S. Department of Agriculture to remove the cash requirement for food stamps, but to no avail. As a growing number of counties changed from federal surplus commodities to food stamps in early 1967, the Delta Ministry informed people about how the program worked and assisted them in organizing protests, such as petition campaigns directed at the county boards of supervisors who authorized the switches. Despite rising agricultural unemployment in the Delta, the Ministry reported, "The joint April 1967 figure for people receiving either commodities or food stamp aid shows a drop of almost 64,000 (from 452,894 to 388,979) on the figure for April 1966, when only a handful of counties in Mississippi had adopted the food stamp program.

Clearly, most of the 64,000 people who needed and were receiving food last year, are not receiving it this year because they can't afford to pay for food stamps." Most of the counties that had adopted food stamps had a much lower participation rate than those localities that distributed surplus commodities.[49]

The problems associated with food stamps and the dire economic and health problems of poor Mississippians received national attention when the U.S. Senate Subcommittee on Employment, Manpower, and Poverty conducted a hearing in Jackson, chaired by Senator Joseph Clark of Pennsylvania, at which Marian Wright explained the deleterious effects of the food stamp program. Clark and subcommittee member Robert F. Kennedy accepted her invitation to visit the Delta to see people begging because they lacked sufficient food. The two senators toured the Delta with Wright, Thelma Barnes, and Amzie Moore, the Mississippi chairman of the Commission on the Delta Ministry. Clark called the conditions he witnessed "savage and barbarous." Kennedy described the poverty he saw as "as great as any in the country." After its visit to Mississippi, the subcommittee tried without success to persuade the administration of President Lyndon B. Johnson to declare an emergency in the state and to provide free food stamps for the neediest residents.[50]

However, the hearing in Jackson and Kennedy and Clark's visit to the Delta received national media coverage that focused attention on poverty in Mississippi, produced a string of national newspaper articles, and brought the Delta Ministry several thousand dollars in donations. In May, six doctors financed by the New York–based Field Foundation examined several hundred African American children at Head Start centers in six Mississippi counties, including the Delta counties of Humphreys and Leflore. The doctors' widely publicized report, *Children in Mississippi*, detailed the extensive poverty and health problems observed. Rebuffed in their subsequent efforts to persuade federal agencies to launch an extensive aid program for the state, the six doctors met with Clark and Kennedy, who scheduled them to appear at a further round of the subcommittee's hearings, which were held in Washington, D.C., in July. By the time the hearing convened, Orville Freeman, secretary of the U.S. Department of Agriculture, had reduced food stamp prices for the very poor, but the measure did not help those who lacked any cash income.[51]

Opposition from Mississippi's senators, James O. Eastland and John C. Stennis, and Delta Congressman Jamie Whitten deterred the Johnson administration from undertaking a significant revision of the program. The president and his officials did not wish to offend the three Mississippians, whose seniority and committee memberships, especially Whitten's chairmanship of the House Appropriations Subcommittee on Agriculture, gave them the power to derail the administration's other legislative programs. Despite further private and senatorial efforts and inquiries, the food stamp program was not sufficiently liberalized to bring a sharp rise in participation until the 1970s.[52]

The Delta Ministry consistently urged the federal government to broaden participation in the food stamp program by providing free food stamps to the neediest. The Ministry also used donations from sympathizers to buy food stamps for black and white Delta families without income. Barnes administered the effort, which became a priority in her welfare and relief work. In the six months preceding November 1967, national publicity regarding hunger conditions in Mississippi had resulted in nineteen thousand dollars in donations to the Ministry for its relief program; most of the money was used to buy food stamps for three thousand people. Some of the donors were northern blacks, many of whom gave money in response to an appeal for Mississippi made by the African American magazine *Jet*. The African Methodist Episcopal Church became the first black American denomination to give the Ministry significant aid, sending five thousand dollars for food stamps and thirty thousand pounds of food for distribution to the Delta's hungry in November 1967.[53]

In addition to providing direct aid, the Ministry sought to improve the dietary and purchasing habits of the poor. Barnes established a nutritional clinic in Glen Allan, Washington County, that taught its enrollees how to plan well-balanced diets and how to spend their food stamps economically. Gort operated a similar program in Tallahatchie County.[54]

Welfare and relief, the Delta Ministry recognized, provided the poor with only some respite from their dire economic circumstances. The implementation of the federal minimum wage law had exacerbated a long-term problem of mass agricultural unemployment in the Delta that had been caused by federal payments to planters to reduce their cotton acreage, mechanization, and growing use of herbicides. In its 1967 annual report, the Delta Ministry concluded that it had to "contribute more toward the economic development of the Black Community."[55]

The Delta Ministry's involvement in economic development during the year had featured two main aspects: DOC and Freedomcrafts. After months of delay, DOC had finally received funding from OEO and the Ford Foundation and begun a self-help housing and job training program in late 1967. Begun with Ministry funding at Strike City in 1965 before spreading to Freedom City, Edwards, Shaw, and West Point a year later, Freedomcrafts had become "virtually self-supporting." Jake Ayers became full-time director of Freedomcrafts in January 1967, succeeding Bob Beech, in line with the Ministry's goal of empowering local people. Ayers, age forty-six, lived in his hometown of Glen Allan, where he had helped to organize a CDGM Head Start center in 1965. He joined CDGM's board of directors and participated in its campaign to maintain OEO funding. Ayers's activism cost him his job at the Greenville Mill, where he had worked for a decade.[56]

Freedomcrafts included wood cooperatives that made furniture and toys for CDGM's Head Start centers and a candy making cooperative in Edwards that filled orders for northern sympathizers. However, Freedomcrafts was undercapitalized and provided employment for fewer than fifty people. Lack of capital also afflicted the Poor People's Corporation, a group of twelve sewing and leather goods cooperatives located around Mississippi. Founded by SNCC activist Jesse Morris in 1965, the corporation employed 110 people and marketed their goods through the Liberty House in Jackson and another store in New York City. The Delta Ministry provided space at Mount Beulah where the corporation could train its workers.[57]

It became clear to the Ministry that the cooperative movement would not provide a viable source of employment for African Americans displaced from Delta agriculture or an economic base for the black community. Harry Bowie concluded after the 1967 election that without such a base, black elected officials would soon become dependent on whites at the expense of the needs of the African American community. Consequently, Bowie began to consider ways of creating black-owned, self-sustaining businesses with sound capitalization. He presented a tentative economic development proposal to the Commission on the Delta Ministry in November 1967 that envisaged the creation of a nonprofit corporation that would capitalize new black-owned businesses and provide them with advice and training. Bowie developed his ambitious proposal during the next few months and, with the commission's approval, initiated what became a frustrating process of seeking funding from the NCC and its member denominations.[58]

However, the Delta Ministry's financial position had stabilized. The Ministry ended 1967 within its NCC-approved budget for the year, but its previous overspending still left it $57,491 in debt to the NCC's Division of Christian Life and Mission. The division refused the Commission on the Delta Ministry's request to cancel the Ministry's debt, and the commission instead approved a 1968 budget of $305,000, which included debt repayment. Consequently, the Ministry remained on a tight budget that limited its program and, as before, required that its staff spend considerable time raising funds for items outside the approved budget, such as Freedom City.[59]

To help raise money, the Delta Ministry hired Henry L. Parker as director of interpretation in January 1968. Like Bowie, Parker was a black Episcopalian minister from New Jersey. College educated in North Carolina, Boston, and New York, he had received his theological training at Harvard Divinity School. After his 1957 ordination, Parker had pastored churches in Detroit and Little Rock. He

African American alderman, Robert Dean Gray, in a special election that resulted from a renewed SEC boycott.[67]

The boycott began in May 1968 to protest the firing of Eddie Lucas, the principal of the local black elementary school, and black high school teacher Joseph Delaney for their civil rights activities. Lucas had managed Kermit Stanton's successful 1967 campaign for the Bolivar County Board of Supervisors. Black elementary and high school students boycotted classes, and the SEC organized a very effective boycott of white-owned downtown stores. The Delta Ministry assisted the students and the SEC, headed by L. C. Dorsey. A thirty-year-old former sharecropper, Dorsey had worked with Brooks on voter registration and citizenship education in Bolivar County since 1965. Employed by the OEO-funded Tufts-Delta Health Center in Mound Bayou, Dorsey was immune to white economic pressure. The SEC ended the boycott after four months when Shelby agreed to the group's demands for improved local services, an end to repressive policing, and employment of African Americans by the fire department. However, the school board refused to rehire Lucas and Delaney. Lucas had joined the Delta Ministry as director of the Bolivar County Project in June, leaving Brooks more time to concentrate on his duties as the Ministry's acting director. A white alderman resigned to allow Robert Dean Gray, a former teacher, to stand for election, thereby giving African Americans representation in Shelby's town government, as the protesters had demanded.[68]

Gray's election was facilitated in part by Delta Ministry workshops in Shelby during the year, which had increased voter registration and knowledge of the political system. The workshops also generated support and a county structure for the Loyal Democrats of Mississippi, which challenged the regular, virtually all-white Democratic Party for the right to represent Mississippi at the 1968 Democratic Party National Convention in Chicago.[69]

Formed in late June 1968, the Loyalists comprised the MFDP, the state NAACP, and the Mississippi Young Democrats, a group of white moderates led by Hodding Carter III. The Mississippi AFL-CIO and two African American organizations, the Mississippi Teachers Association and the Prince Hall Masons, later joined the Loyalists. Often bitter rivals, the MFDP and the NAACP and Young Democrats formed an uneasy coalition based on mutual need. The MFDP lacked statewide organization, had little money, and enjoyed limited support beyond the Delta. It could not mount a serious challenge to the regular Mississippi Democrats without the participation of the better organized NAACP and Young Democrats, which also had more resources than did the MFDP. The black-white coalition of Mississippi moderates, for their part, needed the legitimacy for a challenge to the regular Democrats that only the MFDP, after its performance at Atlantic City four years earlier, could provide.[70]

The Delta Ministry supported the MFDP and in consequence worked on behalf of the Loyalists as they held precinct, county, and state conventions to select a delegation for Chicago, following national party procedures. Brooks contended that a successful challenge by the Loyalists would help break the hold on politics possessed "by a few white interests" and that black representation could not be left solely to the NAACP. The MFDP and the Delta Ministry had to be involved, he argued, as a means of bringing the problems of "the poorest of the poor and the most isolated of the rural people" to "the national forum of the party in power."[71]

Lawrence Guyot argued that MFDP members should comprise half the Loyalist delegation, but the Freedom Democrats had to settle for less than a quarter. Brooks, who shared the MFDP's commitment to creating an independent black political force, objected when the Loyalists chose whites to fill nearly half the delegation. Brooks contended that white Mississippians did not merit such representation, since most of the state's white electorate would not vote for the national party's likely presidential nominee, Hubert Humphrey, but instead for independent George Wallace, the segregationist former governor of Alabama. According to Charles Evers, Brooks "hated seeing whites among us" and Bowie, like Guyot, was not "exactly hoping to work alongside whites." However, Curtis Wilkie, a white journalist based in Clarksdale, recalled that Bowie made an appeal at the Loyalist state convention in Jackson for acceptance of a racially balanced delegation in the interests of unity. An integrated delegation, with Thelma Barnes and Ed King among its members, went to the national convention.[72]

The Ministry sent a task force of Harry Bowie, Joseph Harris, and Charley Horwitz to Chicago "to help coordinate church support for the loyalist challenge." With little success, it also urged the Democratic Party's Platform Committee to ensure that the poor participated fully in antipoverty and welfare programs, to secure federal support for industrial location in the South, to support parity of welfare standards across the country, and to guarantee a national standard of living. The Loyalist challenge succeeded in displacing the regulars, who had only one African American, Dr. Gilbert Mason, in their delegation. A coalition of moderate blacks and whites controlled the Loyalists. The MFDP continued to run candidates in state and municipal elections.[73]

"Hinds County," the Delta Ministry reported, "had the best White participation in the Loyalist challenge of any county in the state," partly as a result of staff work in the white community. The Ministry had discovered that "the violence and shock which followed" the murder of Martin Luther King Jr. had made it "possible to do meaningful work in the Mississippi white community (and even the white church) for the first time in four years." Consequently, the Ministry helped organize a November 1968 statewide conference about racism and poverty that was attended by eighty Mississippians, most of them white. The conference resulted in the founding of the Greater Jackson Area Committee, which opened a youth center in a poor white neighborhood and for the first time involved poor whites in local OEO projects. During the next two years, the Ministry worked with the committee, which also became involved with whites in Hattiesburg, Vicksburg, Starkville, and Oxford.[74]

Youth work constituted another aspect of the Delta Ministry's program that began in 1968. Barnes had been trying to defuse gang rivalries in Greenville since 1967, but the Ministry had lacked any funds for the work. With thirty thousand dollars from the WCC's King Memorial Fund, the Ministry hired Dan Smith, a young black former high school teacher from Indianola, in Sunflower County, to create a youth program that sought to develop youth leadership through workshops, to involve young African Americans in community struggles for equality, and to encourage young blacks to complete their education. Although black youths were involved in some local protests in the late 1960s, the Ministry concluded in 1971 that "perhaps the only real achievement" of the program had occurred on college campuses. Many colleges had agreed to offer black studies programs. A protest by Mississippi Valley State College students in Itta Bena, Leflore County, had forced a relaxation of stringent campus regulations and increased studies in black history, and an American Civil Liberties Union lawsuit had ended state restrictions governing campus invitations to outside speakers.[75]

In its main program areas of welfare, education, citizenship education, and economic development, the Delta Ministry increasingly during the late 1960s provided technical support as much as material aid. Partly a recognition that the Ministry lacked the financial resources to conduct significant direct assistance programs of its own, the move was consistent with its established policy of assisting black Mississippians in devising and implementing solutions of their own design. The changed conditions of the late 1960s, the Ministry explained, meant that the "days of being simply dreamers, the days of seeking liberal sympathy are over. The day of the technician has been thrust upon us."[76]

Richard Nixon's 1968 election as president brought to power a Republican administration that was less sympathetic toward civil rights and antipoverty advocacy groups than its predecessor had been. As African Americans increasingly secured basic rights, such as access to formerly white schools and political representation, the struggle for equality required greater technical help to make these gains effective. Blacks needed assistance to challenge deficiencies in welfare provision and school funding, to make black elected officials effectual, and to facilitate sustainable, long-term economic development. Owen Brooks and Harry Bowie, appointed by the NCC as the Ministry's director and associate director in September 1968, promoted the Delta Ministry's increasing concentration on supplying technical support.[77]

The change in emphasis was least effective in the Ministry's welfare and relief program, which the Ministry tried to reorient from mainly providing material assistance to enabling the poor to assert their rights to state and federal aid. Solomon Gort reported that the Ministry gave food to 1,000 families and provided food stamps for 1,500 more across a dozen counties in 1968, a tiny fraction of those who needed help. The Ministry also provided technical assistance for welfare recipients in fair-hearing cases and helped organize Mississippi chapters of the National Welfare Rights Organization (NWRO), encouraged their activities, and worked with their state office. Formed in 1967 by George Wiley, formerly CORE's associate director, the NWRO sought to make welfare more responsive to the needs of the poor by improving their access to assistance and securing a guaranteed national income. But the NWRO had little impact in Mississippi and, with some exceptions, it was difficult to mobilize the poor to organize for change. Referring to Hinds and Warren Counties, Charley Horwitz reported in May 1970, "The welfare movement here died out after it was organized a few years ago."[78]

The Delta Ministry escalated its direct relief program in response to natural disasters such as tornadoes and the devastation caused along the Gulf Coast by Hurricane Camille in August 1969. The Ministry joined twenty-one other advocacy groups in forming the Combined Community Organization Disaster Committee, which brought direct assistance to the hurricane's victims, challenged racial discrimination in relief programs, and sought, without success, to ensure government involvement of the poor "in planning for rebuilding."[79]

Involvement in the committee illustrated the Ministry's increasing emphasis on working with other groups and coalitions to address problems that affected the poor across Mississippi. In 1969, Brooks and Barnes joined thirty other Mississippi residents in sending telegrams to President Nixon, federal agency officials, and twenty-four U.S. senators and representatives, urging them to restructure the food stamp program to make it more accessible to the poor. In February 1970, the Delta Ministry helped form the Action Committee for Poor People, which challenged Governor Williams's veto of five million dollars in federal grants for countywide Head Start programs in Coahoma, Hinds, Sunflower, and Washington Counties. Comprising the Ministry, the NAACP, the MFDP, almost all of the state's Head Start agencies, and many other community and civil rights organizations, the committee persuaded Robert H. Finch, secretary of the U.S. Department of Health, Education, and Welfare, to override the veto and restore funding to the programs, which served nearly 3,700 poor children and employed 716 people.[80]

During the same year, the Ministry helped organize the Mississippi United Front, a coalition of thirty civil rights, poverty, and community organizations. The coalition turned its attention to the STAR program, which had come under the control of a biracial board of conservative African Americans and moderate whites that excluded the poor from decision making. A December 1970 NAACP investigation uncovered evidence of racial discrimination in STAR's federally funded statewide adult basic education and job training program. Brooks participated in the restructuring of STAR's board of directors that followed in 1971 and served as the board's secretary. OEO continued to fund the program until the Nixon administration abolished both the federal agency and STAR in 1973.[81]

The Delta Ministry also collaborated with other groups to achieve quality education for African Americans. The Ministry continued to support local protests by black communities but also offered technical assistance to progressive lawyers' groups, such as the NAACP Legal Defense and Educational Fund and North Mississippi Rural Legal Services, as they filed suit against segregated education. Rims Barber resumed the mantle of education director after Ed King left the Ministry in the late summer of 1968 to focus on his MFDP work. Barber compiled evidence of segregated education patterns to strengthen lawyers' cases. In October 1969, the Supreme Court ruled in *Alexander v. Holmes County Board of Education* that thirty Mississippi school districts should desegregate immediately. Implemented peacefully in January and February 1970, the decision helped ensure that 250,000 children attended integrated school systems by mid-February.[82]

School desegregation did not in itself ensure equal education because of racial discrimination within integrated schools, black children's need to catch up on the education previously denied them, the demotion and displacement of black principals and teachers, and the departure of white students and teachers to private segregated schools, particularly in the Delta. Consequently, the Delta Ministry provided advice and technical support to improve the quality of education for African American children and to encourage community control of schools. The Ministry also helped recruit college students to provide summer tutoring for black children in several communities and assisted in the development of adult basic education classes. The Ministry researched and disseminated information about the courts' school desegregation rulings, school board functions and elections, and scholarship and fellowship programs. In June 1969 it gathered and presented evidence to the U.S. Senate Subcommittee on Education that Mississippi was misusing thirty-five million dollars in federal funds, received under Title I of the 1965 Elementary and Secondary Education Act, to replace rather than supplement state spending on educational services for deprived children. As a result, HEW ordered Mississippi to comply by September 1970. The Ministry's complaints to federal and state agencies also ensured that Mississippi school districts gave free or reduced-price lunches to thousands of needy schoolchildren as required by U.S. Department of Agriculture regulations.[83]

The Delta Ministry worked closely with Mississippi State Representative Robert Clark, a former schoolteacher, who made education one of his key concerns. Because Clark was Mississippi's only African American legislator, blacks across the state wrote to him, seeking his help. To ease the burden, the Ministry provided Clark with administrative and technical support. It also assisted other black officials whose election it had helped make possible through its citizenship education program.[84]

Armed with ten thousand dollars from the UPCUSA and from the Southern Regional Council, an Atlanta-based biracial group that promoted racial equality, the Ministry registered five thousand people in nine counties in preparation for May and June 1969 municipal elections and provided workshops for campaign workers and candidates. More than 120 African Americans ran for office, but only 21 achieved election in formerly white-controlled communities. Charles Evers became mayor of Fayette, in southwestern Mississippi, accompanied into office by five black aldermen. The Delta Ministry added two thousand new voters during a subsequent registration drive for elections "in places with special charters such as Greenville, Indianola, and Yazoo City." Thelma Barnes campaigned as an independent for one of the three seats available on the Greenville City Council in December 1969, alongside two other African American candidates, the Reverend E. E. Evans and Lewis R. Hill. However, low black turnout combined with some black voting for white candidates to result in their resounding defeat.[85]

Although African American registration in Mississippi had grown from 35,000 in 1965 to 281,000 in 1969, white registration also had increased during this time—from 433,000 to 672,000—in response to black political activity. White bloc voting, state legislation to dilute the impact of African American votes, and continued intimidation of black voters restricted the number of black elected officials to only seventy-two in 1970.[86]

With Delta Ministry assistance, the Lawyers' Committee for Civil Rights under Law and the Lawyers' Constitutional Defense Committee filed suits alleging unfair electoral practices. A major breakthrough occurred in *Allen v. State Board of Elections* (1969), in which the U.S. Supreme Court gave the federal government authority under the 1965 Voting Rights Act to review state legislation that diluted the impact of minority votes. In the immediate term, the decision, despite significant resistance, led to a reversal of the shift to at-large county supervisor elections, a reversal of the change from elected to appointed county school superintendents, and the repeal of legislation that had increased qualifying requirements for independent candidates. The *Allen* ruling also helped to persuade the U.S. Congress to extend the Voting Rights Act when it expired in 1970. In the long term, the *Allen* decision enabled civil rights lawyers to overturn most of the remaining discriminatory legislation enacted by the Mississippi Assembly in 1966 and established that voting-law changes in any state had to be first cleared with the U.S. Justice Department.[87]

The Delta Ministry believed that if African American politicians and voters were to be effective, they needed to have a firm economic base in the community that rendered them independent from white control. With insufficient resources directly to fund economic development, the Ministry continued in the late 1960s to assist the cooperatives of Freedomcrafts and the Poor People's Corporation by connecting them with sources of support and sometimes by providing them with financial aid.[88]

Brooks also focused the Ministry's economic development efforts on Mound Bayou in Bolivar County, where he had served as the Ministry's county project director between 1965 and 1968. An all-black town founded in 1887, Mound Bayou was incorporated and self-governing and had a population of 1,380. Brooks saw in Mound Bayou a base that was independent from whites and from which African Americans in northern Bolivar County could be aided. Consequently, the Ministry decided to provide technical support that would aid Mound Bayou's development and build on its earlier work in the town.[89]

Back in 1965, Brooks had undertaken a field survey for the Tufts-Delta Health Center in Mound Bayou during the center's planning stage. The idea of Count D. Gibson Jr. and Jack Geiger of Tufts University School of Medicine in Massachusetts, the center's origins lay in Geiger's organization of a demonstration health project with the MCHR and the Delta Ministry in Holmes County during 1965. Geiger obtained an OEO grant for Tufts to open a health center in a northern urban ghetto and another in the rural south that would serve the needs of the poor. Tufts opened the Columbia Point Health Center in Boston in December 1965 and, with a $1,168,000 grant, began operating the Mound Bayou center in 1967. Both institutions functioned on the understanding that ill health among the poor was rooted in the social order. Consequently, Geiger explained, the "centers carry out the idea that health services are valuable not only in themselves but as a point of entry for other kinds of effort, such as economic development, education, job training, housing, and so on." The centers hired local residents and involved them in improving their communities. The Tufts initiative became the model for an OEO-funded national program of neighborhood health centers.[90]

The center in Mound Bayou had forty-four professional and technical staff, thirty-two of them African American. Many of the personnel were from Bolivar County. The center also employed local black people in subprofessional positions, such as nurses' aides, and it operated a work-study program for high school students. During the first two years of its existence, the center treated without charge more than eight thousand patients, many of whom would otherwise have been unable to obtain care. Staff members made more than ten thousand home visits, mostly to the rural poor. In addition to providing medical care, the center maintained an environmental team that drained foul water and dug safe wells for drinking water, installed septic tanks and sanitary privies in homes, repaired and fumigated houses, and cleaned up garbage dumps. The health center also used an OEO grant to start the North Bolivar County Farm Cooperative, Inc.[91]

Owen Brooks and L. C. Dorsey, a leader in the Shelby boycott, helped to organize the cooperative, which began planting vegetables on 158 acres in April 1968. Five hundred families who were too poor to buy food stamps worked on the farm and in its freezing operation, which stored food for the winter. They received payment in cash and food. The cooperative fed more than 4,500 malnourished people within its first year. After a period of training, Dorsey became the cooperative's director. Unlike many other cooperatives established in Mississippi during the 1960s, the North Bolivar County Farm Cooperative endured through the 1970s.[92]

Aside from its work with the cooperative, the Ministry assisted in the organization of a Mound Bayou community hospital that merged two small, poorly equipped fraternal hospitals to make them eligible for federal funds. With technical assistance from the Ministry, the community hospital developed proposals that secured a $1.7 million OEO grant to develop its programs. The Mound Bayou Community Hospital operated independently of the Tufts-Delta Health Center and provided free hospitalization and dental care for the indigent in Bolivar, Coahoma, Sunflower, and Washington Counties. The health care industry became Mound Bayou's largest employer.[93]

The Delta Ministry worked with the indigenous Mound Bayou Development Corporation to create other sources of employment. Formed in 1963, the non-profit corporation had failed to bring industry to Mound Bayou, but with the Delta Ministry's help, the organization secured a twenty-seven-thousand-dollar Economic Development Administration technical assistance grant in 1968. Aided by the grant and by money that the Delta Ministry raised from private sources, the corporation bought land for an industrial park and started its first business, the Mound Bayou Brikcrete Factory, in August 1969. The corporation also supported the Delta Merchants' Cooperative Warehouse. Established by ninety small merchants from six Delta counties, the cooperative bought and stored groceries and dry goods to reduce costs and therefore prices for poor black consumers.[94]

Brooks served on the corporation's board of directors, which also included Kermit Stanton, who served on the Bolivar County Board of Supervisors. The Delta Ministry brought the outside contacts needed to attract resources to Mound Bayou, securing technical assistance to write a proposal for the Economic Development Administration that resulted in a $500,000 grant and a $125,000 loan to replace the town's antiquated water system. Brooks worked closely with Mayor Earl Lucas, a member of the Commission on the Delta Ministry, and town aldermen, all of whom the Ministry had helped achieve election in June 1969 on a reform platform. The Ministry subsequently located assistance that enabled the new town government to revise its tax records and reform council procedures.[95]

Despite the Ministry's assistance, the Mound Bayou Development Corporation found it difficult to attract business investors and thus created few jobs. The brikcrete factory, which made a cheap substitute for bricks and concrete blocks, employed only five people. Freedomcrafts and Poor People's Corporation cooperatives also employed relatively few people, and these bodies had begun to run into economic difficulties. The decline of CDGM removed the major market for the toys and furniture produced by Freedomcrafts wood cooperatives. The Poor People's Corporation sustained unprofitable cooperatives by using monies from those that made a profit, thereby preventing the corporation from building sufficient investment capital.[96]

Bowie concluded that cooperatives did not work, but his efforts to attract funds for a nonprofit corporation that would finance black-owned and -managed small businesses failed to attract sufficient financial support from NCC denominations and charitable foundations. Bowie realized that too many community action groups in Mississippi were competing with each other for a very limited amount of money. Consequently, only a small number of disparate projects received funding although the Delta needed a coordinated approach to job creation. In an attempt to overcome the problem, Bowie initiated meetings between rival advocacy groups that resulted in the June 1969 creation of the Delta Foundation. Comprising representatives from the Ministry and thirteen community organizations, the foundation was a nonprofit corporation that lent start-up money through its profit-holding company, Delta Enterprises, to labor-intensive, profit-oriented small businesses that would create employment for low-income Deltans. Most of the Delta Foundation's funds were grants and loans from federal government agencies, but it also received donations from the Ford Foundation and several major denominations. The Delta Foundation provided technical assistance to help prospective companies formulate business plans and helped entrepreneurs secure funds.[97]

Bowie and Brooks served on the Delta Foundation's board of directors, which launched its first enterprise, Fine Vines, a blue jeans manufacturing company, in December 1970. Begun with a $346,000 loan provided by the First National Bank of Greenville and guaranteed by the federal Small Business Administration, the company operated from the barracks of the deactivated Greenville Air Force Base. Within a year of opening, Fine Vines increased its workforce from fifteen to sixty African Americans.[98]

The company's success justified the Delta Foundation's policy of providing capital to businesses that had a reasonable chance of becoming established, profitable, and self-sustaining but would ordinarily have difficulty in getting business loans from banks. By focusing on small-scale industrial development, the Delta Foundation also recognized that small farming communities could not compete against big agribusiness. The Delta Ministry's support of the Delta Foundation reflected a realization that the earlier, idealistic commitments to cooperatives and to Freedom City were not practical or sustainable projects over the longer term. The Delta Foundation provided the kind of sustained commitment to economic development that had been one of the Ministry's founding goals, since the foundation reinvested profits by starting new businesses and supporting community projects. In its first twenty-six years, the Foundation created six thousand jobs, but it lacked the resources to make any significant impact on Delta unemployment, which was a consequence of macroeconomic forces beyond the foundation's influence.[99]

Despite advances made in job creation, school desegregation, voter registration, and black officeholding in Mississippi, it was clear that many years of sustained effort, together with a massive input of financial resources, would be needed to achieve significant advances toward the achievement of genuine racial equality. However, in 1971, the NCC made severe cuts in its staff and program budgets as donations from member denominations fell because of their shrinking membership and declining commitment to social activism. The National Council had little choice but to slash the Delta Ministry's budget in the spring of 1971, cutting its staff to four people.[100]

The largest civil rights group in Mississippi in the late 1960s, the Delta Ministry operated projects in eight counties. It conducted programs in welfare and relief, citizenship, education, economic development, and youth work. The Ministry distributed food, cash for food stamps, and clothing to the needy and encouraged them, albeit with little success, to organize effective welfare rights groups. Aware that it lacked the resources to make any significant impression on poverty, the Ministry urged the federal government to liberalize the food stamp program, registered thousands of voters, and educated them in the political process. The Ministry trained many African American candidates, helped raise campaign funds, and assisted the candidates who won election to office. Although its youth program had limited impact, the Ministry also helped the young by working to desegregate schools and improve the quality of public education. Much of the Ministry's work was done alongside or in support of other groups. Under Owen Brooks's direction, the Ministry increasingly provided technical support and participated in coalitions that addressed statewide problems. Its work in Mound Bayou and with the Delta Foundation epitomized the organization's new direction. However, some Delta Ministry staff disagreed with and felt threatened by the change, which culminated in their protest at being terminated when the NCC severely cut the Ministry's budget in 1971.

CHAPTER NINE

Internal Dissension and Crisis

Significant divisions developed within the Delta Ministry in the late 1960s. By late 1967, the majority of the Ministry's staff were black Mississippians, true to the project's intention of developing local leadership. A black Mississippian majority also sat on the reconstituted Commission on the Delta Ministry. Despite its reorganization in 1966, the Ministry continued to suffer from loose administration. Many of the Delta Ministry's staff also believed that the organization overlooked indigenous personnel and instead relied on northern staff to facilitate a new emphasis on providing technical support to community advocacy groups that addressed multicounty and statewide issues. The staff divided into two factions: the first comprised northerners Owen Brooks, Harry Bowie, Rims Barber, and Charley Horwitz, and the second included the remaining members of staff, all but two of them black Mississippians. The disgruntled majority believed that Brooks, the Ministry's director, neglected county projects and behaved autocratically. They also claimed that Brooks undermined the Ministry's effectiveness by his reluctance to work with moderate black and white Mississippians. A drastic cut in the Ministry's budget by the financially strapped NCC in 1971 brought festering staff conflict into the open. To reduce expenditure, Brooks, with the National Council's endorsement, fired those not engaged in technical support roles. The Ministry shrank to a biracial staff of four northerners.[1]

Reorganized in line with the recommendations of the NCC's Evaluation Committee, the new Commission on the Delta Ministry met in March 1967. The new thirty-one-member commission initially included a slight minority of native Mississippians, most of them African American. Most of its other members represented denominations that contributed to the Ministry's budget. Paul O. Madsen, associate executive secretary and secretary of the Division of Church Missions of the American Baptist Home Mission Societies, served as chairman in place of Bishop Paul Moore Jr., who remained on the commission. Amzie Moore, a veteran NAACP activist from Cleveland, in Bolivar County, served in the new position of Mississippi chairman, which was designed to ensure greater input from Mississippians. He and Madsen also sat on an Executive Committee that included five commission members from Mississippi and four from elsewhere. The Executive Committee assumed the commission's powers between its biannual meetings, meeting every two months or more frequently, as circumstances demanded.[2]

Just under half of the commission's members attended its March 1967 meeting. Absenteeism also plagued its second meeting in November, despite the addition of further members from inside and outside Mississippi, and poor attendance dogged subsequent meetings of both the commission and its Executive Committee. Denominational representatives who did not attend commission meetings because of their geographical distance from Mississippi sometimes sent substitutes. The lack of continuity occasioned by absenteeism and "rotating proxies" inevitably undermined the commission's effectiveness.[3]

Many Mississippi members also did not regularly attend commission meetings, despite the efforts made to include them and the fact that, unlike in previous years, meetings were held only in Greenville. Drawn mostly from among civil rights activists, especially the MFDP, Mississippi members often felt a primary commitment to their own organizations and lacked the time and in some cases the inclination to become significantly involved in the commission. During the second half of the 1960s, Mississippi's civil rights workers increasingly focused on parochial interests, such as federally funded local programs and local elections, at the expense of the larger issues that concerned the Ministry. When they did attend meetings, black Mississippians seldom spoke. Some of them felt intimidated by the nature of the proceedings and believed that their lack of education placed them at a disadvantage compared to the experienced NCC and denominational administrators who dominated the commission's meetings.[4]

Owen Brooks, who had been appointed the Delta Ministry's acting director in September 1966, recalled that Amzie Moore tried to control the Ministry. When Brooks refused to allow this, Moore attempted to discredit the director in the eyes of the NCC and told the National Council to fire Brooks. The NCC refused, but Brooks's leadership also came under fire from the UPCUSA, which, as the Ministry's second-largest financial supporter, after the Methodist Church, had considerable influence.[5]

Bryant George, director of internal operations and administration at the UPCUSA's Board of National Missions and a member of the Commission on the Delta Ministry, severely criticized Brooks's abilities and strongly opposed his being appointed director. George wrote in a January 1967 internal UPCUSA memorandum, "Our position has been that Brooks has done nothing to demonstrate that he has the ability to give the Delta Ministry the leadership it needs in Mississippi, (relating meaningfully to CDGM, MACE [Mississippi Action for Community Education] and the Freedom Democratic Party as well as the churches there) and relating it within the life and interpreting it within the life of the communions that support it. Indeed, he seems to clam up whenever anybody asks him what they intend to do and how they intend to do it."[6]

Although it was true that Brooks was, as staff member Bruce Hilton wrote, "hostile to any discussion of the Christian faith as a motivating force in DM" and, therefore, perhaps an unsuitable ambassador to church groups, he had achieved considerable success as director of the Bolivar County Project. Still only four months into his role as the Delta Ministry's acting director, Brooks had not yet had time to develop a coherent vision for the Ministry.[7]

In early 1967, Brooks enjoyed the support of most of the staff, and they wanted him appointed director. Barber, director of the Ministry's education program and Yazoo County Project, explained to the UPCUSA's Board of National Missions, "Mr. Brooks has taken the reins of the DM at a critical time, and has dealt with its continuing problems with increasing administrative ability, even though his hands were somewhat tied. . . . He is the one person, in the eyes of the staff, who could best set us on a path that would give us again a position of strength in Mississippi. Mr. Borrks [sic] could provide that leadership that would enable the DM to provide assistance for grass roots leadership, as he has a fine reputation for this in Bolivar County and throughout the Delta."[8]

Meeting in November 1967, the Commission on the Delta Ministry expressed its confidence in Brooks and asked the NCC's Division of Christian Life and Mission to appoint him director. However, UPCUSA opposition to Brooks encouraged the division to defer making a decision about the Delta Ministry's directorship, with the result that Brooks remained acting director while the National Council searched for an acceptable alternative. Some members of the NCC also believed that Brooks's reputation for militancy and his status as a layman might deter denominations from giving financial support to the Ministry. There were also concerns about Brooks's administrative ability. South Carolina author James McBride Dabbs, who had joined the reorganized Commission on the Delta Ministry on behalf of the PCUS, reported to his denomination that "As much as I admire Owen Brooks . . . , he seems more like a doer than a manager."[9]

Dabbs also believed that the commission was "too loosely connected" to the Delta Ministry's activities. Frustrated by the "lack of clarity in administrative procedure," Madsen resigned from the commission in October 1967. It remained without a chairman for several months.[10]

Andrew Young, executive vice president of the SCLC, became the commission's new chairman in May 1968. Young had been the National Council's original choice for the Ministry's directorship in 1964, but he had chosen instead to join the SCLC. His appointment to the commission reflected the NCC's long-held confidence in Young's ability as well as a desire to appoint an African American as the commission's leader.[11]

The staff that Young met at his first commission meeting in June 1968 comprised a large black Mississippian majority, which reflected both the Ministry's founding aim of fostering indigenous black leadership and reductions in its northern white staff caused by changing program priorities and budgetary restraints. The Ministry had thirty-two salaried and subsistence staff. Of its twenty-eight African American personnel, only Owen Brooks from Massachusetts and Harry Bowie and Henry Parker from New Jersey, were non-Mississippians. Three of the four white staff members were northerners—the exception was Ed King from Vicksburg, Mississippi. Only six of the Ministry's staff were clergymen, which reflected the Ministry's increasingly secular orientation.[12]

Eleven of the Ministry's indigenous black staffers presented a resolution to Young and the Commission on the Delta Ministry at the June meeting. The petitioners included project directors from five counties (Thelma Barnes [Washington], Solomon Gort Jr. [Tallahatchie], Clarence Hall Jr. [Issaquena and Sharkey], and Joseph Harris [Sunflower]); Jake Ayers of Freedomcrafts; Burnett Jacobs, the former administrator of the Mount Beulah Center; and five secretarial staff members. Concerned by the Ministry's history of forced staff terminations caused by budget cuts, they asked that "personnel assignments be made on a three-year appointment basis" and that "persons to be terminated because of budgetary reasons be given a 12-month notice in writing." The resolution urged the Delta Ministry to redeploy Jacobs, who had lost his post when the UPCUSA took over the lease of Mount Beulah from the NCC in May and had as a result been served with notice of termination by the Ministry. The staff explained, "Once an individual identifies with employment on the staff of the Delta Ministry in Mississippi[,] chances for any other employment in the state is almost nil."[13]

The resolution also demanded budgetary changes and improvements in the Delta Ministry's leadership. Its signatories called for the Delta Ministry to have "a guaranteed annual operational budget" and for each of its county projects to have "a designated budget geared to its individual need based on population and program." Disappointment with the ineffectiveness of the Commission on the Delta Ministry was evident in a call for the commission to "become actively involved in the total work of the Delta Ministry and not a 'paperwork' commission." Confident that Brooks lacked sufficient support in the NCC's Division of Christian Life and Mission, the disgruntled staff called either for Brooks to be appointed director or, preferably, for the appointment of "a Black Mississippian who is involved with the work of the Delta Ministry and who understands the problems with which we are confronted."[14]

Insufficient denominational financial support had troubled the Ministry since its inauguration, made planning difficult, and caused staffers insecurity about their positions. The discontent of some of the indigenous staff with Brooks, and the Commission on the Delta Ministry's support for him, lay partly in his management style but above all in his attempt to reshape the Ministry. Since 1967, Brooks had tried to transform the Delta Ministry from a group of uncoordinated county projects to a focused, cohesive program that fostered black economic development, educational opportunity, and independent political power. Aware that some members of the NCC's Division of Christian Life and Mission opposed giving Brooks the directorship, some of the Ministry's staff had undermined his efforts by appealing over his head to division members to support and fund their particular projects. They also refused to redirect county projects to facilitate the new direction Brooks charted.[15]

Intelligent and articulate, Brooks was also intense and reserved. He had little time for small talk. Single-minded, Brooks was direct and sometimes tactless in his dealings with others. He seemed to revel in an abrasive style that was not always appropriate to the situation. Those who signed the June 1968 staff resolution considered Brooks "overbearing, dominating, and dictatorial" and complained that he "seldom allowed Project Directors to run their Projects as they saw fit." Since the Delta Ministry's creation, county project directors had exercised near autonomy in their operations. They had come to expect the Delta Ministry and the NCC to provide resources for their activities without controlling or supervising them. The Ministry's loosely organized structure reflected SNCC's early influence, a distrust of authority and bureaucratic control, and a desire to develop local leadership and respond creatively to the needs of local people as the situation demanded. The diversity of the Ministry's activities had often required staff to take on several roles, often simultaneously. Flexibility, adaptability, and the capacity for independent action and decision making had become necessary hallmarks of Delta Ministry field workers. Inevitably, staff accustomed to operational independence resisted Brooks's attempt to reorient the Ministry and coordinate its various programs.[16]

The divisions within the Ministry also reflected the fact that its new focus on technical support depended on staff with higher educations who had the ability to understand complex technical information. With some exceptions, notably Thelma Barnes, most of the Ministry's indigenous personnel lacked college education, and some had not finished high school. As college-educated northern staff assumed specialist roles—for example, Bowie in economic development and Barber in education—in tune with the Ministry's new direction and emphasis, less educated black Mississippians feared for their continued employment and became hostile. Given that the Ministry had previously terminated several northern white and black Mississippian staff who did not work in priority areas, indigenous black personnel had understandable concerns for the future. Brooks tried to hire black Mississippi professionals to undertake technical roles, but the Ministry's tight budget prevented him from offering sufficiently attractive salaries to those who might otherwise have participated. However, many indigenous African American professionals rejected what they saw as the Ministry's radicalism and would not work for the group or with it as consultants because association with militancy might damage their careers.[17]

Consequently, the Ministry increasingly worked on projects with northern professionals and university professors, who provided the skills necessary to draw up proposals for federal grants to fund the Mound Bayou Development Corporation's projects, the Mound Bayou Community Hospital, and DOC. Local Ministry staff resented their organization's growing dependence on non-Mississippians. Although they recognized that the Ministry should utilize outsiders with technical skills, locals argued that "there is a vast amount of talent, ability, and organization in the communities not being used and developed. The people know what they need better than the 'professionals.'" So deep did the split in the Delta Ministry become that staff in the Greenville office physically divided the space in half, with supporters of Brooks on one side and his opponents, who had coalesced under Barnes's leadership, on the other.[18]

An executive session of the Commission on the Delta Ministry met on the evening of June 10 to consider the resolution adopted by disgruntled black Mississippi staff, but the meeting took no action. Brooks reported to the meeting that he had devised a plan to assure Burnett Jacobs's job security. Brooks's own position remained undecided. Finally in September, Jon Regier, associate general secretary of the NCC's Division of Christian Life and Mission, announced the appointment of Brooks as director and Bowie as associate director of the Delta Ministry. Regier had pushed for Brooks's appointment; like Andrew Young, Regier approved of the new direction in which Brooks had been taking the Ministry. Staff who opposed the appointment had little choice but to accept it. They bitterly resented Young's claim, with which Regier concurred, that no black Mississippians were qualified for the directorship.[19]

Brooks and Bowie complemented each other. Bowie regarded Brooks as "a gadfly" who challenged and questioned his lieutenant. Whereas Bowie was by nature a fixer and a compromiser, Brooks was a tough negotiator who regarded himself as "a purist." However, as Bowie observed, Brooks could make deals when necessary and be pragmatic when the situation demanded it.[20]

Some black Mississippi staff resented the Commission on the Delta Ministry replacing Mississippians on the commission with others from inside and outside the state who shared Brooks's outlook. The new members included Kermit Stanton and Earl Lucas, with whom Brooks had worked closely in Bolivar County and who also served with him on the Mound Bayou Development Corporation's board of directors. Disgruntled staffers believed that Brooks engineered such appointments to bolster his personal position. However, Regier and Young sanctioned the appointments, and they and the new appointees shared Brooks's conviction that the Ministry needed to focus on providing technical support to achieve substantial long-term development in key areas. Many of the members dropped by the commission had been infrequent participants at its meetings, and Amzie Moore, who was also replaced, had been actively trying to discredit Brooks.[21]

NAACP leaders such as Moore and Mississippi field secretary Charles Evers justifiably viewed Brooks as a militant. Brooks opposed whites receiving near equal representation in the Loyalist Democratic Party delegation that went to the Democratic Party's national convention in 1968 and unseated the virtually all-white regular Mississippi delegation. Evers, who favored a fully integrated delegation, told Brooks, "Owen, you don't understand us down here. We aren't going to be as mean to whites as they've been to us." Brooks took a pragmatic view that few Mississippi whites would support the national ticket. He believed that trying to court them in 1968 was unrealistic and that it would be more productive to concentrate on building an independent black political force in Mississippi. As Brooks had anticipated, only about 10 percent of Mississippi's white voters supported the national Democratic Party's nominee, Hubert Humphrey, in the November presidential election.[22]

Evers's comment that Brooks's views had been conditioned by his northern origins indicates another facet of the divide between indigenous Delta Ministry staff who opposed Brooks and those, mainly from the North, who supported him. Brooks, the son of West Indian immigrants, had grown up in Roxbury, an African American neighborhood in Boston. His ghetto upbringing and his family's pride in its origins and culture had given him a positive sense of black identity from an early age. Brooks heard Malcolm X speak in Boston, and he had several friends in the city who were members of the Nation of Islam. He did not become a Muslim, but he absorbed the Nation's ideas about black pride and the need for black community development independent of whites.[23]

Brooks's experience with recalcitrant white racism in Mississippi convinced him that whites would not voluntarily surrender power and that even moderate whites would seek to retain it, particularly by co-opting black leaders. Consequently, he favored developing the African American community's economic and political strength to ensure an independent black voice. Brooks argued that the MFDP best articulated the concerns of black Mississippians. The MFDP, he noted in 1969, had effectively, although not officially, become an independent black political party. Like former SNCC chairman Stokely Carmichael, who had famously called for Black Power during the Meredith March in 1966, Brooks contended that the African American community in Mississippi, the South, and the nation had to work through independent black political organizations and that only from such a strengthened position could it contemplate eventual alliances with others, such as poor whites. He hoped that the MFDP would link up with other African American groups in the South and create a "regional black political structure to select workable political priorities."[24]

Whereas Brooks believed that the MFDP truly represented what most black Mississippians wanted, he was scathing about the NAACP, which he viewed as elitist and concerned only with the interests of the African American middle class. Brooks believed that the NAACP's leaders in Mississippi had been co-opted by white moderates in the Loyalist Democratic Party at the expense of the interests of the state's African American poor. In fact, neither the NAACP nor the MFDP could accurately claim to represent poor black Mississippians. Most of the poor were unaware of or uninterested in the conflicts between the two organizations and gladly accepted assistance from whoever provided it. The majority of black Mississippians wanted to integrate and then work through the state Democratic Party rather than pursue the independent course advocated by Brooks and the MFDP.[25]

Bowie, Barber, and Horwitz, with whom Brooks worked most closely in the Delta Ministry, shared his vision for independent black economic and political development and support for the MFDP. Bowie, like Brooks, was a black northerner. Yet even Barber and Horwitz, both white northerners, favored independent

African American institutions. Significantly, many black Mississippians on the Delta Ministry staff did not support independent black development, despite its advocacy by the Ministry's northern leaders. The black Mississippians were far more willing than the Ministry's leaders, especially Brooks, to work with the NAACP and moderate white Mississippians, and in this they were in tune with majority black opinion in the state. Barnes enjoyed good working relations with local NAACP leaders and the support of moderate whites, such as Hodding Carter III. She went to the Democratic Party's national convention in 1968 as a delegate in the Loyalists' successful challenge to the regular Mississippi delegation.[26]

As Brooks and those closest to him on the staff increasingly worked on multicounty and statewide problems and on technical issues, they had less of a feel for the wishes of local people than did those staffers who worked in the Delta Ministry's county projects. Ministry leaders participated in several coalitions of community organizations in Mississippi that usually focused on single issues. The coalitions drew on the same pool of like-minded organizers and groups and "led to the development of an ingrown leadership group that is in reality a professionalized society of coalescers." Organizers thereby became insular and disconnected, to some extent, from those they sought to help.[27]

Gaile Noble, who spent the summer of 1968 as a Delta Ministry volunteer, recalled that during the Shelby school boycott, Delta Ministry leaders, including Barber, favored the strengthening of African American schools as transmitters of black consciousness and culture. However, Shelby's black community demonstrated instead for integrated schools, and the Ministry, committed to following the wishes of local people, deferred to them. When the MFDP's Executive Board debated the conditions under which the party might join the Loyalist delegation, black northern Delta Ministry staff argued that the Freedom Democrats should participate only if all their terms were accepted. However, the majority of the Mississippians present voted down the idea as unrealistic. Despite its leadership's reservations about the NAACP, the Ministry worked with the organization in such areas as voter registration and school desegregation, in concert with local wishes.[28]

Some black Mississippians on the Ministry's staff and commission favored the direction charted by Brooks. Mississippi civil rights worker Joyce Ladner's observation that indigenous black activists in her state who favored Stokely Carmichael's call for Black Power saw it in practical rather than ideological terms also applied to some Delta Ministry staff. "The locals," Ladner contended, "felt that Negroes would be able to acquire certain rights only through the control of their economic and political institutions." They believed that efforts to achieve black rights by working with whites had failed—for example, the Mississippi Summer

Project, the MFDP's attempt to be seated at the 1964 Democratic Party National Convention, and attempts to forge alliances with sympathetic northern groups.[29]

Brooks chose to focus much of his and the Delta Ministry's efforts on Mound Bayou not only because this all-black town offered some protection from whites for the development of economic and health programs affecting the black poor of northwest Mississippi but also because its history of African American landownership and self-government had given blacks there a sense of their own efficacy. By contrast, many African Americans elsewhere in the Delta, with the noticeable exception of landowners in Mileston, in Holmes County, had been dependent on whites all their lives; consequently, it was harder to motivate them to take action in support of their interests. Some of the Delta Ministry's black Mississippi staff resented Brooks for redirecting the Ministry's priorities and finances toward Mound Bayou and Bolivar County, where he had been project director, at the expense of other counties and projects.[30]

His belief in the necessity of developing black economic and political power through black community institutions sometimes brought accusations that Brooks favored separatism. He responded in 1969, "I have no quarrels with separatists except that I don't know what the calendar is for that. So until the calendar is properly described and until black people stand up and say they're big and bad enough to get this thing done themselves, the white people aren't going to hand blacks nothing . . . neither money nor land or anything. I just can't participate in that trickery. It's a nice concept. Theoretically it might even work. But I'm convinced that at this stage no one can operate outside the system."[31]

The Ministry's commitment to militancy and to economic development under Brooks's leadership was evident in its support for the Black Manifesto, drawn up by the National Black Economic Development Conference. Ministry staff helped plan the conference, which met in Detroit in April 1969, and participated in its deliberations. The Ministry approved of the Manifesto's demands for five hundred million dollars in reparations from white Protestant and Catholic churches and Jewish synagogues, money that the conference would use for the development of black communities. However, the Ministry disassociated itself from the manifesto's "rhetoric of revolution." A Gallup poll found that only 21 percent of African Americans and 2 percent of whites supported the manifesto's demands. Most of America's white denominations and Jewish organizations rejected the manifesto. By the end of the summer of 1969, the National Black Economic Development Conference had raised less than twenty-five thousand dollars from church sources, although some denominations later disbursed a few hundred thousand dollars to the conference and to the African American community through other outlets.[32]

Hostile white response to the manifesto accelerated an already discernible decline in financial contributions from predominantly white mainstream denominations and by local churches to the NCC. The trend continued into the next decade. Membership in mainline churches had begun falling in the mid-1960s in response to their support for the African American struggle for equality and involvement in other social issues. Those who left mainline denominations sometimes abandoned organized religion altogether, while others joined more conservative denominations, such as the Southern Baptist Convention, which had no affiliation with the NCC and mostly avoided social action. Between 1965 and 1975, membership fell by 17 percent in the Protestant Episcopal Church, 12 percent in the UPCUSA, 10 percent in the United Methodist Church, and 12 percent in the United Church of Christ, the denominations that had constituted the backbone of the Delta Ministry's domestic financial support during the 1960s.[33]

Falling denominational numbers and contributions to the NCC had an immediate impact on the Ministry. The Commission on the Delta Ministry reported in November 1969 that "many denominations had not lived up to their pledges," and three of the churches had warned that they would cut their contributions to the Ministry by between 10 and 20 percent. Young sent out appeals for financial support to the NCC's major denominations, but they did not yield additional money. Brooks and Parker went on a fund-raising tour of Western Europe, an area that they reported provided 60 percent of the Delta Ministry's total funding. NCC denominations contributed $143,662 to the Ministry in 1969. The National Council's Division of Christian Life and Mission transferred a further $49,500 to the Ministry from denominational funds it had received that were not committed elsewhere. Nevertheless, the Ministry ended the year with a deficit. The NCC approved a Ministry budget of $316,000 for 1970, $10,000 of which had to be applied toward the deficit incurred during the previous year.[34]

To keep within the Delta Ministry's budget, Brooks had to deny staff their annual salary increases in 1970, and in March he warned of imminent staff cuts. Eddie Lucas, director of the Bolivar County Project, closed the Cleveland office in April. Brooks shut the Sunflower County office in May. Sunflower County Project Director Joseph Harris, Brooks recalled, preferred to work with local civil rights activist Fannie Lou Hamer rather than to focus on building a sustainable organization in the county. Harris helped Hamer organize the ill-fated Freedom Farm cooperative in 1969 and served as its manager after leaving the Delta Ministry.[35]

Apart from closing its offices in Cleveland and Sunflower, the Ministry also faced the possibility of losing Mount Beulah. Affected by a decline in membership and contributions, in May 1970 the UPCUSA relinquished the lease it had assumed on Mount Beulah from the NCC and abandoned plans to use the site for an adult community college to serve the poor. The Presbyterians had been unable to obtain foundation funding for the proposed college, and repair of Mount Beulah's dilapidated buildings drained resources. The Presbyterians withdrew in the expectation that the UCMS, Mount Beulah's owners, would either lease or sell the site to the Federation of Southern Cooperatives (FSC), which agreed to allow existing programs housed there to continue. The Delta Ministry supported the idea and made a nationwide appeal that generated 2,539 petitions to the UCMS, pleading for it to keep the site for black people and not to sell it to white Mississippians. However, the FSC would accept Mount Beulah only as a gift, a loss the UCMS was unwilling to sustain. The UCMS allowed the Delta Ministry to retain its Mount Beulah office under an NCC lease, but the Ministry's budgetary difficulties forced it to withdraw from the site on March 31, 1971. During the summer, the UCMS sold Mount Beulah to the African Methodist Episcopal Church.[36]

Internal strife continued to plague the Delta Ministry as it struggled to maintain operations in an unfavorable financial climate. Finance officer Roger Smith, a white minister from Pennsylvania, claimed that the Ministry excluded him and female staff members from staff meetings between July and November 1970 that focused on planning the Ministry's direction in the new decade. Sarah Johnson, an African American resident of Greenville who had served as Henry Parker's secretary since April 1968, claimed that Brooks was "a male chauvinist" who was not interested in the opinions of female staff. Chauvinism was not confined to Brooks. Barnes recalled that although young black men on the staff had wanted an African American director appointed after Art Thomas's resignation, they had opposed her getting the post because she was a woman. To compensate for Brooks's administrative shortcomings, Regier had made Barnes the new director's administrative assistant. The exclusion of Smith from staff meetings resulted from his close association with Barnes, who was a focal point for those opposed to Brooks.[37]

Aside from her administrative duties, Barnes continued to direct and raise funds for Freedom City. She became increasingly frustrated as Brooks downgraded Freedom City as a Ministry priority and channeled much of the Ministry's energy and money toward Bolivar County, particularly Mound Bayou. Consequently, Barnes took a one-year leave of absence from the Ministry beginning in October 1970.[38]

The remaining women on the Delta Ministry staff boycotted the November 1970 meeting of the Commission on the Delta Ministry in Greenville in protest at their exclusion from recent staff meetings. Although commission members noted the women's absence, it brought little discussion. Consequently, ten of the Ministry's fourteen permanent staffers called for a full staff meeting, which occurred at Mount Beulah in December. The ten staff members, with Johnson prominent among them, presented Brooks and Bowie with a memorandum that listed twenty-five grievances. The petitioners complained about their exclusion from staff meetings and about the Ministry's growing reliance on non-Mississippians, which, they argued, undermined its original goal of helping local people fulfill their potential by creating an organization that would eventually be staffed and led by indigenes.[39]

Brooks addressed each of the concerns and promised to take proper corrective action. The National Division of the United Methodist Church had reduced its funding of the NCC's Division of Christian Life and Mission, through which it also contributed to the Delta Ministry, by more than half during 1970, which made cuts in the Ministry's budget very likely. Aware of the possibility of such cuts, the staff asked during the meeting if there would be any reductions in their number in the near future. Brooks told the meeting that there would be no reductions in the Ministry's staff and that if cuts in funding forced anyone to leave, he and Jon Regier would be the first to go.[40]

The meeting cleared the air, but on January 26, 1971, Brooks summarily fired Johnson for alleged insubordination and then denied her a hearing. With the agreement of Henry Parker, her supervisor, Johnson had refused to do some additional work for Freedom City, as Brooks had ordered; suffering from a medical complaint, she had gone home after completing her normal day's work. Unaware that she had gone on sick leave and with Parker away at a speaking engagement, Brooks fired Johnson for disobeying his orders and walking off the job. Although Parker returned and supported Johnson and they explained the circumstances to Brooks, the director refused to reinstate her. Brooks's action was symptomatic of the domineering manner in which he ran the Ministry and his tendency to ride roughshod over staff with whom he disagreed.[41]

Johnson wrote to Regier, asking for a hearing. Six other staffers also wrote to Regier in support of Johnson. A week later, Regier denied Johnson's request. By refusing a hearing, Johnson replied, Regier and Brooks were "a part of the worst kind of colonialism. You, the white slave master and Mr. Brooks, the black house nigger—keeping the field nigger (me) in line. What you have done to me is exactly what I expected to receive from any other racist agency, but not the church." Regier wrote to Johnson's supporters on February 11 that Brooks had acted "well within National Council personnel policy" and announced that there would be "substantial reductions" in the Ministry's staff. Four days later, Brooks disclosed that five of the six staff members who had supported Johnson would be terminated because the NCC had cut the Ministry's budget to $150,000 for the year, more than half its 1970 budget.[42]

Brooks explained at a February 23 staff meeting that all project directors had to be terminated, along with Smith and Parker. Brooks denied that the decision, which he claimed had been made by the NCC in New York, was connected to the terminated staffers' support for Johnson. No indigenous staff remained except for Solomon Gort, who had defended Johnson but received his salary from the American Baptist Home Mission Societies; Kattie Kingdom, who oversaw the Ministry's welfare program in Greenville; and two secretaries, Jean Phillips and Maxine Maxwell. Phillips resigned in protest at the end of the meeting. Apart from Gort, Kingdom, and Maxwell, Brooks was left with a staff of Bowie, associate director; Barber, education director; and Horwitz, Hinds County Project director.[43]

Calling themselves the Concerned Staff of the Delta Ministry, the terminated staff members and their remaining supporters on the staff sent Regier a telegram. They called for "new leadership" for the Ministry, explained that they were "disturbed by the continual repressive actions" of its present leadership, and alleged that there had been a "constant threat of intimidation of the staff by the director and lack of concern by the associate director." The Concerned Staff cited Johnson's termination and denial of a hearing as part of a pattern of repression and asserted, "The purpose of justice, love and equality for the liberation of the poor has been lost." They called for the Ministry to be reorganized "to bring it closer to the people and to the Christian ethic."[44]

According to the Concerned Staff, the NCC denied that its headquarters in New York had ordered the Delta Ministry's project directors to be fired and instead maintained that Brooks had made the decision. The Concerned Staff argued that Brooks had been inconsistent in retaining Horwitz, since he was a project director. To them, it seemed more than a coincidence that Brooks had retained Bowie, Barber, and Horwitz, who had not supported Johnson and remained silent about her case, and fired most of those who had stood by her.[45]

The telegram to Regier and subsequent letters to the Commission on the Delta Ministry led to a March 6 meeting of the Concerned Staff, Brooks, Regier, and the commission. The night before the meeting, the Concerned Staff issued a press release that summed up their accumulated grievances against Brooks. They alleged that the Ministry was "characterized by decisions made without consultation, by the downgrading and dehumanizing of staff members, by bypassing of project directors, by irregularities and inequities in the use of funds, by a lack of trust and opportunity for native Mississippians, and by a constant aura of tension, criticism and exploitation." Only five of the commission's thirty-three members attended the meeting, at which the Concerned Staff pressed Johnson's case and called for Brooks's dismissal. Regier again denied that Johnson had a right to a hearing.[46]

The Concerned Staff believed that Regier was deliberately trying to downplay the affair. They noted that although Brooks had informed Regier why Johnson was fired, NCC personnel staff in New York were told only that she had been terminated because of budget cuts. Furthermore, the Concerned Staff later discovered that Johnson was entitled to a hearing under NCC regulations and that Regier had misinformed the group. Regier's conduct after the March 6 meeting also suggested a desire to hush up the matter. He told reporters that no demands had been made for Brooks's dismissal, described the complaints of the Concerned Staff as "just a bit of a problem," and maintained that the Delta Ministry was not in crisis. Regier said that the record of the March 6 meeting would be forwarded to the Commission on the Delta Ministry, which would "take the proper action, if any, on this little matter" at its next meeting at the end of the month.[47]

A *New York Times* reporter in Greenville characterized the struggle within the Ministry as a "power struggle rooted in ideological differences" between "a leadership sympathetic to black separatism and a staff committed to interracial cooperation." The newspaper misinterpreted as separatism the commitment of the Ministry's remaining staff to building up independent black economic and political power; in fact, those who remained regarded independent institutions as simply the most effective means of empowering the African American community, given white Mississippi's resistance to racial equality. Although Brooks certainly distrusted moderate white and black Mississippians, the fact that he and the NCC kept Barber and Horwitz, both white, on the staff indicates that the issue was one of strategy, not separatism. Horwitz tried to involve both races in civil rights work, and Barber had officiated at Mississippi's first legal interracial marriage in August 1970.[48]

In terminating county project directors and other staff, Brooks had acted in accordance with recommendations made by Art Thomas, the Delta Ministry's former director. On January 14, 1971, Regier had appointed Thomas to evaluate the Ministry and make suggestions regarding its future direction, given the necessity of cutting its budget. Issued on February 1, Thomas's report firmly endorsed the abilities and initiative of Brooks, Bowie, Barber, and Horwitz, whom Thomas called the core staff, and their key statewide functions "as initiators, trouble-shooters, and reference resources for other groups." Thomas argued that the four men formed "a flexible, competent team, able to function in many program areas with diverse groups." He recommended ending county projects and retaining only the four men as the Delta Ministry's staff, with necessary administrative support. It was not surprising that Thomas as a former director would endorse the broad-range solution favored by the Ministry's current leaders. But far from being a knee-jerk reaction to financial crisis as the Concerned Staff understandably maintained, the NCC's reorientation of the Ministry was a considered move.[49]

The Concerned Staff presented their complaints to what they expected to be a meeting of the full Commission on the Delta Ministry at the end of March. However, only twelve commission members were present throughout the two-day meeting. Chairman Andrew Young attended only part of the proceedings. The Concerned Staff asked to have Brooks dismissed, Johnson given a hearing, and terminated staff reemployed, with pay cuts for all Ministry personnel to accommodate its reduced budget. The Concerned Staff also called for the restructuring of the Ministry and the commission. Under their proposals, the positions of director and associate director would be abolished in favor of a coordinator with limited powers, and commission members would be selected democratically from among local people. The Ministry would work more closely with local communities and their organizations. It would reach out to local white churches, some of which, the Concerned Staff believed, now exhibited a willingness to engage in dialogue but were spurned by the Ministry.[50]

The commission decided that Brooks had been wrong in dismissing Johnson without a hearing and "delinquent in some aspects of his administration." The members urged "him to be more sensitive to staff inter-relationships" but nevertheless recommended his retention as director. At the commission's urging, the NCC reinstated Johnson, but, satisfied with her vindication after a subsequent personal hearing, she declined to return to her post. Staff reductions, the Commission concluded, had been "made in line with necessary budget limitations and without cause to punish staff for personal differences." Strongly influenced by Thomas's report, the commission endorsed the direction in which Brooks had led the Ministry and hoped that it would continue "the development of Freedom Village, Delta Foundation, and the supportive role played to people and agencies throughout the state." In its final recommendation, the commission urged its own replacement "by the creation of an independent Board of Directors composed of a majority of state representatives which would be related" to the NCC. Seemingly a victory for the Concerned Staff, the recommendation also fitted with demands long made by the UPCUSA and the PCUS for reform of the commission to make it more effective and representative of black Mississippians.[51]

Disappointed by the commission's support for Brooks, Gort and Maxwell resigned. Gort claimed that the Ministry's leadership had "demonstrated an unwillingness to relinquish its colonialistic hold on Mississippi and the appointed staff." The Reverend Vernon Howell, the American Baptist Convention's representative on the commission, said that his convention supported Gort's resignation decision and that it would continue to support his work in Tallahatchie County. Maxwell stated that the "initial operation of the Delta Ministry has been defeated." Barnes sent a telegram of support to the Concerned Staff, declaring that the commission's action "represents the failure of the ministry to live up to its original aims and objectives to help underprivileged and deprived Mississippians determine their own destiny." Ruth Brent, a white Methodist from Greenville who had served on the commission since its beginning, resigned because it had not "paid attention" to the Concerned Staff and done "something about the present leadership." In a press release, Brooks conceded that "in my own passionate concern for the poor and oppressed and because of the great sense of urgency I feel, I have made errors in judgment and may have overreacted to what I felt to be unwarranted criticism."[52]

Outraged by the commission's decision, Jake Ayers and Jean Phillips took their protest to the next meeting of the NCC's Division of Christian Life and Mission, in May 1971. They urged the division to replace Brooks with a capable Mississippian who would run the Ministry according to the wishes of the Concerned Staff. The division rejected this plea and argued that the proposed board of directors would, by including a majority of Mississippians, ensure that the views of local people were fully reflected in the Ministry's operations. The recommendations of the Commission on the Delta Ministry became NCC policy. Financial necessity had forced the National Council to choose between the Ministry's leadership group, which favored statewide involvement and the provision of technical support, and indigenous staff, who wished to continue the projects that had been under way in a few counties for several years.[53]

Although Brooks ran the Delta Ministry autocratically and lacked diplomatic skills, it would not be accurate, as the Concerned Staff believed, to attribute the diminution of its staff and the retention of Bowie, Barber, and Horwitz to the director's personal preferences. Facing the necessity of reducing staff to accommodate a huge budget cut, Brooks, Thomas, and Regier concluded that the Ministry could not afford to maintain local projects and would be most effective, given the financial situation, in acting on a statewide basis as a provider of technical support in the key areas of politics, economic development, education, and welfare. The Ministry's reduction to a completely northern staff base was a regrettable but expedient decision. Yet this state of affairs also demonstrated that for all the effort devoted to promoting the development of local people and local leadership in Mississippi, the Ministry had ultimately failed to achieve that goal within its own organization. With a staff of four northerners and diminishing denominational support, the Ministry struggled to survive in the more conservative national political climate of the 1970s, which ended the supply of federal funds that had underpinned so many of its initiatives during the 1960s.

CHAPTER TEN

Winding Down

After its early 1971 budget and staff crisis, the Delta Ministry focused almost solely on providing technical and research assistance in legislative matters, economic development, education, and welfare. A board of directors replaced the Commission on the Delta Ministry. Black Mississippians, rather than the NCC and representatives from member denominations, played the major governing role on the board. The Ministry became independent of NCC control, with the status of a related movement, but continued to receive donations from several national denominations to sustain the reduced operations. By the mid-1970s, however, the Ministry had few remaining sources of support. Unwilling to abandon the cause to which he had devoted much of his adult life, Owen Brooks continued the Ministry, often as little more than a one-man operation. Brooks also worked for two African American congressmen whose elections from the Delta's Second Congressional District the Ministry had helped make possible through its many years of work. After leaving the Ministry, several former staff members continued to work in Mississippi on behalf of the poor and excluded. They and the many other staff and hundreds of volunteers who had served in the state since 1964 had the satisfaction of knowing that they had contributed to some notable political, economic, and social change, but many of the original problems remained.[1]

Reduced to four workers plus two administrative support staffers, the

Delta Ministry continued to be very active, despite operating during 1971 on an NCC-approved budget of only $150,000. According to journalist Neal R. Peirce, in the early 1970s the Ministry remained "the only broad-scaled social action agency working with Mississippi's blacks."[2]

Brooks, the Delta Ministry's director, stayed at its Greenville office, which he shared with Freedom Village. Brooks concentrated primarily on assisting the development of Mound Bayou as it applied for federal and private grants to improve facilities and to create businesses through the Mound Bayou Development Corporation. He sat on the corporation's board of directors, where he worked closely with Mayor Earl Lucas, who had been elected with Ministry support in 1969. Most of an extensive sewerage and water installation project in Mound Bayou was completed during 1971, paid for by federal funds secured with the Delta Ministry's technical assistance. The federal government insisted that to continue to receive federal funding, the Mound Bayou Community Hospital and the Delta Health Center had to merge and consolidate their overlapping services into one program. Consequently, Brooks assisted in the merger process, which began in 1971, and in May 1972, he became chairman of the board of directors of the newly established Delta Community Hospital.[3]

With less success, Brooks and the Delta Ministry also engaged in welfare rights organizing in Washington County. Both the United Methodist Church and the UPCUSA refused the Ministry's requests for grants to support self-help classes and community workshops designed to inform people of eligibility requirements for welfare, training, and housing programs. Despite limited funds, the welfare rights program helped more than five hundred families obtain welfare benefits, arranged welfare hearings for sixty-two people, and distributed emergency relief to several hundred families in Washington and surrounding counties.[4]

Although based in Greenville, Brooks also worked on issues that extended beyond the Delta. He served as secretary of the board of directors of STAR, a statewide OEO-funded vocational training program sponsored by the Catholic Diocese of Natchez-Jackson. The board met in Jackson, which had also become the location of the Delta Ministry's other office.[5]

In May 1971, less than two months after closure of its office at Mount Beulah, the Ministry opened a full-time office in the state's capital to "better coordinate state-wide research and development efforts." Harry Bowie, the Ministry's associate director, and the remaining core staff, Rims Barber and Charley Horwitz, occupied the Jackson office. The three men focused primarily on broad-range issues, which necessitated proximity to the state government and state agencies. The Ministry provided "technical assistance to community organizers and citizenship education groups," "advocacy development around issues of Day Care and Medical programs," and "consultant services in the formation and funding of community projects." It also continued its earlier involvement in education by furnishing research assistance for groups concerned with monitoring school desegregation and providing "technical assistance for community groups on educational issues and programs."[6]

The Jackson office enabled the Delta Ministry to work closely with Robert Clark, the state's only African American legislator. The Ministry, especially Barber, provided Clark with essential administrative and research support, particularly in preparing bills. Acknowledging Barber's key role, Clark commented, "I didn't know how to draft legislation. I didn't have time to do the research." However, in the early 1970s strong opposition in the Mississippi Assembly often defeated Clark's proposals, many of which dealt with improving education. Apart from assisting Clark, the Ministry worked with advocacy groups and sympathetic Mississippi legislators in unsuccessful attempts to reform the electoral process, provide state aid for day care centers, and widen access to welfare benefits.[7]

Clark won reelection in 1971 by only 364 votes. African Americans won fifty offices in the 1971 state elections, more than double the number achieved four years earlier. Yet the result was disappointing for the black community and the Delta Ministry, since 309 black candidates had stood for election. Furthermore, almost all of the offices secured were minor posts. More than 70 percent of eligible whites voted, and they did so mostly as a bloc. Although black voter turnout increased from previous years, it remained at less than half of those eligible. Apathy, fear, economic dependence on whites, and intimidation restricted African American turnout and accounted for some blacks supporting white candidates. In his campaign for governor, Charles Evers received greater black support than did any other black office seeker, but he secured only 22 percent of the total vote in the November general election. Despite the year's disappointing results, Mississippi had 117 black elected officials after the elections, more than any other state.[8]

The Delta Ministry had lacked staff and money to provide significant support to African American candidates, including those of its longtime ally, the MFDP. Poorly financed, the Freedom Democrats still entered more than forty people in the 1971 elections. They enjoyed little success. Harry Bowie concluded that many black voters considered civil rights leaders and activists to be insufficiently qualified for office. Political scientist Lester Salamon argued that successful African American candidates in Mississippi elections between 1965 and 1970 "were generally not as active in the movement as the losers; they tended more to be latecomers who joined the movement after much of the personal danger had subsided but who quickly rose to the top thanks to their command of the traditional sources of prestige, and perhaps to the support they received from whites." Brooks observed that African Americans elected to office after the civil rights movement had benefited from the opportunities it had created but had not, for the most part, been participants in the struggle and felt no commitment to it.[9]

While Bowie and Barber devoted part of their time to political and legislative issues, Horwitz, formerly director of the Ministry's Hinds County Project, continued his involvement in the county. The Delta Ministry had raised funds to help support 750 African American garbage workers in Jackson who had declared a strike in June 1970 to support their demands for higher pay, better working conditions, and union recognition. The strike ended after three weeks, and the city entered negotiations. When talks failed, Horwitz helped raise six thousand dollars from the UPCUSA in November 1972 to help the union fund a protracted lawsuit it had filed against Jackson authorities.[10]

Although the garbage workers failed, another organizing effort among pulpwood workers enjoyed success. The Southern Conference Educational Fund, a civil rights organization based in Louisville, Kentucky, began organizing black and white workers at the Masonite Corporation's plant in Laurel, Mississippi, in 1967. The effort resulted in the establishment of the Gulf Coast Pulpwood Association, which recruited slowly until 1971, when Masonite reduced the price it paid to the timber cutters and haulers who supplied its pulpwood. Two hundred independent haulers began a strike, which quickly spread under the association's leadership to yards across southern Mississippi. By November, more than three thousand black and white workers had joined the action, now in its tenth week. Evers secured relief for the workers, including NAACP emergency funds. The strikers included blacks and whites in roughly equal numbers, and some were former Ku Klux Klansmen or onetime Klan sympathizers. In a show of gratitude for its support, eighty-four white strikers joined the NAACP. The Delta Ministry played a less publicized role than the NAACP in raising money for the striking workers. After thirteen weeks, Masonite met the strikers' demands, and other wood dealers across the state followed suit. After the strike, the Ministry continued to support the organizing work of the Gulf Coast Pulpwood Association and raised money for it from NCC denominations.[11]

With its small staff, the Ministry could not undertake community organizing. Financial constraints also restricted its economic development program to providing technical assistance for Mound Bayou and Freedom City and participating in the Delta Foundation. Bowie, who had played a key role in establishing the foundation and had headed the Ministry's economics and citizenship education programs, left the Delta Ministry in 1972, joining the Southern Regional Council as associate director in charge of program development and commuting from his home in Mississippi to the council's Atlanta offices. His departure after eight years of service constituted a significant loss for the Ministry. However, Bowie continued to represent the Ministry on the board of the Delta Foundation, and he subsequently joined the Ministry's board of directors.[12]

When the commission on the Delta Ministry recommended its replacement by an independent board of directors, it did so because commission members believed that many of those who served were located too far from Mississippi to be aware of problems festering within the Ministry and that too few of them took an active role in overseeing the program. The reorganization, completed in 1972, strengthened representation from secular African American advocacy groups within Mississippi. Earl Lucas chaired the new board, which drew two-thirds of its members from within Mississippi.[13]

Despite the changes, the board suffered from the same problems that had afflicted its predecessor. High turnover among members and absenteeism from meetings left the Delta Ministry's staff, as before, determining policy, trying to raise funds, and undertaking administration. The Mississippi groups represented on the board tended to regard the Ministry as a mechanism through which they could obtain funds from outside the state rather than as an agency that could pursue a limited agenda in Mississippi.[14]

At the suggestion of the NCC and with the approval of the Delta Ministry's board of directors, the Ministry became a related movement of the National Council in 1972. As such, the Ministry determined its own policies and program but remained eligible for credit from the National Council, which also administered pension dues and payroll. Related-movement status allowed donations to the Ministry to remain tax deductible, but the Ministry had to raise "financial support for its budget." The Ministry adopted a budget of $175,000 in 1972. Although the National Division of the United Methodist Church had ceased funding the Ministry's regular budget by 1973, the division offered some help in balancing the budget. The Ministry also received contributions from the denomination's Women's Division through 1976 and from the UPCUSA throughout the 1970s. The UPCUSA, the PCUS, and the United Methodist Church's Commission on Religion and Race also made donations to Freedom City.[15]

The Delta Ministry found it difficult to raise funds in the 1970s as many of its former northern white sympathizers had become weary of supporting the African American struggle for equality. These former supporters often believed that since so much time and money had been spent on the civil rights movement, the problems either had been or should have been solved. The NCC increasingly focused on other issues, where outcomes could be achieved more quickly and visibly. With falling membership and financial support, the National Council's member denominations continued to decrease their contributions to the NCC and the

Delta Ministry. Whites were also less willing to support the Ministry with African Americans leading it. A layman with a secular orientation, Owen Brooks was not well placed to solicit denominational support, and his advocacy of independent black politics also alienated whites.[16]

Robert Clark chaired the Mississippi delegation to the National Black Political Convention held in Gary, Indiana, in March 1972, with Brooks serving as the delegation's secretary. The Delta Ministry "helped coordinate the planning and transportation" of the convention's Mississippi contingent. Attended by more than three thousand delegates representing every stripe of black opinion except for some NAACP leaders, the meeting was the largest black convention in American history. It called for proportional representation, economic reparations, land and housing reform, free child care, community health centers, national health insurance, community control of schools, improved public education and public transportation, and a guaranteed minimum annual income. However, policy disagreements soon fractured the diverse group. Meetings in 1974 and 1976 of the National Black Political Assembly, which the convention had established, drew fewer and fewer people, with the result that by 1977 the assembly had fewer than three hundred members nationwide.[17]

The MFDP, which the Delta Ministry had done so much to support, also disintegrated. The members of the racially balanced Loyalist Democrat delegation kept their seats at the Democratic Party's 1972 national convention at Miami despite a challenge from the regular Mississippi Democrats, who had retained control of the state party machinery. However, only three of the MFDP delegates to the Atlantic City convention in 1964, Fannie Lou Hamer, Winson Hudson, and Aaron Henry, served as Loyalist delegates in Miami, and Henry's ties with the Freedom Democrats had ended many years earlier. With neither money nor influence, the MFDP withered away, marking the end of the Delta Ministry's hopes that the Freedom Democrats would represent and serve the interests of poor blacks.[18]

Pushed back on the political front, the Ministry faced a tough battle to maintain federal funding for the Delta Community Hospital and Health Center in Mound Bayou after Governor William Waller vetoed its $5.5 million annual grant from OEO in June 1972. Waller disliked the presence of civil rights activists on the hospital's staff and programs. He claimed erroneously that the hospital had facilities that did not meet state requirements, duplicated services available elsewhere, and lacked a valid license. As chairman of the hospital's board of directors, Brooks led the fight to persuade OEO to override the governor's veto. At stake was health care for 128,000 poor people in Bolivar, Coahoma, Sunflower, and Washington Counties.[19]

While the Delta Community Hospital and Health Center waited to be re-funded, Brooks secured a loan from a Greenville bank that kept the hospital in operation and saved it from closure. The hospital's struggle for funding received editorial support from the *Washington Post*, which argued that "the Mound Bayou program deserves to be financed and it deserves to be run by the black community in the area." The *Memphis Commercial Appeal* also supported the facility because it was "opening up modern health care to tens of thousands who had not been getting it." OEO overruled Governor Waller's veto and restored the center's fund-ing and did so again after a subsequent Waller veto. The American Public Health Association, a private organization of health care professionals, recommended that the hospital remain in operation.[20]

Aware that the hospital lacked modern equipment, the Delta Ministry tried to raise funds to upgrade the facility. In addition to his duties as chairman of its board of directors, Brooks acted as the hospital's project director until one could be hired. In February 1973, the State Commission on Health Care denied the hos-pital a renewal of its license and ordered its closure. Although Brooks declined to run again for chairman of the hospital's board of directors in April, he remained on the board as it challenged the state's action through the courts. An out-of-court settlement allowed the hospital to continue functioning while it renovated its facilities using OEO funds. Despite the phasing out of OEO by the Nixon admin-istration in 1973, the hospital maintained federal funding for several years but at a reduced level that had to be supplemented by private funds. Withdrawal of fed-eral funding and an order from the State Commission on Health Care to build a new facility or shut down forced the July 1983 closure of the hospital, which had become outdated. However, the Delta Health Center remained in operation, supported by federal funds, and serving as Mound Bayou's largest employer, with two hundred staff members.[21]

In addition to working on behalf of the Delta Community Hospital and Health Center, Brooks and the Delta Ministry supported efforts to modernize Mound Bayou and develop industry in the town. The Ministry had helped raise funds to launch the Mound Bayou Brikcrete Factory in 1969, but the factory was not a success and ran deficits in the early 1970s. With technical assistance from the Ministry that secured loans from the federal Small Business Administration and banks and a forty-thousand-dollar grant from the United Methodist Church's National Division, the Mound Bayou Development Corporation built a bicycle factory at its industrial park in 1974. The factory created fifteen jobs, surviving but not thriving. Despite the Ministry's efforts, Mound Bayou could not generate sufficient jobs for its young people, who, like their contemporaries in the rest of the Delta, continued to migrate north in search of employment.[22]

With Delta Ministry support, Mound Bayou obtained foundation and federal grants that enabled it to build a park and a neighborhood services building and to acquire its first fire and garbage vehicles. Nevertheless, the Delta Ministry reported in June 1973 that Mound Bayou was struggling to stay "alive." A University of Mississippi report on Mound Bayou that year concluded that "there is too low a tax base so there is not a lot of money going into city government. Without the money the city is unable to provide a great number of government services. Industry is not attracted to Mound Bayou because of this lack of city services and without industry you cannot have a high tax base."[23]

Similar problems afflicted other small Mississippi towns such as Bolton, in Hinds County, where the Delta Ministry also provided technical assistance. Populated by eight hundred people, nearly 67 percent of them African American, Bolton had few resources. Charley Horwitz had worked with black community leaders prior to a 1969 town election in which African Americans had won three of the five seats on the board of aldermen. However, Bolton's white mayor frustrated the black majority's efforts—his veto could be overridden only by four aldermanic votes. Four years later, Bennie Thompson, one of the African American aldermen elected in 1969, became mayor, leading a full slate of black candidates to victory in the city council elections. Vice chairman of the Delta Ministry's board of directors, Thompson received the Ministry's support. With its help, Bolton "retained a city planner, secured property maps and a reassessment of property, and prepared [a] community development proposal."[24]

The Ministry provided technical assistance to the town over the next two years, an effort that culminated in the U.S. Department of Housing and Urban Development's 1975 grant of $146,700 so that Bolton could improve water and sewer systems, create a park, and provide housing assistance. The grant nearly quadrupled the town's budget. Federal funding built a city hall and fire station, a day care center, and forty housing units. The money also paid for renovation of other dwellings, ending Bolton's problem of large-scale substandard housing.[25]

Horwitz's work on behalf of Thompson's mayoralty campaign in 1973 was one of his last actions while on the Delta Ministry staff. He left the Ministry in July to attend law school in Washington, D.C. His departure brought the Ministry's staff, boosted by the recruitment of James Smith in March, back down to three. Smith, from Jackson, had participated in a Delta Ministry–related project in 1967 and had later worked for the Rhode Island Welfare Rights Organization. Funded by a grant from the New York Foundation, he restarted the Ministry's welfare rights organizing program.[26]

In 1973, a limited rapprochement occurred between the Delta Ministry and the staff whose jobs had been cut two years earlier. Sarah Johnson, who had successfully appealed her firing by Owen Brooks in 1971, ran for a seat on the Greenville City Council in a special election. Johnson enjoyed the support of the Concerned Staff of the Delta Ministry, whose members had formed a rival organization, the Delta Resources Committee (DRC), after their termination from the Ministry. The DRC focused on community mobilization, voter registration, antidiscrimination suits, and support of black electoral candidates in nine Delta counties. Thelma Barnes, who had been on a year's absence from the Delta Ministry during the 1971 crisis, also served on the DRC, which sustained itself through donations, mainly from the United Methodist Church.[27]

The Delta Ministry supported Johnson's campaign, and she and Brooks spoke to each other for the first time in two years. The only African American candidate in a field of nine, Johnson reached the runoff election, which she lost to Gerald Abraham, 3,516 to 2,358. The *Delta Democrat-Times,* which had endorsed Johnson, estimated that she picked up 8 percent of the white vote. With high turnout, the electorate divided overwhelmingly along racial lines, although neither candidate had made race-based appeals for support. "It can only be concluded," the *Delta Democrat-Times* editorialized, "that the whites voted out of racial fear rather than interest in good government." Although 49 percent of Greenville's population was African American, the city still had no black council members. However, Johnson later secured a seat on the city council in the regular election.[28]

As Johnson took office, the Delta Ministry prepared to celebrate its tenth anniversary. Held at New York's Cathedral of St. John the Divine, courtesy of New York Bishop Paul Moore Jr., the former chairman of the Commission on the Delta Ministry, the June 1974 celebration gathered together many past and present NCC executives. As much a fund-raising effort as a commemoration of the Ministry's achievements, the event's sponsors included former critics John M. Allin, recently elected presiding bishop of the Protestant Episcopal Church, and Hodding Carter III. Attended by one thousand people, the celebration gave a misleading impression of the Ministry's current support. Many of those who witnessed the celebration regarded the Ministry with nostalgia and had little commitment to its future. Phil Young of the UPCUSA, who had served on the Ministry's board of directors and on the Commission on the Delta Ministry, commented privately, "Concerned support by powerful denominational actors is not available for DM; the 'ten year Commitment' has long since expired. Denominational offices and officers no longer give Mississippi absolute priority. They care neither more— nor less—about Mississippi than they do about Pawtucket, Rhode Island."[29]

Owen Brooks explained to the New York gathering that the Delta Ministry's emphases now lay in providing advice and legal resources to communities confronting postdesegregation education problems, establishing and operating day care centers, providing health and medical services, developing industry and small businesses, and assisting small municipalities in revenue sharing. With federal funds for many social service programs withdrawn by the Nixon administration and federal monies now distributed directly to state governments through revenue sharing, Brooks explained, deprived African American communities in Mississippi had become increasingly reliant on "their own initiatives" and meager resources.[30]

However, the Delta Ministry helped black communities to apply for whatever funds were still available. It assisted Unita Blackwell, a SNCC veteran and participant in the 1966 Greenville Air Force Base occupation, in incorporating Mayersville, in Issaquena County, in 1976, allowing the town, which had fewer than five hundred inhabitants, to apply for federal funds. Appointed the town's first mayor on an interim basis, Blackwell was elected a year later, the county's first black mayor and the state's first black female mayor. Incorporation subsequently brought Mayersville a federally financed five-hundred-thousand-dollar sewerage system to replace the open sewers and an equal sum in other improvement grants. Blackwell remained mayor until stepping down in 1993.[31]

A former member of the MFDP's executive committee, Blackwell nevertheless worked cooperatively with the NAACP. However, Brooks's long-standing difficult relationship with the Mississippi NAACP continued. Although the Delta Ministry had included Aaron Henry among those it honored at its New York celebration, Brooks launched a fierce denunciation of the NAACP state president two years later. Brooks accused Henry of capitulating "to racism and the oppression of your people" by attending a dinner honoring Mississippi Senator James O. Eastland's long congressional career. By attending, Brooks wrote in an open letter to Henry, "You have done irreparable damage to the cause." Henry argued that he had participated because Eastland had agreed to support a three-million-dollar scholarship fund-raising drive for poor law students, irrespective of race, at the University of Mississippi. Furthermore, according to Henry, in recent years Eastland had "supported more civil rights legislation than [at] anytime in his life." Brooks, he complained, was "a racist against the white community." In fact, rather than being a racist, Brooks was unwilling to bury the hatchet with those who had oppressed African Americans for decades and had recently modified their positions only as a matter of political expedience. Eastland hoped to be reelected in 1978 and, with 60.7 percent of Mississippi's African Americans registered by 1976, he knew that he would need black votes.[32]

The regular Mississippi Democrats also recognized political reality after the Loyalists had been seated at consecutive national conventions, and the two groups merged in 1976. The unified delegation was cochaired by Aaron Henry and regular white Democrat Tom Riddell. The Delta Ministry criticized the merger because the convention delegation included whites pledged to George C. Wallace, the former segregationist governor of Alabama, and underrepresented African Americans given their strength in the party.[33]

Disappointed by political developments, the Ministry was also in financial crisis, plagued by persistent deficits. In response, the NCC discontinued its line of credit in May 1976, leaving the Ministry with only two hundred dollars in the bank. Brooks urgently appealed to supporters, but responses barely managed to keep the Ministry afloat. Although its activities were much reduced, the Ministry secured a grant from the Atlanta-based Voter Education Project to conduct a five-week voter registration campaign in Washington County in the fall of 1976.[34]

Conscious of the Delta Ministry's precarious financial situation, in 1977 Barber joined the Jackson office of the Children's Defense Fund, which Marian Wright had opened several years earlier. Barber had been working on racial discrimination in special education placement with a member of the fund's Jackson staff who transferred to Washington, D.C., at the end of 1976. He accepted an invitation to take over the project so that he could remain active in Mississippi.[35]

Brooks continued the Ministry with whatever money and assistance he could muster. In 1977, the Ministry began a demonstration program, funded by the United Methodist Church's Board of Global Ministries, to teach poor Washington County families "how to plan, purchase and consume economical and nutritious, low budget meals." With support from charitable foundations, the program broadened to provide free seeds for the poor, to run a demonstration garden that supplied free vegetables to those without gardens, and to help to find housing for evicted people and jobs for the unemployed. The small-scale program assisted more than two hundred families in the late 1970s. Brooks conceded in 1979 that "with the money available we are not able to help people in a meaningful way [to] find jobs or increase their income."[36]

In October 1982, the Delta Ministry opened a cooperative grocery store for the poor in Greenville that had 250 members. The store priced goods lower than local stores and about the same as supermarkets. It also provided short-term grants and loans to prevent utilities from cutting service, gave canned goods to the hungry, and aided homebound elderly people. The NCC, the United Methodist Church, and the Wild Geese Foundation, a Dutch organization, provided start-up funds for the store.[37]

Spearheaded by L. C. Dorsey, criminal justice and prison reform constituted the Delta Ministry's other major concern in the late 1970s and early 1980s. Dorsey, a former sharecropper who had worked with Owen Brooks since 1966, joined the Ministry in the late 1970s, becoming associate director after Barber's departure.

She had earned a master's degree in social work from the State University of New York at Stony Brook in 1973 before returning to Mississippi to attend the University of Mississippi Law School for a year. Moving to Jackson, Dorsey became administrative director of the Mississippi Prisoners' Defense Committee. Henry also appointed her chairperson of the Mississippi NAACP's Prison Affairs Committee.[38]

Working part time with Brooks, Dorsey focused primarily on death row prisoners. She found lawyers for condemned inmates and publicized cases of brutal treatment. Dorsey became state director of the Southern Coalition on Jails and Prisons, a nine-state organization that called for prison reform, an end to the death penalty, and a moratorium on prison building. According to activist and writer Tom Dent, she "performed with such tenacity that her investigations and the legal suits that ensued virtually transformed the brutal Mississippi prisons into an acceptable modern system." Dorsey also secured a grant for a Delta Ministry project to help female victims of domestic violence. She left the Ministry and Mississippi in 1983 to study for a doctorate in social work at Howard University in Washington, D.C.[39]

Brooks continued the Delta Ministry as a one-man operation. He worked on Mike Espy's successful 1986 campaign for the Second Congressional District, redrawn by federal court order in 1981 to encompass the Delta. Espy became the first African American from Mississippi to serve in the U.S. Congress since 1883. Brooks subsequently became an aide to Espy and then to his successor, Bennie Thompson, elected after Espy became secretary of agriculture in the first Clinton administration. Friends found Brooks a teaching position at a northern university, but he refused to accept it, preferring instead to remain a community activist. In the mid-1990s, Brooks maintained a Delta Ministry office in Greenville. He devoted his time to an oral history project and to working with African American youth in an effort to combat the growing drug problem.[40]

During the 1990s, several former Ministry staffers continued to work on behalf of Mississippi's poor. Executive director of the Delta Foundation since 1985, Harry Bowie oversaw the foundation's operations from an office in Greenville. With support from the Methodist Church, Thelma Barnes and Roger Smith also maintained an office in Greenville, engaging in community work and developing a family life center. After completing her doctorate, L. C. Dorsey returned to Bolivar County, where she served as director of the Delta Health Center for a few years before moving to the Department of Social Work at Jackson State University. Rims Barber was also in Jackson. When the Jackson office of the Children's Defense Fund closed in 1989, Barber began the Mississippi Human Services Agenda with his own resources. Friends and supporters rallied round to help raise money for his new one-man venture, which survived despite its very limited funds. Located in an office a few blocks from the state capitol, Barber monitored and advised the state legislature, disseminated information to advocacy groups, and assisted black educational and development programs.[41]

Delta Ministry veterans noted some significant changes in Mississippi but were also keenly aware that many race and poverty problems remained to be tackled. Barber noted that de jure segregation had ended and racial violence abated. Blacks and whites shopped together in malls. Several hundred African American lawyers and doctors practiced in the state. However, half a million African Americans, Barber observed, remained mired in poverty, and some still lived in shotgun shacks in the Delta. Although overt racism had disappeared from Mississippi politics, it had reappeared in the code phrases, such as opposition to welfare, that conservative politicians used in appeals to white voters. Life had improved for many African Americans, Barber concluded, but much remained to be done.[42]

Owen Brooks lamented the decline of activism in Mississippi since the 1960s and contended that capitalism prevented progress. He argued that the "people with the power to create social change don't *want* social change. They want 'better race relations.' The situation in Mississippi is *not* better, although for many *individuals* things are much better." African Americans had access to public accommodations and were routinely employed in downtown stores and banks, but there were insufficient jobs to make a dent in the Delta's poverty. Brooks noted that de facto segregation had replaced de jure segregation, particularly in the Delta, where African Americans attended the public schools and all but a few whites attended private academies. Whites retained the sources of economic and political power. They controlled the public school system but felt little commitment toward it in heavily black areas, since white children were privately educated.[43]

L. C. Dorsey argued that African Americans had not been truly accepted as equals. In practice, most churches and schools in Mississippi remained segregated, and students self-segregated themselves within officially desegregated schools and universities. Public school teachers directed black students to courses that prepared them for low-skilled jobs. There was little integrated dating in the Delta and little social interaction between the region's blacks and whites. Both races, Dorsey observed, tended to vote in racially defined blocs. Although Mississippians had elected black officials, they were often, she believed, corrupted by power and did not serve the interests of those who had voted for them. Although Dorsey did not specify any names, some of Espy's former supporters believed that he neglected his black constituents and was preoccupied with seeking higher office. White politicians, Dorsey noted, catered to the concerns of those who had elected them.[44]

Although the majority of black people wanted to work, Thelma Barnes observed, the low-skilled jobs available paid less in wages and benefits than welfare entitlements. They could not, she explained, "*afford* to work," even though Mississippi welfare payments were the lowest in the nation. Desegregation, Barnes maintained, had included one major drawback: it had led to a decline in black-owned businesses, since segregation no longer forced blacks to patronize such establishments. Consequently, less money stayed within the African American community as blacks spent their money at white-owned businesses.[45]

Harry Bowie agreed that integration had brought the loss of some family-owned African American businesses, and only a few black-owned downtown businesses opened up. Although Brooks regarded capitalism as an impediment to black progress, the Delta Foundation had created six thousand jobs in twenty-six years by lending money to profit-oriented businesses. By contrast, cooperatives begun in the 1960s had long since failed. Nevertheless, large-scale industrial employers would not, for the most part, locate in heavily black areas and create the jobs that Delta blacks so desperately needed. Northern industry opened plants in predominantly white areas of Mississippi, where schools and infrastructure were better and the inhabitants less likely to join unions. Heavily black areas of the state had attracted only employers who required minimal skills and paid minimum wage. These enterprises frequently relocated to Mexico or other foreign countries to further reduce labor costs.[46]

School desegregation, Bowie believed, had not brought African Americans the skills they needed for well-paid employment. In fact, integration adversely affected black education in Mississippi by removing many of the black counselors, coaches, and bandleaders who had served as role models for their students and had infused them with the importance of educational achievement. Bowie noted a growing contempt for education, part of a wider trend in American society, and a lack of motivation to move ahead. He believed that since the late 1970s, a welfare mentality had taken hold among many of Mississippi's poor blacks, who believed that the government owed them everything. The civil rights movement, Bowie contended, had unwittingly encouraged such dependency by helping to bring federally funded antipoverty programs into poor communities and by encouraging the poor to claim welfare entitlements.[47]

Dorsey lamented the disappearance of a philosophy of mutual aid, responsibility, self-help, and unity that she believed had characterized much of the black community before the civil rights movement and had helped sustain the movement in the 1960s: "We have become fragmented and changed our personal values away from our commitment to the community. Most churches are no longer a part of the community or concerned about the community as a whole. There is a falling away of that sense of togetherness, of belonging, of having meaning and purpose, of having your life be a part of a group of people." Although the pattern she identified was part of a trend discernible in much of American society, Dorsey also traced its origins to developments that occurred in the aftermath of the civil rights movement.[48]

In Dorsey's view, although necessary, federal poverty programs had also been divisive. Local white and black leaders sought access to and control of the funds and jobs these programs provided. Federal and local authorities used these new sources of patronage to divide the black community by co-opting some of its leaders, including some formerly in the civil rights movement, and other favored blacks. People who had benefited from the opportunities opened up by the movement pursued their own economic self-interests, refusing to risk their newfound gains by challenging oppression. Dorsey cautioned, "We will not survive if we depend on Washington to solve our problem, or if we talk ourselves into thinking we are helpless to do anything about the powers around us."[49]

The breakdown in community and growing emphasis on individualism also manifested itself in crime. Dorsey told Tom Dent, "Now I worry about crime in a way I never did before. Crime is directly connected with unemployment, but there is also an alienation among young people—a concern with the materialistic: cars, sneakers, clothes. Drugs have accentuated this process by clouding and obscuring concepts of success." Dorsey contended that families no longer inculcated values into their children and gave them the guidance they needed. Consequently, "we have children relying on their own, taking wild directions from their peers, and winding up seeking someone that can give them direction, discipline and the love they never had."[50]

Statistical evidence and contemporary newspaper reports support and augment the analysis of Delta Ministry veterans. Persistent challenges by civil rights lawyers from the 1960s through to the early 1980s gradually dismantled barriers that diluted the impact of African American votes. Participant-observer Frank Parker of the Jackson office of the Lawyers' Committee for Civil Rights under Law noted that across Mississippi, single-member legislative districts had replaced multimember districts, at-large elections for county boards of supervisors and school boards had ended, racial gerrymandering of electoral districts for county supervisors had been overturned, and most city councils had abandoned at-large elections.[51]

As a result, by 1988 Mississippi had 646 black elected officials, the most of any state in the country. These officials included U.S. Congressman Mike Espy, a state supreme court justice, 22 state legislators, 68 county supervisors, more than 25 mayors, and 282 city councilors. Like the Delta Ministry veterans, Parker noted that systematic white violence designed to control African Americans had subsided and overt racist campaigning to win electoral office had ended. He added that African American votes sometimes determined the outcome of statewide elections, such as Ray Mabus's narrow 1987 gubernatorial victory. Furthermore, evidence showed that white racial attitudes were softening. A 1981 poll found that 68 percent of white Mississippians favored school integration, 60 percent open housing, and 67 percent the Voting Rights Act. More moderate whites increasingly replaced the old generation of segregationist state legislators.[52]

Black elected officials often had a significant impact on policy, particularly at the state level, where they headed several committees, worked with white moderates, and had the votes to influence or block the adoption of major legislation. Robert Clark, chairman of the House Education Committee, and other black state legislators played a crucial role in passing the 1982 Education Reform Act, which restored compulsory school enrollment (abandoned in the 1950s as a defense against desegregation), improved teacher certification requirements, brought state-funded kindergartens to every district, and made several other reforms to improve the public school system. By 1993, the number of black legislators had moved beyond tokenism, with forty-two in office, 24 percent of the Mississippi Assembly. Clark became speaker pro tem of the House, its second in command, and African Americans headed several key House committees.[53]

By 1988, forty-three of Mississippi's eighty-two counties had at least one African American serving on their boards of supervisors, and blacks controlled five boards. The city councils was the largest single category of black elected officials. With some success, African American officeholders solicited federal and other grants to improve local services and infrastructure. Between 1968 and 1981, federal agencies spent more than two hundred million dollars on housing in the Delta, with the result that almost half of the 37,398 housing units black Deltans occupied in 1980 had been built since 1960.[54]

However, Parker noted important limits to the changes that had occurred in Mississippi. African American candidates typically won election only from districts that were at least 65 percent black in population—in the Delta, sometimes as much as 80 percent. Of the more than six hundred black elected officials in 1988, just over twenty constituted exceptions to the 65 percent rule. Several reasons account for the phenomenon. First, the vast majority of whites would not vote for any black candidate, regardless of platform. Second, continued northern migration of young adult African Americans, particularly from the Delta, made the black voting age population proportionately smaller than the black share of the total population. Third, African Americans were less likely to register to vote than were whites and were less likely to vote when registered. Fourth, Mississippi's requirement that voters had to register for federal, state, and county elections and then register separately for municipal elections reduced black registration, and white officials often failed to make African Americans aware of the dual registration requirement. Fifth, disproportionately employed in low-income jobs and paid an hourly wage, blacks were less able to take time off work to register than were whites. Sixth, transportation to county courthouse registration offices presented a further problem, since 27.8 percent of black Mississippi households had no motor vehicle at home for private use, compared to only 6.76 percent of white families. Finally, regardless of race, the poor typically registered and voted less frequently than did other social groups.[55]

Although systematic white racial violence had abated, instances of violence and terrorism still occurred. Racists vandalized Congressman Espy's Madison home and defaced it with racial insults. Parker, like Barber, noted that some white politicians resorted to code phrases to make race-based appeals. In 1982 and 1984, Republican Webb Franklin narrowly defeated Robert Clark for the Second Congressional District by courting white voters in this way. Although black votes could influence and in close contests determine the outcome of statewide elections, they could not offset a large white vote such as that which secured Republican Trent Lott a U.S. Senate seat in 1988.[56]

Despite some evidence of changing white attitudes, many white Mississippians remained opposed to racial change. Mississippi held a referendum in 1987 to consider repealing the state constitution's prohibition of interracial marriage. Although the U.S. Supreme Court's decision in *Loving v. Virginia* (1967) had made the provision unenforceable, 48 percent of Mississippi's voters favored keeping the restriction. Two years later, Mississippi held a referendum to consider repeal of the poll tax, once used to disenfranchise black voters. Even though the poll tax had been invalidated as a consequence of the Voting Rights Act of 1965, 42 percent of the voters supported the tax's retention.[57]

Despite electing hundreds of officeholders, at no level of the political system did African Americans achieve representation proportionate to their share of the voting age population (33 percent in 1990). The problem was especially acute at the county level, where in 1988 African Americans constituted only 17 percent of Mississippi's 410 county supervisors. Majority black counties in the Delta particularly suffered from low African American representation, with only one black supervisor per county in Bolivar, Coahoma, Sunflower, and Washington Counties. Delta whites sought to maintain control of municipalities by ensuring that federally funded housing intended for African Americans was built outside corporate limits. White-controlled municipalities also refused to annex African American residential areas.[58]

Once elected, black politicians often did not produce the changes their voters wanted. African American state legislators were too few in number to enact legislation without white support, and measures that appealed primarily to blacks often had difficulty in finding white allies. Members of the black caucus in the state assembly did not always agree on issues or vote as a bloc. Some African Americans regarded Congressmen Espy, who projected a moderate image in his successful electoral campaigns and won some white support, as too amenable to white planters and catfish farmers. Although local black officials tried to improve their communities, whites frequently opposed such efforts. Even when African Americans had control of governing bodies—only five county boards of supervisors in 1988—they were often powerless to make significant change because low tax bases restricted the ability to finance improvements.[59]

Political influence and federal support brought black Mississippians some advances in education. But de facto school segregation remained commonplace. In 1980, 23.6 percent of black students attended predominantly white schools, and 36.7 percent attended schools that were at least 90 percent black, a figure that increased to 38.7 percent in 1987. Even in desegregated schools, whites and blacks tended not to mix. Furthermore, white teachers and education officials disproportionately placed black students in special education classes and separated the races using ability grouping and tracking. Nevertheless, African Americans had made considerable progress. The median educational attainment of Mississippi's blacks increased from 6 years in 1960 to 9.4 years in 1980. In 1980, 33 percent of the state's African American adults were high school graduates, up from 7.6 percent twenty years earlier, and 60 percent of those aged between eighteen and twenty-four had finished high school. However, many black Mississippians continued to be left behind. Former CDGM staff member Polly Greenberg claimed in 1990 that less than 20 percent of the state's black high school students were enrolled in classes that "could prepare them for any but dead-end jobs." A third of Mississippi's adult population, some 400,000 people, had fewer than eight years of school education. In 1989, only 24 percent of the state's black high school graduates finished the academic core curriculum.[60]

Although income levels for African Americans continued to lag far behind those enjoyed by Mississippi's white population, increased education and opportunities reduced the disparity. By 1980, black median income had increased from 33 percent to 52 percent of white family income but was still only $9,013. Thirty-nine percent of all African American families were mired in poverty in 1980, compared with 83 percent in 1960. Affected by the decline in black businesses after desegregation and the rise of agribusiness, the percentage of nonwhites who were business owners, managers, professionals, and small farmers fell from 18 percent in 1960 to 12.4 percent twenty years later, although the overall number of people in the category grew by 5,500. In 1988, the black Mississippi unemployment rate was 14.7 percent, compared to 8.4 percent for the state as a whole and 5.4 percent across the nation. More than half of Mississippi's black children, almost 200,000 people, were living in poverty in 1990. According to historian John Dittmer, "In the early 1990s Mississippi still led the nation in poverty, infant mortality, and illiteracy."[61]

The Delta fared worst of all. According to historian James C. Cobb, "Transfer payments were the chief source of income in all Delta counties in the 1980s." Some Delta planters still did not pay their farm workers minimum wage, either by underpaying them or by overcharging them for rent, utilities, and advances for the winter, when no work was available. Tunica County was the nation's second-poorest county in 1980, surpassed only by Kalawao County, Hawaii, a leper colony of 144 people. Holmes County, located partially in the Delta, was not far behind at fifth-poorest. Unemployment in Delta counties ranged from 20 percent to 50 percent. Infant mortality in four counties exceeded twenty-five per thousand births in 1984, higher than the rates in Panama, Cuba, and Malaysia. During the 1980s, 40,000 people migrated to northern cities from the Delta in search of work.[62]

Congressman Espy regarded catfish as a means of creating prosperity in the Delta region, introducing National Catfish Day to promote the industry. Although a few Delta planters had experimented with catfish in the 1960s, large-scale development of catfish ponds became significant only during the 1980s. By the end of the decade, catfish had displaced cotton as the Delta's most profitable activity. Catfish farming required large capital outlays, but banks would not lend African Americans start-up funds. Consequently, whites dominated the ownership and management of the industry, which generated $350 million in 1990.[63]

Catfish plants employed African American women to gut and filet the fish and black men to pack and load. Poorly paid and subject to exhausting ten-hour shifts, industrial injury, and intrusive management that drove them to work faster, many catfish workers likened their existence to slavery or to working in the cotton fields. The fast pace and repetitive nature of production line work led some women accidentally to cut themselves with filet knives, and some women developed carpal tunnel syndrome, a painful condition afflicting the arm. Many companies routinely fired injured workers without compensation.[64]

Delta Pride, a huge processor cooperative in Indianola that was owned by 160 Mississippi farmers, treated its workers particularly harshly. Rose Ross, fired by Delta Pride after developing carpal tunnel syndrome, said, "Delta Pride is just like in slavery time. Somebody always standing over you, telling you what to do. If you get hurt, that's just one more black nigger gone and another one coming to get crippled." L. C. Dorsey, director of the Delta Health Center, commented, "It's very much like the sharecroppers 30 years ago. Cotton was king. The owners of the plantations were making a killing, and we weren't making anything." At Delta Pride, white male supervisors allowed black women one five-minute bathroom break a day, and the women were timed. Supervisors sometimes even followed women into the bathroom. Some supervisors also pressured female workers to sleep with their bosses.[65]

Catfish processing plants, including Delta Pride, frequently resisted union organizing, and some even closed their plants rather than accept unions. Despite Delta Pride's opposition, the United Food and Commercial Workers successfully organized the company's workers in 1986 and subsequently negotiated a three-year contract. In 1990, unable to reach agreement with Delta Pride on the terms of a new contract, union members began a bitter thirteen-week strike that was marked by violence on both sides. The launch of a nationwide boycott of Delta Pride catfish led the company to agree to a settlement.[66]

Despite the Delta's high unemployment rate, catfish plants had high labor turnover because of the poor pay and working conditions. Another potential source of employment arose in the early 1990s when Coahoma, Tunica, and Washington were among several counties bordering the Mississippi River that legalized gambling in hopes of generating prosperity. However, the corporations that subsequently built casinos in the Delta provided only menial jobs for local blacks and took most profits out of the region.[67]

Federal and state attempts to revitalize the Delta fell by the wayside. By 1992, the Lower Mississippi Delta Development Center was on the brink of closure. Formed two years earlier to initiate public-private partnerships for development projects along the Mississippi River, it had achieved nothing. Four of the seven states that were to pay its operating costs had withheld funds. Mississippi Governor Ray Mabus argued that his state's budgetary difficulties prevented it from paying its share.[68]

The center had been created to implement recommendations made by the Lower Mississippi Delta Development Commission. Appointed by Congress in 1988 at the prompting of the region's senators and representatives, the commission spent eighteen months studying the area. Chaired by Arkansas Governor Bill Clinton, the all-white commission formulated a ten-year economic development plan that included improving education, health care, and flood control. However, its recommendations did not receive federal funding since President George Bush and congressional leaders gave priority to reducing a federal deficit that had reached $150 billion. Aware that many white Delta politicians had once opposed antipoverty programs, Congressman Mike Espy told reporters, "When the money was available back in the '60s, we had so much obstruction to these kind of things, and that's why we never had it. There were people who did not want the situation to change. Now that the people have come together, the money is in short supply."[69]

By the 1990s, life in some Delta urban areas resembled that in the northern ghettoes from which the Delta Ministry had intended to save black Mississippians. As plantation work had receded, African Americans had increasingly migrated to Delta towns. Some of the migrants moved into new federal housing. Fearing black political control, whites often sold their homes and left town. As whites departed, tax bases dropped and retail sales slumped. Stores geared to affluent whites closed, leaving vacant buildings and new establishments— used furniture and clothing shops, small groceries, juke joints, and storefront churches—that catered to a low-income population. Social problems associated with northern ghettoes, such as high levels of armed violence, burglary, drug abuse, and gang warfare, became common. Several small Delta towns, including Drew, Moorhead, Rosedale, and Sunflower, imposed nightly curfews with the intention of keeping youngsters off the streets and out of trouble.[70]

The situation was perhaps worst in Greenville, where the Ministry had begun its first Delta program. Journalist Richard Schweid reported in 1992 that "gangs, supported by crack sales, have sprung up in Greenville, and cocaine arrests are constantly being made throughout the Delta, in small towns with populations of only a couple thousand." Greenville experienced "drive-by gang killings" and had "the second highest per capita crime rate in the South, next to Miami." Opportunities for African American children were extremely limited. Activist Malcolm Walls told Schweid that "The public school system in Greenville is terrible— it's 90 percent black and totally underfunded, while the white kids go to private academies."[71]

Scaled back in the early 1970s, the Delta Ministry targeted its efforts toward furnishing technical support for selected local communities and organizations. It provided essential aid to Robert Clark, Mound Bayou, Bolton, and Mayersville. Affected by a growing national mood of economic conservatism and declension from the African American struggle for equality, the NCC's member denominations and the federal government increasingly withdrew the financial support that had made so many of the Ministry's projects possible. Although the Ministry lacked the resources to engage in community organizing or to promote significant economic development, its legacy could be seen in the Delta Foundation and in the growth of black elected officials in the Delta, some of whom had been directly associated with the Ministry. Owen Brooks and several former Ministry staff continued their work in Mississippi during the 1980s and 1990s. Unfortunately, the

Delta remained beset by many of the same problems that the Ministry had been founded to address thirty-five years earlier. Poverty, high infant mortality, inferior schools, adult illiteracy, high unemployment, a poorly educated and low-skilled workforce, and lack of industry continued to characterize the region, and young black adults continued to migrate north in search of opportunity. New problems, such as drugs and gang warfare, had also arisen. However, the persistence of deprivation in the Delta should not obscure the Ministry's tenacious long-term efforts and positive contributions.

CHAPTER ELEVEN

Conclusion

In the tradition of SNCC and CORE, and inspired by the biblical call to a servant ministry, the Delta Ministry sought to empower the poor, oppressed, and disenfranchised and to enable them to realize self-chosen goals. Specifically, the NCC charged the Ministry with facilitating relief, community building, literacy, economic development, and reconciliation in the Delta, with shorter-lived projects in Hattiesburg and McComb. The Ministry acted as an enabler rather than as a leadership organization. Content to work with and form alliances with other civil rights and advocacy groups, to create and then set free new organizations and enterprises, and to take a role behind the scenes, the Delta Ministry seldom received the credit its efforts deserved. The Ministry was significantly involved in many of Mississippi's key civil rights incidents and issues in the second half of the 1960s, became the largest civil rights organization in the South, and survived, in attenuated form, beyond the decade as the only widely focused group concerned with the state's impoverished African American population.

From the outset, the Delta Ministry lacked adequate finances to fulfill every facet of its ambitious mandate, and throughout its history, it endured periodic budget crises that restricted its activities and curtailed some of its programs. Even if the Delta Ministry had been fully funded for the ten-year operation originally intended by the NCC, it would have encountered considerable difficulty in achieving its goals because of their magnitude and because of opposition from white Mississippians. As it was, the Ministry never enjoyed sufficient funding from the NCC's member denominations, and without crucial support from members of the WCC, the Ministry would not have survived its first years.

Despite its financial problems, the Delta Ministry had a significant impact on Mississippi, particularly the Delta, and should be credited with some important achievements. With the withdrawal of SNCC and CORE from Mississippi in the mid-1960s, the Ministry became the largest civil rights organization in the state, and by 1967 it had more field staff than any other group operating in the South. Hodding Carter III, a persistent critic of the Ministry, conceded in 1968 that "there has been no other [more] effective civil rights and poverty organization in Mississippi. They have been a key factor in pulling in federal money to Mississippi[,] and they have really been the only organization working with the very poor."[1]

The Ministry widened distribution of federal surplus commodities to all of Mississippi's counties by pressuring state and federal government. It induced counties that had not joined the commodities program to partake by threatening to undertake distribution. By participating in the occupation of the Greenville Air Force Base, the Ministry drew federal attention to the plight of the poor and forced Mississippi to implement Operation Help. When Mississippi counties switched from federal surplus commodities to food stamps, the Ministry began a long and ultimately successful campaign to increase their availability to more of the poverty-stricken. In some areas, the Ministry also trained food stamp recipients to use their stamps efficiently and to ensure balanced, nutritious meals. In the second half of the 1960s, the Ministry dispensed food and clothing, donated by sympathetic denominations and individuals, and in 1982 it established a cooperative grocery store for Greenville's poor.

In several ways, the Ministry played a key role in expanding health care for tens of thousands of impoverished Mississippians. It supported the work of the MCHR and Jack Geiger's pioneering work in Holmes County, which became the model for neighborhood community health centers in Mississippi and across the nation. The Ministry worked with local communities, Tom Levin, and OEO to develop CDGM, which provided health checks for the young children it served. DOC and Freedom City, both created by the Delta Ministry, provided medical examinations and health advice for their participants. Owen Brooks conducted fieldwork for what became the Tufts-Delta Health Center in Mound Bayou, and he worked with the Mound Bayou Community Hospital. Between them, the two facilities provided health care for thousands of poor people in four counties who could not otherwise have afforded it. Brooks assisted in the merger of the programs in 1972, and he played a major part in their campaigns to maintain funding against the opposition of Governor William Waller and white Mississippi health officials.

Aware that African Americans needed political influence if they were to make progress against hostile white-elected state governments and governors, the Delta Ministry consistently engaged in citizenship education training, voter registration, and the development of local leaders as part of its community development mandate. It registered more than seventy thousand African Americans, trained many black political candidates, assisted black elected officials, and helped develop local leaders, such as Thelma Barnes, L. C. Dorsey, and Kermit Stanton. In the late 1960s and 1970s, the Ministry provided essential research and administrative aid to Robert Clark, Mississippi's first African American legislator since Reconstruction. Although progress in electing blacks to office was slow, the problem reflected less deficiencies in the Delta Ministry's approach than the strength of white opposition, divisions in the African American community, and political inexperience among black voters. Even so, since 1971, Mississippi has had more black elected officials than any other state. Extensive and lengthy litigation overturned Mississippi's discriminatory electoral and legislative mechanisms in the late 1970s and early 1980s, enabling the number of black officials to increase significantly and the Delta to elect Mississippi's first black congressman since 1883, Mike Espy. Nevertheless, African Americans continued to be underrepresented at all levels of the political system.

Education was another aspect of the Ministry's community building effort. Whatever its difficulties with financial accounting and record keeping, CDGM served thousands of deprived children in innovative education programs and provided satisfying and comparatively well paid jobs for hundreds of unskilled African Americans. Delta Ministry staffers worked hard to challenge continued school segregation and discrimination in education by encouraging black parents to file lawsuits and gathering evidence that aided litigation. The Ministry achieved a major success by uncovering Mississippi's misuse of funds under Title I of the Elementary and Secondary Education Act and forcing redress. Despite the Ministry's efforts, even in the 1980s and 1990s public schools in heavily black districts often lacked adequate facilities. Delta whites often educated their children in private schools but, for the most part, maintained control of the public system, which remained underfunded.

The Delta Ministry's efforts to initiate a large-scale literacy program for adults through the Diebold Group failed. Unwilling to wait for Diebold to refine its program, the federal government instead chose to fund STAR, sponsored by the Catholic Diocese of Natchez-Jackson. In the late 1960s, DOC contributed to literacy training in a few areas by operating an adult education program.

Launched by the Delta Ministry in 1965, DOC spent two frustrating years pursuing federal and foundation financial support before it succeeded. Concerned primarily with equipping Freedom City residents with the skills to build their own houses and to provide job training for Delta residents, DOC never achieved sufficient funding to become a major program, and it later became dogged by poor administration and infighting.

To provide displaced agricultural workers with some source of income, in 1965 the Delta Ministry created Freedomcrafts, which developed into a series of cooperatives in different parts of Mississippi. Reliant on CDGM and northern sympathizers for its markets, Freedomcrafts cooperatives began to fail when those markets dried up in the late 1960s and early 1970s.

Convinced that only profit-driven, market-oriented businesses could prosper, Harry Bowie worked with other community organizations in Mississippi to create the Delta Foundation in 1969. Designed to ensure long-term economic development, the foundation provided start-up funds for small businesses that could not otherwise obtain funding and were labor-intensive. The foundation generated six thousand jobs in its first twenty-six years. However, its efforts, like those of the Delta Ministry, made little impression on the Delta's massive unemployment problem, which was caused by large-scale agricultural change and the unwillingness of most industries to locate plants in the Delta. Without a massive injection of federal resources and investment from industry, the Ministry could have achieved little more.

Apart from problems caused by constraints on its budget, white opposition, and macroeconomic forces, the Delta Ministry experienced failures produced by its own strategic mistakes. The Ministry's support for the striking tractor drivers at Tribbett and the fledgling MFLU in 1965 failed to recognize the economic reality that agricultural strikes had little chance of success because mechanization and chemicals had massively reduced demand for labor. The Delta Ministry's efforts to support and encourage economic self-help, such as handicraft cooperatives and Freedom City, although understandable given the lack of obvious alternatives for those driven off the land, inevitably failed because of low market demand and the low skill levels of the workers involved. Conceived initially as a form of kibbutz, Freedom City arose in practice out of a desperate need to provide a home for displaced African Americans who had been temporarily housed at Mount Beulah. Although some of Freedom City's uniformly poorly educated and unskilled inhabitants overcame the burdens placed on them by a lifetime of deprivation and dependence, most were unable to adjust to Freedom City's demands for self-support and self-governance.

Most of the Ministry's efforts and the gains it made were directed to and intended to benefit the African American poor. The Ministry had far less success in reaching out to the white community and failed in its aim of reconciling the races. Even during its planning stage, the Ministry faced opposition from many white Mississippi and southern clergymen in the NCC. Mississippi bishops John M. Allin of the Protestant Episcopal Church and Edward J. Pendergrass of the Methodists waged extensive campaigns to undermine the Delta Ministry.

After its launch, the Ministry repeatedly tried to explain its mission and win support from Mississippi's white denominational leaders and local churches, but these early attempts met mostly with hostility and rejection. In part, the effort reflected a certain naïveté among the NCC that communication and support could easily be created on the basis of what those involved in creating the Ministry saw as a self-evident need. While white churchmen's frequent charges that the Delta Ministry ignored them cannot be substantiated, its staff's largely adverse early experiences with the state's white clergymen hardened attitudes toward the white Christian population.

At the same time, many Ministry staffers had little understanding of the strong segregationist pressures that Mississippi's white denominational leaders and clergymen faced from their churches, notwithstanding the fact that some church officials undoubtedly shared a commitment to Jim Crow. Bishop Paul Moore Jr. later confessed that some NCC ministers who served in Mississippi displayed a kind of self-righteousness based on the morality of their cause that led them to exhibit little patience with those who disagreed with the reformers or their methods. Mississippi's white clergy conceived of reconciliation in terms of establishing cordial relations between the races that left in abeyance the issue of entrenched racial discrimination, while the Delta Ministry argued correctly that genuine reconciliation between the races could occur only under conditions of racial equality.

However, the Ministry alienated even the more moderate elements of white Mississippi, such as Hodding Carter II and III and increasingly the NAACP, by supporting direct action and the MFDP. The Delta Ministry compounded the problem by being disingenuous about its relationship with the Freedom Democrats. Although the NCC barred the Ministry from engaging in partisan political activity, in practice the Ministry operated a de facto alliance with the MFDP. Regarding the party as a political successor to SNCC and representative of the interests and wishes of most African Americans, the Delta Ministry failed to recognize that however true this may have been in 1964, the party subsequently failed to create a statewide organization and maintain widespread support. Although the Ministry also worked on behalf of non-MFDP black candidates, such as NAACP leader Charles Evers, and cooperated with the NAACP in voter registration drives, the group still retained a misplaced faith in the representative nature of the MFDP.

Brooks's continued faith in the MFDP, along with that of the other college-educated northerners with whom he worked mostly closely in the Delta Ministry—Harry Bowie, Rims Barber, and Charley Horwitz—contributed to the developing alienation of the remaining, mostly indigenous black Ministry staff. Brooks and his core staff favored independent black politics and thought that experience justified their belief that middle-class African American and white moderates would not represent the interests of the black poor, with whom the Delta Ministry had always been most concerned. The core staff believed, as Black Power advocates proclaimed, that the black community first needed to develop its own economic and political power base before it could enter into alliances with other groups, such as poor whites. Brooks focused much of his effort on securing federal and foundation resources to improve the infrastructure of Mound Bayou, one of Mississippi's few all-black towns. The new direction he charted required the core staff to provide the technical assistance necessary to secure resources to develop such black community institutions as schools and businesses and to challenge discriminatory practices by federal and state agencies.

Indigenous staff, who coalesced as the Concerned Staff of the Delta Ministry, were far more willing to work with the NAACP and with black and white moderates. Group members accused Brooks of neglecting their abilities and projects, and they resented his overbearing, autocratic management style. The Concerned Staff charged Brooks with denying them positions of leadership for which they believed they were suited and with relying instead on northern, college-educated staff to undertake the technical-support roles that had become the Ministry's new direction after 1966. While Brooks and his core staff focused on technical issues and joint efforts with other community advocacy groups to address statewide problems, black indigenous staff, who, for the most part, possessed limited education, continued to work on local projects.

The split within Delta Ministry ranks was already well advanced when the 1971 budget cuts brought the Ministry's division into the open. With the National Council's agreement, Brooks terminated most of the indigenous staff and decided to concentrate the Ministry's efforts on the technical support role that he and the core staff had developed. Mississippians left on the staff resigned in protest when the NCC refused to redress the grievances of the Concerned Staff or to restore their employment.

With just four core staff members—Brooks, Bowie, Barber, and Horwitz—and a much-reduced program, the Delta Ministry focused on technical and research support concerning politics, economic development, education, and welfare. Given its shrunken staff base and budget, the Ministry performed its role well. It helped secure grants and loans that developed the ageing, dilapidated infrastructure of Mound Bayou, Bolton, and Mayersville. The Ministry also continued to provide Robert Clark with essential assistance.

However, the board of directors that replaced the Commission on the Delta Ministry in 1972 suffered from the same chronic absenteeism that had undermined its predecessor. The greater representation accorded native Mississippians also weakened rather than strengthened the Ministry. Many board members regarded the Delta Ministry simply as a source of funds for their favored projects. Reflecting a national disengagement from racial issues and its own financial difficulties, the National Council ended its direct control of and financial responsibility for the Delta Ministry by according it the status of a related movement. Some denominations continued to support the Delta Ministry and to contribute to its reduced budgets and projects. Federal grants, the other major source for the Ministry's projects and spinoff organizations, became increasingly scarce during the 1970s in response to a more conservative fiscal climate, widespread disenchantment with government activism, and mounting national indifference to the plight of African Americans.

By 1977, Bowie, Horwitz, and Barber had left the Delta Ministry because of its financial difficulties. Thereafter, the Ministry frequently functioned as little more than a one-man operation maintained by Owen Brooks. L. C. Dorsey worked with Brooks on prison and criminal justice issues, but she too left the Ministry in 1983 and pursued a doctorate in social work. Dorsey later returned to Mississippi and became director of the Delta Health Center. Brooks and several key former Delta Ministry staff, including Barber, Barnes, Bowie, and Roger Smith, remained active in the state, working on behalf of the poor and excluded.

Although the Ministry had contributed to a degree of significant change in Mississippi, particularly in black political participation and representation, and had helped improve welfare and educational provision and access, many of the problems it had been founded to address remained. At the turn of the century, the Delta remained bedeviled by poverty, illiteracy, health problems, poor educational opportunities, a low skills base, and little industry, while drug abuse and gang violence brought new problems to the region. That the Delta Ministry could not solve the Delta's predicament should not be surprising given its magnitude, but the Ministry helped improve the lives of or at least lessen the burden for many thousands of the region's inhabitants. Given the resources available to it, the Ministry could have done little more.

NOTES

Abbreviations

AEDNY	Archives of the Episcopal Diocese of New York, Cathedral of St. John the Divine
Barber Papers	Rims Barber Papers, L. Zenobia Coleman Library, Tougaloo College
Beech Papers	Robert L. Beech Papers, Bovey, Minnesota
Bishop's Office	Bishop's Office, J. B. Cain Archives of Mississippi Methodism, Millsaps-Wilson Library, Millsaps College
Blake Papers	Eugene Carson Blake Papers, Presbyterian Historical Society
Board of National Missions (PCUSA) Records	Board of National Missions Records (PCUSA)—Division of Church Strategy and Development Records, 1871–1972, Presbyterian Historical Society
Bowie Papers	Harry J. Bowie Papers, Wisconsin Historical Society
Bunche Oral History Collection	Ralph J. Bunche Oral History Collection, Oral History Department, Moorland-Spingarn Research Center, Howard University
Carter Papers	Hodding Carter and Betty Werlein Carter Papers, Mitchell Memorial Library, Mississippi State University
Church and Society Records, UMC	Church and Society Records, United Methodist Church Archives—GCAH, Drew University
CORAR Records	Board of Christian Education—Commission on Religion and Race (CORAR) and Board of National Missions—Council on Church and Race (COCAR) Records, 1963–71, Presbyterian Historical Society
Cox Collection	A. Eugene Cox Collection, Mitchell Memorial Library, Mississippi State University
Dabbs Papers	James McBride Dabbs Papers, #3816, Southern Historical Collection, Wilson Library, University of North Carolina at Chapel Hill
DCLM	Division of Christian Life and Mission
Delta Ministry Papers, Atlanta	Delta Ministry Papers, Martin Luther King Jr. Center for Nonviolent Social Change
Delta Ministry Papers, Starkville	Delta Ministry Papers, Mitchell Memorial Library, Mississippi State University
Derian Papers	Patt Derian Papers, Mitchell Memorial Library, Mississippi State University
ESCRU Papers	Episcopal Society for Cultural and Racial Unity Papers, Martin Luther King Jr. Center for Nonviolent Social Change

Field and Mulford Collection	Connie Field and Marilyn Mulford Collection, L. Zenobia Coleman Library, Tougaloo College
Grigg Papers	Wendell R. Grigg Papers, North Carolina Baptist Historical Collection, Z. Smith Reynolds Library, Wake Forest University
Hamer Papers	Fannie Lou Hamer Papers, Amistad Research Center, Tulane University
Henry Papers	Aaron Edd Henry Papers, L. Zenobia Coleman Library, Tougaloo College
Holloman Papers	Garland H. Holloman Papers, Mitchell Memorial Library, Mississippi State University
Horwitz Papers	Charles Horwitz Papers, L. Zenobia Coleman Library, Tougaloo College
Humphrey Papers	John D. Humphrey Papers, Mitchell Memorial Library, Mississippi State University
Johnson Family Papers	Paul B. Johnson Family Papers, McCain Library and Archives, University of Southern Mississippi
King Papers	Edwin King Papers, L. Zenobia Coleman Library, Tougaloo College
Levin Papers	Tom Levin Papers, Martin Luther King Jr. Center for Nonviolent Social Change
MFDP Papers	Mississippi Freedom Democratic Party Papers, Martin Luther King Jr. Center for Nonviolent Social Change
MOHC	Mississippi Oral History Collection, L. Zenobia Coleman Library, Tougaloo College
Montreat	Department of History, Presbyterian Church (U.S.A.), Montreat, North Carolina
NCC Archives	National Council of Churches Archives, Presbyterian Historical Society
Neigh Papers	Kenneth G. Neigh Papers, Speer Library, Princeton Theological Seminary
Romaine Papers	Anne Romaine Papers, Martin Luther King Jr. Center for Nonviolent Social Change
Reuther and Carliner Collection	UAW International Affairs Department, Victor Reuther and Lewis Carliner Collection, Wayne State University
SCLC Papers	Southern Christian Leadership Conference Papers, Martin Luther King Jr. Center for Nonviolent Social Change
SNCC Papers	Student Nonviolent Coordinating Committee Papers, Martin Luther King Jr. Center for Nonviolent Social Change
SOHP	Southern Oral History Program
Thomas Papers	Arthur C. Thomas Papers, Martin Luther King Jr. Center for Nonviolent Social Change
UCMS Papers	United Christian Missionary Society Papers, Disciples of Christ Historical Society
UMC	United Methodist Church
Wacker Papers	Daniel J. Wacker Papers, Wisconsin Historical Society

WHS   Wisconsin Historical Society
Winham Papers   Alfred R. Winham Papers, Martin Luther King Jr. Center for
     Nonviolent Social Change

CHAPTER ONE. The Origins and Creation of the Delta Ministry

1. *National Council of the Churches of Christ in the U.S.A.;* Findlay, *Church People,* 13–17, 22–31, 33–38, 48–65, 77; "Proposal for a Program of Community Development among the Residents of the Delta Area of the State of Mississippi," n.d., no folder, box 5, Thomas Papers; "Statement Adopted by the General Board, National Council of Churches, May 19, 1954, Chicago, Illinois Re Decision of the U.S. Supreme Court on Segregation in the Public Schools," folder 4, box 15, and Robert W. Spike, "Report of the Executive Director to the Commission on Religion and Race of the National Council of Churches," July 26, 1963, 1–5, folder 4, box 15, and minutes, Commission on Religion and Race, NCC, October 22, 1963, 3–5, 8–9, and exhibit B, folder 8, box 15, series 2, Reuther and Carliner Collection.

2. Haggerty and Thomson, eds., *National Council,* 63, 87; Findlay, *Church People,* 28–29.

3. *National Council of the Churches of Christ in the U.S.A.;* Haggerty and Thomson, eds., *National Council,* 87; Kirstein, "What the NCC Is and Does," 42.

4. "The Rev. Dr. Jon L. Regier," folder 125, box 115, SNCC Papers; H. J. Pratt, *Liberalization,* 37, 264.

5. R. W. Spike, *Civil Rights Involvement,* 10; Findlay, *Church People,* 29–30.

6. Noble, "Delta Ministry," 139–40, 143; R. W. Spike, *Civil Rights Involvement,* 6; R. W. Spike, "Gospel, World, and Church"; *National Council of the Churches of Christ in the U.S.A.;* Arthur C. Thomas to Paul Moore Jr., February 1, 1965, folder 42, box 12, Delta Ministry Papers, Atlanta; Sumner, *Episcopal Church's History,* 135; Findlay, *Church People,* 30.

7. Williams, *Where;* Williams, *What;* Cox, *Secular City;* Cox, "*Secular City* 25 Years Later," 1028; Wieser, ed., *Planning;* Noble, "Delta Ministry," 139–43; Findlay, *Church People,* 30.

8. Williams, *Where,* 24, 31–34; Cox, *Secular City,* 126; Cox, "*Secular City* 25 Years Later," 1025–26 (quotation on p. 1026); Silk, "Rise," 295–96; Noble, "Delta Ministry," 141–43.

9. Cox, "*Secular City* 25 Years Later," 1027–28; Findlay, *Church People,* 30, 44 n.69; Cook, *Sweet Land,* 98–108.

10. Cook, *Sweet Land,* 98, 112–37.

11. "Statement Adopted by the General Board, National Council of Churches, May 19, 1954, Chicago, Illinois Re Decision of the U.S. Supreme Court on Segregation in the Public Schools," folder 4, box 15, series 2, Reuther and Carliner Collection; "Resolution on the Sit-in Demonstrations," June 2, 1960, folder 511, box 6, Grigg Papers; Fey, "Freedom Rides," 766–77; Haselden, "Religion and Race," 133–35; "An Appeal to the Conscience of the American People," 135; Ahmann, ed., *Race;* Findlay, *Church People,* 22–23, 25–26, 32–33; T. Branch, *Parting the Waters,* 630–31.

12. Haselden, "Religion and Race," 134; M. L. King Jr., *Why We Can't Wait,* 47–95 (first quotation on p. 92); H. J. Pratt, *Liberalization,* 158 (third quotation), 160–61 (second quotation on p. 161).

13. *Minutes of the General Assembly of the Presbyterian Church in the United States of America,* 1963, 141–42 (quotation on p. 142); H. J. Pratt, *Liberalization,* 161; Cook, *Sweet Land,* 133; Findlay, *Church People,* 33, 35. For an account of Blake's life, see Brackenridge, *Eugene Carson Blake.*

14. R. W. Spike, *Civil Rights Involvement,* 9–10 (quotations on p. 9); *New York Times,* May

26, 1963; H. J. Pratt, *Liberalization*, 162; Noble, "Delta Ministry," 3; P. Spike, *Photographs*, 31; T. Branch, *Parting the Waters*, 809–13; Schlesinger, *Robert Kennedy*, 355–60.

15. R. W. Spike, *Civil Rights Involvement*, 10; H. J. Pratt, *Liberalization*, 162; "A Report of the President's Temporary Committee of Six on Race," 1–4 (first and third quotations on p. 3; second quotation on p. 1), folder 125, box 115, SNCC Papers; minutes, Commission on Religion and Race, NCC, January 16, 1964, exhibit A, folder 10, box 5, series 2, Reuther and Carliner Collection.

16. "A Report of the President's Temporary Committee of Six on Race," 4, folder 125, box 115, SNCC Papers; minutes, Commission on Religion and Race, NCC, June 28, 1963, 1, folder 2, box 15, minutes, Commission on Religion and Race, NCC, October 22, 1963, p. 1, folder 8, box 15, and minutes, Commission on Religion and Race, NCC, January 16, 1964, 1–3, folder 10, box 15, series 2, Reuther and Carliner Collection; Robert W. Spike, "Report of the Commission on Religion and Race," NCC, October 14, 1963, 2, folder "Staff Meetings," box 3, Thomas Papers; R. W. Spike, *Civil Rights Involvement*, 10; *New York Times*, February 15, 1964; Findlay, *Church People*, 35.

17. Memorandum, James C. Moore to Robert W. Spike, September 12, 1963, 1–2, RG 95, folder 16, box 15, Blake Papers; S. C. Rose, "N.C.C. Visits Clarksdale," 1104–6; S. C. Rose, "NCC Visit to Clarksdale Poses Hard Questions," 28–29; R. W. Spike, *Civil Rights Involvement*, 10, 12; *Clarksdale Press Register*, August 8, 1963; Dittmer, *Local People*, 120–23, 165–67, 176–77.

18. Minutes, Commission on Religion and Race, NCC, June 28, 1963, 9, folder 125, box 115, SNCC Papers; *Clarksdale Press Register*, August 8, 1963; R. W. Spike, *Civil Rights Involvement*, 12 (quotation).

19. P. Spike, *Photographs*, 31 (quotations); *New York Times*, October 18, 1966; Findlay, *Church People*, 35–36.

20. R. W. Spike, *Civil Rights Involvement*, 6–8, 11, 14–16 (first quotation on p. 16); Robert W. Spike, "Report of the Executive Director to the Commission on Religion and Race of the National Council of Churches," July 26, 1963, 1–5, folder 4, box 15, Robert W. Spike, "Report of the Executive Director," September 5, 1963, 1–6, 9 (second quotation), folder 7, box 15, and minutes, Commission on Religion and Race, NCC, October 22, 1963, 3–5, folder 8, box 15, series 2, Reuther and Carliner Collection; Robert W. Spike, "Report of the Commission on Religion and Race," October 14, 1963, 4, 9, folder "Staff Meetings," box 3, Thomas Papers; *New York Times*, August 29, 1963; R. W. Spike, *Freedom Revolution*, 106–8; Hedgeman, *Trumpet Sounds*, 168–82, 194–95; H. J. Pratt, *Liberalization*, 168–72; Clark, "National Council of Churches' Commission," 256–57, 262; Brackenridge, *Eugene Carson Blake*, 103–4; Findlay, *Church People*, 48–65.

21. Andrew J. Young to Robert W. Spike, April 25, 1961, folder 5, box 30, Highlander Research and Education Center Records, WHS; Andrew J. Young to Martin Luther King Jr., Hosea Williams, Albert Sampson, and Bob Green (first quotation), n.d., folder 9, box 43, "Voter Registration in the Mississippi Delta," n.d., folder 8, box 141, "Mississippi Report SCLC Field Secretary," January 1963, folder 5, box 141, Andrew J. Young to the Reverend and Mrs. James Bevel, February 21, 1963, folder 5, box 141, Andrew J. Young to Truman Douglass and Wesley A. Hotchkiss, June 10, 1964, 1–3 (second quotation on p. 1), folder 14, box 136, Andrew J. Young to Wesley A. Hotchkiss, July 20, 1964, folder 14, box 136, and memorandum, Wesley A. Hotchkiss to Truman B. Douglass, August 14, 1964, folder 14, box 136, SCLC Papers; Johns, *Refinement*; *Memphis Commercial Appeal*, May 13, 1968; Noble, "Delta

Ministry," 50; Fairclough, *To Redeem the Soul*, 68–70, 91–92; Garrow, *Bearing the Cross*, 150–51, 161, 163–64, 197, 225; Dittmer, *Local People*, 90–138; Carson, *In Struggle*, 45–50.

22. Memorandum, Henry A. McCanna to David R. Hunter, November 20, 1964, 2 (quotation), RG 5, folder 9, box 16, NCC Archives; Findlay, *Church People*, 113–14; Dittmer, *Local People*, 90–115.

23. "Proposal for a Program of Community Development among the Residents of the Delta Area of the State of Mississippi," n.d., 4–5 (quotation on p. 4), no folder, box 5, Thomas Papers; Henry A. McCanna to Hal DeCell, June 2, 1964, folder 5, box II-A, Cox Collection; memorandum, Henry A. McCanna to David R. Hunter, November 20, 1964, RG 5, folder 9, box 16, NCC Archives; "Report of the Executive Director," Commission on Religion and Race, NCC, January 16, 1964, 2, folder "Staff Meetings," box 3, Thomas Papers; "What Is COFO?" COFO publication 6, 2, folder 199, box 103, SNCC Papers; Hilton, *Delta Ministry*, 32–34; Dittmer, *Local People*, 118–20; Meier and Rudwick, *CORE*, 178–79, 269–72. The eight denominations that had pastors or judicatorial executives at the LeMoyne meeting were the Methodist Church, the Lutheran Church in America, the Protestant Episcopal Church, the Church of the Brethren, the American Baptist Convention, the UPCUSA, the United Church of Christ, and the Mennonite Brethren ("Proposal for a Program of Community Development among the Residents of the Delta Area of the State of Mississippi," n.d., 4–5, no folder, box 5, Thomas Papers). The white Methodist Church in Mississippi sent only representatives, rather than its highest officials, to the meeting at LeMoyne College. The PCUS declined to send any representatives ("Report of the National Council of Churches Study Committee," 8, folder "Anti-Communism, 1952–1964 and undated," no box, Holloman Papers; Patrick D. Miller to Jon L. Regier, April 29, 1964, folder "Delta Current—up," box 5, Thomas Papers).

24. Jon L. Regier to Patrick D. Miller, May 5, 1964, folder "Delta Current—up," box 5, and "Proposal for a Program of Community Development among the Residents of the Delta Area of the State of Mississippi," n.d., no folder, box 5, Thomas Papers; Hilton, *Delta Ministry*, 34.

25. Cobb, *Most Southern Place*, viii, 3–5, 82, 98–124, 154–56, 184–205, 255, 266; Alewine, "Changing Characteristics," 29–37; Noble, "Delta Ministry," 37; "Proposal for a Program of Community Development among the Residents of the Delta Area of the State of Mississippi," n.d., no folder, box 5, Thomas Papers. Ten counties—Bolivar, Coahoma, Humphreys, Issaquena, Leflore, Quitman, Sharkey, Sunflower, Tunica, and Washington— lie entirely within the Yazoo-Mississippi Delta. Holmes and Tallahatchie Counties lie partially in the Delta (Cobb, *Most Southern Place*, 335 n.1; Dittmer, *Local People*, 130).

26. "The Mississippi Delta (Part I)," COFO publication 2, October 1963, 4, folder 150, box 99, and "The Mississippi Delta (Part II)," COFO publication 3, November 1963, 3–4, tables 3, 6, folder 150, box 99, SNCC Papers; Alewine, "Changing Characteristics," 32; "Proposal for a Program of Community Development among the Residents of the Delta Area of the State of Mississippi," n.d., 1–2, no folder, box 5, Thomas Papers; Noble, "Delta Ministry," 33, 35, 37, 41–42; Cobb, *Most Southern Place*, 254, 262–67.

27. "Mississippi Delta (Part II)," COFO publication 3, November 1963, 3, tables 3, 4, folder 150, box 99, SNCC Papers.

28. "Mississippi Delta (Part I)," COFO publication 2, October 1963, 11, folder 150, box 99, SNCC Papers; Noble, "Delta Ministry," 49; Lewis, "Negro Voter," 336–39; Bass and DeVries,

Transformation, 192, 203 (quotations); Garrow, *Protest at Selma,* 11; Colby, "Voting Rights Act," 125–26, 128.

29. Minutes, Commission on Religion and Race, NCC, November 5, 1964, 4, RG 6, folder 14, box 2, NCC Archives; "Report of the Executive Director," Commission on Religion and Race, NCC, January 16, 1964, 2–3, folder "Staff Meetings," box 3, Thomas Papers; "W.C.C. Sends Mission," 660; E. King, "Mississippi," 79 (inconsistent pagination); *Jackson Clarion-Ledger,* December 19, 1963; R. H. Edwin Espy to W. A. Visser 't Hooft, January 2, 1964, RG 5, folder 33, box 16, R. H. Edwin Espy to W. A. Visser 't Hooft, January 9, 1964, RG 6, folder 16, box 2, and W. A. Visser 't Hooft to R. H. Edwin Espy, January 15, 1964 (quotation), RG 6, folder 16, box 2, NCC Archives.

30. *Information Bulletin* [Mississippi Association of Methodist Ministers and Laymen] 1 (March 1964): 4; "General Board Action Concerning *A Ministry among the Residents of the Delta Area of the State of Mississippi,*" February 26, 1964, 1, (first quotation) and exhibit A, 1–5 (second quotation on p. 3; third quotation on p. 4), folder 14, box 12, Delta Ministry Papers, Atlanta; NCC press release, March 3, 1964, folder 125, box 115, SNCC Papers; Findlay, *Church People,* 48–65.

31. "General Board Action Concerning *A Ministry among the Residents of the Delta Area of the State of Mississippi,*" February 26, 1964, 1, (fourth quotation on p. 1) and exhibit A, 1–5 (first and second quotations on p. 4; third quotation on p. 5), folder 14, box 12, Delta Ministry Papers, Atlanta; John M. Allin to John B. Morris, July 6, 1964, folder 39, box 57, ESCRU Papers; *Jackson Daily News,* December 4, 1965.

32. Jon L. Regier to A. Dale Fiers, June 10, 1964, folder "Commission on Mount Beulah Regarding Mississippi Delta Ministry," RG 4, UCMS Papers, box DHM 9; "Progress Report to the General Board of the National Council of Churches on the Delta Ministry," June 5, 1964, 1–2, folder "National Council of Churches (Delta Ministry)," Bishop's Office.

33. R. W. Spike, "Report of the Executive Director," Commission on Religion and Race, NCC, September 5, 1963, 2–3, folder 7, box 15, John M. Pratt, "Report on the Release of 57 Prisoners in Mississippi," August 20, 1963, folder 6, box 15, and John M. Pratt, "Report on Legal Procedures and Bail," February 20, 1964, folder 9, box 15, series 2, Reuther and Carliner Collection; memorandum, John M. Pratt to "Representatives of Denominational Religion and Race Staffs," October 21, 1963, folder 125, box 115, SNCC Papers; Findlay, *Church People,* 79–80.

34. "Statement by Rev. Dr. Jon L. Regier, Chief of Staff, Emergency Commission on Religion and Race, National Council of Churches," June 18, 1963, folder 125, box 115, SNCC Papers; Dittmer, *Local People,* 118–19.

35. Meier and Rudwick, *CORE,* 269; Dittmer, *Local People,* 157–65; Fairclough, *To Redeem the Soul,* 194–95.

36. Sinsheimer, "Freedom Vote," 217–44; Dittmer, *Local People,* 200–207; Carson, *In Struggle,* 46, 77–78, 97–98; Walton, *Black Political Parties,* 91; R. W. Spike, *Civil Rights Involvement,* 13 (quotation). Bob Moses' background and role in the civil rights movement in Mississippi are discussed in Burner, *And Gently He Shall Lead Them.*

37. Robert J. Stone, "Interim Report: Clergy Participation with Council of Federated Organizations, Hattiesburg, Mississippi," February 18, 1964, RG 301.9, folder 17, box 8, minutes of Adjunct Staff Council of Commission on Religion and Race, UPCUSA, February 26, 1964, 7, RG 301.9, folder 7, box 1, Gayraud S. Wilmore to Robert W. Spike, March 5, 1964,

RG 301.9, folder 11, box 8, Executive Committee meeting of the Commission on Religion and Race, UPCUSA, May 6, 1964, 5, RG 301.9, folder 9, box 1, and "Report of the Executive Director and Staff," June 1, 1964, 2, RG 301.9, folder 16, box 1, CORAR Records; John M. Pratt, "Report on Legal Procedures and Bail," February 20, 1964, 2–3, folder 9, box 15, and minutes, Commission on Religion and Race, NCC, February 21, 1964, 5–6, folder 12, box 15, series 2, Reuther and Carliner Collection; Robert W. Spike, "Report to the Commission on Religion and Race," February 21, 1964, 4, folder "Commission Meetings," box 3, Thomas Papers; "Churchmen and the Challenge," *Commission on Religion and Race Reports* [NCC], vol. 1, no. 4, n.d.; Robert L. Beech, "Report and Evaluation, Hattiesburg, September 1964–September 1965," 1, folder 74, box 6, Delta Ministry Papers, Starkville; Minear, "Hattiesburg," 1115–16; Dittmer, *Local People,* 180–84, 219–24.

38. Gayraud S. Wilmore to Robert W. Spike, March 5, 1964, RG 301.9, folder 11, box 8, and "Report of the Executive Director and Staff," June 1, 1964, 2, RG 301.9, folder 16, box 1, CORAR Records; "Delta Ministry Fact Sheet," January 1965, appendix A, folder "Delta Ministry—Minutes, Budgets, Fact Sheets—1965," box 1, Humphrey Papers; minutes, Commission on Religion and Race, NCC, February 21, 1964, 3, 5, folder 12, box 15, and Arthur C. Thomas, "Report of the Associate Director of Community Action," June 29, 1964, folder 13, box 15, series 2, Reuther and Carliner Collection; Arthur C. Thomas, "Report to the Commission on Canton, Mississippi," n.d., folder "Commission Meetings," box 3, Thomas Papers; *Religion and Race Memo* [UPCUSA] 1 (April 27, 1964): 2; Greenberg, *Devil,* 27; Dittmer, *Local People,* 221–24; Meier and Rudwick, *CORE,* 274–75.

39. DeMuth, "Summer," 104; Sutherland, "Cat and Mouse Game," 106; Dittmer, *Local People,* 244; Carson, *In Struggle,* 118–21; Perlstein, "Teaching Freedom," 297–324; Meier and Rudwick, *CORE,* 270–71, 273.

40. Minutes, Commission on Religion and Race, NCC, January 16, 1964, 6, folder 10, box 15, minutes, Commission on Religion and Race, NCC, March 26, 1964, 3–4, folder 10, box 15, and John M. Pratt, "Report from the Counsel to the Commission on Religion and Race," June 29, 1964, folder 13, box 15, series 2, Reuther and Carliner Collection; Bruce Hanson and Arthur C. Thomas, "Report on the Commission's Role in Mississippi, Summer 1964," n.d., RG 6, folder 14, box 2, NCC Archives; Robert W. Spike, "The Report of the Executive Director to the Commission on Religion and Race," NCC, September 15, 1964, 1, folder "Proposals on Delta Ministry," box 3, Thomas Papers; *National Council of Churches' Commission on Religion and Race,* 7; "Summary Report Commission on Religion and Race, June 5, 1964–December 3, 1964," 1–4 (quotation on p. 3), folder "National Council of Churches (Delta Ministry)," Bishop's Office; "The Mississippi Summer Project and the NCC," *Commission on Religion and Race Reports* [NCC], vol. 1, no. 1, n.d.; "A Statement on the Mississippi Summer Program of the Commission on Religion and Race, National Council of Churches," n.d., folder 125, box 115, SNCC Papers; "Role of the National Council of Churches in the Mississippi Summer Project," 10–14.

41. Warren H. McKenna to Arthur Lichtenberger, August 17, 1964, folder 1, box 15, and Warren H. McKenna to "Vestry Wardens and Friends," December 1, 1964, folder 5, box 15, Delta Ministry Papers, Atlanta; "Delta Ministry Fact Sheet," January 1965, appendix A, folder "Delta Ministry—Minutes, Budgets, Fact Sheets—1965," box 1, Humphrey Papers; Arthur C. Thomas, "Report of the Associate Director of Community Action," June 29, 1964, 2, folder 13, box 15, series 2, Reuther and Carliner Collection; Owen H. Brooks,

interview by Robert Wright, September 24, 1968, 20, Bunche Oral History Collection; Shattuck, *Episcopalians and Race*, 92, 141.

42. Fruchter, "Mississippi," 76–77; Meier and Rudwick, *CORE*, 278–79, 394; Carson, *In Struggle*, 115–21; "General Board Action Concerning *A Ministry among the Residents of the Delta Area of the State of Mississippi*," February 26, 1964, exhibit 4, 1–5, folder 14, box 12, Delta Ministry Papers, Atlanta.

43. Carson, *In Struggle*, 149; Meier and Rudwick, *CORE*, 340–42.

44. Meier and Rudwick, *CORE*, 174; Dittmer, *Local People*, 246–52, 418; Carson, *In Struggle*, 117; Cagin and Dray, *We Are Not Afraid*. For a full-length study of the summer project, see N. Mills, *Like a Holy Crusade*. About eight hundred of the new African American registrants lived in Panola County, where a voter registration suit had eased the registration process by eliminating most of the sections of the application test (Warren, *Who Speaks*, 115).

45. Robert W. Spike, "Statement Presented to Credentials Committee of the 1964 Democratic National Convention," August 22, 1964, RG 5, folder 33, box 16, NCC Archives; Robert W. Spike, "The Report of the Executive Director to the Commission on Religion and Race," NCC, September 15, 1964, 3, folder "Proposals on Delta Ministry," box 3, Thomas Papers; Dittmer, *Local People*, 272–75, 279–83, 285–96; Walton, *Black Political Parties*, 80–81, 91–102; Warren, *Who Speaks*, 117 (quotation). For a history of the MFDP, see McLemore, "Mississippi Freedom Democratic Party."

46. Forman, *Making*, 390–95; Dittmer, *Local People*, 282–83, 296–302, 341–43, 498 n.9; Draper, "Mississippi Movement," 358–61; Henry with Curry, *Aaron Henry*, 184–97, 200; Holt, *Summer*, 168–76; Walton, *Black Political Parties*, 102–3, 114–15. According to historian Eric R. Burner, the NCC "intimated that it would cut off funding for MFDP and COFO programs if the Freedom Democrats did not go along" (*And Gently He Shall Lead Them*, 186). Some ideological differences later emerged between the MFDP and the NAACP, but they had little to do with class. While the MFDP opposed U.S. involvement in the Vietnam War and tended to favor independent black politics in the second half of the 1960s, the NAACP supported the war and preferred to work with moderate whites to reconstitute the Democratic Party in Mississippi (Lawson, *In Pursuit*, 93–94, 321 n.17).

47. P. Spike, *Photographs*, 85–86, 92–96; "Rough Minutes of a Meeting Called by the National Council of Churches to Discuss the Mississippi Project," September 18, 1964, folder 125, box 125, SNCC Papers; Minnis, "Mississippi Freedom Democratic Party," 268–72; Forman, *Making*, 396, 399–405; Findlay, *Church People*, 115–16, 132–33 n.12.

48. "Progress Report to the General Board of the National Council of Churches on the Delta Ministry," June 5, 1964, 1–3 (quotations on p. 2), folder "National Council of Churches (Delta Ministry)," Bishop's Office. Bruce Hilton, who authored an account of the Ministry after leaving its staff, wrote of the nine denominations that endorsed the Delta Ministry, "it eventually became clear that some of them had quite different ideas of how best to help the poor" (*Delta Ministry*, 36). The Southern Baptist Convention, the largest white denomination in Mississippi, was not a member of the NCC (Odle, "Southern Baptists," 1, 4).

49. John M. Allin to William L. Hargrave, May 20, 1964, folder "Education," box 3, Thomas Papers; John M. Allin to John B. Morris, July 6, 1964, folder 39, box 57, ESCRU Papers; *Hattiesburg American*, June 5, 1964 (quotation); "Mississippi Methodism," 6; Hilton, *Delta Ministry*, 35, 163–64; P. Moore Jr., *Take a Bishop*, 18.

50. Robert W. Spike to D. Dale Fiers, May 25, 1964, RG 4, folder "Mt. Beulah," box DHM 9, UCMS Papers; Jon L. Regier to A. Dale Fiers, June 10, 1964, and "Executive Session," June 16, 17, 1964, RG 4, folder "Commission on Mount Beulah Regarding Mississippi Delta Ministry," box DHM 9, UCMS Papers; memorandum, Arthur C. Thomas to Jon L. Regier, September 1, 1964, folder "Delta—Working Papers," box 3, and Arthur C. Thomas to A. Dale Fiers, September 16, 1964, folder "Education," box 3, Thomas Papers; "Main Points of Lease Agreement between Delta Ministry and the United Christian Missionary Society," February 1, 1965, folder 35, box 5, minutes, Administrative Committee, Division of Home Missions, NCC, October 7, 1964, 2–4, folder 24, box 4, "Excerpt from the Minutes of the Executive Board," Division of Home Missions, NCC, October 8–9, 1964, folder 22, box 4, and résumé, February 1969, attached to Robert L. Beech to "Dear Jon," March 14, 1969, folder 10, box 21, Delta Ministry Papers, Atlanta; Andrew J. Young to Truman Douglass, June 10, 1964, folder 14, box 136, and Wesley A. Hotchkiss to Andrew J. Young, August 31, 1964, folder 14, box 136, SCLC Papers; Robert W. Spike to Eugene Carson Blake, August 13, 1964, RG 95, folder 16, box 15, Blake Papers; R. H. Edwin Espy to Arthur C. Thomas, November 24, 1964, RG 6, folder 5, box 10, memorandum, Jon L. Regier to R. H. Edwin Espy, September 1, 1964 (quotation), RG 5, folder 9, box 16, memorandum, Jon L. Regier to Arthur C. Thomas, n.d., RG 6, folder 5, box 10, and memorandum, Jon L. Regier to Helen F. Kindt, February 24, 1965, RG 11, folder 3, box 8, NCC Archives; Medelman, "Mission," 16–18; Hilton, *Delta Ministry,* 41–42.

51. Harry J. Bowie, interview by Robert Wright, August 8, 1968, 1, 3, Bunche Oral History Collection; "The Delta Ministry," n.d., in folder "Delta Ministry Program," box 3, Beech Papers; *New York Herald Tribune,* September 26, 1964; "Report from McComb," *Delta Ministry* 1 (November 1964): 6; "Ministers in McComb," 32; Boyd, "Battle," 1398, 1400, 1402, 1404; *PARR* [United Presbyterian Synod of Pennsylvania] 2 (November 20, 1964): 1–2, folder 12, box 21, Delta Ministry Papers, Atlanta; "Magnolia," 18; Oniki, "How Then Can We Witness?" 37–38; Harry J. Bowie, interview by author, September 5, 1996; Dittmer, *Local People,* 99–115, 265–71, 303–14.

52. Warren H. McKenna to Arthur Lichtenberger, August 17, 1964, folder 1, box 15, Wilmina Rowland to W. P. Steven, December 28, 1964, folder 11, box 15, minutes, Administrative Committee, Division of Home Missions, NCC, October 7, 1964, 1–2, 4, folder 24, box 4, and minutes, Executive Board, Division of Home Missions, NCC, October 8–9, 1964, 9, folder 24, box 4, Delta Ministry Papers, Atlanta; "Delta Ministry Fact Sheet," January 1965, appendix A, folder "Delta Ministry—Minutes, Budgets, Fact Sheets—1965," box 1, and "Suggested Principles for Structuring the Delta Ministry," n.d., folder "Delta Ministry Background Reports—1964," box 1, Humphrey Papers; "National Council Board Speaks Out," 3; "W.C.C. Sends Mission," 660; Wilmina Rowland to Kenneth G. Neigh, October 4, 1964, folder "Fan Mail," box 6, Thomas Papers; *Delta Democrat-Times,* October 18, 1964, clipping in folder 1431-2-3:07, Church and Society Records, UMC; Schulz, "Delta Ministry," 34; memorandum, William A. Carhart to Stephen A. Feke, March 7, 1966, RG 11, folder 3, box 8, NCC Archives; Hilton, *Delta Ministry,* 45–46. The United Church of Christ gave ten thousand dollars to the Delta Ministry in 1964 ("Member Denominations Income," attached to "Agenda, Commission on the Delta Ministry, March 31–April 1, 1966," folder 1431-2-3:05, Church and Society Records, UMC).

53. "A Proposal for a Common Discipline of the Delta Ministry Staff," appendix B

(quotations), attached to memorandum, Jon L. Regier to R. H. Edwin Espy, September 1, 1964, RG 5, folder 9, box 16, NCC Archives; Noble, "Delta Ministry," 148–49.

54. Medelman, "Mission," 18.

55. Memorandum, Arthur C. Thomas to Jon L. Regier, September 1, 1964, 2 (first quotation), folder "Delta—Working Papers," box 3, Thomas Papers; "A Proposal for a Common Discipline of the Delta Ministry Staff," appendix B (second and third quotations), attached to memorandum, Jon L. Regier to R. H. Edwin Espy, September 1, 1964, RG 5, folder 9, box 16, NCC Archives; "Delta Ministry Fact Sheet," January 1965, appendix A, folder "Delta Ministry—Minutes, Budgets, Fact Sheets—1965," box 1, Humphrey Papers; Findlay, *Church People,* 118.

56. "A Proposal for a Common Discipline of the Delta Ministry Staff," appendix B (first quotation), attached to memorandum, Jon L. Regier to R. H. Edwin Espy, September 1, 1964, RG 5, folder 9, box 16, NCC Archives; Thomas Weiser, "Report on Conversations with the Staff of the Delta Ministry of the NCC, May 14–15, 1965," July 13, 1965, 2, folder "Commission Executive Committee—July 19, 1965," box 6, Thomas Papers; Gort, "Negro Church," 46–47 (second quotation on p. 46); Hilton, *Delta Ministry,* 157–59, 161–74, 181–85; Findlay, *Church People,* 156; Dittmer, *Local People,* 75, 124, 134, 165; Payne, *I've Got the Light,* 191.

CHAPTER TWO. External Relations, Internal Policy, 1964–1965

1. "Subcommittee Reports to the Evaluation Committee of the Delta Ministry Commission, National Council of Churches," May 6, 1966, folder 9, box 43, SCLC Papers; "Report of the Evaluation Committee on the Mississippi Delta Ministry of the General Board of the National Council of Churches," May 16, 1966, and Paul Moore Jr., "Report of the Delta Ministry (*With Special Reference to the Evaluation Committee Report*)," May 27, 1966, 1–4, 6, folder 44, box 3, Delta Ministry Papers, Starkville; Bruce Hilton to J. Irwin Miller, May 10, 1966, and "The Delta Ministry's Financial Situation," August 10, 1966, RG 11, folder 4, box 8, NCC Archives.

2. John M. Allin to John B. Morris, July 6, 1964, folder 39, box 57, ESCRU Papers; John M. Allin to William L. Hargrave, May 20, 1964, folder "Education," box 3, John M. Allin to David R. Hunter, November 16, 30, 1964, folder "White Mississippi—Episcopalians 1964–1965," box 6, David R. Hunter to John M. Allin, November 25, 1964, folder "White Mississippi—Episcopalians 1964–1965," box 6, and Arthur E. Walmsley to Paul Moore Jr., August 18, 1965, folder "Bishop Paul Moore," box 1, Thomas Papers; memorandum, Arthur Walmsley to "Mr. Turner" et al., November 4, 1964, and memorandum, Arthur Walmsley to "Dr. Hunter," November 23, 1964, RG 5, folder 17, box 19, NCC Archives; "Episcopal Church and the National Council of Churches," 5 (quotation); "Church Consecrates 11 New Bishops," 3; Virgil A. Sly to M. Maurice Grove, January 27, 1965, RG 4, folder "Mt. Beulah," box DHM 9, UCMS Papers. Allin ranked below the diocesan bishop of Mississippi, Duncan Gray Sr., but because Gray was ill, the bishop coadjutor took charge of diocesan affairs during the controversy about the Delta Ministry's inauguration (Shattuck, *Episcopalians and Race,* 263 n.31).

3. Shattuck, *Episcopalians and Race,* 149–50; Sumner, *Episcopal Church's History,* 37, 39; E. King, "Mississippi," 15, 20–21; Cunningham, *Agony,* 122; *Journal of the General Convention of the Protestant Episcopal Church in the United States of America,* 1964, 190–91 (quotation on

p. 191); David R. Hunter to John M. Allin, October 30, 1964, and John M. Allin to David R. Hunter, November 4, 1964, folder 28, box 1, Delta Ministry Papers, Atlanta; Haggerty and Thomson, eds., *National Council*, 63. For an alternative but less credible interpretation that "Allin's questions about the Delta Ministry arose more from the concerns of a critic than an obstructionist," see Alvis, "Racial Turmoil," 89–96 (quotation on pp. 95–96).

4. Arthur Lichtenberger to R. H. Edwin Espy, October 12, 1964 (first quotation), and memorandum, Daniel Corrigan to Jon L. Regier, October 10, 1964 (subsequent quotations), folder 26, box 1, Delta Ministry Papers, Atlanta.

5. Jon L. Regier to Daniel Corrigan, October 28, 1964 (quotations), folder 26, box 1, Delta Ministry Papers, Atlanta; memorandum, Jon L. Regier to Paul O. Madsen, December 4, 1964, 1–2, folder "Delta Ministry Background Reports—1964," box 1, Humphrey Papers.

6. John M. Allin to David R. Hunter, November 4, 1964, folder 28, box 1, Delta Ministry Papers, Atlanta.

7. Memorandum, Jon L. Regier to Paul O. Madsen, December 4, 1964, 1–4 (quotations on p. 3), folder "Delta Ministry Background Reports—1964," box 1, Humphrey Papers.

8. David R. Hunter to John M. Allin, November 10, 25, December 9, 1964, and John M. Allin to David R. Hunter, November 16, 30, 1964, folder "White Mississippi—Episcopalians 1964–1965," box 6, Thomas Papers.

9. *Delta Democrat-Times*, October 22, 24, 1965; *Memphis Commercial Appeal*, October 19, 1965; Warren H. McKenna to W. Appleton Lawrence, December 14, 1964 (quotations), folder 6, box 15, Delta Ministry Papers, Atlanta; Grover C. Bagby to Francis B. Stevens, November 1, 1965, folder 1431-2-3:05, Church and Society Records, UMC.

10. *Episcopal Society for Cultural and Racial Unity Newsletter* January 10, 1965, 1; *New York Times*, February 7, 18, 1965; "Report on Special Order of Business Requested by the Presiding Bishop. Annual Meeting of the Executive Council. Seabury House, Greenwich, Conn., February 17, 1965," folder "White Mississippi—Episcopalians 1964–1965," box 6, Thomas Papers; Shattuck, *Episcopalians and Race*, 146–47, 151–52.

11. Minutes, Executive Board, Division of Home Missions, NCC, October 8–9, 1964, 9, folder 24, box 4, and "General Board Action Concerning *A Ministry among the Residents of the Delta Area of the State of Mississippi*," February 26, 1964, exhibit 4, 5–6, folder 25, box 4, Delta Ministry Papers, Atlanta; memorandum, William A. Carhart to Stephen A. Feke, March 7, 1966, RG 11, folder 3, box 8, and Bruce Hilton to J. Irwin Miller, May 10, 1966, 1, RG 11, folder 4, box 8, NCC Archives; "Background Material from Subcommittee on Administration of the Delta Ministry," February 28–March 1, 1966, 1–2, 2B, 2D, in "Subcommittee Reports to the Evaluation Committee of the Delta Ministry Commission, National Council of Churches," May 6, 1966, folder 9, box 43, SCLC Papers; *Los Angeles Times*, March 5, 1967; Wood, "Unanticipated Consequences," 518; "Two Divisions of Board of Missions," 14.

12. A. D. Owings to *Jackson Clarion-Ledger*, May 16, 1964; letters from Eade Anderson and Dwyn M. Mounger to *Jackson Clarion-Ledger*, June 10, 1964; *Hattiesburg American*, June 5, 1964; *Minutes of the One-Hundred-Fourth General Assembly of the Presbyterian Church in the United States*, 1964, 83–84 (quotations on p. 83), 170–71; memorandum, R. H. Edwin Espy to Jon L. Regier, April 7, 1964, RG 4, folder 23, box 31, NCC Archives; *Information Bulletin* [Mississippi Association of Methodist Ministers and Laymen] 1 (June 1964): 4; *Minutes of Presbytery of Central Mississippi*, 1964, 5–6, 14; "Information Re: I. The Mississippi Summer

Program; II. The Mississippi Delta Project; III. Relationship of Presbyterians, U.S.," n.d., 2, folder "Greenville Air Force Base," box 6, Thomas Papers.

13. Patrick D. Miller to Jon L. Regier, April 29, 1964, and Jon L. Regier to Patrick D. Miller, May 5, 1964, folder "Delta Current—up," box 5, Thomas Papers; Street, "Mississippi Delta Project," 7.

14. *Minutes of the One-Hundred-Fifth General Assembly of the Presbyterian Church in the United States,* 1965, 163–64 (quotation on p. 164); *Memphis Commercial Appeal,* April 26, 1965; *Jackson Daily News,* June 14, 1967; *Delta Democrat-Times,* June 14, 1967; Chauncey, "Should We Support the Delta Ministry?" 24; Colin W. Williams to George A. Chauncey, December 13, 1966, RG 38, folder "Delta Ministry (1)," box 1, Office of Church and Society Records, PCUS, Montreat; "Background Material from Subcommittee on Administration of the Delta Ministry," February 28–March 1, 1966, 2D, in "Subcommittee Reports to the Evaluation Committee of the Delta Ministry Commission, National Council of Churches," May 6, 1966, folder 9, box 43, SCLC Papers.

15. *New York Times,* April 28, 1964; *Washington Post,* October 2, 1966; "S.E. Jurisdictional Conference," 1 (quotations); "Board of Missions Divisions Allocate Funds to Delta Ministry," *Methodists Make News,* October 7, 1966, in folder 1431-2-3:07, Church and Society Records, UMC.

16. "Mississippi Methodism," 4, 6; *North Mississippi Conference Journal of the North Mississippi Annual Conference,* 1964, 50, 131; "Study Committee, National Council of Churches, Mississippi Annual Conference," 2; *Information Bulletin* [Mississippi Association of Methodist Ministers and Laymen] 1 (September 1964): 1; "Old Wounds Reopened," 239; Stevens, "Sign of Change," 8–9, 14; E. R. Branch, "Born of Conviction," 47–48, 109, 139–40, 163, 172–74; Herbers, "Churches and Race," 11, 14.

17. *Jackson Clarion-Ledger/Jackson Daily News,* July 1, 1984; Bagby, "Race Relations," 4–5; Billings, *Segregation,* 23; E. King, "Mississippi," 20, 169–70 (inconsistent pagination); E. R. Branch, "Born of Conviction," 165; Dittmer, *Local People,* 226; B. F. Smith to Marvin A. Franklin, June 9, 1964, and Marvin A. Franklin to B. F. Smith, June 15, 1964, folder "Delta Council—Correspondence 1964," box 1, Humphrey Papers; "Memorandum on the Delta Ministry," B. F. Smith to Evaluation Committee on the Delta Ministry, National Council of Churches, n.d., "Delta Ministry File," Leesha Faulkner Civil Rights Collection, in possession of the author; Henry A. McCanna to Edward J. Pendergrass, July 22, 1964 (quotation), folder "National Council of Churches (Delta Ministry)," Bishop's Office.

18. "Resolution Adopted by the Official Board of the First Methodist Church, Starkville, Mississippi," July 19, 1964 (quotation), folder "Northeast Mississippi Churches, 1964," box 1, and V. B. Montgomery to [NCC] Commission on Religion and Race, October 7, 1964, folder "Desegregation in Miss., 1964 Misc. Articles," box 1, Humphrey Papers; "Report of the National Council of Churches Study Committee," 6–9, folder "Anti-Communism, 1952–1964 and undated," no box, Holloman Papers; Hilton, *Delta Ministry,* 35.

19. James Hand Jr., "A Delta Reaction to Delta Ministry," *Deer Creek Pilot,* June 26, 1964; Henry A. McCanna to James Hand Jr., June 19, 1964 (quotations), folder "Delta Current—up," box 5, Thomas Papers; E. R. Branch, "Born of Conviction," 159.

20. "Memorandum on the Delta Ministry," B. F. Smith to Evaluation Committee on Delta Ministry, National Council of Churches, n.d., 1 (quotation), "Delta Ministry File," Leesha Faulkner Civil Rights Collection, in possession of the author; "The Mississippi

Delta Ministry: A Blue Print for Communist Control," *Information Bulletin* [Mississippi Association of Methodist Ministers and Laymen] 1 (October 1964): 1; memorandum, Henry A. McCanna to David R. Hunter, November 20, 1964, RG 5, folder 9, box 16, NCC Archives.

21. Memorandum, Henry A. McCanna to David R. Hunter, November 20, 1964, 2 (first quotation), RG 5, folder 9, box 16, NCC Archives; *Jackson Clarion-Ledger*, September 10, 1965; Henry A. McCanna to Edward J. Pendergrass, September 21, 1964, folder "National Council of Churches (Delta Ministry)," Bishop's Office; Pendergrass, "Progress," 7; *North Mississippi Conference Journal of the North Mississippi Annual Conference*, 1966, 88, 119–20 (second quotation on p. 120); *Journal of the Upper Mississippi Conference of the United Methodist Church, The Eightieth Annual Session*, 1969, 66–67; Graham, *Mississippi Circuit Riders*, 191–92.

22. *Jackson Clarion-Ledger*, January 29, 1965; "Some Facts about Mount Beulah," folder 61, box 3, Horwitz Papers; "What Is Mount Beulah?" *Delta Ministry* 2 (October 1965): 2; "Ad Hoc Committee to Save Mt. Beulah," folder 6, box 4, Amzie Moore Papers, WHS; Robert W. Spike to A. Dale Fiers, May 25, 1964, and "Executive Session," January 26–27, 1965, RG 4, folder "Mt. Beulah," box DHM 9, UCMS Papers; Jon L. Regier to A. Dale Fiers, June 10, 1964, and "Executive Session," June 16, 17, 1964, RG 4, folder "Commission on Mount Beulah regarding Mississippi Delta Ministry," box DHM 9, UCMS Papers; minutes, Executive Board, Division of Home Missions, NCC, October 8–9, 1964, 10, folder 24, box 4, and minutes, International Convention Coordinating Committee on Moral and Civil Rights, October 14, 1964, folder 10, box 15, Delta Ministry Papers, Atlanta.

23. *Jackson Clarion-Ledger*, January 29, 1965; "Executive Session," January 26–27, 1965, and attached "A Joint Report to the Congregational and the Official Board of the First Christian Church, Jackson, Miss.," December 8, 1964, Virgil A. Sly to Jon L. Regier, January 27, 1965, and Virgil A. Sly to W. H. Edds, January 5, 1965, RG 4, folder "Mt. Beulah," box DHM 9, UCMS Papers; "Main Points of Lease Agreement between Delta Ministry and the United Christian Missionary Society," February 1, 1965, folder 35, box 5, Delta Ministry Papers, Atlanta.

24. Arthur C. Thomas, "Suggested Principles for Structuring the Delta Ministry," August 17, 1964, appendix A, 1 (quotation), attached to memorandum, Jon L. Regier to R. H. Edwin Espy, September 1, 1964, RG 5, folder 9, box 16, and memorandum, Jon L. Regier to Arthur C. Thomas, n.d., RG 6, folder 5, box 10, NCC Archives; minutes, Commission on the Delta Ministry, January 22, 1965, 2–3, folder "Delta Ministry—Minutes, Budgets, Fact Sheets—1965," box 1, Humphrey Papers; Jon L. Regier to Marshal L. Scott, December 31, 1964, RG 95, folder 2, box 22, Blake Papers; minutes, Commission on the Delta Ministry, April 2, 1965, 3, 5, folder 35, box 1, Delta Ministry Papers, Atlanta; Paul Moore Jr., "The Delta Ministry Comes of Age," 5, folder "Articles—1965," box "B P. Moore w/Delta Min," Paul Moore Jr. Papers, AEDNY; *Delta Democrat-Times*, August 22, 1965.

25. P. Moore Jr., *Presences*, 3–131 (quotations on p. 122), 136, 164, 169; Paul Moore Jr., to Jon L. Regier, December 4, 1964, folder "Delta Commission Membership," box 6, Thomas Papers; Paul O. Madsen to Paul Moore Jr., December 21, 1964, RG 5, folder 9, box 16, NCC Archives; Shattuck, *Episcopalians and Race*, 91–92.

26. P. Moore Jr., *Presences*, 136, 138–40, 164, 169, 177–80; Shattuck, *Episcopalians and Race*, 142–43; "Bishop Paul Moore, Jr., Appointed Chairman of Commission," *Delta Ministry* 1 (January 1965): 1–2 (quotation on p. 1).

27. Paul O. Madsen to Paul Moore Jr., December 21, 1964, RG 5, folder 9, box 16, NCC

Archives; Jon L. Regier to Marshal L. Scott, December 31, 1964, RG 95, folder 2, box 22, Blake Papers; draft minutes, Commission on the Delta Ministry, January 22, 1965, 6–7, folder 34, box 12, Delta Ministry Papers, Atlanta; minutes, Commission on the Delta Ministry, January 22, 1965, 1, folder "Delta Ministry—Minutes, Budgets, Fact Sheets—1965," box 1, Humphrey Papers; "Members of the Commission on the Delta Ministry," attached to "Schedule for Commission Meeting of the Delta Ministry, April 2–3, 1965," folder "Delta Ministry, Correspondence, Memos, Jan. 1965–March 1966," box 8, Levin Papers; Pierce, "Mission," 94, 96; Waldron, *Hodding Carter,* 160–61 (first quotation on p. 160), 286; Polly A. Robinson, "Report on Greenville, Mississippi," August 9, 1964, 1 (second quotation), folder "Polly Robinson's Report," box 6, Thomas Papers. Organized in 1962 to promote "respect for all men regardless of race, color, or creed," the Mississippi Council comprised "white liberals and middle-class Black political activists" (Cunnigen, "Men and Women," 116 [first quotation], 328 n.70 [second quotation]).

28. "Report of the Executive Director and Staff," June 1, 1964, 2, RG 301.9, folder 16, box 1, CORAR Records; Mae Yoho Ward application to Ministers Project, August 5, 1964, folder 9, box 8, draft minutes, Commission on the Delta Ministry, January 22, 1965, 3 (quotation), folder 34, box 12, and Arthur C. Thomas to Paul Moore Jr., February 1, 1965, folder 42, box 12, Delta Ministry Papers, Atlanta; Robert L. Beech, "Report from Hattiesburg August 4–11, 1964," folder "Reports and Reactions," box 1, Beech Papers; minutes, Commission on the Delta Ministry, January 22, 1965, 1, 2, 5, folder "Delta Ministry—Minutes, Budgets, Fact Sheets—1965," box 1, Humphrey Papers; *New York Society of Clinical Psychologists, Inc., Newsletter* 13 (winter 1965): 2; Wiles, "Medical Mission"; memorandum, Bryant George to Kenneth G. Neigh, May 31, 1966, folder "Delta Ministry," box 16, Neigh Papers; A. Dale Fiers to "The Christian Churches in Mississippi," January 8, 1963, 1, RG 4, folder "Mt. Beulah–Jackson Carl Braden Situation," box DHM 9, UCMS Papers.

29. Draft minutes, Commission on the Delta Ministry, January 22, 1965, 7 (quotation), folder 34, box 12, Delta Ministry Papers, Atlanta; "January to May 1965," *Commission on Religion and Race Reports* [NCC] 1 (spring 1965): 1; *Student Voice,* October 28, 1964, 1–2, 4, December 1964, 1–4; minutes, Commission on Race and Religion, NCC, June 11, 1965, 4, RG 11, folder 22, box 6, Robert W. Spike to "Commission on Religion and Race of the National Council of Churches," December 22, 1964, RG 6, folder 32, box 47, and "Resolution on the Mississippi Freedom Democratic Party," June 11, 1965, RG 6, folder 1, box 48, NCC Archives; Dittmer, *Local People,* 338–41, 351–52, 497 n.1; Walton, *Black Political Parties,* 105–13, 235–36; McLemore, "Mississippi Freedom Democratic Party," chap. 4. The NCC's Commission on Religion and Race argued that the five Mississippi congressmen should not be seated but did not support Devine, Gray, and Hamer's attempt to replace three of the representatives without a fresh election in which African Americans would be free to vote (Robert W. Spike to "Commission on Religion and Race of the National Council of Churches," December 22, 1964, RG 6, folder 32, box 47, NCC Archives; "A Call to Action," n.d., folder 13, box 161, SNCC Papers).

30. Minutes, Commission on the Delta Ministry, January 22, 1965, 4, folder "Delta Ministry—Minutes, Budgets, Fact Sheets—1965," box 1, Humphrey Papers; draft minutes, Commission on the Delta Ministry, January 22, 1965, 1–16, folder 34, box 12, and Arthur C. Thomas to Paul Moore Jr., February 1, 1965, folder 42, box 12, Delta Ministry Papers, Atlanta.

31. "A Proposal for the Delta Ministry Academy to be located at Mt. Beulah, Edwards, Mississippi," RG 4, folder 35, box 31, NCC Archives; minutes, Executive Board, Division of Home Missions, NCC, October 8–9, 1964, 10, folder 24, box 4, Delta Ministry Papers, Atlanta; minutes, Commission on the Delta Ministry, January 22, 1965, 4–5, folder "Delta Ministry—Minutes, Budgets, Fact Sheets—1965," box 1, Humphrey Papers.

32. Minutes, Commission on the Delta Ministry, January 22, 1965, 5, and "Delta Ministry Fact Sheet," January 1965, 2, folder "Delta Ministry—Minutes, Budgets, Fact Sheets—1965," box 1, Humphrey Papers; H. Jack Geiger to Arthur C. Thomas, July 27, 1965, folder 10, box 12, Delta Ministry Papers, Atlanta; H. Jack Geiger to Arthur C. Thomas, February 1, 1965, and attached Johnny E. Parham Jr. to Arthur C. Thomas, June 25, 1965, folder "Winik Fund—MCHR Program," box 1, and "Report of the Executive Committee," December 2–3, 1965, 9 (quotation), no folder, box 4, Thomas Papers; Dittmer, *Local People*, 335.

33. Minutes, Commission on the Delta Ministry, January 22, 1965, 1, folder "Delta Ministry—Minutes, Budgets, Fact Sheets—1965," box 1, Humphrey Papers; Arthur C. Thomas, "An Open Letter to Bishop Pendergrass of the Methodist Church, Mississippi," May 15, 1966, 2, folder 35, box 3, Delta Ministry Papers, Starkville.

34. John M. Allin to David R. Hunter, November 4, 1964, folder 28, box 1, Delta Ministry Papers, Atlanta; John M. Allin to Edward J. Pendergrass, January 28, 1965 (first quotation), folder "National Council of Churches (Delta Ministry)," Bishop's Office; *Journal of the One-Hundred-Thirty-Ninth Annual Council of the Diocese of Mississippi*, 1966, 74 (second quotation). The Commission on the Delta Ministry reported that the participants at the meeting included "7 Mississippi judicatory officials and other Mississippians" (minutes, Commission on the Delta Ministry, April 2, 1965, 1, folder 35, box 1, Delta Ministry Papers, Atlanta).

35. *Delta Democrat-Times*, June 4, 1965 (quotation); "Report, Study Committee Mississippi Annual Conference, The Methodist Church," RG 5, folder 4, box 21, NCC Archives; "Report of the National Council of Churches Study Committee," 4, folder "Anti-Communism, 1952–1964 and undated," no box, Holloman Papers.

36. "Report of the National Council of Churches Study Committee," 7–9 (first quotation on p. 9; second quotation on p. 7; subsequent quotations on p. 8), folder "Anti-Communism, 1952–1964 and undated," no box, Holloman Papers.

37. Garland H. Holloman to Grover C. Bagby, August 21, 1965, 1–5 (first quotation on p. 5; second quotation on p. 3), folder "Delta Ministry Correspondence, 1964–1966," box 1, Humphrey Papers; Francis B. Stevens to Grover C. Bagby, August 16, 1965, 1–5 (third quotation on p. 4), folder 1431-2-3:05, Grover C. Bagby to Leslie E. Drake, March 18, 1966, folder 1431-2-3:06, Grover C. Bagby to Lorenz M. Schultz, March 22, 1966, folder 1431-2-3:05, and Francis B. Stevens to Grover C. Bagby, August 30, 1965, 1–3 (fourth quotation on pp. 1–2), folder 1431-2-3:05, Church and Society Records, UMC.

38. Edward J. Pendergrass to R. H. Edwin Espy, August 27, 1965, and Edward J. Pendergrass to John D. Humphrey, September 3, 1965 (first quotation), folder "Delta Ministry Correspondence, 1964–1966," box 1, Humphrey Papers; *Jackson Clarion-Ledger*, September 10, 1965 (second quotation); Rogers, "Keynote Address," 1–2; "Response to Letter of Bishop Pendergrass, dtd. 8-27-65," folder "White Mississippi—Methodists 1964–1965," box 6, and memorandum, Alfred R. Winham to Arthur C. Thomas, March 13, 1966, 3, folder "White Mississippi—1966," box 6, Thomas Papers.

39. "About the Von Hoffman 'Interview,' " 1–2 (quotation on p. 2), folder 13, box 1, Horwitz Papers; Paul Moore Jr. to John E. Hines, May 14, 1965, folder "White Mississippi—Episcopalians 1964–1965," box 6, Thomas Papers.

40. "Greenville Mill: A Report on Discrimination in Employment," *Delta Ministry* 1 (January 1965): 3; *Delta Democrat-Times*, February 12, 1965; Hattyn H. Eiland to Edward J. Pendergrass, February 5, 1965, folder "National Council of Churches (Delta Ministry), Bishop's Office; Francis B. Stevens to Edward J. Pendergrass, April 27, 1965, 2–3 (quotation on p. 2), folder "Delta Ministry Correspondence, 1964–1966," box 1, Humphrey Papers; Hilton, *Delta Ministry*, 49–52.

41. *Delta Democrat-Times*, December 29, 1964, March 1, 25, May 4, 5, 6 (quotation), October 24, 1965; *Chicago Daily News*, July 28, 1965; minutes, Commission on the Delta Ministry, April 2, 1965, 5–6, folder 35, box 1, Delta Ministry Papers, Atlanta; memorandum, Larry Walker to Executive Committee, Delta Ministry Commission, May 7, 1965, RG 301.9, folder 14, box 8, CORAR Records; "About the Von Hoffman 'Interview,' " folder 13, box 1, Horwitz Papers; James L. Robertson, "A Memorandum Concerning the Policies and Procedures of the Delta Ministry," April 15, 1966, appendix B in James L. Robertson, "To Whom It May Concern," folder "Delta Ministry—Misc.—1964–66," box 1, Humphrey Papers.

42. Paul Moore Jr. and Arthur C. Thomas, "Report to the Program Board, DCLM," June 1–2, 1965, 3 (quotation), folder 34, box 12, Delta Ministry Papers, Atlanta; "Response to Letter of Bishop Pendergrass, dtd. 8-27-65," folder "White Mississippi—Methodists 1964–1965," box 6, Thomas Papers; Rims K. Barber, interview by author, August 22, 1996; Dittmer, *Local People*, 342–43, 498 n.9; Walton, *Black Political Parties*, 115.

43. "Commission on the Delta Ministry," folder 9, box 43, SCLC Papers; "Response to Letter of Bishop Pendergrass, dtd. 8-27-65," folder "White Mississippi—Methodists 1964–1965," box 6, Thomas Papers; Warren H. McKenna to Robert Hall, May 5, 1965, folder 15, box 28, Delta Ministry Papers, Atlanta; Robert L. Beech, interview by author, June 30, 1998; Walton, *Black Political Parties*, 116–17, 172, 174.

44. *Holyoke Transcript-Telegram*, July 7, 1964; "Appendix A, Biographical Data—Delta Ministry Staff," folder 39, box 2, Delta Ministry Papers, Atlanta; Paul Moore Jr. and Arthur C. Thomas, "Report to the Program Board, DCLM," June 1–2, 1965, 2, folder 34, box 12, Delta Ministry Papers, Atlanta; *Jackson Daily News*, April 12, 1965.

45. Jon L. Regier to Virgil Sly, March 12, 1965, folder 6, box 12, Paul Moore Jr. and Arthur C. Thomas, "Report to the Program Board, DCLM," June 1–2, 1965, folder 34, box 12, and minutes, Commission on the Delta Ministry, April 2, 1965, 2–3, 6–7, folder 35, box 1, Delta Ministry Papers, Atlanta; "Commission on the Delta Ministry, Outline of Director's Report," July 19, 1965, 2, folder "Delta Ministry—Minutes, Budgets, Fact Sheets—1965," box 1, Humphrey Papers; Hilton, *Delta Ministry*, 165; Dittmer, *Local People*, 343–44; Meier and Rudwick, *CORE*, 340–42.

46. Minutes, Commission on the Delta Ministry, April 2, 1965, 2–3, folder 35, box 1, Delta Ministry Papers, Atlanta; memorandum, Henry A. McCanna to H. Leroy Brininger, May 6, 1965, RG 11, folder 3, box 8, NCC Archives; memorandum, Henry A. McCanna to Burrill Crohn, Jon L. Regier, and Arthur C. Thomas, July 15, 1965, "The Delta Ministry Commission," n.d., Burrill Crohn to David Bushnell, September 28, 1965, and Henry A. McCanna to Theodore M. Berry, January 25, 1966, folder "Diebold," box 1, Thomas Papers; Paul Moore

Jr., "Report of the Delta Ministry (*With Special Reference to the Evaluation Committee Report*),"
May 27, 1966, 3, folder 44, box 3, Delta Ministry Papers, Starkville.

47. "Preliminary Proposal for the Establishment of Mississippi Freedom Corps," folder
28, box 6, Delta Ministry Papers, Atlanta; Curtis Hayes, "Freedom Corps," 1–7, Owen H.
Brooks, "Bolivar County Report," 3–4, Alfred R. Winham, "Mt. Beulah Report March 21st
to July 15th 1965," 3, and Frederick S. Lowry, "Mount Beulah July 15th to September 15th,
1965," 1, in "Staff Reports, Commission on the Delta Ministry," October 1, 1965, folder "Staff
Reports, October 1, 1965," box 1, Humphrey Papers; Hilton, *Delta Ministry,* 60–63; Dittmer,
Local People, 106–7, 113–14; Meier and Rudwick, *CORE,* 340–42.

48. Greenberg, *Devil,* 3–33, 782–85; Alfred R. Winham, "Mt. Beulah Report March 21st
to July 15th 1965," 4, in "Staff Reports, Commission on the Delta Ministry," October 1, 1965,
folder "Staff Reports, October 1, 1965," box 1, Humphrey Papers.

49. "Background Material from Subcommittee on the Relationship of Child Development Group of Mississippi and Delta Ministry," March 9–10, 1966, 2, in "Subcommittee Reports to the Evaluation Committee of the Delta Ministry Commission, National Council
of Churches," May 6, 1966, folder 9, box 43, SCLC Papers; "Oral History Memoir of Dr. Tom
Levin," July 1, 1965, 1–3, 11–17, folder "History, Oral—Interviewee Tom Levin, July 1965,"
box 3, Levin Papers; Arthur C. Thomas to "Members of the Board, Child Development
Group of Mississippi," April 20, 1965, folder 27, box 12, Delta Ministry Papers, Atlanta;
Arthur C. Thomas to Walter Reuther, April 26, 1965, folder "Child Development Group
of Mississippi 1965," box 5, Thomas Papers; Greenberg, *Devil,* 3–28, 782–85.

50. Minutes, Executive Committee, Commission on the Delta Ministry, July 19, 1965, 5,
folder "Delta Ministry—Minutes, Budgets, Fact Sheets—1965," box 1, Humphrey Papers;
Greenberg, *Devil,* 32–34, 715, 798–99; Dittmer, *Local People,* 369.

51. "Background Material from Subcommittee on the Relationship of Child Development Group of Mississippi and Delta Ministry," March 9–10, 1966, 1, 3, in "Subcommittee Reports to the Evaluation Committee of the Delta Ministry Commission, National
Council of Churches," May 6, 1966, folder 9, box 43, SCLC Papers; Greenberg, *Devil,* 27,
50–51, 58, 260, 683. Delta Ministry staff also organized a Head Start program in Greenville
and Pike County and assisted CDGM in Hattiesburg (Thelma P. Barnes, "Involvement in
the Head Start Program in Greenville," 1–4, Robert L. Beech, "Report and Evaluation—
Hattiesburg, September 1964–September 1965," 6, and Harry J. Bowie, "McComb Report,"
p. 3, in "Staff Reports, Commission on the Delta Ministry," October 1, 1965, folder "Staff
Reports, October 1, 1965," Humphrey Papers).

52. Greenberg, *Devil,* 53, 224–25, 241, 260, 302, 304; minutes, Executive Committee of the
Commission on the Delta Ministry, July 19, 1965, 5–6, folder "Delta Ministry—Minutes,
Budgets, Fact Sheets—1965," box 1, Humphrey Papers; "Why Was the Child Development
Group Attacked?" *Delta Ministry* 2 (October 1965): 4–5; "Report of the Executive Commit-
tee," December 2–3, 1965, 9, no folder, box 4, Thomas Papers; Dittmer, *Local People,* 369–70;
Colby, "Black Power," 591.

53. Greenberg, *Devil,* 58, 224–25, 302, 337, 427; "Confidential Report to the Executive
Committee, Commission on the Delta Ministry," October 1, 1965, folder 22, box 30, Delta
Ministry Papers, Atlanta; *Jackson Clarion-Ledger,* June 26, July 27, October 15, 1965; *Jackson
Daily News,* June 26, July 1, 27, 28, September 3, October 12, 13, 14, 15, 19, 1965; "Mt. Beulah

Christian Center," in "The Delta Ministry," n.d., folder "Delta Ministry Program," box 3, Beech Papers; "Bishop's Annual Thanksgiving Offering to Be for Delta Ministry Mount Beulah Project," *Together* 11 (December 1967): A-4. The Delta Ministry had charged CDGM $30,710 for the orientation conference, an amount that the OEO claimed included an over-payment of $12,338 (exhibit A, OEO Audit Report, July 31, 1965, attached to "Confidential Report to the Executive Committee, Commission on the Delta Ministry," October 1, 1965, folder 22, box 30, Delta Ministry Papers, Atlanta; memorandum, Bryant George to Kenneth G. Neigh, February 24, 1966, RG 301.7, folder 3, box 44, Board of National Missions [PCUSA] Records).

54. Greenberg, *Devil*, 427, 442–53; memorandum, Bryant George to Kenneth G. Neigh, February 24, 1966, RG 301.7, folder 3, box 44, Board of National Missions (PCUSA) Records; H. Leroy Brininger to James H. Heller, September 9, 1966, RG 11, folder 5, box 8, NCC Archives. In response to renewed pressure from Stennis, in October 1966 OEO denied CDGM's appli-cation for a third grant. Instead, OEO granted three million dollars to Mississippi Action for Progress, Inc. (MAP), to begin taking over the state's Head Start program from CDGM, and OEO promised additional funds. Formed specifically at the request of OEO, MAP com-prised a coalition of moderate, middle-class African Americans and whites led by Aaron Henry and Hodding Carter III. With the support of the NCC and liberal white allies in the North, CDGM secured a third and final grant of nearly five million dollars to operate a reduced program through 1967 in fourteen counties not assigned to MAP. Anxious to focus resources on the Vietnam War and to placate conservative critics of its antipoverty pro-gram, the Johnson administration cut twenty-five million dollars from the national Head Start budget in 1968. As a result, Mississippi lost one-quarter of its Head Start funding (Greenberg, *Devil*, 311–12, 601–24, 626–46, 655–57, 664, 667–78; Dittmer, *Local People*, 377–82).

55. "Background Material from Subcommittee on Mt. Beulah Conference Center," 2, in "Subcommittee Reports to the Evaluation Committee of the Delta Ministry Commis-sion, National Council of Churches," May 6, 1966, folder 9, box 43, SCLC Papers; "Staff Reports, Commission on the Delta Ministry," October 1, 1965, folder "Staff Reports, Octo-ber 1, 1965," box 1, Humphrey Papers; Cook, *Sweet Land*, 148; Robert L. Beech to Clinton D. Morrison, December 29, 1965, folder "Copies of Correspondence Sent Out II," box 1, and "The Delta Ministry," n.d., folder "Delta Ministry Program," box 3, Beech Papers; "About the People from the Delta," August 17, 1965, folder 2, box 81, Myles Horton to Harry J. Bowie, September 8, 1965, folder 2, box 81, "Voter Education Workshop, Edwards, Mis-sissippi, December 13–17, 1965," "Citizenship Education Workshop—December 13 thru 17, 1965," and C. Conrad Browne to Harry J. Bowie, December 21, 1965, folder 5, box 81, High-lander Research and Education Center Records, WHS; minutes, Citizenship Committee Meeting, Commission on the Delta Ministry, September 30, 1965, 1, folder "Commission Meeting—Oct. 1, 1965," box 3, Thomas Papers; Glen, *Highlander*, 3, 158–59, 171, 185–206, 254–56. During its first year, the Delta Ministry had "played a major part in the registration of ten thousand new Negro voters in four counties" ("What the Delta Ministry Is," 23).

56. Memorandum, W. Webb Burke to Clovis Williams, March 3, 1971, Leesha Faulkner Civil Rights Collection, in possession of the author; Owen H. Brooks, interview by Tom Dent, August 18, 1978, MOHC; Ullman, "In Darkest America," 177; Owen H. Brooks, interview by Robert Wright, September 21, 1968, 1–4, 20–22, Bunche Oral History Collection; "Delta Ministry Staff (as of December 1, 1966)," folder "D.M. Fact Sheet," no box, Winham Papers;

Robert L. Beech to Roger Walke, November 19, 1965, folder "Correspondence Sent Out II," box 1, Beech Papers; Owen H. Brooks, "Bolivar County Report," and Solomon Gort Jr., "Field Activities in Greenville, July 15, 1965 to September 4, 1965," in "Staff Reports, Commission on the Delta Ministry," October 1, 1965, folder "Staff Reports, October 1, 1965," box 1, Humphrey Papers; Henry A. McCanna, "A Ministry of Deliverance," folder 10, box 47, and Clarence Hall Jr., "Fidelity Bond Application," July 18, 1967, folder 38, box 45, Delta Ministry Papers, Atlanta. Although McKenna left St. John's Church in Roxbury in 1952, he stayed in contact with Brooks. Before joining the Delta Ministry in 1964, McKenna pastored St. John's Church in Holbrook, within twenty miles of Boston (Warren H. McKenna to "Vestry Wardens and Friends," December 1, 1964, folder 5, box 15, Delta Ministry Papers, Atlanta; Shattuck, *Episcopalians and Race,* 92, 141).

57. Minutes, Executive Committee, Commission on the Delta Ministry, July 19, 1965, 1, 3, and "Commission on the Delta Ministry, Outline of Director's Report," July 19, 1965, 1, folder "Delta Ministry—Minutes, Budgets, Fact Sheets—1965," box 1, Bruce Hilton, "The Information Program," and Frederick S. Lowry, "Mount Beulah July 15th to September 15th, 1965," in "Staff Reports, Commission on the Delta Ministry," October 1, 1965, folder "Staff Reports, October 1, 1965," box 1, Humphrey Papers; "Delta Ministry Staff (as of December 1, 1966)," folder "D.M. Fact Sheet," no box, Winham Papers.

58. Warren H. McKenna, "Volunteer Program," in "Staff Reports, Commission on the Delta Ministry," October 1, 1965, folder "Staff Reports, October 1, 1965," box 1, Humphrey Papers; Roger A. Smith et al., "From Democracy to Dictatorship: The Delta Ministry, 1968–1972," n.p., folder "Delta Ministry Board, 1970–1973," box 9, Derian Papers; Rims K. Barber application to Ministers Project, July 20, 1964, folder 7, box 8, Delta Ministry Papers, Atlanta; Rims K. Barber application to the Delta Ministry, n.d., RG 301.9, folder 18, box 8, CORAR Records; "Delta Ministry Staff (as of December 1, 1966)," folder "D.M. Fact Sheet," no box, Winham Papers; C. O. Chinn Sr. et al., "Madison County Project," folder "Project Directors Meeting," box 6, Thomas Papers.

59. Tut Tate et al., to "Dear Friends," March 15, 1966, folder 6, box II-A, Cox Collection; Bruce Hilton to J. Irwin Miller, May 10, 1966, 2 (quotation), RG 11, folder 4, box 8, NCC Archives.

60. *Delta Democrat-Times,* May 31, June 10, 11, 1965; *New York Times,* June 7, 1965; Robert L. Beech to "Dear Friend and Co-Worker," October 13, 1965, folder "Bob Beech," box 3, Thomas Papers; "Background Material from Subcommittee on Administration of the Delta Ministry," February 28–March 1, 1966, 2, 2A, and "Background Material from Subcommittee on Mt. Beulah Conference Center," 4, in "Subcommittee Reports to the Evaluation Committee of the Delta Ministry Commission, National Council of Churches," May 6, 1966, folder 9, box 43, SCLC Papers; Noble, "Delta Ministry," 74–75, 94.

61. Alfred R. Winham, "Field Staff Quarterly Report," July 1, 1966, folder "Reports— Unified Field Staff," no box, memorandum, Alfred R. Winham to Warren H. McKenna, July 21, 1966, folder "Memo (Miss).—Trips," no box, and Alfred R. Winham to "Your Grace," November 5, 1966, folder "Letters—Pers.," no box, Winham Papers; Delta Ministry press release, September 7, 1965, folder 3, box 19, minutes, Delta Opportunity Association, September 20, 1965, folder 7, box 45, and Theodore M. Berry to Clarence Hall Jr., March 28, 1967, folder 39, box 45, Delta Ministry Papers, Atlanta; minutes, Commission on the Delta Ministry, November 16–17, 1967, 5, folder 62, box 3, Delta Ministry Papers,

Starkville; "Report of the Executive Committee," December 2–3, 1965, 8–9, no folder, box 4, Thomas Papers; Hilton, *Delta Ministry,* 124, 136, 207–18.

62. Steven McNichols and Arthur C. Thomas, "Mississippi: A Crisis in Hunger," August 6, 1965, folder "USDA/NSA Commodity Proposal," box 1, Irving Pearson, "Report to NCC, Commission on Religion and Race," February 13, 1964, 8, no folder, box 5, "Authority to Act: Crisis in Hunger" (quotation), attached to Stephen Arons to Arthur C. Thomas, October 5, 1965, folder "National Student Association," box 1, Thomas Papers; minutes, Commission on the Delta Ministry, April 2, 1965, 1–2, folder 35, box 1, draft minutes, Commission on the Delta Ministry, January 22, 1965, 11–12, folder 34, box 12, Paul Moore Jr. and Arthur C. Thomas, "Report to the Program Board, DCLM," June 1–2, 1965, 1, folder 34, box 12, and "We Have No Government," February 1, 1966, 3, folder 47, box 9, Delta Ministry Papers, Atlanta; "Material Resources Program," in "The Delta Ministry," n.d., folder "Delta Ministry Program," box 3, Beech Papers; minutes, Commission on the Delta Ministry, January 22, 1965, 4, minutes, Executive Committee, Commission on the Delta Ministry, July 19, 1965, 3, and "Commission on the Delta Ministry, Outline of Director's Report," July 19, 1965, 1, folder "Delta Ministry—Minutes, Budgets, Fact Sheets—1965," box 1, Humphrey Papers.

63. Henry A. McCanna to Orville Freeman, November 19, 1965, RG 5, folder 10, box 16, NCC Archives; "Fact Sheet (Background on Poor Peoples' Use of Greenville AFB)," folder 6, box 4, Amzie Moore Papers, WHS; *Delta Ministry Reports,* February 1966, n.p.; "We Have No Government," February 1, 1966, 3, folder 47, box 9, Delta Ministry Papers, Atlanta; Charles E. Cobb, "Report on the Poor People's Conference, Mount Beulah, Mississippi," folder 71, box 170, SNCC Papers; "Report of the Executive Committee," December 2–3, 1965, 7, no folder, box 4, and Orville F. Freeman to Henry A. McCanna, December 9, 1965, folder "O.E.O. Mississippi Food Program," box 1, Thomas Papers. Under the Food Stamp program, the poor bought stamps to buy food in approved stores and received further stamps at no charge to make additional purchases ("Facts about the Food Stamp Program in Mississippi," January 1967, 1, folder 41, box 26, Hamer Papers).

64. Minutes, Commission on the Delta Ministry, April 2, 1965, 3, folder 35, box 1, Delta Ministry Papers, Atlanta; "General Board Action Concerning *A Ministry among the Residents of the Delta Area of the State of Mississippi,*" February 26, 1964, exhibit 4, 5–6, folder 25, box 4, and "Proposal for a Grant to the Delta Ministry of the National Council of the Churches of Christ in the U.S.A. for Community and Economic Development," folder 21, box 6, Delta Ministry Papers, Atlanta; Paul Moore Jr., "Report of the Delta Ministry (*With Special Reference to the Evaluation Committee Report*)," May 27, 1966, 3, 6, folder 44, box 3, Delta Ministry Papers, Starkville; Robert L. Beech to "Dear Friend and Co-Worker," October 13, 1965, folder "Bob Beech," box 3, and "Report of the Executive Committee," December 2–3, 1965, 10, no folder, box 4, Thomas Papers; Bruce Hilton to J. Irwin Miller, May 10, 1966, 2 (quotations), and "The Delta Ministry's Financial Situation," August 10, 1966, RG 11, folder 4, box 8, NCC Archives; minutes, Finance Committee, Commission on the Delta Ministry, July 19, 1965, 1–3, folder "D.M. Reports," no box, Winham Papers; "Commission on the Delta Ministry, Outline of Director's Report," July 19, 1965, 2, folder "Delta Ministry—Minutes, Budgets, Fact Sheets—1965," box 1, and Edward J. Pendergrass to R. H. Edwin Espy, August 27, 1965, 2, folder "Delta Ministry Correspondence, 1964–1966," box 1, Humphrey Papers; "Background Material from Subcommittee on Administration of the Delta Ministry," February 28–March 1, 1966, 1–2, 2A–D, in "Subcommittee Reports to the Evaluation Committee of

the Delta Ministry Commission, National Council of Churches," May 6, 1966, folder 9, box 43, SCLC Papers; Noble, "Delta Ministry," 74–75; Pendergrass, "Bishop's Column," 2; John F. Anderson Jr. to Truman B. Douglass, July 6, 1966, RG 38, folder "Delta Ministry (1)," box 1, Office of Church and Society Records, PCUS, Montreat.

CHAPTER THREE. Hattiesburg, 1964–1967

1. "Report and Evaluation, Hattiesburg, September 1964–September 1965," 1–14 (quotation on p. 1) and attached "Thoughts on the Future of Hattiesburg: A Working Paper," 1–2, in "Staff Reports, Commission on the Delta Ministry," October 1, 1965, folder "Staff Reports, October 1, 1965," box 1, Humphrey Papers; Robert L. Beech, "Report from Hattiesburg," *Delta Ministry* 1 (November 1964): 4–5; Blanchard, "Delta Ministry," 338; Robert L. Beech to Howard Hammerman, March 3, 1966, untitled folder, box 1, Robert L. Beech to Clinton D. Morrison, December 29, 1965, folder "Copies of Correspondence Sent Out II," box 1, and Robert L. Beech to "Dear Friends of Vernon Dahmer," March 4, 1966, folder "Dahmer," box 3, Beech Papers; minutes, Executive Committee, Commission on the Delta Ministry, July 31, 1967, 2, folder 47, box 3, Delta Ministry Papers, Starkville; Robert L. Beech, interview by author, June 27, 30, 1998.

2. "Fact Sheet: Hattiesburg, Mississippi" (quotation), folder 124, box 98, SNCC Papers; "Sketches of Delta Ministry Project Sites," attached to "Special Delta Ministry Activities," folder 1431–2–3:05, Church and Society Records, UMC.

3. "Fact Sheet: Hattiesburg, Mississippi," folder 124, box 98, SNCC Papers; *Hattiesburg American,* July 16, 1965; unidentified press clipping, February 11, 1965, folder "February 1965," box 6, Beech Papers; Dittmer, *Local People,* 179–80; Lawson, *Black Ballots,* 272–74, 412 n.91. Although the U.S. Civil Rights Commission reported that twelve blacks were registered in 1961, the U.S. Justice Department claimed that there were about twenty-five ("Fact Sheet: Hattiesburg, Mississippi," folder 124, box 98, SNCC Papers; Lawson, *Black Ballots,* 412 n.91).

4. "Another Murder in Mississippi," *Delta Ministry* 3 (January 1966): n.p.; "Vernon Dahmer," in *Free at Last,* 86; Hilton, *Delta Ministry,* 27; Dittmer, *Local People,* 180–81; T. Branch, *Pillar of Fire,* 52–53, 58–59.

5. Blanchard, "Delta Ministry," 338; SNCC press release, "Negro Woman Qualifies for Mississippi Senate Seat," April 10, 1964, folder 169, box 101, SNCC Papers; Victoria Gray Adams, interview by David Levine, January 19, 1998, summary in possession of the author; "Synopsis of Conference between Rev. Robert L. Beech and Robert H. Janover Regarding 'False Pretenses' Charge against Rev. Beech—Hattiesburg, Miss.—July 16–17, 1964," folder "Business Correspondence Hattiesburg Project the Delta Ministry Part II," box 1, Beech Papers; T. Branch, *Pillar of Fire,* 61; Current, "Death," 109; Dittmer, *Local People,* 181–83.

6. Victoria Gray Adams, interview by David Levine, January 19, 1998; Dittmer, *Local People,* 182–84, 219–20. Taylor Branch contends that Lynd registered seven African Americans (*Pillar of Fire,* 63).

7. *Mississippi Free Press,* January 18, 1964; Wilmore, *Black and Presbyterian,* 73; SNCC press release, "Hattiesburg 'Freedom Day' Set for January 22," January 18, 1964, folder 169, box 101, SNCC Papers; Gittings, "Clergymen Demonstrate," 30; *Student Voice,* January 20, 1964, 1; John B. Morris to "Participants in the Hattiesburg Mission," January 18, 1964, folder 1, box 59, ESCRU Papers; Robert J. Stone, "Interim Report: Clergy Participation with Council of

Federated Organizations, Hattiesburg, Mississippi," February 18, 1964, 2, RG 301.9, folder 17, box 8, CORAR Records; *Hattiesburg American,* January 22, 1964; T. Branch, *Pillar of Fire,* 70, 216; Dittmer, *Local People,* 219–20. For a detailed description of Freedom Day, see Zinn, *SNCC,* 102–22.

8. Gittings, "Clergymen Demonstrate," 30; John B. Morris "To Participants in the Hattiesburg Mission," January 18, 1964, folder 1, box 59, and "Clergy Participation Freedom Day, January 22, 1964, Hattiesburg, Mississippi," 1–3, folder 3, box 59, ESCRU Papers; *Student Voice,* January 20, 1964, 1; Robert J. Stone, "Interim Report, Clergy Participation with Council of Federated Organizations, Hattiesburg, Mississippi," February 18, 1964, 1–2, RG 301.9, folder 17, box 8, and "Report of the Executive Director and Staff," June 1, 1964, 2, RG 301.9, folder 16, box 1, CORAR Records; *Minutes of the General Assembly of the United Presbyterian Church in the United States of America,* 1966, 412; T. Branch, *Pillar of Fire,* 215. UPCUSA minister James H. Fenner came to Hattiesburg from his home in Texarkana, Texas ("Clergy Participation Freedom Day, January 22, 1964, Hattiesburg, Mississippi," 3, folder 3, box 59, ESCRU Papers).

9. T. Branch, *Pillar of Fire,* 214; Robert J. Stone, "Interim Report, Clergy Participation with Council of Federated Organizations, Hattiesburg, Mississippi," February 18, 1964, 2, RG 301.9, folder 17, box 8, CORAR Records; Robert W. Spike, "Report to the Commission on Religion and Race," February 1, 1964, 4, RG 6, folder 31, box 47, NCC Archives; "Churchmen and the Challenge," *Commission on Religion and Race Reports* [NCC], vol. 1, no. 4, n.d.; minutes, Commission on Religion and Race, NCC, February 21, 1964, 5–6, folder 12, box 15, series 2, Reuther and Carliner Collection.

10. *Hattiesburg American,* January 22, 1964; "The Delta Ministry—Hattiesburg," 1, folder "NCC Delta Ministry," box 33, Social Action Collection, WHS; "Churchmen and the Challenge," *Commission on Religion and Race Reports* [NCC], vol. 1, no. 4, n.d.; memorandum, Robert W. Spike to "Denominational Race Staff People," March 11, 1964, 2, RG 4, folder "Delta Project," box DHM 9, UCMS Papers; Gittings, "Clergymen Demonstrate," 30–33; Zinn, *SNCC,* 109–14. Reporters from the NBC and ABC television networks and from northern newspapers covered Freedom Day (*Hattiesburg American,* January 22, 1964). Away from the protest, police arrested Oscar Chase, a SNCC volunteer, for leaving the scene of an incident after his car had lightly bumped into a truck without causing any damage. Police stood idly by while a fellow prisoner beat Chase unconscious in jail (Zinn, "Incident," 501–2).

11. John M. Pratt, "Report on Legal Procedures and Bail," February 20, 1964, 2–3, folder 9, box 15, series 2, Reuther and Carliner Collection; Robert W. Spike, "Report to the Commission on Religion and Race," February 21, 1964, 4, RG 6, folder 31, box 47, NCC Archives; *Hattiesburg American,* January 23, 25, February 4, 1964; *Student Voice,* February 3, 1964, 1, 3, March 3, 1964, 2, May 26, 1964, 4; Gayraud S. Wilmore Jr. to Lawrence Guyot, April 14, 1964, RG 301.9, folder 17, box 8, CORAR Records; "Clergy Participation Freedom Day, January 22, 1964, Hattiesburg, Mississippi," 1–3, folder 3, box 59, ESCRU Papers; "Hattiesburg Project Second Week Participants January 26–February 1, 1964; Third Week Participants February 2–8, 1964; Fourth Week Participants February 9–15, 1964," folder 169, box 101, SNCC Papers; Zinn, *SNCC,* 117–21. The nine ministers, including one African American, each received a four-month sentence and two-hundred-dollar fine. Released on bail, they appealed their convictions. However, in March the clergymen pleaded no contest and accepted four-hundred-dollar fines from Forrest County Judge William Haralson rather

than face a prolonged and expensive legal battle (Carlson, "Presbyterian Ministers," 27; Carlson, "Hattiesburg," 26; *Hattiesburg American,* March 10, 1964).

12. Carlson, "Presbyterian Ministers," 27; COFO press releases, "Beatings Follow Fourth Integration Attempt at Lea's Restaurant" and "Four Rights Workers Beaten after Attending Assault Hearings," folder "Sworn Written Application for Registration," no box, Beech Papers; "Freedom Candidates Mississippi," RG 301.9, folder 4, box 9, and Robert J. Stone, "A Brief Review of Recent Developments in CORAR's Mississippi Program," April 22, 1964, 1, RG 301.9, folder 16, box 1, CORAR Records; *Religion and Race Memo* [UPCUSA] 1 (April 27, 1964): 3; *Student Voice,* April 28, 1964, 1, 4, May 26, 1964, 1, 4; "Act Two," 36. Smith appealed his thirty-day sentence and $125 fine. He received a $250 fine and a further $10 fine for sitting in the African American section of the segregated courtroom and refusing to move (Carlson, "Hattiesburg," 26; *Hattiesburg American,* March 10, 1964). Federal appellate courts eventually overturned Mississippi's antipicketing law (T. Branch, *Pillar of Fire,* 220).

13. Gayraud S. Wilmore Jr. to Robert W. Spike, March 5, 1964, RG 301.9, folder 11, box 8, and "Report of the Executive Director and Staff," June 1, 1964, 2, RG 301.9, folder 16, box 1, CORAR Records; "Ministers in Hattiesburg, Mississippi, January–May, 1964," folder "Volunteers—Delta Ministry," box 1, Beech Papers; Gayraud S. Wilmore Jr. to Eugene Carson Blake, May 4, 1964, RG 95, folder 18, box 15, Blake Papers; *Minutes of the General Assembly of the United Presbyterian Church in the United States of America,* 1966, 410.

14. *Student Voice,* April 28, 1964, 2, July 22, 1964, 1; "Communication from Executive Secretary," February 25, 1964, RG 301.9, folder 16, box 1, minutes, Adjunct Staff Council of Commission on Religion and Race, UPCUSA, February 26, 1964, 7, RG 301.9, folder 7, box 1, Robert J. Stone, "A Brief Review of Recent Developments in CORAR's Mississippi Program," April 22, 1964, 1, RG 301.9, folder 16, box 1, Gayraud S. Wilmore Jr. to Lawrence Guyot, April 14, 1964, RG 301.9, folder 17, box 8, minutes, Executive Committee, Commission on Religion and Race, UPCUSA, May 6, 1964, 5, RG 301.9, folder 9, box 1, "Freedom Candidates Mississippi," RG 301.9, folder 4, box 9, and minutes, Commission on Religion and Race, UPCUSA, June 2–3, 1964, 12, RG 301.9, folder 3, box 1, CORAR Records; *Religion and Race Memo* [UPCUSA] 1 (April 27, 1964): 3; Jerry DeMuth, "Mission in Mississippi," 10, attached to Jerry DeMuth to Robert L. Beech, August 19, 1964, folder "Reports, (R. B.) and Reactions Summer 1964 Hattiesburg, Mississippi," box 1, Robert L. Beech to James S. Leslie, December 6, 1965, folder "Copies of Correspondence Sent Out II," box 1, Robert L. Beech to the *Herald,* April 23, 1964, folder "News + Corresp.—race," box 3, Gayraud S. Wilmore Jr. to Robert L. Beech, April 24, 1964, folder "News + Corresp.—race," box 3, Robert L. Beech, "A Letter to All My Friends," May 17, 1964, folder "Hugh's Paper," box 3, and Robert L. Beech, "Hattiesburg Ministers' Project, June 13–23, 1964," folder "Reports and Reactions," no box, Beech Papers; T. Branch, *Pillar of Fire,* 269–70; "Appendix A, Biographical Data—Delta Ministry Staff," folder 39, box 2, and résumé, February 1969, attached to Robert L. Beech to "Dear Jon," March 14, 1969, folder 10, box 21, Delta Ministry Papers, Atlanta; Medelman, "Mission," 16–17; Robert L. Beech, interview by author, June 27, 1998.

15. Robert L. Beech, "Report from Hattiesburg, Week of May 18–23," May 24, 1964, 1–3, folder "Reports and Reactions," box 1; Robert L. Beech, "Report from Hattiesburg, May 25–June 2 [1964]," 1 (quotation), folder "Reports and Reactions," box 1, "Synopsis of Conference between Rev. Robert L. Beech and Robert H. Janover Regarding 'False Pretenses' Charge against Rev. Beech—Hattiesburg, Miss.—July 16–17, 1964," folder "Business Cor-

respondence Hattiesburg Project The Delta Ministry Part II," box 1, Beech Papers; Jerry DeMuth, "Mission in Mississippi," 4–6, attached to Jerry DeMuth to Robert L. Beech, August 19, 1964, folder "Reports, (R. B.) and Reactions Summer 1964 Hattiesburg, Mississippi," box 1, and "White Community Contacts," n.d., folder "White Community Contact," box 3, Beech Papers; Kremer, "Good News," 44; Robert L. Beech, "Report from Hattiesburg, October 21–November 9, 1964," 2, folder 3, box 21, Delta Ministry Papers, Atlanta; Sanford R. Leigh to Robert J. Stone, May 30, 1964, RG 301.9, folder 17, box 8, CORAR Records.

16. *Hattiesburg American,* February 22, 24, 1964; J. Moore, "Hattiesburg and Central Illinois," 340–41; unidentified press clipping, December 25, 1964, folder "Hattiesburg— Kamper Park Report," no box, Clyde C. Bryan to H. B. Munson, August 11, 1964, folder "Business Correspondence Hattiesburg Ministers' Project Part I," box 1, Robert L. Beech to W. H. Lockwood, April 27, 1965, folder "Letters, Copies of Business Correspondence, The Delta Ministry Hattiesburg Project," box 1, "White Community Contacts," n.d., folder "White Community Contact," box 3, Robert L. Beech, "Hattiesburg Ministers' Project, June 13–23, 1964," folder "Reports and Reactions," no box, and John E. Fawcett, "A Layman's Report from Mississippi," March 1965, 4, folder "Hattiesburg—1965–1966," no box, Beech Papers; Kremer, "Good News," 46; Robert J. Stone to Edler G. Hawkins, July 28, 1964, RG 301.9, folder 17, box 8, Robert J. Stone to John T. Mathison, March 1, 1965, RG 301.9, folder 17, box 8, and minutes, Executive Committee, Commission on Religion and Race, UPCUSA, November 13, 1964, 2 (quotation), RG 301.9, folder 9, box 1, CORAR Records; Jacobs and Boyd, "Christian Witness," 4.

17. Minear, "Hattiesburg," 115; Jerry DeMuth, "Mission in Mississippi," 10, attached to Jerry DeMuth to Robert L. Beech, August 19, 1964, folder "Reports, (R. B.) and Reactions Summer 1964 Hattiesburg, Mississippi," box 1, Beech Papers; Harry J. Bowie, interview by Tom Dent, May 28, 1979, MOHC; "Divisions of Board of Missions," 6; "Ministers Project Orientation," 3 (quotation), folder 548, box 11, King Papers; Wilmore, *Black and Presbyterian,* 73; E. King, "Religious Observations," 5–7.

18. Jerry DeMuth, "Mission in Mississippi," 2–4 (quotations on p. 3), attached to Jerry DeMuth to Robert L. Beech, August 19, 1964, folder "Reports, (R. B.) and Reactions Summer 1964 Hattiesburg, Mississippi," box 1, Beech Papers.

19. Robert L. Beech to Pat Hornaday, June 10, 1964 (quotation), Pat Hornaday to Robert L. Beech, June 22, 1964, and Robert L. Beech to Gayraud S. Wilmore Jr., June 29, 1964, RG 301.9, folder 13, box 8, CORAR Records; Robert L. Beech, "Report from Hattiesburg, June 3–12, 1964," 1, folder "Reports and Reactions," no box, Beech Papers; *Student Voice,* April 28, 1964, 2, June 2, 1964, 1, 4; "Votes for Freedom Candidates in Official Elections, 1962–1966," attached to Freedom Information Service to "Dear Community Leader or Organizer," July 30, 1966, folder 2, box 2, Bowie Papers. Both SNCC's unofficial figures and those cited by historian Hanes Walton Jr. accord Victoria Gray 4,314 votes and John Cameron 1,071 votes (*Student Voice,* June 9, 1964, 1; Walton, *Black Political Parties,* 93, 235).

20. Robert L. Beech, "Report from Hattiesburg, June 3–12, 1964," 2, Robert L. Beech, "Report from Hattiesburg, July 14–24[,] 1964," 1–2, and Robert L. Beech, "Report from Hattiesburg, August 4–11, 1964," folder "Reports and Reactions," no box, Beech Papers; "Profiles of Typical Freedom Schools" (quotation), n.d., folder 4, box 1, Bowie Papers; Robert L. Beech, "Report from Hattiesburg," *Delta Ministry* 1 (November 1964): 4.

21. Robert L. Beech, "Report from Hattiesburg, October 21–November 9, 1964," 1, folder 3, box 21, Delta Ministry Papers, Atlanta; Robert L. Beech, "Report from Hattiesburg, July 14–24[,] 1964," 1, folder "Reports and Reactions," no box, Robert L. Beech, "Report from Hattiesburg, September 1–October 20 [1964]," 1, folder "Reports and Reactions," no box, Kathleen W. Henderson, "Mississippi—August 2–10, 1964," 4, folder "Reports and Reactions," box 1, and Robert L. Beech to George Pierce, April 27, 1965, folder "Letters, Copies of Business Correspondence, The Delta Ministry Hattiesburg Project," box 1, Beech Papers; Robert L. Beech, "Report from Hattiesburg, for NCC Staff Meeting, Covering October–November 20 [1964]," 1, folder 548, box 11, King Papers; Robert L. Beech, "Report from Hattiesburg," *Delta Ministry* 1 (November 1964): 4; Kremer, "Good News," 44; *Student Voice*, August 5, 1964, 2–3; Minear, "Hattiesburg," 1115.

22. Robert L. Beech, "Report from Hattiesburg, June 23–30, 1964," July 2, 1964, 1–2 (quotations on p. 2), folder 2, box 59, ESCRU Papers; Robert L. Beech, "Hattiesburg Ministers' Project, June 13–23, 1964," Robert L. Beech, "Report from Hattiesburg, July 1–14[,] 1964," 2, and Robert L. Beech, "Report from Hattiesburg, July 14–24[,] 1964," 1, folder "Reports and Reactions," no box, Beech Papers; T. Shaw, "Report to Greenwood and Atlanta," July 11, 1964, folder "Reports (R. B.) and Reactions Summer 1964 Hattiesburg, Mississippi," box 1, Beech Papers; *Milwaukee Journal*, August 3, 1964; *Jackson Clarion-Ledger*, March 29, 1966; Jacobs and Boyd, "Christian Witness," 4.

23. Robert L. Beech, "Report from Hattiesburg, July 1–14[,] 1964," 1–2, folder "Reports and Reactions," no box, Robert L. Beech, "Report from Hattiesburg, July 24–August 3 [1964]," 3, folder "Reports and Reactions," no box, Robert L. Beech, "Report from Hattiesburg[,] August 12–19, 1964," folder "Reports and Reactions," box 1, and "Synopsis of Conference between Rev. Robert L. Beech and Robert H. Janover Regarding 'False Pretenses' Charge against Rev. Beech—Hattiesburg, Miss.—July 16–17, 1964," folder "Business Correspondence Hattiesburg Project The Delta Ministry Part II," box 1, Beech Papers; *Hattiesburg American*, July 10, 1964.

24. Robert L. Beech, "Report from Hattiesburg[,] July 24–August 3 [1964]," 2 (first quotation), and John Cameron, "Report from Hattiesburg, August 24–September 1 [1964]" (second quotation), folder "Reports and Reactions," no box, Beech Papers; Jerry DeMuth, "Mission in Mississippi," 5–7, attached to Jerry DeMuth to Robert L. Beech, August 19, 1964, folder "Reports, (R. B.) and Reactions Summer 1964 Hattiesburg, Mississippi," box 1, and Robert L. Beech to Roger Walke, February 8, 1965, folder "Letters, Copies of Business Correspondence, The Delta Ministry Hattiesburg Project," box 1, Beech Papers.

25. "Report from Hattiesburg, June 23–30, 1964," 2, folder 2, box 59, ESCRU Papers; Jerry DeMuth, "Mission in Mississippi," 5, attached to Jerry DeMuth to Robert L. Beech, August 19, 1964, folder "Reports, (R. B.) and Reactions Summer 1964 Hattiesburg, Mississippi," box 1, and Robert L. Beech, "Hattiesburg Ministers' Project, June 13–23, 1964," folder "Reports and Reactions," no box, Beech Papers; Robert L. Beech "Report from Hattiesburg," *Delta Ministry* 1 (November 1964): 4; Robert L. Beech, "Report and Evaluation—Hattiesburg, September 1964–September 1965," 2, in "Staff Reports, Commission on the Delta Ministry," October 1, 1965, folder "Staff Reports, October 1, 1965," box 1, Humphrey Papers; Holt, *Summer*, 339.

26. Robert L. Beech to Gayraud S. Wilmore Jr., June 29, 1964, RG 301.9, folder 13, box 8, and Gayraud S. Wilmore Jr. to Jon L. Regier, August 28, 1964, RG 301.9, folder 11, box

8, CORAR Records; Robert L. Beech to John Cameron, November 16, 1964, folder 1, box 21, Delta Ministry Papers, Atlanta; Robert L. Beech to Jesse Morris, November 28, 1964, folder "Letters, Copies of Business Correspondence, the Delta Ministry Hattiesburg Project," box 1, Robert L. Beech to E. C. Reckard, November 19, 1965, folder "Copies of Correspondence Sent Out II," box 1, and Robert L. Beech, "Report from Hattiesburg, August 12–19, 1964" (quotation), folder "Reports and Reactions," box 1, Beech Papers.

27. Robert L. Beech, "Report and Evaluation—Hattiesburg, September 1964–September 1965," 1 (quotation), in "Staff Reports, Commission on the Delta Ministry," October 1, 1965, folder "Staff Reports, October 1, 1965," box 1, Humphrey Papers; Robert L. Beech, "Report from Hattiesburg, September 1–October 20 [1964]," 1, folder "Reports and Reactions," no box, Beech Papers; Robert L. Beech, "Report from Hattiesburg, October 21–November 9, 1964," 1, folder 3, box 21, Delta Ministry Papers, Atlanta; Robert L. Beech, "Report from Hattiesburg, for NCC Staff Meeting, Covering October–November 20 [1964]," 1, 3, folder 548, box 11, King Papers.

28. Sanford R. Leigh, "Hattiesburg General Report, Fall, 1964," October 24, 1964, 3–7, folder 126, box 50, SNCC Papers; Robert L. Beech, "Report from Hattiesburg, for NCC Staff Meeting, Covering October–November 20 [1964]," 1, folder 548, box 11, King Papers; Robert L. Beech to Jesse Morris, November 28, 1964, folder "Letters, Copies of Business Correspondence, The Delta Ministry Hattiesburg Project," box 1, Robert L. Beech, "Report from Hattiesburg, September 1–October 20 [1964]," 1, folder "Reports and Reactions," no box, Beech Papers; Robert L. Beech, "Report from Hattiesburg, October 21–November 9, 1964," 1–2, folder 3, box 21, Delta Ministry Papers, Atlanta; "Churchmen and the Challenge," *Commission on Religion and Race Reports* [NCC], vol. 1, no. 4, n.d.

29. Robert L. Beech, "Report from Hattiesburg, for NCC Staff Meeting Covering October–November 20 [1964]," 3 (first quotation), folder 548, box 11, King Papers; Robert L. Beech, interview by author, June 27, 1998; Sanford R. Leigh, "Hattiesburg General Report, Fall, 1964," October 24, 1964, 5–7 (second quotation on p. 5), folder 126, box 50, SNCC Papers; Robert L. Beech, "Report from Hattiesburg, September 1–October 20 [1964]," 1, folder "Reports and Reactions," no box, Beech Papers.

30. Robert L. Beech, interview by author, June 27, 1998; Sanford R. Leigh, "Hattiesburg General Report, Fall, 1964," October 24, 1964, 1–2 (first and second quotations on p. 1), folder 126, box 50, SNCC Papers; Robert L. Beech to E. C. Reckard, November 19, 1965, folder "Copies of Correspondence Sent Out II," box 1, Beech Papers.

31. Robert L. Beech, "Report from Hattiesburg, September 1–October 20 [1964]," 1–2 (first and second quotations on p. 1), folder "Reports and Reactions," no box, Robert L. Beech to Bruce M. Stewart, October 29, 1964 (third quotation), folder "Letters, Copies of Business Correspondence, The Delta Ministry Hattiesburg Project," box 1, and Robert L. Beech to James S. Leslie, December 6, 1965, folder "Copies of Correspondence Sent Out II," box 1, Beech Papers. The Beeches' fourth son, Doug, was born in Hattiesburg on December 29, 1964 (résumé, February 1969, 3, attached to Robert L. Beech to "Dear Jon," March 14, 1969, folder 10, box 21, and "Appendix A, Biographical Data—Delta Ministry Staff," folder 39, box 2, Delta Ministry Papers, Atlanta).

32. Robert L. Beech to Drew Pearson, January 4, 1965, folder 4, box 21, Delta Ministry Papers, Atlanta; Robert L. Beech, "Report from Hattiesburg, September 1–October 20 [1964]," 2, folder "Reports and Reactions," no box, Beech Papers.

33. Robert L. Beech to John Doar, February 9, 1965, folder "Letters, Copies of Business Correspondence, The Delta Ministry Hattiesburg Project," box 1, and Robert L. Beech, "Report from Hattiesburg, September 1–October 20 [1964]," 2, folder "Reports and Reactions," no box, Beech Papers; "ssoc Sponsors Christmas Project," 2.

34. "Report from Hattiesburg," *Delta Ministry* 1 (January 1965): 6; Robert L. Beech, "Report from Hattiesburg, October 21–November 9, 1964," 1–2 (quotations on p. 1), folder 3, box 21, Delta Ministry Papers, Atlanta; Robert L. Beech to Donald Blanchette, February 10, 1965, folder "Letters, Copies of Business Correspondence, The Delta Ministry Hattiesburg Project," box 1, and unidentified press clipping, January 22, 1965, folder "January 1965," no box, Beech Papers.

35. Drew Pearson, "Hoping to Build Some Bridges" (press clipping), folder "Hattiesburg—Kamper Park Report," no box, Beech Papers; "Report from Hattiesburg," *Delta Ministry* 1 (January 1965): 6.

36. *Hattiesburg American,* January 22 (first quotation), March 31, 1965; Robert L. Beech to Roger Walke, February 8, 1965, folder "Letters, Copies of Business Correspondence, The Delta Ministry Hattiesburg Project," box 1, Robert L. Beech to Donald Blanchette, February 10, 1965 (second quotation), folder "Letters, Copies of Business Correspondence, The Delta Ministry Hattiesburg Project," box 1, unidentified press clipping, January 22, 1965, folder "January 1965," no box, and "Statement by Dick Kelly Concerning the Beating after the Citizen's Council Meeting Jan. 21, 1965," folder "Hattiesburg—Kamper Park Report," no box, Beech Papers. The case came before the courts a second time. However, the defendants did not attend, thereby forfeiting the small bonds they had paid and escaping punishment (Robert L. Beech to Donald Blanchette, February 10, 1965, folder "Letters, Copies of Business Correspondence, The Delta Ministry Hattiesburg Project," box 1, Beech Papers). Beech and his family became subject to further harassment in January 1965, when a stink bomb placed under their home forced them to vacate it temporarily. "Three and a half weeks later," Beech wrote, "there is still a very noticeable odor throughout the whole house, and especially beneath it" (Beech to Roger Walke, February 8, 1965, folder "Letters, Copies of Business Correspondence, The Delta Ministry Hattiesburg Project," box 1, Beech Papers).

37. "Report from Hattiesburg," *Delta Ministry* 1 (February 1965): 5; unidentified press clipping, February 23, 1965, folder "February 1965," box 6, Beech Papers.

38. "A Layman's Report from Mississippi, February 1965," 3, folder "Hattiesburg—1965–1966," no box, Beech Papers; "Report from Hattiesburg," *Delta Ministry* 1 (January 1965): 5; "Report from Hattiesburg," *Delta Ministry* 1 (February 1965): 5.

39. "Designated Gifts for Work in Hattiesburg," *Delta Ministry* 1 (November 1964): 5; Robert L. Beech, "Report and Evaluation—Hattiesburg, September 1964–September 1965," 13–14, in "Staff Reports, Commission on the Delta Ministry," October 1, 1965, folder "Staff Reports, October 1, 1965," box 1, Humphrey Papers.

40. "Authority to Act: Crisis in Hunger," attached to Stephen Arons to Arthur C. Thomas, October 5, 1965, folder "National Student Association," box 1, Thomas Papers; Robert L. Beech to Orville Freeman, May 14, 1965, folder "Letters, Copies of Business Correspondence, The Delta Ministry Hattiesburg Project," box 1, and Orville Freeman to Robert L. Beech, July 1, 1965, folder "Forrest Co.," no box, Beech Papers.

41. Barbara Woodard, "Mission to Mississippi," folder "Hattiesburg—1965–1966," no

box, Beech Papers; "Fact Sheet: Hattiesburg, Mississippi," folder 124, box 98, SNCC Papers; Robert L. Beech, "Report and Evaluation—Hattiesburg, September 1964–September 1965," 10–11, in "Staff Reports, Commission on the Delta Ministry," October 1, 1965, folder "Staff Reports, October 1, 1965," box 1, Humphrey Papers.

42. Robert L. Beech, "Report and Evaluation—Hattiesburg, September 1964–September 1965," 1, 3 (quotations), in "Staff Reports, Commission on the Delta Ministry," October 1, 1965, folder "Staff Reports, October 1, 1965," box 1, Humphrey Papers; *Hattiesburg American*, July 16, 1965; Robert L. Beech to M. J. Sanderson, July 5, 1965, folder "Letters, Copies of Business Correspondence, The Delta Ministry Hattiesburg Project," box 1, and Robert L. Beech to E. C. Reckard, November 19, 1965, folder "Copies of Correspondence Sent Out II," box 1, Beech Papers; Bruce Hilton to James L. Holloway, June 23, 1966, folder 10, box 19, Delta Ministry Papers, Atlanta; Daniel J. Wacker, "A Mississippi Journal, July, 1965," section on "Voter Registration," n.p., folder 5, box 1, Wacker Papers.

43. Robert L. Beech, "Report and Evaluation—Hattiesburg, September 1964–September 1965," 2 (quotations), 4, in "Staff Reports, Commission on the Delta Ministry," October 1, 1965, folder "Staff Reports, October 1, 1965," box 1, Humphrey Papers; Sanford R. Leigh, "Hattiesburg General Report, Fall, 1964," October 24, 1964, 4, 9, folder 126, box 50, SNCC Papers; Robert L. Beech, interview by author, June 30, 1998; Dittmer, *Local People*, 338–39, 343.

44. Robert L. Beech to Herbert McKinstry, June 26, 1965, folder "Letters, Copies of Business Correspondence, The Delta Ministry Hattiesburg Project," box 1, Beech Papers; unidentified press clipping in "Scrapbook of Clippings Concerning Civil Rights, Especially the Struggle in Mississippi, 1965, March 16–August 18," microfilm reel 1, Bowie Papers; *Hattiesburg American*, June 2, 1965; Daniel J. Wacker, "A Mississippi Journal, July, 1965," 5 (quotation), folder 5, box 1, Wacker Papers; Dittmer, *Local People*, 369.

45. Robert L. Beech, "Report and Evaluation—Hattiesburg, September 1964–September 1965," 6–8, and attached "Thoughts on the Future of Hattiesburg: A Working Paper," 1, in "Staff Reports, Commission on the Delta Ministry," October 1, 1965, folder "Staff Reports, October 1, 1965," box 1, Humphrey Papers; Robert L. Beech to D. Kumetat, June 2, 1965, Robert L. Beech to M. J. Sanderson, July 5, 1965, and Lee Baum to "Dear Eleanor," July 20, 1965, folder "Letters, Copies of Business Correspondence, The Delta Ministry Hattiesburg Project," box 1, Beech Papers; "Report from Hattiesburg, August 1–14, 1965," 1, folder "Hattiesburg—Kamper Park Report," no box, and "Yearly Report, September, 1965 to September, 1966," 6, folder "Forrest Co.," no box, Beech Papers; Kremer, "Mississippi Revisited," 24; *Hattiesburg American*, September 3, 1965.

46. Robert L. Beech, "Report and Evaluation—Hattiesburg, September 1964–September 1965," 4 (quotation), in "Staff Reports, Commission on the Delta Ministry," October 1, 1965, folder "Staff Reports, October 1, 1965," box 1, Humphrey Papers; David Nesmith to "Dear Friend," July 19, 1965, David Nesmith to "Dear Friends," July 25, August 10, 20, 25, 1965, folder "Hattiesburg—1965–1966," no box, Beech Papers; Bob Beech, "Hattiesburg," *Delta Ministry* 2 (September 1965): 2; Daniel J. Wacker, "A Mississippi Journal, July, 1965," 12–13, folder 5, box 1, Wacker Papers.

47. Robert L. Beech, "Report and Evaluation—Hattiesburg, September 1964–September 1965," 7 (second quotation), in "Staff Reports, Commission on the Delta Ministry," October 1, 1965, folder "Staff Reports, October 1, 1965," box 1, Humphrey Papers; *Hattiesburg*

American, July 27, September 2 (first quotation), 3, 1965; *Jackson Clarion-Ledger,* September 8, 1965. Segregationists founded a private school, the Forrest County School Foundation, Inc., that enabled white students to evade desegregation, which affected five of Hattiesburg's eight white public elementary schools (press clipping, August 31, 1965, folder "Newspaper scrapbook, August 1965," no box, Beech Papers; *Hattiesburg American,* September 2, 1965; Robert L. Beech, "Report and Evaluation—Hattiesburg, September 1964–September 1965," 7, in "Staff Reports, Commission on the Delta Ministry," October 1, 1965, folder "Staff Reports, October 1, 1965," box 1, Humphrey Papers).

48. Robert L. Beech to Clinton D. Morrison, December 29, 1965, folder "Copies of Correspondence Sent Out II," box 1, Beech Papers; Robert L. Beech, "Report and Evaluation—Hattiesburg, September 1964–September 1965," 2–4, 11, (second and third quotations) and attached "Thoughts on the Future of Hattiesburg: A Working Paper," 1 (first quotation), in "Staff Reports, Commission on the Delta Ministry," October 1, 1965, folder "Staff Reports, October 1, 1965," box 1, Humphrey Papers.

49. Robert L. Beech, "Report and Evaluation—Hattiesburg, September 1964–September 1965," 1–3 (quotation on p. 3), and attached "Thoughts on the Future of Hattiesburg: A Working Paper," 1, in "Staff Reports, Commission on the Delta Ministry," October 1, 1965, folder "Staff Reports, October 1, 1965," box 1, Humphrey Papers.

50. Robert L. Beech, "Greetings from Christmastown, Mississippi!" December 15, 1965, no folder, no box, untitled, undated, and unsigned statement concerning FSO, folder "CDGM-CAP," no box, Robert L. Beech, "Ways in Which the Church Should Be Involved in Hattiesburg, Miss. during 1966," 2, folder "Forrest Co.," no box, and "Yearly Report, September, 1965 to September, 1966," 1–5, folder "Forrest Co.," no box, Beech Papers; *Hattiesburg American,* July 22, 1966; "WATS Line Report—for DM Staff," January 3, 1967 (quotation), folder 33, box 3, Delta Ministry Papers, Atlanta.

51. *Hattiesburg American,* January 10, 1966; Robert L. Beech to Drew Pearson, February 10, 1966, folder "Copies of Correspondence Sent Out II," box 1, Beech Papers; "Another Murder in Mississippi," *Delta Ministry* 3 (January 1966): n.p.; "Vernon Dahmer," *Free at Last,* 86; Cagin and Dray, *We Are Not Afraid,* 12, 245–47, 266, 283, 382. Three of the Klansmen received life sentences for Dahmer's murder and another man ten years for arson. Bowers escaped punishment after four trials ended in hung juries. However, he and six others were convicted in October 1967 of violating the civil rights of Schwerner and the two men who had been murdered alongside him, James Chaney and Andrew Goodman. Bowers served six years of a ten-year sentence. He was finally convicted of Dahmer's murder in August 1998 and given a life sentence (Peters, "32 Years"; Cagin and Dray, *We Are Not Afraid,* 382, 452). On Bowers's life, see Marsh, *God's Long Summer,* 49–81.

52. Arthur C. Thomas to Jon L. Regier, January 24, 1966, folder "Correspondence Received IV," box 1, David Emmons, untitled, January 25, 1966 (quotations), folder "Dahmer," box 3, and Robert L. Beech to "Dear Friends of Vernon Dahmer," March 4, 1966, folder "Dahmer," box 3, Beech Papers; *Jackson Daily News,* January 11, 12, 13, 1966; *Hattiesburg American,* January 15, 1966; Gloster B. Current to Robert L. Beech, February 4, 1966, and Robert L. Beech to Gloster B. Current, March 4, 1966, folder "Hattiesburg—Dahmer," box 3, Thomas Papers.

53. David Emmons, untitled, January 25, 1966 (quotation), folder "Dahmer," box 3, Beech Papers; *Jackson Daily News,* January 13, 1966.

54. Robert L. Beech to Ernest Norquist, January 26, 1966 (first, second and third quotations), and Robert L. Beech to Frederick C. Maier, February 9, 1966 (fourth quotation), folder "Copies of Correspondence Sent Out II," box 1, Beech Papers; Robert L. Beech to "Dear Friends of Vernon Dahmer," March 4, 1966, folder "Dahmer," box 3, Beech Papers; Robert L. Beech to Gloster B. Current, March 4, 1966, folder "Hattiesburg—Dahmer," box 3, Thomas Papers. Beech's accusations against the NAACP were substantiated by Dahmer's sister, Mrs. Beard, who wrote to Roy Wilkins that although the NAACP's Hattiesburg chapter had responded negatively to Dahmer's proactive ideas during his lifetime, after his death, its members had "sought to redeem themselves by standing arrayed in the glory of his sacrifice." She praised the effectiveness of the Delta Ministry's work in Hattiesburg and contrasted it with the inadequacies of the local NAACP. Beard concluded her letter by warning Wilkins that the "jealousy and prejudice exhibited by our brothers here cannot superside the hazards that beset us today" (Greenberg, *Devil*, 422–24; first quotation on p. 423, second quotation on p. 424).

55. Gloster B. Current to Robert L. Beech, February 4, 1966, J. C. Fairley to Jon L. Regier, March 25, 1966, and Robert L. Beech to Gloster B. Current, April 1, 1966, folder "Hattiesburg—Dahmer," box 3, Thomas Papers; Gloster B. Current to Robert L. Beech, March 11, 1966 (quotation), untitled folder, box 1, Gloster B. Current to Robert L. Beech, May 10, 1966, untitled folder, box 1, and J. C. Fairley to Jon L. Regier and Robert L. Beech, April 20, 1966, folder "Forrest Co.," no box, Beech Papers.

56. Current, "Death," 109; David Emmons, untitled, January 25, 1966, and Robert L. Beech to "Dear Friends of Vernon Dahmer," March 4, 1966, 1–3 (quotations on p. 2), folder "Dahmer," box 3, Beech Papers.

57. Robert L. Beech to "Dear Friends of Vernon Dahmer," March 4, 1966, 1–3 (first quotation on p. 2; third, fourth, and fifth quotations on p. 3), folder "Dahmer," box 3, and Robert L. Beech to Howard Hammerman, March 3, 1966 (second quotation), untitled folder, box 1, Beech Papers.

58. Robert L. Beech to Carl R. Scovel, April 21, 1966, folder "Keep For Reference No. II," box 1, Robert L. Beech to Howard Hammerman, March 3, 1966, untitled folder, box 1, Robert L. Beech to "Dear Friends of Vernon Dahmer," March 4, 1966, 3–4, folder "Dahmer," box 3, "Yearly Report, September, 1965 to September, 1966," 2, folder "Forrest Co.," no box, memorandum, Robert L. Beech to "Anyone Interested in Following Through," n.d., 5, folder "Proposal Beech," no box, and Robert L. Beech to Martin B. Olsen, June 1, 1966, folder "Keep For Reference No. II," box 1, Beech Papers; Arthur C. Thomas to Jon L. Regier, April 22, 1966, folder "Budget Measures 1966," box 3, Thomas Papers.

59. Robert L. Beech to E. C. Reckard, January 26, 1966, Robert L. Beech to Frederick C. Maier, February 9, 1966, Robert L. Beech to R. H. Beech, February 14, 1966, 1–2 (second quotation on p. 2), and Robert L. Beech to Drew Pearson, February 10, 1966, folder "Copies of Correspondence Sent Out II," box 1, Beech Papers; Robert L. Beech to William H. Bickel, August 5, 1966, untitled folder, box 1, Beech Papers; *New York Times,* January 11, 1966; *Jackson Daily News,* January 11, 1966; *Hattiesburg American,* January 15, 1966 (first quotation).

60. Robert L. Beech to Robert T. Clark, October 29, 1966, untitled folder, box 1, Robert L. Beech to "Dear Friends of Vernon Dahmer," March 4, 1966, 3–4, folder "Dahmer," box 3, and memorandum, Robert L. Beech to "Anyone Interested in Following Through," n.d., 5, folder "Proposal Beech," no box, Beech Papers. According to a *New York Times* report,

the new Dahmer home, built on the site of the old, remained "partly finished" six years later (*New York Times*, December 24, 1972). Before his death, Dahmer and Beech had been discussing the idea of creating a log cabin business as part of the Delta Ministry's desire to create small black-owned businesses in the Hattiesburg area that would provide African Americans with jobs and training (Robert L. Beech to R. H. Beech, February 14, 1966, 1–2, folder "Copies of Correspondence Sent Out II," box 1, and Robert L. Beech to Carl R. Scovel, April 21, 1966, folder "Keep For Reference No. II," box 1, Beech Papers).

61. Robert L. Beech, "Sale of the Old Bay Springs School Property in Kelly Settlement, Forrest County, Miss., Formerly Owned by the Dahmer Family," April 19, 1966, folder "Bob Beech," box 3, Thomas Papers; Benjamin E. Smith to Jim Heller, May 24, 1966, folder "Beard Property," box 3, and Robert L. Beech to "Editor, *Hattiesburg American*," February 3, 1967, folder "CDGM-CAP," no box, Beech Papers.

62. Robert L. Beech to Carl R. Scovel, April 21, 1966, and Robert L. Beech to Marshal Scott, January 3, 1967, folder "Keep For Reference No. II," box 1, Beech Papers; Robert L. Beech to Henry A. McCanna, August 28, 1967, Robert L. Beech to "Dear Sam," September 7, 1967, and Robert L. Beech to John M. Adams, October 6, 1967, untitled folder, box 1, Beech Papers; minutes, Executive Committee, Commission on the Delta Ministry, July 31, 1967, 2 (quotation), folder 47, box 3, Delta Ministry Papers, Starkville; Sue Geiger to Mary Bolljahn, February 10, 1968, folder 31, box 19, Delta Ministry Papers, Atlanta. While at Mary Holmes Junior College, a UPCUSA institution, Beech designed, persuaded the Presbyterian Board of National Missions to fund, and worked in the Clay County Community Development Program, which included a child development center, four cooperatives, a youth center, and a tutorial program. Beech left Mississippi in 1968 to study at Harvard University. He explained that as African Americans "were moving toward self-determination and a new self-identity, my presence was unavoidably a frustration," résumé, February 1969, 3–4 (quotation on p. 4), 8, attached to Robert L. Beech to "Dear Jon," March 14, 1969, folder 10, box 21, Delta Ministry Papers, Atlanta; Robert L. Beech to "Dear Dave," February 17, 1968, and Robert L. Beech to "Dear John & family," April 25, 1968, untitled folder, box 1, Beech Papers; Robert L. Beech, "Position Paper," n.d., folder "Proposal Beech," no box, Beech Papers.

63. Barbara Woodard, "Mission to Mississippi," 2, folder "Hattiesburg—1965–1966," no box, Beech Papers; Robert L. Beech to R. H. Beech, February 14, 1966, 1–2, folder "Copies of Correspondence Sent Out II," box 1, Robert L. Beech to Carl R. Scovel, April 21, 1966, folder "Keep For Reference No. II," box 1, Robert L. Beech to William H. Bickel, August 5, 1966, untitled folder, box 1, and Robert L. Beech to "Dear Walden," May 11, 1967, untitled folder, box 1, Beech Papers; Robert L. Beech, "Report and Evaluation—Hattiesburg, September 1964–September 1965," 5, 9, in "Staff Reports, Commission on the Delta Ministry," October 1, 1965, folder "Staff Reports, October 1, 1965," Humphrey Papers.

64. Robert L. Beech to Hank Bierstecker, March 22, 1967, and Robert L. Beech to "Dear Walden," May 11, 1967, untitled folder, box 1, Beech Papers.

65. Robert L. Beech, "Report and Evaluation—Hattiesburg, September 1964–September 1965," 2–3, in "Staff Reports, Commission on the Delta Ministry," October 1, 1965, folder "Staff Reports, October 1, 1965," box 1, Humphrey Papers; *Hattiesburg American*, June 24, 1965; "WATS Line Report—for DM Staff," January 3, 1967, folder 33, box 3, Delta Ministry Papers, Atlanta; Robert L. Beech to "Dear Friends of Vernon Dahmer," March 4, 1966, 1–

3, folder "Dahmer," box 3, Robert L. Beech to "Dear Andy," May 11, 1967, untitled folder, box 1, "Yearly Report, September, 1965 to September, 1966," 1, 3–5, folder "Forrest Co.," no box, Robert L. Beech to William Zurden, July 28, 1966, folder "CDGM-CAP," box 1, untitled, undated statement, folder "CDGM-CAP," box 1, and memorandum, Robert L. Beech to "Forrest-Stone Opportunities Inc. Board, Staff, & Committees," October 3, 1966, folder "Headstart," no box, Beech Papers.

66. Robert L. Beech to "Dear Friends of Vernon Dahmer," March 4, 1966, 1–3, folder "Dahmer," box 3, and "Yearly Report, September, 1965 to September, 1966," 4–5 (first quotation on p. 5), folder "Forrest Co.," no box, Beech Papers; Morrison, *Black Political Mobilization*, 49; Robert L. Beech, "A Proposal for a Study and Work Program," April 26, 1967, attached to Robert L. Beech to Gayraud S. Wilmore Jr., April 26, 1967, 1 (second and third quotations), RG 301.9, folder 7, box 14, CORAR Records.

CHAPTER FOUR. McComb, 1964–1966

1. "Biographical Sketch," folder 46, box 4, Delta Ministry Papers, Starkville; "McComb," attached to Harry J. Bowie to Myles Horton, August 25, 1965, folder 2, box 81, Highlander Research and Education Center Records, WHS; Harry J. Bowie to Drew Pearson, March 11, 1966, folder 2, box 1, and "McComb Report," n.d., 1–3, folder 10, box 1, Bowie Papers; "McComb," *Delta Ministry* 2 (September 1965): n.p.; Arthur C. Thomas to Jon L. Regier, April 22, 1966, folder "Budget Measures 1966," box 3, Thomas Papers.

2. "Sketches of Delta Ministry Project Sites," attached to "Special Delta Ministry Activities," folder 1431–2–3:05, Church and Society Records, UMC; Harry J. Bowie, interview by Tom Dent, May 28, 1979, MOHC; Hayden, *Revolution*, 9; Feagans, "Voting," 3; Cunnigen, "Men and Women," 304–7 n.21; Dittmer, *Local People*, 99–101.

3. Moses, "Mississippi," 8–12; Hayden, *Revolution*, 5, 7–15, 17–24; Feagans, "Voting," 3–4; *Student Voice*, January 14, 1964, 1–2; Forman, *Making*, 223–31; Zinn, *SNCC*, 66–71; Dittmer, *Local People*, 101–108; Payne, *I've Got the Light*, 111–17, 120; T. Branch, *Parting the Waters*, 330–31, 486–87, 492–500, 503–4, 507–9; Carson, *In Struggle*, 46–48; Burner, *And Gently He Shall Lead Them*, 36–40, 43–56.

4. Cunnigen, "Men and Women," 305–7 n.21; Forman, *Making*, 227–28, 232–33; Moses, "Mississippi," 8, 10–14; Hayden, *Revolution*, 11, 17–21, 23–27; Zinn, *SNCC*, 68–69, 74–76; Dittmer, *Local People*, 106–8, 110–14; Payne, *I've Got the Light*, 117–20, 124–28; T. Branch, *Parting the Waters*, 498, 500, 511–14, 519–20, 522–23; Carson, *In Struggle*, 48–50; Burner, *And Gently He Shall Lead Them*, 53, 59–63, 65; Feagans, "Voting," 3.

5. *Student Voice*, June 1962, 4; Moses, "Mississippi," 12–13, 15; Hayden, *Revolution*, 16, 25–27; Forman, *Making*, 231; Zinn, *SNCC*, 71–74, 76–77; Dittmer, *Local People*, 109, 114; Payne, *I've Got the Light*, 121–24, 128; T. Branch, *Parting the Waters*, 509–11, 520–22, 559–60; Burner, *And Gently He Shall Lead Them*, 57–58, 65–67.

6. *Student Voice*, January 14, 1964, 1; *McComb Enterprise-Journal*, December 12, 1984; Dittmer, *Local People*, 265–66.

7. *Student Voice*, January 14, 1964, 1; Payne, *I've Got the Light*, 121–23, 299–300; Dittmer, *Local People*, 109, 215; T. Branch, *Parting the Waters*, 509–11, 520–22, 921; Burner, *And Gently He Shall Lead Them*, 58–59.

8. *Student Voice*, July 15, 1964, 1, 4; "Civil Rights: Conflict but Encouragement," 21; "Min-

ister Counselors as of 21 July 1964," folder 11, box 23, MFDP Papers; Boyd, "Battle," 1398, 1400; W. Rowland, "How It Is," 340; H. Carter [II], *So the Heffners Left McComb*, 29–30, 43, 97; Johnston, *Mississippi's Defiant Years*, 315; Harry J. Bowie, interview by Jack Bass and Walter DeVries, March 31, 1974, 3, SOHP #4007; "List of Clergy and Seminarians Participating in the Mississippi Project at McComb during the Week from September 28 to October 4, 1964," October 5, 1964, attached to Frederick S. Lowry to "Dear John," October 9, 1964, box 59, folder 8, ESCRU Papers; *McComb Enterprise-Journal*, December 12, 1984; "Delta Ministry Fact Sheet," January 1965, appendix A, folder "Delta Ministry—Minutes, Budgets, Fact Sheets—1965," box 1, Humphrey Papers; Davies, "J. Oliver Emmerich," 2, 5, 9–10; Dittmer, *Local People*, 266–68.

9. Boyd, "Battle," 1402; "Ministers, Adult Laymen Recruited By National Council of Churches for Work in Mississippi Summer Project—June 15 to Sept 1, 1964," folder 38, box 2, "Ministers and Adult Laymen Recruited by NCC for Work in *Mississippi Summer Project* (Participants Listed by State)," folder 21, box 8, and "Ministers and Adult Laymen Recruited by the National Council of Churches for Work in the Mississippi Summer Project," folder 21, box 8, Delta Ministry Papers, Atlanta; *Episcopal Society for Cultural and Racial Unity Newsletter* 24 (November 8, 1964): 2; H. Carter [II], *So the Heffners Left McComb*, 9–142; Johnston, *Mississippi's Defiant Years*, 312–16; Emmerich, *Two Faces*, 133; T. Branch, *Pillar of Fire*, 394; Dittmer, *Local People*, 305.

10. H. Carter [II], *So the Heffners Left McComb*, 97; Harry J. Bowie, interview by Jack Bass and Walter DeVries, March 31, 1974, 3, SOHP #4007; Harry J. Bowie, interview by Robert Wright, August 8, 1968, 1–3, Bunche Oral History Project; Harry J. Bowie, interview by Tom Dent, June 10, 1979, MOHC; Harry J. Bowie, interview by author, September 5, 1996; "Delta Ministry Fact Sheet," January 1965, appendix A, folder "Delta Ministry—Minutes, Budgets, Fact Sheets—1965," box 1, Humphrey Papers; Shattuck, *Episcopalians and Race*, 143.

11. *McComb Enterprise-Journal*, December 12, 1984; W. Rowland, "How It Is," 340; "McComb Report," n.d., 2, folder 10, box 1, Bowie Papers; *Student Voice*, August 5, 1964, 2–3; "Freedom School Data," n.d., folder 4, box 1, Bowie Papers; Dittmer, *Local People*, 268–69.

12. "McComb Report," 1, folder 10, box 1, Bowie Papers; *I. F. Stone's Weekly*, October 5, 1964; Dittmer, *Local People*, 269.

13. *I. F. Stone's Weekly*, October 5, 1964; W. Rowland, "How It Is," 342; Dittmer, *Local People*, 270.

14. *Student Voice*, September 23, 1964, 2, 3; *Episcopal Society for Cultural and Racial Unity Newsletter* 24 (November 8, 1964): 2; *New York Herald-Tribune*, September 26, 1964; *I. F. Stone's Weekly*, October 5, 1964; *McComb Enterprise-Journal*, December 12, 1984; Johnston, *Mississippi's Defiant Years*, 317; Boyd, "Battle," 1400; W. Rowland, "How It Is," 342; William S. Rowling, "An Appeal—A Response: Experience in McComb, Mississippi, September 25–27," *PARR* [United Presbyterian Synod of Pennsylvania] 2 (November 20, 1964): 2; "Shame," 14; "Magnolia," 18; T. Branch, *Pillar of Fire*, 494–95; Dittmer, *Local People*, 104, 306–7.

15. "Shame," 14; T. Branch, *Pillar of Fire*, 497 (quotation); Dittmer, *Local People*, 308.

16. *New York Herald-Tribune*, September 26, 1964; "Shame," 14; "Statement by the Commission on Religion and Race of the National Council of Churches, September 25, 1964," *Information Bulletin* [Mississippi Association of Methodist Ministers and Laymen] 1 (October 1964): 1–2; *McComb Enterprise-Journal*, December 12, 1984; Dittmer, *Local People*, 308–9

(quotation on p. 309); T. Branch, *Pillar of Fire*, 497–98, 504; Davies, "J. Oliver Emmerich," 10–18.

17. William S. Rowling, "An Appeal—A Response: Experience in McComb, Mississippi, September 25–27," *PARR* [United Presbyterian Synod of Pennsylvania] 2 (November 20, 1964): 2; "Ministers in McComb," 32; *Religion and Race Memo* [UPCUSA], October 5, 1964; Robert L. Beech, "Report from Hattiesburg, September 1–October 20 [1964]," folder "Reports by Ministers," no box, Beech Papers; Robert W. Spike, "Report of the Executive Director," November 5, 1964, 2, RG 6, folder 14, box 2, NCC Archives; minutes, International Convention Coordinating Committee on Moral and Civil Rights, October 14, 1964, 1, folder 10, box 15, Delta Ministry Papers, Atlanta; Harry J. Bowie, interview by Tom Dent, May 28, 1979, MOHC; *McComb Enterprise-Journal*, December 12, 1984; Greenberg, *Devil*, 728.

18. *Religion and Race Memo* [UPCUSA], October 5, 1964; "Magnolia," 18; *McComb Enterprise-Journal*, September 29, 1964 (quotations); Boyd, "Battle," 1402, 1404.

19. "List of Ministers in McComb from Sept. 1 to Jan. 5, 1965," folder 10, box 1, Bowie Papers; Robert L. Beech to Brewer Burnett, October 8, 1964 (quotation), folder "Letters, Copies of Business Correspondence, The Delta Ministry Hattiesburg Project," box 1, Beech Papers; "Ministers in McComb," 32; Harbison, "Oh, Freedom," 24–26.

20. Dittmer, *Local People*, 309–10.

21. *Jackson Daily News*, October 2, 1964; *Student Voice*, November 25, 1964, 1 (quotations), 4; "The Eleven McComb Bombers," folder 10, box 1, Bowie Papers; Dittmer, *Local People*, 310–11; *New York Times*, January 19, 1966.

22. J. Frederick McKirachan, "Ministerial Mission to McComb[,] Mississippi, October 19–29, 1964," 1–6, RG 301.9, folder 38, box 9, CORAR Records; memorandum, Betty Garman to "Friends of SNCC, Campus Contacts . . . and Others . . . ," October 27, 1964, 1 (quotation), folder 8, box 59, ESCRU Papers; Harbison, "Oh, Freedom," 24. The food-handling charges were later dismissed (Harry J. Bowie to Drew Pearson, March 11, 1966, folder 2, box 1, Bowie Papers).

23. Memorandum, Betty Garman to "Friends of SNCC, Campus Contacts . . . and Others . . . ," October 27, 1964, 1, 3, folder 8, box 59, ESCRU Papers; Harbison, "Oh, Freedom," 24–26 (quotations on p. 24); J. Frederick McKirachan, "Ministerial Mission to McComb[,] Mississippi, October 19–29, 1964," 2, 6, RG 301.9, folder 38, box 9, CORAR Records; Robert L. Beech to Bruce M. Stewart, October 29, 1964, and Robert L. Beech to J. Raymond Sikkel, October 30, 1964, folder "Letters, Copies of Business Correspondence, The Delta Ministry Hattiesburg Project," box 1, Beech Papers; Robert L. Beech, "Report from Hattiesburg, for NCC Staff Meeting, Covering October–November 20 [1964]," 3, folder 548, box 11, King Papers; Harry J. Bowie to Drew Pearson, March 11, 1966, and attachments, and Harry J. Bowie to William Carhart, March 11, 1966, folder 2, box 1, Bowie Papers; "List of Ministers in McComb from Sept. 1 to Jan. 5, 1965," folder 10, box 1, Bowie Papers. The charges against all those arrested on October 26 and 27 were dismissed in February 1966 with the payment of costs (Harry J. Bowie to Drew Pearson, March 11, 1966, folder 2, box 1, Bowie Papers).

24. "Ministers in McComb," 32 (first and second quotations); Boyd, "Battle," 1398, 1402 (third quotation); Harry J. Bowie, interview by Tom Dent, May 28, 1979, MOHC; "Divisions of Board of Missions," 6.

25. "Report on McComb, Mississippi," September 29, 1964, folder 14, box 59, ESCRU

Papers; Harbison, "Oh, Freedom," 25 (quotation); "List of Ministers in McComb from Sept. 1 to Jan. 5, 1965," folder 10, box 1, Bowie Papers; Dittmer, *Local People,* 266.

26. "Card File of Personnel Involved in the Delta Ministers' Project, McComb County [*sic*], Mississippi, ca. 1964–1967; and Names and Identifications of Local Residents Involved," microfilm, Bowie Papers; "McComb Report," n.d., 3, folder 10, box 1, Bowie Papers; Boyd, "Battle," 1402.

27. Emmerich, *Two Faces,* 135–50 (first quotation on p. 138), 147–50; *Lexington Advertiser,* November 26, 1964 (subsequent quotations); Dittmer, *Local People,* 312.

28. *Memphis Commercial Appeal,* November 21, 1964; *New York Times,* November 19, 1964; Dittmer, *Local People,* 312–13.

29. "List of Ministers in McComb from Sept. 1 to Jan. 5, 1965," folder 10, box 1, Bowie Papers; "Mccomb Volunteers," n.d., folder "Volunteers—Delta Ministry," box 1, Beech Papers; "Report from McComb," *Delta Ministry* 1 (February 1965): 9.

30. B. L. Smith, "Meanwhile in Mississippi," 39; "Report from McComb," *Delta Ministry* 1 (January 1965): 7 (quotations); Dittmer, *Local People,* 313–14.

31. William D. Bennett, "Visit to McComb, Mississippi, November 16–20, 1964," folder 12, box 21, Delta Ministry Papers, Atlanta; Dittmer, *Local People,* 313–14, 341–44 (quotation on p. 342).

32. Dittmer, *Local People,* 322–23; Walton, *Black Political Parties,* 104–5, 235–36.

33. *Mississippi Freedom Democratic Party Newsletter* 2 (April 4, 1965): 2, folder 2, box 2, Robert W. Ostrow to Barbara Brandt, March 23, 1965, and attached "Bail Report—March 23, 1965," folder 2, box 1, and Harry J. Bowie to Drew Pearson, March 11, 1966, folder 2, box 1, Bowie Papers; *Student Voice,* March 5, 1965, 2; "Report from McComb," *Delta Ministry* 1 (February 1965): 9; Blanchard, "Delta Ministry," 338.

34. "The Mississippi Freedom Democratic Party Is Your Party . . . ," n.d., folder 2, box 2, "The Election in McComb—A Report," n.d., folder 3, box 2, *Mississippi Freedom Democratic Party Newsletter* 2 (April 4, 1965): 6, and "Platform," n.d. (quotation), folder 2, box 2, and "McComb Report," n.d., 2, folder 10, box 1, Bowie Papers; "Report from McComb," *Delta Ministry* 1 (February 1965): 9.

35. "The Election in McComb—A Report," n.d., 2, folder 3, box 2, Bowie Papers; "McComb" (quotation), attached to Harry J. Bowie to Myles Horton, August 25, 1965, folder 2, box 81, Highlander Research and Education Center Records, WHS.

36. Harry J. Bowie to Charles McNiell, May 10, 1965 (quotation), folder 8, box 1, and "The Election in McComb—A Report," n.d., 2, folder 3, box 2, Bowie Papers; Harry J. Bowie to Myles Horton, August 25, 1965, folder 2, box 81, Highlander Research and Education Center Records, WHS.

37. "McComb Report," 2, folder 10, box 1, Bowie Papers; memorandum, "Southwest Mississippi Opportunities, Inc., and Southwest Child Development Council," November 14, 1966, folder 6, box 139, Johnson Family Papers.

38. Dorothy Jean Tucker, "Case History of All the Children at the Table of France," and Mr. and Mrs. Frank Tucker to "Dear Sir," n.d., Sweet Home Center, McComb, Mississippi, reel 12, CDGM Records, WHS.

39. *Interchurch News,* October 1965 (first quotation), folder 594, box 11, King Papers; "Mccomb Volunteers," n.d., folder "Volunteers—Delta Ministry," box 1, Beech Papers; Harry J. Bowie to Conard Pyle, July 13, 1965, folder 8, box 1, and "McComb Report," n.d., 3 (second,

third, and fourth quotations), folder 10, box 1, Bowie Papers; Daniel J. Wacker, "A Mississippi Journal, July, 1965," 6, folder 5, box 1, Wacker Papers.

40. Daniel J. Wacker, "A Mississippi Journal, July, 1965," appendix, "Voter Registration," folder 5, box 1, Wacker Papers; "Political Picture—Voter Registration," attached to Harry J. Bowie to Myles Horton, August 25, 1965, folder 2, box 81, Highlander Research and Education Center Records, WHS; "McComb Report," n.d., 1, folder 10, box 1, Bowie Papers; "New Form, New Votes," *Delta Ministry* 1 (August 1965): 3; *Jackson Clarion-Ledger/Jackson Daily News,* August 15, 1965; *Jackson Clarion-Ledger,* August 18, 1965; Lawson, *In Pursuit,* 14–15. By 1967, 10,016 African Americans, 75 percent of those eligible, were registered voters in Pike County (Morrison, *Black Political Mobilization,* 49). Mississippi still required voters in state and local elections to have paid two years of poll taxes. The Twenty-fourth Amendment to the U.S. Constitution, adopted in 1964, had outlawed poll taxes in federal elections. The U.S. attorney general initiated litigation that ended the poll tax in nonfederal elections in 1966 ("What You Should Know about Poll Taxes," n.d., folder 3, box 2, Bowie Papers; Lawson, *Black Ballots,* 82, 290; Lawson, *Running,* 111).

41. L. E. Cole Jr., "Southwest Mississippi Opportunity, Inc.," October 24, 1966, 1, folder 5, box 139, Johnson Family Papers; *McComb Enterprise-Journal,* December 12, 1984.

42. *Jackson Daily News,* August 27, 1965; *McComb Enterprise-Journal,* August 10, 30, September 8, 1965, clippings in "Scrapbook of Clippings Concerning Civil Rights, Especially the Struggle in Mississippi, 1965, March 16–Aug. 18," microfilm reel 1, Bowie Papers; "McComb Report," n.d., 3, folder 10, box 1, and William Ard and Mary Lee Ard to Nicholas Katzenbach, n.d., folder 6, box 2, Bowie Papers.

43. "McComb Report," n.d., 2, folder 10, box 1, Bowie Papers; "McComb," attached to Harry J. Bowie to Myles Horton, August 25, 1965, folder 2, box 81, Highlander Research and Education Center Records, WHS; "McComb," *Delta Ministry Reports* 2 (September 1965): n.p.

44. Minutes of the first membership meeting of the Poor People's Corporation, August 29, 1965, 1, 3–6, folder 82, box 125, and minutes of the second membership meeting of the Poor People's Corporation, November 28, 1965, 1–2, folder 150, box 116, SNCC Papers; Owen H. Brooks, "Report on the Delta Ministry, 1967," folder 32, box 3, Delta Ministry Papers, Atlanta; Sutherland, "Mississippi Summer," 213–14; *New York Times,* March 5, 1967; "McComb Report," n.d., 2, folder 10, box 1, Bowie Papers; E. Coopersmith to Harry J. Bowie, January 18, February 2, 1966, receipt signed by Clementeen Joseph, February 5, 1966, attached to memorandum, Roger A. Smith to William A. Carhart, February 21, 1966, and William A. Carhart to Roger A. Smith, February 25, 1966, folder 5, box 2, Bowie Papers; "McComb," attached to Harry J. Bowie to Myles Horton, August 25, 1965, folder 2, box 81, Highlander Research and Education Center Records, WHS.

45. "Report from McComb," *Delta Ministry* 1 (February 1965): 9; Harry J. Bowie to Conard Pyle, July 13, 1965, folder 8, box 1, and Henry W. Sawyer III to Alvin Bronstein, December 29, 1966, folder 6, box 1, Bowie Papers; Day, " 'Justice Place,' " 27; *Delta Ministry Reports,* February 1969, 2, October 1969, 2; *McComb Enterprise-Journal,* December 12, 1984; L. E. Cole Jr., "South Mississippi Opportunities, Inc.," November 7, 1966, 2–4, and L. E. Cole Jr., "Reverend Harry K. [*sic*] Bowie, Pike County, Mississippi," November 21, 1966, folder 6, box 139, Johnson Family Papers; Harry J. Bowie, interview by author, September

5, 1996; Dittmer, *Local People*, 60. For a history of the Sovereignty Commission, see Katagiri, *Mississippi State Sovereignty Commission.*

46. Arthur C. Thomas to Harry J. Bowie, April 20, 1966, folder 49, box 12, Delta Ministry Papers, Atlanta; Arthur C. Thomas to Jon L. Regier, April 22, 1966, folder "Budget Measures 1966," box 3, Thomas Papers; Robert L. Beech to Gayraud S. Wilmore Jr., October 22, 1966, folder "Keep For Reference No. II," box 1, Beech Papers; *Delta Ministry Reports,* June 1966, 1, November 1966, 2; minutes, Executive Committee Commission on the Delta Ministry, July 31, 1967, 2, folder 47, box 3, and "Biographical Sketch," folder 46, box 4, Delta Ministry Papers, Starkville; "Delta Ministry Staff (as of December 1, 1966)," folder "D.M. Fact Sheet," no box, Winham Papers; L. E. Cole Jr., "Southwest Mississippi Opportunity, Inc.," October 24, 1966, 1–3, and L. E. Cole Jr., "Southwest Mississippi Opportunity, Inc.," October 28, 1966, 2, folder 5, box 139, Johnson Family Papers; *McComb Enterprise-Journal,* December 12, 1984.

47. Aylene Quin to Daniel J. Wacker, February 10, 1967 (quotation), folder 2, box 1, Wacker Papers; memorandum, David R. Bowen to Theodore M. Berry, October 7, 1966, folder "Head Start Project, 1966," box 1, Bowie Papers; OEO press release, "OEO Builds Community Action in Mississippi," October 11, 1966, RG 301.7, folder 19, box 45, Board of National Missions (PCUSA) Records; Greenberg, *Devil,* 588, 617–20, 635–36; Dittmer, *Local People,* 368–79; *Memphis Commercial Appeal,* January 9, 1970; Munford, "White Flight," 25 n.49.

48. *McComb Enterprise-Journal,* December 12, 1984.

CHAPTER FIVE. Greenville and the Delta, 1964–1966

1. F. Davis, "The Delta," 41–43; "Staff Reports, Commission on the Delta Ministry," October 1, 1965, folder "Staff Reports, October 1, 1965," box 1, Humphrey Papers. Mechanical cotton pickers accounted for 68 percent of Delta cotton harvested in 1964 and between 85 and 90 percent the following year, cutting the number of people involved in picking cotton from 10,500 to 6,938 and nearly halving the total number of pickers' workdays (*Delta Democrat-Times,* February 10, 1966; *Memphis Commercial Appeal,* February 10, 1966).

2. "Purchase of Headquarters for the Delta Ministry" (first quotation), attached to "Excerpt from the Minutes of Executive Board, Division of Home Missions, National Council of Churches," October 8–9, 1964, folder 22, box 4, Delta Ministry Papers, Atlanta; "Sketches of Delta Ministry Project Sites" (second and third quotations), attached to "Special Delta Ministry Activities," folder 1431–2-3:05, Church and Society Records, UMC; *Short History;* Waldron, *Hodding Carter,* 160–61, 286; H. Carter [II], "Our Town," 203–4; U.S. Commission on Civil Rights, *Justice in Jackson,* 2:283–86, 290, 292–94, 298–99, 301; Polly A. Robinson, "Report on Greenville, Mississippi," August 9, 1964, 2, folder "Polly Robinson's Report," box 6, Thomas Papers; F. Davis, "The Delta," 43; Lord, *Past,* 233.

3. Chafe, *Civilities;* U.S. Commission on Civil Rights, *Justice in Jackson,* 2:294–95; Wilmina Rowland, "Four Months in Mississippi," 1 (quotation), folder "Reports and Reactions," box 1, Beech Papers; W. Rowland, "How It Is," 340; Wilmina Rowland to J. Randolph Taylor, October 27, 1964, folder 42, box 21, Delta Ministry Papers, Atlanta.

4. "The Greenville Project," in "The Delta Ministry," folder "Delta Ministry Program," box 3, and Wilmina Rowland, "Four Months in Mississippi," 1–2 (quotation on

p. 1), folder "Reports and Reactions," box 1, Beech Papers; H. Carter [II], "Our Town," 206; Waldron, *Hodding Carter,* 311–12; "Sketches of Delta Ministry Project Sites," attached to "Special Delta Ministry Activities," folder 1431–2-3:05, Church and Society Records, UMC; "All Merit Award," *Delta Ministry* 1 (February 1965): 6; *Delta Democrat-Times,* January 19, 1965; U.S. Commission on Civil Rights, *Justice in Jackson,* 2:285; Everett W. Mac-Nair and Mrs. MacNair to "Warren McKenna, Graede Poulard, and NCC Office," August 19, 1964, folder 1, box 15, and Harold I. Cammer and Ralph Shapiro to H. C. Anderson, July 23, 1965, folder 4, box 4, Delta Ministry Papers, Atlanta; Hilton, "Delta Ministry," 6.

5. *Delta Democrat-Times,* October 18, 1964, January 29, 1965; Hilton, *Delta Ministry,* 39, 44–46; "Staff Salaries," folder "Budget Measures 1966," box 3, and Wilmina Rowland to Kenneth G. Neigh, October 4, 1964, folder "Fan Mail," box 6, Thomas Papers; Jacobs, "More Notebook," 6; "Weekly Report of Herbert Edwards," November 10–17, 1964, folder 34, box 2, Laurice M. Walker, "The Delta Ministry Staff Report," November 10, 1964, folder 32, box 2, and "Appendix A, Biographical Data—Delta Ministry Staff," folder 39, box 2, Delta Ministry Papers, Atlanta; Wilmina Rowland, "Four Months in Mississippi," 1 (quotation), folder "Reports and Reactions," box 1, Beech Papers.

6. "Mrs. Thelma Barnes: Candidate for Representative, 1st Congressional District—Mississippi," folder 42, box 1, Delta Ministry Papers, Starkville; Thelma P. Barnes, "Fidelity Bond Application," July 18, 1967, folder 38, box 45, Delta Ministry Papers, Atlanta; "Divisions of Board of Missions," 6; Thelma P. Barnes, interview by author, September 5, 1996.

7. Thelma P. Barnes, interview by author, September 5, 1996; Henry L. Parker to Richard Soeken, June 6, 1969, 1, folder 1, box 3, Delta Ministry Papers, Starkville; Hilton, *Delta Ministry,* 39–40, 64; J. M. Wilzin to National Council of Churches, November 10, 1964, folder 37, box 2, Delta Ministry Papers, Atlanta; *Delta Democrat-Times,* December 29, 1964 (quotations); Jon L. Regier to Hodding Carter III, December 28, 1964, folder "Delta Commission Membership," box 6, and "Rough Draft—Contacts with White Community," n.d., 2, folder "White Mississippi—1966," box 6, Thomas Papers.

8. Laurice M. Walker, "Greenville Project Report, September 15, 1964–September 15, 1965," 1, in "Staff Reports, Commission on the Delta Ministry," October 1, 1965, folder "Staff Reports, October 1, 1965," box 1, Humphrey Papers; Wilson, "Delta Ministry," 18; "The Greenville Project," in "The Delta Ministry," folder "Delta Ministry Program," box 3, Beech Papers; Hilton, *Delta Ministry,* 46; W. Rowland, "How It Is," 340 (first and second quotations); Polly A. Robinson, "Report on Greenville, Mississippi," August 9, 1964, 3, folder "Polly Robinson's Report," box 6, Thomas Papers; Wilmina Rowland, "Four-Month Report, Sept. 15, 1964 to January 14, 1965," n.d. (third quotation), folder 19, box 7, Delta Ministry Papers, Atlanta.

9. Wilmina Rowland to R. H. Edwin Espy, November 30, 1964, folder 42, box 21, Paul M. Thompson to Wilmina Rowland, November 30, 1964, folder 42, box 21, Wilmina Rowland to Paul M. Thompson, December 1, 1964, folder 42, box 21, and Laurice M. Walker to Ned O'Gorman, December 29, 1964, folder 44, box 21, Delta Ministry Papers, Atlanta; Hilton, *Delta Ministry,* 168.

10. Laurice M. Walker, "Greenville Project Report, September 15, 1964–September 15, 1965," 1, in "Staff Reports, Commission on the Delta Ministry," October 1, 1965, folder "Staff

Reports, October 1, 1965," box 1, Humphrey Papers; W. Rowland, "How It Is," 340 (first quotation); Wilmina Rowland, "Four-Month Report, Sept. 15, 1964 to January 14, 1965," n.d. (second, third, and fourth quotations), folder 19, box 7, and "Five Days with Delta Ministry in Greenville, Miss.," n.d., 2–4, folder 23, box 3, Delta Ministry Papers, Atlanta; Polly A. Robinson, "Report on Greenville, Mississippi," August 9, 1961, 1, folder "Polly Robinson's Report," box 6, Thomas Papers.

11. Wilson, "Delta Ministry," 18.

12. Wilmina Rowland, "Four-Month Report, Sept. 15, 1964 to January 14, 1965," n.d. (first and second quotations), folder 19, box 7, Herbert Edwards to "Dear Fellow Ministers," January 5, 1965, folder 21, box 7, and "Weekly Report of Herbert Edwards," November 10–17, 1964 (third quotation), folder 34, box 2, Delta Ministry Papers, Atlanta; "Reflections on Greenville, Mississippi," n.d., 11, folder "Reports and Reactions," box 1, Beech Papers; Everett W. MacNair, "Memorandum on the Financial Problem of Friendship Baptist Church," August 20, 1964, folder "Fan Mail," box 6, Thomas Papers; *Delta Democrat-Times,* January 29, 1965; Owen H. Brooks, interview by Tom Dent, August 18, 1978, MOHC.

13. "Weekly Report of Herbert Edwards," November 10–17, 1964 (quotations), folder 34, box 2, Delta Ministry Papers, Atlanta; Thelma P. Barnes, "Field Activities in Greenville," 1–2, in "Staff Reports, Commission on the Delta Ministry," October 1, 1965, folder "Staff Reports, October 1, 1965," box 1, Humphrey Papers.

14. "Weekly Report of Herbert Edwards," November 10–17, 1964 (first quotation), folder 34, box 2, and Laurice M. Walker, "Delta Ministry Staff Report," November 10, 1964, (second quotation), folder 32, box 2, Delta Ministry Papers, Atlanta; Wilson, "Delta Ministry," 18; Hilton, *Delta Ministry,* 45–46; Laurice M. Walker, "Greenville Project Report, September 15, 1964–September 15, 1965," 4, and Thelma P. Barnes, "Field Activities in Greenville," 1, in "Staff Reports, Commission on the Delta Ministry," October 1, 1965, folder "Staff Reports, October 1, 1965," box 1, Humphrey Papers; "Background Statement," RG 301.9, folder 14, box 8, CORAR Records; *Delta Democrat-Times,* March 12, 1965.

15. Matthew J. Page to John W. Spencer, June 30, 1965, folder 14, box 23, and "Report of Wilmina Rowland for October 25–31, 1964," 2–3 (quotation on p. 2), folder 32, box 2, Delta Ministry Papers, Atlanta; Polly A. Robinson, "Report on Greenville, Mississippi," August 9, 1964, 5, folder "Polly Robinson's Report," box 6, Thomas Papers; Noble, "Delta Ministry," 110 n.52.

16. Laurice M. Walker, "Greenville Project Report, September 15, 1964–September 15, 1965," 3 (quotation), in "Staff Reports, Commission on the Delta Ministry," October 1, 1965, folder "Staff Reports, October 1, 1965," box 1, Humphrey Papers; *Delta Democrat-Times,* January 31, 1965; Hilton, *Delta Ministry,* 49–50.

17. "Greenville Mill: A Report on Discrimination in Employment," *Delta Ministry* 1 (January 1965): 3; Hilton, *Delta Ministry,* 49–50; Laurice M. Walker, "The Delta Ministry Staff Report," November 10, 1964, folder 32, box 2, Delta Ministry Papers, Atlanta; *Sunday Herald Tribune,* March 28, 1965.

18. "Greenville Mill," *Delta Ministry* 1 (February 1965): 1; *Delta Democrat-Times,* January 19, 31 (quotation), 1965; *Sunday Herald Tribune,* March 28, 1965.

19. Laurice M. Walker, "Greenville Project Report, September 15, 1964–September 15, 1965," 3, in "Staff Reports, Commission on the Delta Ministry," October 1, 1965, folder "Staff Reports, October 1, 1965," box 1, Humphrey Papers; *Delta Democrat-Times,* January 20, 31 (first

quotation), February 12 (second quotation), May 7, 1965; U.S. Commission on Civil Rights, *Justice in Jackson,* 2:282.

20. *Delta Democrat-Times,* January 27 (first quotation), February 28, March 1 (second and third quotations), 25, 1965. The attempt to picket Wilcox's home was largely symbolic: the picketers warned Police Chief Burnley of their intentions, were turned back by the police, and did not try to return to the residence (*Delta Democrat-Times,* February 28, March 2, 1965).

21. *Delta Democrat-Times,* March 23, 24, 25 (quotations), 26, April 1, 1965.

22. Minutes, Commission on the Delta Ministry, January 22, 1965, 1, folder "Delta Ministry—Minutes, Budgets, Fact Sheets—1965," box 1, Humphrey Papers; minutes, Commission on the Delta Ministry, April 2, 1965, 1, folder 35, box 1, Delta Ministry Papers, Atlanta; Arthur C. Thomas to Hodding Carter III, May 6, 1965 (quotations), attached to "Background Statement," folder "Hodding Carter—1965," box 6, Thomas Papers.

23. "The Delta Ministry 1965," *Commission on Religion and Race Reports* [NCC] 1 (spring 1965); "Greenville Mill," *Delta Ministry* 1 (June 1965): 1–2; "Background Statement" (first, second, third and fourth quotations), RG 301.9, folder 14, box 8, CORAR Records; *Delta Democrat-Times,* April 16, 27, May 7, 14 (fifth quotation), 1965; Arthur C. Thomas to Hodding Carter III, May 6, 1965, attached to "Background Statement," folder "Hodding Carter—1965," box 6, and Paul Moore Jr. to John E. Hines, May 14, 1965, 1, folder "White Mississippi—Episcopalians 1964–1965," box 6, Thomas Papers; Hilton, *Delta Ministry, 53.*

24. Hilton, *Delta Ministry, 53;* Paul Moore Jr. to R. H. Edwin Espy, August 10, 1965, folder "Bishop Paul Moore," box 1, and Paul Moore Jr. to John E. Hines, May 14, 1965, 1 (quotation), folder "White Mississippi—Episcopalians 1964–1965," box 6, Thomas Papers; *Delta Democrat-Times,* May 7, 1965.

25. James L. Robertson, "A Memorandum Concerning the Policies and Procedures of the Delta Ministry," April 15, 1966, appendix B in James L. Robertson, "To Whom It May Concern," folder "Delta Ministry—Misc.—1964–66," box 1, Humphrey Papers; "Background Material from Subcommittee on Overall Program of the Mississippi Delta Ministry," March 13–14, 1966, 11 (quotation), in "Subcommittee Reports to the Evaluation Committee of the Delta Ministry Commission, National Council of Churches," May 6, 1966, folder 9, box 43, SCLC Papers.

26. *Delta Democrat-Times,* May 4, 5 (first and second quotations), 6 (third quotation), 1965; *Chicago Daily News,* July 28, 1965; *Memphis Commercial Appeal,* July 30, 1965; *Atlanta Journal and Constitution,* August 1, 1965; "Reconciliation through Anger," 70–71; "Criticism of the Delta Ministry—Fair and Foul," folder 22, box 10, Delta Ministry Papers, Starkville.

27. Memorandum, Larry Walker to Executive Committee, the Delta Ministry Commission, May 7, 1965 (quotation), RG 301.9, folder 14, box 8, CORAR Records; memorandum attached to Arthur C. Thomas to "Members of the Commission on the Delta Ministry," August 17, 1965, folder 34, box 1, Delta Ministry Papers, Atlanta; James L. Robertson, "A Memorandum Concerning the Policies and Procedures of the Delta Ministry," April 15, 1966, appendix B in James L. Robertson, "To Whom It May Concern," folder "Delta Ministry—Misc.—1964–66," box 1, Humphrey Papers.

28. Memorandum (first quotation), attached to Arthur C. Thomas to "Members of the Commission on the Delta Ministry," August 17, 1965, folder 34, box 1, Delta Ministry Papers, Atlanta; *Delta Democrat-Times,* May 5, 1965 (second quotation).

29. *Delta Democrat-Times,* July 2, 1965 (quotations).

30. *Student Voice,* April 30, 1965, 1, June 6, 1965, 1, 4; Sutherland, "Mississippi Summer," 213; "Shaw, Mississippi: New Sounds in the Delta," 1–2, folder 564, box 11, King Papers; *National Guardian,* June 12, 1965; *Christian Science Monitor,* April 30, 1966; "Mississippi Freedom Labor Union," n.d., folder 102, box 113, SNCC Papers; *Memphis Commercial Appeal,* April 15, 1965.

31. "Nothin' to Lose," 33, 36; "Report from Hattiesburg," *Delta Ministry* 1 (January 1965): 6; Hilton, *Delta Ministry,* 68–70.

32. Hilton, *Delta Ministry,* 70–72; Howell, *Freedom City,* 81–89; *New York Times,* July 25, 1966; *Chicago Daily News,* July 29, 1965; *Delta Democrat-Times,* May 31, 1965.

33. *Delta Democrat-Times,* May 30, 1967; "Reconciliation through Anger," 70 (first, second and third quotations); "Bob Beech of the Delta Ministry Staff Meeting with Presbyterian Leaders in Jackson, Mississippi," November 7, 1966, 25 (fourth quotation), RG 38, folder "Delta Ministry—Bob Beech," box 1, Office of Church and Society Records, PCUS, Montreat; Wilson, "Delta Ministry," 17–18; Henry A. McCanna to David G. Forsberg, August 24, 1965, folder "White Mississippi—Methodists 1964–1965," box 6, Thomas Papers; *Memphis Commercial Appeal,* July 30, 1965 (fifth quotation); "Criticism of the Delta Ministry—Fair and Foul," 1–3 (sixth quotation on p. 3), folder 22, box 10, Delta Ministry Papers, Starkville; Laurice M. Walker to Lorenz M. Schultz, June 21, 1965, folder 47, box 21, Delta Ministry Papers, Atlanta; Sutherland, "Mississippi Summer," 213. A *Newsweek* report explicitly claimed that Walker shouted, "Your enemy is the white man" to the Andrews workers and condemned the "man in the big white house" ("Nothin' to Lose," 36).

34. A. L. Andrews to James Green, May 31, 1965, folder 49, box 21, Delta Ministry Papers, Atlanta; *Delta Democrat-Times,* June 1, 4, 8, 1965; *New York Times,* June 4, 7, 1965; *Memphis Commercial Appeal,* June 20, 1965; Alfred R. Winham, "Mt. Beulah Report March 21st to July 15th 1965," in "Staff Reports, Commission on the Delta Ministry," October 1, 1965, folder "Staff Reports, October 1, 1965," box 1, Humphrey Papers; "Mississippi Plantation Strikers," 6.

35. Hilton, *Delta Ministry,* 74–75; *Jackson Clarion-Ledger,* June 1, 1965; "Writ of Injunction," June 1, 1965, folder 49, box 21, Delta Ministry Papers, Atlanta; statement by Isaac Foster, August 9, 1965, statement by T. B. Green, n.d., and statement by Isaac Foster, John Henry Sylvester, and Mack Ingram, August 9, 1965, folder 50, box 21, Delta Ministry Papers, Atlanta; "Freedom Now," folder 26, box 8, and Arthur C. Thomas to Paul Moore Jr., August 12, 1965, folder 42, box 12, Delta Ministry Papers, Atlanta; *Delta Democrat-Times,* June 1, 4, 8, 10, July 30, August 5, 9, 10, 1965; *New York Herald Tribune,* June 6, 1965; *New York Times,* June 7, 1965; *Memphis Commercial Appeal,* July 30, 1965.

36. *Delta Democrat-Times,* June 20, 24, 1965; Laurice M. Walker to Greater Portland Council of Churches, June 30, 1965, folder 5, box 17, and Warren H. McKenna to Daniel J. Kaufman, August 13, 1965, folder 7, box 16, Delta Ministry Papers, Atlanta; "Heat . . . Five Continents . . . That Time Article . . . New Voters," *Delta Ministry* 1 (August 1965): 1–2; *Jackson Daily News,* August 28, 1965; *National Guardian,* March 5, 1966; Hilton, "Delta Ministry," 7; Hilton, *Delta Ministry,* 75.

37. *Memphis Commercial Appeal,* February 10, 1966 (quotation); *Delta Democrat-Times,* February 10, 1966.

38. *Memphis Commercial Appeal,* February 10, 1966; *New York Times,* November 18, 1965; *Delta Democrat-Times,* February 10, 1966; Cobb, *Most Southern Place,* 255–56 (first and second quotations on p. 255); Sutherland, "Mississippi Summer," 213; memorandum, Margaret

Lauren to "Northern Offices," n.d., and attached "Minutes of Statewide Meeting—MFLU—September 4 [1965]," folder 102, box 113, and George Shelton Jr., "Mississippi Freedom Labor Union," n.d., folder 102, box 113, SNCC Papers; "Authority to Act: Crisis in Hunger," attached to Stephen Arons to Arthur C. Thomas, October 5, 1965, folder "National Student Association," box 1, Thomas Papers; Dittmer, *Local People,* 364.

39. "Tent City," supplement to *Delta Ministry* 2 (September 1965); Hilton, "Delta Ministry," 6–7; Curtis Hayes, "Freedom Corps," 5, in "Staff Reports, Commission on the Delta Ministry," October 1, 1965, folder "Staff Reports, October 1, 1965," box 1, Humphrey Papers; *New York Times,* November 17, 1965, April 4, 5, 1966; "Worth Noting," *Delta Ministry* 2 (December 1965): 4; Warren H. McKenna to Thomas A. Kerr Jr., January 18, 1966, and Warren H. McKenna to J. W. Spradling, July 22, 1966, folder 44, box 17, Delta Ministry Papers, Atlanta; "How 'Freedomcrafts' Came to Be," n.d., folder "Freedom Crafts," no box, and memorandum, Robert L. Beech to "Anyone Interested in Following Through," n.d., 2, folder "Proposal Beech," no box, Beech Papers; untitled Sovereignty Commission report, February 12, 1966, Leesha Faulkner Civil Rights Collection, in possession of the author; Howell, *Freedom City,* 89; *Memphis Commercial Appeal,* January 1, 1966; "Background Material from Subcommittee on Overall Program of the Mississippi Delta Ministry," March 13–14, 1966, 11, in "Subcommittee Reports to the Evaluation Committee of the Delta Ministry Commission, National Council of Churches," May 6, 1966, folder 9, box 43, SCLC Papers; Thomas Griffin, "Greenville," February 3, 1966, folder 119, box 98, SNCC Papers; *Delta Ministry Reports,* October 1966, 1 (quotation), November 1966, 1; S. J. Rowland Jr., "Tough Mission," 24; Hilton, *Delta Ministry,* 75–76.

40. Claude Ramsay, "A Report on the Delta Farm Strike," August 16, 1965, folder "FLU-Strike," box 6, Thomas Papers; *New York Herald Tribune,* September 12, 1965.

41. James L. Robertson, "A Memorandum Concerning the Policies and Procedures of the Delta Ministry," April 15, 1966, appendix B (first quotation), in James L. Robertson, "To Whom It May Concern," folder "Delta Ministry—Misc.—1964–66," box 1, Humphrey Papers; *Memphis Commercial Appeal,* July 30, 1965 (second quotation). Page told Delta Ministry volunteer Gaile Noble that the Ministry comprised "a group of unbalanced radicals preaching revolution who have upset all we have accomplished" (Noble, "Delta Ministry," 173 [quotation]; Gaile P. Noble, résumé, attached to "Gaile P. Noble to Father Henry Parker," January 9, 1969, folder 63, box 2, Delta Ministry Papers, Starkville).

42. *Delta Democrat-Times,* June 25, July 4 (first quotation), August 8, 1965; Grover C. Bagby to Dorsey Allen, August 9, 1965, folder "Delta Ministry—Correspondence—1964–66," and James L. Robertson, "A Memorandum Concerning the Policies and Procedures of the Delta Ministry," April 15, 1966, appendix B in James L. Robertson, "To Whom It May Concern," folder "Delta Ministry—Misc.—1964–66," box 1, Humphrey Papers; Grover C. Bagby to Joseph Wroten, August 19, 1965, folder 1431–2–3:05, Church and Society Records, UMC; Hodding Carter II to Allen E. Johnson, January 6, 1966 (second quotation), folder "Correspondence 1966: J," box 25, Carter Papers.

43. Hilton, *Delta Ministry,* 55 (quotation); *Delta Democrat-Times,* June 9, 1965; Grover C. Bagby to Joseph Wroten, August 19, 1965, folder 1431–2–3:05, Church and Society Records, UMC. Greenville stores did not adhere to the May 1965 equal employment statement until the NAACP launched a monthlong boycott in June 1966 (*Lexington Advertiser,* June 23, 1966; Waldron, *Hodding Carter,* 312–13).

44. "Rough Draft—Contacts with White Community," n.d., 2, folder "White Mississippi—1966," box 6, Thomas Papers.

45. *Delta Democrat-Times,* June 24 (first and second quotations), August 15 (third quotation), 1965; Wilson, "Delta Ministry," 18 (fourth quotation); Wilmina Rowland, "Four-Month Report, Sept. 15, 1964 to January 14, 1965," n.d., folder 19, box 7, Delta Ministry Papers, Atlanta

46. *New York Herald Tribune,* August 22, 1965; *Delta Democrat-Times,* July 2, August 6, 8 (second and third quotations), 1965; Hilton, "It Shows the Church Cares," 54 (first quotation); Hilton, "Delta Ministry," 5, 7–8. Ginny Hilton, a registered nurse, also lent her expertise to the Ministry by conducting hygiene and nutrition classes in Winstonville and by helping local people there establish a Freedom School ("Medical Committee—Report—Greenville, September 13–October 15, 1965," folder 30, box 29, Delta Ministry Papers, Atlanta; Hilton, *Delta Ministry,* 80).

47. *Delta Democrat-Times,* May 30, 1967; Thelma P. Barnes, "Involvement in the Head Start Program in Greenville," 1–4 (first quotation on p. 4; second quotation on p. 3), in "Staff Reports, Commission on the Delta Ministry," October 1, 1965, folder "Staff Reports, October 1, 1965," box 1, Humphrey Papers; memorandum, Tom Levin to "All Committee Chairmen, Central Administration," July 29, 1965, folder 10, box 29, Delta Ministry Papers, Atlanta; Noble, "Delta Ministry," 110.

48. Solomon Gort Jr., "Field Activities in Greenville, July 15, 1965 to September 4, 1965" (quotations), and Laurice M. Walker, "Greenville Project Report, September 15, 1964–September 15, 1965," 3, in "Staff Reports, Commission on the Delta Ministry," October 1, 1965, folder "Staff Reports, October 1, 1965," box 1, Humphrey Papers; "The Greenville Project," in "The Delta Ministry," folder "Delta Ministry Program," box 3, Beech Papers; *Jackson Daily News,* August 27, 1965; Henry A. McCanna, "A Ministry of Deliverance," folder 10, box 47, Delta Ministry Papers, Atlanta; Hilton, *Delta Ministry,* 58–59.

49. "Report of the Executive Committee," December 2–3, 1965, 9–10, no folder, box 4, Thomas Papers; "Delta Ministry Staff (as of December 1, 1966)," folder "D.M. Fact Sheet," no box, Winham Papers; Owen H. Brooks, "Bolivar County Report," 1–5 (first, third, and fourth quotations on p. 2; second quotation on p. 1), and Curtis Hayes, "Freedom Corps," 1–7, in "Staff Reports, Commission on the Delta Ministry," October 1, 1965, folder "Staff Reports, October 1, 1965," box 1, Humphrey Papers; Hilton, *Delta Ministry,* 26, 80.

50. Owen H. Brooks, "Bolivar County Report," 3–4, and Curtis Hayes, "Freedom Corps," 1–2, 4, 6–7, in "Staff Reports, Commission on the Delta Ministry," October 1, 1965, folder "Staff Reports, October 1, 1965," box 1, Humphrey Papers.

51. Owen H. Brooks, "Bolivar County Report," 4, and Curtis Hayes, "Freedom Corps," 4, in "Staff Reports, Commission on the Delta Ministry," October 1, 1965, folder "Staff Reports, October 1, 1965," box 1, Humphrey Papers; "The Bolivar County Project," in "The Delta Ministry," folder "Delta Ministry Program," box 3, Beech Papers; memorandum, Roger A. Smith to Herman L. Ellis, February 7, 1967, folder 17, box 13, and Solomon Gort Jr. to "Dear Community-Interest Chairmen," September 9, 1966, 1–2 (quotation on p. 1), folder 32, box 23, Delta Ministry Papers, Atlanta.

52. *New York Times,* September 8, 1965; *Memphis Commercial Appeal,* September 8, 1965, November 28, 1967; *Jackson Clarion-Ledger,* September 8, 1965; "Committee to Support Our Delta (Project SOD) Action Program," September 14, 1965, attached to Thelma P. Barnes to

Henry S. Reuss, September 25, 1965, folder 4, box 45, minutes, DOC, June 3, 1967, 1, folder 34, box 45, and "Steering Committee, Delta Opportunity Corporation," n.d., folder 29, box 47, Delta Ministry Papers, Atlanta; "Statement to Press Conference, Jackson, Mississippi, by Theodore M. Berry, Director, Community Action Programs, OEO," April 7, 1966, 2, folder "D.O.C. Self-Help Housing Program," box 1, Thomas Papers; Hilton, *Delta Ministry,* 207–13; Lemann, *Promised Land,* 314–17, 320. The ten counties were Coahoma, Bolivar, Sunflower, Leflore, Washington, Sharkey, Yazoo, Madison, Tallahatchie, and Issaquena ("Anti-Poverty Funds Sought to Assist Delta," *Interchurch News* 7 [October 1965]: 1). On Coahoma Opportunities, see Hill, "Power and Change."

53. Clarence Hall Jr., and Thelma P. Barnes, "EDA—Project # 04-6-09027," n.d., folder 5, box 20, Thelma P. Barnes to Henry S. Reuss, September 25, 1965, and attached "Committee to Support Our Delta (Project SOD) Action Program," folder 4, box 45, Thelma P. Barnes to Francis Walter, December 14, 1965, folder 2, box 45, and Arthur C. Thomas to John H. Betz, April 21, 1966, folder 3, box 45, Delta Ministry Papers, Atlanta; *Delta Democrat-Times,* October 4, 1965 (quotation); Hilton, *Delta Ministry,* 136, 212–13; Barbara A. Shapiro to Ferdinand H. Pease, November 18, 1966, RG 11, folder 5, box 32, NCC Archives; Harry J. Bowie, interview by Robert Wright, August 8, 1968, 33, Bunche Oral History Collection; minutes, Commission on the Delta Ministry, November 16–17, 1967, folder 62, box 3, Delta Ministry Papers, Starkville.

54. "Delta Ministry Staff (as of December 1, 1966)," folder "D.M. Fact Sheet," no box, Winham Papers; "Staff Salaries," folder "Budget Measures 1966," box 3, Thomas Papers; Clarence Hall Jr., and Thelma P. Barnes, "EDA—Project # 04-6-09027," n.d., folder 5, box 20, "Committee to Support Our Delta (Project SOD) Action Program," September 14, 1965, attached to Thelma P. Barnes to Henry S. Reuss, September 25, 1965, folder 4, box 45, and Clarence Hall Jr., "Fidelity Bond Application," July 18, 1967, folder 38, box 45, Delta Ministry Papers, Atlanta; Hilton, "Delta Ministry," 8; Hilton, *Delta Ministry,* 214–15.

55. Laurice M. Walker, "Greenville Project Report, September 15, 1964–September 15, 1965," 2, and Thelma P. Barnes, "Field Activities in Greenville," 1, in "Staff Reports, Commission on the Delta Ministry," October 1, 1965, folder "Staff Reports, October 1, 1965," box 1, Humphrey Papers; "Report of School Desegregation Committee Meeting May 17, 1965," folder 16, box 23, Delta Ministry Papers, Atlanta; Blanchard, "Delta Ministry," 338; H. Carter [II], "Our Town," 202; *Delta Democrat-Times,* January 17, 1965, reprinted in *Lexington Advertiser,* January 21, 1965; *Delta Democrat-Times,* January 22, August 15, 1965.

56. "The Greenville Project" (quotation), in "The Delta Ministry," folder "Delta Ministry Program," box 3, Beech Papers; "Summary of Meeting of the School Desegregation Committee of the Herbert Lee Memorial Community Center with the Greenville School Board," March 8, 1965, folder 16, box 23, Joe Bivins and Charles Moore, "Statement to the Press," May 18, 1965, folder 16, box 23, and Marian E. Wright to Francis Keppel, April 5, May 21, 1965, folder 14, box 23, Delta Ministry Papers, Atlanta; *Delta Democrat-Times,* March 23, 1965; *Jackson Daily News,* July 21, 1965; Thelma P. Barnes, "Field Activities in Greenville," 1, in "Staff Reports, Commission on the Delta Ministry," October 1, 1965, folder "Staff Reports, October 1, 1965," box 1, Humphrey Papers.

57. Laurice M. Walker to Arthur C. Thomas, August 10, 1965 (quotation), folder "Project Directors Meeting," box 6, Thomas Papers; "Delta Ministry Staff (as of December 1, 1966),"

folder "D.M. Fact Sheet," no box, Winham Papers; Thelma P. Barnes, interview by author, September 5, 1996.

58. Waldron, *Hodding Carter,* 315; *Delta Democrat-Times,* October 24 (first quotation), 27 (second quotation), 1965; Hilton, *Delta Ministry,* 216.

59. "Appendix A, Biographical Data—Delta Ministry Staff," 2, folder 39, box 2, and minutes, Commission on the Delta Ministry, April 2, 1965, 4, folder 35, box 1, Delta Ministry Papers, Atlanta; Laurice M. Walker, "Greenville Project Report, September 15, 1964–September 15, 1965," 5, in "Staff Reports, Commission on the Delta Ministry," October 1, 1965, folder "Staff Reports, October 1, 1965," box 1, Humphrey Papers.

60. "Authority to Act: Crisis in Hunger," attached to Stephen Arons to Arthur C. Thomas, October 5, 1965, folder "National Student Association," box 1, and "Report of the Executive Committee," NCC, December 2–3, 1965, 7, no folder, box 5, Thomas Papers; *Delta Democrat-Times,* November 25, 1965, February 8, 1966.

61. "Statement of Special Conditions Governing Grant #9418," November 23, 1965, folder "O.E.O., Mississippi Food Program," box 1, and untitled document, folder "Draft," box 2, Thomas Papers; "Fact Sheet (Background on Poor Peoples' Use of Greenville AFB)," folder 6, box 4, Amzie Moore Papers, WHS; "We Have No Government," February 1, 1966, 3–4, folder 47, box 9, Delta Ministry Papers, Starkville; Howell, *Freedom City,* 27; Hilton, *Delta Ministry,* 81–82; *New York Times,* November 18, 1965, February 6, 1966; *Delta Ministry Reports,* February 1966, n.p.; *Memphis Commercial Appeal,* February 4, 10, 1966; Alewine, "Changing Characteristics," 37.

62. "Telegram to President Lyndon Baines Johnson," January 29, 1966, folder 6, box 138, Johnson Family Papers; *Delta Ministry Reports,* February 1966, n.p.; "Events at the Air Base," n.d., folder 635, box 12, King Papers; "Sequence of Events Leading to Greenville Air Force Base 'Live-in' on February 1, 1966," folder "Greenville Air Force Base," box 6, Thomas Papers; F. Davis, "The Delta," 43; *Washington Post,* February 1, 1966; *Memphis Commercial Appeal,* February 1, 1966; Hilton, *Delta Ministry,* 90–96. Seven Delta Ministry staff and volunteers participated in the occupation (Hilton, *Delta Ministry,* 88).

63. "Sequence of Events Leading to Greenville Air Force Base 'Live-in' on February 1, 1966," folder "Greenville Air Force Base," box 6, Thomas Papers; Paul Moore Jr., "Report of the Delta Ministry (*With Special Reference to the Evaluation Committee Report*)," May 27, 1966, 2–3, folder 44, box 3, Delta Ministry Papers, Starkville; *Memphis Commercial Appeal,* February 8, 1966; Owen H. Brooks, interview by Robert Wright, September 24, 1968, 26–28, Bunche Oral History Collection. Moore recalled in his memoirs that he opposed the occupation of the air base. Nevertheless, he publicly stood by the Ministry and refused to condemn its participation (P. Moore Jr., *Presences,* 182; Paul Moore Jr. to John D. Humphrey, March 1, 1966, folder "Bruce Hilton," box 1, Thomas Papers).

64. "Why We Are Here at the Greenville Air Force Base," January 31, 1966, folder "Notes Concerning the Delta Ministry, 1964–1966," box 52, Carter Papers; "Sequence of Events Leading to Greenville Air Force Base 'Live-in' on February 1, 1966," folder "Greenville Air Force Base," box 6, Thomas Papers; "Events at the Air Base," folder 635, box 12, King Papers; *Delta Ministry Reports,* February 1966, n.p.; *New York Times,* February 2, 1966; *Delta Democrat-Times,* February 1, 1966; "The Poor People's Fund: 'We're Beginning a New Future,'" folder 71, box 170, SNCC Papers; "Through the Long, Hot Summer . . . ," n.d., n.p.,

folder "Articles—1965," box "BP. Moore w/Delta Min.," Paul Moore Jr. Papers, AEDNY; Hilton, *Delta Ministry*, 91, 97–112.

65. *Jackson Daily News*, February 3, 5, 15, 1966; *Delta Democrat-Times*, February 2 (quotation), 15, 16, 1966; *Memphis Commercial Appeal*, February 2, 11, 1966.

66. Nicholas Katzenbach, "Memorandum for the President: Civil Rights, Mississippi," February 14, 1966 (quotation), White House Central Files, Ex HU 2/St 24, box 27, Lyndon Baines Johnson Presidential Library; *Delta Democrat-Times*, February 6, 1966; *New York Times*, February 2, 1966; *Memphis Commercial Appeal*, February 4, 1966; "Statement to Press Conference, Jackson, Mississippi, by Theodore M. Berry, Director, Community Action Programs, OEO," April 7, 1966, 1, folder "D.O.C. Self-Help Housing Program," box 1, and Paul Moore Jr. to John D. Humphrey, March 1, 1966, folder "Bruce Hilton," box 1, Thomas Papers; Aiken, *Cotton Plantation South*, 255; *Jackson Daily News*, April 1, 25, 1966; Dittmer, *Local People*, 368, 374–75; minutes, Evaluation Committee, Mississippi Delta Ministry, January 21, 1966, 1–5, folder 9, box 43, SCLC Papers. The second CDGM grant enabled CDGM to operate five centers for 420 children in Greenville, with Barnes again serving as community chairperson. Page, who maintained cordial relations with Barnes, served as chairman of Mid-Delta Education Association, Inc., a competing Head Start program in Washington County that OEO also funded. The association, supported by Mayor Pat Dunne, county officials, and the *Delta Democrat-Times*, later became part of MAP. Formed in September 1966 by black and white moderates acting at OEO's behest, MAP operated an OEO-funded Head Start program that rivaled CDGM's. Hodding Carter III and Aaron Henry served on MAP's board of directors (*Jackson Daily News*, November 4, 1965; *Delta Democrat-Times*, February 22, March 28, 29, 1966, June 5, 20, 1968; Noble, "Delta Ministry," 110; Dittmer, *Local People*, 377–82, 388).

67. "New City (for Staff Discussion Only)," 1 (quotation), folder 25, box 6, Delta Ministry Papers, Atlanta; "Background Material from Subcommittee on Administration of the Delta Ministry," February 28–March 1, 1966, 4, in "Subcommittee Reports to the Evaluation Committee of the Delta Ministry Commission, National Council of Churches," May 6, 1966, folder 9, box 43, SCLC Papers; "Through the Long, Hot Summer . . . ," n.d., n.p., folder "Articles—1965," box "BP. Moore w/Delta Min.," Paul Moore Jr. Papers, AEDNY; Hilton, *Delta Ministry*, 112–15; "400 Acres of Delta Farmland Bought for Poor Delta Negroes," April 7, 1966, folder 151, box 4, King Papers; "Delta Agency Buys 400 Acres," 17.

CHAPTER SIX. Under Investigation

1. "Report of the Evaluation Committee on the Mississippi Delta Ministry of the General Board of the National Council of Churches," May 16, 1966, folder 44, box 3, Delta Ministry Papers, Starkville; "Report of the Special Committee to Study the Relationship of the National Division to the Delta Ministry," September 26, 1966, folder 1431–2–3:08, Church and Society Records, UMC; "Divisions of Board of Missions," 5–6; "Goals for the Delta Ministry," July 7, 1966, folder 231, box 6, Barber Papers; R. H. Edwin Espy to Paul Moore Jr., May 20, 1966, RG 5, folder 9, box 16, and Paul Moore Jr. to Irwin Miller, August 8, 1966, RG 11, folder 4, box 8, NCC Archives; "Delta Ministry: Report to the Executive Committee of DCLM," September 16, 1966, 6, RG 38, folder "Delta Ministry (1)," box 1, Office of Church and Society Records, PCUS, Montreat.

2. "Report of the Executive Committee," December 2–3, 1965, 10 (quotations), no folder, box 4, Thomas Papers; "General Board Action Concerning *A Ministry among the Residents of the Delta Area of the State of Mississippi*," February 26, 1964, exhibit 4, 5, folder 14, box 12, Delta Ministry Papers, Atlanta; memorandum, William A. Carhart to Stephen A. Feke, April 12, 1966, RG 11, folder 4, box 8, NCC Archives; Hilton, *Delta Ministry*, 72–75.

3. Minutes, Evaluation Committee, Mississippi Delta Ministry, January 21, 1966, 3 (first quotation), folder "Evaluation Committee Correspondence," box 5, Thomas Papers; Edward J. Pendergrass to R. H. Edwin Espy, August 27, 1965, 2, folder 1431-2-3:05, Church and Society Records, UMC; Pendergrass, "Bishop's Column," 2; John F. Anderson Jr. to Truman B. Douglass, July 6, 1966 (second quotation), RG 38, folder "Delta Ministry (1)," box 1, Office of Church and Society Records, PCUS, Montreat; *Minutes of the One-Hundred-Fifth General Assembly of the Presbyterian Church in the United States,* 1965, 163–64; *Minutes of the One-Hundred-Sixth General Assembly of the Presbyterian Church in the United States,* 1966, 93, 177–78 (third quotation on p. 178).

4. "Methodist Mission Board," n.p.; Billings, *Segregation,* 32; Peggy Billings, "I Saw for Myself . . . ," in "What This Packet Is All About," folder 42, box 2, Horwitz Papers; Peggy Billings to Bruce Hilton, November 24, 1965, and unsigned to Peggy Billings, February 12, 1966, folder 2, box 19, Delta Ministry Papers, Atlanta; Peggy Billings to "Frogmore Conference Participants," June 14, 1966, folder 1431-2-3:08, Church and Society Records, UMC; White, "Delta Ministry Is Greatest," 24.

5. "Report of the Evaluation Committee on the Mississippi Delta Ministry of the General Board of the National Council of Churches," May 16, 1966, 1–3, folder 44, box 3, Delta Ministry Papers, Starkville; Baker, *Brooks Hays,* 116, 132–33, 160–73; minutes, Commission on the Delta Ministry, January 22, 1965, 1, folder "Delta Ministry—Minutes, Budgets, Fact Sheets—1965," box 1, Humphrey Papers; Grover C. Bagby to Lorenz M. Schultz, March 22, 1966, 1, folder 1431-2-3:05, Church and Society Records, UMC; memorandum, Bruce Hilton to Arthur C. Thomas, n.d., folder 49, box 12, Delta Ministry Papers, Atlanta; Paul Moore Jr. to Dale Fiers, May 18, 1966, folder "Bishop Paul Moore," box 1, Thomas Papers.

6. "Report of the Evaluation Committee on the Mississippi Delta Ministry of the General Board of the National Council of Churches," May 16, 1966, 1–3, folder 44, box 3, Delta Ministry Papers, Starkville; White, "Delta Ministry Is Greatest," 24; Paul Moore Jr. to Dale Fiers, May 18, 1966 (quotations), folder "Bishop Paul Moore," box 1, Thomas Papers.

7. "Report of the Evaluation Committee on the Mississippi Delta Ministry of the General Board of the National Council of Churches," May 16, 1966, 3 (quotations), folder 44, box 3, Delta Ministry Papers, Starkville.

8. Edward J. Pendergrass, "Statement about the Delta Ministry," 2–3 (first and second quotations on p. 2; third, fourth, fifth, sixth and seventh quotations on p. 3), in "What This Packet Is All About," folder 42, box 2, Horwitz Papers; John D. Humphrey to Paul Moore Jr., February 22, 1966, folder "Delta Ministry Correspondence, 1964–1966," box 1, Humphrey Papers.

9. Edward J. Pendergrass, "Statement about the Delta Ministry," 3–5 (first quotation on p. 4; second, third and fourth quotations on p. 5), in "What This Packet Is All About," folder 42, box 2, Horwitz Papers.

10. Edward J. Pendergrass, "Statement about the Delta Ministry," 5–6 (first and second quotations on p. 5; third quotation on p. 6), in "What This Packet Is All About," folder 42, box 2, Horwitz Papers.

11. Edward J. Pendergrass, "Statement about the Delta Ministry," 1–6, in "What This Packet Is All About," folder 42, box 2, Horwitz Papers; "Mission Divisions," 23; "Report to the Seventh General Assembly, National Council of the Churches of Christ in the U.S.A.," December 4–9, 1966, 34, folder 24, box 2, 1972 addendum, Cox Collection; Grover C. Bagby to Lee Ranck, June 28, 1966, folder 1431–2–3:05, "Missions' Division Rejects Unilateral Action, Vote $70,000 to NCC Delta Ministry," *Michigan Christian Advocate*, October 27, 1966, folder 1431–2–3:07, and "Report of the Special Committee to Study the Relationship of the National Division to the Delta Ministry," September 26, 1966, 1–6, folder 1431–2–3:08, Church and Society Records, UMC.

12. Bishop Paul Moore Jr., "A Total Ministry," February 4, 1966, 1–2 (first and second quotations on p. 1; third quotation on p. 2), in "What This Packet Is All About," folder 42, box 2, Horwitz Papers.

13. "An Open Letter to Bishop Pendergrass of the Methodist Church, Mississippi from the Rev. Arthur C. Thomas, Director, the Delta Ministry," May 15, 1966, 1–4 (first quotation on p. 2; second quotation on p. 3), in "What This Packet Is All About," folder 42, box 2, Horwitz Papers; John Mudd to "Evaluation Committee—Delta Ministry," May 25, 1966, no folder, box 5, Thomas Papers.

14. "What about the Charge That DM Has Made No Effort toward Reconciliation?" "What about the Charge That the D.M. Program Is Not Ecumenical in Nature?" "What about the Charge That the D.M. Program Is Segregated?" "What about the Charge That DM's Theory of Self-Determination Is an Illusion?" and "What about the Charge That the Delta Ministry Program Is Primarily One of Political Action[?]" (quotation), all in "What This Packet Is All About," folder 42, box 2, Horwitz Papers; memorandum, Alfred R. Winham to Arthur C. Thomas, March 13, 1966, 3, folder "White Mississippi—1966," box 6, Thomas Papers.

15. "Report of the Evaluation Committee on the Mississippi Delta Ministry of the General Board of the National Council of Churches," May 16, 1966, 8, folder 44, box 3, Delta Ministry Papers, Starkville; "Background Material from Subcommittee on Administration of the Delta Ministry," February 28–March 1, 1966, 1, 4, in "Subcommittee Reports to the Evaluation Committee of the Delta Ministry Commission, National Council of Churches," May 6, 1966, folder 9, box 43, SCLC Papers; memorandum, William A. Carhart to Stephen A. Feke, April 12, 1966 (quotation), Arthur C. Thomas to Jon L. Regier, April 22, 1966, and Bruce Hilton to J. Irwin Miller, May 10, 1966, RG 11, folder 4, box 8, NCC Archives; memorandum, Stephen A. Feke to R. H. Edwin Espy, April 20, 1966, folder "Budget Memos 1966," box 3, Thomas Papers. A donation from a Delta Ministry sympathizer in the Midwest saved Winham's position for the remainder of the year (Alfred R. Winham to Myron W. Fowell, September 1, 1966, folder "'65–'67 Letters—Mass.," no box, and Owen H. Brooks to Alfred R. Winham, January 2, 1967, no folder, no box, Winham Papers).

16. "Report of the Evaluation Committee on the Mississippi Delta Ministry of the General Board of the National Council of Churches," May 16, 1966, 5–7 (quotation on p. 5), folder 44, box 3, Delta Ministry Papers, Starkville.

17. Robert L. Beech to David McAlpin, June 1, 1966, untitled folder, box 1, Beech Papers;

"Report of the Evaluation Committee on the Mississippi Delta Ministry of the General Board of the National Council of Churches," May 16, 1966, 7–8 (quotations on p. 7), folder 44, box 3, Delta Ministry Papers, Starkville.

18. "Report of the Evaluation Committee on the Mississippi Delta Ministry of the General Board of the National Council of Churches," May 16, 1966, 7–8 (quotation on p. 8), folder 44, box 3, Delta Ministry Papers, Starkville 7–8.

19. "Report of the Evaluation Committee on the Mississippi Delta Ministry of the General Board of the National Council of Churches," May 16, 1966, 8–10 (first and second quotations on p. 9; third quotation on p. 10), folder 44, box 3, Delta Ministry Papers, Starkville.

20. Paul Moore Jr., "Report of the Delta Ministry (*With Special Reference to the Evaluation Committee Report*)," May 27, 1966, 1–6 (quotations on p. 2), folder 44, box 3, Delta Ministry Papers, Starkville.

21. Paul Moore Jr. to John D. Humphrey, March 1, 1966 (quotation), folder "Delta Ministry Correspondence—1964–1966," box 1, Humphrey Papers; "Delta Ministry Staff (as of December 1, 1966)," folder "D.M. Fact Sheet," no box, Winham Papers.

22. Francis B. Stevens to Grover C. Bagby and Don Calume, November 22, 1965, and Francis B. Stevens to Grover C. Bagby, June 6, 1966, folder 1431-2-3:05, Church and Society Records, UMC; P. Moore Jr., *Take a Bishop*, 18 (quotation).

23. Paul Moore Jr. to John E. Hines, May 14, 1965, folder "White Mississippi—Episcopalians 1964–1965," box 6, and Arthur C. Thomas, "Statement to the Evaluation Committee," n.d., 1–4 (first quotation on p. 2; second quotation on p. 3), no folder, box 1, Thomas Papers.

24. Paul Moore Jr. to R. H. Edwin Espy, August 10, 1965, folder "Bishop Paul Moore," box 1, and "Delta Ministry Work in Cities," April 8, 1966, folder "Bob Beech," box 3, Thomas Papers; "Criticism of the Delta Ministry—Fair and Foul," folder 22, box 10, Delta Ministry Papers, Starkville; "Yearly Report, September, 1965 to September, 1966," 2–5, folder "Forrest Co.," no box, Beech Papers; "Life in the Delta Ministry," 8.

25. "Staff Reports, Commission on the Delta Ministry," October 1, 1965, folder "Staff Reports, October 1, 1965," box 1, Humphrey Papers; Warren H. McKenna to C. Richard Cox, March 8, 1966, folder 18, box 17, Delta Ministry Papers, Atlanta.

26. Paul Moore Jr., "Report of the Delta Ministry (*With Special Reference to the Evaluation Committee Report*)," May 27, 1966, 2–3 (quotations on p. 2), folder 44, box 3, Delta Ministry Papers, Starkville; minutes, Commission on the Delta Ministry, April 2, 1965, 5–6, folder 35, box 1, Delta Ministry Papers, Atlanta; R. H. Edwin Espy to "Dear Friends," April 8, 1965, RG 95, folder 2, box 22, Blake Papers; Owen H. Brooks, interview by Robert Wright, September 24, 1968, 26–27, Bunche Oral History Collection.

27. "Background Material from Subcommittee on Overall Program of the Mississippi Delta Ministry," March 13–14, 1966, 12 (first quotation), in "Subcommittee Reports to the Evaluation Committee of the Delta Ministry Commission, National Council of Churches," May 6, 1966, folder 9, box 43, SCLC Papers 12; C. Richard Cox, "2½ Weeks in the Delta Ministry" (second quotation), n.d., folder 1431-2-3:05, Church and Society Records, UMC.

28. Paul Moore Jr., "Report of the Delta Ministry (*With Special Reference to the Evaluation Committee Report*)," May 27, 1966, 3 (quotation), folder 44, box 3, Delta Ministry Papers,

Starkville; "Background Material from Subcommittee on Administration of the Delta Ministry," February 28–March 1, 1966, 1–2, 2D, 4, in "Subcommittee Reports to the Evaluation Committee of the Delta Ministry Commission, National Council of Churches," May 6, 1966, folder 9, box 43, SCLC Papers. The Evaluation Committee reported capital expenditure at Mount Beulah as $24,990 ("Background Material from Subcommittee on Administration of the Delta Ministry," February 28–March 1, 1966, 2, in "Subcommittee Reports to the Evaluation Committee of the Delta Ministry Commission, National Council of Churches," May 6, 1966, folder 9, box 43, SCLC Papers).

29. Paul Moore Jr., "Report of the Delta Ministry (*With Special Reference to the Evaluation Committee Report*)," May 27, 1966, 4–6 (quotations on p. 5), folder 44, box 3, Delta Ministry Papers, Starkville.

30. Minutes, Program Board, Division of Christian Life and Mission, NCC, May 26–27, 1966, 9, no folder, box 1, Thomas Papers; minutes, Commission on the Delta Ministry, January 22, 1965, 1, folder "Delta Ministry—Minutes, Budgets, Fact Sheets—1965," box 1, Humphrey Papers; Pierce, "Mission," 96; "Address by Marian Wright to General Board," June 2–3, 1966, 1–3 (first quotation on p. 1; second quotation on p. 3), folder 1431-2-3:08, Church and Society Records, UMC.

31. "NCC General Board Debates Delta," 46; "Divisions of Board of Missions," 6.

32. "Actions of the General Board—June 2, 1966 Regarding Report of the Evaluation Committee on the Mississippi Delta Ministry of the General Board of the National Council of Churches, May 16, 1966," folder "Delta Ministry—Correspondence—1964–1966," box 1, Humphrey Papers.

33. "Actions of the General Board—June 2, 1966 Regarding Report of the Evaluation Committee on the Mississippi Delta Ministry of the General Board of the National Council of Churches, May 16, 1966," folder "Delta Ministry—Correspondence—1964–1966," box 1, Humphrey Papers"; minutes, Executive Committee, Division of Christian Life and Mission, NCC, June 2, 1966, 1–4, no folder, box 1, Thomas Papers; "Commission on the Delta Ministry," July 6, 1966, 1, folder 35, box 3, Delta Ministry Papers, Starkville; "Delta Ministry: Report to the Executive Committee of DCLM," September 16, 1966, 3–5, and "Report on the Delta Ministry," December 2, 1966, 3–6, RG 38, folder "Delta Ministry (1)," box 1, Office of Church and Society Records, PCUS.

34. *Delta Ministry Reports,* June 1966, 1; "Delta Ministry: Report to the Executive Committee of DCLM," September 16, 1966, 3–6, RG 38, folder "Delta Ministry (1)," box 1, Office of Church and Society Records, PCUS, Montreat; memorandum, Arthur C. Thomas to Colin Williams, June 24, 1966, no folder, box 1, Thomas Papers; Robert L. Beech to Martin B. Olsen, June 1, 1966, folder "Keep For Reference No. II," box 1, and Robert L. Beech to Ron Babb, June 30, 1966, untitled folder, box 1, Beech Papers.

35. Owen H. Brooks, interview by Robert Wright, September 24, 1968, 32–33, Bunche Oral History Collection; Arthur C. Thomas to "Dear Friend," n.d., folder "Delta Ministry Correspondence—1964–1966," box 1, Humphrey Papers; *Jackson Daily News,* June 8, 13, 1966; *New York Times,* June 27, 1966; *Lexington Advertiser,* June 30, 1966; Lawson, *In Pursuit,* 49–62.

36. "Goals for the Delta Ministry," July 7, 1966, 1–7 (quotation on p. 2), folder 231, box 6, Barber Papers; J. Edward Carothers to Kenneth G. Neigh, July 1, 1966, folder "Delta Ministry," box 6, Neigh Papers; minutes, Executive Committee, Division of Christian Life and Mission, NCC, July 7, 1966, 3, no folder, box 1, Thomas Papers.

37. "Report of the Evaluation Committee on the Mississippi Delta Ministry of the General Board of the National Council of Churches," May 16, 1966, 4–5, 7 (first and second quotations), folder 44, box 3, Delta Ministry Papers, Starkville; "Goals for the Delta Ministry," July 7, 1966, 2–3 (third, fourth and fifth quotations on p. 3), folder 231, box 6, Barber Papers.

38. "Goals for the Delta Ministry," July 7, 1966, 4–6, folder 231, box 6, Barber Papers.

39. "Goals for the Delta Ministry," July 7, 1966, 6–7 (quotation on p. 7), folder 231, box 6, Barber Papers.

40. "General Board Action Concerning *A Ministry among the Residents of the Delta Area of the State of Mississippi*," February 26, 1964, exhibit 4, 4–5, folder 14, box 12, Delta Ministry Papers, Atlanta.

41. R. H. Edwin Espy to Paul Moore Jr., May 20, 1966, RG 5, folder 9, box 16, and Paul Moore Jr. to Irwin Miller, August 8, 1966, 2 (quotations), RG 11, folder 4, box 8, NCC Archives; Warren H. McKenna to Paul Moore Jr., July 12, 1966, folder 42, box 12, Delta Ministry Papers, Atlanta; Alfred R. Winham to Paul Moore Jr., July 13, 1966, folder "Letters—General," no box, Winham Papers; "Delta Ministry: Report to the Executive Committee of DCLM," September 16, 1966, 6, RG 38, folder "Delta Ministry (1)," box 1, Office of Church and Society Records, PCUS, Montreat. After leaving the Delta Ministry, Thomas ran a Model Cities program in Trenton, New Jersey, part of President Johnson's Great Society program of domestic reform (Greenberg, *Devil,* 773).

42. Memorandum, Robert L. Beech to Arthur C. Thomas, Warren H. McKenna, Jon L. Regier, Paul Moore Jr., and Gayraud S. Wilmore Jr., May 16, 1966 (first and second quotations), and Harry J. Bowie to Jon Regier, May 24, 1966 (third and fourth quotations), folder "Bob Beech," box 3, Thomas Papers; Warren H. McKenna to Paul Moore Jr., July 12, 1966 (fifth quotation), folder 42, box 12, Delta Ministry Papers, Atlanta; "Report to the Seventh General Assembly, National Council of the Churches of Christ in the U.S.A.," December 4–9, 1966, 34, folder 24, box 2, 1972 addendum, Cox Collection.

43. Memorandum, Bryant George to Kenneth G. Neigh, May 31 (first and second quotations), July 6 (third quotation), 1966, folder "Delta Ministry," box 16, Neigh Papers; minutes, Commission on Religion and Race, UPCUSA, June 8, 1966, 2–3, RG 301.9, folder 11, box 1, CORAR Records; memorandum, Bryant George to Marshal Scott, February 10, 1967 (fourth quotation), RG 301.7, folder 3, box 46, Board of National Missions (PCUSA) Records.

44. "Delta Ministry's Support," December 1, 1966, folder 13, box 4, Delta Ministry Papers, Starkville; Marshal L. Scott to Robert L. Beech, October 5, 1966, folder "Keep For Reference No. II," box 1, Beech Papers; *Minutes of the General Assembly of the United Presbyterian Church in the United States of America,* 1967, 512; *Delta Democrat-Times,* September 30, 1966; *Washington Post,* October 2, 1966 (quotations); "Divisions of Board of Missions," 6.

45. "Delta Ministry: Report to the Executive Committee of DCLM," September 16, 1966, 6, RG 38, folder "Delta Ministry (1)," box 1, Office of Church and Society Records, PCUS, Montreat; Hilton, *Delta Ministry,* 129–30; Rims K. Barber, interview by author, August 22, 1996; Alfred R. Winham to "Dear Fallen Comrade," September 10, 1966 (first quotation), folder "'65–'67 Letters—Mass.," Winham Papers; Colin W. Williams to "Dear Delta Commission Member," October 4, 1966, 3 (second quotation), RG 301.9, folder 15, box 8, CORAR Records; Warren H. McKenna to Paul Moore, Jr., July 12, 1966, folder 42, box 12, and Thelma P. Barnes to Paul Moore Jr., July 11, 1966, folder 31, box 23, Delta Ministry Papers, Atlanta.

46. Memorandum, A. Dudley Ward to Grover C. Bagby, June 14, 1966 (quotations), folder 1431–2–3:06, memorandum, Grover C. Bagby to Dudley Ward, September 15, 1966, folder 1431–2–3:06, and Grover C. Bagby to W. Kenneth Pope, July 11, 1966, folder 1431–2–3:05, Church and Society Records, UMC; A. Dudley Ward to Eugene Carson Blake, October 29, 1963, RG 95, folder 16, box 15, Blake Papers; "Divisions of Board of Missions," 5.

47. "Report of the Special Committee to Study the Relationship of the National Division to the Delta Ministry," September 26, 1966, 1–6 (first quotation on pp. 4–5), folder 1431–2–3:08, and Paul Hardin Jr. to A. Raymond Grant, A. Dudley Ward, W. Kenneth Pope, and Grover C. Bagby Jr., October 18, 1966, and attached untitled statement by College of Bishops, Southeastern Jurisdiction, October 11, 1966 (second quotation), folder 1431–2–3:05, Church and Society Records, UMC; "Divisions of Board of Missions," 5–6; "Bishop and Cabinet Oppose Grant," 1; Lawrence, "On Being Consistent," 2; "Delta Ministry's Support," December 1, 1966, folder 13, box 4, Delta Ministry Papers, Starkville.

48. Chauncey, "Should We Support the Delta Ministry?" 24; memorandum, George A. Chauncey, "Re: FREEDOM CITY of the Delta Ministry," November 21, 1966, RG 38, folder "Norton Committee Report on Delta Ministry," box 1, Office of Church and Society Records, PCUS, Montreat.

49. "Delta Ministry's Support," December 1, 1966, folder 13, box 4, Delta Ministry Papers, Starkville; "Delta Ministry's Support," December 1, 1966, folder 13, box 14, and "Sources of Financial Support for the Budget of the Delta Ministry, National Council of Churches, for 1966," folder 2, box 19, Delta Ministry Papers, Atlanta; "Report on the Delta Ministry," December 2, 1966, 2, RG 38, folder "Delta Ministry (1)," box 1, A. Dudley Ward, "Report of the Budget and Finance Committee," October 5–7, 1966, 2, RG 38, folder "Delta Ministry (2)," box 1, and "Subject to Audit, Delta Ministry 1966," January 23, 1967, RG 38, folder "Delta Ministry, Basic Papers," box 1, Office of Church and Society Records, PCUS, Montreat; "WATS Line Report—for D.M. Staff," December 13, 1966, 1–2 (quotation on p. 1), folder 16, box 26, and memorandum, Colin W. Williams to Delta Ministry Staff, December 1, 1966, folder 1, box 26, Hamer Papers; *New York Times,* December 3, 1966.

50. Colin W. Williams to George A. Chauncey, December 13, 1966, RG 38, folder "Delta Ministry (1)," Office of Church and Society Records, PCUS, Montreat; "Delta Ministry Staff (as of December 1, 1966)," folder "D.M. Fact Sheet," no box, Winham Papers; "Report of the Delta Ministry," February 17–18, 1967, 1, folder 247, box 5, King Papers; "WATS Line Report—for D.M. Staff," December 13, 1966, 1 (quotation), folder 16, box 1, and memorandum, Colin W. Williams to Delta Ministry Staff, December 1, 1966, folder 1, box 26, Hamer Papers; *Delta Democrat-Times,* September 20, 1966.

51. "Report on the Delta Ministry," December 2, 1966, 3–6, RG 38, folder "Delta Ministry (1)," box 1, Office of Church and Society Records, PCUS, Montreat.

52. Chester Higgins, "Pretty Girl, 17, 'With Mean Streak' Starts Movement," *Jet,* n.d., 20, folder 29, box 2, Delta Ministry Papers, Starkville; *Delta Ministry Reports,* February 1967, 2; Mrs. John E. Fawcett, "A Week in Mississippi—from April 10 to April 17, 1965, Newsletter #3," folder "Hattiesburg—1965–1966," no box, Beech Papers; *Providence (Rhode Island) Journal,* August 31, 1966; Erle Johnston Jr., memorandum to file, August 19, 1966, and attached list of eighteen demands, Erle Johnston Jr., "Edwards, Mississippi" report, August 25, 1966 (quotation), and Tom Scarbrough, "Edwards, Mississippi" report, August 30, 1966, folder 3, box 139, Johnson Family Papers; A. L. Hopkins, report, October 27, 1966, folder 5, box 139, Johnson Family Papers.

53. "Delta Ministry Staff (as of February 1, 1967)," folder 13, box 1, Horwitz Papers; "Proposal for the Freedom Information Service," November 15, 1965, 13, folder 17, box 2, and Charles Horwitz, "Hinds County," 1, in Owen H. Brooks, "Report on the Delta Ministry, 1967," folder 32, box 3, Delta Ministry Papers, Atlanta; minutes of the second membership meeting of the Poor People's Corporation, November 28, 1965, 5, folder 150, box 116, SNCC Papers; Arthur C. Thomas to Jon L. Regier, April 22, 1966, folder "Budget Measures 1966," box 3, Thomas Papers; Tut Tate et al. to "Dear Friends," March 15, 1966, folder 6, box II-A, Cox Collection; Bruce Hilton to J. Irwin Miller, May 10, 1966, RG 11, folder 4, box 8, NCC Archives; "Delta Ministry: Report to the Executive Committee of DCLM," September 16, 1966, 5, RG 38, folder "Delta Ministry (1)," box 1, Office of Church and Society Records, PCUS, Montreat.

54. Charles Horwitz, "Hinds County," 1 (second quotation), in Owen H. Brooks, "Report on the Delta Ministry, 1967," folder 32, box 3, Delta Ministry Papers, Atlanta; *Jackson Daily News,* June 13, 1966; Chester Higgins, "Pretty Girl, 17, 'With Mean Streak' Starts Movement," *Jet,* n.d., 14–21 (first quotation on p. 20), folder 29, box 2, Delta Ministry Papers, Starkville; untitled Mississippi State Sovereignty Commission report, August 20, 1966, and Erle Johnston Jr., "Edwards, Mississippi" report, August 25, 1966, 1, folder 3, box 139, Johnson Family Papers.

55. Charles Horwitz, "Hinds County," 3, in Owen H. Brooks, "Report on the Delta Ministry, 1967," folder 32, box 3, Delta Ministry Papers, Atlanta; "How 'Freedomcrafts' Came to Be," n.d., folder "Freedom Crafts," no box, Beech Papers; Martha Thompson to "Dear Friend," n.d., folder 48, box 3, Horwitz Papers; "Passing Scene," 1530; "About That Candy," 461; *Vicksburg Citizens' Appeal* 3 (January 4, 1967), folder 59, box 2, Delta Ministry Papers, Starkville; "WATS Line Report for DM Staff," March 16, 1967, folder 6, box 4, Amzie Moore Papers, WHS.

56. Charles Horwitz, "Hinds County," 1, in Owen H. Brooks, "Report on the Delta Ministry, 1967," folder 32, box 3, Delta Ministry Papers, Atlanta; Tom Scarbrough, "Edwards, Mississippi" report, August 30, 1966, folder 3, box 139, Erle Johnston Jr. to Clark E. Robbins, September 1, 1966, folder 4, box 139, A. L. Hopkins, "Investigation in Edwards, Mississippi . . . ," October 6, 1966, 1–2, folder 5, box 139, and A. L. Hopkins, "Investigation in Hinds, Warren, and Madison Counties," November 3, 1967, 1–2, folder 2, box 141, Johnson Family Papers; *Delta Ministry Reports,* February 1967, 2; Johnston, *Mississippi's Defiant Years,* 334; Frederick S. Lowry, "Mount Beulah July 15th to September 15th, 1965," 3, in "Staff Reports, Commission on the Delta Ministry," October 1, 1965, folder "Staff Reports, October 1, 1965," box 1, Humphrey Papers.

57. "Delta Ministry: Report to the Executive Committee of DCLM," September 16, 1966, 3, 6, RG 38, folder "Delta Ministry (1)," box 1, Office of Church and Society Records, PCUS, Montreat; memorandum, Gayraud S. Wilmore Jr. to "Members of the Executive Committee," July 18, 1966, 1, and memorandum, Gayraud S. Wilmore Jr. to "Members of the Executive Committee," August 2, 1966, 1–2, RG 301.9, folder 15, box 8, CORAR Records; *Delta Ministry Reports,* October 1966, 1, November 1966, 1.

58. Memorandum, Gayraud S. Wilmore to "Members of the Executive Committee," July 18, 1966, folder "Delta Ministry," box 16, Neigh Papers; Robert L. Beech, "Report from Hattiesburg, July 14–24[,] 1964," 2, folder "Reports and Reactions," no box, Beech Papers; *Delta Ministry Reports,* November 1966, 2, February 1967, 1; Owen H. Brooks to John Stachel, November 22, 1966 (quotation), folder 77, box 1, Delta Ministry Papers, Starkville.

59. *Delta Ministry Reports,* May 1966, 2; Owen H. Brooks to John Stachel, November 22, 1966 (quotation), folder 77, box 1, Delta Ministry Papers, Starkville; Curtis Hayes, "Freedom Corps," 1–2, in "Staff Reports, Commission on the Delta Ministry," October 1, 1965, folder "Staff Reports, October 1, 1965," box 1, Humphrey Papers; "Delta Ministry: Report to the Executive Committee of DCLM," September 16, 1966, 5, RG 38, folder "Delta Ministry (1)," box 1, Office of Church and Society Records, PCUS, Montreat; "Delta Ministry Staff (as of February 1, 1967)," folder 13, box 1, Horwitz Papers; Joseph Lewis Harris, résumé, November 24, 1969, folder 11, box 2, and R. H. Edwin Espy to Joseph Lewis Harris, January 9, 1967, folder 1, box 26, Hamer Papers; Ullman, "In Darkest America," 179–80.

60. Robert L. Beech to Beryl Ramsay, October 29, 1966 (first quotation), folder "Keep For Reference No. II," box 1, Beech Papers; "Delta Ministry: Report to the Executive Committee of DCLM," September 16, 1966, 5–6, RG 38, folder "Delta Ministry (1)," box 1, Office of Church and Society Records, PCUS, Montreat; Alfred R. Winham to "Your Grace," November 5, 1966, 2 (second quotation), folder "Letters—Pers.," no box, Winham Papers.

61. "Delta Ministry Staff (as of December 1, 1966)," folder "D.M. Fact Sheet," no box, Winham Papers; *New York Times,* March 7, 1971; Noble, "Delta Ministry," 10, 75; "Subject to Audit, Delta Ministry 1966," January 23, 1967, RG 38, folder "Delta Ministry, Basic Papers," Office of Church and Society Records, PCUS, Montreat.

CHAPTER SEVEN. Freedom City

1. "New Community," n.d., folder "Com. Network," no box, Winham Papers; *Delta Democrat-Times,* January 2, 1970; *New York Times,* July 25, 1966; Sarah H. Johnson, interview by Thomas Healy, September 10, 1978, Mississippi Oral History Program of the University of Southern Mississippi, 12–13; *Jackson Clarion-Ledger,* December 17, 1980.

2. Sam H. Franklin Jr. to Robert L. Beech, February 8, 1965, folder "Correspondence III," box 1, Beech Papers; Silver, *Mississippi,* 36–37; Campbell, *Providence.*

3. Chancey, "Demonstration Plot"; K'Meyer, *Interracialism.*

4. Minutes, Executive Committee, Commission on the Delta Ministry, July 19, 1965, 5, folder "D.M. Reports," no box, Winham Papers; Hilton, *Delta Ministry,* 112 (quotation); David DeRienzis revised by Ralph Galt, "'Moshav' or Coop Farm Plan for Mississippi," n.d., attached to "Proposal: The Development of a Cooperative Farming Village," n.d., folder 41, box 1, Delta Ministry Papers, Atlanta.

5. "Proposal: The Development of a Cooperative Farming Village," n.d., folder 41, box 1, Delta Ministry Papers, Atlanta.

6. Thomas R. Hughes to Arthur C. Thomas, July 1, 1965, memorandum, Joseph G. Knapp to Robert G. Lewis, June 23, 1965, memorandum, George S. Tolley to Robert G. Lewis, June 24, 1965, 1–2 (quotation on p. 2), memorandum, Larry Brock to "Administrator, Rural Community Development Service," n.d., and memorandum, Robert G. Lewis to Thomas R. Hughes, n.d., attached to memorandum, "Administrator," to Robert G. Lewis, n.d., folder "Agriculture Co-op Village," box 2, Thomas Papers. The department did not mention the successful Mileston Farms Project in Holmes County, created by the Farm Security Administration in 1938. Located on 9,350 acres of land, by 1943 the project had created 106 small black-owned farms and a cooperative that included a cotton gin and a store. Relatively immune to white economic intimidation, Mileston farmers invited SNCC to be-

gin a voter registration project in 1963. Holmes County soon became a stronghold of the MFDP. In 1967, the county elected Robert Clark to the Mississippi assembly, the first African American state legislator since Reconstruction (Aiken, *Cotton Plantation South*, 161; Salamon, "Time Dimension," 130–32, 141–47, 166, 182). The Delta Ministry worked with Mileston's black community. In cooperation with the MCHR, the Ministry created the Holmes County Health Improvement Association, based in Mileston, and a health demonstration clinic in the town. There is no evidence that the legacy of the Mileston Farms Project influenced the Ministry's creation of Freedom City (H. Jack Geiger to Arthur C. Thomas, July 27, 1965, folder 10, box 12, Delta Ministry Papers, Atlanta; "The Medical Program," in "The Delta Ministry," n.d., folder "Delta Ministry Program," box 3, Beech Papers).

7. Memorandum, J. Oscar Lee to Jon L. Regier, June 18, 1965, and memorandum, J. Oscar Lee to Arthur C. Thomas, August 3, 1965, folder "Agriculture Co-op Village," box 2, Thomas Papers; "Report to the Seventh General Assembly, National Council of the Churches of Christ in the U.S.A.," December 4–9, 1966, 34, folder 24, box 2, 1972 addendum, Cox Collection; Wright, Aronson, and Mudd, "Proposed," 42–46; minutes, Executive Committee, Commission on the Delta Ministry, July 19, 1965, 1, folder "D.M. Reports," no box, Winham Papers.

8. Minutes, Executive Committee, Commission on the Delta Ministry, July 19, 1965, 5, folder "D.M. Reports," no box, Winham Papers; Sutherland, "Mississippi Summer," 213; "Commission on the Delta Ministry, Outline of Director's Report," July 19, 1965, 3 (quotation), folder 10, box 27, Delta Ministry Papers, Atlanta.

9. *Delta Ministry Reports*, February 1966, n.p. (quotation); "Through the Long, Hot Summer . . . ," n.d., n.p., folder "Articles—1965," box "BP. Moore w/Delta Min.," Paul Moore Jr. Papers, AEDNY.

10. Hilton, *Delta Ministry*, 104–8, 115 (quotation); "Background Material from Subcommittee on Administration of the Delta Ministry," February 28–March 1, 1966, 4, in "Subcommittee Reports to the Evaluation Committee of the Delta Ministry Commission, National Council of Churches," May 6, 1966, folder 9, box 43, SCLC Papers; "Through the Long, Hot Summer . . . ," n.d., n.p., folder "Articles—1965," box "BP. Moore w/Delta Min.," Paul Moore Jr. Papers, AEDNY.

11. *Delta Democrat-Times*, June 17, 1970; Arthur C. Thomas to John H. Betz, April 21, 1966, and attached John H. Betz to Arthur C. Thomas, April 11, 1966, folder 3, box 45, Delta Ministry Papers, Atlanta; "Application for Community Action Program," March 1, 1966, no folder, no box, Winham Papers.

12. Hilton, *Delta Ministry*, 113 (quotations); "New City (for Staff Discussion Only)," n.d., folder 25, box 6, Delta Ministry Papers, Atlanta; Harry J. Bowie, interview by author, September 5, 1996; Thelma P. Barnes, interview by author, September 5, 1996.

13. Hilton, *Delta Ministry*, 129; "New City (for Staff Discussion Only)," n.d., 1–4 (first quotation on p. 1; third, fifth, and sixth quotations on p. 2; fourth quotation on p. 4), folder 25, box 6, Delta Ministry Papers, Atlanta; "New Community," 3 (second quotation), in "A New Approach in Community Development," May 1, 1966, folder "New Community Program Resources," box 3, Thomas Papers.

14. "New City (for Staff Discussion Only)," n.d., 2 (quotations), folder 25, box 6, Delta Ministry Papers, Atlanta.

15. "New City (for Staff Discussion Only)," n.d., 2–3 (first and third quotations on p. 3;

second quotation on p. 2), folder 25, box 6, Delta Ministry Papers, Atlanta; Carmichael and Hamilton, *Black Power.*

16. "Statement to Press Conference, Jackson, Mississippi, by Theodore M. Berry, Director, Community Action Programs, OEO," April 7, 1966, 2 (quotations), and Noel H. Klores to Clarence Hall Jr., n.d., folder "D.O.C. Self-Help Housing Program," box 1, Thomas Papers.

17. Hilton, *Delta Ministry,* 129; Robert L. Beech to Carl R. Scovel, April 21, 1966, 1, folder "Keep For Reference No. II," box 1, Beech Papers; Harry J. Bowie, interview by author, September 5, 1996; Warren H. McKenna to Irving Fain, March 16, 1966, no folder, box 2, Thomas Papers; Clarence Hall Jr. to Noel H. Klores, April 27, 1966, and Noel H. Klores to Clarence Hall Jr., May 4, 1966, folder "D.O.C. Self-Help Housing Program," box 1, Thomas Papers; "Five Days with Delta Ministry in Greenville, Miss.," n.d., 4, folder 23, box 3, and Warren H. McKenna to Alfred Schroeder, June 9, 1966, folder 35, box 16, Delta Ministry Papers, Atlanta; "400 Acres of Delta Farmland Bought for Poor Delta Negroes," April 7, 1966, "Black Folder," box 12, Delta Ministry Papers, Starkville; *Delta Democrat-Times,* April 29, 1966; *New York Times,* July 25, 1966; memorandum, Ferdinand H. Pease to Stephen A. Feke, November 14, 1966, William A. Carhart to Irving Fain, November 15, 1966, and Barbara A. Shapiro to Ferdinand H. Pease, November 18, 1966, RG 11, folder 5, box 32, NCC Archives; Clarence Hall Jr. to Noel H. Klores, April 27, 1966 (quotation), no folder, no box, Winham Papers; McEachran, "Freedom City," 11.

18. Warren H. McKenna to David H. McAlpin Jr., June 9, 1966, folder 35, box 16, Delta Ministry Papers, Atlanta; Alfred R. Winham, "Field Staff Quarterly Report," July 1, 1966, folder "Reports—Unified Field Staff," no box, and memorandum, Alfred R. Winham to Warren McKenna, July 21, 1966, folder "Memo (Miss).—Trips," no box, Winham Papers; *Delta Democrat-Times,* April 29, 1966 (quotation).

19. "Through the Long, Hot Summer . . . ," n.d., n.p., folder "Articles—1965," box "BP. Moore w/Delta Min.," Paul Moore Jr. Papers, AEDNY; untitled, n.d., folder 8, box 46, Warren H. McKenna to Alfred Schroeder, June 9, 1966, folder 35, box 16, and untitled, undated two-page account of Freedom City's financial arrangements, folder 8, box 46, Delta Ministry Papers, Atlanta; "Delta Ministry Staff Meeting," February 23–24, 1967, 2, 6, folder 224, box 5, King Papers; Hilton, *Delta Ministry,* 112; Howell, *Freedom City,* 51.

20. *New York Times,* July 25, 1966; Howell, *Freedom City,* 43–45 (first quotation on p. 45), 83, 85–89; "Through the Long, Hot Summer . . . ," n.d., n.p., folder "Articles—1965," box "BP. Moore w/Delta Min.," Paul Moore Jr. Papers, AEDNY.

21. Howell, "Freedom City," 226–27; Howell, *Freedom City,* 22, 44–45 (first and second quotations on p. 44), 49–50 (third quotation on p. 50).

22. "Delta Ministry: Report to the Executive Committee of DCLM," September 16, 1966, 4, RG 38, folder "Delta Ministry (1)," box 1, Office of Church and Society Records, PCUS, Montreat; Thelma P. Barnes to Roy P. Huddleston, September 20, 1966, 1, folder 32, box 23, and unsigned letter to Thomas G. Uter, April 22, 1966, folder 29, box 23, Delta Ministry Papers, Atlanta; *Delta Democrat-Times,* July 19, 1966; *New York Times,* July 25, 1966.

23. *New York Times,* July 25, 1966 (first, second, and third quotations); Thelma P. Barnes, interview by author, September 5, 1996; Warren H. McKenna to Robert Powell, July 13, 1966 (fourth quotation), folder 36, box 16, Delta Ministry Papers, Atlanta.

24. "Report of the Evaluation Committee on the Mississippi Delta Ministry of the

General Board of the National Council of Churches," May 16, 1966, 9, folder 44, box 3, Delta Ministry Papers, Starkville; "Report on the Delta Ministry," December 2, 1966, 1–4, RG 38, folder "Delta Ministry (1)," box 1, Office of Church and Society Records, PCUS, Montreat; Warren H. McKenna to Alfred Schroeder, June 9, 1966, Warren H. McKenna to David H. McAlpin Jr., June 9, 1966, and draft "The Delta Ministry in Mississippi: What You Can Do to Help," n.d., folder 35, box 16, Delta Ministry Papers, Atlanta; *Delta Democrat-Times,* July 19, 1966 (quotation); *Memphis Commercial Appeal,* July 19, 1966.

25. Rims K. Barber, interview by author, September 3, 1996; memorandum, Sue Geiger to H. Newton Hudson, July 31, 1967, folder 94, box 6, Delta Ministry Papers, Starkville; Naomi Long to "Dear Teacher," April 30, 1966, folder 2, box 22, and Rims K. Barber, "Education—June to September" (quotation), in Owen H. Brooks, "Report on the Delta Ministry, 1967," folder 32, box 3, Delta Ministry Papers, Atlanta; Hilton, "Pioneering," 12; "Delta Ministry: Report to the Executive Committee of DCLM," September 16, 1966, 5, RG 38, folder "Delta Ministry (1)," box 1, Office of Church and Society Records, PCUS, Montreat; "Delta Ministry Staff (as of December 1, 1966)," folder "D.M. Fact Sheet," no box, Winham Papers.

26. *Delta Ministry Reports,* October 1966, 1; Hilton, *Delta Ministry,* 125–27; Rims K. Barber, "Education—June to September," in Owen H. Brooks, "Report on the Delta Ministry, 1967," folder 32, box 3, Delta Ministry Papers, Atlanta; Howell, *Freedom City,* 51, 68; Rims K. Barber, interview by author, September 3, 1996.

27. Hilton, "Pioneering," 11–12; Hilton, *Delta Ministry,* 127; "Delta Ministry: Report to the Executive Committee of DCLM," September 16, 1966, 5, RG 38, folder "Delta Ministry (1)," box 1, Office of Church and Society Records, PCUS, Montreat; "Delta Ministry Staff (as of December 1, 1966)," folder "D.M. Fact Sheet," no box, Winham Papers; *Delta Democrat-Times,* April 20, 1967.

28. *Delta Democrat-Times,* July 19, 1966; Alfred R. Winham to "Dear Jack," September 14, 1966 (first quotation), folder "'65–'67 Letters—Mass.," no box, Winham Papers; Hilton, *Delta Ministry,* 122–23; Thelma P. Barnes to Roy P. Huddleston, September 20, 1966 (second and third quotations), folder 32, box 23, Delta Ministry Papers, Atlanta.

29. Marian E. Wright to Thelma P. Barnes, September 15, 1966, folder 5, box 24, minutes, DOC, November 6, 1966, 1–4, folder 14, box 27, minutes, DOC, December 12, 1966, 2, folder 23, box 45, and minutes, DOC, December 29, 1966, 1–2, folder 23, box 45, Robert Holmes Jr. to Howard W. Hallman, March 7, 1969, folder 4, box 47, and Clarence Hall Jr. and Thelma P. Barnes, "EDA—Project # 04–6–09027," n.d., folder 5, box 20, Delta Ministry Papers, Atlanta; Alfred R. Winham to "Your Grace," November 5, 1966, folder "Letters—Pers.," no box, and David G. Colwell to R. Sargent Shriver, December 2, 1966, folder "Letters—General," no box, Winham Papers; Hilton, *Delta Ministry,* 125.

30. *Delta Ministry Reports,* October 1966, 1; Howell, *Freedom City,* 90–91; Hilton, *Delta Ministry,* 109–10, 123–24; "Freedom Crafts Nativity Set," n.d., no folder, no box, Winham Papers; McEachran, "Freedom City," 12, 14; "Delta Ministry Staff Meeting," February 23–24, 1967, 2, 6, folder 224, box 5, King Papers; *Delta Democrat-Times,* July 16, 1967.

31. "Delta Ministry Staff (as of December 1, 1966)," folder "D.M. Fact Sheet," no box, Winham Papers; *Delta Ministry Reports,* October 1966, 1; *Delta Democrat-Times,* July 16, 1967; Ullman, "In Darkest America," 180 (first quotation); Hilton, *Delta Ministry,* 128 (second quotation).

32. *Delta Ministry Reports,* October 1966, 1, November 1966, 1; Robert L. Beech to Miles Cooper, October 27, 1966, untitled folder, box 1, Beech Papers; "Delta Ministry Staff (as of December 1, 1966)," folder "D.M. Fact Sheet," no box, Winham Papers; "Delta Ministry: Report to the Executive Committee of DCLM," September 16, 1966, 5, RG 38, folder "Delta Ministry (1)," box 1, Office of Church and Society Records, PCUS, Montreat.

33. Alfred R. Winham to William P. Thorp, November 11, 1966, folder 37, box 20, Delta Ministry Papers, Atlanta; Hilton, *Delta Ministry,* 124–25.

34. Thelma P. Barnes to Roy P. Huddleston, September 20, 1966, 2 (quotation), folder 32, box 23, Delta Ministry Papers, Atlanta; *Delta Ministry Reports,* October 1966, 1; Robert L. Beech to Beryl Ramsay, October 29, 1966, folder "Keep For Reference No. II," box 1, Beech Papers.

35. *Delta Ministry Reports,* November 1966, 1; Alfred R. Winham to Charles E. Cobb, November 23, 1966, 1–3 (quotation on p. 1), folder "Letters—C.C.S.A.," no box, Winham Papers.

36. Clarence Hall Jr. to R. Sargent Shriver, November 10, 1966, and attached Noel H. Klores to Clarence Hall Jr., n.d., folder 36, box 47, and minutes, DOC, November 13, 1966, 2, folder 13, box 27, Delta Ministry Papers, Atlanta; Grover C. Bagby to Lorenz M. Schultz, March 22, 1966, folder 1431–2–3:05, Church and Society Records, UMC; *Delta Ministry Reports,* November 1966, 1; Alfred R. Winham to Charles E. Cobb, November 23, 1966, folder "Letters—C.C.S.A.," no box, Winham Papers.

37. *Delta Ministry Reports,* November 1966, 1; Alfred R. Winham to Charles E. Cobb, November 23, 1966, 1, folder "Letters—C.C.S.A.," no box, Winham Papers; memorandum, George A. Chauncey, "Re: FREEDOM CITY of the Delta Ministry," November 21, 1966, RG 38, folder "Norton Committee Report on Delta Ministry," box 1, Office of Church and Society Records, PCUS, Montreat; Chauncey, "Should We Support the Delta Ministry?" 24; "Christmas at Freedom City—A Report," December 9, 1966, folder 19, box 3, Delta Ministry Papers, Atlanta. The Methodist Church sent $5,000 and the Evangelical United Brethren Church $1,300 for the emergency at Freedom City (memorandum, George A. Chauncey, "Re: FREEDOM CITY of the Delta Ministry," November 21, 1966, RG 38, folder "Norton Committee Report on Delta Ministry," box 1, Office of Church and Society Records, PCUS, Montreat).

38. Alfred R. Winham to Charles E. Cobb, November 23, 1966, 1, folder "Letters—C.C.S.A.," no box, Winham Papers; memorandum, George A. Chauncey, "Re: FREEDOM CITY of the Delta Ministry," November 21, 1966, RG 38, folder "Norton Committee Report on Delta Ministry," box 1, Office of Church and Society Records, PCUS, Montreat; Howell, *Freedom City,* 53; *Delta Democrat-Times,* November 13, 1966.

39. Howell, *Freedom City,* 53; "Delta Ministry Staff (as of December 1, 1966)," folder "D.M. Fact Sheet," no box, Winham Papers; "Report on the Delta Ministry," December 2, 1966, 3–4, RG 38, folder "Delta Ministry (1)," box 1, Office of Church and Society Records, PCUS, Montreat; Alfred R. Winham to Robert Eubanks, December 6, 1966 (quotation), folder 13, box 20, Delta Ministry Papers, Atlanta; Noble, "Delta Ministry," 92.

40. *National Observer,* December 26, 1966.

41. *New York Times,* December 3, 1966; "Christmas at Freedom City—A Report," December 9, 1966, folder 19, box 3, Delta Ministry Papers, Atlanta.

42. *Delta Democrat-Times,* December 19, 1966 (quotation); Hilton, *Delta Ministry,* 135.

43. Alfred R. Winham to Charles E. Cobb, January 13, 1967, folder "Letters—C.C.S.A.,"

no box, Winham Papers; *Delta Ministry Reports,* February 1967, 1–2, March 1967, 2; Ullman, "In Darkest America," 178; "Delta Ministry Staff Meeting," February 23–24, 1967, 2, folder 224, box 5, King Papers.

44. "Delta Ministry Staff Meeting," February 23–24, 1967, 2 (first quotation), 5–6 (second quotation on p. 6), folder 224, box 5, King Papers.

45. *Memphis Commercial Appeal,* January 16, 1967 (quotations); Evers and Szanton, *Have No Fear,* 145, 147.

46. Minutes, Commission on the Delta Ministry, March 27–28, 1967, p. 4 (quotation), folder 12, box 2, Theodore M. Berry to Clarence Hall Jr., March 28, 1967, folder 39, box 45, and DOC, "Proposal to the Ford Foundation," April 1967, folder 10, box 46, Delta Ministry Papers, Atlanta; *Delta Ministry Reports,* April 1967, 1; *Delta Democrat-Times,* March 29, 1967.

47. U.S. Congress, Senate, Subcommittee on Employment, Manpower, and Poverty of the Committee on Labor and Public Welfare, *Examination of the War on Poverty,* pt. 2: *Jackson, Mississippi,* 90th Cong., 1st sess., April 10, 1967; Noble, "Delta Ministry," 13, 88; Kotz, *Let Them Eat Promises,* 2–3; *New York Times,* April 12, 1967; "YES, America," 1; Simeon Booker, "In Mississippi Starts Action," *Jet,* n.d., 15–21, folder 21, box 24, Delta Ministry Papers, Atlanta; Howell, *Freedom City,* 74–75; Ullman, "In Darkest America," 178 (quotation).

48. Ullman, "In Darkest America," 178. Having sent the Delta Ministry $11,108 from the Wild Goose Committee in March, the WCC forgot it had done so and mistakenly sent the same sum again in April. Rather than try to claw the money back, the World Council decided to subtract it from future donations it received for the Ministry (Wim J. Schot to Bruce Hilton, May 17, 1967, no folder, box 48, Delta Ministry Papers, Atlanta).

49. DOC, "Proposal to the Ford Foundation," April 1967, folder 10, box 46, Thelma P. Barnes to Alice B. Thomas, June 2, 1967, folder 10, box 24, Thelma P. Barnes to Maude Alexander, June 5, 1967, folder 10, box 24, Doris Smith to Thelma P. Barnes, July 5, 1967, folder 17, box 24, Moses T. Carstarphen Jr., July 11, 1967, folder 17, box 24, and Booker, "In Mississippi Starts Action," 15–21, folder 21, box 24, Delta Ministry Papers, Atlanta; memorandum, Ferdinand H. Pease to William A. Carhart, May 22, 1967, RG 11, folder 5, box 32, Henry A. McCanna to Louis Winnick, May 29, 1967, RG 6, folder 25, box 8, and "Memorandum of Understanding," June 5, 1967, RG 6, folder 25, box 8, NCC Archives.

50. Cobb, *Most Southern Place,* 255–56; Thelma P. Barnes to Maude Alexander, June 5, 1967 (quotation), folder 10, box 24, Delta Ministry Papers, Atlanta; *Delta Democrat-Times,* July 16, 1967.

51. Howell, *Freedom City,* 71–73 (first quotation on p. 73); Hilton, *Delta Ministry,* 137–38; *Delta Democrat-Times,* July 16, 1967 (second quotation); S. Geiger, "How Freedom City Overcame," 34.

52. Memorandum, Sue Geiger to H. Newton Hudson, July 31, 1967, 1–3 (first quotation on p. 1; second and third quotations on p. 3), folder 94, box 6, Delta Ministry Papers, Starkville; *Delta Democrat-Times,* January 19, 1970; "WATS Line Report—for DM Staff," March 16, 1967, folder 6, box 4, Amzie Moore Papers, WHS. Both the STAR and MDTA programs in Greenville provided enrollees with living allowances. In July 1967, four of Freedom City's men were enrolled as trainees in STAR and three in MDTA. Bradford argued that both programs trained African Americans for jobs that did not exist and therefore provided no solution to their problems (*Delta Democrat-Times,* July 16, 1967).

53. Unsigned to "Dear Vic," August 16, 1967, folder 23, box 19, John F. Anderson Jr. to

Jon L. Regier, August 17, 1967, folder 30, box 13, Thelma P. Barnes to Delwyn R. Rayson, October 14, 1967, folder 6, box 39, Owen H. Brooks to Bruce Hilton, May 1, 1967, folder 9, box 13, and Louis Winnick to Henry A. McCanna, October 4, 1967, 1–2 (quotation on p. 1), folder 40, box 45, Delta Ministry Papers, Atlanta; memorandum, Owen H. Brooks to John F. Anderson Jr., n.d., attached to Owen H. Brooks to John F. Anderson Jr., September 29, 1967, RG 1, folder "NCC Delta Ministry," box 10, Executive Secretary Correspondence Files, 1953–73, PCUS, Montreat; Robert L. Beech to Harvey G. Cox, September 28, 1967, untitled folder, box 1, Beech Papers; minutes, Commission on the Delta Ministry, November 16–17, 1967, 5, folder 62, box 3, Delta Ministry Papers, Starkville.

54. Minutes, Commission on the Delta Ministry, November 16–17, 1967, 5, folder 62, box 3, Delta Ministry Papers, Starkville; *Memphis Commercial Appeal* clipping, November 28, 1967, in "OEO" vertical file, Special Collections, Mitchell Memorial Library, Mississippi State University; "Agency Capabilities," n.d., 1, folder 12, box 47, Delta Ministry Papers, Atlanta; "Report on the Delta Ministry to the Program Board of the Division of Christian Life and Mission," 4, November 27, 1967, folder 1431-2-3:08, Church and Society Records, UMC.

55. Minutes, Commission on the Delta Ministry, November 16–17, 1967, 5, folder 62, box 3, Delta Ministry Papers, Starkville; "Report on the Delta Ministry to the Program Board of the Division of Christian Life and Mission," November 27, 1967, 5, folder 1431-2-3:08, Church and Society Records, UMC; Myer, *Sabotage,* 4–5.

56. "Agency Capabilities," n.d., 1, folder 12, box 47, Delta Ministry Papers, Atlanta; *Delta Ministry Reports,* January 1968, 2; Thelma P. Barnes to Aurilla Peterson, February 14, 1968, folder 9, box 39, David Payton, "Counseling Report," 7–8, in "Delta Opportunities Corporation: A Half Year of Progress," n.d., folder 40, box 13, and DOC, "Proposal to the Ford Foundation," April 1967, 3–5, folder 10, box 46, Delta Ministry Papers, Atlanta; Thelma P. Barnes, "Delta Opportunities Corporation," n.d., 1, folder 12, box 9, Delta Ministry Papers, Starkville; "Delta Opportunities," 1.

57. "Agency Capabilities," n.d., 2–4, folder 12, box 47, Delta Ministry Papers, Atlanta; Thelma P. Barnes, "Delta Opportunities Corporation," n.d., 1–3, folder 12, box 9, Delta Ministry Papers, Starkville; D. LaVonne Morgan, "Educational Report," 1–3, and David Payton, "Counseling Report," 8, in "Delta Opportunities Corporation: A Half Year of Progress," n.d., folder 40, box 13, Delta Ministry Papers, Atlanta; Morgan, "G.E.D. Candidates Successful," 1; "HEP Candidates," 1.

58. "Agency Capabilities," n.d., 1–2, folder 12, box 47, Delta Ministry Papers, Atlanta.

59. "Ground Breaking Ceremony, Freedom Village Housing Complex," May 31, 1968, and minutes, Commission on the Delta Ministry, June 10–11, 1968, 4, RG 4, folder "Delta Ministry April 1, '68—March 31, '69," box DHM 8, UCMS Papers; Thelma P. Barnes, "Delta Opportunities Corporation," n.d., 1–2 (first quotation on p. 2), folder 12, box 9, Delta Ministry Papers, Starkville; Thelma P. Barnes to Sandra K. Land, July 23, 1968, folder 19, box 39, Thelma P. Barnes to "Dear Friends," July 25, 1968, 1–2 (second quotation on p. 1), folder 21, box 46, and "Agency Capabilities," n.d., 1, 4–5, folder 12, box 47, Delta Ministry Papers, Atlanta; Barnes, "Money Changes Faces," 29, 31; Gordon A. Hanson to George W. Long, February 15, 1968, RG 1, folder "NCC Delta Ministry," box 10, Executive Secretary Correspondence Files, 1953–73, PCUS, Montreat; Murray, "World Council," 880; minutes, Delta Ministry Steering Committee, September 3, 1968, 2, folder 10, box 43, SCLC Papers.

60. Harry J. Bowie, "Economic Development," in "Report of the Delta Ministry—1968," folder 40, box 3, Delta Ministry Papers, Atlanta; "Facts about Delta Opportunities Corporation," January 31, 1969, folder 42, box 46, and Thelma P. Barnes to Joseph N. Peacock, December 13, 1968, folder 16, box 39, Delta Ministry Papers, Atlanta.

61. Gaile P. Noble, résumé, attached to Gaile P. Noble to Father Henry Parker, January 9, 1969, folder 63, box 2, Delta Ministry Papers, Starkville; Noble, "Delta Ministry," 91–93 (quotation on p. 92).

62. OEO press release, "Delta Opportunities Corporation, Mississippi," n.d., folder 10, box 47, and "DOC: A Progress Report," May 1969, 1–2, folder 40, box 46, Delta Ministry Papers, Atlanta; *Delta Ministry Reports,* January 1969, 1; "DOC Prescribes Poverty Cure," 3.

63. McKinley C. Martin, "Executive Director's Report," 3, in "Progress Report," August 2, 1969, folder 38, box 46, Clarence Hall Jr. et al. to "Dear Friend," April 25, 1969, folder 14, box 14, minutes, DOC, May 3, 1969, 2, folder 32, box 6, minutes, DOC, October 4, 1969, 3, folder 27, box 27, and Thelma P. Barnes to Cecil P. E. Pottieger, October 17, 1969, folder 13, box 27, Delta Ministry Papers, Atlanta; "DOC: A Progress Report," March 1969, RG 4, folder "Delta Ministry April 1, '68—March 31, '69," box DHM 8, UCMS Papers; "DOC Prescribes Poverty Cure," 3. The Methodist Church and the Evangelical United Brethren Church had merged in April 1968 to form the United Methodist Church (Taft, "Racial Birth Pangs," 34).

64. *Delta Ministry Reports,* September 1969, 1, November–December 1969, 2, October–November 1970, 1; McKinley C. Martin, "Executive Director's Report," 1, 4, in "Progress Report," August 2, 1969, folder 38, box 46, minutes, DOC, October 4, 1969, 2, folder 27, box 27, and Bruce Hanson to Jane Hinchcliffe Mavity, September 17, 1970, no folder, box 48, Delta Ministry Papers, Atlanta; "The Delta Ministry Report—1969," 10, folder 7, box 4, Delta Ministry Papers, Starkville; minutes, DOC, September 5, 1970, 2, 4, folder 7, box 27, Hamer Papers; Myer, *Sabotage,* 5; *Delta Democrat-Times,* June 18, 1970 (quotation); Howard R. Dressner to R. H. Edwin Espy, October 28, 1970, RG 6, folder 25, box 8, NCC Archives; *Jackson Clarion-Ledger,* December 17, 1980. The name change from Freedom City to Freedom Village indicated the intention to continue house construction on an 80-acre section known as Freedom Village, with the remaining 320 acres of Freedom City leased out for agriculture (Myer, *Sabotage,* 4).

65. Memorandum, Andrew L. Smith to "DOC Board," April 27, 1970, folder 12, box 27, Hamer Papers; *Delta Democrat-Times,* June 16, 17, 18, 1970.

66. *Delta Democrat-Times,* June 17, 1970; *Memphis Commercial Appeal,* June 18, 1970 (quotation).

67. *Delta Democrat-Times,* June 18, 1970.

68. *Delta Democrat-Times,* June 18, 1970; *Memphis Commercial Appeal,* June 18, 1970 (quotation); Martin, "Executive Director's Report," 1–4, in "Progress Report," August 2, 1969, folder 38, box 46, Delta Ministry Papers, Atlanta.

69. *Delta Democrat-Times,* October 2, 1970; Thelma P. Barnes, interview by author, September 5, 1996.

70. Memorandum, David M. Frank to H. C. Redmond, January 15, 1971 (quotation), folder 4, box 27, Hamer Papers; Sarah H. Johnson, interview by Thomas Healy, September 10, 1978, 12; Myer, *Sabotage,* 5.

71. *Delta Ministry Reports,* January 1971, 2, March 1971, 1, May 1971, 1, March 1973, 2; "Freedomcraft Ceramics Catalogue 1972," 1st ed., no folder, no box, Beech Papers; *Minutes of the*

General Assembly of the United Presbyterian Church in the United States of America, 1973, 684–85 (quotations on p. 684); undated *Delta Ministry Reports,* 1, no folder, no box, Winham Papers; Myer, *Sabotage,* 7.

72. "Special Report: The 1973 Flood," "Delta Ministry" vertical file, McCain Library and Archives, University of Southern Mississippi; *Delta Ministry Reports,* March 1973, 2, November 1973, 1, November 1974, 2, April 1976, 2; Myer, *Sabotage; Journal of the Women's Division of the Board of Global Ministries of the United Methodist Church,* 1975, xv–11; Schweid, *Catfish,* 179; *Jackson Clarion-Ledger,* December 17, 1980 (quotations), October 1, 1982; Sarah H. Johnson, interview by Thomas Healy, September 10, 1978, 12.

CHAPTER EIGHT. Changing Focus, 1967–1971

1. Owen H. Brooks, "Report on the Delta Ministry, 1967," folder 32, box 3, and "Report of the Delta Ministry—1968," folder 40, box 3, Delta Ministry Papers, Atlanta; "The Delta Ministry Report—1969," folder 7, box 4, Delta Ministry Papers, Starkville; *Memphis Commercial Appeal,* April 2, 1971.

2. *New York Times,* February 7, 1967; *Delta Ministry Reports,* February 1967, 1; Carson, *In Struggle,* 209–11, 215–26, 229, 231, 235–41; Meier and Rudwick, *CORE,* 414–17, 419.

3. *New York Times,* February 7, 1967; "Proposal for a Grant to the Delta Ministry of the National Council of the Churches of Christ in the U.S.A. for Community and Economic Development," folder 21, box 6, and "Introduction," in Owen H. Brooks, "Report on the Delta Ministry, 1967," folder 32, box 3, Delta Ministry Papers, Atlanta; "Subject to Audit, Delta Ministry 1966," January 23, 1967, RG 38, folder "Delta Ministry, Basic Papers," box 1, and Colin W. Williams to George A. Chauncey, February 7, 1967, RG 38, folder "Norton Committee Report on Delta Ministry," box 1, Office of Church and Society Records, PCUS, Montreat; "The Delta Ministry," n.d., 1, folder "National Council of the Churches of Christ in the U.S.A.," box 33, Social Action Collection, WHS; Alfred R. Winham to Myron W. Fowell, September 1, 1966, folder " '65–'67 Letters—Mass.," no box, and Owen H. Brooks to Alfred R. Winham, January 2, 1967, no folder, no box, Winham Papers.

4. *Minutes of the One-Hundred-Seventh General Assembly of the Presbyterian Church in the United States,* 1967, 176–77, 185–86; John F. Anderson Jr. to Truman B. Douglass, August 16, 1966, RG 38, folder "Delta Ministry (3), box 1, George A. Chauncey to Robert P. Douglass, November 17, 1966, Robert P. Douglass to Alex Hunter, November 30, 1966, Special Committee of the Council on Church and Society [Norton Committee], "Report and Recommendations on the Delta Ministry," n.d., 1–6 (first quotation on p. 4; second quotation on pp. 4–5), and George A. Chauncey to Colin W. Williams, January 27, February 14, 1967, RG 38, folder "Norton Committee Report on Delta Ministry," box 1, Office of Church and Society Records, PCUS, Montreat; Special Committee of the Council on Church and Society [Norton Committee], "Report and Recommendations on the Delta Ministry," n.d., appendix A, folder 520, Dabbs Papers; Chauncey, "Should We Support the Delta Ministry?" 23–24; "Panel Urges Support," 4.

5. George A. Chauncey to Colin W. Williams, February 14, 1967, 1–2 (first and second quotations on p. 1), RG 38, folder "Norton Committee Report on Delta Ministry," box 1, Office of Church and Society Records, PCUS, Montreat; minutes, Committee on Church Extension, Synod of Mississippi, March 30, 1967, 1–2 (third quotation on p. 1), and minutes,

Delta Ministry Committee, Board of Church Extension, May 20, 1967, 1–2, RG 1, folder "Delta Ministry Committee," box 7, Executive Secretary Correspondence Files, 1953–73, PCUS, Montreat.

6. Robert L. Beech, "Report from Hattiesburg, July 14–24[,] 1964," folder "Reports and Reactions," no box, Beech Papers; Robert L. Beech to Gayraud S. Wilmore Jr., October 22, 1966, and memorandum, Colin W. Williams to Edward E. Williams, November 7, 1966, RG 301.9, folder 15, box 8, CORAR Records; minutes, Commission on the Delta Ministry, November 16–17, 1967, 4 (first quotation), folder 62, box 3, Delta Ministry Papers, Starkville; Harry J. Bowie, "Citizenship Education Program," 1 (second quotation), in Owen H. Brooks, "Report on the Delta Ministry, 1967," folder 32, box 3, and Owen H. Brooks to S. E. Weissman, September 29, 1967, folder 13, box 19, Delta Ministry Papers, Atlanta; *Delta Ministry Reports,* February 1967, 1.

7. Joseph Lewis Harris, "Sunflower County," 1, in Owen H. Brooks, "Report on the Delta Ministry, 1967," folder 32, box 3, Delta Ministry Papers, Atlanta; "WATS Line Report—for D.M. Staff," December 13, 1966, folder 16, box 26, Hamer Papers; *Delta Ministry Reports,* February 1967, 2; "Proposed Editorial or Feature Story for Jackson Daily News to Be Picked up and Distributed by Wire Service," n.d., Leesha Faulkner Civil Rights Collection, in possession of the author; Lawson, *In Pursuit,* 99–101; Owen H. Brooks to John Stachel, November 22, 1966, folder 77, box 1, Delta Ministry Papers, Starkville.

8. Joseph Lewis Harris, "Sunflower County," 1, in Owen H. Brooks, "Report on the Delta Ministry, 1967," folder 32, box 3, Delta Ministry Papers, Atlanta; *Delta Ministry Reports,* May 1967, 2; Dittmer, *Local People,* 411–13; Lawson, *In Pursuit,* 101–2; McLemore, "Mississippi Freedom Democratic Party," 353–54, 363, 370. The MFDP filed suit for a new election in the town of Sunflower. However, the suit failed for lack of sufficient evidence and because federal election observers had found no irregularities (Walton, *Black Political Parties,* 123–24).

9. Rims K. Barber, "Yazoo County," 1, in Owen H. Brooks, "Report on the Delta Ministry, 1967," folder 32, box 3, Delta Ministry Papers, Atlanta; Curtis Hayes, "Freedom Corps," 1, in "Staff Reports, Commission on the Delta Ministry," October 1, 1965, folder "Staff Reports, October 1, 1965," box 1, Humphrey Papers; Noble, "Delta Ministry," 126. Fear prevented anyone from renting a house in Yazoo City to Barber (Hilton, *Delta Ministry,* 220).

10. Bruce Hilton to Frank Heard, June 30, 1967, folder 11, box 7, Delta Ministry Papers, Atlanta; minutes, Executive Committee, Commission on the Delta Ministry, July 31, 1967, 2, folder 47, box 3, Delta Ministry Papers, Starkville; Robert L. Beech to Harvey G. Cox, September 28, 1967, 1 (quotation), no folder, box 1, Beech Papers; "Report on the Delta Ministry to the Program Board of the Division of Christian Life and Mission," November 27, 1967, 1, RG 38, folder "Delta Ministry (2)," box 1, Office of Church and Society Records, PCUS, Montreat.

11. Owen H. Brooks to Mary Dale, June 14, 1967, RG 4, folder "Delta Ministry—NCC & UCMS Re: Mount Beulah Campus," box DHM 8, UCMS Papers; memorandum, Henry A. McCanna to Jon L. Regier, July 12, 1967, folder 41, box 5, minutes, ad hoc committee meeting to save Mount Beulah, August 16, 22, 1967, folder 41, box 5, and "Report of Meeting to Discuss Delta Ministry Lease Arrangement at Mount Beulah," July 12, 1967, folder 42, box 5, Delta Ministry Papers, Atlanta; minutes, Executive Committee, Commission on the Delta Ministry, July 31, 1967, 1, folder 47, box 3, Delta Ministry Papers, Starkville; minutes, Executive

Committee, Delta Ministry Commission, August 18, 1967, 1, RG 38, folder "Delta Ministry (2)," box 1, Office of Church and Society Records, PCUS, Montreat; Charles Horwitz et al. to "Mr. Moore," August 12, 1967, folder 6, box 4, Amzie Moore Papers, WHS.

12. Charles Horwitz et al. to "Mr. Moore," August 12, 1967, folder 6, box 4, Amzie Moore Papers, WHS; minutes, ad hoc committee meeting to save Mount Beulah, August 16, 22, 1967, folder 41, box 5, Delta Ministry Papers, Atlanta; Robert L. Beech to John M. Adams, October 6, 1967, untitled folder, box 1, Beech Papers; John W. Kalas to John F. Else, April 24, 1970, RG 301.7, folder 5, box 46, Board of National Missions (PCUSA) Records; untitled two-page fact sheet in RG 4, folder "Facts about Mt. Beulah," box DHM 9, UCMS Papers; minutes, Commission on the Delta Ministry, March 5, 1969, 5, folder 520, Dabbs Papers.

13. Noble, "Delta Ministry," 72, 76; "Introduction," 1, in Owen H. Brooks, "Report on the Delta Ministry, 1967," folder 32, box 3, Delta Ministry Papers, Atlanta.

14. Dan H. Barfield to "Dear Friends," August 5, 1967, folder 22, box 18, Delta Ministry Papers, Atlanta; see letters in folder 67, box 2, folders 3, 10, and 12, box 3, and folder 83, box 5, Delta Ministry Papers, Starkville.

15. *Minutes, The Synod of Mississippi of the Presbyterian Church, U.S., The One Hundred Thirty-Seventh Annual Session*, 1967, 109–11, 136–38 (first through fifth quotations on p. 137; sixth quotation on p. 138).

16. Unidentified press clipping, June 13, 1967 (first quotation), in folder 19, box 1, 1972 addendum, Cox Collection; *Delta Democrat-Times*, June 13, 1967 (second quotation); *Minutes, The Synod of Mississippi of the Presbyterian Church, U.S., The One-Hundred-Thirty-Seventh Annual Session*, 1967, 136.

17. *Minutes of the One-Hundred-Seventh General Assembly of the Presbyterian Church in the United States*, 1967, 84–85 (quotation on p. 85), 176–77, 183–86.

18. Memorandum, J. A. [John F. Anderson Jr.] to Henry A. McCanna, June 20, 1967, RG 1, folder "NCC Delta Ministry," box 10, Executive Secretary Correspondence Files, 1953–73, PCUS, Montreat; *Jackson Daily News*, June 14, 1967 (quotation); John F. Anderson Jr. to Jon L. Regier, August 17, 1967, folder 30, box 13, Delta Ministry Papers, Atlanta. The Board of Christian Education had donated three thousand dollars to the Delta Ministry during 1967, before the meeting of the General Assembly (Chauncey, "Should We Support the Delta Ministry?" 24).

19. *Minutes, The Synod of Mississippi of the Presbyterian Church, U.S., The One Hundred Thirty-Seventh Annual Session*, 1967, 138–41 (quotation on p. 139); *Minutes, The Synod of Mississippi of the Presbyterian Church in the U.S., The One Hundred Thirty-Eighth Annual Session*, 1968, 35–36, 68–70; *Minutes, The Synod of Mississippi of the Presbyterian Church in the U.S., The One Hundred Thirty-Ninth Annual Session*, 1969, 82–83; *Minutes, The Synod of Mississippi of the Presbyterian Church in the U.S., The One Hundred Fortieth Annual Session*, 1970, 46, 80–81; *Minutes, The Synod of Mississippi of the Presbyterian Church in the U.S., The One Hundred Forty-First Annual Session*, 1971, 64–66; *Minutes, The Synod of Mississippi of the Presbyterian Church in the U.S., The One Hundred Forty-Third Annual Session*, 1973, 18, 52–55.

20. Memorandum, Owen H. Brooks to John F. Anderson Jr., n.d., folder 45, box 13, Delta Ministry Papers, Atlanta; minutes, Executive Committee, Commission on the Delta Ministry, July 31, 1967, 4, folder 47, box 3, Delta Ministry Papers, Starkville.

21. Rims K. Barber, "Education—June to September," 1 (first quotation), in Owen H. Brooks, "Report on the Delta Ministry, 1967," folder 32, box 3, and minutes, Commission on

the Delta Ministry, March 27–28, 1967, 3 (second quotation), folder 12, box 2, Delta Ministry Papers, Atlanta; Bolton, "Last Stand," 329–30, 333–35.

22. Rims K. Barber, "Education—June to September," 1 (quotation), in Owen H. Brooks, "Report on the Delta Ministry, 1967," folder 32, box 3, Delta Ministry Papers, Atlanta.

23. Hilton, *Delta Ministry,* 126–27; Rims K. Barber, "Education—June to September," 2 (quotation), Edwin King, "Education Program," 1, Owen H. Brooks, "Citizenship Education," 1, and Clarence Hall Jr., "Issaquena County," 2, in Owen H. Brooks, "Report on the Delta Ministry, 1967," folder 32, box 3, Delta Ministry Papers, Atlanta; "Draft of a Proposal for Support of an Emergency Tutorial Program in Mississippi," n.d., folder 35, box 18, Delta Ministry Papers, Atlanta; "Delta Ministry Staff Meeting," February 23–24, 1967, 1–2, folder 224, box 5, King Papers; minutes, Commission on the Delta Ministry, November 16–17, 1967, 2–3, folder 62, box 3, and "BTCM Bulletin," fall 1966, folder 22, box 5, Delta Ministry Papers, Starkville.

24. Brooks, "Citizenship Education," 1, in Owen H. Brooks, "Report on the Delta Ministry, 1967," folder 32, box 3, Delta Ministry Papers, Atlanta; "A Brief History of the Shelby Problems," and untitled six-page description of the Shelby boycott, folder 254, box 6, Barber Papers.

25. Hilton, *Delta Ministry,* 178; Edwin King, interview by author, September 2, 1996; "Rev. Edwin King, Freedom Vote's Unofficial Candidate for Lt. Governor," n.d., folder 11, box 2, Romaine Papers; Edwin King, "Growing Up in Mississippi in a Time of Change," in *Mississippi Writers,* ed. Abbott, 2:375–80 (quotation on p. 380).

26. "Rev. Edwin King, Freedom Vote's Unofficial Candidate for Lt. Governor," n.d., folder 11, box 2, Romaine Papers; Marsh, *God's Long Summer,* 122–26; Edwin King, interview by author, September 2, 1996; T. Branch, *Pillar of Fire,* 121–22.

27. Marsh, *God's Long Summer,* 126–51, 195, 234, n.34; T. Branch, *Pillar of Fire,* 121–22, 264–65; "Divided Flocks," 1470; Edwin King, interview by author, September 2, 1996; "Divisions of Board of Missions," 6; Wren, "Insider," 28; Dittmer, *Local People,* 202–5, 288, 296–97, 394; Walton, *Black Political Parties,* 91, 95, 236; Owen H. Brooks to William Spofford, May 9, 1967, folder 15, box 13, Delta Ministry Papers, Atlanta.

28. Edwin King, interview by author, September 2, 1996; Owen H. Brooks to William Spofford, May 9, 1967 (quotation), folder 15, box 13, Delta Ministry Papers, Atlanta.

29. Edwin King, "Education Program," 1 (first quotation), in Owen H. Brooks, "Report on the Delta Ministry, 1967," folder 32, box 3, Delta Ministry Papers, Atlanta; minutes, Commission on the Delta Ministry, November 16–17, 1967, 3 (second quotation), folder 62, box 3, Delta Ministry Papers, Starkville; Noble, "Delta Ministry," 206.

30. Edwin King, "Education Program," 1, and Harry J. Bowie, "Citizenship Education Program," 1–2, in Owen H. Brooks, "Report on the Delta Ministry, 1967," folder 32, box 3, Delta Ministry Papers, Atlanta; Dittmer, *Local People,* 416.

31. Harry J. Bowie, interview by Robert Wright, August 8, 1968, 26, Bunche Oral History Collection; Owen H. Brooks to William B. Spofford, August 2, 1967, folder 15, box 13, Henry A. McCanna to Thomas Y. Minniece, September 15, 1967, folder 30, box 13, and Joseph Lewis Harris to Alex Capron, December 29, 1967, folder 26, box 13, Delta Ministry Papers, Atlanta; "Mississippians United to Elect Negro Candidates," *Mississippi Freedom Democratic Party Newsletter* 1 (October 1, 1967): 1; "The Delta Ministry Citizenship Education," n.d., 4 (first quotation), folder 7, box 10, and minutes, Commission on the Delta

Ministry, November 16–17, 1967, 4 (second quotation), folder 62, box 3, Delta Ministry Papers, Starkville; Joseph Lewis Harris to Sandra Nystrom, January 3, 1968, folder 6, box 5, Hamer Papers.

32. Thomas Y. Minniece to "Gentlemen," September 7, 1967, folder 30, box 13, Henry A. McCanna to Thomas Y. Minniece, September 15, 1967 (quotation), folder 30, box 13, minutes, Mississippians United Steering Committee, August 4 [1967], folder 22, box 5, and Charles Horwitz, "Hinds County," 1–2, in Owen H. Brooks, "Report on the Delta Ministry, 1967," folder 32, box 3, Delta Ministry Papers, Atlanta; Thomas Y. Minniece to Henry A. McCanna, October 11, 1967, and Henry A. McCanna to Thomas Y. Minniece, October 24, 1967, RG 1, folder "NCC Delta Ministry," box 10, Executive Secretary Correspondence Files, 1953–73, PCUS, Montreat; *Jackson Clarion-Ledger,* June 8, 1967; *Delta Democrat-Times,* May 30, 1967; Noble, "Delta Ministry," 86, 165, 206; Hilton, *Delta Ministry,* 147–48; Dittmer, *Local People,* 420.

33. *Memphis Commercial Appeal,* January 16, March 31, 1967; Walton, *Black Political Parties,* 115–16, 122, 237; Dittmer, *Local People,* 410.

34. *Memphis Commercial Appeal,* January 16, 1967 (first quotation); McEachran, "Freedom City," 13 (second quotation); memorandum, Erle Johnston Jr. to "Governor Paul B. Johnson, Chairman, Members of the State Sovereignty Commission," March 13, 1967, folder 2, box 140, Johnson Family Papers; Walton, *Black Political Parties,* 123.

35. *Delta Ministry Reports,* October 1966, 1–2, April 1967, 2 (quotation); Rims K. Barber, interview by author, August 22, 1996; Dittmer, *Local People,* 353–62.

36. *Memphis Commercial Appeal,* March 31, 1967; Owen H. Brooks et al. to "Dear Friend," (first and second quotations) folder 26, box 13, Delta Ministry Papers, Atlanta; Guyot and Thelwell, "Toward Independent Political Power," 246–48, 252–54 (third quotation on p. 252; fourth quotation on p. 254); Dittmer, *Local People,* 394, 414–15.

37. Owen H. Brooks et al. to "Dear Friend" (quotations), folder 26, box 13, Delta Ministry Papers, Atlanta; Walton, *Black Political Parties,* 125.

38. Glen, *Highlander,* 256; Harry J. Bowie, "Citizenship Education Program," 1–2 (first quotation on p. 1), and Owen H. Brooks, "Citizenship Education," 1, in Owen H. Brooks, "Report on the Delta Ministry, 1967," folder 32, box 3, untitled list of campaign workers for Joseph H. Bivins, n.d., folder 6, box 24, and Joseph H. Bivins to "Dear Friend," September 6, 1967, folder 6, box 24, and "Mississippi[ans] United to Elect Negro Candidates Annual Financial Report," folder 30, box 5, Delta Ministry Papers, Atlanta; Owen H. Brooks, interview by Tom Dent, August 18, 1978, MOHC; minutes, Commission on the Delta Ministry, November 16–17, 1967, 4 (second quotation), folder 62, box 3, and "To Get That Power," n.d., folder 33, box 5, and "Delta Ministry Staff (as of February 1, 1967)," folder 13, box 4, Delta Ministry Papers, Starkville; "Mississippians United—$5,000," 1; "Candidates," 1; Ted Weiss, "Campaigning in the Black Belt," folder 2, box 141, Johnson Family Papers; L. C. Dorsey, interview by author, September 4, 1996; *Delta Democrat-Times,* October 3, 17, 1967.

39. "Negro Election Victories in Mississippi—1967," n.d., folder 17, box 32, Hamer Papers; *Delta Ministry Reports,* November 1967, 1; Garland, "A Taste of Triumph for Black Mississippi," 25–28, 30, 32; Dittmer, *Local People,* 416; Glen, *Highlander,* 256.

40. "Negro Election Victories in Mississippi—1967," 1–2, folder 17, box 32, Hamer Papers; Parker, *Black Votes Count,* 69, 72–75; Dittmer, *Local People,* 415–16; Owen H. Brooks et al., to "Dear Friend," n.d., folder 33, box 5, Delta Ministry Papers, Starkville; "Washing-

ton County Political Handbook," n.d., 3, folder 47, box 28, Delta Ministry Papers, Atlanta. While John Dittmer lists black registration as 181,233 in the fall of 1967 (24 percent of Mississippi's registered voters), Frank Parker records 263,754 African Americans as registered (59.8 percent of those eligible and 28 percent of the state's electorate) (Dittmer, *Local People*, 415; Parker, *Black Votes Count*, 31).

41. Parker, *Black Votes Count*, 34–37, 72, 74; "Negro Election Victories in Mississippi—1967," 1–2, folder 17, box 32, Hamer Papers.

42. Parker, *Black Votes Count*, 76; Dukes, "Marion County News," 2; "Negro Election Victories in Mississippi—1967," n.d., 2 (quotation), folder 17, box 32, Hamer Papers; Rims K. Barber, "Yazoo County," 2, in Owen H. Brooks, "Report on the Delta Ministry, 1967," folder 32, box 3, and Thelma P. Barnes to Darnell J. Blackett, September 19, 1967, folder 22, box 24, Delta Ministry Papers, Atlanta; *Delta Ministry Reports*, June 1967, 1, November 1967, 1.

43. Minutes, Commission on the Delta Ministry, November 16–17, 1967, 3–5, 7, folder 62, box 3, Delta Ministry Papers, Starkville.

44. Solomon Gort Jr., "Welfare and Relief," 1, Thelma P. Barnes, "Report of Staff Activities," 1, 3, and Charles Horwitz, "Hinds County," 1, in Owen H. Brooks, "Report on the Delta Ministry, 1967," folder 32, box 3, Delta Ministry Papers, Atlanta; Thelma P. Barnes to Benjamin Matthews, September 8, 1967, folder 22, box 24, and Thelma P. Barnes to Samuel Adams, June 5, 1967, folder 26, box 38, Delta Ministry Papers, Atlanta.

45. Minutes, Commission on the Delta Ministry, November 16–17, 1967, 5 (quotation), 7, folder 62, box 3, Delta Ministry Papers, Starkville.

46. H. Carter III, "Negro Exodus," 26, 120; Alewine, "Changing Characteristics," 38–39; Dunbar, *Our Land Too*, 14–15; minutes, Commission on the Delta Ministry, March 27–28, 1967, 1–2, folder 12, box 2, Delta Ministry Papers, Atlanta; Lemann, *Promised Land*, 319; Cobb, *Most Southern Place*, 256.

47. Schulman, *From Cotton Belt to Sunbelt*, 191–92; Kotz, *Let Them Eat Promises*, 45, 52–56; Dunbar, *Our Land Too*, 76–77; "Facts about the Food Stamp Program in Mississippi," January 1967, folder 41, box 26, Hamer Papers; John A. Baker to Henry A. McCanna, March 28, 1966, folder "Commission Meeting—March 31, 1966," box 5, Thomas Papers; "What's Wrong with Food Stamps," February 16, 1967, no folder, no box, Winham Papers.

48. "What's Wrong with Food Stamps," February 16, 1967, no folder, no box, Winham Papers; "Facts about the Food Stamp Program in Mississippi," January 1967, folder 41, box 26, Hamer Papers; Dunbar, *Our Land Too*, 79–83 (quotation on p. 82).

49. Henry A. McCanna to John A. Baker, February 21, 1966, folder "O.E.O. Mississippi Food Program," box 1, Thomas Papers; "Report of the Delta Ministry," February 17–18, 1967, 4–5, folder 247, box 5, and "Hunger in the Mississippi Delta" (quotation), folder 204, box 4, King Papers; Kotz, *Let Them Eat Promises*, 4.

50. U.S. Congress, Senate, Subcommittee on Employment, Manpower, and Poverty of the Committee on Labor and Public Welfare, *Examination of the War on Poverty*, pt. 2: *Jackson, Mississippi*, 90th Cong., 1st sess., April 10, 1967; *Delta Ministry Reports*, May 1967, 2 (quotations); *New Orleans Times-Picayune*, April 11, 1967; Kotz, *Let Them Eat Promises*, 1–7, 17, 48–49, 65–69.

51. *Washington Post*, July 9, 1967; *Delta Ministry Reports*, July 1967, 1; Brenner et al., "Children in Mississippi," in Southern Regional Council, *Hungry Children*, 1–27; *New York Times*,

June 17, July 31, 1967; Coles, *Farewell,* 95–97, 145–46; Kotz, *Let Them Eat Promises,* 7–11, 35–36, 69, 72–77, 81–82; U.S. Congress, Senate, Subcommittee on Employment, Manpower, and Poverty of the Committee on Labor and Public Welfare, *Examination of the War on Poverty: First Session on Hunger and Malnutrition in America,* 90th Cong., 1st sess., July 11–12, 1967.

52. Kotz, *Let Them Eat Promises,* 68–69, 83–102; Cobb, *Most Southern Place,* 259, 261; Schulman, *From Cotton Belt to Sunbelt,* 192. Removal of a "requirement that food stamp recipients pay 30 percent of the stamps' face value" added one hundred thousand Mississippians to the program in 1978 (*Jackson Clarion-Ledger,* November 27, 1989).

53. "Concerned Mississippians for Hunger and Poverty" to Richard M. Nixon et al., March 7, 1969, folder 12, box 5, Hamer Papers; *Delta Democrat-Times,* March 12, 1969; memorandum, Thelma P. Barnes to "Concerned Mississippians for Hunger and Poverty," May 9, 1969, folder 217, box 6, Owen H. Brooks to William C. Smith, May 22, 1969, folder 216, box 6, Rims K. Barber to George McGovern, October 17, 1969, folder 216, box 6, and George McGovern to Rims K. Barber, November 13, 1969, folder 216, box 6, and Owen H. Brooks to Grace Olivarez, "Proposal," May 29, 1971, folder 44, box 2, Barber Papers; press release by the MFDP and the Delta Ministry, May 21, 1969, and attached "A Position on Hunger," folder 10, box 20, MFDP Papers; *Delta Ministry Reports,* July 1967, 1, March 1969, 1; Frederick S. Lowry to the Reverend and Mrs. John F. Else, October 3, 1967, folder 20, box 18, Thelma P. Barnes to D. C. Choy, May 15, 1967, folder 33, box 38, Thelma P. Barnes to Samuel Adams, June 5, 1967, folder 26, box 38, Thelma P. Barnes to Mr. and Mrs. Frank Hamilton, May 24, 1967, folder 34, box 38, Frederick S. Lowry to Dwight Blough, August 23, 1967, folder 46, box 28, Thelma P. Barnes to Simeon Booker, June 14, 1967, folder 16, box 24, and NCC press release, November 16, 1967, folder 19, box 1, Delta Ministry Papers, Atlanta; Delta Ministry to "Dear Friend," September 1967, folder 1431–2–3:07, Church and Society Records, UMC; minutes, Commission on the Delta Ministry, November 16–17, 1967, 4, folder 62, box 3, Delta Ministry Papers, Starkville.

54. Minutes, Commission on the Delta Ministry, November 16–17, 1967, 5, folder 62, box 3, Delta Ministry Papers, Starkville; Roger A. Smith to J. H. Dames, December 12, 1967, folder 1, box 39, Thelma P. Barnes to Joseph B. Lawson, January 9, 1968, folder 30, box 39, and Thelma P. Barnes to Albert W. McCollough, February 28, 1968, folder 30, box 39, Delta Ministry Papers, Atlanta; "Report on the Delta Ministry to the Program Board of the Division of Christian Life and Mission," November 27, 1967, 3, folder 1431–2–3:08, Church and Society Records, UMC.

55. "Summary," 1, in Owen H. Brooks, "Report on the Delta Ministry, 1967," folder 32, box 3, Delta Ministry Papers, Atlanta.

56. "Economic Development Programs," 1 (quotation), in Owen H. Brooks, "Report on the Delta Ministry, 1967," folder 32, box 3, Delta Ministry Papers, Atlanta; minutes, Commission on the Delta Ministry, November 16–17, 1967, 5, folder 62, box 3, Delta Ministry Papers, Starkville; "How 'Freedomcrafts' Came to Be," folder "Freedom Crafts," no box, and memorandum, Robert L. Beech to Donovan Smucker, September 27, 1967, folder "M. Holmes Ed. Dev. Prog. (M.H.C.)," no box, Beech Papers; *Delta Ministry Reports,* November 1966, 1, February 1967, 2; Nevin, "Struggle," 108, 110, 112; Roger A. Smith et al., "From Democracy to Dictatorship: The Delta Ministry, 1968–1972," unpaged section, folder "Delta Ministry Board, 1970–1973," box 9, Derian Papers.

57. Minutes, Delta Ministry staff meeting, February 23–24, 1967, 2, box 5, and "WATS Line

Report—for DM Staff," March 16, 1967, folder 224, box 5, King Papers; Thelma P. Barnes to William A. McAllister, May 22, 1967, folder 9, box 40, memorandum, Owen H. Brooks to John F. Anderson Jr., n.d., folder 45, box 13, and "Economic Development Programs," 1, in Owen H. Brooks, "Report on the Delta Ministry, 1967," folder 32, box 3, Delta Ministry Papers, Atlanta; Jeff Coburn to Frank Teagle, August 21, 1967, no folder, no box, Winham Papers; Jake Ayers to John M. Musser, December 14, 1967, folder "Freedom Crafts," no box, and "Liberty Outlet House Catalogue," folder "The Poor People's Corporation," no box, Beech Papers; *Poor People's Corporation Newsletter,* March 25, 1968, folder 39, box 26, Hamer Papers; Sutherland, "Mississippi Summer," 214; *New York Times,* March 5, 1967; Crawford, "Grassroots Activism," 24–25.

58. Harry J. Bowie, interview by Tom Dent, June 10, 1979, MOHC; minutes, Commission on the Delta Ministry, November 16–17, 1967, 5–7, folder 62, box 3, and minutes, Executive Committee, Commission on the Delta Ministry, January 30, 1968, 2–3, folder 49, box 3, Delta Ministry Papers, Starkville; "Economic Development Programs," 1–2, in Owen H. Brooks, "Report on the Delta Ministry, 1967," folder 32, box 3, and minutes, Commission on the Delta Ministry, June 10–11, 1968, 4–5, folder 13, box 2, Delta Ministry Papers, Atlanta.

59. Minutes, Commission on the Delta Ministry, November 16–17, 1967, 6–7, folder 62, box 3, and minutes, Executive Committee, Commission on the Delta Ministry, January 30, 1968, 3, folder 49, box 3, Delta Ministry Papers, Starkville.

60. Henry L. Parker to Owen H. Brooks, December 11, 1967, folder 11, box 13, Delta Ministry Papers, Atlanta; "A Different Perspective," n.d., folder 52, box 9, Delta Ministry Papers, Starkville; Roger A. Smith et al., "From Democracy to Dictatorship: The Delta Ministry, 1968–1972," unpaged section, folder "Delta Ministry Board, 1970–1973," box 9, Derian Papers; Noble, "Delta Ministry," 78; Shattuck, *Episcopalians and Race,* 77–78; "Opening Doors to Opportunity," 48–49, 52, 54.

61. Lawson, *In Pursuit,* 103; Walton, *Black Political Parties,* 127–28; Dittmer, *Local People,* 420; *Delta Ministry Reports,* March 1968, 1.

62. Mississippians United to Elect Negro Candidates, press release, n.d., folder 27, box 5, "Mississippi[ans] United to Elect Negro Candidates Annual Financial Report," n.d., folder 30, box 5, and minutes, Commission on the Delta Ministry, June 10–11, 1968, 3, folder 13, box 2, Delta Ministry Papers, Atlanta; Noble, "Delta Ministry," 16, 110; Parker, *Black Votes Count,* 41–51; Owen H. Brooks and Harry J. Bowie to Arthur Walmsley, April 17, 1968, folder 6, box 28, Hamer Papers; *Journal of the Upper Mississippi Conference of the United Methodist Church, The Seventy-Ninth Annual Session,* 1968, 29.

63. Minutes, Commission on the Delta Ministry, June 10–11, 1968, 3, folder 13, box 2, and Harry J. Bowie, "Citizenship Education" (quotation), in "Report of the Delta Ministry—1968," folder 40, box 3, Delta Ministry Papers, Atlanta; Murray, "World Council," 880; minutes, Delta Ministry Steering Committee, September 3, 1968, 2, folder 10, box 43, SCLC Papers.

64. Fager, *Uncertain Resurrection,* 15–19; "People Invited to 'Dr. King—Miss. State-Wide Leaders Meeting' on February 14th and 15th," n.d., folder 9, box 178, memorandum, Leon Hall to Hosea Williams, February 19, 1968, folder 9, box 178, and memorandum, Leon Hall to Hosea Williams, March 4, 1968, folder 10, box 178, SCLC Papers; Freeman, "Mule Train," 91–93; Owen H. Brooks, interview by Robert Wright, September 24, 1968, 49–50 (quotation

on p. 50), Bunche Oral History Collection; Tut Tate, Leon Hall, and Joe Harris to Joseph Lewis Harris, March 27, 1968, folder 37, box 26, Hamer Papers.

65. Fager, *Uncertain Resurrection*, 19–20, 32–142; *Delta Ministry Reports*, May 1968, 1; Poor People's Campaign press release, April 22, 1968, folder 39, box 26, Hamer Papers; minutes, Delta Ministry Steering Committee, September 3, 1968, 2, folder 10, box 43, and memorandum, Leon Hall to Hosea Williams, March 4, 1968, folder 10, box 178, SCLC Papers; Delta Ministry, "Too Late to Wait: Report from Mississippi," summer 1968, folder 224, box 5, King Papers; minutes, Commission on the Delta Ministry, June 10–11, 1968, 5, folder 13, box 2, and Thelma P. Barnes to Frederick S. Lowry, June 18, 1968, folder 17, box 39, Delta Ministry Papers, Atlanta.

66. *Delta Ministry Reports*, June 1968, 2; L. C. Dorsey to the *Delta Democrat-Times*, June 12, 1968; Thelma P. Barnes to William Mueller, June 18, 1968 (quotation), folder 36, box 40, Delta Ministry Papers, Atlanta; Noble, "Delta Ministry," 104.

67. Harry J. Bowie, "Citizenship Education," in "Report of the Delta Ministry—1968," folder 40, box 3, and "Gray Elected to City Gov't," *Voice of the Black Youth* 1 (November 9, [1968]): 7, folder 47, box 7, Delta Ministry Papers, Atlanta; Delta Ministry, press release, "First Black Man Elected to City Government in Mississippi since Reconstruction," October 31, 1968, folder 255, box 6, Barber Papers; *Delta Democrat-Times*, September 1, 1968.

68. *Delta Ministry Reports*, May 1968, 2, September–October 1968, 2; *Delta Democrat-Times*, May 6, 16, 23, 24, 31, June 2, 3, 7, 9, 21, August 14, 16, September 1, 1968; "A Brief History of the Shelby Problems," memorandum, Rims K. Barber to Charles Spivey, August 27, 1968, and "Shelby—Boycott of Schools," n.d., folder 254, box 6, Barber Papers; L. C. Dorsey, interview by author, September 4, 1996; Abbott, ed., *Mississippi Writers*, 2:698; minutes, Commission on the Delta Ministry, June 10–11, 1968, 5, folder 13, box 2, Delta Ministry Papers, Atlanta; Noble, "Delta Ministry," 15. According to Harry Bowie, the "economic boycott in Shelby yielded 14 jobs and a new atmosphere more conducive to economic development" (Harry J. Bowie, "Economic Development," in "Report of the Delta Ministry—1968," folder 40, box 3, Delta Ministry Papers, Atlanta).

69. Harry J. Bowie, "Citizenship Education," and Harry J. Bowie, "Economic Development," in "Report of the Delta Ministry—1968," folder 40, box 3, Delta Ministry Papers, Atlanta.

70. "Constitution of the Young Democratic Clubs of Mississippi," August 9, 1964, COFO, press release, "National Young Democrats Refuse to Charter State Youth Group[,] Young Democratic Clubs of Mississippi to Continue Organizing," April 20, 1965, and Carolyn Stevens, "Malicious Attack on Young Democrats Exposed," n.d., folder 10, box 1, Bowie Papers; "A Call for Support of the Young Democratic Clubs of Mississippi," n.d., and *The Young Democratic Clubs of Mississippi* 1 (April 1965): 1–2, 21–30, folder "MFDP Summer Project," no box, Beech Papers; "Memo on Young Democratic Clubs of Mississippi (YDCM)," n.d., folder 51, box 28, Delta Ministry Papers, Atlanta; *Jackson Clarion-Ledger*, August 15, 1965, October 7, 1966; Sutherland, "Mississippi Summer," 212; *Lexington Advertiser*, May 5, 1966, October 5, 1967, July 18, 1968; Hodding Carter III, interview by Robert Wright, September 23, 1968, 1–2, 14–15, Bunche Oral History Collection; *Memphis Commercial Appeal*, March 19, 1967; *Delta Democrat-Times*, July 14, 1968; Simpson, "Birth," 27–42; Dittmer, *Local People*, 347–49, 378, 390, 418–21; Noble, "Delta Ministry," 134–36; K. Mills, *This Little Light*, 216–25, 231.

71. Harry J. Bowie, "Citizenship Education," in "Report of the Delta Ministry—1968,"

folder 40, box 3, Delta Ministry Papers, Atlanta; Harry J. Bowie to Aaron Henry, August 2, 1968, folder 1670, box 99, Henry Papers; Owen H. Brooks, "The Mississippi Challenge: A Delta Ministry Position Paper," August 1968, 1–2 (quotations on p. 1), folder 44, box 8, Delta Ministry Papers, Starkville; Owen H. Brooks, interview by Robert Wright, September 24, 1968, 43–45, Bunche Oral History Collection.

72. McLemore, "Mississippi Freedom Democratic Party," 441; Simpson, "Birth," 40–44; K. Mills, *This Little Light*, 224–25; Evers and Szanton, *Have No Fear*, 238 (quotations); Henry with Curry, *Aaron Henry*, 226; *Lexington Advertiser*, August 22, 29, 1968.

73. Owen H. Brooks to Charles Spivey, August 2, 1968 (quotation), folder 38, box 13, Delta Ministry Papers, Atlanta; "Delta Ministry's Submitted Testimony to Democratic Platform Committee," August 20, 1968, folder 1431-2-3:05, Church and Society Records, UMC; *Lexington Advertiser*, August 22, 1968; Walton, *Black Political Parties*, 128–30; Edwin King, interview by author, September 2, 1996. The regulars had selected three African American delegates—Charles Evers, Dr. Matthew J. Page, and Dr. Gilbert Mason—but not content with such tokenism, Evers and Page had resigned (Dittmer, *Local People*, 420).

74. Harry J. Bowie, "Citizenship Education" (first quotation), in "Report of the Delta Ministry—1968," folder 40, box 3, and minutes, Commission on the Delta Ministry, June 10–11, 1968, 6–7 (second quotation on p. 6; third quotation on pp. 6–7), folder 13, box 2, Delta Ministry Papers, Atlanta; Charles Horwitz, "Year End Report, 1969, from Hinds County Delta Ministry Project," folder 14, box 1, and Charles Horwitz, "Hinds County Delta Ministry Project Report," May 13, 1970, 1, folder 61, box 3, Horwitz Papers.

75. Minutes, Commission on the Delta Ministry, June 10–11, 1968, 7, folder 13, box 2, and John D. Smith, "Youth," in "Report of the Delta Ministry—1968," folder 40, box 3, Delta Ministry Papers, Atlanta; minutes, Delta Ministry Steering Committee, September 3, 1968, 2, folder 10, box 43, SCLC Papers; Noble, "Delta Ministry," 124; "Proposal Draft the Delta Ministry," n.d., 9 (quotation), folder "Mississippi Delta Ministry January 1971," box 2, Thomas Papers; "The Delta Ministry Report—1969," 4–5, folder 7, box 4, Delta Ministry Papers, Starkville; *Delta Ministry Reports*, February 1969, 1; K. Mills, *This Little Light*, 239–40; Morrison, *Black Political Mobilization*, 137; Keady, *All Rise*, 115.

76. "Report of the Delta Ministry—1968," folder 40, box 3, Delta Ministry Papers, Atlanta; "The Delta Ministry Report—1969," 1–10 (quotation on p. 1), folder 7, box 4, Delta Ministry Papers, Starkville.

77. Rims K. Barber, interview by author, August 22, 1996; "Report of the Delta Ministry—1968," folder 40, box 3, Delta Ministry Papers, Atlanta; "The Delta Ministry Report—1969," 1–10, folder 7, box 4, and minutes, Commission on the Delta Ministry, September 23–24, 1968, 7, folder 4, box 4, Delta Ministry Papers, Starkville.

78. Minutes, Ad Hoc Committee, Commission on the Delta Ministry, June 16, 1968, 3, folder 10, box 43, SCLC Papers; minutes, Executive Committee, Commission on the Delta Ministry, January 30, 1968, 2, folder 49, box 3, and "The Delta Ministry Report—1969," 7, folder 7, box 4, Delta Ministry Papers, Starkville; *Delta Ministry Reports*, May 1968, 2, March 1969, 1; Solomon Gort Jr., "Welfare and Relief," in "Report of the Delta Ministry—1968," folder 40, box 3, minutes, Commission on the Delta Ministry, June 10–11, 1968, 3–4, folder 13, box 2, and "NOW! A Brief History of the National Welfare Rights Organization," folder 10, box 5, Delta Ministry Papers, Atlanta; M. F. Davis, *Brutal Need*, 43–45; Charles Horwitz, "Year End Report, 1969, from Hinds County Delta Ministry Project," 2, folder

14, box 1, Charles Horwitz, "Hinds County Delta Ministry Project Report," May 13, 1970, 2–3 (quotation on p. 2), folder 61, box 3, and Kattie Kingdom, "Proposal for Welfare Rights Organization Funds, Washington County Branch," January 20, 1972, folder "Current Delta Ministry," no box, Horwitz Papers.

79. "The Delta Ministry Report—1969," 5–6 (quotation on p. 6), folder 7, box 4, Delta Ministry Papers, Starkville; Kattie Kingdom, "Proposal for Welfare Rights Organization Funds, Washington County Branch," January 20, 1972, folder "Current Delta Ministry," no box, and statement of Owen H. Brooks to Special Subcommittee on Disaster Relief of the Senate Committee on Public Works, January 9, 1970, folder 27, box 2, Horwitz Papers; minutes, Commission on the Delta Ministry, November 12–13, 1969, 1, 5–6, RG 4, folder "Delta Ministry April 1, '68–March 31, '69," box DHM 8, UCMS Papers; Combined Community Organization Disaster Committee, press release, September 3, 1969, and "Report and Recommendations of the Combined Community Organization Disaster Committee Regarding Conditions of the Refugees and Hurricane Camille Victims at Camp Shelby and the Miss. Gulf Coast," September 18, 1969, folder 218, box 6, Barber Papers; *Delta Democrat-Times,* August 21, 1969; *Delta Ministry Reports,* September 1969, 2, November–December 1969, 1, January 1970, 2; *Memphis Commercial Appeal,* January 9, 1970.

80. "Concerned Mississippians for Hunger and Poverty," to Richard M. Nixon et al., March 7, 1969, folder 12, box 5, Hamer Papers; minutes, Steering Committee, Action Committee for Poor People, February 28, 1970, and attached "Demands to Secretary of Health, Education, and Welfare Robert Finch," no folder, box 48, Delta Ministry Papers, Atlanta; *Delta Ministry Reports,* February 1970, 1–2; *Delta Democrat-Times,* February 15, 20, March 1, 10, 1970; "Mississippi Head Starts Vetoed by Governor," n.d., and *HEW News,* March 10, 1970, folder 213, box 6, Barber Papers; Owen H. Brooks to Robert Finch, February 17, 1970, folder 30, box 2, and minutes, Mississippi United Front, April 3, 1970, folder 57, box 3, Horwitz Papers; *Jackson Northside Reporter,* June 25, 1970.

81. Charles Horwitz, "News from Mt. Beulah, Hinds County," n.d., and minutes, Mississippi United Front, April 3, 1970, folder 57, box 3, Horwitz Papers; *Jackson Northside Reporter,* June 25, 1970; *Delta Democrat-Times,* August 8, November 8, 1971; Richard Polk to "Members and Board of Directors, STAR, Inc.," November 2, 1971, and attached "Resumes of Nominees for Officers of State Board—STAR, Inc.," filed under "STAR, Inc. Minutes, January 13, 1969–April 21, 1973," and Al Rhodes Jr. to Joseph O. Brunini, March 1, 1973, filed under "STAR, Inc. Correspondence, February 20, 1969–May 1, 1973," Archives of the Catholic Diocese of Jackson; "Findings and Recommendations of NAACP Public Hearing Panel on STAR, Inc.," December 9, 1970, folder 1644, box 98, Henry Papers.

82. Minutes, Executive Committee, Commission on the Delta Ministry, January 30, 1968, 2, folder 49, box 3, Delta Ministry Papers, Starkville; "Education: A Delta Ministry Priority," n.d., folder 292, box 6, and Ed King, "Education Report Delta Ministry," June 11, 1968, folder 321, box 7, King Papers; Rims K. Barber, "Education," in "Report of the Delta Ministry—1968," folder 40, box 3, Delta Ministry Papers, Atlanta; Sarah H. Johnson, interview by Thomas Healy, September 10, 1978, 13–14; Edwin King, interview by author, September 2, 1996; Bass, *Unlikely Heroes,* 313–15; Munford, "White Flight," 12, 14; *Delta Ministry Reports,* January 1970, 1; W. F. Minor, "Mississippi Schools," 31–36; Keady, *All Rise,* 106.

83. W. F. Minor, "Mississippi Schools," 33–36; Munford, "White Flight," 16, 21, 23–24; Bolton, "Last Stand," 341–50; M. Lowry II, "Schools," 175–76, 178; Keady, *All Rise,* 106–11; Rims

K. Barber, "Education," in "Report of the Delta Ministry—1968," folder 40, box 3, Delta Ministry Papers, Atlanta; "The Delta Ministry—A Proposal, Education in Mississippi, Spring, 1970," folder 7, box 10, and "The Delta Ministry Report—1969," 1–4, folder 7, box 4, Delta Ministry Papers, Starkville; "Education—A Statement of Priorities, the Delta Ministry, November 1969," folder 11, box 43, SCLC Papers; *Washington Post,* June 21, 1969; *Memphis Commercial Appeal,* June 25, 1969; *Delta Democrat-Times,* June 26, July 13, 31, 1969; *Delta Ministry Reports,* September 1969, 1, November–December 1969, 1–2, January 1970, 1, February 1970, 2, January 1971, 1.

84. *Memphis Commercial Appeal,* November 9, 1967; "Clark Seated," 1, 6; *Delta Ministry Reports,* May 1971, 2; Rims K. Barber, interview by author, August 22, 1996; Trillin, "State Secrets," 63–64; "The Delta Ministry Report—1969," 8, folder 7, box 4, Delta Ministry Papers, Starkville.

85. "The Delta Ministry Report—1969," 7–8 (quotation on p. 8), folder 7, box 4, Delta Ministry Papers, Starkville; *Delta Democrat-Times,* October 30, December 2, 9, 1969; *Memphis Commercial Appeal,* December 10, 1969.

86. *Delta Ministry Reports,* April 1970, 1; Salamon and Van Evera, "Fear," 1290.

87. "The Delta Ministry Report—1969," 8, folder 7, box 4, Delta Ministry Papers, Starkville; Parker, *Black Votes Count,* 80–82, 91–101, 170–73, 180–84, 186–88; Rhodes, "Enforcing the Voting Rights Act," 709, 711–14.

88. Harry J. Bowie, "Economic Development," in "Report of the Delta Ministry—1968," folder 40, box 3, Delta Ministry Papers, Atlanta; Harry J. Bowie, interview by Tom Dent, June 10, 1979, MOHC.

89. Harry J. Bowie, "Economic Development," in "Report of the Delta Ministry—1968," folder 40, box 3, Delta Ministry Papers, Atlanta; Hall, "Stir of Hope," 67; *National Observer,* December 26, 1966; H. M. Rose, "The All-Negro Town," 363–64, 367; Couto, *Ain't Gonna Let Nobody Turn Me Round,* 275. Mound Bayou's origins are described in Hermann, *Pursuit.*

90. L. C. Dorsey, interview by author, September 4, 1996; U.S. Congress, Senate, Subcommittee on Employment, Manpower, and Poverty of the Committee on Labor and Public Welfare, *Examination of the War on Poverty: First Session on Hunger and Malnutrition in America,* 90th Cong., 1st sess., July 11–12, 1967, 262–63, 303–11; H. Jack Geiger to Arthur C. Thomas, July 27, 1965, folder 10, box 12, Delta Ministry Papers, Atlanta; H. Jack Geiger to David R. Minter, May 30, 1967, folder 21, box 2, 1971 addendum, Cox Collection; Sardell, *U.S. Experiment,* 51–53, 59; Couto, *Ain't Gonna Let Nobody Turn Me Round,* 274–75; J. Geiger, "Health Center," 68–71, 75–77, 81 (quotation); Hall, "Stir of Hope," 69–70, 73, 76–77; Mc-Carthy, "Hunger," 10–11; James, "Tufts-Delta"; Maloney, "Tufts Comprehensive Community Health Action Program," 109–12.

91. J. Geiger, "Health Center," 70, 77, 81; Hall, "Stir of Hope," 67, 70, 73, 76–78; James, "Tufts-Delta," 438–45; OEO press release, "OEO Grant to Assist Mississippi Food Cooperative," May 15, 1968, no folder, no box, Winham Papers; McCarthy, "Hunger," 8–9, 11; Dorsey, *Freedom Came,* 35.

92. J. Geiger, "Health Center," 81; Hall, "Stir of Hope," 67, 77–78; James, "Tufts-Delta," 444–45; OEO press release, "OEO Grant to Assist Mississippi Food Cooperative," May 15, 1968, no folder, no box, Winham Papers; McCarthy, "Hunger," 8–9, 11; L. C. Dorsey, interview by author, September 4, 1996; Dorsey, *Freedom Came,* 35; Dent, *Southern Journey,* 353–55.

93. "What You Should Know about the New Community Hospital," n.d., folder 11,

box 28, minutes, special meeting, Mound Bayou Community Hospital Nomination and Election Committee, May 10, 1967, folder 11, box 28, "Mound Bayou: U.S. Largest Negro Town," n.d., 2, folder 9, box 28, Harry J. Bowie, "Economic Development," in "Report of the Delta Ministry—1968," folder 40, box 3, and Pinkye M. Myles, "Health Service Report," in "The Delta Opportunities Corporation's Board and Staff Present to the Commission of the Delta Ministry," March 6, 1969, 19, folder 29, box 46, Delta Ministry Papers, Atlanta; H. Jack Geiger to David R. Minter, May 30, 1967, folder 21, box 2, 1971 addendum, Cox Collection; J. Geiger, "Health Center," 76; U.S. Congress, Senate, Subcommittee on Employment, Manpower, and Poverty of the Committee on Labor and Public Welfare, *Examination of the War on Poverty: First Session on Hunger and Malnutrition in America,* 90th Cong., 1st sess., July 11–12, 1967, 265, 294; *Memphis Commercial Appeal,* July 21, 1972; Owen H. Brooks, interview by Tom Dent, August 18, 1978, MOHC.

94. "Mound Bayou: U.S. Largest Negro Town," n.d., 2, 4A, folder 9, box 28, and "The Mound Bayou Development Corporation, Organizers of the Delta Merchants' Cooperative," n.d., folder 10, box 28, and Harry J. Bowie, "Economic Development," in "Report of the Delta Ministry—1968," folder 40, box 3, Delta Ministry Papers, Atlanta; "The Delta Ministry Report—1969," 9, folder 7, box 4, and W. Ralph Heller Jr., "Christmas in the South," n.d., 5, folder 54, box 11, Delta Ministry Papers, Starkville; minutes, Commission on the Delta Ministry, November 12–13, 1969, 5, RG 4, folder "Delta Ministry April 1, '68–March 31, '69," box DHM 8, UCMS Papers; *Delta Democrat-Times,* August 28, 1969, August 2, 1970; *Delta Ministry Reports,* September 1969, 1, October 1969, 2; McCanna, "A Ministry of Deliverance," 39.

95. "Mound Bayou Development Corporation Proposal for Financial Assistance," folder 8, box 28, and minutes, Delta Ministry monthly staff meeting, July 14, 1970, 3, folder 45, box 3, Delta Ministry Papers, Atlanta; Daniel B. Mitchell to Jon L. Regier, March 24, 1971, folder 6, box 37, Black Economic Research Center Records, 1969–1980, Schomburg Center for Research in Black Culture, New York Public Library; *Delta Ministry Reports,* January 1969, 2, September 1969, 1; minutes, Commission on the Delta Ministry, November 12–13, 1969, 1, RG 4, folder "Delta Ministry April 1, '68–March 31, '69," box DHM 8, UCMS Papers; "The Delta Ministry Report—1969," 8, folder 7, box 4, Delta Ministry Papers, Starkville; Owen H. Brooks, interview by Tom Dent, August 18, 1978, MOHC; L. C. Dorsey, interview by author, September 4, 1996.

96. Minutes, Commission on the Delta Ministry, November 12–13, 1969, 5, RG 4, folder "Delta Ministry April 1, '68–March 31, '69," box DHM 8, UCMS Papers; *Delta Democrat-Times,* August 2, 1970; Charles Horwitz, "Hinds County Delta Ministry Project Report," May 13, 1970, 2, folder 61, box 3, Horwitz Papers; Harry J. Bowie, interview by Tom Dent, June 10, 1979, MOHC.

97. "The Delta Ministry Report—1969," 9, folder 7, box 4, and "Delta Foundation," n.d., folder 33, box 3, Delta Ministry Papers, Starkville; Harry J. Bowie, interview by Tom Dent, June 10, 1979, MOHC; minutes, Commission on the Delta Ministry, November 12–13, 1969, 4–5, RG 4, folder "Delta Ministry April 1, '68–March 31, '69," box DHM 8, UCMS Papers; memorandum, Thomas W. Wahmann to RBF Files, October 28, 1970, folder "Delta Ministry Board 1970–1973," box 9, Derian Papers; memorandum, Charles F. Bound to GLIC, September 4, 1970, 1–2, folder "Delta Ministry—Bishop Moore," box "Delta Ministry Files," Paul Moore Jr. Papers, AEDNY; Millsaps, "Putting the System to Work," 9; *Delta Democrat-Times,* July 2, 1970; *Jackson Advocate,* July 18, 1970.

98. Memorandum, Thomas W. Wahmann to RBF Files, October 28, 1970, 1, folder "Delta Ministry Board, 1970–1973," box 9, Derian Papers; *Wall Street Journal,* October 2, 1984; *Delta Ministry Reports,* October–November 1970, 2, November 1971, 1; Millsaps, "Putting the System to Work," 10–11; *Jackson Clarion-Ledger,* October 1, 1982.

99. Harry J. Bowie, interview by Tom Dent, June 10, 1979, MOHC; Harry J. Bowie, interview by author, September 5, 1996.

100. *Delta Ministry Reports,* March 1971, 1; memorandum from Steve Brimigion, May 11, 1971, RG 6, folder 19, box 4, NCC Archives; Isserman and Kazin, *America Divided,* 245–46; L. C. Dorsey, interview by author, September 4, 1996.

CHAPTER NINE. Internal Dissension and Crisis

1. Hilton, *Delta Ministry,* 17; "Report of the Delta Ministry," February 17–18, 1967, 1, folder 16, box 13, Delta Ministry Papers, Atlanta; minutes, Commission on the Delta Ministry, September 23–24, 1968, 7, folder 4, box 4, Delta Ministry Papers, Starkville; Roger A. Smith et al., "From Democracy to Dictatorship: The Delta Ministry, 1968–1972," folder "Delta Ministry Board, 1970–1973," box 9, Derian Papers; *Delta Democrat-Times,* March 7, 9, April 1, 1971; Arthur C. Thomas, "A Report on the Delta Ministry," February 1, 1971, and memorandum, members, Delta Ministry Commission, to Executive Committee, Division of Christian Life and Mission, March 31, 1971, 1–2, folder "Mississippi Delta Ministry, January 1971," box 2, Thomas Papers; minutes, Executive Committee, Division of Christian Life and Mission, NCC, May 12, 1971, 8–9, RG 6, folder 19, box 4, NCC Archives.

2. "Report of the Delta Ministry," February 17–18, 1967, 1, folder 16, box 13, minutes, Commission on the Delta Ministry, March 27–28, 1967, 1, 3, folder 12, box 2, and Paul O. Madsen to Owen H. Brooks, July 24, 1967, folder 14, box 13, Delta Ministry Papers, Atlanta; "Commission on the Delta Ministry March 1967," folder 46, box 3, Delta Ministry Papers, Starkville; "WATS Line Report—for DM Staff," March 16, 1967, folder 224, box 5, King Papers; memorandum, Owen H. Brooks and Henry A. McCanna to "Members and Friends of the Commission on the Delta Ministry," April 5, 1967, folder "Delta Ministry—Correspondence—1964–1966," box 1, Humphrey Papers.

3. Minutes, Commission on the Delta Ministry, March 27–28, 1967, 1, folder 12, box 2, and minutes, Commission on the Delta Ministry, June 10–11, 1968, 1, folder 13, box 2, Delta Ministry Papers, Atlanta; memorandum, Owen H. Brooks and Henry A. McCanna to "Members and Friends of the Commission on the Delta Ministry," April 5, 1967, folder "Delta Ministry—Correspondence—1964–1966," box 1, Humphrey Papers; "Commission on the Delta Ministry June 1967," folder 13, box 1, Horwitz Papers; minutes, Executive Committee, Commission on the Delta Ministry, July 31, 1967, 1, folder 47, box 3, minutes, Commission on the Delta Ministry, November 16–17, 1967, 1, folder 62, box 3, and minutes, Executive Committee, Commission on the Delta Ministry, January 30, 1968, 1, folder 49, box 3, Delta Ministry Papers, Starkville; minutes, Executive Committee, Commission on the Delta Ministry, August 18, 1967, 1, RG 38, folder "Delta Ministry (2)," box 1, Office of Church and Society Records, PCUS, Montreat; minutes, Ad Hoc Committee, Commission on the Delta Ministry, June 16, 1968, 2 (quotation), folder 10, box 43, SCLC Papers.

4. Minutes, Commission on the Delta Ministry, March 27–28, 1967, 1, folder 12, box 2, and minutes, Commission on the Delta Ministry, June 10–11, 1968, 1, folder 13, box 2, Delta Ministry Papers, Atlanta; memorandum, Owen H. Brooks and Henry A. McCanna

to "Members and Friends of the Commission on the Delta Ministry," April 5, 1967, folder "Delta Ministry—Correspondence—1964–1966," box 1, Humphrey Papers; "Commission on the Delta Ministry June 1967," folder 13, box 1, Horwitz Papers; minutes, Executive Committee, Commission on the Delta Ministry, July 31, 1967, 1, folder 47, box 3, minutes, Commission on the Delta Ministry, November 16–17, 1967, 1, folder 62, box 3, minutes, Executive Committee, Commission on the Delta Ministry, January 30, 1968, 1, folder 49, box 3, and minutes, Commission on the Delta Ministry, September 23–24, 1968, 7, folder 4, box 4, Delta Ministry Papers, Starkville; minutes, Executive Committee, Commission on the Delta Ministry, August 18, 1967, 1, RG 38, folder "Delta Ministry (2)," box 1, Office of Church and Society Records, PCUS, Montreat; "Proposal Draft the Delta Ministry," n.d., 2–4, folder "Mississippi Delta Ministry, January 1971," box 2, Thomas Papers; Noble, "Delta Ministry," 59.

5. *Delta Democrat-Times,* September 20, 1966; "Delta Ministry Staff (as of February 1, 1967)," folder 13, box 1, Horwitz Papers; Owen H. Brooks, interview by Tom Dent, August 18, 1978, MOHC.

6. "Commission on the Delta Ministry March 1967," folder 46, box 3, Delta Ministry Papers, Starkville; memorandum, Bryant George to Daniel Little, January 19, 1967 (quotation), RG 301.7, folder 3, box 46, Board of National Missions (PCUSA) Records. Tom Levin, CDGM's first director, described the Head Start program in the summer of 1965 as a project of Mississippi Action for Community Education (MACE). He envisaged MACE as an umbrella group for projects that would be created with federal and charitable foundation funds. MACE first received foundation funding in September 1966, when it obtained twenty-five thousand dollars for program development from the Merrill Foundation. With support from the Ford Foundation, MACE began training community organizers in seven Delta counties during 1968. Harry J. Bowie worked with Ed Brown, MACE's director, to establish the Delta Foundation in 1969 (Greenberg, *Devil,* 19, 196, 664–65; "Director's Report to the Board and Friends of CCAP [Citizens' Crusade against Poverty]," December 31, 1968, 5, folder "Citizens' Crusade," box 4, Neigh Papers; Harry J. Bowie, interview by Tom Dent, June 10, 1979, MOHC).

7. Hilton, *Delta Ministry,* 158.

8. Marshal L. Scott to Bryant George, February 7, 1967, RG 301.9, folder 7, box 14, CORAR Records; Rims K. Barber, "Education—June to September," and Rims K. Barber, "Yazoo County," in Owen H. Brooks, "Report on the Delta Ministry, 1967," folder 32, box 3, Delta Ministry Papers, Atlanta; Rims K. Barber to Dan Little, n.d. (quotation), RG 301.7, folder 3, box 46, Board of National Missions (PCUSA) Records.

9. "Report on the Delta Ministry to the Program Board of the Division of Christian Life and Mission," November 27, 1967, 7, RG 38, folder "Delta Ministry (2)," box 1, Office of Church and Society Records, PCUS, Montreat; minutes, Commission on the Delta Ministry, November 16–17, 1967, 1, folder 62, box 3, Delta Ministry Papers, Starkville; memorandum, Bryant George to Marshal Scott, February 10, 1967, RG 301.7, folder 3, box 46, Board of National Missions (PCUSA) Records; Noble, "Delta Ministry," 186; John F. Anderson Jr. to James McBride Dabbs, April 10, 1967, folder 520, Dabbs Papers; James McBride Dabbs to John F. Anderson Jr., June 30, 1968 (quotation), RG 1, folder "NCC Delta Ministry," box 10, Executive Secretary Correspondence Files, 1953–73, PCUS, Montreat.

10. James McBride Dabbs to John F. Anderson Jr., June 30, 1968 (first quotation), RG 1,

folder "NCC Delta Ministry," box 10, Executive Secretary Correspondence Files, 1953–73, PCUS, Montreat; Paul O. Madsen to Jon L. Regier, October 19, 1967 (second quotation), RG 6, folder 13, box 6, NCC Archives.

11. *Delta Ministry Reports,* May 1968, 1; Andrew J. Young to Truman Douglass and Wesley A. Hotchkiss, June 10, 1964, folder 14, box 136, SCLC Papers; Robert W. Spike to Eugene Carson Blake, August 13, 1964, RG 95, folder 16, box 15, Blake Papers.

12. Minutes, Commission on the Delta Ministry, June 10–11, 1968, 1–2, folder 13, box 2, and Henry L. Parker to Owen H. Brooks, December 11, 1967, folder 11, box 13, Delta Ministry Papers, Atlanta; Howell, *Freedom City,* 117; "Delta Ministry Staff (as of February 1, 1967)," folder 13, box 1, Horwitz Papers; "A Different Perspective," n.d., folder 52, box 9, Delta Ministry Papers, Starkville; Edwin King, "Growing Up in Mississippi in a Time of Change," in *Mississippi Writers,* ed. Abbott, 2:374, 377–80.

13. Joseph Lewis Harris et al., "Resolution," June 9, 1968 (quotations), folder 13, box 2, Delta Ministry Papers, Atlanta; "Delta Ministry Staff (as of February 1, 1967)," folder 13, box 1, Horwitz Papers; John W. Kalas to John F. Else, n.d., RG 301.7, folder 5, box 46, Board of National Missions (PCUSA) Records.

14. Joseph Lewis Harris et al., "Resolution," June 9, 1968 (quotations), folder 13, box 2, Delta Ministry Papers, Atlanta; Roger A. Smith et al., "From Democracy to Dictatorship: The Delta Ministry, 1968–1972," 1, folder "Delta Ministry Board, 1970–1973," box 9, Derian Papers; Noble, "Delta Ministry," 186.

15. Roger A. Smith et al., "From Democracy to Dictatorship: The Delta Ministry, 1968–1972," 2, folder "Delta Ministry Board, 1970–1973," box 9, Derian Papers; "Report of the Delta Ministry—1968," folder 40, box 3, Delta Ministry Papers, Atlanta; Noble, "Delta Ministry," 17–18, 23–24, 183–87.

16. Noble, "Delta Ministry," 17–18, 23–24, 61–65, 68–69, 184; Edwin King, interview by author, September 2, 1996; Howell, *Freedom City,* 126; K. Mills, *This Little Light,* 225; Roger A. Smith et al., "From Democracy to Dictatorship: The Delta Ministry, 1968–1972," 2 (quotations), folder "Delta Ministry Board, 1970–1973," box 9, Derian Papers.

17. Noble, "Delta Ministry," 64–69, 176, 181–83; Robert L. Beech to Harvey G. Cox, September 28, 1967, untitled folder, box 1, Beech Papers.

18. Noble, "Delta Ministry," 68–69, 184; Roger A. Smith et al., "From Democracy to Dictatorship: The Delta Ministry, 1968–1972," i, iv–v, 1–2, 19 (quotation), folder "Delta Ministry Board, 1970–1973," box 9, Derian Papers.

19. Memorandum, Andrew J. Young to "Staff of the Delta Ministry," July 26, 1968, folder 11, box 26, Hamer Papers; minutes of Ad Hoc Committee, Commission on the Delta Ministry, June 16, 1968, 4, folder 10, box 43, SCLC Papers; minutes, Commission on the Delta Ministry, September 23–24, 1968, 7, folder 4, box 4, Delta Ministry Papers, Starkville; Roger A. Smith et al., "From Democracy to Dictatorship: The Delta Ministry, 1968–1972," 1, 26, folder "Delta Ministry Board, 1970–1973," box 9, Derian Papers; Noble, "Delta Ministry," 24, 174, 181, 187.

20. Harry J. Bowie, interview by Tom Dent, June 10, 1979, MOHC.

21. "Commission on the Delta Ministry," November 15, 1968, RG 301.7, folder 4, box 46, Board of National Missions (PCUSA) Records; *Delta Ministry Reports,* January 1969, 2; "Mound Bayou Development Corporation Proposal for Financial Assistance," folder 8, box 28, Delta Ministry Papers, Atlanta; Roger A. Smith et al., "From Democracy to Dicta-

torship: The Delta Ministry, 1968–1972," 14, folder "Delta Ministry Board, 1970–73," box 9, Derian Papers; Noble, "Delta Ministry," 24, 56–57, 59.

22. Noble, "Delta Ministry," 23–24, 197; Evers and Szanton, *Have No Fear,* 238 (quotation); K. Mills, *This Little Light,* 224–25.

23. Owen H. Brooks, "Black Politics in the South," n.d., 1, Department of Humanities Records, Massachusetts Institute of Technology, Institute Archives and Special Collections, The Libraries, Massachusetts Institute of Technology (hereinafter cited as Department of Humanities Records, MIT); Noble, "Delta Ministry," 24; Owen H. Brooks, interview by Tom Dent, August 18, 1978, MOHC; Owen H. Brooks, interview by Robert Wright, September 4, 1968, 4, Bunche Oral History Collection.

24. Owen H. Brooks, "Black Politics in the South," n.d., 2–13 (quotation on p. 7), Department of Humanities Records, MIT; Carmichael and Hamilton, *Black Power*; Carson, *In Struggle,* 199–204, 206–11. The Delta Ministry reported that at the Freedom Democrats' convention in January 1969, "The FDP declared that it will not apply for formal recognition as a political party, but attempt to maintain its status as the pressure group that most represents the poor of the State" (*Delta Ministry Reports,* January 1969, 1).

25. Owen H. Brooks, interview by Robert Wright, September 24, 1968, 45–46, 48, Bunche Oral History Collection; Noble, "Delta Ministry," 174–76; Fortenberry and Abney, "Mississippi Unreconstructed," 494; Draper, "Mississippi Movement," 360–61.

26. "Recommendations and Procedures to Reorganize Mississippi Freedom Democratic Party from the County to the State," n.d., folder 54, box 3, Horwitz Papers; Noble, "Delta Ministry," 16, 22, 135, 183–84, 206–7; Ladner, "What Black Power Means," 135; *New York Times,* March 7, 1971; Draper, "Mississippi Movement," 360–61; Howell, *Freedom City,* 78. Horwitz served on the MFDP's executive committee, which was otherwise almost entirely black (minutes, Executive Committee of the Mississippi Freedom Democratic Party, March 9, 1969, 1, folder 54, box 3, Horwitz Papers).

27. "Proposal Draft the Delta Ministry," n.d., 5 (quotation), folder "Mississippi Delta Ministry, January 1971," box 2, Thomas Papers.

28. Gaile P. Noble, résumé, attached to "Gaile P. Noble to Father Henry Parker," January 9, 1969, folder 63, box 2, Delta Ministry Papers, Starkville; Noble, "Delta Ministry," 206–7; "Education: A Delta Ministry Priority," folder 292, box 6, King Papers; *Delta Ministry Reports,* October 1966, 2; Hilton, "Whatever Happened," 3.

29. Ladner, "What Black Power Means," 135, 142–47 (quotation on p. 146), 151–52; Carson, *In Struggle,* 222–23; Payne, *I've Got the Light,* 63–64.

30. Owen H. Brooks, interview by Tom Dent, August 18, 1978, MOHC; Harry J. Bowie, interview by Jack Bass and Walter DeVries, March 31, 1974, 36–39, SOHP #4007; Salamon, "Time Dimension," 129–31, 155–82; Thelma P. Barnes, interview by author, September 5, 1996.

31. *New York Times,* March 7, 1971; *Jackson Clarion-Ledger,* June 6, November 6, 1971; Owen H. Brooks, "Black Politics in the South," n.d., 13–14 (quotation), Department of Humanities Records, MIT.

32. Hilton, "Whatever Happened," 3; *Delta Ministry Reports,* April–May 1969, 3; "Manifesto to the White Christian Churches and the Jewish Synagogues in the United States of America and All Other Racist Institutions," April 26, 1969, folder 298, box 4, Grigg Papers; Forman, *Making,* 543–50; minutes, Commission on the Delta Ministry, November 12–13,

1969, 2–3 (quotation on p. 3), RG 4, folder "Delta Ministry April 1, '68–March 31, '69," box DHM 8, UCMS Papers; Gallup, *Gallup Poll*, 3:2200; "James Forman's Black Manifesto," 605; Wilmore, *Black Religion*, 233–43; H. J. Pratt, *Liberalization*, 188–206; Findlay, *Church People*, 199–220; "Black Manifesto's Birthday," 37.

33. "DCLM Program and Budget—1969," n.d., RG 6, folder 21, box 4, and memorandum, Jon L. Regier to DCLM Executive Committee, February 18, 1969, RG 6, folder 20, box 4, NCC Archives; *Memphis Commercial Appeal*, September 28, 1969; Findlay, *Church People*, 222–23; H. J. Pratt, *Liberalization*, 201; Isserman and Kazin, *America Divided*, 245–46; Wood, "Unanticipated Consequences," 517 n.15.

34. Minutes, Commission on the Delta Ministry, November 12–13, 1969, 2–3 (quotation on p. 2), RG 4, folder "Delta Ministry April 1, '68–March 31, '69," box DHM 8, UCMS Papers; Andrew J. Young to Kenneth Kuntz, November 10, 1969, and Kenneth A. Kuntz to Andrew J. Young, November 25, 1969, RG 4, folder "Delta Ministry April 1, '69–March 31, '70," box DHM 8, UCMS Papers; "Delta Ministry Aides Toured Europe as Fund Raisers," *American Baptist News Service*, December 23, 1969, folder 22, box 1, Delta Ministry Papers, Starkville; Delta Ministry Expense and Income Statement, April 27, 1970, folder 27, box 11, and Jon L. Regier to Owen H. Brooks, March 11, 1970, folder 7, box 14, Delta Ministry Papers, Atlanta.

35. Memorandum, Owen H. Brooks to "Delta Ministry Staff," March 3, 1970, folder 7, box 14, Delta Ministry Papers, Atlanta; Eddie Lucas to Amzie Moore, March 11, 1970, folder 6, box 4, Amzie Moore Papers, WHS; memorandum, "Delta Ministry Finance Office" to Joseph Lewis Harris, May 8, 1970, folder 12, box 26, and memorandum, Owen H. Brooks to Joseph Lewis Harris, January 23, 1970, folders 13, box 26, Hamer Papers; Owen H. Brooks, interview by Tom Dent, August 18, 1978, MOHC; Noble, "Delta Ministry," 123–24; K. Mills, *This Little Light*, 259–72; Lee, *For Freedom's Sake*, 147–62.

36. Thomas J. Liggett to "Dear Friend," April 29, 1970, and Wade D. Rubick to Albert O. Kean, April 30, 1970, RG 4, folder "Mrs. Mary Dale's File on Mt. Beulah," box DHM 8, UCMS Papers; Thomas J. Griffin, "The Mt. Beulah Situation: A Report," July 6, 1970, RG 4, folder "Mt. Beulah Proposals for the Use of Property," box DHM 8, UCMS Papers; Russell Harrison, "National Council of Churches: Delta Ministry & Mt. Beulah," February 17, 1971, RG 4, folder "Delta Ministry—NCC & UCMS Re: Mount Beulah Campus," box DHM 8, UCMS Papers; John W. Kalas to John F. Else, n.d., and Kenneth G. Neigh to Edward N. McNulty, April 30, 1970, RG 301.7, folder 5, box 46, Board of National Missions (PCUSA) Records; Philip H. Young to Richard E. Murdoch, June 15, 1970, and "SOS Mount Beulah Delta Ministry Special Appeal," March 1970, folder "Mount Beulah," box 13, Neigh Papers; letters to the editor from Thomas J. Liggett and Owen H. Brooks, *Christian Century* 87 (June 3, 1970): 704–5; *Delta Ministry Reports*, April 1970, 1; H. Bruce Bowser, "Report: A Recent Meeting Concerning the Mount Beulah Property," April 16–17, 1970, RG 4, folder "Mt. Beulah—Federation of Southern Cooperatives Mississippi Christian Missy. Conv," box DHM 9, UCMS Papers; "Petitions," n.d., RG 4, untitled folder, box DHM 9, UCMS Papers; press release, June 23, 1971, RG 4, folder "Mt. Beulah—1971," box DHM 9, UCMS Papers; minutes, Delta Ministry monthly staff meeting, July 14, 1970, 3, folder 45, box 3, Delta Ministry Papers, Atlanta; *Memphis Commercial Appeal*, January 30, 1971.

37. Roger A. Smith et al., "From Democracy to Dictatorship: The Delta Ministry, 1968–1972," 2, and unpaged section, folder "Delta Ministry Board, 1970–1973," box 9, Derian Papers; Sarah H. Johnson, interview by Thomas Healy, September 10, 1978, 15 (quotation);

Thelma P. Barnes, interview by author, September 5, 1996. The minutes of the Delta Ministry's staff meeting in July 1970 indicate that women attended and participated. The available sources do not contain minutes for staff meetings in October and November 1970 (Minutes, Delta Ministry Monthly Staff Meeting, July 14, 1970, folder 45, box 3, Delta Ministry Papers, Atlanta).

38. Thelma P. Barnes, interview by author, September 5, 1996; *Delta Democrat-Times,* October 2, 1970.

39. Roger A. Smith et al., "From Democracy to Dictatorship: The Delta Ministry, 1968–1972," 3–4, folder "Delta Ministry Board, 1970–1973," box 9, Derian Papers.

40. Roger A. Smith et al., "From Democracy to Dictatorship: The Delta Ministry, 1968–1972," 3–4, folder "Delta Ministry Board, 1970–73," box 9, Derian Papers; *Journal of the Women's Division of the Board of Global Ministries of the United Methodist Church,* 335; Sarah H. Johnson, interview by Thomas Healy, September 10, 1978, 16.

41. *Delta Democrat-Times,* March 7, 1971; Roger A. Smith et al., "From Democracy to Dictatorship: The Delta Ministry, 1968–1972," 3–4, 23–24, folder "Delta Ministry Board, 1970–1973," box 9, Derian Papers; Sarah H. Johnson, interview by Thomas Healy, September 10, 1978, 15–16.

42. *New York Times,* March 7, 1971 (second quotation); *Delta Democrat-Times,* March 7 (third quotation), 9 (first quotation); Roger A. Smith et al., "From Democracy to Dictatorship: The Delta Ministry, 1968–1972," 4–5, folder "Delta Ministry Board, 1970–1973," box 9, Derian Papers; *Delta Ministry Reports,* March 1971, 1; "Delta Ministry Restructured," 2.

43. Roger A. Smith et al., "From Democracy to Dictatorship: The Delta Ministry, 1968–1972," 5–8, folder "Delta Ministry Board, 1970–1973," box 9, Derian Papers; *Delta Democrat-Times,* March 7, 1971; *New York Times,* March 7, 1971; "Charlie" to Anne Braden, n.d., folder 33, box 2, Horwitz Papers; McCanna, "A Ministry of Deliverance," 39; minutes, Delta Ministry monthly staff meeting, July 14, 1970, 1–2, folder 45, box 3, Delta Ministry Papers, Atlanta.

44. *Delta Democrat-Times,* March 7, 1971 (quotations). The terminated staff included Mississippians Jake Ayers, Berdia Coleman, and Homer Crawford and northerners Henry Parker and Roger Smith. Although not signatories to the telegram, Sarah Johnson and secretary Jeanne Smith were also members of the Concerned Staff. Ayers served as the group's chairman (Roger A. Smith et al., "From Democracy to Dictatorship: The Delta Ministry, 1968–1972," 8, folder "Delta Ministry Board, 1970–1973," box 9, Derian Papers; *Delta Democrat-Times,* March 7, 1971).

45. Roger A. Smith et al., "From Democracy to Dictatorship: The Delta Ministry, 1968–1972," 5–6, folder "Delta Ministry Board, 1970–1973," box 9, Derian Papers.

46. *Delta Democrat-Times,* March 7, 1971 (quotation); Roger A. Smith et al., "From Democracy to Dictatorship: The Delta Ministry, 1968–1972," 8–11, folder "Delta Ministry Board, 1970–1973," box 9, Derian Papers; *New York Times,* March 7, 1971.

47. Roger A. Smith et al., "From Democracy to Dictatorship: The Delta Ministry, 1968–1972," 8–10, folder "Delta Ministry Board, 1970–1973," box 9, Derian Papers; *Delta Democrat-Times,* March 9, 1971 (quotations). Brooks confirmed to reporters that at the meeting the Concerned Staff had called for his dismissal (*New York Times,* March 7, 1971).

48. *New York Times,* March 7, 1971 (quotations); "Charlie" to Anne Braden, n.d., folder 33, box 2, Horwitz Papers. On August 17, 1970, Barber presided over the marriage of Roger

Mills, a twenty-four-year-old white Mississippian, to Berta Linson, an African American, at a black Methodist church in Jackson (Johnston, *Mississippi's Defiant Years,* 410).

49. Jon L. Regier to Arthur C. Thomas, January 14, 1971, and Arthur C. Thomas, "A Report on the Delta Ministry," February 1, 1971 (quotations), folder "Mississippi Delta Ministry, January 1971," box 2, Thomas Papers; Roger A. Smith et al., "From Democracy to Dictatorship: The Delta Ministry, 1968–1972," 6, folder "Delta Ministry Board, 1970–1973," box 9, Derian Papers.

50. Roger A. Smith et al., "From Democracy to Dictatorship: The Delta Ministry, 1968–1972," 12–19, folder "Delta Ministry Board, 1970–1973," box 9, Derian Papers; Sarah H. Johnson, interview by Thomas Healy, September 10, 1978, 16; memorandum, members, Delta Ministry Commission, to Executive Committee, Division of Christian Life and Mission, March 31, 1971, 1–2, folder "Mississippi Delta Ministry, January 1971," box 2, Thomas Papers.

51. Memorandum, members, Delta Ministry Commission, to Executive Committee, Division of Christian Life and Mission, March 31, 1971, 1–2 (first, second, and fifth quotations on p. 2; third and fourth quotations on p. 1), and Arthur C. Thomas, "A Report on the Delta Ministry," February 1, 1971, folder "Mississippi Delta Ministry, January 1971," box 2, Thomas Papers; Sarah H. Johnson, interview by Thomas Healy, September 10, 1978, 16; memorandum, Philip H. Young to David Ramage Jr., October 20, 1969, E. Eugene Huff to Jon L. Regier, November 10, 1969, and Jon L. Regier to David Ramage Jr. November 24, 1969, RG 301.7, folder 3, box 46, Board of National Missions (PCUSA) Records; John F. Anderson Jr. to Jon L. Regier, August 21, 1968, RG 1, folder "NCC Delta Ministry," box 10, Executive Secretary Correspondence Files, 1953–73, PCUS, Montreat.

52. *Delta Democrat-Times,* April 1, 1971 (quotations); Roger A. Smith et al., "From Democracy to Dictatorship: The Delta Ministry, 1968–1972," 20–22, folder "Delta Ministry Board, 1970–1973," box 9, Derian Papers.

53. Minutes, Executive Committee, Division of Christian Life and Mission, NCC, May 12, 1971, 8–9, RG 6, folder 19, box 4, NCC Archives.

CHAPTER TEN. Winding Down

1. *Delta Ministry Reports,* May 1972, 2; "The Delta Ministry—1972," 1–4, attached to minutes, Delta Ministry Board, January 31, 1972, folder "Delta Ministry Board, 1970–1973," box 9, Derian Papers; Philip H. Young to Robert A. Roof, February 17, 1972, and memorandum, Philip H. Young to Arthur M. Tennies, June 4, 1973, RG 301.7, folder 3, box 46, Board of National Missions (PCUSA) Records; Rims K. Barber, interview by author, August 22, 1996; L. C. Dorsey, interview by author, September 4, 1996; Harry J. Bowie, interview by Jack Bass and Walter DeVries, March 31, 1974, 1–2, SOHP #4007; Harry J. Bowie, interview by author, September 5, 1996; Thelma P. Barnes, interview by author, September 5, 1996; *DRC Mississippi Newsletter* 13 (December 1985): 1–2, 4.

2. Peirce, *Deep South States,* 232 (quotation); *Delta Ministry Reports,* May 1971, 1; Rims K. Barber, interview by author, August 22, 1996.

3. "The Delta Ministry—1972," 1, 4, attached to minutes, Delta Ministry Board, January 31, 1972, folder "Delta Ministry Board, 1970–1973," box 9, Derian Papers; *Memphis Commercial Appeal,* July 21, 1972; *Delta Ministry Reports,* n.d., Winham Papers; press release by Board of Directors, Delta Community Hospital and Health Center, July 5, 1972, 1, RG

301.7, folder 3, box 46, Board of National Missions (PCUSA) Records; K. H. Smith to Ernest C. Moss Jr., June 6, 1972, folder "Delta Ministry—Bishop Moore," box "Delta Ministry Files," Paul Moore Jr. Papers, AEDNY. The connection between the Delta Health Center and its founder, Tufts University, had been severed in November 1970 by the North Bolivar County Health and Civic Improvement Association, which administered the center and represented local people (*Jackson Clarion-Ledger*, November 15, 1971; "Brief History of the Delta Health Center 1970–1972, and of the Events Leading to Merger with the Mound Bayou Community Hospital in a New Corporation Beginning March 1, 1972," 1, folder 1428, box 87, Henry Papers).

4. "The Delta Ministry—1972," 1, 3, attached to minutes, Delta Ministry Board, January 31, 1972, folder "Delta Ministry Board, 1970–1973," box 9, Derian Papers; Charles Horwitz to Betsy K. Ewing, December 17, 1971, Betsy K. Ewing to Owen H. Brooks, December 22, 1971, and Philip H. Young to Owen H. Brooks, January 3, 1972, and Kattie Kingdom, "Proposal for Welfare Rights Organization Funds, Washington County Branch," January 20, 1972, folder "Current Delta Ministry," no box, Horwitz Papers.

5. "The Delta Ministry—1972," 1, 4, attached to minutes, Delta Ministry Board, January 31, 1972, folder "Delta Ministry Board, 1970–1973," box 9, Derian Papers; *Delta Democrat-Times*, August 8, November 8, 1971.

6. *Delta Ministry Reports*, May 1971, 1 (first quotation); "The Delta Ministry—1972," 1–4 (second, third, and fourth quotations on p. 1; fifth quotation on p. 3), attached to minutes, Delta Ministry Board, January 31, 1972, folder "Delta Ministry Board, 1970–1973," box 9, Derian Papers.

7. *Jackson Clarion-Ledger*, November 27, 1989 (quotation); "The Delta Ministry—1972," 1–4, attached to minutes, Delta Ministry Board, January 31, 1972, and "The Delta Ministry, Involvement in Legislative Issues," 1–2, attached to minutes, Delta Ministry Board, April 17, 1972, folder "Delta Ministry Board, 1970–1973," box 9, Derian Papers; *Delta Ministry Reports*, January 1971, 2, May 1971, 2; *Memphis Commercial Appeal*, February 21, 1971.

8. K. Mills, *This Little Light*, 287–89; Salamon, "Mississippi Post-Mortem," 45–47; Salamon and Van Evera, "Fear," 1290; Evers and Szanton, *Have No Fear*, 271; Loewen, "Continuing Obstacles," 32–37; Lawson, *In Pursuit*, 179–89. According to political scientist Sam Kernell, Evers won 23 percent of the vote in the gubernatorial election (Kernell, "Comment," 1309 n.6, 1315). Historian Steven Lawson writes that fifty-one African Americans won elections in 1971 (Lawson, *In Pursuit*, 188).

9. Walton, *Black Political Parties*, 129; K. Mills, *This Little Light*, 287–90; Salamon, "Leadership and Modernization," 617, 623–46 (quotation on p. 644); Owen H. Brooks, interview by Tom Dent, August 18, 1978, MOHC.

10. "Delta Ministry Action Memo," July 1970, no folder, no box, Winham Papers; minutes, Delta Ministry monthly staff meeting, July 14, 1970, 2, folder 45, box 3, Delta Ministry Papers, Atlanta; *Delta Ministry Reports*, August–September 1970, 2, January 1971, 2; memorandum, Charles Horwitz to Philip H. Young, August 20, 1972, Charles Horwitz to Philip H. Young, September 12, 1972, memorandum, Philip H. Young to "Emergency Fund for Legal Aid," September 29, 1972, and Charles Horwitz to Wilbur K. Cox Jr., December 11, 1972, RG 301.7, folder 3, box 46, Board of National Missions (PCUSA) Records.

11. *Delta Ministry Reports*, September 1971, 1, November 1971, 1, March 1972, 2, November 1973, 2; "Strike," 9; Peirce, *Deep South States*, 224–25; Riches, *Civil Rights Movement*, 138–39;

Evers and Szanton, *Have No Fear,* 273; Charles Horwitz to James Simmons and Bob Zellner, February 19, 1972, and "DM Project Application," n.d., 2, folder "Current Delta Ministry," no box, Horwitz Papers.

12. Harry J. Bowie, interview by Jack Bass and Walter DeVries, March 31, 1974, 1–2, SOHP #4007; Harry J. Bowie, interview by Tom Dent, June 10, 1979, MOHC.

13. Memorandum, Members, Delta Ministry Commission to Executive Committee, Division of Christian Life and Mission, March 30–31, 1971, and memorandum, "The Special Committee of the Delta Ministry Commission" to the Executive Committee of the Division of Christian Life and Mission, April 21, 1971, RG 6, folder 19, box 4, NCC Archives; *Delta Ministry Reports,* May 1972, 2; minutes, Delta Ministry Board, April 17, 1972, 1, folder "Delta Ministry Board, 1970–1973," box 9, Derian Papers.

14. Memorandum, Philip H. Young to Lucius Walker Jr., March 4, 1974, RG 301.7, folder 3, box 46, Board of National Missions (PCUSA) Records; minutes, Delta Ministry Board, April 17, 1972, 1, and minutes, Executive Committee, Delta Ministry, October 7, 1972, 3, folder "Delta Ministry Board, 1970–1973," box 9, Derian Papers.

15. Minutes, Delta Ministry Board, January 31, 1972, 1–2, and attached "Statement Concerning Possible Relationships of Programs to the National Council of Churches," and memorandum, Jon L. Regier to Owen H. Brooks, April 14, 1972, folder "Delta Ministry Board, 1970–1973," box 9, Derian Papers; John W. Brown to Owen H. Brooks and Rims K. Barber, April 30, 1976 (quotation), folder "Delta Ministry," box "Delta Ministry Files," Paul Moore Jr. Papers, AEDNY; memorandum, Philip H. Young to Arthur M. Tennies, June 4, 1973, RG 301.7, folder 3, box 46, Board of National Missions (PCUSA) Records; *Minutes of the General Assembly of the United Presbyterian Church in the United States of America,* 1973, 684–85, 817, 819; 1974, 781; 1975, 569; 1977, 531; 1978, 322; 1979, 360; 1980, 260; *Journal, Spring Meeting of the Women's Division of the Board of Global Ministries of the United Methodist Church,* 1975, 25, 261; *Journal, Fourth Annual Meeting of the Women's Division of the Board of Global Ministries of the United Methodist Church,* 1975, 35, 117, 120, 335–36; *Delta Ministry Reports,* n.d., no folder, no box, Winham Papers; *Delta Ministry Reports,* March 1973, 2.

16. Rims K. Barber, interview by author, August 22, 1996; L. C. Dorsey, interview by author, September 4, 1996.

17. *Delta Ministry Reports,* March 1972, 1; Marable, *Race, Reform, and Rebellion,* 122–23, 133, 137; Lawson, *Running,* 141–42.

18. *Delta Ministry Reports,* March 1972, 1–2; K. Mills, *This Little Light,* 295–96; Parker, *Black Votes Count,* 148–49; Lawson, *In Pursuit,* 196–200.

19. Press release, "Waller Calls Mound Bayou Hospital a National Scandal," n.d., 1–4, folder "Delta Ministry—Bishop Moore," box "Delta Ministry Files," Paul Moore Jr. Papers, AEDNY; *Memphis Commercial Appeal,* July 21, 1972; *Delta Ministry Reports,* August 1972, 1; press release by Board of Directors, Delta Community Hospital and Health Center, July 5, 1972, 1–3, RG 301.7, folder 3, box 46, Board of National Missions (PCUSA) Records; unidentified press clipping, n.d., folder "Current Delta Ministry," no box, Horwitz Papers; unidentified press clipping, n.d., folder 1428, box 87, Henry Papers.

20. Press release, "Waller Calls Mound Bayou Hospital a National Scandal," n.d., 2, folder "Delta Ministry—Bishop Moore," box "Delta Ministry Files," Paul Moore Jr. Papers, AEDNY; Harry J. Bowie, interview by Tom Dent, June 10, 1979, MOHC; *Washington Post,* July 18, 1972 (first quotation) in "Cities and Towns—'Mound Bayou'" vertical file, Special

Collections, Mitchell Memorial Library, Mississippi State University; *Memphis Commercial Appeal,* July 25 (second quotation), 29, 1972, February 15, May 23, 1973; *Delta Ministry Reports,* October 1972, 1, December 1972, 1.

21. "Mound Bayou's Crisis," *Time,* November 25, 1974, in "Mound Bayou Hospital" vertical file, Special Collections, Mitchell Memorial Library, Mississippi State University; *Delta Ministry Reports,* March 1973, 1, June 1973, 1, November 1973, 1; "'We Need More Doctors,'" 30–31; *Memphis Commercial Appeal,* February 15, April 11, August 3, 1973; *Delta Democrat-Times,* September 14, 1973; *Jackson Clarion-Ledger,* October 11, 1973, August 17, 1984.

22. *Delta Ministry Reports,* October 1972, 1, December 1972, 1, June 1973, 1, November 1973, 1, April 1974, 2; Owen H. Brooks, interview by Tom Dent, August 18, 1978, MOHC; *Journal, Fourth Annual Meeting of the Women's Division of the Board of Global Ministries of the United Methodist Church,* 1975, 335–36.

23. *Delta Ministry Reports,* March 1973, 1, June 1973, 1 (quotations).

24. Charles Horwitz, "Year End Report, 1969, from Hinds County Delta Ministry Project," 1, folder 14, box 1, Horwitz Papers; Morrison, *Black Political Mobilization,* 16, 53–54, 60, 62–65, 68–70, 79–93; *Delta Ministry Reports,* May 1973, 1, June 1973, 1, November 1973, 1 (quotation), April 1974, 2; Parker, *Black Votes Count,* 165–66.

25. *Delta Ministry Reports,* December 1975, 1; Parker, *Black Votes Count,* 165–66.

26. Charles Horwitz to "Dear Delta Ministry Board Member," July 6, 1973, folder "Delta Ministry Board, 1970–1973," box 9, Derian Papers; *Delta Ministry Reports,* March 1973, 1; "The Delta Ministry Ten Year Celebration," June 10, 1974, folder "Hold," box 3, Thomas Papers.

27. Owen H. Brooks, interview by Tom Dent, August 18, 1978, MOHC; Sarah H. Johnson, interview by Thomas Healy, September 10, 1978, 15–17; memorandum, Philip H. Young to Arthur C. Tennies, June 4, 1973, RG 301.7, folder 3, box 46, Board of National Missions (PCUSA) Records; Jake B. Ayers Sr. to Lucius Walker Jr., July 9, 1973, and "Delta Resources Committee, September 1973–September 1974," n.d., 1–4, folder "Delta Resources Committee Non-Funded Proposal 1972–1973," box 34, Interreligious Foundation for Community Organization Papers, Schomburg Center for Research in Black Culture, New York Public Library; *DRC Mississippi Newsletter* 13 (December 1985): 1–2, 4.

28. Owen H. Brooks, interview by Tom Dent, August 18, 1978, MOHC; Sarah H. Johnson, interview by Thomas Healy, September 10, 1978, 1 (biography), 17; *Delta Democrat-Times,* January 24, 31, October 3 (quotation), 1973; "Analysis of Greenville City Council Special Election," n.d., folder 9, box 1, Barber Papers; U.S. Commission on Civil Rights, *School Desegregation,* 11.

29. "The Delta Ministry Ten Year Celebration," June 10, 1974, folder "Hold," box 3, Thomas Papers; "Delta Ministry's Tenth Year," 694; Sumner, *Episcopal Church's History,* 177; Owen H. Brooks to Paul Moore Jr., April 8, 1974, folder "Delta Ministry—Bishop Moore," box "Delta Ministry Files," Paul Moore Jr. Papers, AEDNY; Bryant George to Jon L. Regier, November 19, 1968, and memorandum, Philip H. Young to Lucius Walker Jr., March 7, 1974, 1–5 (quotation on p. 1), RG 301.7, folder 3, box 46, Board of National Missions (PCUSA) Records; minutes, Delta Ministry Board, April 17, 1972, 2, and minutes, Delta Ministry Board, November 10, 1972, 1, folder "Delta Ministry Board, 1970–1973," box 9, Derian Papers.

30. "Delta Ministry after Ten Years," 4; *Delta Ministry Reports,* n.d., 2 (quotation), "Delta Ministry" vertical file, Special Collections, Mitchell Memorial Library, Mississippi State University.

31. "We Have No Government," February 1, 1966, folder 635, box 12, King Papers; *Jackson Clarion-Ledger,* September 27, 1981; Dent, *Southern Journey,* 370–71, 380; Morrison, *Black Political Mobilization,* 95, 99–122; *Memphis Commercial Appeal,* May 5, 1986.

32. "We Have No Government," February 1, 1966, folder 635, box 12, King Papers; Morrison, *Black Political Mobilization,* 108; "The Delta Ministry Ten Year Celebration," June 10, 1974, folder "Hold," box 3, Thomas Papers; Owen H. Brooks to Aaron Henry, March 10, 1976, 1–2 (first quotation on p. 1; second quotation on p. 2) and attached clippings from the *Delta Democrat-Times,* March 11, 1976, and unidentified and undated (third and fourth quotations), folder "Delta Ministry," box "Delta Ministry Files," Paul Moore Jr. Papers, AEDNY; Parker, *Black Votes Count,* 31; Alt, "Impact," 374. Aware that most African American voters opposed him, Eastland subsequently decided not to run for reelection in 1978 and retired to his plantation in Sunflower County (Bass, *Unlikely Heroes,* 332).

33. Foster, "Time," 189–90; Lamis, *Two-Party South,* 52; *Delta Ministry Reports,* April 1976, 1; Bass and DeVries, *Transformation,* 207–8. The Ministry complained that the new unified one-hundred-member state Democratic Party executive committee had only twenty-seven African Americans and included fifty-three people pledged to Wallace. The twenty-four-member Mississippi national convention delegation, the Ministry observed in April 1976, had eight blacks and eleven Wallace supporters. Jimmy Carter won the Democratic Party's presidential nomination and Mississippi in his successful election campaign (*Delta Ministry Reports,* April 1976, 1; Lamis, *Two-Party South,* 52).

34. *Journal, Spring Meeting of the Women's Division of the Board of Global Ministries of the United Methodist Church,* 1975, 25, 261; Owen H. Brooks to Paul Moore Jr., May 4, 1976, folder "Delta Ministry," box "Delta Ministry Files," Paul Moore Jr. Papers, AEDNY; *Delta Ministry Reports,* September 1976, 1.

35. Rims K. Barber, interview by author, August 22, 1996; Greenberg, *Devil,* 734, 793.

36. *Delta Ministry Reports,* March 1977, 1 (first quotation); *Memphis Commercial Appeal,* June 21, 1979 (second quotation).

37. *Memphis Commercial Appeal,* February 13, 1983.

38. *Delta Ministry Reports,* March 1977, 1; "The Delta Ministry Ten Year Celebration," June 10, 1974, folder "Hold," box 3, Thomas Papers; Abbott, ed., *Mississippi Writers,* 2:698; L. C. Dorsey, interview by author, September 4, 1996; L. C. Dorsey to Mr. and Mrs. L. C. Morrow, May 19, 1981, folder 1670, box 99, Henry Papers; Henry with Curry, *Aaron Henry,* 229–31.

39. Abbott, ed., *Mississippi Writers,* 2:698; L. C. Dorsey, interview by author, September 4, 1996; Dent, *Southern Journey,* 367 (quotation).

40. L. C. Dorsey, interview by author, September 4, 1996; Rims K. Barber, interview by author, August 22, 1996; B. Minor, "Congressman Espy," 1; Parker, *Black Votes Count,* 90–91; Dent, *Southern Journey,* 366, 379; Greenberg, *Devil,* 768, 774.

41. Harry J. Bowie, interview by author, September 5, 1996; Thelma P. Barnes, interview by author, September 5, 1996; K. Mills, *This Little Light,* 292, 323; L. C. Dorsey, interview by author, September 4, 1996; Rims K. Barber, interview by author, August 22, 1996; *Jackson Clarion-Ledger,* November 27, 1989; Trillin, "State Secrets," 63–64; Greenberg, *Devil,* 727–28, 734–35.

42. Rims K. Barber, interview by author, August 22, 1996.

43. Greenberg, *Devil,* 773–74 (quotation on p. 773); Dent, *Southern Journey,* 366, 379; Owen H. Brooks, interview by Tom Dent, August 18, 1978, MOHC.

44. L. C. Dorsey, interview by Clarity Educational Productions, Inc., January 23, 1990, 18, 23–25, 28, Field and Mulford Collection; Dorsey, *Freedom Came*, 38; Greenberg, *Devil*, 768–69; Dittmer, *Local People*, 426.

45. Greenberg, *Devil*, 726–27 (quotation on p. 727); *Memphis Commercial Appeal*, May 5, 1986.

46. Harry J. Bowie, interview by Tom Dent, May 28, June 10, 1979, MOHC; Harry J. Bowie, interview by author, September 5, 1996; Greenberg, *Devil*, 733, 737; Dent, *Southern Journey*, 353–55; *Jackson Clarion-Ledger*, December 1, 1991.

47. Harry J. Bowie, interview by Tom Dent, May 28, 1979, MOHC.

48. L. C. Dorsey, "Harder Times Than These," in *Mississippi Writers*, ed. Abbott, 2:170–73 (quotation on p. 172).

49. Dorsey, "Harder Times Than These," in *Mississippi Writers*, ed. Abbott, 2:173 (quotation); L. C. Dorsey, interview by Clarity Educational Productions, Inc., January 23, 1990, 20–23, Field and Mulford Collection.

50. Dent, *Southern Journey*, 349, 367–68 (first quotation on p. 368); Dorsey, "Harder Times Than These," in *Mississippi Writers*, ed. Abbott, 2:172 (second quotation).

51. Parker, *Black Votes Count*, 4, 198.

52. Parker, *Black Votes Count*, 2, 143–47, 157, 199–203; *Jackson Clarion-Ledger*, October 23, 1988.

53. Parker, *Black Votes Count*, 130–36, 146–47; *Jackson Clarion-Ledger*, May 31, 1991, January 8, 1992; Greenberg, *Devil*, 759, 771; Dittmer, *Local People*, 427; Orey, "Black Legislative Politics," 804, 806–7, 811.

54. Parker, *Black Votes Count*, 158, 162–63; Aiken, *Cotton Plantation South*, 322–23; *Jackson Clarion-Ledger*, December 17, 1980.

55. Parker, *Black Votes Count*, 136–40, 204–6; Orey, "Black Legislative Politics," 802, 811. Estimates of voter registration vary. A federal district court ruled in 1987 that as a result of discriminatory registration procedures, 54 percent of eligible blacks and 79 percent of eligible whites were registered in Mississippi. However, political scientist David C. Colby claims that 68.2 percent of eligible blacks and 91.4 percent of eligible whites were registered in 1984. Historian Steven F. Lawson lists eligible black voter registration as 77.1 percent in 1984 (Parker, *Black Votes Count*, 205; Colby, "Voting Rights Act," 130; Lawson, *Running*, 223).

56. *Jackson Clarion-Ledger*, November 9, 1984; B. Minor, "Congressman Espy," 1; Parker, *Black Votes Count*, 91, 199–202; Dittmer, *Local People*, 426; Greenberg, *Devil*, 771; Lamis, *Two-Party South*, 56–57; Cobb, *Most Southern Place*, 273.

57. Parker, *Black Votes Count*, 203; Wallenstein, "*Loving v. Virginia*," 326; Lawson, *Running*, 111.

58. Greenberg, *Devil*, 772; Parker, *Black Votes Count*, 157, 159; Aiken, *Cotton Plantation South*, 326–27.

59. Parker, *Black Votes Count*, 135–36, 140, 158, 165; Dittmer, *Local People*, 426; Greenberg, *Devil*, 768–69; T. J. Davis Jr., "Blacks' Political Representation," 155, 157–58.

60. Orfield, *Public School Desegregation*, 8, 51; Parker, "Protest, Politics, and Litigation," 694–95; Greenberg, *Devil*, 759–60 (quotation on p. 759).

61. *Jackson Clarion-Ledger*, July 1, 1984; Parker, "Protest, Politics, and Litigation," 700–701; Greenberg, *Devil*, 737; Dittmer, *Local People*, 427 (quotation).

BIBLIOGRAPHY

Primary Sources

Journals and Minutes

Journal, Fourth Annual Meeting of the Women's Division of the Board of Global Ministries of the United Methodist Church, 1975.

Journal of the General Convention of the Protestant Episcopal Church in the United States of America, 1964.

Journal of the One Hundred Thirty-Ninth Annual Council of the Diocese of Mississippi [Protestant Episcopal Church], 1966.

Journal, Spring Meeting of the Women's Division of the Board of Global Ministries of the United Methodist Church, 1975.

Journal of the Upper Mississippi Conference of the United Methodist Church, The Seventy-Ninth Annual Session, 1968.

Journal of the Upper Mississippi Conference of the United Methodist Church, The Eightieth Annual Session, 1969.

Journal of the Women's Division of the Board of Global Ministries of the United Methodist Church, 1975.

Minutes of the General Assembly of the United Presbyterian Church in the United States of America, 1963, 1966, 1967, 1973–75, 1977–80.

Minutes of the One-Hundred-Fourth General Assembly of the Presbyterian Church in the United States, 1964.

Minutes of the One-Hundred-Fifth General Assembly of the Presbyterian Church in the United States, 1965.

Minutes of the One-Hundred-Sixth General Assembly of the Presbyterian Church in the United States, 1966.

Minutes of the One-Hundred-Seventh General Assembly of the Presbyterian Church in the United States, 1967.

Minutes of Presbytery of Central Mississippi [Presbyterian Church in the United States], 1964.

Minutes, The Synod of Mississippi of the Presbyterian Church, U.S., The One Hundred Thirty-Seventh Annual Session, 1967.

Minutes, The Synod of Mississippi of the Presbyterian Church in the U.S., The One Hundred Thirty-Eighth Annual Session, 1968.

Minutes, The Synod of Mississippi of the Presbyterian Church in the U.S., The One Hundred Thirty-Ninth Annual Session, 1969.

Minutes, The Synod of Mississippi of the Presbyterian Church in the U.S., The One Hundred Fortieth Annual Session, 1970.

Minutes, The Synod of Mississippi of the Presbyterian Church in the U.S., The One Hundred Forty-First Annual Session, 1971.

Minutes of the Synod of Mississippi of the Presbyterian Church in the United States, The One Hundred Forty-Third Annual Session, 1973.

North Mississippi Conference Journal of the North Mississippi Annual Conference [Methodist Church], 1964, 1966.

Archival Collections

Archives of the Catholic Diocese of Jackson, Mississippi
  STAR, Inc. Correspondence. February 20, 1969–May 1, 1973
  STAR, Inc. Minutes. January 13, 1969–April 21, 1973
Archives of the Episcopal Diocese of New York, Cathedral of St. John the Divine, New York
  Paul Moore Jr. Papers
Archives of Labor and Urban Affairs, Wayne State University, Detroit, Michigan
  UAW International Affairs Department, Victor Reuther and Lewis Carliner Collection
Amistad Research Center, Tulane University, New Orleans
  Fannie Lou Hamer Papers
J. B. Cain Archives of Mississippi Methodism, Millsaps-Wilson Library, Millsaps College, Jackson, Mississippi
  Bishop's Office
L. Zenobia Coleman Library, Tougaloo College, Tougaloo, Mississippi
  Rims Barber Papers
  Aaron Edd Henry Papers
  Charles Horwitz Papers
  Edwin King Papers
Department of History, Presbyterian Church (U.S.A.), Montreat, North Carolina
  Executive Secretary Correspondence Files, 1953–73, Presbyterian Church in the United States
  Office of Church and Society Records, Presbyterian Church in the United States
Disciples of Christ Historical Society, Nashville, Tennessee
  United Christian Missionary Society Papers
Institute Archives and Special Collections, The Libraries, Massachusetts Institute of Technology, Cambridge
  Department of Humanities Records, Massachusetts Institute of Technology
Lyndon Baines Johnson Library, Austin, Texas
  White House Central Files
Martin Luther King Jr. Center for Nonviolent Social Change, Atlanta
  Delta Ministry Papers
  Episcopal Society for Cultural and Racial Unity Papers
  Tom Levin Papers
  Mississippi Freedom Democratic Party Papers
  Anne Romaine Papers
  Southern Christian Leadership Conference Papers
  Student Nonviolent Coordinating Committee Papers

Arthur C. Thomas Papers
Alfred R. Winham Papers
McCain Library and Archives, University of Southern Mississippi, Hattiesburg
"Delta Ministry" vertical file
Paul B. Johnson Family Papers
Mitchell Memorial Library, Mississippi State University, Starkville
Hodding Carter and Betty Werlein Carter Papers
"Cities and Towns—'Mound Bayou'" vertical file
A. Eugene Cox Collection
Delta Ministry Papers
"Delta Ministry" vertical file
Patt Derian Papers
John D. Humphrey Papers
Garland H. Holloman Papers
"Mound Bayou Hospital" vertical file
"OEO" vertical file
North Carolina Baptist Historical Collection, Z. Smith Reynolds Library, Wake Forest
University, Winston-Salem, North Carolina
Wendell R. Grigg Papers
Presbyterian Historical Society, Philadelphia
Eugene Carson Blake Papers
Board of Christian Education—Commission on Religion and Race (CORAR) and Board
of National Missions—Council on Church and Race (COCAR) Records, 1963–71
Board of National Missions (Presbyterian Church in the United States of America)—
Division of Church Strategy and Development Records, 1871–1972
National Council of Churches Archives
Schomburg Center for Research in Black Culture, New York Public Library, New York
Black Economic Research Center Records, 1969–1980
Interreligious Foundation for Community Organization Papers
Southern Historical Collection, Wilson Library, University of North Carolina at Chapel
Hill
James McBride Dabbs Papers, #3816
Speer Library, Princeton Theological Seminary, Princeton, New Jersey
Kenneth G. Neigh Papers
United Methodist Church Archives—GCAH, Drew University, Madison, New Jersey
Church and Society Records
Wisconsin Historical Society, Madison
Harry J. Bowie Papers
Child Development Group of Mississippi Records
Highlander Research and Education Center Records
Amzie Moore Papers
Social Action Collection
Daniel J. Wacker Papers

Oral Histories and Interviews

ORAL HISTORIES

Ralph J. Bunche Oral History Collection, Oral History Department, Moorland-Spingarn Research Center, Howard University, Washington, D.C.

Harry J. Bowie, interview by Robert Wright, August 8, 1968

Owen H. Brooks, interview by Robert Wright, September 24, 1968

Hodding Carter III, interview by Robert Wright, September 23, 1968

Connie Field and Marilyn Mulford Collection, L. Zenobia Coleman Library, Tougaloo College, Tougaloo, Mississippi

L. C. Dorsey, interview by Clarity Educational Productions, Inc., January 23, 1990

Tom Levin Papers, Martin Luther King Jr. Center for Nonviolent Social Change, Atlanta

Oral History Memoir of Dr. Tom Levin, unidentified interviewer, July 1, 1965

Mississippi Oral History Collection, L. Zenobia Coleman Library, Tougaloo College, Tougaloo, Mississippi

Harry J. Bowie, interview by Tom Dent, May 28, June 10, 1979

Owen H. Brooks, interview by Tom Dent, August 18, 1978

The Mississippi Oral History Program of the University of Southern Mississippi, Hattiesburg

Sarah H. Johnson, interview by Thomas Healy, September 10, 1978. Vol. 243 (1978)

The Southern Oral History Program #4007, Wilson Library, University of North Carolina at Chapel Hill

Harry J. Bowie, interview by Jack Bass and Walter DeVries, March 31, 1974

INTERVIEWS

Victoria Gray Adams, by David Levine, January 19, 1998, summary in possession of the author

Rims K. Barber, by author, August 22, September 3, 1996

Thelma P. Barnes, by author, September 5, 1996

Robert L. Beech, by author, June 27, 30, 1998

Harry J. Bowie, by author, September 5, 1996

L. C. Dorsey, by author, September 4, 1996

Edwin King, by author, September 2, 1996

Pamphlets

A Short History of Greenville. Greenville, Miss.: Chamber of Commerce, n.d.

Billings, Peggy. *Segregation in the Methodist Church*. Cincinnati: Board of Missions—The Methodist Church, 1967.

Hayden, Tom. *Revolution in Mississippi*. N.p., n.d.

Johns, R. Elizabeth. *Refinement by Fire*. N.p., n.d.

Myer, Joe. *The Sabotage of Freedom Village*. Foreword by Clay L. Cochran. Studies in Bad Housing in America, 3. Washington, D.C.: Rural Housing Alliance, 1974.

The National Council of Churches' Commission on Religion and Race. N.p., n.d.

The National Council of Churches of Christ in the U.S.A.: What It Is, What It Does. New York:

Department of Publication Services for the Office of Communication, National Council of Churches, n.d.

Spike, Robert W. *Civil Rights Involvement: Model for Mission.* Detroit: Detroit Industrial Mission, 1965.

U.S. Government Documents

Alewine, Ralph W., Jr. "The Changing Characteristics of the Mississippi Delta." In U.S. Department of Labor, Manpower Administration, "Farm Labor Developments," May 1968, mimeo, 29–40.

U.S. Commission on Civil Rights. *Justice in Jackson, Mississippi: Hearings Held in Jackson, Miss., February 16–20, 1965.* Vol 2. New York: Arno Press and the *New York Times,* 1971.

———. *School Desegregation in Greenville, Mississippi.* Washington, D.C.: U.S. Government Printing Office, 1977.

U.S. Congress, Senate, Subcommittee on Employment, Manpower, and Poverty of the Committee on Labor and Public Welfare. *Examination of the War on Poverty,* pt. 2: *Jackson, Mississippi,* 90th Cong., 1st sess., April 10, 1967.

———. *Examination of the War on Poverty: First Session on Hunger and Malnutrition in America.* 90th Cong., 1st sess., July 11–12, 1967.

Miscellaneous

Robert L. Beech Papers, in possession of Beech, Bovey, Minnesota.

King, Edwin. "Mississippi: The White Church and Social Crisis." Unpublished manuscript in possession of the author.

———. "Religious Observations." Unpublished manuscript in possession of the author.

Leesha Faulkner Civil Rights Collection, in possession of the author.

Magazines, Newsletters, Newspapers

American Baptist News Service, December 23, 1969
Atlanta Journal and Constitution, August 1, 1965
Chicago Daily News, July 28, 1965
Christian Science Monitor, April 30, 1966
Clarksdale (Mississippi) Press Register, August 8, 1963
Commission on Religion and Race Reports [National Council of Churches], 1964–65
Deer Creek (Mississippi) Pilot, June 26, 1964
Delta (Mississippi) Democrat-Times, 1964–71, 1973
Delta Ministry, November 1964–January 1966
Delta Ministry Reports, February 1966–March 1977; published sporadically
The DRC Mississippi Newsletter, December 1985
Episcopal Society for Cultural and Racial Unity Newsletter, 1964–65
Hattiesburg (Mississippi) American, 1964–66
HEW News, March 10, 1970
Holyoke (Massachusetts) Transcript-Telegram, July 7, 1964

Information Bulletin [Mississippi Association of Methodist Ministers and Laymen], 1964

Information Service [National Council of Churches], June 1964

Jackson (Mississippi) Advocate, July 18, 1970

Jackson (Mississippi) Clarion-Ledger, 1963–67, 1971, 1973, 1980–82, 1984, 1988–93

Jackson (Mississippi) Daily News, 1965–67

Jackson (Mississippi) Northside Reporter, June 25, 1970

Lexington (Mississippi) Advertiser, November 26, 1964, January 21, 1965, May 6, June 23, 30, 1966, August 22, 29, 1968

Los Angeles Times, March 5, 1967

McComb (Mississippi) Enterprise Journal, August 10, 30, September 8, 1965, December 12, 1984

Memphis Commercial Appeal, 1964–73, 1979, 1983, 1986

Methodists Make News, October 7, 1966

Michigan Christian Advocate, October 27, 1966

Milwaukee Journal, August 3, 1964

Mississippi Free Press, January 18, 1964

Mississippi Freedom Democratic Party Newsletter, April 4, 1965, October 1, 1967

National Guardian, June 12, 1965, March 5, 1966

National Observer, December 26, 1966

New Orleans Times-Picayune, April 11, 1967

New York Herald Tribune, September 26, 1964, June 6, August 22, September 12, 1965

New York Society of Clinical Psychologists, Inc., Newsletter, winter 1965

New York Times, 1963–67, 1971–72

PARR [United Presbyterian Synod of Pennsylvania], November 20, 1964

Providence (Rhode Island) Journal, August 31, 1966

Religion and Race Memo [United Presbyterian Church in the United States of America], April 27, October 5, 1964

I. F. Stone's Weekly, October 5, 1964

Sunday Herald Tribune, March 28, 1965

Wall Street Journal, October 2, 1984

Washington Post, February 1, October 2, 1966, July 9, 1967, June 21, 1969, July 18, 1972

Books

Abbott, Dorothy, ed. *Mississippi Writers: Reflections of Childhood and Youth.* Vol. 2, *Nonfiction.* Jackson and London: University Press of Mississippi, 1986.

Ahmann, Mathew, ed. *Race: Challenge to Religion.* Chicago: Regnery, 1963.

Carmichael, Stokely, and Charles V. Hamilton. *Black Power: The Politics of Liberation in America.* New York: Vintage, 1967.

Carson, Clayborne, ed. *The Student Voice, 1960–1965: Periodical of the Student Nonviolent Coordinating Committee.* Westport, Conn., and London: Meckler, 1990.

Carter, Hodding, [II]. *So the Heffners Left McComb.* Garden City, N.Y.: Doubleday, 1965.

Coles, Robert. *Farewell to the South.* Boston and Toronto: Little, Brown, 1972.

Cox, Harvey. *The Secular City: Secularization and Urbanization in Theological Perspective.* New York: Macmillan, 1965.

Cunningham, W. J. *Agony at Galloway: One Church's Struggle with Social Change.* Jackson: University Press of Mississippi, 1980.

Dent, Tom. *Southern Journey: A Return to the Civil Rights Movement.* New York: William Morrow, 1997.

Dorsey, L. C. *Freedom Came to Mississippi.* New York: Field Foundation, 1977.

Dunbar, Tony. *Our Land Too.* Introduction by Robert Coles. New York: Pantheon, 1971.

Emmerich, J. Oliver. *Two Faces of Janus: The Saga of Deep South Change.* Jackson: University and College Press of Mississippi, 1973.

Evers, Charles, and Andrew Szanton. *Have No Fear: The Charles Evers Story.* New York: Wiley, 1997.

Fager, Charles. *Uncertain Resurrection: The Poor People's Washington Campaign.* Grand Rapids, Mich.: Eerdmans, 1969.

Forman, James. *The Making of Black Revolutionaries.* 1972; Seattle: Open Hand, 1985.

Gallup, George H. *The Gallup Poll: Public Opinion, 1935–1971.* Vol. 3, *1959–1971.* New York: Random House, 1972.

Greenberg, Polly. *The Devil Has Slippery Shoes: A Biased Biography of the Child Development Group of Mississippi.* 1969; Washington, D.C.: Youth Policy Institute, 1990.

Hedgeman, Anna Arnold. *The Trumpet Sounds: A Memoir of Negro Leadership.* New York: Holt, Rinehart, and Winston, 1964.

Henry, Aaron, with Constance Curry. *Aaron Henry: The Fire Ever Burning.* Introduction by John Dittmer. Jackson: University Press of Mississippi, 2000.

Hilton, Bruce. *The Delta Ministry.* London: Macmillan, 1969.

Holt, Len. *The Summer That Didn't End: The Story of the Mississippi Civil Rights Project of 1964.* New preface by Julian Bond. New York: Da Capo, 1992.

Howell, Leon. *Freedom City: The Substance of Things Hoped For.* Richmond, Va.: John Knox, 1969.

Johnston, Erle. *Mississippi's Defiant Years, 1953–1973: An Interpretive Documentary with Personal Experiences.* Foreword by William F. Winter. Forest, Miss.: Lake Harbor, 1990.

Keady, William C. *All Rise: Memoirs of a Mississippi Federal Judge.* Boston: Recollections Bound, 1988.

King, Martin Luther, Jr. *Why We Can't Wait.* New York: Mentor, 1964.

Kotz, Nick. *Let Them Eat Promises: The Politics of Hunger in America.* Introduction by George S. McGovern. Englewood Cliffs, N.J.: Prentice-Hall, 1969.

Lord, Walter. *The Past That Would Not Die.* London: Hamish Hamilton, 1966.

Moore, Paul, Jr. *Take a Bishop Like Me.* New York: Harper and Row, 1979.

———. *Presences: A Bishop's Life in the City.* New York: Farrar, Strauss, and Giroux, 1997.

Silver, James W. *Mississippi: The Closed Society.* New York: Harcourt, Brace, and World, 1964.

Spike, Paul. *Photographs of My Father.* New York: Knopf, 1973.

Spike, Robert W. *The Freedom Revolution and the Churches.* New York: Association Press, 1965.

Warren, Robert Penn. *Who Speaks for the Negro?* New York: Random House, 1965.

Wieser, Thomas, ed. *Planning for Mission: Working Papers on the Quest for Missionary Communities.* New York: U.S. Conference for the World Council of Churches, 1966.

Williams, Colin W. *Where in the World?* New York: Friendship Press, 1963.

———. *What in the World?* New York: Friendship Press, 1963.

Wilmore, Gayraud S. *Black and Presbyterian: The Heritage and the Hope.* Philadelphia: Geneva Press, 1983.

Zinn, Howard. *SNCC: The New Abolitionists.* 2d ed. Boston: Beacon Press, 1965.

Articles

"About That Candy." *Christian Century* 84 (April 12, 1967): 461.

"Act Two in the Mississippi Power Play." *Presbyterian Life* 17 (May 15, 1964): 36.

Alexander, Michael. "Fishy Business." *Southern Exposure* 14 (September–December 1986): 32–34.

"An Appeal to the Conscience of the American People." *Christian Century* 80 (January 30, 1963): 135.

"Anti-Poverty Funds Sought to Assist Delta." *Interchurch News* 7 (October 1965): 1.

Bagby, Grover C. "Race Relations and Our Concern." *Methodist Story,* January 1965, pp. 3–5.

Barnes, Thelma. "Money Changes Faces in the Delta." *Church Woman,* August–September 1968, pp. 29, 31.

Bates, Eric. "The Kill Line." *Southern Exposure* 19 (fall 1991): 23–29.

———. "Parting the Waters." *Southern Exposure* 19 (fall 1991): 34–36.

———. "Something as One." *Southern Exposure* 19 (fall 1991): 30–33.

"Bishop and Cabinet Oppose Grant to Delta Ministry." *Mississippi Methodist Advocate,* October 5, 1966, pp. 1, 8.

"Bishop's Annual Thanksgiving Offering to Be for Delta Ministry Mount Beulah Project." *Together* 11 (December 1967): A4–A5.

"Black Manifesto's Birthday: Frosting on the Cake?" *Christianity Today* 14 (May 22, 1970): 37.

Blanchard, Eric D. "The Delta Ministry." *Christian Century* 82 (March 17, 1965): 337–38.

Boyd, Malcolm. "The Battle of McComb." *Christian Century* 81 (November 11, 1964): 1398, 1400, 1402, 1404.

Brenner, Joseph, Robert Coles, Alan Mermann, Milton J. E. Senn, Cyril Walwyn, and Raymond Wheeler. "Children in Mississippi." In Southern Regional Council, *Hungry Children,* 1–27. Atlanta: Southern Regional Council, 1967.

"Candidates." *Mississippi Newsletter* [Freedom Information Service] 30 (September 15, 1967): 1.

Carlson, Paul R. "Presbyterian Ministers to Appeal Sentence in Hattiesburg." *Presbyterian Life* 17 (March 1, 1964): 27–28.

———. "Hattiesburg: Trial and Debate." *Presbyterian Life* 17 (April 1, 1964): 26.

Carter, Hodding [II]. "Our Town Is Conservative." *Virginia Quarterly Review* 41 (spring 1965): 202–6.

Carter, Hodding, III. "The Negro Exodus from the Delta Continues." *New York Times Magazine,* March 10, 1968, pp. 26, 117–21.

Chauncey, George A. "Should We Support the Delta Ministry?" *Presbyterian Survey* 57 (June 1967): 23–24.

"The Church Consecrates 11 New Bishops." *Christian Advocate* 8 (July 30, 1964): 3.

"Civil Rights: Conflict but Encouragement." *Presbyterian Life* 17 (August 1, 1964): 20–21.

"Clark Seated—No Challenge Made." *Mississippi Newsletter* [Freedom Information Service] 42 (January 5, 1968): 1, 6.

Cox, Harvey. "*The Secular City* 25 Years Later." *Christian Century* 107 (November 7, 1990): 1025–29.

Current, Gloster B. "Death in Mississippi." *Crisis* 73 (February 1966): 103–9, 125.

Davis, Foster. "The Delta: Rich Land and Poor People." *Reporter* 34 (March 24, 1966): 41–43.

Day, A. Garnett, Jr. " 'Justice Place' in the Delta." *World Call*, February 1966, pp. 25–27.

"Delta Agency Buys 400 Acres to Aid Negro Home-Building." *Religious News Service*, April 12, 1966, pp. 17.

"Delta Ministry after Ten Years Finds Oppression Garbed in New Clothes." *Episcopal New Yorker*, June 1974, p. 4.

"Delta Ministry Restructured." *Race Relations Reporter* 2 (June 21, 1971): 2–3.

"Delta Ministry's Tenth Year." *Christian Century* 91 (July 3–10, 1974): 694.

"Delta Opportunities: Job Training." *Mississippi Newsletter* [Freedom Information Service] 48 (February 16, 1968): 1.

DeMuth, Jerry. "Summer in Mississippi: Freedom Moves in to Stay." *Nation* 199 (September 14, 1964): 104–5, 108–10.

"Divided Flocks in Jackson." *Christian Century* 80 (November 27, 1963): 1469–70.

"Divisions of Board of Missions Allocate $130,000 to Delta Ministry." *Central Christian Advocate* 141 (December 1, 1966): 5–6.

"DOC Prescribes Poverty Cure." *Rural Opportunities* 4 (May 1969): 3, 8.

Dukes, Lucille. "Marion County News." *Mississippi Newsletter* [Freedom Information Service] 30 (September 15, 1967): 2.

"The Episcopal Church and the National Council of Churches." *Church News: Episcopal Diocese of Mississippi*, June 1964, pp. 5–6.

Feagans, Janet. "Voting, Violence, and Walkout in McComb." *New South* 16 (October 1961): 3–4, 11.

Fey, Harold E. "Freedom Rides at N.C.C." *Christian Century* 78 (June 21, 1961): 766–67.

Garland, Phyl. "A Taste of Triumph for Black Mississippi." *Ebony* 23 (February 1968): 25–28, 30, 32.

Geiger, Jack. "Health Center in Mississippi." *Hospital Practice* 4 (February 1969): 68–71, 75–77, 81.

Geiger, Sue. "How Freedom City Overcame." *World Outlook* 58 (February 1968): 32–34.

Gittings, James A. "Clergymen Demonstrate in Hattiesburg, Mississippi." *Presbyterian Life* 17 (February 15, 1964): 30–33.

Gort, Solomon, Jr. "The Negro Church in Mississippi: Its Potential and Dynamic in View of Social Change." *Risk* 4 (1968): 45–53.

Guyot, Lawrence, and Mike Thelwell. "Toward Independent Political Power." *Freedomways* 6 (summer 1966): 246–54.

Hall, Richard. "A Stir of Hope in Mound Bayou." *Life* 66 (March 28, 1969): 67–70, 73, 76–78, 81.

Harbison, Janet. "Oh, Freedom." *Presbyterian Life* 17 (December 1, 1964): 24–26.

Haselden, Kyle. "Religion and Race." *Christian Century* 80 (January 30, 1963): 133–35.

"HEP Candidates." *DOC News* 1 (March 29, 1968): 1.

Herbers, John. "The Churches and Race in Mississippi." *Concern* 6 (February 1, 1964): 11, 14.

Hilton, Bruce. "The Delta Ministry." *Church and Home* 3 (February 1, 1966): 4–8.

———. "Pioneering in World of the Delta." *Methodist Woman* 27 (September 1966): 10–12.

———. "It Shows the Church Cares." *Together* 11 (January 1967): 53–55.

———. "Whatever Happened to the Delta Ministry?" *Tempo*, May 15, 1969, p. 3.

Howell, Leon. "Freedom City: Mississippi's New Community." *Christianity and Crisis* 26 (October 17, 1966): 226–28.

Jacobs, William J. "More Notebook on Our Own Congo." *Ave Maria* 101 (January 30, 1965): 5–9.

Jacobs, William J., and Malcolm Boyd. "Christian Witness to Christian Failure." *Ave Maria* 101 (January 16, 1965): 1, 3–6.

"James Forman's Black Manifesto." *America* 120 (May 24, 1969): 605.

James, Andrew. "Tufts-Delta Administers Environmental Treatment." *Journal of Environmental Health* 31 (March–April 1969): 437–45.

Kirstein, John A. "What the NCC Is and Does." *Presbyterian Survey* 54 (December 1964): 41–42.

Kremer, Barbara G. "Good News in Mississippi." *Episcopalian* 129 (September 1964): 42–47.
———. "Mississippi Revisited." *Episcopalian* 130 (December 1965): 24–26, 41–42.

Lawrence, Roy. "On Being Consistent." *Mississippi Methodist Advocate*, October 12, 1966, p. 2.

"Life in the Delta Ministry." *WRFD Commentator*, March 18, 1966, pp. 7–8.

"Magnolia: Mississippi Denies Clerics Common Courtesy." *Churchman*, November 1964, p. 18.

Maloney, William F. "The Tufts Comprehensive Community Health Action Program." *Journal of the American Medical Association* 202 (October 30, 1967): 109–12.

McCanna, Henry A. "A Ministry of Deliverance." *Mission*, January 1969, p. 39.

McCarthy, Colman. "Hunger Runs a Co-op." *Communities in Action* 5 (February 1969): 8–11.

McEachran, Angus. "Freedom City, Mississippi." *Ave Maria* 105 (April 22, 1967): 10–15.

Medelman, Judy. "Mission to Mississippi." *Twin Citian* 7 (March 1965): 16–18.

"Methodist Mission Board Considers Delta Ministry." *News from the Board of Missions of the Methodist Church*, May 3, 1966, n.p.

Millsaps, Betty. "Putting the System to Work." *NAM Reports* 19 (July 29, 1974): 9–11.

Minear, Lawrence. "Hattiesburg: Toward Reconciliation." *Christian Century* 81 (September 9, 1964): 1115–16.

"Ministers in McComb." *Presbyterian Life* 17 (November 1, 1964): 32.

Minnis, Jack. "The Mississippi Freedom Democratic Party: A New Declaration of Independence." *Freedomways* 5 (spring 1965): 264–78.

Minor, Bill. "Congressman Espy from Mississippi." *Southern Changes* 8 (December 1986): 1–3.

Minor, W. F. "Mississippi Schools in Crisis." *New South* 25 (winter 1970): 31–36.

"Mission Divisions: No Delta Ministry Action." *Christian Advocate* 10 (May 19, 1966): 23.

"Mississippi Methodism Turns a Corner." *Together* 9 (April 1965): 3–4, 6, 9–10.

"Mississippi Plantation Strikers Backed by Delta Ministry." *Witness* 50 (June 24, 1965): 6.

"Mississippians United—$5,000." *Mississippi Newsletter* [Freedom Information Service] 30 (September 15, 1967): 1.

Moore, Joanna. "Hattiesburg and Central Illinois." *Christian Century* 81 (March 11, 1964): 340–41.

Morgan, D. LaVonne. "G.E.D. Candidates Successful." *DOC News* 1 (June 26, 1968): 1.

Moses, Bob. "Mississippi: 1961–1962." *Liberation* 14 (January 1970): 6–17.

Murray, Geoffrey. "World Council." *Christian Century* 85 (July 3, 1968): 880.

"National Council Board Speaks Out on Major Issues." *United Church Herald* 7 (August 1, 1964): 3.

"NCC General Board Debates Delta, Vietnam." *World Outlook* 56 (August 1966): 46.

Nevin, David. "Struggle That Changed Glen Allan." *Life* 63 (September 29, 1967): 108, 110, 112.

"Nothin' to Lose." *Newsweek* 65 (June 21, 1965): 33, 36.

Odle, Joe T. "Southern Baptists and the National Council of Churches." *Baptist Record* 85 (June 25, 1964): 1, 4.

"Old Wounds Reopened." *America* 112 (February 20, 1965): 239.

Oniki, S. Garry. "How Then Can We Witness?" *Social Action* 31 (November 1964): 35–38.

"Opening Doors to Opportunity." *Nation's Business,* April 1970, pp. 48–49, 52, 54.

"Panel Urges Support of Delta Ministry." *Presbyterian Journal* 25 (February 8, 1967): 4–5.

"The Passing Scene." *Christian Century* 83 (December 14, 1966): 1530.

Pendergrass, Edward J. "The Bishop's Column." *Mississippi Methodist Advocate,* February 23, 1966, p. 2.

————. "Progress in Mississippi." *Classmate* 73 (June 1966): 7.

Peters, Sandra. "32 Years to Justice." Available at http://gbgm-umc.org/Response/articles/dahmer.html [consulted June 28, 2001].

Pierce, Ponchitta. "The Mission of Marian Wright." *Ebony* 21 (June 1966): 94–97, 100, 102–4, 106–8.

"Reconciliation through Anger." *Time* 86 (July 2, 1965): 70–71.

Rogers, Nat S. "Keynote Address for Meeting of Mississippi Methodist Action Crusade, 'Are Ye Able.'" *Mississippi Methodist Advocate,* September 15, 1965, pp. 1–2.

"The Role of the National Council of Churches in the Mississippi Summer Project." *Social Action* 31 (November 1964): 10–14.

Rose, Stephen C. "NCC Visit to Clarksdale Poses Hard Questions." *Presbyterian Life* 16 (September 1, 1963): 28–29.

————. "N.C.C. Visits Clarksdale." *Christian Century* 80 (September 11, 1963): 1104–6.

Rowland, Stanley J., Jr. "Tough Mission in Mississippi." *Presbyterian Life* 9 (November 15, 1966): 24–25.

Rowland, Wilmina. "How It Is in Mississippi." *Christian Century* 82 (March 17, 1965): 340, 342.

"S.E. Jurisdictional Conference." *Mississippi Methodist Advocate* 17 (July 29, 1964): 1.

Salamon, Lester. "Mississippi Post-Mortem: The 1971 Elections." *New South* 27 (winter 1972): 43–47.

"Shame: Whites' Responsibility for Order Asked by Group." *Churchman,* November 1964, p. 14.

Schulz, Larold K. "The Delta Ministry." *Social Action* 31 (November 1964): 30–35.

Schweid, Richard. "Down on the Farm." *Southern Exposure* 19 (fall 1991): 15–21.

Smith, Bardwell L. "Meanwhile in Mississippi." *Commonweal* 82 (April 2, 1965): 39–42.

Spike, Robert W. "Gospel, World, and Church." *Theology Today* 22 (July 1965): 163–72.

"SSOC Sponsors Christmas Project in Mississippi." *Newsletter: Southern Student Organizing Committee* 2 (January 1965): 2.

Stevens, Francis B. "A Sign of Change in Mississippi Methodism." *Concern* 7 (September 1, 1965): 8–9, 14.

Street, T. Watson. "The Mississippi Delta Project." *Presbyterian Outlook* 146 (June 29, 1964): 7.

"Strike." *The Drummer* 1 (Christmas 1971): 9.

"Study Committee, National Council of Churches, Mississippi Annual Conference." *Mississippi Methodist Advocate*, September 19, 1964, p. 2.

Sutherland, Elizabeth. "The Cat and Mouse Game." *Nation* 199 (September 14, 1964): 105–8.

———. "Mississippi Summer of Discontent." *Nation* 201 (October 11, 1965): 212–15.

Taft, Adon. "Racial Birth Pangs for United Methodists." *Christianity Today* 12 (May 10, 1968): 34.

Trillin, Calvin. "State Secrets." *New Yorker*, May 29, 1995, pp. 54–64.

"Two Divisions of Board of Missions Allocate $130,000 to Delta Ministry." *Louisiana Methodist*, October 13, 1966, p. 14.

Ullman, Victor. "In Darkest America." *Nation* 205 (September 4, 1967): 177–80.

"W.C.C. Sends Mission to Mississippi Delta." *Christian Century* 81 (May 20, 1964): 660.

"'We Need More Doctors': Official in All Black Town." *Jet* 43 (February 15, 1973): 30–31.

"What the Delta Ministry Is." *Classmate* 73 (June 1966): 23.

White, Willmon L. "Delta Ministry Is Greatest, BUT. . . ." *Christian Advocate* 10 (June 30, 1966): 24.

Wiles, V. McKinley. "Medical Mission to Mississippi." *Freedomways* 5 (spring 1965): 314–17.

Wilson, Leland. "The Delta Ministry: Reconciliation through Anger?" *Messenger* [Church of the Brethren], October 14, 1965, pp. 16–19.

Wren, Christopher S. "An 'Insider' Stays to Fight." *Look*, September 8, 1964, pp. 27–28.

Wright, Marion, Henry Aronson, and John Mudd, "Proposed: A Kibbutz in Mississippi." *New South* 21 (winter 1966): 42–46.

"YES, America, There Are HUNGRY PEOPLE in Miss." *Mississippi Newsletter* [Freedom Information Service] 8 (April 14, 1967): 1.

Zinn, Howard. "Incident in Hattiesburg." *Nation* 198 (May 18, 1964): 501–4.

SECONDARY SOURCES

Books

Aiken, Charles S. *The Cotton Plantation South since the Civil War*. Baltimore and London: Johns Hopkins University Press, 1998.

Baker, James T. *Brooks Hays*. Macon, Ga.: Mercer University Press, 1989.

Bass, Jack. *Unlikely Heroes*. 1981; Tuscaloosa and London: University of Alabama Press, 1990.

Bass, Jack, and Walter DeVries, *The Transformation of Southern Politics: Social Change and Political Consequence since 1945*. New York: Basic Books, 1976.

Brackenridge, R. Douglas. *Eugene Carson Blake: Prophet with Portfolio*. New York: Seabury, 1978.

Branch, Taylor. *Parting the Waters: America in the King Years, 1954–63*. New York: Simon and Schuster, 1988.

———. *Pillar of Fire: America in the King Years, 1963–65*. New York: Simon and Schuster, 1998.

Burner, Eric R. *And Gently He Shall Lead Them: Robert Parris Moses and Civil Rights in Mississippi*. New York and London: New York University Press, 1994.

Cagin, Seth, and Philip Dray, *We Are Not Afraid: The Story of Goodman, Schwerner, and Chaney and the Civil Rights Campaign for Mississippi*. New York: Macmillan, 1988.

Campbell, Will D. *Providence*. Atlanta: Longstreet Press, 1992.

Carson, Clayborne. *In Struggle: SNCC and the Black Awakening of the 1960s*. Cambridge and London: Harvard University Press, 1981.

Chafe, William H. *Civilities and Civil Rights: Greensboro, North Carolina, and the Black Struggle for Freedom*. New York: Oxford University Press, 1980.

Cobb, James C. *The Most Southern Place on Earth: The Mississippi Delta and the Roots of Regional Identity*. New York and Oxford: Oxford University Press, 1992.

Cook, Robert. *Sweet Land of Liberty? The African-American Struggle for Civil Rights in the Twentieth Century*. London and New York: Longman, 1998.

Couto, Richard A. *Ain't Gonna Let Nobody Turn Me Round: The Pursuit of Racial Justice in the Rural South*. Philadelphia: Temple University Press, 1991.

Davis, Martha F. *Brutal Need: Lawyers and the Welfare Rights Movement, 1960–1973*. New Haven and London: Yale University Press, 1993.

Dittmer, John. *Local People: The Struggle for Civil Rights in Mississippi*. Urbana and Chicago: University of Illinois Press, 1994.

Fairclough, Adam. *To Redeem the Soul of America: The Southern Christian Leadership Conference and Martin Luther King, Jr.* Athens and London: University of Georgia Press, 1987.

Findlay, James F., Jr. *Church People in the Struggle: The National Council of Churches and the Black Freedom Movement, 1950–1970*. New York and Oxford: Oxford University Press, 1993.

Free at Last: A History of the Civil Rights Movement and Those Who Died in the Struggle. Montgomery, Ala.: Civil Rights Education Project, Southern Poverty Law Center, n.d.

Garrow, David J. *Protest at Selma: Martin Luther King Jr. and the Voting Rights Act of 1965*. New Haven and London: Yale University Press, 1978.

———. *Bearing the Cross: Martin Luther King, Jr., and the Southern Christian Leadership Conference*. New York: Morrow, 1986.

Glen, John M. *Highlander: No Ordinary School*. 2d ed. Knoxville: University of Tennessee Press, 1996.

Graham, John H. *Mississippi Circuit Riders, 1865–1965*. Nashville: Parthenon, 1967.

Haggerty, Donald L., and Alan Thomson, eds. *National Council of the Churches of Christ in the United States of America: A Guide to the NCC Archives, 1950–1972*. Philadelphia: Presbyterian Historical Society, 1984.

Hermann, Janet Sharp. *The Pursuit of a Dream*. New York and Oxford: Oxford University Press, 1981.

Isserman, Maurice, and Michael Kazin. *America Divided: The Civil War of the 1960s*. New York and Oxford: Oxford University Press, 2000.

Katagiri, Yasuhiro. *The Mississippi State Sovereignty Commission: Civil Rights and States' Rights*. Jackson: University Press of Mississippi, 2001.

K'Meyer, Tracy Elaine. *Interracialism and Christian Community in the Postwar South: The Story of Koinonia Farm*. Charlottesville and London: University Press of Virginia, 1997.

Lamis, Alexander P. *The Two-Party South*. 2d exp. ed. New York and Oxford: Oxford University Press, 1990.

Lawson, Steven F. *Black Ballots: Voting Rights in the South, 1944–1969*. New York: Columbia University Press, 1976.

————. *In Pursuit of Power: Southern Blacks and Electoral Politics, 1965–1982.* New York: Columbia University Press, 1985.

————. *Running for Freedom: Civil Rights and Black Politics in America since 1941.* 2d ed. New York: McGraw-Hill, 1997.

Lee, Chana Kai. *For Freedom's Sake: The Life of Fannie Lou Hamer.* Urbana and Chicago: University of Illinois Press, 1999.

Lemann, Nicholas. *The Promised Land: The Great Black Migration and How It Changed America.* New York: Vintage, 1992.

Marable, Manning. *Race, Reform, and Rebellion: The Second Reconstruction in Black America, 1945–1990.* 2d ed. Basingstoke: Macmillan, 1991.

Marsh, Charles. *God's Long Summer: Stories of Faith and Civil Rights.* Princeton: Princeton University Press, 1997.

Meier, August, and Elliott Rudwick. *CORE: A Study in the Civil Rights Movement, 1942–1968.* 1973; Urbana and Chicago: University of Illinois Press, 1975.

Mills, Kay. *This Little Light of Mine: The Life of Fannie Lou Hamer.* New York: Plume, 1993.

Mills, Nicolaus. *Like a Holy Crusade: Mississippi 1964—The Turning of the Civil Rights Movement in America.* Chicago: Elephant, 1993.

Morrison, Minion K. C. *Black Political Mobilization: Leadership, Power, and Mass Behavior.* Albany: State University of New York Press, 1987.

Orfield, Gary. *Public School Desegregation in the United States, 1968–1980.* Washington, D.C.: Joint Center for Political Studies, 1983.

Parker, Frank R. *Black Votes Count: Political Empowerment in Mississippi after 1965.* Foreword by Eddie N. Williams. Chapel Hill and London: University of North Carolina Press, 1990.

Payne, Charles M. *I've Got the Light of Freedom: The Organizing Tradition and the Mississippi Freedom Struggle.* Berkeley, Los Angeles, and London: University of California Press, 1995.

Peirce, Neal R. *The Deep South States of America: People, Politics, and Power in the Seven Deep South States.* New York: Norton, 1974.

Pratt, Henry J. *The Liberalization of American Protestantism: A Case Study in Complex Organizations.* Detroit: Wayne State University Press, 1972.

Riches, William T. Martin. *The Civil Rights Movement: Struggle and Resistance.* Basingstoke: Macmillan, 1997.

Sardell, Alice. *The U.S. Experiment in Social Medicine: The Community Health Center Program, 1965–1986.* Pittsburgh: University of Pittsburgh Press, 1988.

Schlesinger, Arthur M., Jr. *Robert Kennedy and His Times.* 1978; New York: Ballantine Books, 1979.

Schulman, Bruce J. *From Cotton Belt to Sunbelt: Federal Policy, Economic Development, and the Transformation of the South, 1938–1980.* New York and Oxford: Oxford University Press, 1991.

Schweid, Richard. *Catfish and the Delta: Confederate Fish Farming in the Mississippi Delta.* Berkeley, Calif.: Ten Speed, 1992.

Shattuck, Gardiner H., Jr. *Episcopalians and Race: Civil War to Civil Rights.* Lexington: University Press of Kentucky, 2000.

Sumner, David E. *The Episcopal Church's History, 1945–1985.* Wilton, Conn.: Morehouse-Barlow, 1987.

Waldron, Ann. *Hodding Carter: The Reconstruction of a Racist.* Chapel Hill, N.C.: Algonquin, 1993.

Walton, Hanes, Jr. *Black Political Parties: An Historical and Political Analysis.* New York: Free Press, 1972.

Wilmore, Gayraud S. *Black Religion and Black Radicalism: An Interpretation of the Religious History of African Americans.* 3d rev. ed. Maryknoll, N.Y.: Orbis, 1998.

Articles

Alt, James E. "The Impact of the Voting Rights Act on Black and White Voter Registration in the South." In *Quiet Revolution in the South: The Impact of the Voting Rights Act, 1965–1990,* edited by Chandler Davidson and Bernard Grofman, 351–77. Princeton: Princeton University Press, 1994.

Alvis, Joel L., Jr. "Racial Turmoil and Religious Reaction: The Rt. Rev. John M. Allin." *Historical Magazine of the Protestant Episcopal Church* 50 (March 1981): 83–96.

Bolton, Charles C. "The Last Stand of Massive Resistance: Mississippi Public School Integration, 1970." *Journal of Mississippi History* 61 (winter 1999): 329–50.

Chancey, Andrew S. " 'A Demonstration Plot for the Kingdom of God': The Establishment and Early Years of Koinonia Farm." *Georgia Historical Quarterly* 75 (summer 1981): 321–53.

Clark, Henry. "The National Council of Churches' Commission on Religion and Race: A Case Study of Religion and Social Change." In *American Mosaic: Social Patterns of Religion in the United States,* edited by Phillip E. Hammond and Benton Johnson, 255–65. New York: Random House, 1970.

Colby, David C. "Black Power, White Resistance, and Public Policy: Political Power and Poverty Program Grants in Mississippi." *Journal of Politics* 47 (June 1985): 579–95.

———. "The Voting Rights Act and Black Registration in Mississippi." *Publius: The Journal of Federalism* 16 (fall 1986): 123–37.

Crawford, Vicki Lynn. "Grassroots Activism in the Mississippi Civil Rights Movement." *Sage* 5 (fall 1988): 24–29.

Davies, David R. "J. Oliver Emmerich and the McComb *Enterprise-Journal:* Slow Change in McComb, 1964." *Journal of Mississippi History* 57 (February 1995): 1–23.

Davis, Theodore J., Jr. "Blacks' Political Representation in Rural Mississippi." In *Blacks in Southern Politics,* edited by Laurence W. Moreland, Robert P. Steed, and Tod A. Baker, 149–59. New York; Westport, Conn.; and London: Praeger, 1987.

Draper, Alan. "The Mississippi Movement: A Review Essay." *Journal of Mississippi History* 60 (winter 1998): 355–66.

Fortenberry, Charles N., and F. Glenn Abney. "Mississippi Unreconstructed and Unredeemed." In *The Changing Politics of the South,* edited by William C. Havard, 472–524. Baton Rouge: Louisiana State University Press, 1972.

Foster, E. C. "A Time of Challenge: Afro-Mississippi Political Developments since 1965." *Journal of Negro History* 68 (spring 1983): 185–200.

Freeman, Roland L. "Mule Train: A Thirty-Year Perspective on the Southern Christian Leadership Conference's Poor People's Campaign of 1968." *Southern Cultures* 4 (spring 1998): 91–118.

Fruchter, Norm. "Mississippi: Notes on SNCC." *Studies on the Left,* winter 1965, 74–80.

Grim, Valerie. "The Politics of Inclusion: Black Farmers and the Quest for Agribusiness Participation, 1945–1990s." *Agricultural History* 69 (spring 1995): 257–71.

Kernell, Sam. "Comment: A Re-Evaluation of Black Voting in Mississippi." *American Political Science Review* 67 (1973): 1307–18.

Ladner, Joyce. "What Black Power Means to Negroes in Mississippi." In *The Transformation of Activism,* edited by August Meier, 131–54. Chicago: Aldine, 1970.

Lewis, Earl M. "The Negro Voter in Mississippi." *Journal of Negro Education* 26 (summer 1957): 329–50.

Loewen, James W. "Continuing Obstacles to Black Electoral Success in Mississippi." *Civil Rights Research Review* 9 (fall–winter 1981): 24–38.

Lowry, Mark, II. "Schools in Transition." *Annals of the Association of American Geographers* 63 (June 1973): 167–80.

Munford, Luther. "White Flight from Desegregation in Mississippi." *Integrated Education: Minority Children in Schools* 11 (May–June 1973): 12–26.

Orey, Byron D'Andra. "Black Legislative Politics in Mississippi." *Journal of Black Studies* 30 (July 2000): 791–814.

Parker, Frank R. "Protest, Politics, and Litigation: Political and Social Change in Mississippi, 1965 to Present." *Mississippi Law Journal* 57 (1987): 677–704.

Perlstein, Daniel. "Teaching Freedom: SNCC and the Creation of the Mississippi Freedom Schools." *History of Education Quarterly* 30 (fall 1990): 297–324.

Rhodes, Carroll. "Enforcing the Voting Rights Act in Mississippi through Litigation." *Mississippi Law Journal* 57 (August 1987): 705–37.

Rose, Harold M. "The All-Negro Town: Its Evolution and Function." *Geographical Review* 55 (July 1965): 362–81.

Salamon, Lester M. "Leadership and Modernization: The Emerging Black Political Elite in the American South." *Journal of Politics* 35 (August 1973): 615–46.

———. "The Time Dimension in Policy Evaluation: The Case Study of the New Deal Land-Reform Experiments." *Public Policy* 27 (spring 1979): 129–83.

Salamon, Lester M., and Stephen Van Evera. "Fear, Apathy, and Discrimination: A Test of Three Explanations of Political Participation." *American Political Science Review* 67 (1973): 1288–1306.

Silk, Mark. "The Rise of the 'New Evangelicalism': Shock and Adjustment." In *Between the Times: The Travail of the Protestant Establishment in America, 1900–1960,* edited by William R. Hutchison, 278–99. Cambridge: Cambridge University Press, 1989.

Simpson, William. "The Birth of the Mississippi 'Loyalist Democrats' (1965–1968)." *Journal of Mississippi History* 44 (February 1982): 27–45.

Sinsheimer, Joseph A. "The Freedom Vote of 1963: New Strategies of Racial Protest in Mississippi." *Journal of Southern History* 55 (May 1989): 217–44.

Wallenstein, Peter. "*Loving v. Virginia.*" In *Encyclopedia of African-American Civil Rights: From Emancipation to the Present,* edited by Charles D. Lowery and John F. Marszalek, foreword by David J. Garrow, 326. New York: Greenwood, 1992.

Wood, James R. "Unanticipated Consequences of Organizational Coalitions: Ecumenical Cooperation and Civil Rights Policy." *Social Forces* 50 (1972): 512–21.

Theses and Dissertations

Branch, Ellis Ray. "Born of Conviction: Racial Conflict and Change in Mississippi Methodism, 1945–1983." Ph.D. diss., Mississippi State University, 1984.

Cunnigen, Donald. "Men and Women of Goodwill: Mississippi's White Liberals." Ph.D.
diss., Harvard University, 1987.

Hill, Homer Douglass. "Power and Change in a Mississippi Delta County: Coahoma Opportunities, Incorporated, 1965–1972." Master's thesis, University of Southern Mississippi, 1995.

McLemore, Leslie Burl. "The Mississippi Freedom Democratic Party: A Case Study of
Grass-Roots Politics." Ph.D. diss., University of Massachusetts, 1971.

Noble, Gaile Patricia. "The Delta Ministry: Black Power, Poverty, and Politics in the Mississippi Delta." Master's thesis, Cornell University, 1969.

INDEX

DM = the Delta Ministry

Danville, Va., 8
Davenport, Iowa, 43, 134
De Cell, Hal, 30
Deer Creek Pilot, 30
Delaney, Joseph, 169
Delta. *See* Yazoo-Mississippi Delta
Delta Blues Festival, 147
Delta Community Hospital (and Health
   Center), 198, 202–3. *See also* Delta Health
   Center; Mound Bayou Community
   Hospital
Delta Cooperative Farm, 128
Delta Council, 29, 109, 132
Delta Democrat-Times, 33, 85, 87, 90, 91, 93–94,
   98, 99, 103, 105, 132, 135, 139, 167, 205, 272
   (n. 66). *See also* Carter, Hodding, II;
   Carter, Hodding, III
Delta Enterprises, 177
Delta Foundation, 179, 195, 200, 201, 208, 217,
   222, 302 (n. 6); achievements of, 178, 210,
   222; aims, xii, 177; origins of, 166
Delta Health Center, 198, 203, 208, 216, 225,
   308 (n. 3). *See also* Delta Community
   Hospital (and Health Center); Tufts-
   Delta Health Center
Delta Merchants' Cooperative Warehouse,
   176–77
Delta Ministry: absence of religious
   observation in, 20–21; achievements of,
   xii, 23, 34–35, 45, 46, 67, 68, 82–83, 84, 106,
   112, 149, 178–79, 198–99, 217–18, 219, 220–21,
   222, 225; aims of, ix, x, xi–xii, 9, 12, 16, 21,
   26, 34–35, 45, 46, 67, 82–83, 107, 118–20, 126,
   149, 171–72, 179, 184–85, 196, 197, 198–99,
   205–6, 218, 219, 224–25; board of directors
   of, 197, 201, 204, 205, 225; budget of, 9, 35,
   44, 108, 167, 178, 276 (n. 28); —, deficit and
   cuts of, xii, 45, 107–8, 112, 116, 122–23, 125,
   126, 148, 149, 166, 183–84, 190, 191, 192, 224;
   —, donations and fundraising for, 27, 44,
   121, 133, 138, 150, 153, 197, 201, 290 (n. 18);
   —, funded by wcc, 12, 20, 23, 285 (n. 48);
   —, grants and loans for, 82, 130, 134, 142,
   144, 147, 202, 207, 225; —, support from
   ncc, 113, 117–18, 179, 180, 194–95, 196, 198,
   217, 219–20; divisions within, 130, 180–96,
224, 306 (nn. 37, 44, 47); founding of,
   ix, 1, 3, 4, 7, 8–9, 10–12, 18, 19, 20–21, 22,
   23, 24–26, 33, 34, 231 (n. 23), 234 (n. 48),
   236 (n. 2); headquarters of, 19, 20, 31, 86;
   leadership of, xi, 19, 107, 120–21, 122, 123,
   126, 149, 168, 172, 179, 181–87, 191, 306 (n. 47);
   tenth anniversary celebration of, 205,
   206; volunteers, 20, 43, 55, 59, 60, 63, 64,
   85, 91, 96, 125, 126, 134–35, 136, 138, 150, 151,
   268 (n. 41); —, in city of McComb, 72, 74,
   77, 79–80; —, white, 43, 136
Delta Opportunities Association (DOA),
   102; founding of, 43, 101
Delta Opportunities Corporation (DOC),
   133, 142–43, 185, 220; aims of, 43, 130, 140,
   141–43, 144, 221–22; founding of, xii,
   43–44, 101–102, 270 (n. 52); and Freedom
   City, 127, 130, 131, 132, 135, 137, 138, 139,
   141–42, 143–44, 145, 146, 222; funding of,
   43–44, 45, 102, 140, 144, 145, 146–47, 165,
   222
Delta Pride, 215–16
Delta Resources Committee (DRC), 205
Democratic Party National Convention:
   in 1964, 17, 18, 37–38, 55, 157, 160, 170, 189,
   202, 234 (n. 46); in 1968, 169, 170, 186, 188;
   in 1972, 202
Dennis, Dave, 9, 48
Dent, Tom, 208, 211
DeRienzis, David, 96
Desegregation, of schools. *See* School
   desegregation
Detroit, Mich., 166, 189
Devine, Annie, 34, 240 (n. 29)
Diebold Group, 34–35, 38, 39, 221
Dillon, Matti, 72
Disciples of Christ, 2, 19, 33, 50, 70, 79–80,
   109, 137; donates relief, 34; Mississippi
   Christian Churches, 24, 31, 38; and
   Mount Beulah, 19, 31, 38, 113, 153, 191
Dittmer, John, 17, 215, 293 (n. 40)
Doar, John, 72
Dorsey, L. C., 169, 176, 207–8, 209, 210–11, 221,
   225
Douglass, Truman, 7
Draper, Alan, 18

Millard, James A., Jr., 28

Miller, J. Irwin, 2–3, 5, 6

Miller, Patrick D., 28

Miller, Reuben H., 108

Mills, Roger, 307–8 (n. 48)

Millsaps College, 157

Minniece, Thomas Y., 158–59

Minter, David, 128

Missionary Baptists, 42, 72, 78

Mississippi: antipicketing law, 50, 249 (n. 12); assessment of, in the 1980s and 1990s, 209–18; distinctiveness of, ix, x; state constitution of, 11; voter registration statistics in, 11, 160, 174, 206, 293 (n. 40), 312 (n. 55)

Mississippi Action for Community Education (MACE), 182, 302 (n. 6)

Mississippi Action for Progress (MAP), 244 (n. 54), 272 (n. 66)

Mississippi AFL-CIO, 98, 169

Mississippians United to Elect Negro Candidates, 158, 159, 160, 161, 167

Mississippi Association of Methodist Ministers and Laymen (MAMML), 29, 30. See also Methodist Church; Mississippi Conference of the Methodist Church; North Mississippi Conference of the Methodist Church; Southeastern Jurisdictional Conference of the Methodist Church

Mississippi Baptist State Educational Association, 96

Mississippi Christian Churches (Disciples of Christ), 24, 31, 38. See also Disciples of Christ

Mississippi Conference of the Methodist Church, 109, 137, 157; investigates NCC, 29, 36. See also Methodist Church; Mississippi Association of Methodist Ministers and Laymen; North Mississippi Conference of the Methodist Church; Southeastern Jurisdictional Conference of the Methodist Church

Mississippi Council on Human Relations, 33, 88, 240 (n. 27)

Mississippi Department of Public Welfare, 44, 58–59, 104, 105, 137

Mississippi Freedom Democratic Party (MFDP), 55, 61, 62, 63, 64, 98, 124, 125, 151–52, 161, 167, 170, 173, 187, 199, 281 (n. 6), 289 (n. 8); composition of, xi, 17–18; congressional challenge of, 34, 52–53, 59, 160, 240 (n. 29); at Democratic Party National Convention (1964), 17, 37–38, 55, 157, 160, 189, 202, 234 (n. 46); and DM, xi, 23, 34, 36, 38, 41, 42, 45, 55, 59, 60, 68, 75, 77–79, 83, 100, 104–5, 112, 115, 116, 124, 129, 151, 152, 157, 158, 159, 160, 167, 170, 181, 182, 187, 188, 199, 202, 223–24, 304 (nn. 24, 26); endorsed by Moore, Paul, Jr., 38; endorsed by Spike, 34; excludes Henry, 18, 37–38, 202; founding of, 17; and Freedom Vote (1963), 70; and Freedom Vote (1964), 34, 75, 77–78; and Freedom Vote (1965) in McComb, 78; and Loyal Democrats of Mississippi, 169–70, 187, 202; and NAACP, xi, 17– 18, 37–38, 77, 82, 101, 159, 160, 167, 169–70, 206, 234 (n. 46); nature of xi, 17–18, 38; succeeds COFO, 39; and Vietnam War, 234 (n. 46); weaknesses of, xi, 38, 61, 64, 67, 78–79, 82, 101, 159, 169, 187, 199, 202

Mississippi Freedom Labor Union (MFLU), 95–98, 100, 104, 106, 116, 129, 222, 267 (n. 33). See also Andrews Brothers' Plantation

Mississippi Human Services Agenda, 208–9

Mississippi Methodist Action Crusade, 37

Mississippi Methodist Ministry (MMM), 30–31, 110–11. See also Methodist Church

Mississippi Prisoners' Defense Committee, 208

Mississippi State Sovereignty Commission, 81, 109, 124, 263 (n. 45)

Mississippi Student Union, 58, 60, 61

Mississippi Summer Project, 12–13, 15, 16–17, 20, 23, 29, 31, 32, 33, 38, 43, 50, 53–54, 59, 68, 70–72, 82, 85, 188–89, 234 (n. 44)

statistics for, in Mississippi, 11, 160, 174, 206, 293 (n. 40), 312 (n. 55)

Voting Rights Act (1965), 42, 62, 80, 174, 175, 212, 213

Waker, Rutledge A., 145, 146

Walker, Larry, 21, 98; and Andrews Brothers' Plantation strike, 95–97, 267 (n. 33); background of, 20; and Greenville, Miss., 86, 87, 88, 89, 90–91, 94; joins DM, 20; resigns from DM, 103

Wallace, George C., 170, 207, 311 (n. 33)

Waller, William, 202, 203, 221

Walls, Malcolm, 217

Walmsley, Arthur E., 24

Walthall County, Miss., 69

Walton, Hanes, Jr., 250 (n. 19)

Ward, A. Dudley, 121–22

Ward, Mae Yoho, 33

Warren, R. R., 72, 76

Warren County, Miss., 172

Washington County, Miss., 19, 85, 89, 91, 100, 102, 135, 139, 143, 144, 172, 176, 202, 213, 216, 231 (n. 25), 270 (n. 52), 272 (n. 66); and DM, 43, 95–98, 103–4, 106, 126, 132, 146, 162, 165, 183, 198, 207. *See also* Greenville, Miss.

Washington County Democratic Club, 94

Washington County Employment Committee (WCEC), 90, 91, 93, 98–99

Washington Post, 121, 203

Watkins, Hollis, 48, 160

Watkins, W. H., 74

Wayside, Miss., 132, 139

Weisheit, Eldon, 76

Welfare assistance, and DM, 149, 162, 163, 171, 172, 178–79, 196, 197, 198, 220, 224–25, 294 (n. 52)

Werner, Peter, 54

Western College for Women, 15

Westminster Presbyterian Church, Hattiesburg, Miss., 51, 57

West Point, Miss., 40, 153, 165; and DM, 42, 61, 64, 97, 112, 136, 165. *See also* Clay County, Miss.; Mary Holmes Junior College

White, Lee, 72

White, Mary, 124

Whites, opposition of, to DM, x, 9, 12, 18–19, 21, 22, 23, 24–25, 28, 29–30, 31, 35–37, 40–41, 45, 76, 79–80, 87, 91–92, 93–94, 98, 99–100, 103, 105, 106, 109, 110–12, 114, 116, 121, 122, 131, 151, 153–54, 223, 237 (n. 3), 241 (n. 34)

Whitley, Clifton R., 159

Whitten, James, 164

Wieser, Thomas, 3

Wilcher, Johnnie Lee, 72

Wilcox, W. T., 37, 91, 266 (n. 20)

Wild Geese Foundation, 207. *See also* Wild Goose Committee

Wild Goose Committee, 139, 285 (n. 48). *See also* Wild Geese Foundation

Wiley, George, 109, 172

Wilkie, Curtis, 170

Wilkins, Roy, 62, 256 (n. 54)

William Carey College, 51, 57, 60

Williams, Colin W., 6, 7, 11, 21; ideas of, 3; on McKenna's termination, 121

Williams, John Bell, 109, 167; and veto of Head Start grants, 172–73

Williams, Oliver Lee, 85

Wilmington, N.C., 8

Wilmore, Gayraud S., Jr., 33, 49, 51

Wilson, Ora D., 138, 147

Wilson, Sammy Lee, 138

Winham, Alfred R., 112, 126; background of, 38; and DM, 38, 43, 132, 135, 136, 137, 139, 274 (n. 15); joins DM, 38; praises Brooks, 126; terminated from DM, 112, 150

Winham, Margery, 38

Winstonville, Miss., 101, 269 (n. 46). *See also* Bolivar County, Miss.

Winter, William F., 28, 154

Woman's Division of the Methodist Church, 108, 122. *See also* Methodist Church

Women's Division of the United Methodist Church, 201. *See also* United Methodist Church

Wong, Larry Jack, 49

World Council of Churches (wcc), 21, 28, 42, 140; aims of, 3; and financial support of DM, 9, 12, 20, 27, 44, 122, 134, 144, 167, 171, 219, 285 (n. 48); and founding of DM, 9, 11–12, 22; North American Working Group of, 3, 5; Third Assembly of (1961), 3

Wright, Marian, 168, 207; background of, 33; and DM, 33, 117, 129, 135, 140, 156, 164

Yale Divinity School, 70

Yale University, 14, 32

Yazoo City, Miss., 174, 289 (n. 9). *See also* Yazoo County, Miss.

Yazoo County, Miss., 162; and DM, 152, 156, 182; and DOC, 43, 101, 143, 144, 270 (n. 52); and Freedom Corps, 39, 101, 152. *See also* Yazoo City, Miss.

Yazoo County Voters' League, 152

Yazoo-Mississippi Delta, x, xii–xiii, 1, 8, 19, 20, 21, 25, 30, 33, 35, 39, 42, 44, 46, 64, 84–106, 115, 125, 132, 138, 140, 148, 151, 159, 160, 161, 165, 167, 176–77, 189, 197, 198, 205, 208, 220, 302 (n. 6); assessment of, in the 1980s and 1990s, 209–18, 221, 225; definition of, 231 (n. 25); involvement of SNCC in, 8, 13, 48, 69; nature of, ix, 9–10; problems of, ix, xii–xiii, 7, 10, 11, 37, 84, 104, 127, 128, 163–65, 178, 209–11, 211–14, 215–18, 222, 225, 263 (n. 1)

YMCA, 87

Young, Andrew J., 190; chairs Commission on the Delta Ministry, 168, 183, 186, 195; declines to join DM staff, 19, 183; and founding of DM, 8

Young, Bernadine, 91

Young, Phil, 205

Youth program, of DM, 171, 178, 179